Codification Movement of

PUBLIC CORPORATION LAW

Codification of
Social Enterprise Law

公共主义公司法的法典运动

社会企业法法典编纂

蒋大兴 · 主　编
王首杰　龚浩川 · 副主编

法律出版社
LAW PRESS · CHINA
北京

图书在版编目(CIP)数据

公共主义公司法的法典运动：社会企业法法典编纂／蒋大兴主编. -- 北京：法律出版社，2024
ISBN 978－7－5197－7753－1

Ⅰ. ①公… Ⅱ. ①蒋… Ⅲ. ①公司法－研究－美国 Ⅳ. ①D971.222.9

中国国家版本馆CIP数据核字(2023)第058166号

公共主义公司法的法典运动
——社会企业法法典编纂
GONGGONGZHUYI GONGSIFA DE FADIAN YUNDONG
—SHEHUI QIYEFA FADIAN BIANZUAN

蒋大兴 主编

策划编辑 沈小英
责任编辑 沈小英 张思婕
装帧设计 李 瞻

出版发行 法律出版社
编辑统筹 法治与经济出版分社
责任校对 晁明慧
责任印制 吕亚莉
经 销 新华书店

开本 787毫米×1092毫米 1/16
印张 51.5 **字数** 1170千
版本 2024年1月第1版
印次 2024年1月第1次印刷
印刷 北京中科印刷有限公司

地址:北京市丰台区莲花池西里7号(100073)
网址:www.lawpress.com.cn
投稿邮箱:info@lawpress.com.cn
举报盗版邮箱:jbwq@lawpress.com.cn

销售电话:010－83938349
客服电话:010－83938350
咨询电话:010－63939796

书号:ISBN 978－7－5197－7753－1
定价:360.00元

凡购买本社图书,如有印装错误,我社负责退换。电话:010－83938349

主编简介

蒋大兴

1971年生，湖南省邵阳市人，南京大学法学博士。曾在湖南省邵阳市中级人民法院、南京大学法学院工作，现任北京大学法学院教授、博士生导师，教育部长江学者特聘教授，兼任北京大学中国企业法律风险管理研究中心主任、中国法学会证券法学研究会副会长、中国法学会商法学研究会常务理事、最高人民法院案例指导委员会专家委员、最高人民法院特邀执行咨询专家、国务院国资委法律顾问、北京仲裁委员会与深圳国际仲裁院仲裁员等职。

出版《公司法的展开与评判：方法、判例、制度》《公司法的观念与解释》等著作，在各类法学期刊发表论文100余篇，主持国家社科基金重大项目、国家社科基金重点项目、司法部、最高人民法院、国家发改委、国务院国资委等课题30余项。

副主编简介

王首杰

1980年生，辽宁朝阳人，北京大学法学博士。曾任职于西南政法大学高等研究院，现任西南政法大学人工智能法律研究院副院长，兼任中国证券法学研究会理事。近年主要从事公司法与规制法学研究，在《中国社会科学》《法学评论》《法商研究》等期刊发表法学论文多篇，独立申报并主持中国法学会、北京市法学会课题。

龚浩川

1988年生，吉林长春人，北京大学法学博士。吉林大学法学院副编审、《当代法学》编辑部副主任，兼任吉林大学理论法学研究中心、吉林大学司法数据应用研究中心研究员。曾在《清华法学》《法制与社会发展》《山东大学学报（哲学社会科学版）》等期刊发表论文多篇。主持国家社科基金青年项目，参加国家社科基金重大项目、马工程特别委托项目、中国法学会重点课题等多项。

说明与致谢

近些年，无论是文章报道，[1]还是各种会议论坛，[2]经常能够看到对“社会企业”的讨论。最近，在此基础上，企业社会责任运动又变形或者深化为“ESG（环境、社会和公司治理）”。社会企业在域外发展多年，但并无统一定义。英国商业、创新与技能部认为：社会企业是“并非仅受股东和所有者利益最大化驱使，而是将盈余主要向企业或所在社区进行再投资的企业。”[3]我国香港特别行政区民政事务局在对其进行介绍时指出：“社会企业（社企）没有统一的定义。一般而言，社企是一盘生意，宗旨是要达至特定的社会目的，例如，提供社会所需的服务（如长者支援服务）或产品、为弱势社群创造就业和培训机会、保护环境、运用本身赚取的利润资助辖下的其他社会服务等。”[4]简单来说，它是一个在实现经济效益的同时实现社会效益的企业，[5]双重目标是它与一般商事公司最主要的区别。

社会企业出现的主要原因是现有的各种私人组织在服务社会上的表现难以令人满意。首先，商事企业的传统目标是“营利”或者“股东利益至上”，难以与企业的社会目标兼容，这也被认为是许多企业成为经济和社会丑闻主角的原因。其次，非营利机构虽然在服务社会方面有不错的表现，但其无法向成员分配收益并且在资金使用上受到严格的限制，难以吸引投资。这条需求与供给间的鸿沟催生了社会企业，使其成为政府、企业和非营利机构之外的“第四部门”。[6]

社会企业一方面可以从事营利行为，在公开市场上进行融资并向成员分配利润；另一方面也要确保其行为有利于社会目标的实现。但是，社会企业并非企业与非营利机构的简单相加。在社会企业中，“社会目标”不再是“营利”的附带事项，也不是简单靠慈善捐款就能实现的，社会企业必须同时服务于“社会目标”与“商业

---

1 截至2016年11月10日，在中国知网上篇名中含有“社会企业”的各类文献共有36,803篇。

2 例如，“中国社会企业与社会投资论坛”“全球社会企业家生态论坛”“世界社会企业论坛”等。

3 Department for Business, Innovation and Skills, UK, A GUIDE TO LEGAL FORMS FOR SOCIAL ENTERPRISE, https://www.gov.uk/government/publications/legal-forms-for-social-enterprise-aguide.

4 http://www.social-enterprises.gov.hk/sc/introduction/whatis.html.

5 Joseph W. Yockey, *Does Social Enterprise Law Matter*, 66 Ala. L. Rev. 767 (2015).

6 Thomas Kelley, *Law and Choice of Entity on the Social Enterprise Frontier*, 84 Tul. L. Rev. 337, 338–41 (2009).

目标”这两个“平等的主人”，[1]社会目标须更深层次地融入企业的商业模式之中。[2]

社会企业以其新型的组织模式和良好的功能预期吸引着社会各界的目光，作为法律人，我们更加关注如何通过制度设计来实现社会企业的混合目标。在英国，除可以选择传统的普通合伙、有限合伙和有限公司外，人们还可以通过设立社区利益公司（Community Interest Companies）来创办社会企业。我国香港特别行政区虽然正在大力推动社会企业的创办，但是还没有专门的组织形式和配套的法律。美国 50 个州中超过 30 个进行了专门的社会企业立法，主要有《公共利益公司法》（Benefit Corporation Act）、《微利有限责任公司法》（Low-Profit Limited Liability Company Act）、《社会目的公司法》（Social Purpose Corporations Act）、《公共利益有限责任公司法》（Benefit Limited Liability Companies Act）和可持续商事公司（Sustainable Business Corporation Act），其中公共利益公司的立法最普遍。

美国的社会企业立法有五个特点：第一，突出企业的社会目的。4 种主要社会企业法都要求企业在公司章程中规定“一般公共利益目的”[3]或者“慈善或教育目的”[4]等社会目的。第二，第三方评估和制定年度报告。多数公共利益公司法和社会目的公司法要求公司采用第三方标准对公司的社会效益进行评估，并要求其编制年度报告，对公司社会目的实现情况、存在的阻碍、第三方标准的选取等问题进行说明。第三，异议股东回购请求权。美国一些州的公共利益公司法[5]和社会目的公司法[6]规定，非社会企业转化为社会企业时，异议股东享有股份回购请求权。第四，名称体现企业类型。社会企业法一般要求企业在名称中表明具体的社会企业类型或含有相应的缩写。第五，公共利益实施程序和赔偿责任的豁免。美国各州公共利益公司法为了确保“公共利益目的”的实现，一般会规定“公共利益实施程序”，允许特定主体对公司未追求公共利益目的或董事高级管理人员（以下简称高管）未履行相关义务的情况提起诉讼，但是原则上豁免公司和董事高管的赔偿责任。

以上只是对美国社会企业立法一般特点的概括，由于各州具体情况和各种社会企业类型的不同，具体立法还有许多差异。为了让读者能够对美国的社会企业立法有一个更加全面和详细的了解，我们对美国现存的 4 种典型社会企业立法进行翻译，汇编成《公共主义公司法的法典运动——社会企业法法典编纂》，希望读者可以从中看到，在蓬勃的商事公司发展的另一端，还存在公共主义公司法的法典运动。

在全书的翻译过程中，我主要是承担了选题设计、规范分工等组织工作，本书的具体翻译是由我指导的北京大学法学院的一些博士研究生和硕士研究生完成的，王首杰和龚浩川同学也协助做了大量协调工作。因为后期校对等事宜耗费不少时间，

---

1 Briana Cummings, *Benefit Corporations: How to Enforce a Mandate to Promote the Public Interest*, 112 COLUM. L. REV. 578, 582 (2012).

2 Dana Brakman Reiser, *For-Profit Philanthropy*, 77 FORDHAM L. REV. 2437 (2009).

3 主要为公共利益公司和社会目的公司。

4 主要是微利有限责任公司。

5 例如，美国佛罗里达州、明尼苏达州、华盛顿州等。

6 例如，美国加利福尼亚州。

参与此项工作的学生已离校工作。在此，对他们的辛苦付出表示感谢。

本书具体翻译和校对分工如下：

<table>
<tr><td rowspan="12">翻译（按姓氏笔画排序）</td><td>王首杰</td><td>公共利益公司法</td><td>南卡罗来纳州、田纳西州、犹他州、佛蒙特州、弗吉尼亚州、华盛顿哥伦比亚特区、西弗吉尼亚州</td></tr>
<tr><td rowspan="4">陈毓坤</td><td>公共利益有限责任公司法</td><td>马里兰州</td></tr>
<tr><td>微利有限责任公司</td><td>犹他州、怀俄明州</td></tr>
<tr><td>社会目的公司</td><td>佛罗里达州、得克萨斯州</td></tr>
<tr><td>可持续商事公司</td><td>夏威夷州</td></tr>
<tr><td>金晓文</td><td colspan="2">示范公共利益公司法及其解释性评论</td></tr>
<tr><td rowspan="3">唐夕雅</td><td>公共利益公司法</td><td>科罗拉州、康涅狄格州、特拉华州、内布拉斯加州、内华达州、新罕布什尔州、新泽西州、纽约州、俄勒冈州、宾夕法尼亚州、罗得岛州</td></tr>
<tr><td>微利有限责任公司</td><td>密歇根州、北卡罗来纳州、罗得岛州</td></tr>
<tr><td>社会目的公司</td><td>华盛顿州</td></tr>
<tr><td rowspan="3">龚浩川</td><td>公共利益公司法</td><td>亚利桑那州、阿肯色州、加利福尼亚州、佛罗里达州、爱达荷州、伊利诺伊州、印第安纳州、路易斯安那州、马里兰州、马萨诸塞州、明尼苏达州、蒙大拿州</td></tr>
<tr><td>微利有限责任公司</td><td>伊利诺伊州、路易斯安那州、缅因州</td></tr>
<tr><td>社会目的公司</td><td>加利福尼亚州</td></tr>
<tr><td>校对</td><td colspan="3">龚浩川、王首杰、金晓文</td></tr>
</table>

为了贴近我国立法在法律结构中的表述习惯，以及帮助读者辨识条文之间的梯级层次，译文按照我国读者熟悉的编排体系，降序使用“编、章、节、条、款、项、目”等译名，灵活对应原文的 title，chapter，subchapter，section，subsection， division/paragraph 等层次。例如，section 一般翻译为“节”，若在具体立法中对应内容仅相当于我国法律中“条”，则翻译为“条”。也就是说，无论原文名称如何，译文只求梯级层次的对应，而不论字面是否相符。

当然，由于我们在学识水平和翻译能力上的局限，难免会存在一些错误和疏漏，敬请各位读者批评指正。

2024 年 1 月 1 日

CONTENTS

目　　录

BENEFIT CORPORATION ACT

MODEL BENEFIT CORPORATION LEGISLATION 2
THE STATE OF ARIZONA 42
THE STATE OF ARKANSAS 60
THE STATE OF CALIFORNIA 80
THE STATE OF COLORADO 102
THE STATE OF CONNECTICUT 112
THE STATE OF DELAWARE 132
THE STATE OF FLORIDA 140
THE STATE OF IDAHO 158
THE STATE OF ILLINOIS 180
THE STATE OF INDIANA 200
THE STATE OF LOUISIANA 224
THE STATE OF MARYLAND 244
THE STATE OF MASSACHUSETTS 254
THE STATE OF MINNESOTA 274
THE STATE OF MONTANA 292
THE STATE OF NEBRASKA 312
THE STATE OF NEVADA 332
THE STATE OF NEW HAMPSHIRE 352
THE STATE OF NEW JERSEY 376
THE STATE OF NEW YORK 394
THE STATE OF OREGON 408
THE STATE OF PFNNSYLVANIA 424
THE STATE OF RHODE ISLAND 444

公共利益公司法

示范公共利益公司法及其解释性评论 3
亚利桑那州 43
阿肯色州 61
加利福尼亚州 81
科罗拉州 103
康涅狄格州 113
特拉华州 133
佛罗里达州 141
爱达荷州 159
伊利诺伊州 181
印第安纳州 201
路易斯安那州 225
马里兰州 245
马萨诸塞州 255
明尼苏达州 275
蒙大拿州 293
内布拉斯加州 313
内华达州 333
新罕布什尔州 353
新泽西州 377
纽约州 395
俄勒冈州 409
宾夕法尼亚州 425
罗得岛州 445

THE STATE OF SOUTH CAROLINA 466
THE STATE OF TENNESSEE 490
THE STATE OF UTAH 512
THE STATE OF VERMONT 536
THE STATE OF VIRGINIA 556
WASHINGTON DISTRICT OF COLUMBIA 568
THE STATE OF WEST VIRGINIA 590

LOW-PROFIT LIMITED LIABILITY COMPANY ACT

THE STATE OF ILLINOIS 606
THE STATE OF LOUISIANA 610
THE STATE OF MAINE 614
THE STATE OF MICHIGAN 620
THE STATE OF NORTH CAROLINA 622
THE STATE OF RHODE ISLAND 626
THE STATE OF UTAH 630
THE STATE OF WYOMING 634

SOCIAL PURPOSE CORPORATIONS ACT

THE STATE OF CALIFORNIA 640
THE STATE OF FLORIDA 730
THE STATE OF TEXAS 748
THE STATE OF WASHINGTON 766

南卡罗来纳州 467
田纳西州 491
犹他州 513
佛蒙特州 537
弗吉尼亚州 557
华盛顿哥伦比亚特区 569
西弗吉尼亚州 591

微利有限责任公司法

伊利诺伊州 607
路易斯安那州 611
缅因州 615
密歇根州 621
北卡罗来纳州 623
罗得岛州 627
犹他州 631
怀俄明州 635

社会目的公司法

加利福尼亚州 641
佛罗里达州 731
得克萨斯州 749
华盛顿州 767

BENEFIT LIMITED LIABILITY COMPANIES ACT

THE STATE OF MARYLAND 786

SUSTAINABLE BUSINESS CORPORATION

THE STATE OF HAWAII 796

公共利益有限责任公司法

马里兰州 787

可持续商事公司

夏威夷州 797

BENEFIT CORPORATION ACT

公共利益公司法

MODEL BENEFIT CORPORATION LEGISLATION

With Explanatory Comments[1]

[Chapter] __
Benefit Corporations

[Subchapter]
1. Preliminary Provisions
2. Corporate Purposes
3. Accountability
4. Transparency

[Subchapter] 1
Preliminary Provisions

Section
101. Application and effect of [chapter].
102. Definitions.
103. Incorporation of benefit corporation.
104. Election of benefit corporation status.
105. Termination of benefit corporation status.

---

1 For a detailed discussion of the issues to be considered when preparing legislation for introduction in a state see Clark et al., *The Need and Rationale for the Benefit Corporation* (2011), available at www.benefitcorp.org. See generally, William H. Clark, Jr. and Elizabeth K. Babson, *How Benefit Corporations are Redefining the Purpose of Business Corporations*, 38 WM. MITCHELL L. REV. 817 (2012).

示范公共利益公司法及其解释性评论

示范公共利益公司法及其解释性评论[1]

［章］__
公共利益公司

［节］
1. 初步条款
2. 公司目的
3. 公司责任
4. 透明度

第 1 节
初步条款

条款
第 101 条 ［本章］的适用及效力
第 102 条 定义
第 103 条 公共利益公司的设立
第 104 条 公共利益公司的形态选择
第 105 条 公共利益公司形态的终止

---

1 For a detailed discussion of the issues to be considered when preparing legislation for introduction in a state see Clark et al., *The Need and Rationale for the Benefit Corporation* (2011), available at www.benefitcorp.org. See generally, William H. Clark, Jr. and Elizabeth K. Babson, *How Benefit Corporations are Redefining the Purpose of Business Corporations*, 38 WM. MITCHELL L. REV. 817 (2012).

§101. Application and effect of [chapter].

(a) **General rule.** – This [chapter] shall be applicable to all benefit corporations.

(b) **Application of business corporation law generally.** – The existence of a provision of this [chapter] shall not of itself create an implication that a contrary or different rule of law is applicable to a business corporation that is not a benefit corporation. This [chapter] shall not affect a statute or rule of law that is applicable to a business corporation that is not a benefit corporation.

(c) **Laws applicable.** – Except as otherwise provided in this [chapter], [the enacting state's business corporation law] shall be generally applicable to all benefit corporations. A benefit corporation may be subject simultaneously to this [chapter] and [cite any statutes that provide for the incorporation of a specific type of business corporation, such as a professional corporation or for–profit cooperative corporation]. The provisions of this [chapter] shall control over the provisions of [cite the business corporation law] [and] [cite the professional corporation, cooperative corporation and other relevant laws].

(d) **Organic records.** – A provision of the articles of incorporation or bylaws of a benefit corporation may not limit, be inconsistent with, or supersede a provision of this [chapter].

Comment:

This chapter authorizes the organization of a form of business corporation that offers entrepreneurs and investors the option to build, and invest in, a business that operates with a corporate purpose broader than maximizing shareholder value and that consciously undertakes a responsibility to maximize the benefits of its operations for all stakeholders, not just shareholders. Enforcement of that purpose and responsibility comes not from governmental oversight, but rather from new provisions on transparency and accountability included in this chapter.

The second sentence of subsection (c) makes clear that if a state provides for the incorporation of specialized types of business corporations, such as statutory close corporations, insurance corporations, for–profit cooperative corporations, or professional corporations, those corporations may also be benefit corporations. In the case of a professional corporation, section 201(e) provides a special rule that eliminates any conflict between this chapter and the requirement found in many professional corporation laws that limits the purposes or business of a professional corporation to providing a particular type of professional service.

As a result of subsection (d), a corporation that elects to be subject to this chapter will be subject to all of the provisions of the chapter and will not be able to vary their application to the corporation.

The term "benefit corporation" used in this section is defined in section 102.

第 101 条 ［本章］的适用及效力

（a）**一般规则。**——［本章］适用于所有的公共利益公司。

（b）**商事公司法的一般适用。**——［本章］条款不应为非公共利益公司设定相反或不同的规则。［本章］不影响非公共利益公司有关条文和规则的适用。

（c）**适用的法律。**——除［本章］另有规定外，［各州颁布的商事公司法］适用于公共利益公司。公共利益公司同时受［本章］和［与特殊类型商事公司（如专业公司或营利合作公司）有关规定］的调整。［本章］条款效力优先于［商事公司法］［和］［专业公司与合伙公司有关的法律］的条款。

（d）**组织文件。**——公共利益公司的公司章程或公司章程细则不得限制、违背或取代［本章］的规定。

评论：

本章授权企业家和投资者建立、投资一种公司目的超出股东利益最大化范围的商事公司形式，旨在最大化包括股东在内的所有利益相关者的利益。公司目的的实现和公司责任的履行并非来自政府监督，而是来自本章对透明度和公司责任的规定。

第（c）款第二句表明，如果美国各州颁布了法规调整特殊形式的商事公司，如封闭公司、保险公司、营利合作公司或专业公司，也有可能是公共利益公司。如果属于专业公司，适用第 201（e）款所提供的特定规则，用以消除本章规定与专业公司法规要求的冲突，后者将专业公司的公司目的和公司业务限制为提供某种特定类型的专业服务。

基于第（d）款的规定，选择受本章规定调整的公司适用本章所有条款，不能进行选择性适用。

“公共利益公司”的定义见第 102 条。

§102. Definitions.

The following words and phrases when used in this [chapter] shall have the meanings given to them in this section unless the context clearly indicates otherwise:

"**Benefit corporation**." A business corporation:

(1) that has elected to become subject to this [chapter]; and

(2) the status of which as a benefit corporation has not been terminated.

"**Benefit director**." the director designated as the benefit director of a benefit corporation under section 302.

"**Benefit enforcement proceeding**." Any claim or action or proceeding for:

(1) failure of a benefit corporation to pursue or create general public benefit or a specific public benefit purpose set forth in its articles; or

(2) violation of any obligation, duty, or standard of conduct under this [chapter].

"**Benefit officer**." The individual designated as the benefit officer of a benefit corporation under section 304.

"**General public benefit**." A material positive impact on society and the environment, taken as a whole, assessed against a third-party standard, from the business and operations of a benefit corporation.

"**Independent**." Having no material relationship with a benefit corporation or a subsidiary of the benefit corporation. Serving as benefit director or benefit officer does not make an individual not independent. A material relationship between an individual and a benefit corporation or any of its subsidiaries will be conclusively presumed to exist if any of the following apply:

(1) The individual is, or has been within the last three years, an employee other than a benefit officer of the benefit corporation or a subsidiary.

(2) An immediate family member of the individual is, or has been within the last three years, an executive officer other than a benefit officer of the benefit corporation or a subsidiary.

(3) There is beneficial or record ownership of 5% or more of the outstanding shares of the benefit corporation, calculated as if all outstanding rights to acquire equity interests in the benefit corporation had been exercised, by:

(i) the individual; or

(ii) an entity:

(A) of which the individual is a director, an officer, or a manager; or

(B) in which the individual owns beneficially or of record 5% or more of the outstanding equity interests, calculated as if all outstanding rights to acquire equity interests in the entity had been exercised.

"**Minimum status vote**."

第 102 条　定义

除另有规定外，［本章］出现的用语的含义如下：

“公共利益公司”是指一家商事公司：

（1）选择接受［本章］规定的调整；并且

（2）公共利益公司形态并未终止。

“公共利益董事”是指公共利益公司根据第 302 条规定任命的董事。

“公共利益实施程序”是指因以下行为产生的任何主张、诉讼或程序：

（1）公共利益公司未追求或实现公司章程规定的一般或特定公共利益目的；或者

（2）违反［本章］规定下的任何义务、责任或行为标准。

“公共利益高管”是指公共利益公司根据第 304 条规定任命的高管。

“一般公共利益”是指根据第三方标准，公司的业务和经营在整体上对社会和环境产生的实质性积极影响。

“独立”是指个体与公共利益公司或其子公司没有实质性关系。担任公共利益董事或公共利益高管并不当然丧失独立性。下列情形中，则认为该个体与公共利益公司或其子公司存在实质性关系：

（1）该个体是，或在过去 3 年内是，公共利益公司或其子公司公共利益高管以外的雇员。

（2）该个体的直系亲属是，或在过去的 3 年内是，公共利益公司或其子公司公共利益高管以外的执行高管。

（3）在所有购股权被视为已行使的情况下，下述持有公共利益公司 5% 以上已发行股份的登记股东或实际受益人：

（i）个人；或者

（ii）实体：

（A）该个人是该实体的董事、高管或经理；或者

（B）在所有购股权被视为已行使的情况下，该实体中的个人为持有公共利益公司 5% 以上已发行股份的登记股东或实际受益人。

“最低表决要求”是指：

(1) In the case of a business corporation, in addition to any other required approval or vote, the satisfaction of the following conditions:

(i) The shareholders of every class or series shall be entitled to vote as a [separate voting group] [class] on the corporate action regardless of a limitation stated in the articles of incorporation or bylaws on the voting rights of any class or series.

(ii) The corporate action must be approved by the affirmative vote of the shareholders of each class or series entitled to cast at least two-thirds of the votes that all shareholders of the class or series are entitled to cast on the action.

[(2) In the case of a domestic entity other than a business corporation, in addition to any other required approval, vote, or consent, the satisfaction of the following conditions:

(i) The holders of every class or series of equity interest in the entity that are entitled to receive a distribution of any kind from the entity shall be entitled to vote on or consent to the action regardless of any otherwise applicable limitation on the voting or consent rights of any class or series.

(ii) The action must be approved by the affirmative vote or consent of the holders described in subparagraph (i) entitled to cast at least two-thirds of the votes or consents that all of those holders are entitled to cast on the action.]

"**Publicly traded corporation**." A business corporation that has shares listed on a national securities exchange or traded in a market maintained by one or more members of a national securities association.

"**Specific public benefit**." Includes:

(1) providing low-income or underserved individuals or communities with beneficial products or services;

(2) promoting economic opportunity for individuals or communities beyond the creation of jobs in the normal course of business;

(3) protecting or restoring the environment;

(4) improving human health;

(5) promoting the arts, sciences, or advancement of knowledge;

(6) increasing the flow of capital to entities with a purpose to benefit society or the environment; and

(7) conferring any other particular benefit on society or the environment.

"**Subsidiary**." In relation to a person, an entity in which the person owns beneficially or of record 50% or more of the outstanding equity interests, calculated as if all outstanding rights to acquire equity interests in the entity had been exercised.

"**Third-party standard**." A recognized standard for defining, reporting, and assessing corporate social and environmental performance that is:

(1) Comprehensive because it assesses the effects of the business and its operations

（1）在商事公司中，除其他批准或表决的要求外，还应满足以下条件：

（i）每一类别或系列的股东有权作为一个［独立的投票团体］对公司行为进行投票，即使公司章程或章程细则对某一类别或系列股东的投票权作出了限制。

（ii）公司行为必须获得每个类别或系列有投票权的所有股东至少 2/3 的赞成票才能通过。

［（2）在本州非商事公司的实体中，除其他批准、表决或赞成的要求外，还应满足以下条件：

（i）该实体的每一类别或系列任何权益分配形式下的股权持有者有权对公司行为进行投票，即使存在任何对该类别或系列股东的投票权限制。

（ii）公司行为必须获得第（i）项规定的有投票权的所有股东至少 2/3 的赞成票才能通过。］

“上市公司”是指在美国证券交易所或美国证券协会中的一个或几个成员形成的市场上进行交易的商事公司。

“特定公共利益”包括：

（1）向低收入、低福利人群或社区提供有益的产品或服务；

（2）在正常业务过程中向个人或社区提供创造就业之外的经济机会；

（3）保护或修复环境；

（4）改善人类健康；

（5）促进艺术、科学或知识进步；

（6）促进资本向拥有有利于社会或环境目标的实体流动；以及

（7）提供关于社会或环境的其他特别利益。

“子公司”是指在所有购股权被视为已行使的情况下，该实体 50% 以上已发行的股份的受益所有权或登记所有权被另一实体所拥有。

“第三方标准”是指用于定义、报告和评估公司社会和环境绩效的标准，其应满足以下条件：

（1）综合，根据第 301（a）（1）（ii），（iii），（iv）和（v）目中所列利益评

upon the interests listed in section 301(a)(1)(ii), (iii), (iv) and (v).

(2) Developed by an entity that is not controlled by the benefit corporation.

(3) Credible because it is developed by an entity that both:

(i) has access to necessary expertise to assess overall corporate social and environmental performance; and

(ii) uses a balanced multistakeholder approach to develop the standard, including a reasonable public comment period.

(4) Transparent because the following information is publicly available:

(i) About the standard:

(A) The criteria considered when measuring the overall social and environmental performance of a business.

(B) The relative weightings, if any, of those criteria.

(ii) About the development and revision of the standard:

(A) The identity of the directors, officers, material owners, and the governing body of the entity that developed and controls revisions to the standard.

(B) The process by which revisions to the standard and changes to the membership of the governing body are made.

(C) An accounting of the revenue and sources of financial support for the entity, with sufficient detail to disclose any relationships that could reasonably be considered to present a potential conflict of interest.

Comment:

"Benefit corporation." The provisions of this chapter apply to a business corporation while it has the status of a benefit corporation because its articles contain a statement that it is a benefit corporation. If that statement is deleted as provided in section 105, the corporation will cease to be a benefit corporation immediately upon the effectiveness of the deletion.

"Benefit enforcement proceeding." This definition not only describes the action that may be brought under section 305, but it also has the effect of excluding other actions against a benefit corporation and its directors and officers because section 305(a) provides that "no person may bring an action or assert a claim against a benefit corporation or its directors or officers" with respect to violation of the provisions of this chapter except in a benefit enforcement proceeding.

The obligations that may be enforced through a benefit enforcement proceeding include the obligations of a benefit corporation under section 402(b) to post its benefit reports on its Internet website and to supply copies of its benefit report if it does not have an Internet website. In the case of a failure to provide a copy of a benefit report, a benefit enforcement proceeding to enforce that obligation may only be brought by the persons listed in section

估公司业务和经营绩效。

（2）独立，经非由公共利益公司控制的第三方实体制定。

（3）可信，该标准由满足以下条件的第三方实体制定：

（i）拥有评估公司社会和环境综合绩效所需的专业知识；并且

（ii）使用平衡多方相关者利益的方法制定标准，包括设定合理期间以听取公众意见。

（4）透明，以下信息可公开获取：

（i）有关标准：

（A）衡量企业整体社会和环境绩效时所考虑的指标。

（B）这些指标的相关权重。

（ii）关于标准的制定和修改：

（A）制定和控制修改标准的董事、高管、主要股东和该实体控制人员的身份。

（B）标准修改和控制人员变动的程序。

（C）收入和资金来源的核算，包括充分披露合理认知下存在利益冲突的所有细节。

评论：

"公共利益公司"本章条款适用于因其公司章程表明其为公共利益公司而拥有公共利益公司身份的商事公司。如果此条款根据第 105 条的规定被删除，那么该公司将在该删除行为生效以后立即丧失公共利益公司的身份。

"公共利益实施程序"该定义不但描述了可能由第 305 条引发的公司诉讼，而且具有排除其他针对公共利益公司和其董事、高管的诉讼的效力。基于第 305（a）款的规定，除在公共利益实施程序中，"任何人不得向公共利益公司或其董事、高管提起违反本章规定的诉讼或发表主张"。

公司可以通过公共利益实施程序执行的义务包括根据第 402（b）款的规定在网站上发表其公共利益报告，或者在没有网站的情况下提供其公共利益报告的副本。如果公司不能提供公共利益报告，公共利益实施程序只能由第 305 条中所列的人员提起，而不能由请求提供该报告的主体提起，除非该主体在第 305 条规定下拥有起诉权。

305 and not by the person requesting the copy of the report unless the person otherwise has standing under section 305.

"General public benefit." By requiring that the impact of a business on society and the environment be looked at "as a whole," the concept of general public benefit requires consideration of all of the effects of the business on society and the environment. What is involved in creating general public benefit is informed by section 301(a) which lists the specific interests and factors that the directors of a benefit corporation are required to consider.

"Minimum status vote." An amendment of the articles or a fundamental change that has the effect of changing the status of a corporation so that it either becomes a benefit corporation or ceases to be a benefit corporation must be approved by the minimum status vote. See sections 104 and 105. The purpose of requiring a two-thirds vote under this chapter is to ensure that there is broad shareholder support for an action. This definition will not be needed in states that require a supermajority vote of two-thirds or more for amendments of the articles or fundamental changes.

The second paragraph of the definition extends its policy to other forms of entities so that, for example, a merger of a limited liability company into a benefit corporation must be approved by the members of the limited liability company by at least a two-thirds vote. The second paragraph should be omitted by those states that require a supermajority vote of two-thirds or more by the owners of an unincorporated entity to approve a fundamental change. See, e.g., Uniform Limited Liability Company Act (2006) (Last Amended 2013) §1023, which requires a unanimous vote by the members of a limited liability company to approve a merger.

The two-thirds vote required by the definition is in addition to any other vote required in the case of any particular corporation or other form of entity. If the articles of a corporation were to require, for example, an 80% supermajority vote to approve a merger, a 70% vote to approve a merger of the corporation into a benefit corporation would be sufficient to satisfy the requirement that the merger be approved by the minimum status vote but would not be sufficient for valid approval of the merger.

"Publicly traded corporation." This definition is used in section 302, which makes the requirement of a benefit director mandatory for publicly traded corporations. The definition is patterned after Model Business Corporation Act §1.40(18A) (2010). This definition will not be necessary if the enacting state's business corporation law includes a similar definition.

"Specific public benefit." Every benefit corporation has the purpose under section 201(a) of creating general public benefit. A benefit corporation may also elect to pursue one or more specific public benefit purposes. Since the creation of specific public benefit is optional, paragraph (7) of this definition permits a benefit corporation to identify a specific

“一般公共利益”要求“整体”看待公司对社会和环境的影响，一般公共利益的概念要求考虑公司对社会和环境的所有影响。一般公共利益涉及的内容可参考第301（a）款的规定，其列出了公共利益公司的董事应予考虑的利益和因素。

“最低表决要求”改变公司形态，使公司成为公共利益公司或终止其公共利益公司形态的公司章程修改或公司重大变动，必须满足最低表决要求，见第104条和第105条的规定。本章要求2/3多数决的目的在于确保有足够多的股东支持此类公司行为。美国规定了修改章程或公司重大变动需要2/3或以上绝对多数决的州不需要适用该规定。

此定义的第二段将政策扩展至其他形式的实体，例如，有限责任公司并入公共利益公司必须经有限责任公司的2/3股东绝对多数决通过。第二段可被规定了经被兼并企业2/3多数通过重大变动的州所忽略，例如，美国《统一有限责任公司法》(2006年）（最新修订于2013年）第1023条规定了有限责任公司需要全体一致同意兼并事项。

定义中对2/3多数决的要求需同时满足公司或其他形式的实体对投票权的要求。例如，如果一家公司的章程规定，合并事项需80%的绝对多数通过，那么70%的赞成票满足了该公司并入公共利益公司的最低表决要求，但其不能批准该合并事项。

“上市公司”此定义出现在第302条中，要求上市公司必须任命公共利益董事。此定义依据美国《模范商事公司法》（2010年）第1.40条（第18A章）制定，如果美国各州颁布的商事公司法中有类似的定义，则不再需要此定义。

“特定公共利益”每个公共利益公司都根据第201（a）款的规定设定一般公共利益的目的。公共利益公司可以选择追求一项或多项特定的公共利益目的。由于特定的公共利益的设定是有选择性的，此定义的第（7）项允许一家公共利益公司确定一项与第（1）项至第（6）项规定不同的特定公共利益。

public benefit that is different from those listed in paragraphs (1) through (6).

"Third-party standard." The requirement in section 401 that a benefit corporation prepare an annual benefit report that assesses its performance in creating general public benefit against a third-party standard provides an important protection against the abuse of benefit corporation status. The performance of a regular business corporation is measured by the financial statements that the corporation prepares. But the performance of a benefit corporation in creating general or specific public benefit will not be readily apparent from those financial statements. The annual benefit report is intended to permit an evaluation of that performance so that the shareholders can judge how the directors have discharged their responsibility to manage the corporation and thus whether the directors should be retained in office or the shareholders should take other action to change the way the corporation is managed. The annual benefit report is also intended to reduce "greenwashing" (the phenomenon of businesses seeking to portray themselves as being more environmentally and socially responsible than they actually are) by giving consumers and the general public a means of judging whether a business is living up to its claimed status as a benefit corporation.

The financial support that must be disclosed by an organization if it wishes to make available a third party standard should include investment income, grants, and other types of support in addition to revenue it receives from its operations.

§103. Incorporation of benefit corporation.

A benefit corporation shall be incorporated in accordance with [cite incorporation provisions of the business corporation law], but its articles of incorporation must also state that it is a benefit corporation.

Comment:

This section provides for how a corporation that is being newly formed may elect to be a benefit corporation. Existing corporations may become benefit corporations in the manner provided in section 104.

This chapter only applies to domestic business corporations. A foreign business corporation that has a status in its home jurisdiction similar to the status of a benefit corporation under this chapter is not subject to this chapter and has the status simply of a foreign business corporation for purposes of the state's business corporation law.

The term "benefit corporation" used in this section is defined in section 102.

§104. Election of benefit corporation status.

(a) Amendment. – An existing business corporation may become a benefit corporation under this [chapter] by amending its articles of incorporation so that they contain, in addition to the requirements of [cite section of the business corporation law on the required contents of articles of incorporation], a statement that the corporation is a benefit corporation. In order

“第三方标准”根据第 401 条的规定，公共利益公司依据第三方标准，编写反映其创造一般公共利益的年度公共利益报告，作为防止滥用公共利益公司地位的重要手段。普通的商事公司的绩效通过公司编写的财务报表来衡量，但公共利益公司创造一般和特殊公共利益的绩效不会像财务报表反映的数据一样显而易见。年度的公共利益报告旨在进行绩效的评估，由股东来判断董事行使其责任的状况，以决定是否继续留任该董事，或是否更换经营策略。年度公共利益报告也旨在为顾客或大众判断该公司是否符合其作为公共利益公司的宗旨提供依据，以减少公共利益公司的“漂绿”行为（公司伪装得更加环保或履行了更多社会责任的现象）。

一实体希望达到第三方标准，必须披露资金来源，包括投资收入、拨款，或者其他经营收入以外的资助。

第 103 条　公共利益公司的设立

公共利益公司应当按照［商事公司法关于公司设立的条款］设立，但公司章程必须声明其是公共利益公司。

评论：

本条规定了新设公司可以选择成为一家公共利益公司。已成立的公司可以根据第 104 条的规定转换为公共利益公司。

本章只适用于州内的商事公司。外国的商事公司如在其母国拥有与本章规定的公共利益公司相似的形态，则不受本章规定的调整，而只是依据美国各州的商事公司法拥有外国商事公司的地位。

本条所称的“公共利益公司”的定义规定在第 102 条中。

第 104 条　公共利益公司的形态选择

（a）修改公司章程。——已成立的商事公司可依据［本章］规定转换为公共利益公司，除满足［商事公司法有关公司章程所需内容］的要求外，还需修改公司章程，作出该公司为公共利益公司的声明。公司章程的修改应满足最低表决要求才能生效。

to be effective, the amendment must be adopted by at least the minimum status vote.

(b) **Fundamental transactions.**

(1) Except as provided in paragraph (2), if a domestic entity that is not a benefit corporation is a party to a merger[, consolidation, or conversion] [or the exchanging entity in a share exchange] and the surviving[, new, or resulting] entity in the merger, [consolidation, conversion, or share exchange] is to be a benefit corporation, the [plan of] merger[, consolidation, conversion, or share exchange] must be [adopted] [approved] by the domestic entity by at least the minimum status vote.

(2) Paragraph (1) does not apply in the case of a corporation that is a party to a merger if the shareholders of the corporation are not entitled to vote on the merger pursuant to [cite section of the business corporation law authorizing "short form" mergers].

Comment:

This section provides the procedures for an existing corporation to become a benefit corporation. A corporation that is being newly formed may become a benefit corporation in the manner provided in section 103. Subsection (a) applies to a business corporation that is directly electing to be a benefit corporation by amending its articles of incorporation. Subsection (b) applies when a corporation is becoming a benefit corporation indirectly in the context of a fundamental transaction. In both cases, the change to benefit corporation status must be approved by at least the minimum status vote.

Subsection (b) also applies to a domestic entity that is not a corporation when the entity is a party to a transaction that will result in a benefit corporation. In those situations, a supermajority vote of the owners of the entity is required by subsection (b).

See section 201(d) with respect to changing the identification of a specific public benefit that it is the purpose of a benefit corporation to pursue.

The following terms used in this section are defined in section 102:

"benefit corporation"

"minimum status vote"

§105. Termination of benefit corporation status.

(a) **Amendment.** – A benefit corporation may terminate its status as such and cease to be subject to this [chapter] by amending its articles of incorporation to delete the provision required by section 103 or 104 to be stated in the articles of a benefit corporation. In order to be effective, the amendment must be adopted by at least the minimum status vote.

(b) **Fundamental transactions.** –

(1) Except as provided in paragraph (2), if a [plan of] merger[, consolidation, conversion, or share exchange] would have the effect of terminating the status of a business corporation as a benefit corporation, the [plan] [transaction] must be adopted by at least the minimum status vote in order to be effective.

（b）**重大交易**

（1）除第（2）项的规定外，如果一家本州非公共利益公司是兼并［合并或财产转换］的一方，［或者是股权置换中的一方］，并且在该兼并［合并、财产转换或股权置换］中存续［新设或留存］的实体属公共利益公司，那么此等兼并［合并、财产转换或股权置换］的［计划］须满足最低表决要求才能采用［获准］。

（2）第（1）项不适用于兼并一方的股东根据［商事公司法“简易合并”条款］无权投票的情形。

评论：

本条规定了已成立的公司转换为公共利益公司的程序。新设公司可以根据第103条的规定成为公共利益公司。本条的第（a）款适用于通过修改公司章程选择成为公共利益公司的商事公司。本条的第（b）款适用于通过重大交易间接成为公共利益公司的商事公司。这两种情形中，公司形态向公共利益公司的转换都须满足最低表决要求。

本条的第（b）款同样适用于参与产生公共利益公司交易之前的非公司实体。在这种情况下，第（b）款要求绝对多数的股东投票通过。

参见第201（d）款有关公共利益公司改变作为公司目的的某项特定公共利益的规定。

本节以下用语的定义参见第102条：

“公共利益公司”

“最低表决要求”

第105条　公共利益公司形态的终止

（a）**修改公司章程**。——公共利益公司可通过删除第103条或第104条规定的在公司章程中其作为公共利益公司的声明来终止其公共利益公司的形态并不再受［本章］规定调整。公司章程的修改应满足最低表决要求。

（b）**重大交易**。——

（1）除第（2）项的规定外，如果兼并［合并、财产转换或股权置换］［计划］有终止商事公司作为公共利益公司的效力，该计划［交易］应满足最低表决要求。

(2) Paragraph (1) does not apply in the case of a corporation that is a party to a merger if the shareholders of the corporation are not entitled to vote on the merger pursuant to [cite section of the business corporation law authorizing "short form" mergers].

(3) Any sale, lease, exchange, or other disposition of all or substantially all of the assets of a benefit corporation, unless the transaction is in the usual and regular course of business, shall not be effective unless the transaction is approved by at least the minimum status vote.

Comment:

This section provides the procedures for a benefit corporation to terminate voluntarily its status as a benefit corporation. As with an election of benefit corporation status under section 104, the termination may be accomplished either directly by an amendment of the articles or indirectly through a fundamental transaction.

Subsection (b)(3) provides a special rule for a sale of all or substantially all of the assets of a benefit corporation. Such a transaction will not result in a termination of the status of the corporation as a benefit corporation, but will have effectively the same result since it will terminate the operations of the business. Thus it was considered appropriate to require approval of a sale of assets by the minimum status vote. Whether a sale of assets is in the usual and regular course will be determined under the same standards as apply to that question under the state's business corporation law. See, e.g., Model Business Corporation Act §§12.01 and 12.02.

The following terms used in this section are defined in section 102:

"benefit corporation"

"minimum status vote"

Subchapter 2
Corporate Purpose

Section

201. Corporate purposes.

§201. Corporate purposes.

(a) **General public benefit purpose**. – A benefit corporation shall have a purpose of creating general public benefit. This purpose is in addition to its purpose under [cite section of the business corporation law on the purpose of business corporations].

(b) **Optional specific public benefit purpose**. – The articles of incorporation of a benefit corporation may identify one or more specific public benefits that it is the purpose of the benefit corporation to create in addition to its purposes under [cite section of the business corporation law on the purpose of business corporations] and subsection (a). The identification of a specific public benefit under this subsection does not limit the purpose of

（2）如合并一方的股东根据［商事公司法“简易合并”条款］无权投票，则第（1）项不适用于此情形。

（3）除正常商业往来外，公共利益公司的任何出售、出租、交换或者其他处置全部或主要财产的行为，须满足最低表决要求。

评论：
本条规定了公共利益公司自愿终止的程序。例如，第104条规定了公共利益公司的形态选择程序，公共利益公司的终止通过直接修改公司章程或间接进行实质交易的方式达成。

第（b）（3）项为出售公共利益公司全部或大部分财产的行为的特殊规则。此种交易不会导致公共利益公司状态的终止，但是由于其终止了公司的运营，与公司的终止有相同的效果。因此，该行为要求满足最低表决要求使资产出售生效具有合理性。判断交易是否为正常商业往来适用美国各州商事公司法的评判标准。例如，美国《示范商事公司法》第12.01条和第12.02条的规定。

本节以下用语的定义参见第102条：
“公共利益公司”
“最低表决要求”

第2节
公司目的

条款
第201条　公司目的

第201条　公司目的
（a）**一般公共利益目的**。——公共利益公司应当有服务于一般公共利益的目的。此目的在［商事公司法公司目的条款］之外。

（b）**选择性的特定公共利益目的**。——公共利益公司的章程可以在［商事公司法公司目的条款和］第（a）款外确定一项或多项特定公共利益目的。依据本款设定的特定公共利益目的并不限制公共利益公司在第（a）款规定下设定一般公共利益目的。

a benefit corporation to create general public benefit under subsection (a).

(c) **Effect of purposes.** – The creation of general public benefit and specific public benefit under subsections (a) and (b) is in the best interests of the benefit corporation.

(d) **Amendment.** – A benefit corporation may amend its articles of incorporation to add, amend, or delete the identification of a specific public benefit that it is the purpose of the benefit corporation to create. In order to be effective, the amendment must be adopted by at least the minimum status vote.

(e) **Professional corporations.** – A professional corporation that is a benefit corporation does not violate [cite section of professional corporation law, if any, that restricts the business in which a professional corporation may engage] by having the purpose to create general public benefit or a specific public benefit.

Comment:

Every benefit corporation has the corporate purpose of creating general public benefit. A benefit corporation may also elect to pursue specific public benefits under subsection (b).

Subsection (c) confirms that pursuing general and specific public benefit is in the best interests of the benefit corporation. Because the basic duty of a director is to act in a manner that the director reasonably believes to be in the best interests of the corporation, decisions by the board of directors that promote the creation of general or specific public benefit will satisfy the requirement to act in the best interests of the corporation. If an ordinary business corporation includes in its articles of incorporation a statement of a specific purpose, it is by definition in the best interests of the corporation for the directors to pursue that purpose. Thus the rule in subsection (c) would be the case in any event with respect to specific public benefit purposes, but specific public benefits have been referred to expressly in subsection (c) to avoid the confusion that might result if subsection (c) only referred to the creation of general public benefit.

Some professional corporation statutes provide that a professional corporation may not engage in any business other than rendering the professional service for which it was specifically incorporated. Subsection (e) makes clear that such a limitation will not interfere with a professional corporation electing to be a benefit corporation. In such a case, the professional corporation (such as a law firm, accounting firm, or medical practice) will be limited to providing the professional services for which it was incorporated, but it will be able to provide those services in a manner that creates general public benefit or a specific public benefit (for example, a medical practice that focuses on providing care for low–income individuals).

The following terms used in this section are defined in section 102:

"benefit corporation"

"general public benefit"

（c）**目的效力**。——依据第（a）款和第（b）款规定创设的一般和特定公共利益为公共利益公司最佳利益。

（d）**修改公司章程**。——公共利益公司可以增加、修改或删除公司章程中设定的特定公共利益目的。公司对章程的修改需满足最低表决要求。

（e）**专业公司**。——选择公共利益形态的专业公司并不因其有创设一般或特定公共利益的目的的行为而违反［商事公司法关于专业性公司营业范围的限制］。

评论：

每个公共利益公司都应创设一般公共利益的公司目的。公共利益公司可根据第（b）款的规定选择特定的公共利益目的。

第（c）款规定了一般公共利益目的和特定公共利益目的属于公共利益公司的最佳利益。公司董事最基本的义务是能合理地为公司的最佳利益行事，因此，董事会作出的符合一般公共利益目的和特定公共利益目的的行为，即符合公司最佳利益的行事标准。如果一家普通商事公司的公司章程中包含特定目的，那么公司董事为该目的的实现而行事就符合公司的最佳利益。因此，第（c）款的规定在任何履行特定公共利益目的的情况下都适用，但是第（c）款中明确提及了特定公共利益，以避免只提及一般公共利益可能造成的问题。

某些有关专业公司的法律规定，专业公司不能从事其设立时确定的专业服务以外的服务。第（e）款明确了该规定不会影响专业公司转变为公共利益公司。在这种情形下，专业公司（如律师事务所、会计师事务所或者医疗机构）将被限制只能从事其设立时确定的专业服务，但是该类公司可以通过创造一般公共利益或特定公共利益的方式提供其他服务（例如，一家医疗机构可向低收入个体提供救助）。

本节以下用语的定义参见第 102 条：

“公共利益公司”

“一般公共利益”

"minimum status vote"
"specific public benefit"

Subchapter 3
Accountability

Section
301. Standard of conduct for directors.
302. Benefit director.
303. Standard of conduct for officers.
304. Benefit officer.
305. Right of action.

§301. Standard of conduct for directors.

(a) **Consideration of interests.** – In discharging the duties of their respective positions and in considering the best interests of the benefit corporation, the board of directors, committees of the board, and individual directors of a benefit corporation:

(1) shall consider the effects of any action or inaction upon:

(i) the shareholders of the benefit corporation;

(ii) the employees and work force of the benefit corporation, its subsidiaries, and its suppliers;

(iii) the interests of customers as beneficiaries of the general public benefit or specific public benefit purposes of the benefit corporation;

(iv) community and societal factors, including those of each community in which offices or facilities of the benefit corporation, its subsidiaries, or its suppliers are located;

(v) the local and global environment;

(vi) the short–term and long–term interests of the benefit corporation, including benefits that may accrue to the benefit corporation from its long–term plans and the possibility that these interests may be best served by the continued independence of the benefit corporation; and

(vii) the ability of the benefit corporation to accomplish its general public benefit purpose and any specific public benefit purpose; and

(2) may consider:

[(i) the interests referred to in [cite constituencies provision of the business corporation law if it refers to constituencies not listed above]; and (ii)] other pertinent factors or the interests of any other group that they deem appropriate; but

(3) need not give priority to a particular interest or factor referred to in paragraph (1) or (2) over any other interest or factor unless the benefit corporation has stated in its articles

“最低表决要求”

“特定公共利益”

第3节
公司责任

条款

第301条　董事行为标准
第302条　公共利益董事
第303条　高管行为标准
第304条　公共利益高管
第305条　诉讼权利

第301条　董事行为标准

（a）**利益的考虑。**——在履行各自职责和考虑公共利益公司最佳利益时，公共利益公司的董事会、董事委员会和董事：

（1）其作为或不作为，应当考虑其行为对以下对象的影响：

（i）公共利益公司的股东；

（ii）公共利益公司雇员及其子公司和供应商；

（iii）作为公共利益公司一般或特定公共利益受益者的消费者的利益；

（iv）社区和社会因素，包括公共利益公司及其子公司或供应商办公地或设施所在地的社区；

（v）当地和全球环境；

（vi）公共利益公司的短期和长期利益，包括公共利益公司可能从其长期计划中获得的利益，以及公共利益公司继续保持独立可能产生的最佳利益；以及

（vii）公共利益公司实现其一般和特定公共利益目的的能力；以及

（2）可供参考的其他因素：

[（i）（以上条款虽未涉及，但在商事公司法其他利益相关者条款中所涉及的）利益；以及（ii）] 董事认为合适的其他相关因素或其他群体的利益；但是

（3）除公司章程中赋予特定利益或因素以优先权外，无须给予第（1）项或第（2）项中某个利益或因素优先权。

of incorporation its intention to give priority to certain interests or factors related to the accomplishment of its general public benefit purpose or of a specific public benefit purpose identified in its articles.

(b) **Coordination with other provisions of law**. – The consideration of interests and factors in the manner provided by subsection (a)[:

(1)] does not constitute a violation of [cite provision of the business corporation law on the duties of directors generally] [; and

(2) is in addition to the ability of directors to consider interests and factors as provided in [cite constituencies provision of the business corporation law]].

(c) **Exoneration from personal liability**. – Except as provided in the [articles of incorporation] [bylaws], a director is not personally liable for monetary damages for:

(1) any action or inaction in the course of performing the duties of a director under subsection (a) if the director performed the duties of office in compliance with [cite provision of the business corporation law on the duties of directors generally] and this section; or

(2) failure of the benefit corporation to pursue or create general public benefit or specific public benefit.

(d) **Limitation on standing**. – A director does not have a duty to a person that is a beneficiary of the general public benefit purpose or a specific public benefit purpose of a benefit corporation arising from the status of the person as a beneficiary.

(e) **Business judgments**. – A director who makes a business judgment in good faith fulfills the duty under this section if the director:

(1) is not interested in the subject of the business judgment;

(2) is informed with respect to the subject of the business judgment to the extent the director reasonably believes to be appropriate under the circumstances; and

(3) rationally believes that the business judgment is in the best interests of the benefit corporation.

Comment:

This section is at the heart of what it means to be a benefit corporation. By requiring the consideration of interests of constituencies other than the shareholders, the section rejects the holdings in Dodge v. Ford, 170 N.W. 668 (Mich. 1919), and eBay Domestic Holdings, Inc. v. Newmark, 16 A.3d 1 (Del. Ch. 2010), that directors must maximize the financial value of a corporation.

In a state that has adopted a "constituency statute" directors are authorized to consider the interests of corporate constituencies other than the shareholders, but the directors are not required to do so. Subsection (a) makes it mandatory for the directors of a benefit corporation to consider the interests and factors that they would otherwise simply be permitted to consider in their discretion under the typical constituency statute.

（b）**与其他法律条款的协调**。——对第（a）款中利益和相关因素的考虑［：

（1）］不构成对［商事公司法中董事责任条款］的违反［；并且

（2）是在董事考虑［商事公司法利益相关者条款］规定的利益和相关因素的能力之外。构成［商事公司法利益相关者条款］规定的董事所应考虑利益范围的补充。

（c）**个人责任的免除**。——除［公司章程］［章程细则］另有明确规定外，董事不对以下行为负损害赔偿责任：

（1）依据第（a）款规定履行董事责任的任何作为或不作为，例如，该行为符合［商事公司法董事责任条款］及本条的规定；或者

（2）公共利益公司未能追求或创造一般或特定公共利益。

（d）**董事责任限制**。——董事不对公共利益公司一般或特定社会目的的受益人负责。

（e）**商业判断**。——如果董事的行为满足以下要求，善意进行商业判断的董事被视为已履行本节所规定的义务：

（1）在商业判断过程中不涉及个人利益；

（2）拥有使其在该情形下作出合理商业判断的充分信息；以及

（3）有合理理由认为该商业判断符合公共利益公司的最佳利益。

评论：

本条是形塑公共利益公司的关键。本条通过要求公共利益公司考虑股东以外的利益相关者的利益，推翻了 Dodge v. Ford 案和 eBay Domestic Holdings， Inc. v. Newmark 案中的裁决，即董事必须使公司经济价值最大化。

在颁布了“利益相关者法律”的州，董事被授权可以考虑股东之外的公司利益相关者的利益，但这并不是强制性规定。第（a）款则要求公共利益公司的董事必须考虑在普通商事公司法中可选择性考虑的利益和因素。

Subsection (d) negates any enforceable duty of directors to non–shareholder constituents. But see section 305(b) which permits a benefit corporation to provide in its articles that an identified category of persons may bring a benefit enforcement proceeding. If a benefit corporation were to do so, the identified non–shareholder constituents would be able to allege a breach of duty by the directors under this chapter for failing to pursue or create general or specific public benefit, but subsection (d) would prevent those constituents from alleging a breach of duty to them.

Subsection (e) confirms that the business judgment rule applies to actions by directors under this section. The formulation of the rule is patterned after American Law Institute, Principles of Corporate Governance: Analysis and Recommendations §4.01(c). If the law of the enacting state is not clear that the business judgment rule applies generally to actions by directors of corporations that are not business corporations, consideration should be given to confirming that the rule applies more broadly than just under this chapter. The best interests of the corporation referred to in subsection (e)(3) include the creation of general public benefit and specific public benefit as provided in section 201(c) and the determination of what is in the best interests of the benefit corporation requires consideration of the interests and factors listed in subsection (a).

The following terms used in this section are defined in section 102:

"benefit corporation"

"general public benefit"

"specific public benefit"

"Subsidiary"

§302. Benefit director.

(a) **General rule**. – The board of directors of a benefit corporation that is a publicly traded corporation shall, and the board of any other benefit corporation may, include a director, who:

(1) shall be designated the benefit director; and

(2) shall have, in addition to the powers, duties, rights, and immunities of the other directors of the benefit corporation, the powers, duties, rights, and immunities provided in this [chapter].

(b) **Election, removal, and qualifications**. – The benefit director shall be elected, and may be removed, in the manner provided by [cite provisions of the business corporation law on the election and removal of directors generally]. [Except as provided in subsection (f),] the benefit director shall be an individual who is independent. The benefit director may serve as the benefit officer at the same time as serving as the benefit director. The articles of incorporation or bylaws of a benefit corporation may prescribe additional qualifications of the benefit director not inconsistent with this subsection.

第（d）款否认了任何董事对非股东利益相关者负有可被强制执行的义务。但是第 305（b）款允许公共利益公司在其公司章程中明确某一类群体可以提起公共利益诉讼。如果公共利益公司在公司章程中有明确规定，则该类利益相关者可以对根据本章规定未能追求或创造一般或特定公共利益而违反董事责任的董事提起诉讼，但第（d）款限制这些利益相关者提起违反董事责任的诉讼。

第（e）款明确规定，董事商业判断规则适用于依据本条规定提起的诉讼。本规则参照美国法律研究所发布的《公司治理原则：分析和建议》第 4.01（c）款规定制定。如果美国各州不能明确商业判断规则是否适用于非商事公司的董事，需确认商业判断规则更广泛地适用于本章之外。第（e）（3）项中公司的最佳利益包括依据第 201（c）款创造一般或特定公共利益，在决定何为公司的最佳利益时需考虑本条第（a）款列明的利益和因素。

本节以下用语的定义参见第 102 条：
“公共利益公司”
“一般公共利益”
“特定公共利益”
“子公司”

第 302 条　公共利益董事

（a）**一般规则**。——上市的公共利益公司以及其他形式的公共利益公司的董事会，需包含满足以下要求的董事：

（1）被任命为公共利益董事；并且

（2）除拥有公共利益公司的其他董事的权力、义务、权利和豁免权以外，还有［本章］规定的权力、义务、权利和豁免权。

（b）**任免和资格**。——公共利益董事应当依据［商事公司法董事选任条款］的规定任免。［除第（f）款规定外，］公共利益董事应为独立个体。公共利益董事可同时担任公共利益高管。公共利益公司的章程或章程细则可对公共利益董事的资格作出与本条不一致的规定。

(c) **Annual compliance statement**. – The benefit director shall prepare, and the benefit corporation shall include in the annual benefit report to shareholders required by section 401, the opinion of the benefit director on all of the following:

(1) Whether the benefit corporation acted in accordance with its general public benefit purpose and any specific public benefit purpose in all material respects during the period covered by the report.

(2) Whether the directors and officers complied with sections 301(a) and 303(a), respectively.

(3) If, in the opinion of the benefit director, the benefit corporation or its directors or officers failed to act or comply in the manner described in paragraphs (1) and (2), a description of the ways in which the benefit corporation or its directors or officers failed to act or comply.

(d) **Status of actions**. – The act or inaction of an individual in the capacity of a benefit director shall constitute for all purposes an act or inaction of that individual in the capacity of a director of the benefit corporation.

(e) **Exoneration from personal liability**. – Regardless of whether the articles of incorporation or bylaws of a benefit corporation include a provision eliminating or limiting the personal liability of directors authorized by [cite section of the business corporation law permitting exoneration of directors], a benefit director shall not be personally liable for an act or omission in the capacity of a benefit director unless the act or omission constitutes self–dealing, willful misconduct, or a knowing violation of law.

[(f) **Professional Corporations**. – The benefit director of a professional corporation does not need to be independent.]

Comment:

The statement of the benefit director required by subsection (c) is an important part of the transparency required under this chapter. The perspective of the benefit director on whether the corporation has been successful in pursuing its general and any named specific public benefit purpose will be an important source of information for the shareholders as to whether the directors have adequately discharged their stewardship of the benefit corporation and its resources.

Subsection (d) makes clear that the actions of a benefit director are actions of a director of the benefit corporation and are subject to the same standards as actions of directors generally.

The wording of subsection (e) should be conformed to the provision of the state's business corporation law that permits the shareholders to adopt a provision of the articles of incorporation or bylaws exonerating directors from liability for breach of duty. But unlike existing exoneration provisions, subsection (e) does not require the benefit corporation

（c）**年度合规声明**。——公共利益董事应当编写其对以下事项的意见，公共利益公司应当根据第 401 条的规定将其附于年度公共利益报告中供股东查阅：

（1）在报告所述时间内，公共利益公司是否在所有重要事项上依一般和特定公共利益目的行事。

（2）董事和高管是否分别依第 301（a）款和第 303（a）款的规定行事。

（3）若公共利益董事认为公共利益公司或其董事、高管未能依第（1）项和第（2）项的要求行事，应陈述公共利益公司或其董事、高管未能履行责任的情况。

（d）**行为效力归属**。——公共利益董事在职权范围内的个人作为或不作为应视为公共利益公司董事的行为。

（e）**个人责任免除**。——无论公共利益公司章程或章程细则是否依据［商事公司法董事责任免除条款的规定］删除或限制董事的个人责任，公共利益董事在行使职责时不对其任何作为或不作为承担个人责任，但自我交易或故意违法行为除外。

［（f）**专业性公司**。——对专业公司的公共利益董事的独立性不作要求。］

评论：

第（c）款规定的公共利益董事陈述是本章透明度要求的一个重要组成部分。公共利益董事对公司是否追求其一般和任何其他声明的特定公共利益目的的意见，为股东判断董事是否适当地履行了其管理人责任的重要信息来源。

第（d）款明确规定了公共利益董事的个人行为等同于公共利益公司董事的行为，并普遍地适用董事的行为准则。

第（e）款的表述应当符合美国各州商事公司法的规定，此类规定允许股东通过公司章程或章程细则对违反董事义务的责任进行豁免。但是与现有的豁免条款不同，第（e）款并未要求公共利益公司在公司章程或章程细则中增加此条款。第（e）款规定的免责条款自动适用于所有公共利益董事。

to adopt an implementing provision in the articles or bylaws. Instead the liability shield provided by subsection (e) automatically applies to all benefit directors.

The following terms used in this section are defined in section 102:

"benefit corporation"

"benefit director"

"benefit officer"

"general public benefit"

"independent"

"publicly traded corporation"

"specific public benefit"

§303. Standard of conduct for officers.

(a) **General rule.** – Each officer of a benefit corporation shall consider the interests and factors described in section 301(a)(1) in the manner provided in section 301(a)(3) if:

(1) the officer has discretion to act with respect to a matter; and

(2) it reasonably appears to the officer that the matter may have a material effect on the creation by the benefit corporation of general public benefit or a specific public benefit identified in the articles of incorporation of the benefit corporation.

(b) **Coordination with other provisions of law.** – The consideration of interests and factors in the manner provided in subsection (a) shall not constitute a violation of [cite provision, if any, of the business corporation law on the duties of officers] [the duties of an officer].

(c) **Exoneration from personal liability.** – Except as provided in the [articles of incorporation] [bylaws], an officer is not personally liable for monetary damages for:

(1) an action or inaction as an officer in the course of performing the duties of an officer under subsection (a) if the officer performed the duties of the position in compliance with [cite provision of the business corporation law on the duties of officers] [the duties of an officer] and this section; or

(2) failure of the benefit corporation to pursue or create general public benefit or specific public benefit.

(d) **Limitation on standing.** – An officer does not have a duty to a person that is a beneficiary of the general public benefit purpose or a specific public benefit purpose of a benefit corporation arising from the status of the person as a beneficiary.

(e) **Business judgments.** – An officer who makes a business judgment in good faith fulfills the duty under this section if the officer:

(1) is not interested in the subject of the business judgment;

(2) is informed with respect to the subject of the business judgment to the extent the officer reasonably believes to be appropriate under the circumstances; and

本节以下用语的定义参见第 102 条：
“公共利益公司”
“公共利益董事”
“公共利益高管”
“一般公共利益”
“独立”
“上市公司”

第 303 条 高管行为标准

（a）**一般规则**。——公共利益公司高管应以第 301（a）（3）项中规定的行为标准考虑第 301（a）（1）项中规定的利益和因素，如果：

（1）高管就该行为有自由裁量权；以及

（2）高管有合理理由认为该行为对公共利益公司在章程中创设的一般或特定公共利益有实质性影响。

（b）**与其他法律条款的协调**。——对第（a）款中利益和相关因素的考虑不违反［商事公司法中的高管责任条款的规定］。

（c）**个人责任的免除**。——除［公司章程］［章程细则］中另有规定外，高管不对以下行为承担损害赔偿责任：

（1）依据第（a）款规定履行高管责任过程中的任何作为或者不作为，如果该行为符合［商事公司法高管责任条款］及本条的规定。或者

（2）公共利益公司未能追求或创造一般或特定公共利益的行为。

（d）**高管责任限制**。——高管不对公共利益公司一般或特定公共利益目的的受益人负责。

（e）**商业判断**。——如果董事的行为满足以下要求，善意进行商业判断的董事则视为已履行本条所规定的义务：

（1）在商业判断过程中不涉及个人利益；

（2）拥有使其在该情形下作出合理商业判断的充分信息；

(3) rationally believes that the business judgment is in the best interests of the benefit corporation.

Comment:

As an agent of the corporation, an officer is generally required to follow the instructions of his or her principal. But in those instances where an officer has discretion to act with a respect to a matter, subsection (a) requires the officer to consider the interests of the benefit corporation's constituencies in the same manner as required of the directors by section 301.

This section applies to all of the officers of a benefit corporation and is not limited just to the benefit officer, if any, of the benefit corporation.

Subsection (c) provides an exoneration from personal liability for officers similar to the exoneration provided for directors. If the law of the enacting state is not clear that officers can be exonerated in the same manner as directors, consideration should be given to confirming that officers of business corporations that are not benefit corporations may be exonerated. See also the Comment to section 301(d) with respect to subsection (d).

Subsection (e) confirms that the business judgment rule applies to actions by officers under this section. The formulation of the rule is patterned after American Law Institute, Principles of Corporate Governance: Analysis and Recommendations § 4.01(c). If the law of the enacting state is not clear that the business judgment rule applies generally to actions by officers of corporations that are not business corporations, consideration should be given to confirming that the rule applies more broadly than just under this chapter. The best interests of the corporation referred to in subsection (e)(3) include the creation of general public benefit and specific public benefit under section 201(c) and the determination of what is in the best interests of the benefit corporation requires consideration of the interests and factors listed in section 301(a) (as provided by subsection (a)).

The following terms used in this section are defined in section 102:

"benefit corporation"

"benefit officer"

"general public benefit"

"specific public benefit"

§304. Benefit officer.

(a) **Designation.** – A benefit corporation may have an officer designated the benefit officer.

(b) **Functions.** – A benefit officer shall have:

(1) the powers and duties relating to the purpose of the corporation to create general public benefit or specific public benefit provided:

(i) by the bylaws; or

(ii) absent controlling provisions in the bylaws, by resolution or order of the board of

（3）有合理理由认为该商业判断符合公共利益公司的最佳利益。

评论：

作为公司的代理人，高管普遍地被要求遵守上级指令。但是当高管有权依行为标准行使自由裁量权时，第（a）款要求高管依第 301 条规定的董事行为准则来考虑公共利益公司其他利益相关者的利益。

本条适用于公共利益公司所有的高管，并不仅限于公共利益公司的公共利益高管。

第（c）款规定了与董事责任豁免类似的高管个人责任豁免。如果美国各州立法未明确规定高管责任可像董事责任一样免除，需确认非公共利益公司的商事公司的高管是可以被豁免的，参见第 301（d）款中对第（d）款的评论。

第（e）款确认了在本条下商业判断规则适用于高管。本规则参照美国法律研究所发布的《公司治理原则：分析和建议》第 4.01（c）条制定。在美国，如果各州法律没有明确规定商业判断规则是否普遍适用于非商事公司的公司高管，则应考虑确认该规则的适用范围比本章规定的范围更广。第（e）（3）项中公司的最佳利益包括依据第 201（c）款设定的一般公共利益和特定公共利益，在决定何为公司的最佳利益时需考虑本条第（a）款列明的利益和因素。

本节以下用语的定义参见第 102 条：

"公共利益公司"

"公共利益高管"

"一般公共利益"

"特定公共利益"

第 304 条　公共利益高管

（a）**任命**。——公共利益公司可以将高管任命为公共利益高管。

（b）**职能**。——公共利益高管应当有：

（1）规定于以下文件的创设一般或特定公共利益目的的权力和义务：

（i）公司章程细则；或者

（ii）在公司章程细则中没有规定时，董事会的决议或者命令。

directors.

(2) the duty to prepare the benefit report required by section 401.

Comment:

The designation of a benefit officer is optional. But if a benefit officer is designated, one of the duties of that officer will be to prepare the annual benefit report required by section 401.

The following terms used in this section are defined in section 102:

"benefit corporation"

"benefit officer"

"general public benefit"

"specific public benefit"

§305. Right of action.

(a) **General rule**. – Except in a benefit enforcement proceeding, no person may bring an action or assert a claim against a benefit corporation or its directors or officers with respect to:

(1) failure to pursue or create general public benefit or a specific public benefit set forth in its articles of incorporation; or

(2) violation of an obligation, duty, or standard of conduct under this [chapter].

(b) **Limitation on liability of corporation**. – A benefit corporation shall not be liable for monetary damages under this [chapter] for any failure of the benefit corporation to pursue or create general public benefit or a specific public benefit.

(c) **Standing**. – A benefit enforcement proceeding may be commenced or maintained only:

(1) directly by the benefit corporation; or

(2) derivatively [in accordance with [cite sections of business corporation law on derivative suits]] by:

(i) a person or group of persons that owned beneficially or of record at least 2% of the total number of shares of a class or series outstanding at the time of the act or omission complained of;

(ii) a director;

(iii) a person or group of persons that owned beneficially or of record 5% or more of the outstanding equity interests in an entity of which the benefit corporation is a subsidiary at the time of the act or omission complained of; or

(iv) other persons as specified in the articles of incorporation or bylaws of the benefit corporation.

(d) **Beneficial ownership**. – For purposes of this section, a person is the beneficial owner of shares or equity interests if the shares or equity interests are held in a voting trust

（2）第 401 条要求的编写公共利益报告的义务。

评论：

公共利益高管的任命是可选择的。但是如果公共利益高管被任命，其义务包括编写第 401 条要求的公共利益报告。

本节以下用语的定义参见第 102 条：

“公共利益公司”

“公共利益高管”

“一般公共利益”

“特定公共利益”

第 305 条　诉讼权利

（a）**一般规则**。——非经公共利益实施程序，任何人不得因以下事项向公共利益公司或者其董事、高管提起诉讼或提起主张：

（1）未能追求或创造其在公司章程中陈述的一般或特定公共利益；

（2）违反［本章］规定下的责任、义务或行为标准。

（b）**公司责任的限制**。——公共利益公司不对［本章］规定下任何未能追求或创造一般或特定公共利益的行为承担损害赔偿责任。

（c）**诉讼资格**。——下列情形中，仅以下主体可提起公共利益实施程序：

（1）由公共利益公司直接提起；或者

（2）依据［商事公司法派生诉讼条款］的规定，由以下主体派生提起：

（i）在被诉作为或不作为发生时，持有公共利益公司 2% 以上已发行的某类别或系列股份的个人或群体；

（ii）董事；

（iii）在被诉作为或不作为行为发生时，持有公共利益公司母公司 5% 以上已发行股份的登记股东或实际受益人；或者

（iv）公共利益公司章程或章程细则中规定的其他人员。

（d）**实益所有权**。——为实现本章目的，若股份或者股利由表决权信托或指定第三人代持时，将此人视为该股份和股利的实益所有权人。

or by a nominee on behalf of the beneficial owner.

Comment:

Standing in an action against the directors or officers of a business corporation that is not a benefit corporation for breach of duty is limited in most states just to the corporation or shareholders bringing a derivative suit. This section broadens the categories of persons that can bring a derivative suit to include directors, 5% owners of a parent entity, and other persons to which a benefit corporation grants standing in its articles of incorporation or bylaws. To reduce the possibility of nuisance suits, a shareholder or group of shareholders bringing a derivative suit must own at least 2% of the outstanding shares of the benefit corporation.

This section only applies to actions or claims arising under this chapter. Lawsuits for breaches of duty arising outside of this chapter, or for breach of contract by directors, officers, or the benefit corporation are not subject to this section.

The following terms used in this section are defined in section 102:

"benefit corporation"

"benefit enforcement proceeding"

"general public benefit"

"specific public benefit"

"subsidiary"

Subchapter 4
Transparency

Section

401. Preparation of annual benefit report.

402. Availability of annual benefit report.

§ 401. Preparation of annual benefit report.

(a) **Contents.** – A benefit corporation shall prepare an annual benefit report including all of the following:

(1) A narrative description of:

(i) The ways in which the benefit corporation pursued general public benefit during the year and the extent to which general public benefit was created.

(ii) Both:

(A) the ways in which the benefit corporation pursued a specific public benefit that the articles of incorporation state it is the purpose of the benefit corporation to create; and

(B) the extent to which that specific public benefit was created.

(iii) Any circumstances that have hindered the creation by the benefit corporation of

评论：

对非公共利益公司的商事公司的董事或高管违反职责的行为提起诉讼的权利，在大多数州只能由公司或股东通过派生诉讼行使。本节扩大了可以提起派生诉讼的群体范围，包括母公司 5% 的股权持有者和公共利益公司章程或章程细则中授权的其他人员。为了减少恶意诉讼，提起派生诉讼的股东必须拥有公共利益公司至少 2% 已发行的股份。

本条只适用于依本章规定提起的诉讼或主张。在本章规定之外因违反职责提起的诉讼，因董事、高管或公共利益公司违反合同责任提起的诉讼不受本条规定调整。

本节以下用语的定义参见第 102 条：

“公共利益公司”

“公共利益实施程序”

“一般公共利益”

“特定公共利益”

“子公司”

第 4 节
透明度

条款

第 401 条　年度公共利益报告的编写

第 402 条　年度公共利益报告的提供

第 401 条　年度公共利益报告的编写

（a）**内容**。——公共利益公司的年度公共利益报告应包括以下内容：

（1）对以下事项的说明：

（i）公共利益公司本年度实现一般公共利益的方法和一般公共利益实现的情况。

（ii）同时包括：

（A）公共利益公司追求公司章程中规定的特定公共利益的方法；以及

（B）该特定公共利益实现的情况。

（iii）阻碍公共利益公司创造一般和特定公共利益的情形；

general public benefit or specific public benefit.

(iv) The process and rationale for selecting or changing the third-party standard used to prepare the benefit report.

(2) An assessment of the overall social and environmental performance of the benefit corporation against a third-party standard:

(i) applied consistently with any application of that standard in prior benefit reports; or

(ii) accompanied by an explanation of the reasons for:

(A) any inconsistent application; or

(B) the change to that standard from the one used in the immediately prior report.

(3) The name of the benefit director and the benefit officer, if any, and the address to which correspondence to each of them may be directed.

(4) The compensation paid by the benefit corporation during the year to each director in the capacity of a director.

(5) The statement of the benefit director described in section 302(c).

(6) A statement of any connection between the organization that established the third-party standard, or its directors, officers or any holder of 5% or more of the governance interests in the organization, and the benefit corporation or its directors, officers or any holder of 5% or more of the outstanding shares of the benefit corporation, including any financial or governance relationship which might materially affect the credibility of the use of the third-party standard.

(b) **Change of benefit director.** – If, during the year covered by a benefit report, a benefit director resigned from or refused to stand for reelection to the position of benefit director, or was removed from the position of benefit director, and the benefit director furnished the benefit corporation with any written correspondence concerning the circumstances surrounding the resignation, refusal, or removal, the benefit report shall include that correspondence as an exhibit.

(c) **Audit not required.** – Neither the benefit report nor the assessment of the performance of the benefit corporation in the benefit report required by subsection (a)(2) needs to be audited or certified by a third party.

Comment:

A benefit corporation may change from year to year the standard it uses under subsection (a)(2) for assessing its performance. But if a benefit corporation uses the same standard for assessing its performance in more than one year, the standard must either be applied consistently or the benefit corporation must provide an explanation of the reasons for any inconsistent use of the standard.

Subsection (b) is patterned after Item 5.02(a)(2) of Form 8-K under the Securities Exchange Act of 1934.

（iv）为编写公共利益报告而选择或更换第三方标准的程序和原因。

（2）依据第三方标准对公共利益公司的社会和环境表现的整体评价：

（i）沿用先前公共利益报告中使用的标准；或者
（ii）附一份说明以解释：
（A）适用的差异；或者
（B）与上一份报告中所用的标准相比，使用的标准的差异。
（3）公共利益董事和公共利益高管的姓名和联系地址。

（4）公共利益公司在上一年度支付给每位董事的薪酬。

（5）公共利益董事依第 302（c）款的规定应编写的陈述报告。
（6）设立第三方标准的组织或其董事、高管或 5% 以上管理权利的持有者与公共利益公司或其董事、高管或公共利益公司 5% 以上已发行股份持有者之间关系的声明，包括任何可能影响第三方标准可信度的财务或管理关系。

（b）**公共利益董事的变更**。——在公共利益报告年度内，如果公共利益董事辞职、拒绝连任或被免职，且该公共利益董事与公司有任何书面的涉及辞职、拒绝连任或免职的书信往来，公共利益报告应当将该书信往来的内容作为附件。

（c）**无须审计**。——公共利益报告和依据第（a）（2）项规定编写的公共利益报告中的公共利益公司表现评价书都无须经审计或第三方证明。

评论：
公共利益公司每年可根据第（a）（2）项更换不同的表现评价标准。但如果相同的标准连续使用超过一年，之后若停止对该标准的使用，则须提供未能持续使用的原因。

第（b）款是依据美国《1934 年证券交易法》的 8-K 表格的第 5.02（a）（2）项制定的。

The following terms used in this section are defined in section 102:

"benefit corporation"

"benefit director"

"general public benefit"

"specific public benefit"

"third-party standard"

§402. Availability of annual benefit report.

(a) **Timing of report.** – A benefit corporation shall send its annual benefit report to each shareholder on the earlier of:

(1) 120 days following the end of the fiscal year of the benefit corporation; or

(2) the same time that the benefit corporation delivers any other annual report to its shareholders.

(b) **Internet website posting.** – A benefit corporation shall post all of its benefit reports on the public portion of its Internet website, if any; but the compensation paid to directors and financial or proprietary information included in the benefit reports may be omitted from the benefit reports as posted.

(c) **Availability of copies.** – If a benefit corporation does not have an Internet website, the benefit corporation shall provide a copy of its most recent benefit report, without charge, to any person that requests a copy, but the compensation paid to directors and financial or proprietary information included in the benefit report may be omitted from the copy of the benefit report provided.

(d) **Filing of report.** – Concurrently with the delivery of the benefit report to shareholders under subsection (a), the benefit corporation shall deliver a copy of the benefit report to the [Secretary of State] for filing, but the compensation paid to directors and financial or proprietary information included in the benefit report may be omitted from the benefit report as delivered to the [Secretary of State]. The [Secretary of State] shall charge a fee of $__ for filing a benefit report.

Comment:

Subsection (b) requires a benefit corporation to post all of its annual benefit reports on its website, but subsection (c) only requires that the most recent benefit report be supplied if the benefit corporation does not have a website.

The term "benefit corporation" used in this section is defined in section 102.

"benefit corporation"

"benefit director"

本节以下用语的定义参见第 102 条：

"公共利益公司"

"公共利益董事"

"一般公共利益"

"特定公共利益"

"第三方标准"

第 402 条　年度公共利益报告的提供

（a）**报告的日期**。——公共利益公司应当在以下较早的日期内将公共利益报告送交各股东：

（1）公共利益公司财政年度结束后 120 天内；或者

（2）公共利益公司向其股东送交其他年度报告的同一时间。

（b）**网站发布**。——若条件允许，公共利益公司应当将其所有公共利益报告发布于其网站的公共部分；但可将公共利益报告中董事薪酬和财务、所有权信息删除。

（c）**副本的提供**。——如果公共利益公司没有网站，应向任何索取报告的个人免费提供最新公共利益报告的副本，但可将公共利益报告副本中的董事薪酬和财务、所有权信息删除。

（d）**报告备案**。——根据第（a）款的规定将公共利益报告提交给股东的同时，公共利益公司应当将该公共利益报告提交［州务卿］备案，但可将公共利益报告中董事薪酬和财务、所有权信息在提交［州务卿］的报告中予以删除。［州务卿］应收取 __ 美元作为备案费用。

评论：

第（b）款规定公共利益公司要将其所有公共利益报告上传网站，但是第（c）款规定在公共利益公司没有网站的情况下，可以仅提供最新的公共利益报告。

本节中"公共利益公司"的定义参见第 102 条。

"公共利益公司"

"公共利益董事"

THE STATE OF ARIZONA

Senate

Fifty-first Legislature

First Regular Session

2013

SENATE BILL 1238

Effective date December 31, 2014

AN ACT

AMENDING SECTIONS 10122 AND 101302,ARIZONA REVISED STATUTES; AMENDING TITLE 10, ARIZONA REVISED STATUTES, BY ADDING CHAPTER 22; RELATING TO BENEFIT CORPORATIONS.

Article 1. General Provisions

10-2401. Application and effect of chapter

A. This chapter is applicable to all benefit corporations.

B. The existence of a provision of this chapter does not of itself create an implication that a contrary or different rule of law is applicable to a business corporation that is not a benefit corporation. This chapter does not affect a statute or rule of law that is applicable to a business corporation that is not a benefit corporation.

C. Except as otherwise provided in this chapter, chapters 1, 2, 3, 4, 5, 6, 7, 8, 10, 11, 12, 13, 14, 15, 16 and 17 of this title are generally applicable to all benefit corporations. The specific provisions of this chapter control over the general provisions of chapters 1 through 17 of this title.

D. A benefit corporation may be subject simultaneously to this chapter and chapter 18 or 20 of this title. In that event, the provisions of this chapter control over chapter 18 or 20.

E. A provision of the articles of incorporation or bylaws of a benefit corporation may not

亚利桑那州

亚利桑那州参议院

第 51 届立法机关

第 1 次常规会议

2013 年

第 1238 号参议院议案

生效日 2014 年 12 月 31 日

该法案

修改了亚利桑那州修订法的第 10122 条和第 101302 条；通过增加第 22 章修订亚利桑那州修订法第 10 编；该部分与公共利益公司有关。

第一节 一般规定

第 10-2401 条 本章的适用和效力

A. 本章适用于所有公共利益公司。

B. 本章条款没有为非公共利益公司设定相反的或不同的规则。本章规定不影响非公共利益公司有关条文和规则的适用。

C. 除本章另有规定，本编的第 1、 2、 3、 4、5、6、7、8、10、11、12、13、14、15、16 章和第 17 章的规定适用于公共利益公司。本章特殊条款的效力优先于本编第 1 章至第 17 章的一般条款的效力。

D. 公共利益公司同时受本章和本编的第 18 章或第 20 章的规定调整。在此情况下，本章规定的效力优先于第 18 章或第 20 章的规定。

E. 公共利益公司的公司章程或附带条款不得违背或取代本章的条款。

limit, be inconsistent with or supersede a provision of this chapter.

10-2402. Definitions

In this chapter, unless the context otherwise requires:

1. "Benefit corporation" means a corporation that both:

(a) Has elected to become subject to this chapter.

(b) The status of which as a benefit corporation has not been terminated.

2. "Benefit enforcement proceeding" means any claim or action for either of the following:

(a) The failure of a benefit corporation to pursue or create general public benefit or a specific public benefit purpose set forth in its articles.

(b) A violation of any obligation, duty or standard of conduct under this chapter.

3. "General public benefit" means a material positive impact on society and the environment, taken as a whole, assessed against a third-party standard, from the business and operations of a benefit corporation.

4. "Minimum status vote" means:

(a) In the case of a business corporation, in addition to any other required approval or vote, the satisfaction of the following conditions:

(i) The shareholders of every class or series are entitled to vote as a separate voting group on the corporate action regardless of a limitation stated in the articles of incorporation or bylaws on the voting rights of any class or series.

(ii) The corporate action is approved by vote of the shareholders of each class or series entitled to cast at least two-thirds of the votes that all shareholders of the class or series are entitled to cast on the action.

(b) In the case of a domestic entity other than a business corporation, in addition to any other required approval, vote or consent, the satisfaction of the following conditions:

(i) The holders of every class or series of equity interest in the entity that are entitled to receive a distribution of any kind from the entity are entitled to vote on or consent to the action regardless of any otherwise applicable limitation on the voting or consent rights of any class or series.

(ii) The action is approved by vote or consent of the holders described in item (i) of this subdivision entitled to cast at least two-thirds of the votes or consents that all of those holders are entitled to cast on the action.

5. "Specific public benefit" includes:

(a) Providing low-income or underserved individuals or communities with beneficial products or services.

(b) Promoting economic opportunity for individuals or communities beyond the creation of jobs in the normal course of business.

第 10–2402 条　定义

本章中，除另有规定外：

1. “公共利益公司”是指符合以下条件的公司：

（a）选择接受本章规定调整。

（b）公共利益公司形态并未终止。

2. “公共利益实施程序”是指因以下行为产生的任何主张或诉讼：

（a）公共利益公司未能追求或实现公司章程规定的一般或特定公共利益目的。

（b）公司违反本章规定的任何义务、责任或行为标准。

3. “一般公共利益”是指根据第三方标准，公司的业务和经营在整体上对社会和环境产生的实质性积极影响。

4. “最低表决要求”是指：

（a）在商事公司中，除其他批准或表决的要求外，还应满足以下条件：

（i）每一类别或系列的股东有权作为一个独立的投票团体对公司行为进行投票，即使公司章程或章程细则对某一类别或系列股东作出限制。

（ii）公司行为必须获得每个类别或系列有投票权的所有股东至少 2/3 的投票才能通过。

（b）在本州的非商事公司实体中，除其他批准、表决或赞成的要求外，还应满足以下条件：

（i）该实体的每一类别或系列享有任何权益分配形式的股权持有者有权对公司行为进行投票，即使存在任何对该类别或系列股东的投票权限制。

（ii）公司行为必须获得本项第（i）目规定的有投票权的所有股东至少 2/3 的投票才能通过。

5. “特定公共利益”包括：

（a）向低收入、低福利人群或社区提供有益的产品或服务。

（b）在正常业务过程中向个人或社区提供创造就业之外的经济机会。

(c) Protecting or restoring the environment.

(d) Improving human health.

(e) Promoting the arts, sciences or advancement of knowledge.

(f) Increasing the flow of capital to entities with a purpose to benefit society or the environment.

(g) Conferring any other particular benefit on society or the environment as specified in the benefit corporation's articles of incorporation.

6. "Subsidiary" means, in relation to a person, an entity in which the person owns beneficially or of record fifty per cent or more of the outstanding equity interests.

7. "Supermajority status vote" means:

(a) For a business corporation, in addition to any other required approval or vote, the satisfaction of the following conditions:

(i) The shareholders of every class or series are entitled to vote as a separate voting group on the corporate action regardless of a limitation stated in the articles of incorporation or bylaws on the voting rights of any class or series.

(ii) The corporate action is approved by vote of the shareholders of each class or series entitled to cast at least three-fourths of the votes that all shareholders of the class or series are entitled to cast on the action.

(b) For a domestic entity other than a business corporation, in addition to any other required approval, vote or consent, the satisfaction of the following conditions:

(i) The holders of every class or series of equity interest in the entity that are entitled to receive a distribution of any kind from the entity are entitled to vote on or consent to the action regardless of any otherwise applicable limitation on the voting or consent rights of any class or series.

(ii) The action is approved by vote or consent of the holders described in item (i) of this subdivision entitled to cast at least three-fourths of the votes or consents that all of those holders are entitled to cast on the action.

8. "Third-party standard" means a recognized standard for defining, reporting and assessing corporate social and environmental performance that is:

(a) Comprehensive because it assesses the effect of a business and its operations on the interests listed in section 10-2431, subsection A, paragraph 1.

(b) Developed by an entity that is not controlled by the benefit corporation.

(c) Credible because it is developed by an entity that both:

(i) Has access to necessary expertise to assess overall corporate social and environmental performance.

(ii) Uses a balanced multistakeholder approach to develop the standard, including a reasonable public comment period.

（c）保护或修复环境。

（d）改善人类健康。

（e）促进艺术、科学或知识进步。

（f）促进资本向拥有有利于社会或环境目标的实体流动。

（g）给予公共利益公司章程中规定的关于社会或环境的其他特别利益。

6. “子公司”是指该实体 50% 以上已发行的股份的受益所有权或登记所有权被另一实体所拥有。

7. “绝大多数表决要求”是指：

（a）在商事公司中，除其他批准或表决的要求外，还应满足以下条件：

（i）每一类别或系列的股东有权作为一个独立的投票团体对公司行为进行投票，即使公司章程或章程细则对某一类别或系列股东作出了限制。

（ii）公司行为必须获得每个类别或系列有投票权的所有股东至少 3/4 的投票才能通过。

（b）在本州的非商事公司实体中，除其他批准、表决或赞成的要求外，还应满足以下条件：

（i）该实体的每一类别或系列享有任何权益分配形式的股权持有者有权对公司行为进行投票，即使存在任何对该类别或系列股东的投票权限制。

（ii）公司行为必须获得本项的第（i）目规定的有投票权的所有股东至少 3/4 的投票才能通过。

8. “第三方标准”是指用于定义、报告和评估公司社会和环境绩效的标准，其应满足以下条件：

（a）综合，根据第 10-2431 条第 A 款第 1 项中所列利益评估公司业务和经营绩效。

（b）独立，经非由公共利益公司控制的第三方实体制定。

（c）可信，该标准由满足以下条件的第三方实体制定：

（i）拥有评估公司社会和环境综合绩效所需的专业知识。

（ii）使用平衡多方利益相关者的方法制定标准，包括设定合理期间以听取公众意见。

(d) Transparent because the following information is publicly available about the standard:

(i) The criteria considered when measuring the overall social and environmental performance of a business.

(ii) The relative weightings, if any, of those criteria.

(e) Transparent because the following information is publicly available about the development and revision of the standard:

(i) The identity of the directors, officers, material owners and governing body of the entity that developed and controls revisions to the standard.

(ii) The process by which revisions to the standard and changes to the membership of the governing body are made.

(iii) An accounting of the revenue and sources of financial support for the entity, with sufficient detail to disclose any relationships that could reasonably be considered to present a potential conflict of interest.

10-2403. Incorporation of benefit corporation

A benefit corporation shall be incorporated in accordance with chapter 2, article 1 of this title, except that its articles of incorporation must also state that it is a benefit corporation.

10-2404. Election of benefit corporation status

A. An existing business corporation may become a benefit corporation under this chapter by amending its articles of incorporation so that they contain, in addition to the requirements of section 10–202, a statement that the corporation is a benefit corporation. In order to be effective, the amendment must be adopted by at least the supermajority status vote.

B. If an entity that is not a benefit corporation is a party to a merger or the acquired entity in a share exchange, and the surviving or acquired entity in the merger or share exchange is to be a benefit corporation, the plan of merger or share exchange must be adopted by at least the supermajority status vote.

10-2405. Termination of benefit corporation status

A. A benefit corporation may terminate its status as a benefit corporation and cease to be subject to this chapter by amending its articles of incorporation to delete the provision required by section 10–2403 or 10–2404 to be stated in the articles of a benefit corporation. In order to be effective, the amendment must be adopted by at least the minimum status vote.

B. Any sale, lease, exchange or other disposition of all or substantially all of the assets of a benefit corporation, unless the transaction is in the usual and regular course of business, shall not be effective unless the transaction is approved by at least the minimum status vote.

（d）透明，以下关于标准的信息可公开获取：

（i）衡量企业整体社会和环境绩效时所考虑的指标。

（ii）这些指标的相关权重。

（e）透明，以下关于标准制定和修改的信息可公开获取：

（i）制定和控制修改程序的董事、高管、主要股东和该实体控制人员的身份。

（ii）标准修改和控制人员变动的程序。

（iii）收入和资金来源的核算，包括充分披露合理认知下存在利益冲突的所有细节。

第 10-2403 条　公共利益公司的设立

公共利益公司应当按照本编第 2 章第 1 节的规定设立，但公司章程必须声明其是公共利益公司。

第 10-2404 条　公共利益公司形态的选择

A. 已成立的商事公司可依据本章规定转换为公共利益公司，公司除满足第 10-202 条的要求外，还需修改公司章程，作出该公司为公共利益公司的声明。公司章程的修改应满足最低表决要求。

B. 如果一家非公共利益公司的实体是兼并的一方或股权置换中的收购实体，而且兼并中存续实体或收购实体属公共利益公司，那么此兼并或股权置换的计划至少须满足绝大多数表决要求才能获准。

第 10-2405 条 公共利益公司形态的终止

A. 公共利益公司可通过删除第 10-2403 条或第 10-2404 条规定的在公司章程中的作为公共利益公司的声明来终止其公共利益公司的形态并不再受本章规定调整。公司章程的修改应满足最低表决要求。

B. 除正常商业往来外，公共利益公司的任何出售、出租、交换或者其他处置全部或主要财产的行为，须满足最低表决要求。

10-2406. Merger, interest exchange, conversion, domestication or division; definitions

A. A domestic benefit corporation may be a party to or otherwise undertake A merger, an interest exchange, a conversion, a domestication or a division by complying with chapters 11 and 13 of this title and title 29, chapter 6.

B. If a benefit corporation is to be created in a merger, a conversion, a domestication or a division, the formation of the corporation must otherwise comply with this chapter.

C. If a merger, an interest exchange, a conversion, a domestication or a division would have the effect of terminating the status of a business corporation as a benefit corporation, the plan must be adopted by at least the minimum status vote in order to be effective.

D. For the purposes of this section:

1. "Conversion" means a transaction authorized by title 29, chapter 6, article 4.
2. "Division" means a transaction authorized by title 29, chapter 6, article 6.
3. "Domestication" means a transaction authorized by title 29, chapter 6, article 5.
4. "Interest exchange" means a transaction authorized by title 29, chapter 6, article 3.
5. "Merger" means a transaction authorized by title 29, chapter 6, article 2.
6. "Plan" means a plan of merger, interest exchange, conversion, domestication or division.

Article 2. Corporate Purposes

10-2421. Corporate purposes

A. A benefit corporation shall have a purpose of creating general public benefit. This purpose is in addition to its purpose under section 10–301.

B. The articles of incorporation of a benefit corporation may identify one or more specific public benefits that it is the purpose of the benefit corporation to create in addition to its purposes under section 10–301 and subsection A of this section. The identification of a specific public benefit under this subsection does not limit the obligation of a benefit corporation under subsection A of this section.

C. The creation of general public benefit and a specific public benefit under subsections A and B of this section is in the best interests of the benefit corporation.

D. A benefit corporation may amend its articles of incorporation to add, amend or delete the identification of a specific public benefit that it is the purpose of the benefit corporation to create. In order to be effective, the amendment must be adopted by at least the minimum status vote.

E. A professional corporation that is a benefit corporation does not violate section 10–2211 by having the purpose to create general public benefit or a specific public benefit.

第 10-2406 条　合并，权益置换，转换，本土化或分立；定义

A. 一家本州公共利益公司可以依据本编第 11 章和第 13 章及第 29 编第 6 章的规定成为合并、权益置换、转换、本土化、分立的一方或以其他方式从事上述行为。

B. 如果在合并、转换、本土化或分立后出现公共利益公司，公共利益公司设立必须遵守本章规定。

C. 如果合并、权益置换、转换、本土化或分立将产生终止商事公司的公共利益公司的效力，该计划应满足最低表决要求。

D. 在本节中：

1. “转换”是指第 29 编第 6 章第 4 节授权的交易。
2. “分立”是指第 29 编第 6 章第 6 节授权的交易。
3. “本土化”是指第 29 编第 6 章第 5 节授权的交易。
4. “权益置换”是指第 29 编第 6 章第 3 节授权的交易。
5. “合并”是指第 29 编第 6 章第 2 节授权的交易。
6. “计划”是指合并、权益置换、转换、本土化或分立的计划。

第 2 节　公司目的

第 10-2421 条　公司目的

A. 公共利益公司应当具有服务于一般公共利益的目的。此目的在第 10-301 条的规定之外。

B. 公共利益公司的章程可以在第 10-301 条和本条的第 A 款的规定外确定一项或多项特定公共利益目的。依据本小节设定的特定公共利益目的并不限制本条第 A 款下的公共利益公司义务。

C. 依据本条第 A 款和第 B 款的规定创设的一般和特定公共利益目的为公共利益公司的最佳利益。

D. 公共利益公司可以通过修改章程增加、修改或删除公共利益公司设定的特定公共利益目的。对章程的修改需满足最低表决要求。

E. 选择公共利益形态的专业公司并不因其有创设一般或特定公共利益的目的而违反第 10-2211 条的规定。

Article 3. Accountability

10-2431. Standard of conduct for directors

A. In discharging the duties of their respective positions and in considering the best interests of the benefit corporation, the board of directors, committees of the board and individual directors of a benefit corporation:

1. Shall consider the effects of any action or inaction on:

(a) The shareholders of the benefit corporation.

(b) The employees and workforce of the benefit corporation, its subsidiaries and its suppliers.

(c) The interests of customers as beneficiaries of the general public benefit or specific public benefit purposes of the benefit corporation.

(d) Community and societal factors, including those of each community in which offices or facilities of the benefit corporation, its subsidiaries or its suppliers are located.

(e) The local and global environment.

(f) The short–term and long–term interests of the benefit corporation, including benefits that may accrue to the benefit corporation from its long–term plans and the possibility that these interests may be best served by the continued independence of the benefit corporation.

(g) The ability of the benefit corporation to accomplish its general public benefit purpose and any specific public benefit purpose.

2. May consider the interests referred to in section 10–2702 and other pertinent factors or the interests of any other group that they deem appropriate except that they do not have to give priority to the interests of a particular person or group referred to in this subsection over the interests of any other person or group unless the benefit corporation has stated in its articles of incorporation its intention to give priority to certain interests related to its accomplishment of its general public benefit purpose or of a specific public benefit purpose identified in its articles.

B. The consideration of interests and factors in the manner required by subsection A of this section does not constitute a violation of section 10–830.

C. Except as provided in the articles of incorporation or bylaws and in subsection E of this section, a director is not personally liable for monetary damages for:

1. Any action or inaction in the course of performing the duties of a director under subsection A of this section if the director performed the duties of office in compliance with section 10–830 and this section.

2. Failure of the benefit corporation to pursue or create general public benefit or a specific public benefit.

D. A director does not have a duty to a person that is a beneficiary of the general public

第3节 责任

第10–2431条 董事行为标准

A. 在履行各自职责和考虑公共利益公司的最佳利益时，公共利益公司的董事会、董事委员会和董事：

1. 其作为或不作为，应当考虑行为对以下对象的影响：

（a）公共利益公司的股东。

（b）公共利益公司雇员及其子公司和供应商。

（c）作为公共利益公司一般或特定公共利益受益者的消费者利益。

（d）社区和社会因素，包括公共利益公司及其子公司或供应商办公地或设施所在地的社区。

（e）当地和全球环境。

（f）公共利益公司的短期和长期利益，包括从其长期计划中产生的利益以及这类利益被公共利益公司实现的最好的方式。

（g）公共利益公司实现其一般和特定公共利益目的的能力。

2. 可参考第10–2702条中所涉及的利益以及董事认为合适的其他相关因素或其他群体的利益，但是除公司章程中要求优先考虑特定利益或因素外，无须优先考虑本小节中某个利益或因素。

B. 对本条的第A款中利益和相关因素的考虑不构成对第10–830条规定的违反。

C. 除公司章程、章程细则或本条的第E款另有明确规定外，董事不对以下行为承担损害赔偿责任：

1. 依据本条的第A款履行董事责任的任何作为或不作为行为，在该行为符合第10–830条及本条的规定的情况下。

2. 公共利益公司未能追求或创造一般或特定公共利益。

D. 董事不对公共利益公司一般或特定社会目的的受益人负责。

benefit purpose or a specific public benefit purpose of a benefit corporation arising from the status of the person as a beneficiary.

E. Subsection C of this section does not apply to a director's conflicting interest transaction, as defined in section 10–860, in which the director has directly or indirectly benefitted.

10-2432. Standard of conduct for officers

A. Each officer of a benefit corporation shall consider the interests and factors described in section 10–2431, subsection A, in the manner provided in that subsection, if both of the following apply:

1. The officer has discretion to act with respect to a matter.

2. It reasonably appears to the officer that the matter may have a material effect on the general public benefit or specific public benefit identified in the articles of incorporation of the benefit corporation.

B. The consideration of interests and factors in the manner described in subsection A of this section does not constitute a violation of section 10–842.

C. Except as provided in the articles of incorporation or bylaws, an officer is not personally liable for monetary damages for either of the following:

1. An action or inaction as an officer in the course of performing the duties of an officer under subsection A of this section if the officer performed the duties of the position in compliance with section 10–842 and this section.

2. Failure of the benefit corporation to pursue or create general public benefit or a specific public benefit.

D. An officer does not have a duty to a person that is a beneficiary of the general public benefit purpose or the specific public benefit purpose of a benefit corporation arising from the status of the person as a beneficiary.

E. An officer who makes a business judgment in good faith fulfills the duty under this section if all of the following apply:

1. The officer is not interested in the subject of the business judgment.

2. The officer is informed with respect to the subject of the business judgment to the extent the officer reasonably believes to be appropriate under the circumstances.

3. The officer rationally believes that the business judgment is in the best interests of the benefit corporation.

10-2433. Right of action

A. Except in a benefit enforcement proceeding, a person may not bring an action or assert a claim against a benefit corporation or its directors or officers with respect to either of the following:

1. The failure to pursue or create general public benefit or a specific public benefit set

E. 本条的第 C 款不适用于第 10-860 条规定的董事从中直接或间接获益的利益冲突交易的情形。

第 10-2432 条　高管行为标准

A. 公共利益公司高管应以本款规定的行为标准考虑第 10-2431 条第 A 款中规定的利益和因素，如果：

1. 高管就该行为有自由裁量权。

2. 高管有合理理由认为该行为对公共利益公司在章程中创设的一般或特定公共利益有实质性影响。

B. 对本条第 A 款中规定的利益和相关因素的考虑不违反第 10-842 条的规定。

C. 除公司章程或章程细则中另有规定外，高管不对以下行为承担损害赔偿责任：

1. 依据本条第 A 款履行高管责任过程中的任何作为或者不作为，如果该行为符合第 10-842 条及本条的规定。

2. 公共利益公司未能追求或创造一般或特定公共利益。

D. 高管不对公共利益公司一般或特定公共利益的受益人负责。

E. 如果董事的行为满足以下要求，善意进行商业判断的董事视为已履行本节所规定的义务：

1. 高管在商业判断过程中不涉及个人利益。

2. 高管拥有使其在该情形下作出合理商业判断的充分信息。

3. 高管有合理理由认为该商业判断符合公共利益公司的最佳利益。

第 10-2433 条　诉讼权利

A. 非经公共利益实施程序，任何人不得因以下事项向公共利益公司或者其董事、高管提起诉讼或提起主张：

1. 未能追求或创造在公司章程中陈述的一般或特定公共利益。

forth in its articles of incorporation.

2. The violation of an obligation, duty or standard of conduct under this chapter.

B. A benefit corporation is not liable for monetary damages under this chapter for any failure of the benefit corporation to pursue or create general public benefit or a specific public benefit.

C. A benefit enforcement proceeding may be commenced or maintained only by either of the following:

1. Directly by the benefit corporation.

2. Derivatively in accordance with chapter 7, article 4 of this title by any of the following:

(a) A person or group of persons that owns beneficially or of record at least two per cent of the total number of shares of all classes and series outstanding at the time of the act or omission that is the subject of the complaint.

(b) A director.

(c) A person or group of persons that owns beneficially or of record five per cent or more of the outstanding equity interests in an entity of which the benefit corporation is a subsidiary at the time of the act or omission that is the subject of the complaint.

(d) Other persons as specified in the articles of incorporation or bylaws of the benefit corporation.

D. For the purposes of this section, a person is the beneficial owner of shares or equity interests if the shares or equity interests are held in a voting trust or by a nominee on behalf of the beneficial owner.

Article 4. Transparency

10-2441. Preparation of annual benefit report

A. A benefit corporation shall prepare an annual benefit report that includes all of the following:

1. A narrative description of:

(a) The ways in which the benefit corporation pursued general public benefit during the year and the extent to which general public benefit was created.

(b) Both:

(i) The ways in which the benefit corporation pursued a specific public benefit that the articles of incorporation state is the purpose of the benefit corporation to create.

(ii) The extent to which the specific public benefit was created.

(c) Any circumstances that have hindered the benefit corporation in creating general public benefit or a specific public benefit.

(d) The process and rationale for selecting or changing the third–party standard used to

2. 违反本章规定的责任、义务或行为标准。

B. 公共利益公司不应根据本章规定，因未能追求或创造一般或特定公共利益，承担损害赔偿责任。

C. 下列情形中，以下主体可提起公共利益实施程序：

1. 由公共利益公司直接提起。

2. 依据本编第 7 章第 4 节的规定由以下主体派生提起：

（a）在被诉作为或不作为行为发生时，持有公共利益公司 2% 以上已发行的某类别或系列股份的个人或群体。

（b）董事。

（c）在被诉作为或不作为行为发生时，持有公共利益公司母公司 5% 以上已发行股份的登记股东或实际受益股人。

（d）公共利益公司章程或章程细则中规定的其他人员。

D. 为实现本章目的，若股份或者股利由表决权信托或指定第三人代持，将此人视为该股份和股利的实益所有权人。

第 4 节　透明度

第 10–2441 条　年度公共利益报告的编写

A. 公共利益公司的年度公共利益报告应包括以下内容：

1. 对以下事项的说明：

（a）公共利益公司本年度实现一般公共利益的方法和一般公共利益实现的情况。

（b）同时包括：

（i）公共利益公司实现公司章程中规定的特定公共利益的方法。

（ii）该特定公共利益实现的情况。

（c）阻碍公共利益公司创造一般和特定公共利益的情形。

（d）为编写公共利益报告而选择或更换第三方标准的程序和原因。

prepare the benefit report.

2. An assessment of the overall social and environmental performance of the benefit corporation against a third–party standard that is either of the following:

(a) Applied consistently with any application of that standard in prior benefit reports.

(b) Accompanied by an explanation of the reasons for either of the following:

(i) Any inconsistent application.

(ii) The change to that standard from the one used in the immediately prior report.

3. The compensation paid by the benefit corporation during the year to each director in the capacity of a director.

4. A statement of any connection between the organization that established the third–party standard, or its directors, its officers or any holder of five per cent or more of the governance interests in the organization and the benefit corporation or its directors, its officers or any holder of five per cent or more of the outstanding shares of the benefit corporation, or any other financial or governance relationship that might materially affect the credibility of the use of the third–party standard.

B. Neither the benefit report nor the assessment of the performance of the benefit corporation in the benefit report required by subsection A, paragraph 2 of this section is required to be audited or certified by a third–party standards provider.

10-2442. Availability of annual benefit report

A. A benefit corporation shall send its annual benefit report to each shareholder:

1. Within one hundred twenty days following the end of the fiscal year of the benefit corporation.

2. At the same time the benefit corporation delivers any other annual report to its shareholders.

B. A benefit corporation shall post all of its benefit reports on the public portion of its internet website, if any, except that the compensation paid to directors and financial or proprietary information included in the benefit reports may be omitted from the benefit reports as posted.

C. If a benefit corporation does not have an internet website, the benefit corporation shall provide a copy of its most recent benefit report, without charge, to any person that requests a copy, except that the compensation paid to directors and financial or proprietary information included in the benefit report may be omitted from the copy of the benefit report provided.

D. Concurrently with the delivery of the benefit report to shareholders under subsection A of this section, the benefit corporation shall deliver a copy of the benefit report to the Arizona corporation commission for filing, except that the compensation paid to directors and financial or proprietary information included in the benefit report may be omitted from the benefit report as delivered to the Arizona corporation commission.

2. 依据第三方标准对公共利益公司的社会和环境表现作出的整体评价：

（a）沿用先前公共利益报告中使用的标准。
（b）附一份说明以解释：
（i）适用的差异。
（ii）与上一份报告相比，标准的变化。
3. 公共利益公司在该年度支付给每个董事的薪酬。

4. 设立第三方标准的组织或其董事、高管或 5% 以上管理权利的持有者与公共利益公司或其董事、高管或公共利益公司 5% 以上已发行股份持有者之间关系的声明，或者任何可能影响第三方标准可信度的财务或管理关系。

B. 本条第 A 款第 2 项要求的公共利益公司报告和公共利益公司绩效评估均不需要由第三方标准制定者进行审计或认证。

第 10–2442 条　年度公共利益报告的提供

A. 公共利益公司应当在以下日期内将公共利益报告送交各股东：
1. 公共利益公司财政年度结束后 120 天内。

2. 公共利益公司向其股东送交其他年度报告的同一时间。

B. 若条件允许，公共利益公司应当将其所有公共利益报告发布于其网站的公共部分，但可将公共利益报告中董事薪酬和财务、所有权信息删除。

C. 如果公共利益公司没有网站，应向任何索取报告的个人免费提供最新公共利益报告的副本，但可将公共利益报告副本中董事薪酬和财务、所有权信息删除。

D. 根据本条第 A 款的规定将公共利益报告提交给股东的同时，公共利益公司应当将该公共利益报告提交亚利桑那州公司委员会备案，但可将公共利益报告中有关董事薪酬和财务、所有权的信息在提交亚利桑那州公司委员会的报告中删除。

THE STATE OF ARKANSAS

Act 1388 of the Regular Session

State of Arkansas

89th General Assembly

Regular Session, 2013

HOUSE BILL 1510

APPROVED: 04/19/2013

For An Act To Be Entitled

AN ACT TO ESTABLISH THE ARKANSAS BENEFIT CORPORATION ACT; AND FOR OTHER PURPOSES.

Subtitle

TO ESTABLISH THE ARKANSAS BENEFIT CORPORATION ACT.

BE IT ENACTED BY THE GENERAL ASSEMBLY OF THE STATE OF ARKANSAS:

SECTION 1. Arkansas Code Title 4, is amended to add an additional chapter to read as follows:

阿肯色州

常规会议 1388 号法案

阿肯色州

第 89 届州议会

2013 年常规会议

众议院法案 1510 号

批准提起：2013 年 4 月 19 日

作为一部被授权的法案

一部制定了阿肯色州公共利益公司法的法案；以及其他目的。

副标题

制定阿肯色州公共利益公司法。

由阿肯色州的州议会制定：

第 1 部分　阿肯色州法典第 4 编被修订后增加如下章节：

CHAPTER 36
ARKANSAS BENEFIT CORPORATION ACT

Subchapter 1 — Preliminary Provisions

4-36-101. Title.

This chapter shall be known and may be cited as the "Arkansas Benefit Corporation Act".

4-36-102. Application of chapter.

(a) This chapter shall apply to all benefit corporations.

(b) This chapter does not imply that a contrary statute or rule of law applies to a business corporation that is not a benefit corporation.

(c) (1) Except as otherwise provided in this chapter, the Arkansas Business Corporation Act, § 4–27–101 et seq., is generally applicable to a benefit corporation.

(2) Specific provisions of this chapter shall control over the general provisions of the Arkansas Business Corporation Act, § 4–27–101 et seq.

(3) A benefit corporation may be simultaneously subject to this chapter and other statutes that provide for the incorporation of a specific type of business corporation.

(d) The articles of incorporation or bylaws of a benefit corporation shall not limit, relax, be inconsistent with, or supersede this chapter.

4-36-103. Definitions.

(a) As used in this chapter:

(1) "Benefit corporation" means a business corporation that is subject to this chapter.

(2) "Benefit director" means the director designated as the benefit director of a benefit corporation under § 4–36–302.

(3) "Benefit enforcement proceeding" means a claim or action for:

(A) Failure of a benefit corporation to pursue or create a general public benefit or a specific public benefit purpose as stated in its articles of incorporation; or

(B) Violation of an obligation, duty, or standard of conduct under this chapter;

(4) "Benefit officer" means the individual designated as the benefit officer of a benefit corporation under § 4–36–304.

(5) "General public benefit" means a material positive impact on society and the environment, taken as a whole, assessed against a third–party standard, from the business and operations of a benefit corporation.

(6) (A) "Independent" means having no material relationship with a benefit corporation

第 36 章
阿肯色州公共利益公司法

第 1 节——初步条款

第 4–36–101 条　名称

本章应被称为和引用为《阿肯色州公共利益公司法》。

第 4–36–102 条　本章的适用范围

（a）本章应适用于所有公共利益公司。

（b）本章不为非公共利益公司设定相反的规则。

（c）（1）除本章另有规定外，阿肯色州商事公司法的第 4–27–101 条及以下条款普遍适用于公共利益公司。

（2）本章特殊条款的效力优先于阿肯色州商事公司法的第 4–27–101 条及以下一般条款的规定；

（3）公共利益公司同时受本章和规定特定种类商事公司设立的其他法律调整。

（d）公共利益公司的章程或章程细则不应限制、放宽、违背或取代本章。

第 4–36–103 条　定义

（a）在本章中：

（1）“公共利益公司”是指选择接受本章规定调整的商事公司。

（2）“公共利益董事”是指依据第 4–36–302 条的规定被任命为公共利益公司的公共利益董事的董事。

（3）“公共利益实施程序”是指因以下行为产生的任何主张或诉讼：

（A）公共利益公司未追求或实现公司章程规定的一般或特定公共利益目的；或者

（B）公共利益公司违反本章规定的任何义务、责任或行为标准。

（4）“公共利益高管”是指依据第 4–36–304 条的规定被任命为公共利益公司的公共利益高管的个体。

（5）“一般公共利益”是指根据第三方标准，公司的业务和经营在整体上对社会和环境产生的实质性积极影响。

（6）（A）“独立”是指与公共利益公司或其子公司没有实质性关系。

or a subsidiary of the benefit corporation.

(B) A person shall be independent even if serving as benefit director or benefit officer.

(C) A material relationship between a person and a benefit corporation or its subsidiaries is conclusively presumed to exist if:

(i) The person is, or has been in the last three (3) years, an employee other than a benefit officer of the benefit corporation or a subsidiary of the benefit corporation;

(ii) An immediate family member of the person is, or has been in the last three (3) years, an executive officer other than a benefit officer of the benefit corporation or its subsidiary; or

(iii) There is beneficial or record ownership of five percent (5%) or more of the outstanding shares of the benefit corporation by the person or an association:

(a) Of which the person is a director, an officer, or a manager; or

(b) In which the person owns beneficially or of record five percent (5%) or more of the outstanding equity interests;

(7) "Minimum status vote" means:

(A) In the case of a business corporation, in addition to any other required approval or vote, the satisfaction of the following conditions:

(i) The shareholders of a class or series may vote as a class on the corporate action regardless of a limitation stated in the articles of incorporation or bylaws on the voting rights of the class or series; and

(ii) The corporate action shall be approved by vote of the shareholders of each class or series entitled to cast at least two–thirds (2/3) of the votes that all shareholders of the class or series are entitled to cast on the action.

(B) In the case of a domestic entity other than a business corporation, in addition to any other required approval, vote, or consent, the satisfaction of the following conditions:

(i) The holders of a class or series of equity interest in the entity that are entitled to receive a distribution from the entity may vote on or consent to the action regardless of an otherwise applicable limitation on the voting or consent rights of the class or series; and

(ii) The action shall be approved by vote or consent of the holders described in subdivision (7)(B)(i) of this section entitled to cast at least two–thirds (2/3) of the votes or consents that all of those holders are entitled to cast on the action;

(8) "Specific public benefit" means:

(A) Providing low–income or underserved individuals or communities with beneficial products or services;

(B) Promoting economic opportunity for individuals or communities beyond the creation of jobs in the normal course of business;

(C) Preserving the environment;

(D) Improving human health;

（B）个体担任公共利益董事或公共利益高管后仍具有独立性。

（C）在下列情形中，认为该个体与公共利益公司或其子公司存在实质性关系：

（i）该个体是，或在过去 3 年内是，公共利益公司或其子公司公共利益高管以外的雇员；

（ii）该个体的直系亲属是，或在过去的 3 年内是，公共利益公司或其子公司公共利益高管以外的执行高管；或者

（iii）下述持有公共利益公司 5% 以上已发行股份的受益所有权或登记所有权的人或组织：

（a）该个体是该组织的董事、高管或经理；或者

（b）该组织中的个体为持有公共利益公司 5% 以上已发行股份受益所有权或登记所有权的人；

（7）“最低表决要求”是指：

（A）在商事公司中，除其他批准或表决的要求外，还应满足以下条件：

（i）每一类别或系列的股东可以作为一个类别对公司行为投票，即使公司章程或章程细则对某一类别或系列股东作出了限制；以及

（ii）公司行为必须获得每个类别或系列有投票权的所有股东至少 2/3 的投票才能通过。

（B）在非商事公司的本州实体中，除其他批准、表决或赞成的要求外，还应满足以下条件：

（i）该实体的每一类别或系列享有任何权益分配形式的股权持有者可以对公司行为进行投票，即使存在任何对该类别或系列的投票权限制；以及

（ii）公司行为必须获得本条的第（7）（B）（i）目规定的有投票权的所有股东的至少 2/3 的投票才能通过。

（8）“特定公共利益”是指：

（A）向低收入、低福利人群或社区提供有益的产品或服务；

（B）在正常业务过程中向个人或社区提供除创造就业之外的经济机会；

（C）保护环境；

（D）改善人类健康；

(E) Promoting the arts, sciences, or advancement of knowledge;

(F) Increasing the flow of capital to entities with a public benefit purpose; and

(G) Conferring any other particular benefit on society or the environment;

(9) "Subsidiary" means in relation to a person, an association in which the person owns beneficially or of record fifty percent (50%) or more of the outstanding equity interests; and

(10) "Third-party standard" means a recognized standard for defining, reporting, and assessing corporate social and environmental performance that is:

(A) Comprehensive in that it assesses the effect of the business and its operations on the interests listed in § 4-36-301(a)(1)(B)-(E);

(B) Developed by an organization that is independent of the benefit corporation and satisfies the following:

(i) Not more than one-third (1/3) of the members of the governing body of the organization are representatives of:

(a) An association of businesses operating in a specific industry, the performance of whose members is measured by the standard;

(b) Businesses from a specific industry or an association of businesses in that industry; or

(c) A business whose performance is assessed against the standard; and

(ii) The organization is not materially financed by an association or business described in subdivision (10)(B)(i) of this section;

(C) Credible because the standard is developed by a person that both:

(i) Has access to necessary expertise to assess overall corporate social and environmental performance; and

(ii) Uses a balanced multistakeholder approach, including a public comment period of at least thirty (30) days to develop the standard; and

(D) Transparent because the following information is publicly available:

(i) The standard criteria considered if measuring the overall social and environmental performance of a business;

(ii) The relative weighting factor of those criteria;

(iii) The development and revision of the standard, including:

(a) The identity of the directors, officers, material owners, and the governing body of the organization that developed and controls revisions to the standard; and

(b) The process by which revisions to the standard and changes to the membership of the governing body are made; and

(iv) An accounting of the sources of financial support for the organization, with sufficient detail to disclose a relationship that could reasonably be considered to present a potential conflict of interest.

（E）促进艺术、科学或知识进步；

（F）促进资本向有公共利益目的的实体流动；以及

（G）给予关于社会或环境的其他特别利益；

（9）“子公司”是指该实体50%以上已发行的股份的受益所有权或登记所有权被另一实体所拥有；以及

（10）“第三方标准”是指用于定义、报告和评估公司社会和环境绩效的标准，其应满足以下条件：

（A）综合，根据第4-36-301（a）（1）（B）-（E）分项中所列利益评估公司业务和经营绩效；

（B）独立，“第三方标准”由独立于公共利益公司的组织制定并满足以下条件：

（i）组织管理层1/3以下的成员作为以下主体的代表：

（a）在特定行业经营的企业协会，其成员的绩效由该标准衡量；

（b）特定行业或该行业企业协会中的企业；或者

（c）绩效由该标准评价的企业；以及

（ii）该组织并非由本条中第（10）（B）（i）目规定的协会或企业资助；

（C）可信，该标准由满足以下两点条件的实体制定：

（i）拥有评估公司社会和环境综合绩效所需的专业知识；以及

（ii）使用平衡多方利益相关者的方法制定标准，包括设定至少30天的听取公众意见期间以制定标准；以及

（D）透明，以下信息可公开获取：

（i）衡量企业整体社会和环境绩效时所考虑的标准；

（ii）那些标准的相关权重；

（iii）标准的制定和修改，包括

（a）制定和控制修改标准的董事、高管、主要股东和该实体控制人员的身份；以及

（b）标准修改和控制人员变动的程序；以及

（iv）资金来源的核算，包括充分披露合理认知下存在利益冲突的所有细节。

(b) For purposes of the definitions of "independent" and "subsidiary" in subsection (a) of this section, a percentage of ownership in an entity is computed as if all outstanding rights to acquire equity interests in the association had been exercised.

4-36-104. Formation -- Fees.

(a) A benefit corporation shall be formed under the Arkansas Business Corporation Act, § 4–27–101 et seq., and its articles of incorporation shall state that it is a benefit corporation.

(b) The Secretary of State shall collect filing fees, service fees, and fees for copying when documents are delivered to him or her to be filed under this subchapter and under § 4–27–122.

4-36-105. Election of status.

(a) An existing business corporation may become a benefit corporation under this chapter by amending its articles of incorporation so that they contain, in addition to the requirements of § 4–27–202, a statement that the corporation is a benefit corporation.

(b) To be effective, an amendment shall be adopted by at least the minimum status vote.

(c) If an entity is not a benefit corporation but is a constituent corporation or organization in a merger or conversion with a benefit corporation, the merger or conversion shall be approved by at least the minimum status vote.

4-36-106. Termination of status.

(a) A benefit corporation may end its benefit corporation status and not be subject to this chapter by amending its articles of incorporation to delete the statement in the articles of incorporation required by § 4–36–104 or § 4–36–105 to be stated in the articles of incorporation of a benefit corporation.

(b) To be effective, the amendment shall be adopted by at least the minimum status vote.

(c) If a merger or conversion would have the effect of terminating the status of a business corporation as a benefit corporation, to be effective, the merger or conversion shall be approved by at least the minimum status vote.

(d) A sale, lease, exchange, or other disposition of all or a substantial part of the assets of a benefit corporation, unless the transaction is in the usual and regular course of business, shall not be effective unless the transaction is approved by at least the minimum status vote.

Subchapter 2 — Corporate Purposes

4-36-201. Corporate purposes.

(a) A benefit corporation shall have a purpose of creating a general public benefit and it is in addition to its purpose under § 4–36–103(a)(5).

(b) (1) The articles of incorporation of a benefit corporation may identify one (1) or more

（b）本条第（a）款有关“独立”和“子公司”的定义中，实体的所有权比例应在所有购股权被视为已行使的情况下计算。

第 4-36-104 条　设立——费用

（a）公共利益公司应当依据《阿肯色州商事公司法》第 4-27-101 条及以下条款设立，并且在公司章程中必须声明其是公共利益公司。

（b）当文件依据本节和第 4-27-122 条的规定提交给州务卿备案时，州务卿应收取备案费、服务费和复印费。

第 4-36-105 条　形态选择

（a）已成立的商事公司可依据本章的规定转换为公共利益公司，除满足第 4-27-202 条的要求外，还需修改公司章程，作出该公司为公共利益公司的声明。

（b）公司章程的修改应满足最低表决要求才能生效。

（c）如果一个实体不是公共利益公司而是合并或转换中的公司或组织，该合并或转换应满足最低表决要求。

第 4-36-106 条　形态终止

（a）公共利益公司可通过删除第 4-36-104 条或第 4-36-105 条规定的在公司章程中的声明来终止其公共利益公司的形态并不再受本章规定调整。

（b）公司章程的修改应满足最低表决要求才能生效。

（c）如果合并或转换有终止商事公司的公共利益公司形态的效力，合并或转换应满足最低表决要求才能生效。

（d）除正常商业往来外，公共利益公司出售、出租、置换或者其他处置全部或主要财产的行为，须满足最低表决要求。

第 2 节——公司目的

第 4-36-201 条　公司目的

（a）公共利益公司应当有服务于一般公共利益的目的，并且此目的是在第 4-36-103（a）（5）项规定的目的之外。

（b）（1）公共利益公司的章程可以在第 4-36-103（a）（5）项和本条的第（a）

specific public benefits that it is the purpose of the benefit corporation to pursue in addition to its purposes under § 4–36–103(a)(5) and subsection (a) of this section.

(2) The identification of a specific public benefit under this subsection does not limit the obligation of a benefit corporation under subsection (a) of this section.

(c) The creation of a general public benefit and a specific public benefit under subsections (a) and (b) of this section is in the best interests of the benefit corporation.

(d) (1) A benefit corporation may amend its articles of incorporation to add, amend, or delete the identification of a specific public benefit that it is the purpose of the benefit corporation to pursue.

(2) To be effective, the amendment shall be adopted by at least the minimum status vote.

(e) A professional corporation that is a benefit corporation does not violate the Arkansas Professional Corporation Act, § 4–29–201 et seq., by having the purpose to pursue a general public benefit or a specific public benefit.

Subchapter 3 — Accountability

4-36-301. Standard of conduct for directors.

(a) In discharging the duties of their respective positions and in considering the best interests of the benefit corporation, the board of directors, committees of the board, and individual directors of a benefit corporation:

(1) Shall consider the effects of an action or inaction on:

(A) The shareholders of the benefit corporation;

(B) The employees and work force of the benefit corporation, its subsidiaries, and its suppliers;

(C) The interests of customers as beneficiaries of the general public benefit or specific public benefit purposes of the benefit corporation;

(D) Community and societal factors, including those of each community in which offices or facilities of the benefit corporation, its subsidiaries, or its suppliers are located;

(E) The local and global environment;

(F) The short–term and long–term interests of the benefit corporation, including benefits that may accrue to the benefit corporation from its long–term plans and the possibility that these interests may be best served by the continued independence of the benefit corporation; and

(G) The ability of the benefit corporation to accomplish its general public benefit purpose and a specific public benefit purpose.

(2) May consider other pertinent factors or the interests of a group that they consider appropriate; and

款的目标外确定一项或多项特定公共利益目的。

（2）依据本款规定设定的特定公共利益并不限制公共利益公司在本条的第（a）款规定下的义务。

（c）依据本条的第（a）款和第（b）款规定创设的一般和特定公共利益目的为公共利益公司的最佳利益。

（d）（1）公共利益公司可以增加、修改或删除公司章程中设定的特定公共利益目的。

（2）公司对章程的修改须满足最低表决要求才能生效。

（e） 选择公共利益形态的专业公司并不因其有创设一般或特定公共利益的目的而违反阿肯色州专业公司法第 4-29-201 条及以下条款的规定。

第 3 节——责任

第 4-36-301 条　董事行为标准

（a）在履行各自职责和考虑公共利益公司最佳利益时，公共利益公司的董事会、董事委员会和董事：

（1）其作为或不作为，应当考虑对以下对象的影响：

（A）公共利益公司的股东；

（B）公共利益公司雇员及其子公司和供应商；

（C）作为公共利益公司一般或特定公共利益受益者的消费者的利益；

（D）社区和社会因素，包括公共利益公司及其子公司或供应商办公地或设施所在地的社区；

（E）当地和全球环境；

（F）公共利益公司的短期和长期利益，包括公共利益公司可能从其长期计划中产生的利益，以及公共利益公司继续保持独立可能产生的最佳利益；以及

（G）公共利益公司实现其一般和特定公共利益目的的能力。

（2）可考虑董事认为合适的其他相关因素或其他群体的利益；以及

(3) Need not give priority to the interests of a particular person or group referred to in subdivision (a)(1) or subdivision (a)(2) of this section over the interests of another person or group unless the benefit corporation has stated in its articles of incorporation its intention to give priority to certain interests related to its accomplishment of its general public benefit purpose or of a specific public benefit purpose identified in its articles of incorporation.

(b) The consideration of interests and factors required by subsection (a) of this section does not constitute a violation of § 4–27–801.

(c) A director is not personally liable for monetary damages for:

(1) Action taken as a director if the director performed the duties of office in compliance with § 4–27–801; or

(2) Failure of the benefit corporation to pursue a general public benefit or a specific public benefit.

(d) A director does not have a duty to a person that is a beneficiary of a general public benefit purpose or a specific public benefit purpose of a benefit corporation arising from the status of the person as a beneficiary.

4-36-302. Benefit director.

(a) The board of directors of a benefit corporation may include a director who:

(1) Is designated the benefit director; and

(2) Has the powers, duties, rights, and immunities provided in this subchapter in addition to the powers, duties, rights, and immunities of the other directors of the benefit corporation.

(b) (1) The benefit director is elected and may be removed under § 4–27–803.

(2) The benefit director shall be an independent individual.

(c) The benefit director may serve concurrently as the benefit officer and the benefit director.

(d) The articles of incorporation or bylaws of a benefit corporation may prescribe additional qualifications of the benefit director not inconsistent with this section.

(e) The benefit director shall prepare and the benefit corporation shall include in the annual benefit report to shareholders as required by § 4–36–401 the opinion of the benefit director on:

(1) Whether the benefit corporation acted under its general public benefit purpose and a specific public benefit purpose in all material respects during the period covered by the report;

(2) Whether the directors complied with § 4–36–301(a) and the officers complied with § 4–36–303(a); and

(3) Whether the benefit corporation or its directors or officers failed to comply with this section, including a description of the ways in which the benefit corporation or its directors

（3）除公司章程中优先考虑与实现一般或特定公共利益相关的某种利益外，无须优先考虑本条第（a）（1）项或第（a）（2）项中某个利益或因素。

（b）对本条第（a）款中利益和相关因素的考虑不构成对第 4-27-801 条规定的违反。

（c）董事不对以下行为承担损害赔偿责任：

（1）董事履行职责的行为符合第 4-27-801 条的规定；或者

（2）公共利益公司未能追求或创造一般或特定公共利益。

（d）董事不对公共利益公司一般或特定社会目的的受益人负责。

第 4-36-302 条　公共利益董事

（a）公共利益公司的董事会应包含满足以下要求的董事：

（1）被任命为公共利益董事；并且

（2）除公共利益公司的其他董事的权力、义务、权利和豁免权以外，还有本节规定的权力、义务、权利和豁免权。

（b）（1）公共利益董事应当依据第 4-27-803 条的规定任免。

（2）公共利益董事应为独立个体。

（c）公共利益董事可同时担任公共利益高管。

（d）公共利益公司的章程或章程细则可对公共利益董事的资格作出与本条不一致的规定。

（e）公共利益董事应当编写其对以下事项的意见，公共利益公司应当根据第 4-36-401 条规定将其附于年度公共利益报告中供股东查阅：

（1）在报告所述期间内，公共利益公司是否在所有重要事项上依一般和特定公共利益目的行事；

（2）董事和高管是否分别依第 4-36-301（a）款和第 4-36-303（a）款规定行事；以及

（3）公共利益公司或其董事、高管是否未能依本条要求行事，应包括公共利益公司或其董事、高管未能履行责任的情况。

or officers failed to comply.

(f) The action or inaction of an individual in the capacity of a benefit director is an action or inaction of that individual in the capacity of a director of the benefit corporation.

(g) Regardless of whether the bylaws of a benefit corporation include a provision eliminating or limiting the personal liability of directors authorized by § 4–26–811, a benefit director shall not be personally liable for an act or omission in the capacity of a benefit director unless the act or omission constitutes self–dealing, willful misconduct, or a knowing violation of law.

(h) The benefit director of a professional corporation does not need to be independent.

4-36-303. Standard of conduct for officers.

(a) An officer of a benefit corporation shall consider the interests and factors described in § 4–36–301 if:

(1) The officer has discretion to act with respect to a matter; and

(2) It reasonably appears to the officer that the matter may have a material effect on the creation by the benefit corporation of a general public benefit or a specific public benefit identified in the articles of incorporation of the benefit corporation.

(b) The consideration of interests and factors described in subsection (a) of this section shall not constitute a violation of § 4–27–841.

(c) An officer is not personally liable for monetary damages for:

(1) An action or omission as an officer if the officer performed the duties of the position in compliance with § 4–27–841 and this section; or

(2) Failure of the benefit corporation to pursue a general public benefit or a specific public benefit.

(d) An officer does not have a duty to a person that is a beneficiary of a general public benefit purpose or a specific public benefit purpose of a benefit corporation arising from the status of the person as a beneficiary.

4-36-304. Benefit officer.

(a) A benefit corporation may have an officer designated as the benefit officer.

(b) A benefit officer shall have:

(1) The powers and duties relating to the purpose of the corporation to pursue a general public benefit or a specific public benefit provided:

(A) By the bylaws; or

(B) Absent controlling provisions in the bylaws, by resolutions or orders of the board of directors; and

(2) The duty to prepare the benefit report required by § 4–36–401.

4-36-305. Right of action.

(a) Except in a benefit enforcement proceeding, a person may not bring an action or

（f）个人在公共利益董事的职权范围内的作为或不作为应视为公共利益公司董事的行为。

（g）无论公共利益公司章程细则是否依据第 4-26-811 条规定删除或限制董事的个人责任，公共利益董事在行使职责时不对其任何作为或不作为行为承担个人责任，但自我交易或故意违法行为除外。

（h）专业公司的公共利益董事不需要具有独立性。

第 4-36-303 条　高管行为标准

（a）公共利益公司高管应考虑第 4-36-301 条中规定的利益和因素，如果：

（1）高管就该行为有自由裁量权；以及

（2）高管有合理理由认为该行为对公共利益公司在章程中创设的一般或特定公共利益有实质性影响。

（b）对本条第（a）款中规定的利益和因素的考虑不违反第 4-27-841 条的规定。

（c）高管不对以下行为承担损害赔偿责任：

（1）高管的作为或者不作为，如果该行为符合第 4-27-841 条及本条的规定；或者

（2）公共利益公司未能追求或创造一般或特定公共利益。

（d）高管并不对公共利益公司一般目的或特定社会目的的受益人负责。

第 4-36-304 条　公共利益高管

（a）公共利益公司可以将高管任命为公共利益高管。

（b）公共利益高管应有：

（1）规定于以下文件的创设一般或特定公共利益目的的权力和义务：

（A）公司章程细则；或者

（B）在公司章程细则中没有规定时，董事会的决议或者命令。

（2）第 4-36-401 条要求的公共利益报告的编写义务。

第 4-36-305 条　诉讼权利

（a）非经公共利益实施程序，任何人不得因以下事项向公共利益公司或者其

assert a claim against a benefit corporation or its directors or officers with respect to:

(1) Failure to pursue or create a general public benefit or a specific public benefit stated in its articles of incorporation; or

(2) Violation of a duty or standard of conduct under this chapter.

(b) A benefit corporation shall not be liable for monetary damages under this chapter for the failure of the benefit corporation to pursue a general public benefit or a specific public benefit.

(c) A benefit enforcement proceeding may begin and be maintained only:

(1) Directly by the benefit corporation; or

(2) Derivatively by:

(A) A shareholder;

(B) A director;

(C) A person or group of persons that owns beneficially or of record five percent (5%) or more of the equity interest in an entity of which the benefit corporation is a subsidiary at the time of the action or inaction complained of; or

(D) Other persons as named in the articles of incorporation or bylaws of the benefit corporation.

Subchapter 4 — Transparency

4-36-401. Annual reports.

(a) (1) A benefit corporation shall prepare an annual benefit report and an annual franchise tax report under § 26–54–104.

(2) An annual benefit report shall include:

(A) A narrative description of:

(i) The ways in which the benefit corporation pursued the general public benefit during the year and the extent to which the general public benefit was pursued;

(ii) Both:

(a) The ways in which the benefit corporation pursued a specific public benefit that the articles of incorporation state is the purpose of the benefit corporation to pursue; and

(b) The extent to which that specific public benefit was pursued;

(iii) Circumstances that have hindered the creation by the benefit corporation of a general public benefit or a specific public benefit; and

(iv) The process and rationale for selecting or changing the third–party standard used to prepare the benefit report;

(B) (i) An assessment of the overall social and environmental performance of the benefit corporation against a third–party standard:

(a) Applied consistently with an application of that standard in earlier benefit reports; or

董事、高管提起诉讼或主张：

（1）未能追求或实现其在公司章程中声明的一般或特定公共利益；或者

（2）违反本章规定的义务或行为标准。

（b）公共利益公司不应根据本章的规定，因其未能追求一般或特定公共利益，承担损害赔偿责任。

（c）下列情形中，仅以下主体可提起公共利益实施程序：

（1）由公共利益公司直接提起；或者

（2）由以下主体派生提起：

（A）股东；

（B）董事；

（C）在被诉作为或不作为行为发生时，持有公共利益公司母公司 5% 以上已发行股份的登记股东或实际受益股人；或者

（D）公共利益公司章程或章程细则中规定的其他人员。

第 4 节——透明度

第 4-36-401 条　年度报告

（a）（1）公共利益公司应依据第 26-54-104 条的规定编写年度公共利益报告和年度特许税报告。

（2）年度报告应包括以下内容：

（A）对以下事项的描述：

（i）公共利益公司本年度实现一般公共利益的方法和一般公共利益实现的情况；

（ii）同时包括：

（a）公共利益公司实现公司章程中规定的特定公共利益的方法；以及

（b）该特定公共利益实现的情况；

（iii）阻碍公共利益公司创造一般和特定公共利益的情形；以及

（iv）编写公共利益报告时选择或更换第三方标准的程序和原因；

（B）（i）依据第三方标准对公共利益公司的社会和环境表现作出的整体评价：

（a）沿用先前公共利益报告中使用的标准；或者

(b) Accompanied by an explanation of the reasons for an inconsistent application.

(ii) The assessment does not need to be performed, audited, or certified by a third–party standards provider;

(C) The name of the benefit director and the benefit officer and the address to which correspondence to each of them may be directed;

(D) The compensation paid by the benefit corporation during the year to each director for serving in the capacity of a director;

(E) The statement of the benefit director described in § 4–36–302; and

(F) A statement of the connection between the organization that established the third–party standard or its directors, officers, or a holder of five percent (5%) or more of the governance interests in the organization, and the benefit corporation or its directors, officers, or a holder of five percent (5%) or more of the outstanding shares of the benefit corporation, including a financial or governance relationship that may materially affect the credibility of the use of the third–party standard.

(b) A benefit corporation shall send a benefit report to each shareholder annually:

(1) Before the stated due date of an annual franchise tax under § 26–54–104; or

(2) When the benefit corporation delivers an annual financial report to its shareholders.

(c) (1) A benefit corporation shall post all of its benefit reports on the public part of its Internet website.

(2) The compensation paid to a director and a financial or proprietary informationist included in the benefit reports may be omitted from the benefit reports as posted.

(d) (1) If a benefit corporation does not have a website, the benefit corporation shall provide a copy of its most recent benefit report, without charge, to a person who requests a copy.

(2) The compensation paid to directors and the financial or proprietary informationist included in the benefit report may be omitted from the copy of the benefit report provided.

(e) (1) Concurrently with the delivery of the benefit report to shareholders under subsection (b) of this section, the benefit corporation shall deliver a copy of the benefit report to the Secretary of State for filing.

(2) The compensation paid to directors and the financial or proprietary informationist included in the benefit report may be omitted from the benefit report as delivered to the Secretary of State.

(3) The Secretary of State shall charge a fee of seventy dollars ($70.00) for filing a benefit report.

（b）附一份解释适用标准差异的说明。

（ii）该评价无须第三方标准提供者执行、审计或证明；

（C）公共利益董事和公共利益高管的姓名和联系地址；

（D）公共利益公司在该年度支付给每个董事的薪酬；

（E）第 4-36-302 条规定的公共利益董事的声明；以及

（F）设立第三方标准的组织或其董事、高管或 5% 以上管理权利的持有者，与公共利益公司或其董事、高管或公共利益公司 5% 以上已发行股份持有者之间关系的声明，包括所有可能影响第三方标准可信度的财务或管理关系。

（b）公共利益公司应每年提交给各股东一份公共利益报告：

（1）在第 26-54-104 条规定年度特许税规定的到期日之前；或者

（2）公共利益公司向股东提交财务报告时。

（c）（1）公共利益公司应将所有的公共利益报告公布在其网站的公共部分。

（2）公共利益报告中关于支付给董事和财务信息专家的报酬的信息可以在公布的公共利益报告中删除。

（d）（1）如果公共利益公司没有网站，应向任何想获取报告的个人免费提供最新公共利益报告的副本。

（2）公共利益报告中关于支付给董事和财务信息专家的报酬的信息可以在公布的公共利益报告的副本中删除。

（e）（1）依本条第（b）款规定将公共利益报告提交给股东的同时，公共利益公司应当将该公共利益报告提交州务卿备案。

（2）公共利益报告中关于支付给董事和财务信息专家的报酬的信息可以在提交给州务卿的公共利益报告中删除。

（3）州务卿将收取 70 美元作为公共利益报告备案的费用。

THE STATE OF CALIFORNIA

Assembly Bill No. 361

CHAPTER 728

An act to add Part 13 (commencing with Section 14600) to Division 3 of Title 1 of the Corporations Code, relating to benefit corporations.

[Approved by Governor October 9, 2011. Filed with Secretary of State October 9, 2011.]

Legislative counsel's digest

AB 361, Huffman. Benefit corporations.

Existing law, the General Corporation Law, authorizes and regulates the formation and governance of general corporations. The Nonprofit Corporation Law authorizes the formation and governance of nonprofit public benefit corporations, nonprofit mutual benefit corporations, and nonprofit religious corporations, and specifies the respective purposes for which those corporations may lawfully be formed. Existing law specifies the duties of corporate directors and the rights of shareholders. Existing law does not provide for the formation and governance of benefit corporations.

This bill would authorize and regulate the formation and governance of a new form of corporate entity known as a benefit corporation. The bill would also permit an existing corporation to become a benefit corporation by amendment to its articles of incorporation, as specified, adopted by at least a minimum status vote, as defined, and would permit a corporation to become a benefit corporation through a merger, reorganization, or conversion, or domestic other business entity, as specified.

This bill would define "benefit corporation" to mean a corporation that has been organized under the General Corporation Law and has elected to become subject to the provisions of the bill, as specified. The bill would provide that a benefit corporation may

加利福尼亚州

361 号议会法案

第 728 章

本法案关于公共利益公司，增加在《公司法》的第 1 编下的第 3 分编的第 13 节（始于第 14600 条）。

［2011 年 10 月 9 日由州长批准，2011 年 10 月 9 日由州务卿备案。］

立法建议摘要

AB361，霍夫曼。公共利益公司。

《普通公司法》，现行法律，授权和调整普通公司的成立和治理。《非营利公司法》管理非营利公共利益公司、非营利互惠公司和非营利宗教公司的成立和治理，并明确规定了这些公司各自依法成立的目的。现行法律规定了公司董事和股东的权利。现有法律未规定公共利益公司的成立和治理。

本法案将授权和调整一种被称为公共利益公司的新型公司组织的成立和治理。本法案也允许已成立的公司通过对公司章程进行满足最低表决要求的修改，成为公共利益公司，并且允许公司通过合并、重组或者转换形式变成本法案规定的公共利益公司或者本州其他商业实体。

本法案将“公共利益公司”定义为依据《普通公司法》设立的并选择受本法案条款调整的公司。本法案规定，公共利益公司可以为创造一般公共利益成立，即根据第三方标准在整体上对社会和环境产生的实质性积极影响。本法案也规定公共利

be formed for the purpose of creating general public benefit, defined as a material positive impact on society and the environment, taken as a whole, as assessed against a 3rd–party standard, as defined, that satisfies certain requirements. The bill would also provide that a benefit corporation may identify one or more specific public benefits,as defined, as an additional purpose of the corporation, including, without limitation, providing low–income or underserved individuals or communities with beneficial products or services, promoting economic opportunity for individuals or communities beyond the creation of jobs in the ordinary course of business, preserving the environment, and improving human health.

This bill would require directors to consider the impacts of any action or proposed action upon specified considerations, including, among others,the shareholders and employees, and of customers who are beneficiaries of the general or specific public benefit purposes, and the environment, and would allow directors to consider the impacts of those actions on, among other things, the resources, intent, and conduct of any person seeking to acquire control of the benefit corporation.

This bill would require the board of directors to prepare a specified statement relating to the public benefit purposes of the corporation. The bill would require the benefit corporation to prepare an annual benefit report to include, among other things, a statement indicating whether, in the board's opinion, the benefit corporation failed to pursue its general public benefit and any specific public benefit, a description of the ways in which the benefit corporation pursued those benefits, the extent to which those benefits were created, and the process and rationale for selecting the 3rd–party standard used to prepare the benefit reports, and would require the benefit corporation to file with the Secretary of State a copy of the benefit report together with a filing fee in a specified amount to cover the reasonable regulatory costs associated with maintaining those filings. This bill would include provisions governing the fiduciary duty and liability of an officer or director of a benefit corporation. The bill would provide that the duties of a director or officer, and the general, and any specific, public benefit purpose of a benefit corporation, may be enforced only in a benefit enforcement proceeding, as defined, that would be permitted to be commenced or maintained only as specified.

The people of the State of California do enact as follows:

SECTION 1. Part 13 (commencing with Section 14600) is added to Division 3 of Title 1 of the Corporations Code, to read:

PART 13. BENEFIT CORPORATIONS

Chapter 1. Preliminary Provisions

§ 14600. Applicability of part; Construction with other laws

(a) This part shall be applicable to all benefit corporations.

益公司可以确定一项或多项特定公共利益，作为另外的公司目的，包括但不限于向低收入、低福利人群或社区提供有益的产品或服务，在正常业务过程中向个人或社区提供除创造就业之外的经济机会，保护环境和改善人类健康。

本法案要求董事考虑所有行为或者将要发生的行为对特定因素的影响，包括股东、雇员和受益于一般或者特定公共利益目的的消费者以及环境，同时要求董事考虑这些行为对以下事项的影响，包括资源、目的以及试图获得公共利益公司控制权的任何人的行为。

本法案要求董事会编写一份关于公司公共利益目的的声明。本法案要求公共利益公司编写的年度公共利益报告包括：董事会关于公共利益公司是否未能追求其一般和特定公共利益的意见，公共利益公司追求公共利益方式的描述，公共利益实现的情况，选择编写公共利益报告的第三方标准的过程和原因，以及公共利益公司向州务卿备案公共利益报告的副本。同时提交一定数额的备案费以支付维持备案的合理规制成本。本法案包含规定公共利益公司董事或高管的信义义务和责任的条款。本法案规定了公共利益公司的董事或高管的义务以及一般和特定公共利益目的，其执行仅能按规定提起公共利益实施程序。

加利福尼亚州公民制定如下内容：

第 1 部分　第 13 节（始于第 14600 条）加入公司法第 1 编下的第 3 分编，称为：

第 13 节　公共利益公司

第 1 章　初步条款

第 14600 条　本部分的适用；与其他法律的协调

（a）本部分应适用于所有公共利益公司。

(b) The existence of a provision of this part shall not of itself create any implication that a contrary or different rule of law is or would be applicable to a business corporation that is not a benefit corporation. This part shall not affect any statute or rule of law that is or would be applicable to a corporation that is not a benefit corporation.

(c) The provisions of the General Corporation Law (Division 1 (commencing with Section 100)) shall apply to benefit corporations, except where those provisions are in conflict with or inconsistent with the provisions of this part.

§ 14601. Definitions

As used in this part:

(a) "Benefit corporation" means a corporation organized under the General Corporation Law that has elected to become subject to this part and whose status as a benefit corporation has not been terminated as provided in this part.

(b) "Benefit enforcement proceeding" means a claim or action relating to any of the following:

(1) Failure to pursue the general public benefit purpose of the benefit corporation or any specific public benefit purpose set forth in its articles.

(2) Violation of a duty or standard of conduct imposed on a director pursuant to this part.

(3) Failure of the benefit corporation to deliver or post an annual benefit report as required by Section 14630.

(c) "General public benefit" means a material positive impact on society and the environment, taken as a whole, as assessed against a third-party standard, from the business and operations of a benefit corporation.

(d) "Minimum status vote" means that:

(1) In the case of a corporation, in addition to any other approval or vote required by Division 1 (commencing with Section 100) or the articles of incorporation, both of the following shall apply:

(A) The shareholders of every class or series shall be entitled to vote on the corporate action regardless of any limitation stated in the articles or bylaws on the voting rights of any class or series.

(B) The corporate action shall be approved by the outstanding shares of each class or series by at least two-thirds of the votes, or greater vote if required in the articles of incorporation, that all shareholders of the class or series are entitled to cast on that action.

(2) In the case of a domestic other business entity (Section 167.7), both of the following shall apply in addition to any other approval, vote, or consent required by the statutory law, if any, that principally governs the internal affairs of the entity or any provision of the publicly filed record or document required to form the entity, if any, or of any agreement binding some

（b）本部分条款不应为非公共利益公司设定相反或不同的规则。本部分条款不影响适用于或将适用于非公共利益公司的任何法规或规则。

（c）《普通公司法》[第 1 分编（始于第 100 条）]的条款应适用于公共利益公司，除非该条款与本部分的条款存在冲突或不一致。

第 14601 条　定义

在本部分中：

（a）"公共利益公司"是指依据一般公司法成立的，选择接受本部分规定调整，且公共利益公司形态并未终止的公司。

（b）"公共利益实施程序"是指因以下行为产生的任何主张或诉讼：

（1）未能追求公共利益公司章程规定的一般或特定公共利益目的。

（2）违反本部分规定下董事的义务或行为标准。

（3）公共利益公司未提交或寄送第 14630 条规定的年度公共利益报告。

（c）"一般公共利益"是指根据第三方标准，公司的业务和经营在整体上对社会和环境产生的实质性积极影响。

（d）"最低表决要求"是指：

（1）在公司中，除第 1 分编（始于第 100 条）或公司章程规定的其他批准或表决要求外，表决还应满足以下两个条件：

（A）每一类别或系列的股东有权对公司行为进行投票，即使公司章程或章程细则对某一类别或系列股东作出了限制。

（B）公司行为必须获得每个类别或系列已发行股份有投票权的所有股东至少 2/3 的投票才能通过，或者经公司章程规定的更严格的表决要求通过。

（2）在本州其他商事实体（第 167.7 条）中，除主要调整实体内部事务的法律，约束部分或所有股权持有者协议的规定，设立实体要求的公开登记记录或文件的规定中的其他批准、表决或赞成的要求外，该商事实体的表决应满足以下两个条件：

or all of the holders of equity interests in the entity:

(A) The holders of every class or series of interest in the entity that are entitled to receive a distribution of any kind from the entity regardless of any otherwise applicable limitation on the voting rights of the interest.

(B) The action shall be approved by the vote or consent of the holders described in subparagraph (A) by at least two-thirds of the votes or consents, or greater vote or consent if required in the articles of incorporation, of those holders.

(e) "Specific public benefit" includes all of the following:

(1) Providing low-income or underserved individuals or communities with beneficial products or services.

(2) Promoting economic opportunity for individuals or communities beyond the creation of jobs in the ordinary course of business.

(3) Preserving the environment.

(4) Improving human health.

(5) Promoting the arts, sciences, or advancement of knowledge.

(6) Increasing the flow of capital to entities with a public benefit purpose.

(7) The accomplishment of any other particular benefit for society or the environment.

(f) "Subsidiary" of a person means an entity in which the person owns beneficially or of record 50 percent or more of the outstanding equity interests. For purposes of this definition, a percentage of ownership in an entity shall be calculated as if all outstanding rights to acquire equity interests in the entity had been exercised.

(g) "Third-party standard" means a standard for defining, reporting, and assessing overall corporate social and environmental performance to which all of the following apply:

(1) The standard is a comprehensive assessment of the impact of the business and the business's operations upon the considerations listed in paragraphs (2) to (5), inclusive, of subdivision (b) of Section 14620.

(2) The standard is developed by an entity that has no material financial relationship with the benefit corporation or any of its subsidiaries and that satisfies both of the following requirements:

(A) Not more than one-third of the members of the governing body of the entity are representatives of any of the following:

(i) Associations of businesses operating in a specific industry, the performance of whose members is measured by the standard.

(ii) Businesses from a specific industry or an association of businesses in that industry.

(iii) Businesses whose performance is assessed against the standard.

(B) The entity is not materially financed by an association or business described in subparagraph (A).

（A）该实体的每一类别或系列享有任何权益分配形式的股权持有者有权投票，即使存在任何投票权限制。

（B）该行为必须经第（A）分项规定的股东的至少 2/3 投票通过，或者经公司章程中规定的更严格的表决要求通过。

（e）“特定公共利益”包括以下所有内容：
（1）向低收入、低福利人群或社区提供有益的产品或服务。

（2）在正常业务过程中向个人或社区提供创造就业之外的经济机会。

（3）保护环境。
（4）改善人类健康。
（5）促进艺术、科学或知识进步。
（6）促进资本向有公共利益目的的实体流动。
（7）实现关于社会或环境的其他特别利益。
（f）“子公司”是指该实体 50% 以上已发行的股份的受益所有权或登记所有权被另一实体所拥有。在本定义中，应在所有购股权视为已行使的情况下，计算实体的所有权比例。

（g）“第三方标准”是指用于定义、报告和评估公司社会和环境绩效的标准，其应满足以下条件：
（1）标准是根据第 14620 条的第（b）款的第（2）项至第（5）项所列因素对公司业务和经营绩效的综合评价。

（2）经与公共利益公司或其子公司没有实质性财务关系的实体制定并且满足以下两个要求：

（A）实体管理层作为以下主体代表的成员比例不超过 1/3：

（i）在特定行业经营的企业协会，其成员的绩效由该标准衡量。

（ii）特定行业或该行业的企业协会中的企业。
（iii）绩效由该标准评价的企业。
（B）实体并非由第（A）分项规定的协会或企业资助。

(3) The standard is developed by an entity that does both of the following:

(A) Accesses necessary and appropriate expertise to assess overall corporate social and environmental performance.

(B) Uses a balanced multistakeholder approach, including a public comment period of at least 30 days to develop the standard.

(4) All of the following information regarding the standard is publicly available:

(A) The criteria considered when measuring the overall social and environmental performance of a business.

(B) The relative weightings assigned to the criteria described in subparagraph (A).

(C) The identity of the directors, officers, any material owners, and the governing body of the entity that developed, and controls revisions to, the standard.

(D) The process by which revisions to the standard and changes to the membership of the governing body described in subparagraph (C) are made.

(E) An accounting of the sources of financial support for the entity, with sufficient detail to disclose any relationships that could reasonably be considered to present a potential conflict of interest.

§ 14602. Formation of benefit corporation

A benefit corporation shall be formed in accordance with Chapter 2 (commencing with Section 200) of Division 1 except that the articles shall also state that the corporation is a benefit corporation and shall identify any specific public benefit adopted pursuant to Section 14610.

§ 14603. Corporation as benefit corporation; Requirements; Merger reorganization; Conversion

(a) A corporation may become a benefit corporation under this part by amending the corporation's articles so that the articles contain a statement that the corporation is a benefit corporation. The amendment shall not be effective unless it is adopted by at least the minimum status vote. If the amendment is adopted, a shareholder of the corporation may, by complying with Chapter 13 (commencing with Section 1300) of Division 1, require the corporation to purchase at their fair market value the shares owned by the shareholder which are dissenting shares as defined in subdivision (b) of Section 1300 in accordance with the procedures in that chapter, as if the adoption of the amendment were a reorganization to which that chapter applies.

(b) If a corporation that is not a benefit corporation is a constituent corporation in a merger reorganization or is the acquired corporation in an exchange reorganization, and the surviving corporation in the merger reorganization is to be a benefit corporation or the articles of the acquired corporation are to be amended in the exchange reorganization to provide that it will be a benefit corporation, then the reorganization shall not be effective

（3）由满足以下两个要求的实体制定：

（A）拥有评估公司社会和环境综合绩效所需的专业知识。

（B）使用平衡多方相关者利益的方法制定标准，包括设定至少 30 天听取公众意见的期间以制定标准。

（4）关于标准的以下所有信息可公开获取：

（A）衡量企业整体社会和环境绩效时所考虑的标准。

（B）第（A）分项中标准的相关权重。

（C）该标准中制定和控制修改程序的董事、高管、主要股东和该实体控制人员的身份。

（D）标准修改和第（C）分项规定的控制人员变动的程序。

（E）资金来源的核算，包括充分披露合理认知下存在利益冲突的所有细节。

第 14602 条　公共利益公司的设立

公共利益公司应当依据第 1 分编的第 2 章（始于第 200 条）设立，但公司章程必须声明其是公共利益公司并且依据第 14610 条的规定设定特定公共利益。

第 14603 条　公共利益公司；要求；合并重组；转换

（a）一个公司可依据本部分规定成为公共利益公司，通过修改公司章程，作出该公司为公共利益公司的声明。公司章程的修改应满足最低表决要求。如果修改获准，公司股东可以依据第 1 分编第 13 章（始于第 1300 条）的规定，要求公司以公允价格购买股东的在该章第 1300 条第（b）款定义下的异议股份，修改获准的要求与该章中重组的规定一致。

（b）如果合并重组或股权置换中的收购公司是一家非公共利益公司，而且在合并重组中的存续公司属公共利益公司或者收购公司的章程将在置换重组中将本公司修改为公共利益公司，那么重组须满足最低表决要求才能获准。

unless the reorganization is approved by the corporation or domestic other business entity by at least the minimum status vote.

(c) If a domestic other business entity is a party to a merger reorganization and the surviving corporation in the reorganization is to be a benefit corporation, then the reorganization shall not be effective unless the reorganization is approved by the domestic other business entity by at least the minimum status vote.

(d) If a domestic other business entity is the converting entity (subdivision (d) of Section 1150) in a conversion in which the converted corporation (subdivision (a) of Section 1150) is a benefit corporation, the conversion shall not be effective unless the conversion is approved by the domestic other business entity by at least the minimum status vote.

§ 14604. Termination of status; Effect of reorganization or conversion; Disposition of assets

(a) A benefit corporation may terminate its status as a benefit corporation and cease to be subject to this part by amending the corporation's articles to delete the provision required by Section 14602. The amendment shall not be effective unless the amendment is adopted by at least the minimum status vote. If the amendment is adopted, a shareholder of the corporation may, by complying with Chapter 13 (commencing with Section 1300) of Division 1, require the corporation to purchase at their fair market value the shares owned by the shareholder which are dissenting shares as defined in subdivision (b) of Section 1300 in accordance with the procedures in that chapter.

(b) If a reorganization (Section 181) would have the effect of terminating the status of a corporation as a benefit corporation, the reorganization shall not be effective unless the reorganization is approved by at least the minimum status vote.

(c) If a benefit corporation is the converting corporation (Section 1150) in a conversion (Section 161.9), the conversion shall not be effective unless the conversion is approved by at least the minimum status vote.

(d) A sale, lease, conveyance, exchange, transfer, or other disposition of all or substantially all of the assets of a benefit corporation, unless the transaction is in the usual and ordinary course of business of the benefit corporation, shall not be effective unless the transaction is approved by at least the minimum status vote. If the transaction is approved, a shareholder of the corporation may, by complying with Chapter 13 (commencing with Section 1300) of Division 1, require the corporation to purchase at their fair market value the shares owned by the shareholder which are dissenting shares as defined in subdivision (b) of Section 1300 in accordance with the procedures in that chapter, as if the transaction were a reorganization to which that chapter applies.

（c）如果本州其他商业实体是合并重组的一方并且重组中的存续一方为公共利益公司，那么重组至少须满足最低表决要求才能获准。

（d）如果本州其他商业实体是转换中的转换实体［第 1150 条第（d）款］且转换后的实体［第 1150 条第（d）款］是公共利益公司，那么转换至少须满足最低表决要求才能获准。

第 14604 条　形态终止；重组或转换的效力；财产处分

（a）公共利益公司可通过删除第 14602 条规定的公司章程中其作为公共利益公司的声明来终止其公共利益公司的形态并不再受本部分规定调整。公司章程的修改应满足最低表决要求。如果修改获准，公司股东可依据第 1 分编第 13 章（始于第 1300 条）的规定，要求公司以公允价格购买股东的在该章第 1300 条第（b）款定义下的异议股份。

（b）如果重组（第 181 条）有终止公司的公共利益形态的效力，重组应满足最低表决要求。

（c）如果公共利益公司是转换（第 161.9 条）中的转换公司（第 1150 条），转换应满足最低表决要求。

（d）除公共利益公司的正常商业往来外，公共利益公司的出售、出租、让与、置换、转让或者其他处置全部或主要财产的行为，须满足最低表决要求。如果该交易获准，公司股东可以依据第 1 分编第 13 章（始于第 1300 条）的规定，要求公司以公允价格购买股东在该章第 1300 条第（b）款定义下的异议股份，该交易如同该章中的重组。

Chapter 2. Corporate Purposes

§ 14610. Purpose of benefit corporation; Statement in articles of incorporation; Amendment of articles

(a) A benefit corporation shall have the purpose of creating general public benefit. This purpose is in addition to, and may be a limitation on, the corporation's purpose under Section 206 and any specific purpose set forth in its articles in accordance with subdivision (b).

(b) In addition to the provisions required by Section 202, the articles of incorporation of a benefit corporation shall contain the following statement: "This corporation is a benefit corporation." Notwithstanding subdivision (b) of Section 202, the articles of a benefit corporation may identify one or more specific public benefits that shall be the purpose or purposes of the benefit corporation. The identification of a specific public benefit under this subdivision does not limit the obligation of a benefit corporation to create general public benefit.

(c) The creation of general and specific public benefit as provided in subdivisions (a) and (b) shall be deemed to be in the best interests of the benefit corporation.

(d) A benefit corporation may amend its articles to add, amend, or delete the identification of a specific public benefit that shall be the purpose of the benefit corporation to create. The amendment shall not be effective unless the amendment is adopted by at least the minimum status vote.

Chapter 3. Accountability

§ 14620. Duties of directors, board, or committees; Considerations; Liability

(a) A director shall perform the duties of a director including duties as a member of any committee of the board upon which the director may serve, in good faith, in a manner the director believes to be in the best interests of the benefit corporation and with that care, including reasonable inquiry, as an ordinarily prudent person in a like position would use under similar circumstances.

(b) In discharging their respective duties, and in considering the best interests of the benefit corporation, the board of directors, committees of the board, and individual directors of a benefit corporation shall consider the impacts of any action or proposed action upon all of the following:

(1) The shareholders of the benefit corporation.

(2) The employees and workforce of the benefit corporation and its subsidiaries and suppliers.

(3) The interests of customers of the benefit corporation as beneficiaries of the general or specific public benefit purposes of the benefit corporation.

(4) Community and societal considerations, including those of any community in which offices or facilities of the benefit corporation or its subsidiaries or suppliers are located.

第 2 章　公司目的

第 14610 条　公共利益公司的目标；公司章程中的声明；章程的修改

（a）公共利益公司应当有服务于一般公共利益的目的。此目的在第 206 条规定的公司目的和依据第（b）款规定在公司章程中创设的特别目标之外或对公共利益公司构成限制。

（b）除第 202 条的规定外，公共利益公司的章程应包含以下声明："公司为公共利益公司。"尽管根据第 202 条第（b）款的规定，公共利益公司的章程可以设定一项或多项特定公共利益作为公共利益公司的目标。依据本款规定设定的特定公共利益并不影响公共利益公司履行创设一般公共利益的义务。

（c）依据第（a）款和第（b）款规定创设的一般和特定公共利益目的被视为公共利益公司的最佳利益。

（d）公共利益公司可以通过修改章程增加、修改或删除公司章程中设定的特定公共利益目的。公司对章程的修改需满足最低表决要求。

第 3 章　责任

第 14620 条　董事、董事会或委员会的义务；考虑因素；责任

（a）董事应履行董事义务，包括董事委员会成员的义务，董事应善意地以符合公共利益公司最佳利益的方式来任职，并且履行包括合理调查在内的一般谨慎人在相似情况下的注意义务。

（b）在履行各自职责和考虑公共利益公司最佳利益时，公共利益公司的董事会、董事委员会和董事应当考虑行为或计划中的行为对以下对象的影响：

（1）公共利益公司的股东。

（2）公共利益公司雇员及其子公司和供应商。

（3）作为公共利益公司一般或特定公共利益受益者的消费者的利益。

（4）社区和社会因素，包括公共利益公司及其子公司或供应商办公地或设施所在地的社区。

(5) The local and global environment.

(6) The short–term and long–term interests of the benefit corporation, including benefits that may accrue to the benefit corporation from its long–term plans and the possibility that these interests may be best served by retaining control of the benefit corporation rather than selling or transferring control to another entity.

(7) The ability of the benefit corporation to accomplish its general, and any specific, public benefit purpose.

(c) In discharging their respective duties, the persons described in subdivision (b) may consider any of the following:

(1) The resources, intent, and conduct, including past, stated, and potential conduct, of any person seeking to acquire control of the corporation.

(2) Any other pertinent factors or the interests of any other person or group.

(d) In discharging their respective duties, the persons described in subdivision (a) shall not be required to give priority to any particular factor or the interests of any particular person or group referred to in subdivision (b) or (c) over any other factor or the interests of any other person or group unless the benefit corporation has stated its intention to give priority to a specific public benefit purpose identified in the articles.

(e) In performing the duties of a director, a director shall be entitled to rely on information, opinions, reports, or statements, including financial statements and other financial data, in each case prepared or presented by any of the following:

(1) One or more officers or employees of the benefit corporation whom the director believes to be reliable and competent in the matters presented.

(2) Counsel, independent accountants, or other persons as to matters that the director believes to be within those persons' professional or expert competence.

(3) A committee of the board upon which the director does not serve, as to matters within its designated authority, which committee the director believes to merit confidence, so long as, in any of those cases, the director acts in good faith, after reasonable inquiry when the need therefor is indicated by the circumstances and without knowledge that would cause that reliance to be unwarranted.

(f) A director shall not be liable for monetary damages under this part for any failure of the benefit corporation to create a general or specific public benefit.

(g) A person who performs the duties of a director in accordance with this part shall not be liable for monetary damages for any alleged failure to discharge the person's obligations as a director.

(h) In addition to the limitations provided in subdivisions (f) and (g), the liability of a director for monetary damages may be eliminated or limited in a benefit corporation's articles to the extent provided in paragraph (10) of subdivision (a) of Section 204.

（5）当地和全球环境。

（6）公共利益公司的短期和长期利益，包括可能从其长期计划中获得的利益，以及公共利益公司继续保持独立可能产生的最佳利益，而不是将控制权出让或转卖给其他实体。

（7）公共利益公司实现其一般和特定公共利益目的的能力。

（c）在履行各自义务时，第（b）款规定中的人员可能要考虑以下因素：

（1）寻求获取公司控制权的人的资源、意图和行为，包括过去、现在和未来的行为。

（2）任何其他人或团体的其他相关因素或利益。

（d）在履行各自义务时，除公司章程要求优先考虑特定利益或因素外，第（a）款规定的人无须优先考虑第（b）款 或第（c）款中的某个利益或因素。

（e）在履行董事义务时，董事有权依赖以下主体准备或提供的信息、意见、报告或报表，包括财务报表和其他财务数据：

（1）董事认为在相关事项中可靠并能够胜任的一个或多个公共利益公司的高管或职员。

（2）董事认为相关事项在其专业能力之内的顾问、独立会计或其他人。

（3）董事认为值得信任、相关事项在其权限范围内且该董事不任职的董事委员会，只要董事在情况表明需要时，经过合理的调查，在不知道该信任不可靠的情况下，善意地行事。

（f）董事不对公共利益公司未能创造一般或特定公共利益承担本部分规定下的损害赔偿责任。

（g）依据本部分履行董事义务的人不对未能履行董事义务承担损害赔偿责任。

（h）除第（f）款和第（g）款规定的限制外，公共利益公司章程中董事的损害赔偿责任可以在第 204 条第（a）款第（10）项规定的限度内被消除或限制。

(i) A director shall not have a fiduciary duty to a person that is a beneficiary of the general or specific public benefit purposes of a benefit corporation arising from the status of the person as a beneficiary.

(j) A director of a foreign corporation that is subject to Section 2115 shall not be subject to Section 309 and shall be subject instead to this section if the director of the foreign corporation is subject to duties under its articles of incorporation, bylaws, or the law of its jurisdiction of incorporation similar to the duties of directors under this section.

§ 14621. Benefit report; Statement; Requirements

(a) The board of directors of a benefit corporation shall prepare for inclusion in the annual benefit report to shareholders required by Section 14630, a statement indicating whether, in the opinion of the board of directors, the benefit corporation failed to pursue its general, and any specific, public benefit purpose in all material respects during the period covered by the report.

(b) If, in the opinion of the board of directors, the benefit corporation failed to pursue its general, and any specific, public benefit purpose, the statement required by subdivision (a) shall include a description of the ways in which the benefit corporation failed to pursue its general, and any specific, public benefit purpose.

§ 14622. Duties of Officers; Considerations; Liability

(a) Each officer of a benefit corporation shall consider the interests and factors described in Section 14620 in the manner provided in that section when either of the following applies:

(1) The officer has discretion to act with respect to a matter.

(2) It reasonably appears to the officer that the matter may have a material effect on any of the following:

(A) The creation of a general or specific public benefit by the benefit corporation.

(B) Any of the interests or factors referred to in subdivision (b) of Section 14620.

(b) The consideration by an officer of interests and factors in the manner described in subdivision (a) shall not constitute a violation of the duties of the officer.

(c) An officer shall not be liable for monetary damages under this part for any of the following:

(1) Any action taken as an officer if the officer performed the duties of the position in compliance with this section.

(2) Any failure of the benefit corporation to create a general or specific public benefit.

(d) An officer shall not have a fiduciary duty to a person that is a beneficiary of the general or specific public benefit purposes of a benefit corporation arising from the status of the person as a beneficiary.

（i）董事不对公共利益公司一般或特定社会目的的受益人负责。

（j）如果州外公司的董事在公司章程、章程细则和其设立地法律规定下的义务与本节的董事义务相似，受第 2115 条规定调整的外州公司不应受第 309 条调整而应受本条调整。

第 14621 条　公共利益报告；声明；要求

（a）公共利益董事在第 14630 条规定的提供给股东的年度公共利益报告中应当包含董事会对报告所述时间内公共利益公司是否在所有重要事项上依一般和特定公共利益目的行事的意见。

（b）如果董事会认为公共利益公司未能追求一般和特定公共利益目的，应依第（a）款规定陈述公共利益公司未能追求一般和特定公共利益目的的情况。

第 14622 条　高管义务；考虑因素；责任

（a）当出现以下情况时，公共利益公司高管应根据本条规定的行为标准考虑第 14620 条中规定的利益和因素：

（1）高管就该行为有自由裁量权。
（2）高管有理由认为该行为对以下事项有实质性影响：

（A）公共利益公司创设的一般或特定公共利益。
（B）第 14620 条第（b）款提到的任何利益或因素。
（b）高管对第（a）款中规定的利益和因素的考虑不违反高管义务。

（c）高管不因本部分规定对以下行为承担损害赔偿责任：

（1）符合本条规定的高管行为。

（2）公共利益公司未能追求或创设一般或特定公共利益。
（d）高管不对公共利益公司一般目的或特定社会目的的受益人负责。

§ 14623. Action or claims against benefit corporation or directors; Commencement of benefit enforcement proceeding; Failure to comply with part

(a) No person may bring an action or assert a claim against a benefit corporation or its directors or officers under this chapter except in a benefit enforcement proceeding.

(b) A benefit enforcement proceeding may be commenced or maintained only as follows:

(1) Directly by the benefit corporation.

(2) Derivatively by any of the following:

(A) A shareholder.

(B) A director.

(C) A person or group of persons that owns beneficially or of record 5 percent or more of the equity interests in an entity of which the benefit corporation is a subsidiary.

(D) Other persons as have been specified in the articles or bylaws of the benefit corporation.

(c) A benefit corporation shall not be liable for monetary damages under this part for any failure of the benefit corporation to create a general or specific public benefit.

(d) If the court in a benefit enforcement proceeding finds that a failure to comply with this part was without justification, the court may award an amount sufficient to reimburse the plaintiff for the reasonable expenses incurred by the plaintiff, including attorney's fees and expenses, in connection with the benefit enforcement proceeding.

Chapter 4. Transparency

§ 14630. Benefit report; Contents of report; Posting of report on Internet Web site

(a) A benefit corporation shall deliver to each shareholder an annual benefit report including all of the following:

(1) A narrative description of all of the following:

(A) The process and rationale for selecting the third–party standard used to prepare the benefit report.

(B) The ways in which the benefit corporation pursued a general public benefit during the applicable year and the extent to which that general public benefit was created.

(C) The ways in which the benefit corporation pursued any specific public benefit that the articles state it is the purpose of the benefit corporation to create and the extent to which that specific public benefit was created.

(D) Any circumstances that have hindered the creation by the benefit corporation of a general or specific public benefit.

(2) An assessment of the overall social and environmental performance of the benefit corporation, prepared in accordance with a third–party standard applied consistently with

第 14623 条　向公共利益公司或董事提起诉讼或主张；公共利益实施程序的提起；未能遵守本部分规定

（a）非经公共利益实施程序，任何人不得依据本章规定向公共利益公司或者其董事、高管提起诉讼或提出主张。

（b）下列情形中，以下主体可提起公共利益实施程序：

（1）由公共利益公司直接提起。

（2）由以下主体派生提起：

（A）股东。

（B）董事。

（C）持有公共利益公司母公司 5% 以上已发行股份的登记股东或实际受益人。

（D）公共利益公司章程或章程细则中规定的其他人员。

（c）公共利益公司不对本部分规定下任何未能追求或创造一般或特定公共利益承担损害赔偿责任。

（d）如果在公共利益实施程序中，法院发现公共利益公司或董事未能遵守本部分规定而且没有正当理由，法院可以判决其赔偿原告充足的合理费用，包括与公共利益实施程序相关的律师费用和其他费用。

第 4 章　透明度

第 14630 条　公共利益报告；报告的内容；将报告公布于网站

（a）公共利益公司应提交给股东包含以下内容的年度公共利益报告：

（1）对以下事项的描述：

（A）编写公共利益报告所选择的第三方标准的程序和原因。

（B）公共利益公司本年度追求一般公共利益的方法和一般公共利益实现的情况。

（C）公共利益公司追求公司章程中规定的特定公共利益的方法以及该特定公共利益实现的情况。

（D）阻碍公共利益公司创造一般和特定公共利益的情形。

（2）依据第三方标准对公共利益公司的社会和环境表现进行的整体评价，其应沿用先前公共利益报告中使用的标准或者附一份解释适用差异的说明。该评价无

any application of that standard in prior benefit reports or accompanied by an explanation of the reasons for any inconsistent application. The assessment does not need to be audited or certified by a third party.

(3) The name of each person that owns 5 percent or more of the outstanding shares of the benefit corporation, either beneficially, to the extent known to the benefit corporation without independent investigation, or of record.

(4) The statement required by Section 14621.

(5) A statement of any connection between the entity that established the third-party standard, or its directors, officers, or material owners, and the benefit corporation, or its directors, officers, and material owners, including any financial or governance relationship that might materially affect the credibility of the objective assessment of the third-party standard.

(b) The benefit report shall be sent annually to each shareholder within 120 days following the end of the fiscal year of the benefit corporation or at the same time that the benefit corporation delivers any other annual report to its shareholders.

(c) A benefit corporation shall post all of its benefit reports on the public portion of its Internet Web site, if any, except that the compensation paid to directors and any financial or proprietary information included in the benefit report may be omitted from the benefit report as posted on the Internet Web site.

(d)(1) If a benefit corporation does not have an Internet Web site, the benefit corporation shall provide a copy of its most recent benefit report, without charge, to any person that requests a copy.

(2) The benefit corporation may omit any proprietary or financial information, including, but not limited to, compensation paid to directors, from the copy of a benefit report that the benefit corporation provides pursuant to paragraph (1).

§ 14631. Statement in certificates representing shares of benefit corporation

All certificates representing shares of a benefit corporation shall contain, in addition to any other statements required by the General Corporation Law (Division 1 (commencing with Section 100)), the following conspicuous language on the face of the certificate:

"This entity is a benefit corporation organized under Part 13 (commencing with Section 14600) of Division 3 of Title 1 of the California Corporations Code."

须第三方审计或证明。

（3）拥有公共利益公司5%以上已发行股份的实际收益人或股东的姓名，前者无须公共利益公司单独进行调查即可获知。

（4）第14621条要求的声明。

（5）设立第三方标准的实体或其董事、高管或实际控制人与公共利益公司或其董事、高管或实际控制人之间关系的声明，包括任何可能影响第三方标准可信度的财务或管理关系。

（b）公共利益公司应在公共利益公司财政年度结束后120天内或者公共利益公司向其股东送交其他年度报告的同一时间将公共利益报告送交各股东。

（c）若条件允许，公共利益公司应当将其所有公共利益报告发布于其网站的公共部分，但可将公共利益报告中的董事薪酬和财务、所有权信息删除。

（d）（1）如果公共利益公司没有网站，应向所有索取该报告的个人免费提供最新公共利益报告的副本。

（2）公共利益公司可以删除公共利益报告副本中的任何所有权或财务信息，包括但不限于公共利益公司依据第（1）项支付的董事薪酬。

第14631条　公共利益公司股份证书中的声明

除《普通公司法》［第1分编（始于第100条）］中要求的声明，所有公共利益公司股份证书上应包含以下明确声明：

“该实体为依据《加利福尼亚州法典》第1编第3分编第13节（始于第14600条）成立的公共利益公司。”

THE STATE OF COLORADO

The governor Signed this measure on May 5, 2013

House bill 13–1138

CONCERNING BENEFIT CORPORATIONS, AND, IN CONNECTION THEREWITH, MAKING AN APPROPRIATION.

Be it enacted by the general assembly of the state of Colorado:

Section 1. In Colorado revised statutes, add part 5 to article 101 of title 7 as follows:

Part 5 public benefit corporations

7-101-501. Short title.

This part 5 shall be known and may be cited as the "public benefit corporation act of Colorado".

7-101-502. Law applicable to public benefit corporations – how formed.

This part 5 applies to all public benefit corporations. If a corporation elects to become a public benefit corporation under this part 5 in the manner prescribed in this part 5, it is subject in all respects to the "Colorado business corporation act", articles 101 to 117 of this title, and the "Colorado corporations and associations act", article 90 of this title, except to the extent this part 5 imposes additional or different requirements, in which case such additional or different requirements apply.

7-101-503. Public benefit corporation - definitions - contents of articles of incorporation.

(1) a public benefit corporation is a for–profit corporation organized under and subject to the requirements of the "Colorado business corporation act", articles 101 to 117 of this title, or a domestic cooperative organized under article 55 or 56 of this title that is subject to the "Colorado business corporation act", that is intended to produce a public benefit or public benefits and to operate in a responsible and sustainable manner. To that end, a public benefit corporation shall be managed in a manner that balances the shareholders' pecuniary

科罗拉州

本法案于2013年5月5日由州长签署

众议院法案 13-1138
与公共利益公司以及拨款有关

由科罗拉州州议会颁布：
第1部分 《科罗拉州修订法》，于第7编第101章增加第5节。

第5节 公共利益公司

第7-101-501条 简称
第5节 被称为《科罗拉州公共利益公司法》。

第7-101-502条 公共利益公司法律适用——设立
第5节适用于所有公共利益公司。根据本节选择公共利益形态的公司，受《科罗拉州商事公司法》第101章至第117章和《科罗拉州公司和组织法》第90章的规定调整，第5节中有其他或不同的要求需要适用的情形除外。

第7-101-503条 公共利益公司——定义——公司章程的内容

（1）公共利益公司是指根据《科罗拉州商事公司法》第101节至第117节规定设立的，意图促进公共利益并以负责任的和持续性方式运行的营利性公司或根据《科罗拉州商事公司法》第55节或第56节的规定创立的州内公司。为实现该目的，公共利益公司应平衡股东利益、受公司运营影响的利益相关者利益和公共利益或公司章程确定的公共利益。在公司章程中，公共利益公司应：

interests, the best interest of those materially affected by the corporation's conduct, and the public benefit identified in its articles of incorporation. In its articles of incorporation, a public benefit corporation shall:

(a) identify within its statement of business or purpose pursuant to section 7–103–101 (1) one or more specific public benefits to be promoted by the corporation; and

(b) state at the beginning of the articles of incorporation that it is a public benefit corporation.

(2) "public benefit" means one or more positive effects or reduction of negative effects on one or more categories of persons, entities, communities, or interests other than shareholders in their capacities as shareholders, including effects of an artistic, charitable, cultural, economic, educational, environmental, literary, medical, religious, scientific, or technological nature.

(3) "public benefit provisions" means the provisions of articles of incorporation contemplated by this part 5.

(4) the domestic entity name of a public benefit corporation must, without exception, contain the words "public benefit corporation", the abbreviation " P.B.C.", or the designation "PBC", and otherwise satisfy the requirements of section7–102–102(1) (a).

7-101-504. Certain amendments and mergers - votes required - dissenter's rights.

(1) notwithstanding any other provisions of this part 5 other than subsection (2) of this section, a corporation that is not a public benefit corporation shall not, without the approval of two–thirds of the outstanding shares of each class of shares of the corporation of which there are outstanding shares, whether voting or non–voting:

(a) Amend its articles of incorporation to include a provision authorized by section 7–101–503 (1) ;

(b) Convert into a domestic or foreign public benefit corporation or similar entity; or

(c) Merge with or into another entity if, as a result of the merger, the shares in such corporation would become, or be converted into or exchanged for the right to receive, shares or other equity interests in a domestic or foreign public benefit corporation or similar entity.

(2) the restrictions of this section do not apply before the corporation has received payment for any of its capital stock. In the case of a domestic cooperative formed under article 55 or 56 of this title that is subject to the "Colorado business corporation act", articles 101 to 117 of this title, an ccccaction described in subsection (1) of this section must be approved by vote or consent of the holders of every class or series of equity interest in the entity that are entitled to vote on the action by at least two–thirds of the votes or consents that all of those holders are entitled to cast on the action.

(3) a shareholder of a corporation that is not a public benefit corporation is entitled

（a）根据第 7–103–101（1）款的规定在公司章程中声明公司目的或确定具体公司目的；并且

（b）在公司章程标题中声明其为公共利益公司。

（2）“公共利益”是指对一类或多类群体、实体、社区或其他利益（而非股东），包括但不限于艺术、慈善、文化、经济、教育、环境、文学、医疗、宗教、科学或自然技术等产生积极影响（或减少消极影响）。“公共利益条款”是指根据本节规定在公司章程中涉及的条款。

（3）“公共利益条款”是指根据第 5 节规定在公司章程中涉及的条款。

（4）本州公共利益公司的名称必须包含“公共利益公司”，其缩写为“P.B.C.”或含有“PBC”的标志，符合上述要求的名称则认为其满足第 7–102–102（1）（a）款的规定。

第 7–101–504 条　章程的修改和合并——投票要求——异议权

（1）除第 5 节的本条第（2）款的其他规定外，非公共利益公司的以下行为须获得每一类别股 2/3 以上多数股份的同意，无论是否有投票权：

（a）修改公司章程，使其包含第 7–101–503（1）款规定的条款；

（b）公司转换为本州或外州的公共利益公司或相似实体；或者

（c）与另一个实体合并或并入另一个实体，如果由于合并，该公司的股份将成为或被转换为或置换为接收本州或外州公共利益公司或类似实体的股份或其他股权的权利。

（2）本条的限制性规定不适用于公司在此之前出售股份所获得的资本金。根据本编第 55 章或第 56 章设立的州内公司受《科罗拉州商事公司法》调整，本编第 101 章至第 117 章、本条第（1）款所述的行为必须获得每一类别或系列有投票权的股东的至少 2/3 以上票数的同意。

（3）如果股东根据第（3）款的规定不赞成对公司章程的修改、合并或转换非

to exercise the right to dissent pursuant to article 113 of this title if the shareholder has neither voted in favor of an amendment, merger, or conversion specified in this subsection (3) nor consented thereto in writing pursuant to Section 7–107–104 and holds shares of such corporation immediately before the effective time of:

(a) an amendment to the corporation's articles of incorporation to include a provision authorized by section 7–101–503 (1) (a);

(b) a conversion into a domestic or foreign public benefit corporation or similar entity; or

(c) a merger that would result in the conversion of the corporation's shares into, or exchange of the corporation's shares for, the right to receive shares or other equity interests in a domestic or foreign public benefit corporation or similar entity.

(4) notwithstanding any other provision of this part 5, a corporation that is a public benefit corporation shall not, without the approval of two–thirds of the outstanding shares of each class of shares of the corporation of which there are outstanding shares, whether voting or nonvoting:

(a) amend its articles of incorporation to delete or amend a provision authorized by section 7–101–503 (1) (a);

(b) convert into another domestic or foreign entity that is not a public benefit corporation or similar entity; or

(c) merge with or into another entity if:

(i) as a result of the merger, the shares in such corporation would become, be converted into, or be exchanged for the right to receive shares or other equity interests in a domestic or foreign corporation that is not a public benefit corporation or similar entity; and

(ii) the articles of incorporation or similar governing instrument of the domestic or foreign corporation that is not a public benefit corporation or similar entity do not contain the identical provisions identifying the public benefit pursuant to section 7–101–503 (1).

(5) a nonprofit corporation cannot be a constituent entity in connection with a merger or conversion governed by this section.

7-101-505. Share certificates - notices regarding uncertificated shares.

A share certificate issued by a public benefit corporation must note conspicuously that the corporation is a public benefit corporation formed pursuant to this part 5. A statement sent by a public benefit corporation pursuant to section 7–106–207 must state conspicuously that the corporation is a public benefit corporation formed pursuant to this part 5.

7-101-506. Duties of directors.

(1) the board of directors shall manage or direct the business and affairs of a public benefit corporation in a manner that balances the pecuniary interests of the shareholders, the best interests of those materially affected by the corporation's conduct, and the specific

公共利益公司，亦未根据第 7–107–104 条的规定作出书面同意，则在以下时间之前，持有该公司股票的股东有权根据本编第 113 章的规定行使异议权：

（a）在公司章程中增加第 7–101–503（1）（a）项规定的条款之前；

（b）转换为本州或外州公共利益公司或类似实体之前；或者

（c）在与本州或外州公共利益公司或相似实体合并导致公司股份与前者发生合并或置换之前。

（4）尽管第 5 节另有规定，无论是以投票还是非投票的方式进行，非公共利益公司的以下行为须获得公司每一类别已发行股份 2/3 以上多数股份同意：

（a）根据本条第 7–101–503（1）（a）款的规定修改公司章程；

（b）转换为其他本州或外州非公共利益公司或其他相似实体；

（c）与其他实体合并，如果：

（i）合并的结果会导致该公司股份与本州或其他州非公共利益公司或其他相似实体发生置换；

（ii）本州或外州非公共利益公司或其他相似实体的公司章程或其他类似文件不包含第 7–101–503（1）款规定的条款。

（5）非营利性公司不能成为合并或转换中的存续实体。

第 7–101–505 条　股权证书——无股权证书的通知

公共利益公司颁发的股权证书上必须载明该公司为根据本法第 5 节设立的公共利益公司。公共利益公司根据第 7–106–207 条规定发出的任何通知都应在明显位置声明本公司是根据本节设立的公共利益公司。

第 7–101–506 条　董事义务

（1）董事会在管理公司时必须平衡出资股东利益和公司章程规定的特定公共利益。

public benefit identified in its articles of incorporation.

(2) a director of a public benefit corporation: (a) does not, by virtue of the public benefit provisions of section 7–101–503 (1), have a duty to any person on account of an interest of the person in the public benefit identified in the articles of incorporation or on account of an interest materially affected by the corporation's conduct; and

(b) with respect to a decision implicating the balance requirement in subsection (1) of this section, will be deemed to satisfy the director's fiduciary duties to shareholders and the corporation if the director's decision is both informed and disinterested and not such that no person of ordinary, sound judgment would approve.

(3) the articles of incorporation of a public benefit corporation may include a provision that a disinterested director's failure to satisfy this section does not, for the purposes of section 7–108–401 or article 109 of this title, constitute an act or omission not in good faith or a breach of the duty of loyalty.

7-101-507. Benefit report - definition.

(1) a public benefit corporation shall prepare a report that includes:

(a) a narrative description of:

(i) the ways in which the public benefit corporation promoted the public benefit identified in the articles of incorporation and the best interests of those materially affected by the corporation's conduct;

(ii) any circumstances that have hindered the public benefit corporation's promotion of the identified public benefit and the best interests of those materially affected by the corporation's conduct; and

(iii) the process and rationale for selecting or changing the third–party standard used to prepare the benefit report; and

(b) an assessment of the overall social and environmental performance of the public benefit corporation against a third–party standard:

(i) applied consistently with any application of that standard in prior benefit reports; or

(ii) accompanied by an explanation of the reasons for any inconsistent application. The assessment does not need to be performed, audited, or certified by a third party.

(2) for purposes of subsection (1) of this section, "third–party standard" means a standard for defining, reporting, and assessing the overall corporate social and environmental performance, which standard is developed by an organization that is not controlled by the public benefit corporation or any of its affiliates and that makes publicly available the following information:

(a) the criteria considered when measuring the social and environmental performance of a business, the relative weightings of those criteria, if any, and the process for development and revision of the standard; and

（2）公共利益公司的董事：（a）并不因第 7–101–503（1）款的规定而对任何公司章程中规定的公共利益或受公司行为重大影响的利益的受益人承担个人责任；并且

（b）如果董事行为满足本条第（1）款所规定的平衡各方利益的要求，且董事的决定基于合理信息且无涉私利，则认为董事行为符合其对股东的信义义务；

（3）公共利益公司章程中可以包含免责条款，声明任何非由个人私利导致的不满足本编第 7–108–401 条或第 109 章规定的行为不构成对诚实信用或忠诚义务的违反。

第 7–101–507 条　公共利益报告——定义

（1）公共利益公司编写的公共利益报告应包括以下内容：

（a）对下述事项的说明：

（i）公共利益公司促进公司章程确定的公共利益和受公司行为实质影响群体的最大利益实现的方法；

（ii）阻碍公共利益公司实现公司章程确定的公共利益和受公司行为实质影响群体最大利益的情形；

（iii）为编写公共利益报告而选择或更换第三方标准的程序和原因；以及

（b）依据第三方标准对公共利益公司的社会和环境表现作出的整体评价：

（i）沿用先前公共利益报告中使用的标准；或者

（ii）附一份说明以解释适用标准的差异。公共利益公司表现评价书无须经审计或第三方证明。

（2）为实现本条第（1）款规定的目的，“第三方标准”是指用于定义、报告和评估公司社会和环境绩效的标准，该标准经非由公共利益公司或其子公司控制的第三方实体制定，并且以下信息可公开获得：

（a）衡量企业社会和环境绩效时所考虑的相关指标及其权重，以及标准的制定和修改程序；并且

(b) any material owners of the organization that developed the third–party standard, the members of its governing body and how they are selected, and the sources of financial support for the organization, in sufficient detail to disclose any relationships that could reasonably be considered to compromise its independence.

(3) a public benefit corporation that prepares a report pursuant to this section shall send it to each shareholder.

(4) a public benefit corporation shall post all of its reports prepared pursuant to this section on the public portion of its web site, if any, but the public benefit corporation may omit from the posted reports any financial or proprietary information included in the reports.

(5) if a public benefit corporation does not have a web site, the public benefit corporation shall provide a copy of its most recent report, without charge, to a person that requests a copy, but the public benefit corporation may omit any financial or proprietary information from the copy of the benefit report so provided.

7-101-508. Derivative suits.

(1) shareholders of a public benefit corporation may maintain a derivative lawsuit to enforce the requirements of section 7–101–506 (1) if the shareholders own, individually or collectively, as of the date of instituting a derivative suit, either:

(a) at least two percent of the corporation's outstanding shares; or

(b) in the case of a corporation with shares listed on a national securities exchange, the lesser of two percent of the corporation's outstanding shares or shares of at least two million dollars in market value.

7-101-509. No effect on other corporations.

This part 5 does not affect a statute or rule of law that applies to a corporation that is not a public benefit corporation, except as provided in section 7–101–504.

（b）标准制定方实体控制人员的身份、控制该组织及其成员选任的管理人员、该组织的财政收入来源以及其他影响其独立性的详细信息。

（3）公共利益公司根据本条规定编写的报告应向每位股东递交。

（4）若条件允许，公共利益公司应当将其所有根据本条规定编写的公共利益报告发布于其网站的公共部分；但可将公共利益报告中的财务或所有权信息删除。

（5）如果公共利益公司没有网站，应向所有索取报告的个人免费提供最新的公共利益报告的副本，但可将公共利益报告副本中的财务或所有权信息删除。

第 7–101–508 条　派生诉讼

（1）如果个人或合计持有公共利益公司股份的股东满足以下条件之一，则公共利益公司的股东可以提起派生诉讼以请求执行第 7–101–506（1）款中的规定：

（a）至少持有 2% 的已发行公司股份；或者

（b）在国家级证券市场上市的公司中，至少拥有公司 2% 已发行股份或市值 $2，000，000 的股份。

第 7–101–509 条　本节规定不适用于其他类型的公司

除第 7–101–504 条另有规定外，第 5 节规定不影响非公共利益公司有关条文和规则的适用。

THE STATE OF CONNECTICUT

CHAPTER 604
BENEFIT CORPORATIONS

Sec. 33-1350. Short title: Connecticut Benefit Corporation Act.

Sections 33–1350 to 33–1364, inclusive, shall be known and may be cited as the "Connecticut Benefit Corporation Act".

Sec. 33-1351. Definitions.

As used in this section and sections 33–1352 to 33–1364, inclusive:

(1) "Benefit corporation" means a business corporation (A) that has elected to become subject to the provisions of sections 33–1352 to 33–1364, inclusive, and (B) whose status as a benefit corporation has not been terminated pursuant to section 33–1356.

(2) "Benefit director" means either (A) the director designated as the benefit director of a benefit corporation pursuant to section 33–1359, or (B) a person with one or more of the powers, duties or rights of a benefit director under section 33–1359 to the extent that such person has been granted all or part of the authority to manage the business and affairs of the corporation by a shareholder agreement that complies with section 33–717.

(3) "Benefit enforcement proceeding" means any claim or action for (A) the failure of a benefit corporation to pursue or create a general public benefit or any specific public benefit purpose set forth in its certificate of incorporation, or (B) the violation of any obligation, duty or standard of conduct under sections 33–1352 to 33–1364, inclusive.

(4) "Benefit officer"means the individual designated as the benefit officer of a benefit corporation pursuant to section 33–1361.

(5) "Business corporation" means a corporation whose internal affairs are governed by chapter 601.

(6) "Charitable organization" means any organization that is exempt from federal income tax under Section 501(a) of the Internal Revenue Code of 1986, or any subsequent

康涅狄格州

第 604 章
公共利益公司

第 33–1350 条　简称：公共利益公司法

第 33–1350 条至第 33–1364 条被称为《康涅狄格州公共利益公司法》。

第 33–1351 条　定义

本条以及第 33–1352 条至第 33–1364 条使用的词语含义如下：

（1）“公共利益公司”是指一家商业公司（A）选择接受第 33–1352 条至第 33–1364 条规定调整；并且（B）根据第 33–1356 条的规定，公共利益公司形态并未终止。

（2）“公共利益董事”是指（A）公共利益公司根据第 33–1359 条规定任命的董事，或者（B）根据第 33–717 条规定的股东协议管理经营公司事务，可以行使第 33–1356 条中所规定的公共利益董事权力或权利并承担相应义务的个人。

（3）“公共利益实施程序”是指因以下行为产生的任何主张、诉讼或程序（A）公共利益公司未追求或创设公司章程规定的一般或特定公共利益目的，或者（B）公共利益公司违反第 33–1352 条至第 33–1364 条规定的任何义务、责任或行为标准。

（4）“公共利益高管”是指公共利益公司根据第 33–1361 条任命的高管。

（5）“商事公司”是指公司内部事务受第 601 章规定调整的公司。

（6）“慈善组织”是指根据《1986 年国内税收法典》第 501（a）款的规定或者此后《美国税收法典》新增的或美国财政部明确认可并规定于《1986 年国内税收

corresponding internal revenue code of the United States, as amended from time to time, and that the United States Treasury Department has expressly determined, by letter, to be an organization that is described in Section 501(c)(3) of said Internal Revenue Code.

(7) "General public benefit" means a material positive impact on both society and the environment, taken as a whole, as assessed against a third-party standard, from the business and operations of a benefit corporation.

(8) "Independent" means having no material relationship with a benefit corporation or a subsidiary of the benefit corporation, provided a person who serves as a benefit director or benefit officer does not lack independence solely by serving in such capacity.

(9) "Legacy preservation provision" means a provision in the certificate of incorporation adopted in accordance with section 33-1355.

(10) "Material relationship" means a relationship between a person and a benefit corporation or any of its subsidiaries if any of the following apply: (A) The person is, or has been within the last three years, an employee other than a benefit officer of the benefit corporation or a subsidiary; (B) an immediate family member of the person is, or has been within the last three years, an executive officer other than a benefit officer of the benefit corporation or a subsidiary; or (C) there is beneficial or record ownership of five per cent or more of the outstanding shares of the benefit corporation, calculated on the assumption that all outstanding rights to acquire shares in the benefit corporation had been exercised, by (i) the person, or (ii) an entity (I) of which the person is a director, an officer or a manager; or (II) in which the person owns beneficially or of record five per cent or more of the outstanding equity interests, calculated on the assumption that all outstanding rights to acquire equity interests in the entity had been exercised.

(11) "Minimum status vote" means (A) in the case of a business corporation, in addition to any other required approval or vote, the satisfaction of the following conditions: (i) The shareholders of every class or series shall be entitled to vote as a separate voting group on the corporate action regardless of a limitation stated in the certificate of incorporation or bylaws on the voting rights of any class or series; and (ii) the corporate action is approved by the vote of shareholders of each class or series entitled to cast at least two-thirds of the votes that shareholders of the class or series are entitled to cast on the action; and (B) in the case of a domestic entity other than a business corporation, in addition to any other required approval, vote or consent, the satisfaction of the following conditions: (i) The holders of each class or series of equity interest in the entity that are entitled to receive a distribution of any kind from the entity shall be entitled to vote on or consent to the action regardless of any otherwise applicable limitation on the voting or consent rights of any such class or series; and (ii) the action is approved by the vote or written consent of the holders described in subparagraph (B) (i) of this subdivision entitled to cast at least two-thirds of the votes that all of those holders

法典》第 501（c）（3）项中的免征所得税的任何组织形式。

（7）“一般公共利益”是指根据第三方标准，公司的业务和经营在整体上对社会和环境产生的实质性积极影响。

（8）“独立”是指与公共利益公司或其子公司之间没有实质性关系。担任公共利益董事或公共利益高管并不当然丧失独立性。

（9）“遗产保留条款”是指公司章程中根据第 33–1355 条规定设立的条款。

（10）“实质性关系”是指个体与公共利益公司或其子公司之间存在满足以下条件的关系：（A）该个体是，或在过去 3 年内是，公共利益公司或其子公司除公共利益高管以外的雇员；（B）该个体的直系亲属是，或在过去的 3 年内是，公共利益公司或其子公司除公共利益高管以外的执行高管；或者（C）在所有购股权视为已行使的情况下，该个体是下述持有公共利益公司 5% 以上已发行股份的登记股东或实际受益人：（i）个人，或（ii）实体（Ⅰ）该个人是该实体的董事、高管或经理；或（Ⅱ）在所有购股权视为已行使的情况下，该实体中的个人为持有公共利益公司 5% 以上已发行股份的登记股东或实际受益人。

（11）“最低表决要求”是指（A）在商事公司中，除其他批准或表决的要求外，还应满足以下条件：（i）每一类别或系列的股东有权作为一个独立的投票团体对公司行为进行投票，即使公司章程或章程细则对某一类别或系列股东作出了限制；（ii）公司行为必须获得每个类别或系列有投票权的所有股东至少 2/3 的赞成票才能通过；并且（B）在非商事公司的本州实体中，除其他批准、表决或赞成的要求外，还应满足以下条件：（i）该实体的每一类别或系列享有任何权益分配权利的股权持有者有权对公司行为进行投票，即使存在任何对该类别或系列股东的投票权限制；（ii）公司行为须获得第（B）（i）目规定的有投票权的所有股东至少 2/3 的赞成票才能通过。

are entitled to cast on the action.

(12) "Publicly traded corporation" means a business corporation that has shares listed on a national securities exchange or traded in a market maintained by one or more members of a national securities association.

(13) "Specific public benefit" includes: (A) Providing low-income or underserved individuals or communities with beneficial products or services; (B) promoting economic opportunity for individuals or communities beyond the creation of jobs in the normal course of business; (C) protecting or restoring the environment; (D) improving human health; (E) promoting the arts, sciences or advancement of knowledge; (F) increasing the flow of capital to other benefit corporations or similar entities whose purpose is to benefit society or the environment; and (G) conferring any other particular benefit on society or the environment.

(14) "Subsidiary" means, in relation to a person, an entity in which the person owns beneficially or of record fifty per cent or more of the outstanding equity interests.

(15) "Third-party standard" means a recognized standard for defining, reporting and assessing corporate social and environmental performance that: (A) Assesses the effect of its business and operations upon the interests listed in subparagraphs (B), (C), (D) and (E) of subdivision (1) of subsection (a) of section 33-1358; (B) is developed by an entity that is independent; and (C) makes publicly available the following information about the development and revision of the standard: (i) The identity of the directors, officers, material owners, and the governing body of the entity that developed and controls revisions to the standard; (ii) the process by which revisions to the standard and changes to the membership of the governing body are made; and (iii) an accounting of the revenue and sources of financial support for such entity, with sufficient detail to disclose any relationships that could reasonably be considered to present a potential conflict of interest.

Sec. 33-1352. Construction of statutes.

(a) The provisions of this section and sections 33-1353 to 33-1364, inclusive, shall be applicable to all benefit corporations.

(b) The provisions of this section and sections 33-1353 to 33-1364, inclusive, shall not create an implication that a contrary or different rule of law is applicable to a business corporation that is not a benefit corporation. The provisions of this section and sections 33-1353 to 33-1364, inclusive, shall not affect a statute or rule of law that is applicable to a business corporation that is not a benefit corporation.

(c) Except as otherwise provided in this section and sections 33-1353 to 33-1364, inclusive, the provisions of chapter 601 shall be generally applicable to all benefit corporations. The specific provisions of this section and sections 33-1353 to 33-1364, inclusive, shall control over the general provisions of chapter 601.

(d) A provision of the certificate of incorporation or bylaws of a benefit corporation may

（12）“上市公司”是指在美国证券交易所或美国证券协会中的一个或几个成员形成的市场上进行交易的商业公司。

（13）“特定公共利益”包括：（A）向低收入、低福利人群或社区提供有益的产品或服务；（B）在正常业务过程中向个人或社区提供创造就业之外的经济机会；（C）保护或修复环境；（D）改善人类健康；（E）促进艺术、科学或知识进步；（F）促进资本向有利于社会或环境目标的实体流动；以及（G）为社会或环境提供其他特别的利益。

（14）“子公司”是指在所有购股权被视为已行使的情况下，该实体50%以上已发行的股份的受益所有权或登记所有权被另一实体所拥有。

（15）“第三方标准”是指用于定义、报告和评估公司社会和环境绩效的标准，其应满足以下条件：（A）根据第33-1358条中第（a）（1）（B）、（C）、（D）、（E）项中所列利益评估公司业务和经营绩效；（B）经非由公共利益公司控制的第三方实体独立制定；以及（C）以下信息可公开获取：（i）制定和控制修改程序的董事、高管、主要股东和该实体控制人员的身份；（ii）标准修改和控制人员变动的程序；以及（iii）收入和资金来源的核算，包括充分披露合理认知下存在利益冲突的所有细节。

第33-1352条　对法条的解释

（a）第33-1353条至第33-1364条规定适用于所有公共利益公司。

（b）本条及第33-1353条至第33-1364条规定不应为非公共利益公司设定相反或不同的规则。上述规则不影响非公共利益公司有关条文和规则的适用。

（c）除本条及第33-1353条至第33-1364条另有规定外，第601章的规定适用于所有公共利益公司。本条及第33-1353条至第33-1364条的特别规定效力优先于第601章规定的一般条款。

（d）公共利益公司的公司章程或章程细则不得限制、违背或取代本条及第33-

not limit, be inconsistent with, or supersede a provision of this section or sections 33–1353 to 33–1364, inclusive.

(e) Nothing in this section or sections 33–1353 to 33–1364, inclusive, shall (1) be construed as creating or granting to any person any contractual right to, or proprietary interest in, the income or assets of a benefit corporation by virtue of the fact that he or she may directly or indirectly benefit from the general public benefit or any specific public benefit of a benefit corporation, (2) be construed as imposing or creating a charitable use, interest or restriction on any property or assets of a benefit corporation, or (3) deprive the Attorney General of jurisdiction over a benefit corporation under any other applicable law.

Sec. 33-1353. Incorporation of benefit corporation.

A benefit corporation shall be incorporated in accordance with the provisions of chapter 601 by filing a certificate of incorporation with the office of the Secretary of the State that states that the corporation is a benefit corporation.

Sec. 33-1354. Election of benefit corporation status.

(a) A business corporation that is not a benefit corporation may elect to become a benefit corporation by amending its certificate of incorporation to contain, in addition to matters required by section 33–636, a statement that the corporation is a benefit corporation. Any such amendment to the certificate of incorporation shall be approved by a minimum status vote.

(b) If an entity that is not a benefit corporation is a party to (1) a merger in which (A) the surviving entity will be a benefit corporation, or (B) shares or other equity interests in such entity will be converted into a right to receive shares of a benefit corporation, or (2) a share exchange with a benefit corporation in which the shares or other equity interests of the entity will be exchanged for shares of a benefit corporation, the plan of merger or share exchange shall be approved by a minimum status vote. If an entity other than a business corporation is a party to any such transaction and a minimum status vote by the equity owners of such entity is required for approval of the transaction, the equity owners of such entity shall be entitled to appraisal rights under the procedures set forth in chapter 601 as if the entity were a business corporation.

Sec. 33-1355. Legacy preservation provision.

(a) A benefit corporation may, not earlier than twenty–four months after the date that it became a benefit corporation, adopt a legacy preservation provision by amending its certificate of incorporation to contain a statement that the corporation is subject to a legacy preservation provision. Any such amendment shall be adopted in accordance with the procedures set forth in chapter 601 and shall be approved by the unanimous vote or written consent of the shareholders of every class or series, regardless of any limitation stated in the certificate of incorporation or bylaws on the voting rights of any such class or series.

(b) A dissolved benefit corporation that has adopted a legacy preservation provision

1353 条至第 33-1364 条的规定。

（e）本条及第 33-1353 条至第 33-1364 条的规定不应被解释为，（1）由于某人可能直接或间接受益于公共利益公司的一般或特定公共利益，使其对公共利益公司的收入或资产任何合同权利或财产利益享有任何权益，（2）对公共利益公司的任何财产或资产施加或创设慈善用途、利益或限制，或（3）剥夺首席检察官依其他现行法对公共利益公司享有的司法管辖权。

第 33-1353 条　公共利益公司的设立

公共利益公司应当按照第 601 章的规定，向州务卿递交材料申请设立公共利益公司，并且在公司章程中声明其是公共利益公司。

第 33-1354 条　公共利益公司的形态选择

（a）已成立的商业公司可依据本条规定转变为公共利益公司，除满足商业公司法有关公司章程内容的要求外，还需修改公司章程，作出该公司为公共利益公司的声明。公司章程的修改应满足最低表决要求。

（b）如果一家本州非公共利益公司是（1）实行合并的一方，且（A）存续方将成为公共利益公司，或者（B）该公司的股份或其他股权收益将转换成公共利益公司的股份或收益，或者（2）与公共利益公司进行股份置换，则该兼并、财产转换或股权置换的计划须满足最低表决要求才能获准。如果商业公司以外的实体是任何此类交易的一方，并且该实体的股权所有者需要以最低表决要求来批准该交易，则该实体的股权所有者应有权根据第 601 章规定的程序获得评估权，如同该实体是商业公司一样。

第 33-1355 条　遗产保护条款

（a）在成为公共利益公司之后的 24 个月内，公共利益公司可以通过修改公司章程声明其采用遗产保护条款。无论公司章程或章程细则是否对某一类别或系列的投票权进行限制，该修改必须符合第 601 章规定的程序且获得一致同意或每一类别或系列股东的书面同意。

（b）采用遗产保护条款的已解散的公共利益公司只能向一个或多个（1）慈善

shall distribute its remaining property only to one or more (1) charitable organizations, or (2) other benefit corporations that have adopted a legacy preservation provision.

Sec. 33-1356. Termination of benefit corporation status.

(a) Except for a benefit corporation that adopts a legacy preservation provision, a benefit corporation may terminate its status as such and cease to be subject to the provisions of sections 33–1352 to 33–1364, inclusive, by amending its certificate of incorporation to delete any provision stating that such corporation is a benefit corporation. Any such amendment shall be approved by a minimum status vote.

(b) Except for a benefit corporation that adopts a legacy preservation provision, if a benefit corporation is a party to (1) a merger in which (A) the surviving entity will not be a benefit corporation, or (B) shares of such benefit corporation will be converted into a right to receive shares or other equity interests of an entity that is not a benefit corporation, or (2) a share exchange in which the shares of the benefit corporation will be exchanged for shares or other equity interests of an entity that is not a benefit corporation, the plan of merger or share exchange shall be approved by a minimum status vote.

(c) A benefit corporation that adopts a legacy preservation provision may only be a party to (1) a merger in which (A) the surviving entity will be a benefit corporation that has adopted a legacy preservation provision, or (B) shares of such benefit corporation will be converted into a right to receive shares of a benefit corporation that has adopted a legacy preservation provision, or (2) a share exchange in which the shares of the benefit corporation will be exchanged for shares of a benefit corporation that has adopted a legacy preservation provision, and such merger or share exchange is approved by a minimum status vote.

(d) Except for a benefit corporation that adopts a legacy preservation provision, any sale, lease, exchange or other disposition of assets of a benefit corporation, other than a disposition described in section 33–830, that would leave the benefit corporation without a significant continuing business activity shall be approved by a minimum status vote. A benefit corporation that adopts a legacy preservation provision shall not enter into a sale, lease, exchange or other disposition of its assets, other than a disposition described in section 33–830, unless the disposition is to one or more (1) charitable organizations, or (2) other benefit corporations that have adopted legacy preservation provisions, and such disposition is approved by a minimum status vote.

Sec. 33-1357. Purposes.

(a) A benefit corporation shall have a purpose of creating a general public benefit. Such purpose shall be in addition to any purpose under chapter 601.

(b) The certificate of incorporation of a benefit corporation may identify one or more specific public benefits as a purpose for such benefit corporation to create in addition to any purpose under chapter 601 and subsection (a) of this section. The identification of a specific

机构，或（2）采用遗产保护条款的其他公共利益公司，分配其剩余财产。

第 33–1356 条　公共利益公司形态的终止

（a）除公共利益公司采用遗产保留条款外，还可通过删除第 33–1352 条至第 33–1364 条规定的公司章程中其作为公共利益公司的声明来终止其公共利益公司的形态并不再受上述规定调整。公司章程的修改应满足最低表决要求。

（b）除公共利益公司采用遗产保留条款外，如果公共利益公司是（1）兼并的一方，且（A）存续方将成为非公共利益公司，或者（B）公共利益公司的股份或其他股权收益将转换为非公共利益公司的股份或收益，或者（2）与非公共利益公司进行股份置换，则该兼并、财产转换或股权置换的计划须满足最低表决要求才能获准。

（c）采用遗产保留条款的公共利益公司可能成为（1）兼并的一方，并且（A）在该兼并中，存续方为已采用遗产保留条款的公共利益公司，或（B）该公共利益公司的股份将转换为已采用遗产保留条款的公共利益公司的股份；或者（2）该公司的股份将与已采用遗产保留条款的公共利益公司进行置换，则上述兼并或股权置换须满足最低表决要求。

（d）除公共利益公司已采用遗产保留条款外，公共利益公司的任何出售、出租、交换或者其他第 33–830 条规定之外的影响公共利益公司持续进行商事活动的处置行为，须满足最低表决要求。已采用遗产保留条款的公共利益公司除依据第 33–830 条的规定外，不应进行出售、出租、交换，除非该处置行为是针对（1）慈善组织或（2）其他已采用遗产保留条款的公共利益公司进行，并且满足最低表决要求。

第 33–1357 条　目的

（a）公共利益公司应当具有服务于一般公共利益的目的。此目的在第 601 章规定之外。

（b）公共利益公司的章程可以在第 601 章和本条第（a）款规定之外确定一项或多项特定公共利益目的。依据本款设定的特定公共利益目的并不限制公共利益公司在第（a）款规定下设定一般公共利益目的。

public benefit under this subsection shall not limit the obligation of a benefit corporation under subsection (a) of this section.

(c) The creation of a general public benefit and any specific public benefit under subsections (a) and (b) of this section is in the best interests of the benefit corporation.

(d) A benefit corporation may amend its certificate of incorporation to add, amend or delete the identification of a specific public benefit that it is the purpose of the benefit corporation to create. Any such amendment shall be adopted by a minimum status vote.

Sec. 33-1358. Standards of conduct for directors.

(a) In discharging the duties of their respective positions and considering the best interests of the benefit corporation, the board of directors, any committee of the board and the individual directors of the benefit corporation:

(1) Shall consider the effects of any corporate action or inaction upon:

(A) The shareholders of the benefit corporation;

(B) The employees and workforce of the benefit corporation, its subsidiaries and its suppliers;

(C) The interests of the customers of the benefit corporation as beneficiaries of the general public benefit purpose and any specific public benefit purpose of the benefit corporation;

(D) Community and societal factors, including those of each community in which offices or facilities of the benefit corporation, its subsidiaries or its suppliers are located;

(E) The local and global environment;

(F) The short-term and long-term interests of the benefit corporation, including benefits that may accrue to the benefit corporation from such corporation's long-term plans and the possibility that such interests may be best served by the continued independence of the benefit corporation; and

(G) The ability of the benefit corporation to accomplish its general public benefit purpose and any specific public benefit purpose;

(2) May consider (A) in the circumstances described in subsection (d) of section 33-756, the interests referred to in said subsection, and (B) other pertinent factors or the interests of any other group that the board of directors, any committee of the board and the directors of the benefit corporation deem appropriate; and

(3) Need not give priority to the interests of a particular person or group referred to in subdivision (1) or (2) of this subsection over the interests of any other person or group unless the certificate of incorporation for such benefit corporation states an intention to give priority to certain interests related to the accomplishment of the corporation's general public benefit purpose or of a specific public benefit purpose identified in the corporation's certificate of incorporation.

（c）依据第（a）款和第（b）款规定创设的一般和特定公共利益目的为公共利益公司最佳利益。

（d）公共利益公司可以增加、修改或删除公司章程中设定的特定公共利益目的。公司对章程的修改需满足最低表决要求。

第 33-1358 条　董事行为标准

（a）在履行各自职责和考虑公共利益公司最佳利益时，公共利益公司的董事会、董事委员会和董事：

（1）其作为或不作为，应当考虑对以下对象的影响：

（A）公共利益公司的股东；

（B）公共利益公司雇员及其子公司和供应商；

（C）作为公共利益公司一般或特定公共利益受益者的消费者的利益；

（D）社区和社会因素，包括公共利益公司及其子公司或供应商办公地或设施所在地的社区；

（E）当地和全球环境；

（F）公共利益公司的短期和长期利益，包括公共利益公司可能从其长期计划中获得的利益，以及公共利益公司继续保持独立可能产生的最佳利益；以及

（G）公共利益公司实现其一般和特定公共利益目的的能力；

（2）可供参考的其他因素：以上条款虽未涉及，（A）但在第 33-756 条第（d）款中涉及的利益；以及（B）董事认为合适的其他相关因素或其他群体的利益；以及

（3）除公司章程中规定优先考虑特定利益或因素外，无须优先考虑本条第（1）项或第（2）项中某个利益或因素。

(b) The consideration of interests and factors in the manner required by subsection (a) of this section (1) shall not constitute a violation of section 33–756, and (2) is in addition to the power of directors to consider the interests and factors listed in subsection (d) of section 33–756 in the circumstances described in said subsection.

(c) A director shall not be personally liable for (1) any act or omission in the course of performing the duties of a director under subsection (a) of this section if the director performed the duties of the position in compliance with section 33–756 and this section, or (2) failure of the benefit corporation to pursue or create a general public benefit or any specific public benefit.

(d) A director shall not have a duty to a person who is a beneficiary of the general public benefit purpose or a specific public benefit purpose of a benefit corporation based on the status of such person as a beneficiary.

Sec. 33-1359. Benefit director.

(a) The board of directors of a benefit corporation that is a publicly traded corporation shall, and the board of any other benefit corporation may, include a director who shall (1) be designated the benefit director, and (2) have, in addition to the powers, duties, rights and immunities of the other directors of the benefit corporation, the powers, duties, rights and immunities provided in sections 33–1352 to 33–1364, inclusive.

(b) The benefit director shall be elected, and may be removed, in the manner provided under chapter 601. The benefit director shall be an individual who is independent. The benefit director may serve as the benefit officer at the same time as serving as the benefit director. The certificate of incorporation or bylaws or a shareholder agreement of a benefit corporation may prescribe additional qualifications of the benefit director that are consistent with this subsection.

(c) The benefit director shall prepare, and the benefit corporation shall include in the annual benefit report to its shareholders required by section 33–1363, the opinion of the benefit director on each of the following: (1) Whether the benefit corporation acted in accordance with its general public benefit purpose and any specific public benefit purpose in all material respects during the period covered by the report, (2) whether the directors and officers complied with subsection (a) of section 33–1358 and subsection (a) of section 33–1360, respectively, and (3) if, in the opinion of the benefit director, the benefit corporation or its directors or officers failed to comply with subsection (a) of section 33–1358 or subsection (a) of section 33–1360, a description of the ways in which the benefit corporation or the corporation's directors or officers failed to comply.

(d) The act or omission of an individual in the capacity of a benefit director shall constitute for all purposes an act or omission of that individual in the capacity of a director of the benefit corporation.

（b）对本条第（a）款中利益和相关因素的考虑（1）不构成对第 33–756 条规定的违反；并且（2）构成对第 33–756 条第（d）款规定的补充。

（c）董事不对以下行为承担损害赔偿责任：（1）依据第（a）款履行董事责任的任何作为或不作为行为，如该行为符合第 33–756 条和本条的规定；或者（2）公共利益公司未能追求或创设一般或特定公共利益。

（d）董事不对公共利益公司一般或特定社会目的的受益人负责。

第 33–1359 条　公共利益董事

（a）上市的公共利益公司以及其他形式的公共利益公司的董事会，应当包含满足以下要求的董事：（1）被任命为公共利益董事，并且（2）除拥有公共利益公司的其他董事的权力、义务、权利和豁免权以外，还有第 33–1352 条至第 33–1364 条规定的权力、义务、权利和豁免权。

（b）任免和资格。公共利益董事应当根据第 601 章的规定任免。除第（f）款规定外，公共利益董事应为独立个体。公共利益董事可同时担任公共利益高管。公共利益公司的章程、章程细则或股东协议可对公共利益董事的资格作出与本款规定一致的额外规定。

（c）公共利益董事应当编写其对以下事项的意见，公共利益公司应当根据第 33–1363 条的规定将其附于年度公共利益报告中供股东查阅：（1）在报告所述时间内，公共利益公司是否在所有重要事项上依一般和特定公共利益目的行事；（2）董事和高管是否分别依第 33–1358 条第（a）款和第 33–1360 条第（a）款规定行事；（3）如果公共利益董事认为公共利益公司或其董事、高管未能依第 33–1358 条第（a）款 和第 33–1360 条第（a）款的规定行事，应陈述公共利益公司或其董事、高管未能履行责任的情况。

（d）公共利益董事在职权范围内个人的作为或不作为行为应视为公共利益公司董事的行为。

(e) Regardless of whether the certificate of incorporation of a benefit corporation includes a provision limiting the personal liability of directors, as authorized by chapter 601, a benefit director shall not be personally liable for any act or omission in the capacity of a benefit director unless the act or omission constitutes self–dealing, willful misconduct or a knowing violation of law.

Sec. 33-1360. Standards of conduct for officers.

(a) Each officer of a benefit corporation shall consider the interests and factors described in subsection (a) of section 33–1358 in the manner provided in that subsection if (1) the officer has discretion to act with respect to a matter, and (2) it reasonably appears to the officer that the matter may have a material effect on the creation by the benefit corporation of a general public benefit or any specific public benefit identified in the certificate of incorporation of the benefit corporation.

(b) The consideration of interests and factors in the manner described in subsection (a) of this section shall not constitute a violation of section 33–765.

(c) An officer shall not be personally liable for (1) an act or omission as an officer in the course of performing the duties of an officer under subsection (a) of this section if the officer performed the duties of the position in compliance with section 33–765 and this section, or (2) the failure of the benefit corporation to pursue or create a general public benefit or any specific public benefit.

(d) An officer shall not have a duty to a person that is a beneficiary of the general public benefit purpose or any specific public benefit purpose of a benefit corporation based on the status of such person as a beneficiary.

Sec. 33-1361. Benefit officer.

A benefit corporation may designate a benefit officer. A benefit officer shall have (1) the powers and duties relating to the purpose of the corporation to create a general public benefit or any specific public benefit provided (A) by the bylaws, or (B) absent controlling provisions in the bylaws, by resolutions or orders of the board of directors, and (2) the duty to prepare the benefit report required by section 33–1363.

Sec. 33-1362. Right of action. Benefit enforcement proceeding.

(a) Except in a benefit enforcement proceeding, no person may bring an action or assert a claim against a benefit corporation or its directors or officers with respect to (1) the failure to pursue or create a general public benefit or any specific public benefit identified in its certificate of incorporation, or (2) the violation of an obligation, duty or standard of conduct under sections 33–1352 to 33–1364, inclusive.

(b) A benefit corporation shall not be liable for monetary damages under sections 33–1352 to 33–1364, inclusive, for any failure of the benefit corporation to pursue or create a general public benefit or any specific public benefit.

（e）无论公共利益公司章程或章程细则是否依据第 601 章的规定删除或限制董事的个人责任，公共利益董事在行使职责时不对其任何作为或不作为行为承担个人责任，但自我交易或故意违法行为除外。

第 33–1360 条　高管行为标准

（a）公共利益公司高管应根据第 33–1358 条规定的行为标准考虑第 33–1358 条第（a）款中规定的利益和因素，如果（1）高管就该行为有自由裁量权，以及（2）高管有合理理由认为该行为对公共利益公司在章程中创设的一般或特定公共利益有实质性影响。

（b）对第（a）款中利益和相关因素的考虑不构成对第 33–765 条规定的违反。

（c）高管不对以下行为承担损害赔偿责任：（1）依据第（a）款规定履行高管责任过程中的任何作为或者不作为行为，如该行为符合第 33–765 条及本条的规定；或者（2）公共利益公司未能追求或创造一般或特定公共利益。

（d）高管不对公共利益公司一般目的或特定社会目的的受益人负责。

第 33–1361 条　公共利益高管

公共利益公司（1）可以将高管任命为公共利益高管。公共利益高管创造一般或特定公共利益的权力或义务规定于（A）公司章程细则，或者（B）在公司章程细则中没有规定时，根据董事会的决议或者命令行事。（2）公共利益高管有根据第 33–1363 条的要求编写公共利益报告的义务。

第 33–1362 条　诉讼权利　公共利益实施程序

（a）非经公共利益实施程序，任何人不得因以下事项向公共利益公司或者其董事、高管提起诉讼或提起主张：（1）未能追求或创造其在公司章程中陈述的一般或特定公共利益，或（2）违反第 33–1352 条至第 33–1364 条规定的责任、义务或行为标准。

（b）公共利益公司不对第 33–1352 条至第 33–1364 条规定的任何未能追求或创造一般或特定公共利益的行为承担损害赔偿责任。

(c) A benefit enforcement proceeding may be commenced or maintained only (1) directly by the benefit corporation, or (2) derivatively in accordance with the provisions of chapter 601 by (A) a person or group of persons that owns beneficially or of record not less than five per cent of the total number of shares of a class or series outstanding at the time of the act or omission complained of, (B) a person or group of persons that owns beneficially or of record ten per cent or more of the outstanding equity interests in an entity of which the benefit corporation is a majority-owned subsidiary at the time of the act or omission complained of, or (C) other persons as specified in the certificate of incorporation or bylaws of the benefit corporation.

(d) For purposes of this section, a person is the beneficial owner of shares or equity interests if the shares or equity interests are held in a voting trust or by a nominee on behalf of the beneficial owner.

Sec. 33-1363. Third-party standard. Preparation of annual benefit report.

(a) A benefit corporation shall select a third-party standard by which to assess such corporation's pursuit of a general public benefit and any specific public benefit. Selecting or changing a third-party standard shall require approval by (1) the greater of (A) a majority of all the directors in office when the action is taken, or (B) the number of directors required by the certificate of incorporation or bylaws of the benefit corporation to take action under this section, or (2) the vote or written consent of the shareholders required by the certificate of incorporation or bylaws of the benefit corporation to take action under this section.

(b) A benefit corporation shall prepare an annual benefit report that includes each of the following:

(1) A narrative description of (A) the ways in which the benefit corporation pursued a general public benefit during the year and the extent to which a general public benefit was created; (B) both (i) the ways in which the benefit corporation pursued any specific public benefit identified in the benefit corporation's certificate of incorporation, and (ii) the extent to which such specific public benefit was created; (C) any circumstances that have hindered the creation by the benefit corporation of a general public benefit or any specific public benefit; and (D) the process and rationale for selecting or changing the third-party standard used to prepare the benefit report;

(2) An assessment of the overall social and environmental performance of the benefit corporation against a third-party standard (A) applied consistently with any application of that standard in prior benefit reports, or (B) accompanied by an explanation of the reasons for any inconsistent application or the change to that standard from the standard used in the most recent prior report;

(3) The name of the benefit director and the benefit officer, if any, and the address to which correspondence to the benefit director or the benefit officer may be directed;

（c）公共利益实施程序只能由以下主体提起：（1）由公共利益公司直接提起，或（2）依据第601章的规定由以下主体派生提起：（A）在被诉作为或不作为行为发生时，拥有公共利益公司5%以上已发行的某类别或系列股份的个人或群体；（B）在被诉作为或不作为行为发生时，持有公共利益公司母公司5%以上已发行股份的登记股东或实际受益股人；或（C）公共利益公司章程或章程细则中规定的其他人员。

（d）就本条而言，如果股份或股权由有表决权的信托持有或由代表受益所有人的人名义持有，则该人是股份或股权的实益拥有人。

第33-1363条　第三方标准，年度公共利益报告的编写

（a）公共利益公司应选择第三方标准评估公司一般和特定公共利益的实现情况。选择或更改第三方标准应满足以下要求（1）达到以下标准中更高者：（A）行为发生时获得董事会的多数票或（B）公共利益公司章程或章程细则就本条行为规定的票数要求；或者（2）公司章程或章程细则就本条行为规定的股东表决票数或书面同意的要求。

（b）公共利益公司的年度公共利益报告应包括以下内容：

（1）对以下事项的描述：（A）公共利益公司本年度追求一般公共利益的方法和一般公共利益实现的情况；（B）同时包括（i）公共利益公司追求公司章程中规定的特定公共利益的方法，以及（ii）该特定公共利益实现的情况；（C）阻碍公共利益公司创造一般和特定公共利益的情形；（D）为编写公共利益报告而选择或更换第三方标准的程序和原因；

（2）依据第三方标准对公共利益公司的社会和环境表现作出的整体评价：（A）沿用先前公共利益报告中使用的标准，或者（B）附一份说明解释适用中的差异或与上一份报告相比标准的变化；

（3）公共利益董事和公共利益高管的姓名和联系地址；

(4) The compensation paid by the benefit corporation during the year to each director in his or her capacity as a director;

(5) The opinion of the benefit director described in subsection (c) of section 33–1359; and

(6) A statement of any connection between the organization that established the third–party standard, its directors or officers or any holder of five per cent or more of the voting power or capital interests in the organization, and the benefit corporation, its directors or officers or any holder of five per cent or more of the outstanding shares of the benefit corporation, including any financial or governance relationship that might materially affect the credibility of the use of the third–party standard.

(c) If, during the year covered by a benefit report, a benefit director or benefit officer resigned from or refused to stand for reelection to the position of benefit director or benefit officer, or was removed from the position of benefit director or benefit officer, and the benefit director or benefit officer furnished the benefit corporation with a written statement or correspondence concerning the circumstances surrounding the resignation, refusal or removal, the benefit report shall include that statement or correspondence as an exhibit.

(d) Neither the benefit report nor the assessment of the performance of the benefit corporation in the benefit report required by subdivision (2) of subsection (b) of this section shall be required to be audited or certified by the third–party standards provider.

Sec. 33-1364. Availability of annual benefit report.

(a) A benefit corporation shall send its annual benefit report to each shareholder (1) not later than one hundred twenty days following the end of the fiscal year of the benefit corporation, or (2) at the same time that the benefit corporation delivers any other annual report to its shareholders, whichever is earlier.

(b) A benefit corporation shall post and maintain each annual benefit report on the public portion of its Internet web site, if any, except that the compensation paid to directors and any financial, confidential or proprietary information included in any benefit report may be omitted from the benefit report as posted.

(c) If a benefit corporation does not have an Internet web site, the benefit corporation shall provide a copy of such corporation's most recent benefit report, without charge, to any person who requests a copy, but the compensation paid to directors and any financial, confidential or proprietary information included in any benefit report may be omitted from such copy.

（4）公共利益公司在上一年度支付给每位董事的薪酬。

（5）公共利益董事对第 33-1359 条第（c）款中规定事项的董事意见；以及

（6）设立第三方标准的机构或其董事、高管或 5% 以上管理权利的持有者与公共利益公司或其董事、高管或公共利益公司 5% 以上已发行股份持有者之间关系的声明，包括任何可能影响第三方标准可信度的财务或管理关系。

（c）在公共利益报告年度内，如果公共利益董事辞职、拒绝连任或被免职，且该公共利益董事与公司有任何书面的涉及辞职、拒绝连任或免职的书信往来，公共利益报告应当将该书信往来作为附件。

（d）公共利益报告和依据第（b）款第（2）项规定编写的公共利益报告中的公共利益公司表现评价书无须经审计或第三方证明。

第 33-1364 条　年度公共利益报告的提供

（a）公共利益公司应当在以下日期内尽早地将年度公共利益报告送交各股东：（1）公共利益公司财政年度结束后 120 天内，或者（2）公共利益公司向其股东送交其他年度报告的同一时间。

（b）若条件允许，公共利益公司应当将其所有年度公共利益报告发布于其网站的公共部分，但可将公共利益报告中的董事薪酬和财务、所有权信息删除。

（c）如果公共利益公司没有网站，应向所有索取报告的个人免费提供最新的公共利益报告的副本，但可将公共利益报告副本中的董事薪酬和财务、所有权信息删除。

THE STATE OF DELAWARE

TITLE 8
Corporations

CHAPTER 1. GENERAL CORPORATION LAW

Subchapter XV. Public Benefit Corporations

§ 361 Law applicable to public benefit corporations; how formed.

This subchapter applies to all public benefit corporations, as defined in § 362 of this title. If a corporation elects to become a public benefit corporation under this subchapter in the manner prescribed in this subchapter, it shall be subject in all respects to the provisions of this chapter, except to the extent this subchapter imposes additional or different requirements, in which case such requirements shall apply.

§ 362 Public benefit corporation defined; contents of certificate of incorporation.

(a) A "public benefit corporation" is a for-profit corporation organized under and subject to the requirements of this chapter that is intended to produce a public benefit or public benefits and to operate in a responsible and sustainable manner. To that end, a public benefit corporation shall be managed in a manner that balances the stockholders' pecuniary interests, the best interests of those materially affected by the corporation's conduct, and the public benefit or public benefits identified in its certificate of incorporation. In the certificate of incorporation, a public benefit corporation shall:

(1) Identify within its statement of business or purpose pursuant to § 102(a)(3) of this title 1 or more specific public benefits to be promoted by the corporation; and

(2) State within its heading that it is a public benefit corporation.

(b) "Public benefit" means a positive effect (or reduction of negative effects) on 1 or more categories of persons, entities, communities or interests (other than stockholders in their capacities as stockholders) including, but not limited to, effects of an artistic, charitable, cultural, economic, educational, environmental, literary, medical, religious, scientific or

特拉华州

第八编　公司

第 1 章　《普通公司法》

第 15 节　公共利益公司

第 361 条　公共利益公司法律的适用；公共利益公司的设立

本节规定适用于由本编第 362 条定义的所有公共利益公司。除本节另有规定外，根据本节规定转变为公共利益形态的公司受本章规定调整。

第 362 条　公共利益公司的定义；公司章程的内容

（a）“公共利益公司”是指根据本章规定设立的意图促进公共利益并以负责任的和持续性方式运行的营利性公司。为实现该目的，公共利益公司应平衡股东利益、受公司运营影响的利益相关者利益和公共利益或公司章程确定的公共利益。在公司章程中，公共利益公司应：

（1）根据第 1 编第 102（a）（3）项规定在公司章程中声明公司追求的一般利益或确定一个或多个特定公司利益；并且

（2）在章程标题中表明其为公共利益公司。

（b）“公共利益”是指对一类或多类群体、实体、社区或其他利益（而非股东），包括但不限于艺术、慈善、文化、经济、教育、环境、文学、医疗、宗教、科学或自然技术等产生的积极影响（或减少消极影响）。“公共利益条款”是指根据本节规定在公司章程中涉及的条款。

technological nature. "Public benefit provisions" means the provisions of a certificate of incorporation contemplated by this subchapter.

(c) The name of the public benefit corporation may contain the words "public benefit corporation," or the abbreviation "P.B.C.," or the designation "PBC," which shall be deemed to satisfy the requirements of § 102(a)(l)(i) of this title.

§ 363 Certain amendments and mergers; votes required; appraisal rights.

(a) Notwithstanding any other provisions of this chapter, a corporation that is not a public benefit corporation, may not, without the approval of 2/3 of the outstanding stock of the corporation entitled to vote thereon:

(1) Amend its certificate of incorporation to include a provision authorized by § 362(a)(1) of this title; or

(2) Merge or consolidate with or into another entity if, as a result of such merger or consolidation, the shares in such corporation would become, or be converted into or exchanged for the right to receive, shares or other equity interests in a domestic or foreign public benefit corporation or similar entity.

The restrictions of this section shall not apply prior to the time that the corporation has received payment for any of its capital stock, or in the case of a nonstock corporation, prior to the time that it has members.

(b) Any stockholder of a corporation that is not a public benefit corporation that holds shares of stock of such corporation immediately prior to the effective time of:

(1) An amendment to the corporation's certificate of incorporation to include a provision authorized by § 362(a)(1) of this title; or

(2) A merger or consolidation that would result in the conversion of the corporation's stock into or exchange of the corporation's stock for the right to receive shares or other equity interests in a domestic or foreign public benefit corporation or similar entity.

(c) Notwithstanding any other provisions of this chapter, a corporation that is a public benefit corporation may not, without the approval of 2/3 of the outstanding stock of the corporation entitled to vote thereon:

(1) Amend its certificate of incorporation to delete or amend a provision authorized by § 362(a)(1) or § 366(c) of this title; or

(2) Merge or consolidate with or into another entity if, as a result of such merger or consolidation, the shares in such corporation would become, or be converted into or exchanged for the right to receive, shares or other equity interests in a domestic or foreign corporation that is not a public benefit corporation or similar entity and the certificate of incorporation (or similar governing instrument) of which does not contain the identical provisions identifying the public benefit or public benefits pursuant to § 362(a) of this title or imposing requirements pursuant to § 366(c) of this title.

（c）公共利益公司名称包含“公共利益公司”“P.B.C.”缩写或“PBC”标志的，则认为其满足本编第 102（a）（1）（i）分项的要求。

第 363 条　章程的修改和兼并；投票要求；评估权

（a）虽然本章其他条款另有规定，但是非公共利益公司的以下行为须获得 2/3 以上多数股份的同意：

（1）根据本编第 362（a）（1）项修改公司章程；或

（2）与其他实体合并，如果合并或兼并的结果会导致该公司股份与本州或其他州的公共利益公司或其他相似实体的股份发生置换。

本条的限制性规定不能约束公司在此之前出售股份所获得的资本金，或若为非股份公司，则不能约束在此之前的成员。

（b）非公共利益公司的股东在以下行为生效前持有的股份：

（1）公共利益公司根据本编第 362（a）（1）项规定修改公司章程；或者

（2）兼并或合并将导致公司股份合并或导致公司股份与其他本州或其他州公共利益公司或相似实体的股份发生置换。

（c）虽然本章其他条款另有规定，但是上市公共利益公司未获得有投票权股东 2/3 以上的赞成票，无权进行以下行为：

（1）修改其公司章程，删除或修改由本编第 362（a）（1）项或第 366（c）款规定的条款；或者

（2）与其他实体合并或兼并，如果该公司的股份将转变为或将获得本州或外州非公共利益公司或相似实体的股份或其他股权收入，并且存续公司的公司章程中没有包含本编第 362（a）款或第 366（c）款规定的条款。

(d) Notwithstanding the foregoing, a nonprofit nonstock corporation may not be a constituent corporation to any merger or consolidation governed by this section.

§ 364 Stock certificates; notices regarding uncertificated stock.

Any stock certificate issued by a public benefit corporation shall note conspicuously that the corporation is a public benefit corporation formed pursuant to this subchapter. Any notice sent by a public benefit corporation pursuant to § 151(f) of this title shall state conspicuously that the corporation is a public benefit corporation formed pursuant to this subchapter.

§ 365 Duties of directors.

(a) The board of directors shall manage or direct the business and affairs of the public benefit corporation in a manner that balances the pecuniary interests of the stockholders, the best interests of those materially affected by the corporation's conduct, and the specific public benefit or public benefits identified in its certificate of incorporation.

(b) A director of a public benefit corporation shall not, by virtue of the public benefit provisions or § 362(a) of this title, have any duty to any person on account of any interest of such person in the public benefit or public benefits identified in the certificate of incorporation or on account of any interest materially affected by the corporation's conduct and, with respect to a decision implicating the balance requirement in subsection (a) of this section, will be deemed to satisfy such director's fiduciary duties to stockholders and the corporation if such director's decision is both informed and disinterested and not such that no person of ordinary, sound judgment would approve.

(c) The certificate of incorporation of a public benefit corporation may include a provision that any disinterested failure to satisfy this section shall not, for the purposes of § 102(b)(7) or § 145 of this title, constitute an act or omission not in good faith, or a breach of the duty of loyalty.

§ 366 Periodic statements and third-party certification.

(a) A public benefit corporation shall include in every notice of a meeting of stockholders a statement to the effect that it is a public benefit corporation formed pursuant to this subchapter.

(b) A public benefit corporation shall no less than biennially provide its stockholders with a statement as to the corporation's promotion of the public benefit or public benefits identified in the certificate of incorporation and of the best interests of those materially affected by the corporation's conduct. The statement shall include:

(1) The objectives the board of directors has established to promote such public benefit or public benefits and interests;

(2) The standards the board of directors has adopted to measure the corporation's progress in promoting such public benefit or public benefits and interests;

（d）尽管有上述规定，一家既非公共利益形态也非股份制形态的公司不能与受本章规制的公司进行兼并或合并。

第 364 条　股份证书；无证股情形下的通知书

任何由公共利益公司发行的股份应在明显位置标明该公司是受本节规定调整的公共利益公司。公共利益公司根据本编第 151（f）款发出的任何通知都应在明显位置表明本公司是根据本节规定设立的公共利益公司。

第 365 条　董事义务

（a）公共利益董事应以平衡股东的金钱收益、受公司行为实质影响群体的最大利益以及公司章程规定的特定公共利益的方式管理公司事务。

（b）公共利益公司的董事不应根据公共利益条款或本编第 362（a）款的规定对任何一般公共利益或公司章程中规定的特定公共利益受益人或受公司行为重大影响的利益承担个人责任。如果董事行为满足本条第（a）款所规定的平衡各方利益的要求，且董事的决定基于合理信息且无涉私利，则认为董事的行为符合其对股东的信义义务。

（c）公共利益公司章程可以包含免责条款，声明任何非由个人私利导致的不符合本编第 102(b)(7)项或第 145 条规定的行为不构成对诚实信用或忠诚义务的违反。

第 366 条　定期报表和第三方证书

（a）公共利益公司应在每一份股东会召开通知书中附一份书面通知，声明其为根据本节规定设立的公共利益公司。

（b）公共利益公司应至少每两年向股东提交一份报告，汇报公共利益或公司章程规定的特定公共利益以及受公司行为实质影响群体最佳利益的实现情况。该报告应包括以下内容：

（1）董事会确立的旨在促进上述公共利益的具体目标；

（2）董事会用于评估公司实现公共利益情况的第三方标准；

(3) Objective factual information based on those standards regarding the corporation's success in meeting the objectives for promoting such public benefit or public benefits and interests; and

(4) An assessment of the corporation's success in meeting the objectives and promoting such public benefit or public benefits and interests.

(c) The certificate of incorporation or bylaws of a public benefit corporation may require that the corporation:

(1) Provide the statement described in subsection (b) of this section more frequently than biennially;

(2) Make the statement described in subsection (b) of this section available to the public; and/or

(3) Use a third-party standard in connection with and/or attain a periodic third-party certification addressing the corporation's promotion of the public benefit or public benefits identified in the certificate of incorporation and/or the best interests of those materially affected by the corporation's conduct.

§ 367 Derivative suits.

Stockholders of a public benefit corporation owning individually or collectively, as of the date of instituting such derivative suit, at least 2% of the corporation's outstanding shares or, in the case of a corporation with shares listed on a national securities exchange, the lesser of such percentage or shares of at least $2,000,000 in market value, may maintain a derivative lawsuit to enforce the requirements set forth in § 365(a) of this title.

§ 368 No effect on other corporations.

This subchapter shall not affect a statute or rule of law that is applicable to a corporation that is not a public benefit corporation, except as provided in § 363 of this title.

（3）根据这些标准所确定目标的实现情况；

（4）对公司是否实现其公共利益目标的评估。

（c）公共利益公司章程或章程细则可以要求公司：

（1）高于本条第（b）款规定的每两年一次的频率向股东提交报告；

（2）根据本条第（b）款规定所作的报告可公开获取；并且 / 或者

（3）使用第三方标准评估公司促进一般公共利益、公司章程中规定的特定公共利益以及受公司行为实质影响群体利益的情况。

第 367 条　派生诉讼

个人或合计持有公共利益公司至少 2% 已发行股份的股东，或在国家级证券市场上市的公司中，拥有上述持股比例或至少 $2，000，000 市值股份的股东可以提起诉讼请求执行本编第 365（a）款的规定。

第 368 条　本节规定不适用于其他类型的公司

除第 363 条另有规定外，本节不影响非公共利益公司有关条文和规则的适用。

THE STATE OF FLORIDA

Title XXXVI. Business Organizations. (Chs. 605–623).
Chapter 607. Corporations.
Part III. Benefit Corporations.

§ 607.601. Application and effect of part.

(1) This part applies to a benefit corporation and does not affect a corporation that is not a benefit corporation.

(2) Except as provided in this part, this chapter applies generally to all benefit corporations.

(3) A benefit corporation may be simultaneously subject to this part and to one or more chapters, including chapter 621. In such event, this part takes precedence with respect to a benefit corporation.

(4) Except as authorized by this part, a provision of the articles of incorporation or bylaws of a benefit corporation, or a shareholders agreement among shareholders of a benefit corporation, may not limit, be inconsistent with, or supersede a provision of this part.

§ 607.602. Definitions.

As used in this part, unless the context otherwise requires, the term:

(1) "Benefit corporation" means a corporation that is formed, or has elected to become, subject to this part, the status of which as a benefit corporation has not been terminated.

(2) "Benefit director" means:

(a) The director designated as the benefit director of a benefit corporation under s. 607.608; or

(b) A person with one or more of the powers, duties, or rights of a benefit director to the extent provided in the articles of incorporation or bylaws under s. 607.608.

(3) "Benefit enforcement proceeding" means any claim or action for:

(a) The failure of a benefit corporation to pursue or create general public benefit or a specific public benefit purpose set forth in its articles of incorporation; or

(b) A violation of any obligation, duty, or standard of conduct under this part.

佛罗里达州

第36编 商业组织（第605–623章）
第607章 公司
第3节 公共利益公司

第607.601条 本节的适用和效力

（1）本节适用于公共利益公司并且不对非公共利益公司产生影响。

（2）除本节另有规定外，本章规定适用于所有公共利益公司。

（3）公共利益公司同时受本节和第621章在内的一个或多个章节的规定调整。在这种情况下，本节对于公共利益公司优先适用。

（4）除本节另有授权外，公共利益公司的章程或章程细则，或公共利益公司股东间的股东协议，不得限制、违背或取代本节的条款。

第607.602条 定义

在本节中，除上下文另有规定外，这些用语的含义如下：

（1）“公共利益公司”是指依据本节的规定成立或选择不终止公共利益公司形态的公司。

（2）“公共利益董事”是指：

（a）公共利益公司依据第607.608条规定任命的董事；或者

（b）公共利益公司中依据第607.608条规定享有公司章程或章程细则中规定的权力、权利以及履行义务的人。

（3）“公共利益实施程序”是指因以下行为产生的任何主张或诉讼：

（a）公共利益公司未追求或实现公司章程规定的一般或特定公共利益目的；或者

（b）违反本节规定的任何义务、责任或行为标准。

(4) “Benefit officer” means the individual designated as the benefit officer of a benefit corporation under s. 607.610.

(5) “General public benefit” means a material, positive effect on society and the environment, taken as a whole, as assessed using a third–party standard which is attributable to the business and operations of a benefit corporation.

(6) “Independent” means not having a material relationship with the benefit corporation or a subsidiary of the benefit corporation. A person does not have a material relationship solely by virtue of serving as the benefit director or benefit officer of the benefit corporation or a subsidiary of the benefit corporation. In determining whether a director or officer is independent, a material relationship between an individual and a benefit corporation or any of its subsidiaries will be conclusively presumed to exist, at the time independence is to be determined, if any of the following apply:

(a) The individual is or has been within the prior 3 years an employee, other than a benefit officer, of the benefit corporation or a subsidiary.

(b) An immediate family member of the individual is or has been within the prior 3 years an executive officer, other than a benefit officer, of the benefit corporation or a subsidiary.

(c) When ownership is calculated as if all outstanding rights to acquire equity interests in the benefit corporation had been exercised, there is beneficial or record ownership of 5 percent or more of the outstanding shares of the benefit corporation by:

1. The individual; or

2. An entity:

a. Of which the individual is a director, an officer, or a manager; or

b. In which, when ownership is calculated as if all outstanding rights to acquire equity interests in the entity had been exercised, the individual owns beneficially or of record 5 percent or more of the outstanding equity interests.

(7) “Minimum status vote” means:

(a) In the case of a corporation that is to become a benefit corporation, whether by amendment of the articles of incorporation or by way of or pursuant to a merger, conversion, or share exchange; a benefit corporation whose articles of incorporation are to be amended pursuant to s. 607.606(2); or a benefit corporation that is to cease being a benefit corporation, in addition to any other required approval or vote, the satisfaction of the following conditions:

1. The holders of each class or series of shares shall be entitled to vote as a separate voting group on the corporate action regardless of any limitation on the voting rights of any class or series stated in the articles of incorporation or bylaws.

2. The corporate action is approved by vote of each class or series of shares entitled to vote by at least two–thirds of the total votes of the class or series.

（4）“公共利益高管”是指公共利益公司根据第 607.610 条规定任命的高管。

（5）“一般公共利益”是指根据第三方标准，公司的业务和经营在整体上对社会和环境产生的实质性积极影响。

（6）“独立”是指与公共利益公司或其子公司没有实质性关系。个体担任公共利益公司或其子公司的公共利益董事或公共利益高管并不构成实质性关系。在认定董事或高管是否独立时，若有下列情形，则视为该个体与公共利益公司或其子公司存在实质性关系：

（a）该个体是，或在过去 3 年内是，公共利益公司或其子公司公共利益高管以外的雇员。

（b）该个体的直系亲属是，或在过去的 3 年内是，公共利益公司或其子公司公共利益高管以外的执行高管。

（c）在所有购股权被视为已行使的情况下，下述持有公共利益公司 5% 以上已发行股份的登记股东或实际受益人：

1. 个人；或者

2. 实体：

a. 该个人是该实体的董事、高管或经理；或者

b. 在所有购股权被视为已行使的情况下，该实体中的个人为持有公共利益公司 5% 以上已发行股份的登记股东或实际受益人。

（7）“最低表决要求”是指：

（a）无论是通过修订公司章程还是通过合并、转换或者股权置换方式，某公司要转变为公共利益公司；公共利益公司将根据第 607.606 条规定修订章程；或者公共利益公司将终止公共利益公司形态，除任何其他对批准或表决的要求外，公司还应满足以下条件：

1. 每一类别或系列的股东有权作为一个独立的投票团体对公司行为进行投票，即使公司章程或章程细则对某一类别或系列股东作出了限制。

2. 公司行为必须获得每个类别或系列有投票权的所有股东至少 2/3 的投票才能通过。

(b) In the case of a domestic entity, other than a corporation, which is to be simultaneously converted to a benefit corporation or merged into a benefit corporation, in addition to any other required approval, vote, or consent, the satisfaction of the following conditions:

1. The holders of each class or series of equity interest in the entity who are entitled to receive a distribution of any kind are entitled, as a separate voting group, to vote on or consent to the action regardless of any applicable limitation on the voting or consent rights of any class or series.

2. The action is approved by vote or consent of each class or series of equity interest described in subparagraph 1. who are entitled to vote by at least two-thirds of the votes or consent of the class or series.

(8) "Specific public benefit" includes, but is not limited to:

(a) Providing low-income or underserved individuals or communities with beneficial products or services;

(b) Promoting economic opportunity for individuals or communities beyond the creation of jobs in the normal course of business;

(c) Protecting or restoring the environment;

(d) Improving human health;

(e) Promoting the arts, sciences, or advancement of knowledge;

(f) Increasing the flow of capital to entities that have as their stated purpose the provision of a benefit to society or the environment; and

(g) Any other public benefit consistent with the purposes of the benefit corporation.

(9) "Subsidiary" means, in relation to a person other than an individual, an entity in which a person owns beneficially or of record 50 percent or more of the outstanding equity interests.

(10) "Third-party standard" means a recognized standard for defining, reporting, and assessing the societal and environmental performance of a business which is:

(a) Comprehensive, because it assesses the effect of the business and its operations upon the interests provided in s. 607.607(1)(a)2.–5.

(b) Developed by an entity that is not controlled by the benefit corporation.

(c) Credible, because it is developed by an entity that has access to necessary expertise to assess the overall societal and environmental performance of a business and uses a balanced, collaborative approach to develop the standard, including a period for public comment.

(d) Transparent, because the following information is publicly available:

1. The criteria considered under the standard when measuring the overall societal and environmental performance of a business and the relative weights, if any, of those criteria.

（b）非公司的本州实体要转变为或并入公共利益公司，除其他批准、表决或赞成的要求外，还应满足以下条件：

1. 该实体的每一类别或系列享有任何权益分配权的股权持有者有权作为一个独立的投票团体对公司行为进行投票或表示赞成，即使存在任何对该类别或系列的投票或表决权利的限制。

2. 公司行为必须经第 1 分项规定的每个类别或系列有投票权的股东的至少 2/3 赞成通过。

（8）“特定公共利益”包括但不限于：
（a）向低收入、低福利人群或社区提供有益的产品或服务；

（b）在正常业务过程中向个人或社区提供除创造就业外的经济机会；

（c）保护或修复环境；
（d）改善人类健康；
（e）促进艺术、科学或知识进步；
（f）促进资本向拥有有利于社会或环境目标的实体流动；以及

（g）任何其他与公共利益公司目的一致的公共利益。
（9）“子公司”是指，该实体 50% 以上已发行的股份的受益所有权或登记所有权被另一实体所拥有。

（10）“第三方标准”是指用于定义、报告和评估公司社会和环境绩效的标准，其应满足以下条件：
（a）综合，根据第 607.607（1）（a）2–5 分项中所列利益评估公司业务和经营绩效。

（b）经非由公共利益公司控制的第三方实体制定。
（c）可信，该标准由一个能够获得必要专业知识来评估企业的整体社会和环境绩效的实体，并采用平衡的、合作的方式来制定，包括设定公众意见征询期。

（d）透明，以下信息可公开获取：
1. 衡量企业整体社会和环境绩效时所考虑的指标和这些指标的相关权重。

2. The identity of the directors, officers, material owners, and the governing body of the entity that developed and controlled revisions; the process by which revisions to the standard and changes to the membership of the governing body are made; and an accounting of the revenue and sources of financial support for the entity, with sufficient detail to disclose any relationships that could reasonably be considered to present a potential conflict of interest.

§ 607.603. Incorporation.

To incorporate as a benefit corporation, an incorporator must satisfy the requirements of this chapter, and the articles of incorporation must state that the corporation is a benefit corporation under this part.

§ 607.604. Election of benefit corporation status.

(1) An existing corporation may become a benefit corporation under this part by amending its articles of incorporation to include a statement that the corporation is a benefit corporation under this part. The amendment must be adopted by the minimum status vote.

(2) A plan of merger, conversion, or share exchange must be adopted by the minimum status vote if an entity that is not a benefit corporation is a party to a merger or conversion or if the exchanging entity in a share exchange and the surviving, new, or resulting entity is, or will be, a benefit corporation.

(3) If an entity elects to become a benefit corporation by amendment of the articles of incorporation or by a merger, conversion, or share exchange, the shareholders of the entity are entitled to appraisal rights under and pursuant to ss. 607.1301–607.1333.

§ 607.605. Termination of benefit corporation status.

(1) A benefit corporation may terminate its status as such and cease to be subject to this part by amending its articles of incorporation to delete the provision required under s. 607.603 or s. 607.604. The amendment must be adopted by the minimum status vote.

(2) A plan of merger, conversion, or share exchange which has the effect of terminating the status of a corporation as a benefit corporation must be adopted by the minimum status vote. A sale, lease, exchange, or other disposition of all or substantially all of the assets of a benefit corporation is not effective unless the transaction is approved by the minimum status vote. However, a minimum status vote is not required if the transaction is in the usual and regular course of business, is pursuant to court order, or is a sale pursuant to which all or a substantial portion of the net proceeds of the sale will be distributed to the shareholders within 1 year after the date of the sale.

(3) If a corporation's status as a benefit corporation is terminated pursuant to, shareholders of the corporation are entitled to appraisal rights under and pursuant to ss. 607.1301–607.1333.

§ 607.606. Corporate purpose.

(1) A benefit corporation has the purpose of creating general public benefit. This

2. 制定和控制修改标准的董事、高管、主要股东和该实体控制人员的身份；标准修改和控制人员变动的程序；以及收入和资金来源的核算，包括充分披露合理认知下存在利益冲突的所有细节。

第 607.603 条　设立

为设立公共利益公司，公司发起人必须满足本章的要求，并且必须在公司章程中声明其是本节规定下的公共利益公司。

第 607.604 条　公共利益公司的形态选择

（1）已成立的商事公司可依据本节规定转变为公共利益公司，公司可以通过修改公司章程，作出该公司为本节规定下公共利益公司的声明。公司章程的修改应满足最低表决要求。

（2）若作为非公共利益公司的实体是合并或财产转换中的一方，或股权置换中的置换实体和存续、新设或留存的实体是，或将是公共利益公司，则合并、财产转换或股权置换的方案须满足最低表决要求。

（3）若某实体选择通过修改公司章程或者通过合并、财产转换或者股权置换方式成为公共利益公司，该实体的股东有权依据第 607.1301 条至第 607.1333 条的规定享有股份回购请求权。

第 607.605 条　公共利益公司形态的终止

（1）公共利益公司可通过修改公司章程删除第 607.603 条或第 607.604 条规定要求的条款来终止其公共利益公司的形态并不再受本节规定的调整。该修改应满足最低表决要求。

（2）若公司合并、财产转换或股权置换的计划有终止公司的公共利益公司形态的效力，该计划应满足最低表决要求。一项出售、出租、置换或者其他处置公共利益公司全部或主要财产的行为满足最低表决要求才能生效。但是，若该交易为正常商业往来，依据法院裁决，或出售的全部或主要净收入将在出售后 1 年内分配给股东，则无须满足最低表决要求。

（3）若公司的公共利益公司形态根据第（1）款或第（2）款规定终止，公司的股东依据第 607.1301 条至第 607.1333 条的规定享有股份回购请求权。

第 607.606 条　公司目的

（1）公共利益公司应具有服务于一般公共利益的目的。此目的在第 607.0301

purpose is in addition to its purpose under s. 607.0301.

(2) The articles of incorporation of a benefit corporation may identify one or more specific public benefits as its purpose in addition to its purposes under subsection (1) and s. 607.0301. A benefit corporation may amend its articles of incorporation to add, amend, or delete the identification of a specific public benefit purpose; however, the amendment must be adopted by the minimum status vote. The identification of a specific public benefit under this subsection does not limit the obligation of a benefit corporation under subsection (1).

(3) The creation of general public benefit and a specific public benefit under subsections (1) and (2) is deemed to be in the best interest of the benefit corporation.

(4) A professional corporation that is a benefit corporation does not violate s. 621.08 by having as its purpose the creation of general public benefit or a specific public benefit.

§ 607.607. Standard of conduct for directors.

(1) In discharging their duties and in considering the best interests of the benefit corporation, the directors:

(a) Shall consider the effects of any action or inaction upon:

1. The shareholders of the benefit corporation;

2. The employees and workforce of the benefit corporation, its subsidiaries, and its suppliers;

3. The interests of customers and suppliers as beneficiaries of the general public benefit and any specific public benefit purposes of the benefit corporation;

4. Community and societal factors, including those of each community in which offices or facilities of the benefit corporation, its subsidiaries, or its suppliers are located;

5. The local and global environment;

6. The short-term and long-term interests of the benefit corporation, including benefits that may accrue to the benefit corporation from its long-term plans and the possibility that these interests may be best served by the continued independence of the benefit corporation; and

7. The ability of the benefit corporation to accomplish its general public benefit purpose and each of its specific public benefit purposes, if any.

(b) May consider other pertinent factors or the interests of any other group that they deem appropriate.

(c) Are not required to give priority to the interests of a particular person or group referred to in paragraph (a) or paragraph (b) over the interests of any other person or group, unless the benefit corporation has stated in its articles of incorporation its intention to give priority to certain interests.

(d) Are not required to give equal weight to the interests of a particular person or group referred to in paragraph (a) or paragraph (b) unless the benefit corporation has stated in its

条规定的目的之外。

（2）公共利益公司的章程可以在第（1）款和第 607.0301 条规定外确定一项或多项特定公共利益目的。公共利益公司可以通过修改章程增加、修改或删除已确定的特定公共利益目的；但是，该修改必须满足最低表决要求。依据本款规定确定的特定公共利益目的不限制公共利益公司第（1）项规定的义务。

（3）依据第（1）项和第（2）项规定创设的一般和特定公共利益被视为公共利益公司的最佳利益。

（4）选择公共利益形态的专业公司并不因其有创设一般或特定公共利益的目的而违反第 621.08 条的规定。

第 607.607 条　董事行为标准

（1）在履行各自职责和考虑公共利益公司最佳利益时，董事：

（a）其作为或不作为，应当考虑对以下对象的影响：

1. 公共利益公司的股东；

2. 公共利益公司雇员及其子公司和供应商；

3. 作为公共利益公司一般或特定公共利益受益者的消费者和供应商的利益；

4. 社区和社会因素，包括公共利益公司及其子公司或供应商办公地或设施所在地的社区；

5. 当地和全球环境；

6. 公共利益公司的短期和长期利益，包括从其长期计划中产生的利益以及公共利益公司继续保持独立可能产生的最佳利益；以及

7. 公共利益公司实现其一般和特定公共利益目的的能力。

（b）可以考虑他们认为合适的任何其他相关因素或其他团体的利益。

（c）除公司章程中规定外，无须优先考虑第（a）项或第（b）项中特定的个人或团体的利益。

（d）除公共利益公司在章程中声明了同等对待的意愿外，无须给予第（a）项或第（b）项中的特定人或团体同等待遇。

articles of incorporation its intention to give such equal weight.

(2) Except as provided in the articles of incorporation, a director is not personally liable for monetary damages to the corporation, or to any other person, for the failure of the benefit corporation to pursue or create general public benefit or a specific public benefit. A director is subject to the duties established in s. 607.0830.

(3) Except as provided in the articles of incorporation, a director does not have a duty to a person who is a beneficiary of the general public benefit purpose or any one or more specific public benefit purposes of the benefit corporation.

§ 607.608. Benefit director.

(1) If the articles of incorporation so provide, the board of directors of a benefit corporation may include a director who is designated as the benefit director and, in addition to the powers, duties, rights, and immunities of the other directors of the benefit corporation, has the powers, duties, rights, and immunities provided in this part.

(2) The benefit director shall be elected, and may be removed, in the manner provided by this chapter. Except as provided under subsection (5), the benefit director shall be independent and may serve as a benefit officer. The articles of incorporation or bylaws may prescribe additional qualifications of the benefit director.

(3) Unless the articles of incorporation or bylaws provide otherwise, the benefit director shall prepare, and the benefit corporation shall include in the annual benefit report to shareholders required under s. 607.612, the opinion of the benefit director on the following:

(a) Whether the benefit corporation in all material respects acted in accordance with its general public benefit purpose and any specific public benefit purpose during the period covered by the report.

(b)Whether the directors and officers complied with ss. 607.607(1) and 607.609(1).

(c) Whether the benefit corporation or its directors or officers failed to comply with paragraph (a) or s. 607.607(1) or s. 607.609(1), including a description of the ways in which the benefit corporation or its directors or officers failed to comply.

(4) The action or inaction of an individual in his or her capacity as a benefit director shall constitute for all purposes an action or inaction of that individual in his or her capacity as a director of the benefit corporation.

(5) The benefit director of a corporation formed under chapter 621 is not required to be independent.

§ 607.609. Standard of conduct for officers.

(1) If an officer of a benefit corporation reasonably believes that a matter may have a material effect on the ability of the corporation to create, or the creation by the corporation of, general public benefit or a specific public benefit identified in the articles of incorporation and the officer has discretion to act on the matter, the officer shall consider the interests and

（2）除在公司章程中另有规定外，董事个人不因公共利益公司未能追求或创设一般或特定公共利益对公司或任何其他人承担损害赔偿责任。董事有第 607.0830 条规定的义务。

（3）除章程中另有规定外，董事不对公共利益公司一般或特定利益目的的受益人负责。

第 607.608 条　公共利益董事

（1）若公司章程作出规定，公共利益公司董事会中可以包含被任命为公共利益董事的董事，公共利益董事除有公共利益公司的其他董事的权力、义务、权利和豁免权外，还有本节规定的权力、义务、权利和豁免权。

（2）公共利益董事应当依据本章规定任免。除第（5）款规定外，公共利益董事应当独立并且可担任公共利益高管。公司章程或章程细则可对公共利益董事的任职资格作出其他规定。

（3）除公司章程或章程细则另有规定外，公共利益董事应当编写其对以下事项的意见，公共利益公司应当根据第 607.612 条的规定将报告附于年度公共利益报告中供股东查阅：

（a）在报告所述时间内，公共利益公司是否在所有重要事项上依一般和特定公共利益目的行事。

（b）董事和高管是否分别依第 607.607（1）款和第 607.609（1）款的规定行事。

（c）公共利益公司或其董事或高管是否未能依第（a）项或第 607.607（1）款或第 607.609（1）款的要求行事，包括陈述公共利益公司或其董事、高管未能履行责任的情况。

（4）公共利益董事在其职权范围内的个人作为或不作为行为应视为公共利益公司董事的行为。

（5）依据第 621 章规定成立的公司的公共利益董事不需要是独立的。

第 607.609 条　高管行为标准

（1）若公共利益公司高管有合理理由认为该行为对公共利益公司在章程中确定的一般或特定公共利益的创设和公司的创设能力有实质性影响，并且高管就该行为有自由裁量权，高管应当考虑第 607.607（1）款中规定的利益和因素。

factors provided in s. 607.607(1).

(2) The officer's consideration of interests and factors under subsection (1) does not constitute a violation of s. 607.0841.

(3) Except as provided in the articles of incorporation, an officer is not personally liable for monetary damages to the corporation or to any other person for the failure of the benefit corporation to pursue or create general public benefit or a specific public benefit; however, he or she is subject to s. 607.0841.

(4) Except as provided in the articles of incorporation, an officer does not have a duty to a person who is a beneficiary of the general public benefit purpose or any specific public benefit purpose of the benefit corporation arising from the status of the person as a beneficiary.

§ 607.610. Benefit officer.

(1) A benefit corporation may designate an officer as the benefit officer.

(2) The benefit officer has the powers and duties set forth in the bylaws or determined by the board of directors, which may include, but are not limited to:

(a) Powers and duties relating to the general public benefit or a specific public benefit purpose of the corporation; and

(b) The duty to prepare the annual benefit report required under s. 607.612.

§ 607.611. Right of action.

(1) (a) Except in a benefit enforcement proceeding, no person may bring an action or assert a claim against a benefit corporation or its directors or officers with respect to:

1. A failure to pursue or create a general public benefit or a specific public benefit set forth in its articles of incorporation; or

2. A violation of an obligation, duty, or standard of conduct under this part.

(b) A benefit corporation is not liable for monetary damages under this part for the failure of the benefit corporation to pursue or create general public benefit or a specific public benefit.

(2) A benefit enforcement proceeding may be commenced or maintained only:

(a) Directly by the benefit corporation; or

(b) Derivatively by:

1. A shareholder of record on the date of the action or inaction complained of in the benefit enforcement proceeding;

2. A director;

3. A person or group of persons that owns beneficially or of record 5 percent or more of the outstanding equity interests in an entity of which the benefit corporation is a subsidiary on the date of the action or inaction complained of in the proceeding; or

（2）高管对第（1）款规定的利益和因素的考量不违反第 607.0841 条的规定。

（3）除公司章程中另有规定外，高管不因公共利益公司未能追求或创设一般或特定公共利益对公司或任何其他人承担损害赔偿责任；但是，其应受第 607.0841 条规定的调整。

（4）除公司章程中另有规定外，高管不对公共利益公司一般或特定公共利益目的的受益人负责。

第 607.610 条　公共利益高管

（1）公共利益公司可以将本公司高管任命为公共利益高管。

（2）公共利益高管应当有公司章程细则或者董事会决定确立的权力和义务，包括但不限于：

（a）关于公司一般公共利益或特定公共利益目的权利和义务；以及

（b）编写第 607.612 条要求的公共利益报告的义务。

第 607.611 条 诉讼权利

（1）（a）非经公共利益实施程序，任何人不得因以下事项向公共利益公司或者其董事、高管提起诉讼或主张：

1. 未能追求或创造其在公司章程中声明的一般或特定公共利益；或者

2. 违反本节规定的责任、义务或行为标准。

（b）公共利益公司不对本节规定的任何未能追求或创造一般或特定公共利益的行为承担损害赔偿责任。

（2）仅在下列情形中，以下主体可提起公共利益实施程序：

（a）由公共利益公司直接提起；或者

（b）由以下主体派生提起：

1. 公共利益实施程序中被诉作为或不作为行为发生时登记的股东；

2. 董事；

3. 程序中被诉作为或不作为行为发生时，持有公共利益公司母公司 5% 以上已发行股份的登记股东或实际受益人；或者

4. Any other person who is specified in the articles of incorporation or bylaws of the benefit corporation.

§ 607.612. Preparation of annual benefit report.

(1) Unless it is prepared by a benefit director or a benefit officer, the board of directors shall prepare an annual benefit report. The annual benefit report must include all of the following:

(a) A narrative description of:

1. The ways in which the benefit corporation pursued general public benefit during the year and the extent to which the general public benefit was created.

2. Any circumstance that has hindered the pursuit or creation of general public benefit or a specific public benefit by the benefit corporation.

3. The process and rationale for selecting or changing the third–party standard used to prepare the benefit report.

(b) The name of the benefit director and the benefit officer, if those positions exist, and the respective business addresses to which correspondence may be directed.

(c) If the corporation has a benefit director, the statement as provided in s. 607.608(3).

(d) A statement of any connection between the organization that established the third–party standard, or its directors, officers, or any holder of 5 percent or more of the governance interests in the organization, and the benefit corporation or its directors, officers, or any holder of 5 percent or more of the outstanding shares of the benefit corporation, including any financial or governance relationship that might materially affect the credibility of the use of the third–party standard.

(2) The annual benefit report must be prepared in accordance with a third–party standard that is:

(a) Applied consistently with any previous application in prior annual benefit reports; or

(b) Accompanied by an explanation of the reasons for any inconsistent application or any change in the standard from the immediate prior report.

(3) If, during the year covered by an annual benefit report, a benefit director resigned from, or refused to stand for reelection to, his or her position, or was removed from his or her position, and he or she furnished written correspondence to the benefit corporation concerning the circumstances surrounding his or her departure, that correspondence must be included as an exhibit in the annual benefit report.

(4) The annual benefit report and the assessment of the performance of the benefit corporation in the annual benefit report required under subsection (2) are not required to be audited or certified by a third–party standards provider.

§ 607.613. Availability of annual benefit report.

(1) Each benefit corporation shall send its annual benefit report to each shareholder:

4. 公共利益公司章程或章程细则中规定的其他人员。

第 607.612 条　年度公共利益报告的编写

（1）除非由公共利益董事或高管编写，否则董事会应编写公司年度公共利益报告。年度公共利益报告必须包含以下所有内容：

（a）对以下事项的描述：

1. 公共利益公司本年度追求一般公共利益的方法和实现的情况。

2. 阻碍公共利益公司实现一般和特定公共利益的情形。

3. 为编写公共利益报告而选择或更换第三方标准的程序和原因。

（b）公共利益董事和公共利益高管的姓名和地址。

（c）若公司有公共利益董事，其应依第 607.608（3）款的规定进行声明。

（d）设立第三方标准的组织或其董事、高管或 5% 以上管理权利的持有者与公共利益公司或其董事、高管或公共利益公司 5% 以上已发行股份的持有者之间关系的声明，包括任何可能影响第三方标准可信度的财务或管理关系。

（2）年度公共利益报告必须依据第三方标准编写，即：

（a）沿用先前年度公共利益报告中使用的标准；或者

（b）附一份说明解释与上一份报告的标准相比适用上的差异或变化。

（3）在公共利益报告年度内，如果公共利益董事辞职、拒绝连任或被免职，且该公共利益董事与公司有任何书面的涉及其离职的书信往来，公共利益报告应当将该书信往来作为附件。

（4）年度公共利益报告和依据第（2）款规定编写的公共利益报告中对于公共利益公司表现的评价无须经审计或第三方标准提供者认证。

第 607.613 条　年度公共利益报告的提供

（1）每个公共利益公司应当将其公共利益报告送交各股东：

(a) Within 120 days after the end of the fiscal year of the benefit corporation; or

(b) At the same time that the benefit corporation delivers any other annual report to its shareholders.

(2) A benefit corporation shall post each annual benefit report on the public portion of its website, if any, and it shall remain posted for at least 3 years.

(3) If a benefit corporation does not have a website, the benefit corporation shall provide a copy of its most recent annual benefit report, without charge, to any person who requests a copy.

(4) If a benefit corporation does not comply with the annual benefit report delivery requirement, the circuit court in the county in which the principal office of the benefit corporation is located or, if no office is located in this state, the county in which its registered office is located, may, after a shareholder of the benefit corporation requests a copy, summarily order the corporation to furnish the report. If the court orders the report to be furnished, the court may also order the benefit corporation to pay the shareholder's costs, including reasonable attorney fees, which were incurred in obtaining the order and otherwise enforce his or her rights under this section.

（a）公共利益公司财政年度结束后 120 天内；或者

（b）公共利益公司向其股东送交其他年度报告的同一时间。

（2）若条件允许，公共利益公司应当将其每份公共利益报告发布于其网站的公共部分，并且至少应保留 3 年。

（3）若公共利益公司没有网站，应向所有索取报告的人免费提供最新公共利益报告的副本。

（4）若公共利益公司未遵守年度公共利益报告提交的要求，且该公司在公共利益公司主营业地所在县，或在该州中没有办公室，则在该公司注册地所在县的巡回法院可以在公共利益公司股东要求提供副本后，要求公司提交年度公共利益报告。若法院命令公共利益公司提交报告，则法院也可以命令公共利益公司支付股东的费用，包括为获得此命令和其他行使其本条规定的权利的合理律师费用。

THE STATE OF IDAHO

LEGISLATURE OF THE STATE OF IDAHO

Sixty-third Legislature

First Regular Session-2015

IN THE SENATE

SENATE BILL NO.1076

BY COMMERCE AND HUMAN RESOURCES COMMITTEE

AN ACT RELATING TO BENEFIT CORPORATIONS; AMENDING TITLE , IDAHO CODE, BY THE ADDITION OF A NEW CHAPTER, TITLE, IDAHO CODE, TO PROVIDE A SHORT TITLE AND STATE THE APPLICATION AND EFFECT OF THIS CHAPTER, TO DEFINE TERMS, TO ESTABLISH INCORPORATION REQUIREMENTS FOR BENEFIT CORPORATIONS, TO ESTABLISH THE PROCESS UNDER WHICH BENEFIT CORPORATION STATUS IS ADOPTED, TO ESTABLISH THE PROCESS UNDER WHICH BENEFIT CORPORATION STATUS IS TERMINATED, TO DESCRIBE THE PURPOSES OF BENEFIT CORPORATIONS, TO ESTABLISH STANDARDS OF CONDUCT FOR DIRECTORS, TO PROVIDE THAT CERTAIN BENEFIT CORPORATIONS SHALL HAVE AND OTHERS MAY HAVE A BENEFIT DIRECTOR AND TO ESTABLISH RULES RELATING TO THE BENEFIT DIRECTOR, TO ESTABLISH STANDARDS OF CONDUCT FOR OFFICERS, TO PROVIDE THAT BENEFIT CORPORATIONS MAY HAVE A BENEFIT OFFICER WHO PERFORMS CERTAIN DUTIES, TO PROVIDE RULES FOR BRINGING AN ACTION AGAINST A BENEFIT CORPORATION, TO REQUIRE AN ANNUAL BENEFIT REPORT AND TO REQUIRE THE BENEFIT REPORT BE MADE AVAILABLE TO CERTAIN PERSONS AND THE PUBLIC.

Be It Enacted by the Legislature of the State of Idaho:

SECTION 1. That Title 30, Idaho Code, be, and the same is hereby amended by the

爱达荷州

爱达荷州立法机关

第63届

2015年第1次常规会议

参议院

州参议院法案第1076号

由商务和人力资源委员会提出

本法案涉及公共利益公司；通过增加《爱达荷州法典》下的新的一章修订《爱达荷州法典》中的一编，以规定法条名称和本章的适用范围和效力，确立名词的定义，确立公共利益公司设立的标准，确立采用公共利益公司形态的程序，确立终止公共利益公司形态的程序，描述公共利益公司的目的，确立董事行为的标准，规定某种公共利益公司应当有和其他公共利益公司可以有公共利益董事并且关于公共利益董事的规则，确立高管的行为标准，规定公共利益公司可以有一个履行某种义务的公共利益高管，规定对公共利益公司提起诉讼的规则，要求公司编写年度公共利益报告并且要求将该公共利益报告提供给某些人和公众。

由爱达荷州议会颁布：

第1部分　《爱达荷州法典》第30编增加新的一章作为《爱达荷州法典》第

addition thereto of a NEW CHAPTER, to be known and designated as Chapter 20, Title 30, Idaho Code, and to read as follows:

CHAPTER 20
IDAHO BENEFIT CORPORATION ACT

30-2001. APPLICATION AND EFFECT OF THIS CHAPTER.

(1) This chapter may be known and cited as the "Idaho Benefit Corporation Act."

(2) This chapter shall be applicable to all benefit corporations.

(3) The existence of a provision of this chapter shall not of itself create an implication that a contrary or different rule of law is applicable to a business corporation that is not a benefit corporation. This chapter shall not affect a statute or rule of law that is applicable to a business corporation that is not a benefit corporation.

(4) Except as otherwise provided in this chapter, the Idaho business corporation act shall be generally applicable to all benefit corporations. A benefit corporation may be subject simultaneously to this chapter and other chapters of this title. The provisions of this chapter shall control over other provisions of this title, including chapters 1 and 13 of this title.

(5) A provision of the articles of incorporation or bylaws of a benefit corporation may not limit, be inconsistent with or supersede a provision of this chapter.

30-2002. DEFINITIONS.

In this chapter:

(1) "Benefit corporation" means a business corporation that has elected to become subject to this chapter and the status of which as a benefit corporation has not been terminated.

(2) "Benefit director" means the director designated as the benefit director of a benefit corporation under section 30–2008, Idaho Code.

(3) "Benefit enforcement proceeding" means any claim, action or proceeding for failure of a benefit corporation to pursue or create general public benefit or a specific public benefit purpose as set forth in its articles, or violation of any obligation, duty or standard of conduct under this chapter.

(4) "Benefit officer" means the individual designated as the benefit officer of a benefit corporation under section 30–2010, Idaho Code.

(5) "General public benefit" means a material positive impact on society and the environment, taken as a whole, as assessed under a third–party standard, resulting from the

30 编的第 20 章，内容如下：

第 20 章
爱达荷州公共利益公司法

第 30–2001 条　本章的适用和效力

（1）本章可以被称为《爱达荷州公共利益公司法》。

（2）本章适用于所有的公共利益公司。

（3）本章条款不应为非公共利益公司的商事公司设定相反或不同的规则。本章规定不影响非公共利益公司有关条文和规则的适用。

（4）除本章另有规定外，《爱达荷州商事公司法》应适用于所有的公共利益公司。公共利益公司同时受本章和本编其他章的规定的约束。本章条款的效力应优先于本编的其他章节的条款，包括本编第 1 章和第 13 章。

（5）公共利益公司的章程或章程细则不得限制、违背或取代本章的条款。

第 30–2002 条　定义

在本章中：

（1）“公共利益公司”是指一家选择接受本章规定的调整且公共利益公司形态并未终止的商事公司。

（2）“公共利益董事”是指公共利益公司根据《爱达荷州法典》第 30–2008 条的规定任命的董事。

（3）“公共利益实施程序”是指因公共利益公司未能追求或实现公司章程规定的一般或特定公共利益目的或者违反本章规定的义务、责任或行为标准而提起的主张、诉讼或程序。

（4）“公共利益高管”是指公共利益公司根据第 30–2010 条规定任命的高管。

（5）“一般公共利益”是指根据第三方标准，公司的业务和经营在整体上对社会和环境产生的实质性积极影响。

business and operations of a benefit corporation.

(6) "Independent" means having no material relationship with a benefit corporation or a subsidiary of the benefit corporation; provided however, that serving as a benefit director or benefit officer does not by itself preclude a person from being independent. A material relationship between an individual and a benefit corporation or any of its subsidiaries will be conclusively presumed to exist if any of the following apply:

(a) The individual is or has been within the last three (3) years an employee other than a benefit officer of the benefit corporation or a subsidiary.

(b) An immediate family member of the individual is or has been within the last three (3) years an executive officer other than a benefit officer of the benefit corporation or a subsidiary.

(c) There is beneficial or record ownership of five percent (5%) or more of the outstanding shares of the benefit corporation, calculated as if all outstanding rights to acquire equity interests in the benefit corporation had been exercised, by:

(i) The individual; or

(ii) An entity:

1. Of which the individual is a director, an officer or a manager; or

2. In which the individual owns beneficially or of record five percent (5%) or more of the outstanding equity interests, calculated as if all outstanding rights to acquire equity interests in the entity had been exercised.

(7) "Minimum status vote" means:

(a) In the case of a business corporation, in addition to any other required approval or vote, the satisfaction of the following conditions:

(i) The shareholders of every class or series shall be entitled to vote as a separate voting group on the corporate action regardless of a limitation stated in the articles of incorporation or bylaws on the voting rights of any class or series.

(ii) The corporate action must be approved by vote of the shareholders of each class or series entitled to cast at least two-thirds (2/3) of the votes that all shareholders of the class or series are entitled to cast on the action.

(b) In the case of a domestic entity other than a business corporation, in addition to any other required approval, vote or consent, the satisfaction of the following conditions:

(i) The holders of every class or series of equity interest in the entity that are entitled to receive a distribution of any kind from the entity shall be entitled to vote on or consent to the action regardless of any otherwise applicable limitation on the voting or consent rights of any class or series.

(ii) The action must be approved by vote or consent of the holders entitled to cast at least two-thirds (2/3) of the votes or consents that all of those holders are entitled to cast on

（6）“独立”是指与公共利益公司或其子公司没有实质性的关系；但是担任公共利益董事或者公共利益高管不妨碍其独立性。出现下列情形，则认为该个体与公共利益公司或其子公司存在实质性的关系：

（a）该个体是，或在过去的3年内是，公共利益公司或其子公司的公共利益高管以外的雇员。

（b）该个体的直系亲属是，或在过去的3年内是，公共利益公司或其子公司的公共利益高管以外的执行高管。

（c）在所有购股权被视为已行使的情况下，下述持有公共利益公司5%以上已发行股份的登记股东或实际受益人：

（i）个人；或者

（ii）实体：

1. 该个人是该实体的董事、高管或经理；或者

2. 在所有购股权被视为已行使的情况下，该实体中的个人为持有公共利益公司5%以上已发行股份的登记股东或实际受益人。

（7）“最低表决要求”是指：

（a）在商事公司中，除任何其他对批准或表决的要求外，还应满足以下条件：

（i)每一类别或系列的股东有权作为一个独立的投票团体对公司行为进行投票，即使公司章程或章程细则对某一类别或系列股东的投票权作出了限制。

（ii）公司行为必须获得每一类别或系列有投票权的所有股东的至少2/3的票数才能通过。

（b）在非商事公司的本州实体中，除任何其他对批准、表决或赞成的要求外，还应满足以下条件：

（i）该实体的每个类别或系列的任何权益分配形式下的股权持有者应当有权对公司行为进行投票，即使存在任何对该类别或系列股权持有者的投票权的限制。

（ii）公司行为必须获得有投票权的所有股权持有者的至少2/3的投票或同意才能通过。

the action.

(8) "Publicly traded corporation" means a business corporation that has shares listed on a national securities exchange or traded in a market maintained by one (1) or more members of a national securities association.

(9) "Specific public benefit" includes:

(a) Providing low-income or underserved individuals or communities with beneficial products or services;

(b) Promoting economic opportunity for individuals or communities beyond the creation of jobs in the normal course of business;

(c) Protecting or restoring the environment;

(d) Improving human health;

(e) Promoting the arts, sciences or advancement of knowledge;

(f) Increasing the flow of capital to entities with a purpose to benefit society or the environment; or

(g) Conferring any other particular benefit on society or the environment.

(10) "Subsidiary" means, in relation to a person, an entity in which the person owns beneficially or of record fifty percent (50%) or more of the outstanding equity interests, calculated as if all outstanding rights to acquire equity interests in the entity had been exercised.

(11) "Third-party standard" means a recognized standard for defining, reporting and assessing corporate social and environmental performance that is:

(a) Comprehensive in that it assesses the effect of the business and its operations on the interests listed in section 30-2007(1), Idaho Code;

(b) Developed by an entity that is not controlled by the benefit corporation;

(c) Credible in that it is developed by an entity that both has access to necessary expertise to assess overall corporate social and environmental performance, and uses a balanced multi-stakeholder approach to develop the standard, including a reasonable public comment period; and

(d) Transparent in that information about the standard is publicly available, including information about:

(i) The criteria and weighting of such criteria used in the standard;

(ii) The identity of those who developed or revised the standard; and

(iii) An accounting of the revenue and sources of financial support for the entity that developed the standard, with sufficient detail to disclose any relationships that could reasonably be considered to present a potential conflict of interest.

30-2003. INCORPORATION.

A benefit corporation shall be incorporated in accordance with part 2, chapter 1, title

（8）“上市公司”是指在美国证券交易所或美国证券协会中一个或几个成员形成的市场上进行交易的商事公司。

（9）“特定公共利益”包括：

（a）向低收入或者低福利人群或社区提供有益的产品或服务；

（b）在正常业务过程中向个人或社区提供创造就业之外的经济机会；

（c）保护或修复环境；

（d）改善人类健康；

（e）促进艺术、科学或知识进步；

（f）促进资本向有利于社会或环境目标的实体流动；以及

（g）给予社会或环境其他特别的利益。

（10）“子公司”是指，在所有购股权被视为已行使的情况下，该实体50%以上已发行的股份的受益所有权或登记所有权被另一实体所拥有。

（11）“第三方标准”是指用于定义、报告和评估公司的社会和环境绩效的标准，应满足以下条件：

（a）综合，其在评估《爱达荷州法典》第30-2007（1）款中所列利益的基础上评价公司业务和经营绩效；

（b）其非由公共利益公司控制的第三方实体制定；

（c）可信，制定标准的第三方实体拥有评估公司社会和环境综合绩效所需的专业知识并且使用平衡多方相关者利益的方法，包括设定合理期间以听取公众意见；以及

（d）透明，以下关于标准的信息是公开的：

（i）标准中使用的指标和这些指标的权重；

（ii）制定或修订该标准的人员的身份；和

（iii）对制定标准的机构的收入和资金来源的核算，充分披露在合理认知下存在利益冲突的所有关系。

第30-2003条　设立

公共利益公司应当按照《爱达荷州法典》第30编第1章第2节的规定设立，

30, Idaho Code, but its articles of incorporation must also state that it is a benefit corporation.

30-2004. ELECTION OF BENEFIT CORPORATION STATUS.

(1) An existing business corporation may become a benefit corporation under this chapter by amending its articles of incorporation so that they contain a statement that the corporation is a benefit corporation. In order to be effective, the amendment must be adopted by at least the minimum status vote.

(2) (a) Except as provided in paragraph (b) of this subsection, if a domestic entity that is not a benefit corporation is a party to a merger or conversion or the exchanging entity in an interest exchange and the surviving or converted entity in the merger, conversion or interest exchange is to be a benefit corporation, the plan of merger, conversion or interest exchange must be approved by the domestic entity by at least the minimum status vote.

(b) Paragraph (a) of this subsection does not apply in the case of a corporation that is a party to a merger if the shareholders of the corporation are not entitled to vote on the merger pursuant to section 30–1–1105, Idaho Code.

30-2005. TERMINATION OF STATUS.

(1) A benefit corporation may terminate its status as such and cease to be subject to this chapter by amending its articles of incorporation to delete the provision adopting benefit corporation status. In order to be effective, the amendment must be adopted by at least the minimum status vote.

(2) (a) Except as provided in paragraph (b) of this subsection, if a plan of merger, conversion or share exchange would have the effect of terminating the status of a business corporation as a benefit corporation, the plan must be adopted by at least the minimum status vote in order to be effective.

(b) Paragraph (a) of this subsection does not apply in the case of a corporation that is a party to a merger if the shareholders of the corporation are not entitled to vote on the merger pursuant to section 30–1–1105, Idaho Code.

(3) Any sale, lease, exchange or other disposition of all or substantially all of the assets of a benefit corporation, unless the transaction is in the usual and regular course of business, shall not be effective unless the transaction is approved by at least the minimum status vote.

30-2006. CORPORATE PURPOSES.

(1) A benefit corporation shall have a purpose of creating general public benefit. This purpose is in addition to its purpose under section 30–1–301, Idaho Code.

(2) The articles of incorporation of a benefit corporation may identify one (1) or more specific public benefits that it is the purpose of the benefit corporation to create in addition to its purposes under section 30–1–301, Idaho Code, and subsection (1) of this section. The identification of a specific public benefit under this subsection does not limit the purpose of a benefit corporation to create general public benefit under subsection (1) of this subsection.

但其公司章程必须声明其是公共利益公司。

第 30–2004 条　公共利益公司形态的选择

（1）已成立的商事公司可依据本章的规定成为公共利益公司，该公司需通过修改其公司章程作出该公司为公共利益公司的声明。公司章程的修改应满足最低表决要求。

（2）（a）除本款第（b）项的规定外，如果不具有公共利益公司形态的本州实体是合并、转换或股权置换中的一方，并且在合并、转换或股权置换中，存续或转换的一方为公共利益公司，那么该合并、转换或股权置换计划应满足最低表决要求。

（b）如果合并一方的股东根据《爱达荷州法典》第 30–1–1105 条的规定无权投票，则本款的第（a）项规定不适用于此种情形。

第 30–2005 条　形态的终止

（1）公共利益公司可通过修改公司章程删除有关公共利益公司形态的条款来终止其公共利益公司形态并不再受本章规定的调整。公司章程的修改应满足最低表决要求。

（2）（a）除本款第（b）项的规定外，如果公司合并、财产转换或股权置换的计划有终止商事公司作为公共利益公司的效力，则该计划必须满足最低表决要求。

（b）如果合并一方的股东根据《爱达荷州法典》第 30–1–1105 条的规定无权投票，则本款第（a）项的规定不适用于此种情形。

（3）除正常商业往来外，公共利益公司任何出售、出租、置换或者其他处置全部或者主要财产的行为，须满足最低表决要求。

第 30–2006 条　公司目的

（1）公共利益公司应有服务于一般公共利益的目的。此目的在《爱达荷州法典》第 30–1–301 条规定之外。

（2）公共利益公司的章程可以在《爱达荷州法典》第 30–1–301 条和本条第（1）款的规定之外确定一项或者多项特定的公共利益目的。依据本款规定创设的特定的公共利益目的并不限制公共利益公司根据本条第（1）款的规定设定的一般公共利益目的。

(3) The creation of general public benefit and specific public benefits under subsections (1) and (2) of this section is in the best interests of the benefit corporation.

(4) A benefit corporation may amend its articles of incorporation to add, amend or delete the identification of a specific public benefit that it is the purpose of the benefit corporation to create. In order to be effective, the amendment must be adopted by at least the minimum status vote.

(5) A professional corporation that is a benefit corporation does not violate section 30–1–1303(2), Idaho Code, by having the purpose to create general public benefit or a specific public benefit.

30-2007. STANDARD OF CONDUCT FOR DIRECTORS.

(1) In discharging the duties of their respective positions and in considering the best interests of the benefit corporation, the board of directors, committees of the board and individual directors of a benefit corporation shall consider the effects of any action or inaction on:

(a) The shareholders of the benefit corporation;

(b) The employees of the benefit corporation;

(c) The subsidiaries and suppliers of the benefit corporation;

(d) The interests of customers as beneficiaries of the general public benefit or specific public benefit purposes of the benefit corporation;

(e) Community and social factors, including those of each community in which offices or facilities of the benefit corporation, its subsidiaries, or its suppliers are located;

(f) The local and global environment;

(g) The short–term and long–term interests of the benefit corporation, including benefits that may accrue to the benefit corporation from its long–term plans and the possibility that these interests may be best served by the continued independence of the benefit corporation; and

(h) The ability of the benefit corporation to accomplish its general public benefit purpose and any specific public benefit purpose.

(2) In discharging the duties of their respective positions and in considering the best interests of the benefit corporation, the board of directors, committees of the board and individual directors of a benefit corporation may also consider any other pertinent factors or the interests of any group that they deem appropriate.

(3) The board of directors, committees of the board and individual directors of a benefit corporation need not give priority to a particular interest or factor referred to in subsection (1) or (2) of this section over any other interest or factor unless the benefit corporation has stated in its articles of incorporation its intention to give priority to certain interests or factors related to its accomplishment of its general public benefit or of a specific public benefit

（3）依据本条第（1）款和第（2）款的规定创造的一般和特定公共利益目的应当为公共利益公司的最佳利益。

（4）公共利益公司可以增加、修改或删除公司章程里设定的特定公共利益目的。公司章程的修改需满足最低表决要求。

（5）选择公共利益形态的专业公司并不因其有实现一般或特定公共利益的目的而违反《爱达荷州法典》第30-1-1303（2）款的规定。

第30-2007条 董事行为标准

（1）在履行各自职责和考虑公共利益公司最佳利益时，公共利益公司的董事会、董事委员会和董事应当考虑作为或不作为的行为对以下对象的影响：

（a）公共利益公司的股东；

（b）公共利益公司的雇员；

（c）公共利益公司的子公司和供应商；

（d）作为公共利益公司一般或特定公共利益受益者的消费者的利益；

（e）社区和社会因素，包括公共利益公司、其子公司或其供应商的办公地或设施所在地的社区；

（f）当地和全球环境；

（g）公共利益公司的短期和长期利益，包括从其长期计划中产生的利益以及公共利益公司继续保持独立可能产生的最佳利益；以及

（h）公共利益公司实现其一般和特定公共利益目的的能力。

（2）在履行各自职责和考虑公共利益公司的最佳利益时，公共利益公司的董事会、董事委员会和董事可以考虑他们认为合适的任何其他因素或其他群体的利益。

（3）除公司章程中要求优先考虑特定利益或因素外，公共利益公司的董事会、董事委员会和董事无须优先考虑第（1）款或第（2）款规定中的某个利益或因素。

purpose identified in its articles of incorporation.

(4) The consideration of interests and factors in the manner required by this section does not constitute a violation of section 30–1–830, Idaho Code.

(5) Except as provided in the articles of incorporation, a director is not personally liable for monetary damages for:

(a) Any action or inaction in the course of performing the duties of a director under subsection (1) of this section if the director performed the duties of office in compliance with section 3–1–830, Idaho Code, and this section; or

(b) Failure of the benefit corporation to pursue or create general public benefit or specific public benefit.

(6) A director does not have a duty to a person that is a beneficiary of the general public benefit purpose or a specific public benefit purpose of a benefit corporation arising from the status of the person as a beneficiary.

30-2008. BENEFIT DIRECTOR.

(1) The board of directors of a benefit corporation that is a publicly traded corporation shall, and the board of any other benefit corporation may, include a director who shall be designated the benefit director, and shall have, in addition to the powers, duties, rights and immunities of the other directors of the benefit corporation, the powers, duties, rights and immunities provided in this chapter.

(2) The benefit director shall be elected and may be removed in the manner provided in sections 30–1–803 through 30–1–809, Idaho Code. Except as provided in subsection (6) of this section, the benefit director shall be an individual who is independent. The benefit director may serve as the benefit officer at the same time as serving as the benefit director. The articles of incorporation or bylaws of a benefit corporation may prescribe additional qualifications of the benefit director not inconsistent with this subsection.

(3) The benefit director shall prepare and the benefit corporation shall include in the annual benefit report to shareholders required by section 30–2012, Idaho Code, the opinion of the benefit director on the following:

(a) Whether the benefit corporation acted in accordance with its general public benefit purpose and any specific public benefit purpose in all material respects during the period covered by the report;

(b) Whether the directors and officers complied with sections 30–2007 and 30–2009, Idaho Code, respectively; and

(c) If, in the opinion of the benefit director, the benefit corporation or its directors or officers failed to act or comply in the manner described in paragraphs (a) and (b) of this subsection, a description of the ways in which the benefit corporation or its directors or officers failed to act or comply.

（4）对本条中规定的利益和相关因素的考虑不违反爱达荷州法典第 30–1–830 条的规定。

（5）除公司章程另有明确规定外，董事不对以下行为承担损害赔偿责任：

（a）依据本条第（1）款的规定履行董事责任过程中的任何作为或不作为，若该行为符合《爱达荷州法典》第 3–1–830 条以及本条的规定；或者

（b）公共利益公司未能追求或实现一般或特定公共利益。

（6）董事不对公共利益公司一般或特定社会目的的受益人负责。

第 30–2008 条　公共利益董事

（1）上市的公共利益公司以及其他形式的公共利益公司的董事会应当任命公共利益董事，而且，公共利益董事除有公共利益公司其他董事的权力、义务、权利和豁免外，还有本章规定的权力、义务、权利和豁免权。

（2）公共利益董事应当依据《爱达荷州法典》第 30–1–803 条至第 30–1–809 条的规定进行任免。除本条第（6）款的规定外，公共利益董事应当是独立个体。公共利益董事可以同时担任公共利益高管。公共利益公司的章程或章程细则可以规定与本款规定不一致的公共利益董事资格。

（3）公共利益董事应当编写其对以下事项的意见，公共利益公司应当根据《爱达荷州法典》第 30–2012 条的规定将该意见附于年度公共利益报告中供股东查阅：

（a）在报告所述期间内，公共利益公司是否在所有重要事项上依其一般和特定公共利益目的行事；

（b）董事和高管是否分别依《爱达荷州法典》第 30–2007 条和第 30–2009 条的规定行事。

（c）如果公共利益董事认为公共利益公司、其董事或高管未能依本款第（a）项和第（b）项的规定行事，应在意见中陈述公共利益公司、其董事或高管未能履行责任的情况。

(4) The act or inaction of an individual in the capacity of a benefit director shall constitute for all purposes an act or inaction of that individual in the capacity of a director of the benefit corporation.

(5) Regardless of whether the articles of incorporation or bylaws of a benefit corporation include a provision eliminating or limiting the personal liability of directors authorized by section 30–1–202, Idaho Code, a benefit director shall not be personally liable for an act or omission in the capacity of a benefit director unless the act or omission constitutes self–dealing, willful misconduct or a knowing violation of law.

(6) The benefit director of a professional corporation organized under chapter 13, title 30, Idaho Code, does not need to be independent.

30-2009. STANDARD OF CONDUCT FOR OFFICERS.

(1) Each officer of a benefit corporation shall consider the interests and factors as provided in section 30–2007, Idaho Code, if the officer has discretion to act with respect to a matter, and it reasonably appears to the officer that the matter may have a material effect on the creation by the benefit corporation of general public benefit or a specific public benefit identified in the articles of incorporation.

(2) The consideration of interests and factors as provided in subsection (1) of this section shall not constitute a violation of sections 30–1–841 and 30–1–842, Idaho Code.

(3) Except as provided in the articles of incorporation or bylaws, an officer is not personally liable for monetary damages for:

(a) An action or inaction as an officer in the course of performing the duties of an officer under subsection (1) of this section if the officer performed the duties of the position in compliance with sections 30–1–841 and 30–1–842, Idaho Code, and this section; or

(b) Failure of the benefit corporation to pursue or create general public benefit or specific public benefit.

(4) An officer does not have a duty to a person that is a beneficiary of the general public benefit purpose or a specific public benefit purpose of a benefit corporation arising from the status of the person as a beneficiary.

30-2010. BENEFIT OFFICER.

A benefit corporation may have an officer designated the benefit officer. The benefit officer shall have:

(1) The powers and duties relating to the purpose of the corporation to create general public benefit or specific public benefit provided by the bylaws or, absent controlling provisions by the bylaws, by resolutions or orders of the board of directors; and

(2) The duty to prepare the benefit report required in section 30–2012, Idaho Code.

30-2011. RIGHT OF ACTION.

(1) Except in a benefit enforcement proceeding, no person may bring an action or

（4）公共利益董事在职权范围内的个人作为或不作为的行为应视为该公共利益公司董事的行为。

（5）无论公共利益公司的章程或者章程细则是否依据《爱达荷州法典》第 30-1-202 条的规定删除或限制董事的个人责任，公共利益董事在履行公共利益董事职责时不对其任何作为或不作为行为承担个人责任，但自我交易或故意违法行为除外。

（6）对依据《爱达荷州法典》第 30 编第 13 章的规定成立的专业公司的公共利益董事的独立性不做要求。

第 30-2009 条　高管行为标准

（1）公共利益公司的高管行事应当考虑《爱达荷州法典》第 30-2007 条规定的利益和因素，如果高管就该行为有自由裁量权并且有合理理由认为该行为对公共利益公司实现公司章程中规定的一般或特定公共利益有实质性的影响。

（2）对本条第（1）款规定中利益和相关因素的考虑不违反《爱达荷州法典》第 30-1-841 条和第 30-1-842 条的规定。

（3）除公司章程或章程细则另有明确规定外，高管不对以下行为承担损害赔偿责任：

（a）依据本条第（1）款的规定履行高管责任过程中的任何作为或者不作为，如果该高管依据《爱达荷州法典》第 30-1-841 条和第 30-1-842 条以及本条的规定履行了高管责任；或者

（b）公共利益公司未能追求或创造一般或特定公共利益。

（4）高管不对公共利益公司一般或特定公共利益目的的受益人负责。

第 30-2010 条　公共利益高管

公共利益公司可以将公司高管任命为公共利益高管。公共利益高管应有：

（1）规定于公司章程细则的或者，在公司章程细则中没有规定时根据董事会决议或者命令规定创造一般或特定公共利益目的的权力和义务。

（2）《爱达荷州法典》第 30-2012 条规定的编写公共利益报告的义务。

第 30-2011 条　诉讼权利

（1）非经公共利益实施程序，任何人不得因未能追求或实现在公司章程中声

assert a claim against a benefit corporation or its directors or officers with respect to the corporation's failure to pursue or create general public benefit or a specific public benefit set forth in its articles of incorporation, or the corporation's violation of an obligation, duty or standard of conduct under this chapter.

(2) A benefit corporation shall not be liable for monetary damages under this chapter for any failure of the benefit corporation to pursue or create general public benefit or a specific public benefit.

(3) A benefit enforcement proceeding may be commenced or maintained directly by the benefit corporation, or derivatively by:

(a) A person or group of persons that owned beneficially or of record at least two percent (2%) of the total number of shares of a class or series outstanding at the time of the act or omission complained of;

(b) A director;

(c) A person or group of persons that owned beneficially or of record five percent (5%) or more of the outstanding equity interests in an entity of which the benefit corporation is a subsidiary at the time of the act or omission complained of; or

(d) Other persons as specified in the articles of incorporation or bylaws of the benefit corporation.

(4) For purposes of this section, a person is the beneficial owner of shares or equity interests if the shares or equity interests are held in a voting trust or by a nominee on behalf of the beneficial owner.

30-2012. PREPARATION OF ANNUAL BENEFIT REPORT.

(1) A benefit corporation shall prepare an annual benefit report including the following:

(a) A narrative description of:

(i) The ways in which the benefit corporation pursued general public benefit during the year and the extent to which general public benefit was created;

(ii) The ways in which the benefit corporation pursued a specific public benefit that the articles of incorporation describe as the purpose of the benefit corporation to create, and the extent to which the specific public benefit was created;

(iii) Any circumstances that hindered the creation by the benefit corporation of either general public benefit or specific public benefit; and

(iv) The process and rationale for selecting or changing the third–party standard used to prepare the benefit report.

(b) An assessment of the overall social and environmental performance of the benefit corporation under a third–party standard applied consistently with any application of that standard in prior benefit reports, or accompanied by an explanation of the reasons for any inconsistent application, or the change to that standard from the one used in the immediate

明的一般或特定公共利益，或者违反本章规定的责任、义务或行为标准，向公共利益公司或者其董事、高管提起诉讼或主张。

（2）公共利益公司不对本章规定的任何未能追求或创造一般或特定公共利益的行为承担损害赔偿责任。

（3）公共利益实施程序可以由公共利益公司直接提起，或由以下主体派生提起：

（a）在被诉的作为或不作为行为发生时，拥有公共利益公司 2% 以上某类别或系列已发行股份的个人或团体；

（b）董事；

（c）在被诉的作为或不作为行为发生时，拥有公共利益公司母公司的 5% 以上已发行股份的登记股东或实际受益人；或者

（d）公共利益公司章程或章程细则中规定的其他人员。

（4）为实现本条的目的，某人的股份或者股利为表决权信托或者由指定的第三人代持时，将此人视为该股份和股利的实际所有权人。

第 30–2012 条　年度公共利益报告的编写

（1）公共利益公司的年度公共利益报告应包括以下内容：

（a）对以下事项的说明：

（i）公共利益公司本年度追求一般公共利益的方法和一般公共利益实现的情况；

（ii）公共利益公司追求公司章程中规定的特定公共利益的方法和该特定公共利益实现的情况；

（iii）阻碍公共利益公司实现一般公共利益和特定公共利益的情形；以及

（iv）为编写公共利益报告而选择或更换第三方标准的程序和原因。

（b）依据第三方标准对公共利益公司的社会和环境表现作出的整体评价，沿用先前公共利益报告中使用的标准或者附一份解释以说明使用的不一致或对上一份报告中使用标准的改变。

prior report.

(c) The name of the benefit director and the benefit officer, if any, and the address to which correspondence to each of them may be directed.

(d) The compensation paid by the benefit corporation during the year to each director in the capacity of a director.

(e) The opinion of the benefit director described in section 30–2008(3), Idaho Code.

(f) A statement of any connection between the organization that established the third–party standard, or its directors, officers or any holder of five percent (5%) or more of the governance interests in the organization, and the benefit corporation or its directors, officers or any holder of five percent (5%) or more of the outstanding shares of the benefit corporation, including any financial or governance relationship that might materially affect the credibility of the use of the third–party standard.

(g) If the benefit corporation has dispensed with or restricted the discretion or powers of the board of directors, a description of the persons who exercise the powers, duties, and rights and who have the immunities of the board of directors, and the benefit director.

(2) If, during the year covered by a benefit report, a benefit director resigned from or refused to stand for reelection to the position of benefit director, or was removed from the position of benefit director, and the benefit director furnished the benefit corporation with any written correspondence concerning the circumstances surrounding the resignation, refusal or removal, the benefit report shall include that correspondence as an exhibit.

(3) Neither the benefit report nor the assessment of the performance of the benefit corporation in the benefit report required in subsection (1) of this section needs to be audited or certified by a third party.

30-2013. AVAILABILITY OF ANNUAL BENEFIT REPORT.

(1) A benefit corporation shall send its annual benefit report to each shareholder either one hundred twenty (120) days following the end of the fiscal year of the benefit corporation, or at the same time that the benefit corporation delivers any other annual report to its shareholders, whichever is earlier.

(2) A benefit corporation shall post all of its benefit reports on the public portion of its website, if any; but the compensation paid to directors and financial or proprietary information included in the benefit reports may be omitted from the benefit reports as posted.

(3) If a benefit corporation does not have a website, the benefit corporation shall provide a copy of its most recent benefit report, without charge, to any person who requests a copy, provided however, that the compensation paid to directors and financial or proprietary information included in the benefit report may be omitted from the copy of the benefit report provided.

(4) Concurrently with the delivery of the benefit report to shareholders under subsection

（c）公共利益董事和公共利益高管的姓名、联系地址。

（d）公共利益公司在上一年度支付给每位董事的薪酬。

（e）《爱达荷州法典》第 30–2008（3）款规定的公共利益董事的意见。

（f）设立第三方标准的组织或其董事、高管或 5% 以上管理权利的持有者与公共利益公司或其董事、高管或公共利益公司 5% 以上已发行股份的持有者之间关系的声明，包括任何可能影响第三方标准可信度的财务或管理关系。

（g）如果公共利益公司已经免除或限制董事会的权力，记述行使权力、履行权利、义务和享有豁免权的人和公共利益董事。

（2）在公共利益报告年度内，如果公共利益董事辞职、拒绝连任或被免职，且该公共利益董事与公司有任何书面的涉及辞职、拒绝连任或免职的书信往来，公共利益报告应当将该书信往来作为附件。

（3）公共利益报告和依据本条的第（1）款编写的公共利益报告中的公共利益公司表现评价书都无须经审计或第三方认证。

第 30–2013 条　年度公共利益报告的提供

（1）公共利益公司应当在会计年度结束后 120 天内或者公共利益公司向其股东送交其他年度报告的同一时间尽早地将公共利益报告送交各股东。

（2）若条件允许，公共利益公司应当将其公共利益报告发布于其网站的公共部分；但是可以将公共利益报告中的董事薪酬和财务、所有权信息删除。

（3）如果公共利益公司没有网站，其应向所有索取报告的个人免费提供最新公共利益报告的副本，但是可以将公共利益报告副本中的董事薪酬和财务、所有权信息删除。

（4）在依本条第（1）款的规定将公共利益报告提交给股东的同时，公共利益

(1) of this section, the benefit corporation shall deliver a copy of the benefit report to the secretary of state for filing, provided however, that the compensation paid to directors and financial or proprietary information included in the benefit report may be omitted from the benefit report as delivered to the secretary of state. The secretary of state shall charge a fee for filing a benefit report, such fee to be set in a rule promulgated by the secretary.

公司应当将该公共利益报告提交州务卿备案，但是可以将公共利益报告中的董事薪酬和财务、所有权信息在提交州务卿的报告中删除。州务卿应收取备案费用，该费用由州务卿公布。

THE STATE OF ILLINOIS

SB2897 Enrolled

LRB097 13492 JLS 62053 b

AN ACT concerning business.

Be it enacted by the People of the State of Illinois, represented in the General Assembly:

Article 1. General Provisions

Section 1. Short title.

This Act may be cited as the Benefit Corporation Act.

Section 1.05. Application and effect of the Act.

(a) This Act shall be applicable to all benefit corporations.

(b) The existence of a provision of this Act shall not of itself create an implication that a contrary or different rule of law is applicable to a corporation which is not a benefit corporation. This Act shall not affect a statute or rule of law that is applicable to a business corporation that is not a benefit corporation.

(c) The Business Corporation Act of 1983, as heretofore or hereafter amended, shall be applicable to such benefit corporations, including their organization, and they shall enjoy the powers and privileges and be subject to the duties, restrictions, and liabilities of other corporations, except so far as the same may be limited or enlarged by this Act. If any provision of this Act conflicts with the Business Corporation Act of 1983, this Act shall take precedence.

(d) A provision of the articles of incorporation or bylaws of a benefit corporation may not relax, be inconsistent with, or supersede a provision of this Act.

Section 1.10. Definitions.

As used in this Act, unless the context otherwise requires, the words and phrases defined in this Section shall have the meanings set forth herein.

"Benefit corporation" means a corporation organized under the Business Corporation Act of 1983:

伊利诺伊州

登记为 SB2897
LRB097 13492 JLS 62053 b
关于商业的法案。
由州议会代表伊利诺伊州公民颁布：

第 1 节　一般规定

第 1 条　简称

本法案可以被称为《公共利益公司法》。

第 1.05 条　本法的适用和效力

（a）本法适用于所有的公共利益公司。

（b）本法的条款不应为非公共利益公司的商事公司设定相反或不同的规则。本法不影响非公共利益公司有关条文和规则的适用。

（c）今后修改的《1983 年商事公司法》应适用于此类公共利益公司，包括其组织，并且公共利益公司拥有其他公司的权力和权利也服从于其义务、限制和责任的规定，除非本法另行限制或扩大。如果本法条款与《1983 年商事公司法》冲突，优先适用本法。

（d）公共利益公司的章程或章程细则不得放宽、违背或取代本章的条款。

第 1.10 条　定义

在本法中，除上下文另有规定外，本条中单词和短语含义如下。

“公共利益公司”是指依据《1983 年商事公司法》的规定成立的公司：

(1) which has elected to become subject to this Act; and

(2) whose status as a benefit corporation has not been terminated under Section 2.10.

"Benefit director" means either:

(1) the director designated as the benefit director of a benefit corporation under Section 4.05; or

(2) a person with one or more of the powers, duties, or rights of a benefit director to the extent provided in the bylaws pursuant to Section 4.05.

"Benefit enforcement proceeding" means a claim or action for:

(1) the failure of a benefit corporation to pursue or create general public benefit or a specific public benefit set forth in its articles of incorporation; or

(2) a violation of an obligation, duty, or standard of conduct under this Act.

"Benefit officer" means the individual designated as the benefit officer of a benefit corporation under Section 4.15.

"General public benefit" means a material positive impact on society and the environment, taken as a whole, assessed against a third–party standard, from the business and operations of a benefit corporation.

"Independent" means having no material relationship with a benefit corporation or a subsidiary of the benefit corporation. A person serving as benefit director or benefit officer may be considered independent. For the purposes of this definition, a percentage of ownership in an entity shall be calculated as if all outstanding rights to acquire equity interests in the entity have been exercised. A material relationship between a person and a benefit corporation or any of its subsidiaries will be conclusively presumed to exist if:

(1) the person is, or has been within the last 3 years, an employee other than a benefit officer of the benefit corporation or a subsidiary of the benefit corporation;

(2) an immediate family member of the person is, or has been within the last 3 years, an executive officer other than a benefit officer of the benefit corporation or its subsidiaries; or

(3) there is beneficial or record ownership of 5% or more of the outstanding shares of the benefit corporation by:

(A) the person; or

(B) an entity:

(i) of which the person is a director, an officer, or a manager; or

(ii) in which the person owns beneficially or of record 5% or more of the outstanding equity interests.

"Minimum status vote" means that:

(1) in the case of a corporation, in addition to any other approval or vote required by the Business Corporation Act of 1983, the bylaws, or the articles of incorporation:

(A) the shareholders of every class or series shall be entitled to vote on the corporate

（1）选择接受本法调整；并且

（2）公共利益公司形态并未依据第 2.10 条终止。

“公共利益董事”是指：

（1）公共利益公司依据第 4.05 条的规定任命的董事；或者

（2）有依据第 4.05 条的规定在章程细则中规定的公共利益董事的权力、义务或权利的人。

“公共利益实施程序”是指因以下行为产生的主张或诉讼：

（1）公共利益公司未追求或实现公司章程中规定的一般或特定公共利益目的；或者

（2）公共利益公司违反本法中规定的任何义务、责任或行为标准。

“公共利益高管”是指公共利益公司依据第 4.15 条的规定任命的高管。

“一般公共利益”是指根据第三方标准，公司的业务和经营在整体上对社会和环境产生的实质性积极影响。

“独立”是指与公共利益公司或其子公司没有实质性关系。担任公共利益董事或者公共利益高管仍具有独立性。本定义中对组织一定比例的所有权的计算应当在所有购股权视为已行使的情况下进行。若出现以下情形，则认为个体与公共利益公司或其子公司存在实质性关系：

（1）此人是，或在过去的 3 年内是，公共利益公司或其子公司的除公共利益高管外的雇员；

（2）此人的直系亲属是，或在过去的 3 年内是，公共利益公司或其子公司的除公共利益高管外的执行高管；或者

（3）下述持有公共利益公司 5% 以上已发行股份的登记股东或实际受益人：

（A）个人；或

（B）实体：

（i）该个人是该实体的董事、高管或经理；或

（ii）该个人是持有公共利益公司 5% 以上已发行股份的登记股东或实际受益人。

“最低表决要求”是指

（1）在商事公司中，除《1983 年商事公司法》、公司章程或章程细则中规定的任何其他对批准或表决的要求外：

（A）每一类别或系列的股东应有权对公司行为进行投票，即使公司章程或章

action regardless of a limitation stated in the articles of incorporation or bylaws on the voting rights of any class or series; and

(B) the corporate action shall be approved by vote of the outstanding shares of each class or series entitled to vote by at least two–thirds of the votes that all shareholders of the class or series are entitled to cast on the action; and

(2) in the case of an entity organized under the laws of this State that is not a corporation, in addition to any other approval, vote, or consent required by the statutory law, if any, that principally governs the internal affairs of the entity or any provision of the publicly filed record or document required to form the entity, if any, or of any agreement binding on some or all of the holders of equity interests in the entity:

(A) the holders of every class or series of equity interest in the entity that are entitled to receive a distribution of any kind from the entity shall be entitled to vote on or consent to the action regardless of any otherwise applicable limitation on the voting or consent rights of any class or series; and

(B) the action must be approved by a vote or consent of at least two–thirds of such holders.

"Specific public benefit" means:

(1) providing low–income or underserved individuals or communities with beneficial products or services;

(2) promoting economic opportunity for individuals or communities beyond the creation of jobs in the ordinary course of business;

(3) preserving the environment;

(4) improving human health;

(5) promoting the arts, sciences or advancement of knowledge;

(6) increasing the flow of capital to entities with a public benefit purpose; or

(7) the accomplishment of any other particular benefit for society or the environment.

"Subsidiary" of a person means an entity in which the person owns beneficially or of record 50% or more of the outstanding equity interests. For the purposes of this subsection, a percentage of ownership in an entity shall be calculated as if all outstanding rights to acquire equity interests in the entity have been exercised.

"Third–party standard" means a standard for defining, reporting, and assessing overall corporate, social, and environmental performance that:

(1) is a comprehensive assessment of the impact of the business and the business' operations upon the considerations listed in subdivisions (a)(1)(B) through (a)(1)(E) of Section 4.01;

(2) is developed by an entity that has no material financial relationship with the benefit corporation or any of its subsidiaries;

程细则对任何类别或系列股东的投票权作出了限制；并且

（B）公司行为必须获得每一类别或系列有投票权的所有股东的至少 2/3 的投票才能通过；并且

（2）在依据本州法律成立的非公司组织中，除主要调整组织内部事务或规定组织成立要求的文件或公开备案登记的法律，或约束组织部分或全部股权持有者的协议中的任何其他对批准、表决或赞成的要求外：

（A）该实体的每一类别或系列的任何权益分配形式下的股权持有者应有权对公司行为进行投票，即使存在任何对该类别或系列投票权的限制；并且

（B）公司行为必须获得股权持有者至少 2/3 的投票或赞成才能通过。

“特定公共利益”是指：
（1）向低收入或者低福利人群或社区提供有益的产品或服务；

（2）在正常业务过程中向个人或社区提供创造就业之外的经济机会；

（3）保护环境；
（4）改善人类健康；
（5）促进艺术、科学或知识进步；
（6）促进资本向有公共利益目的的实体流动；或者
（7）实现社会或环境的其他特别利益。

“子公司”是指 50% 以上已发行的股份的受益所有权或登记所有权被另一实体所拥有的实体。在本定义中对组织一定比例的所有权应当在所有购股权视为已行使的情况下计算。

“第三方标准”是指用于定义、报告和评估公司社会和环境绩效的标准，其具有以下特点：
（1）在第 4.01 条的第（a）（1）（B）分项至第（a）（1）（E）分项中所列利益的基础上对公司业务和经营绩效作出的全面评价；

（2）由与公共利益公司或者其子公司没有实质性财务关系的实体制定；

(3) is developed by an entity that is not materially financed by any of the following organizations and not more than one–third of the members of the governing body of the entity are representatives of:

(A) associations of businesses operating in a specific industry, the performance of whose members is measured by the standard;

(B) businesses from a specific industry or an association of businesses in that industry; or

(C) businesses whose performance is assessed against the standard; and

(4) is developed by an entity that:

(A) accesses necessary and appropriate expertise to assess overall corporate social and environmental performance; and

(B) uses a balanced multi–stakeholder approach, including a public comment period of at least 30 days to develop the standard; and

(5) makes the following information regarding the standard publicly available:

(A) the factors considered when measuring the overall social and environmental performance of a business and the relative weight, if any, given to each of those factors;

(B) the identity of the directors, officers, any material owners, and the governing body of the entity that developed, and controls revisions to, the standard, and the process by which revisions to the standard and changes to the membership of the governing body are made; and

(C) an accounting of the sources of financial support for the entity, with sufficient detail to disclose any relationships that could reasonably be considered to present a potential conflict of interest.

Article 2. Formation of Benefit Corporations

Section 2.01. Formation of benefit corporations.

A benefit corporation must be formed in accordance with Article 2 of the Business Corporation Act of 1983. In addition to the formation requirements of that Act, the articles of incorporation of a benefit corporation must state that it is a benefit corporation in accordance with the provisions of this Article.

Section 2.05. Election of status.

(a) A corporation may become a benefit corporation under this Act by amending its articles of incorporation so that they contain a statement that the corporation is a benefit corporation. In order to be effective, the amendment must be adopted by at least the minimum status vote.

(b) For any entity that is a party to a merger or consolidation or is the exchanging entity in a share exchange, where the surviving, new, or resulting entity in the merger,

（3）管理层中不多于 1/3 的成员是以下组织的代表或者非由以下组织实质性资助的实体制定：

（A）经营特定行业的企业协会，其成员的绩效由此标准衡量；

（B）特定行业的企业或者此行业的企业协会；或者

（C）绩效以此标准评价的企业；以及

（4）由满足以下要求的实体制定：

（A）拥有评估公司社会和环境综合绩效所需的专业知识；并且

（B）使用平衡多方利益相关者的方法制定标准，包括设定至少 30 天的听取公众意见期间来制定标准；以及

（5）以下关于标准的信息可以公开获取：

（A）衡量企业总体社会和环境表现时考虑的因素和这些因素的相关权重；

（B）制定和控制修改标准的董事、高管、主要股东和该实体控制人员的身份，标准修改及控制人员变动的程序；以及

（C）收入和资金来源的核算，包括充分披露在合理认知下存在利益冲突的所有关系。

第 2 节　公共利益公司的成立

第 2.01 条　公共利益公司的设定

公共利益公司应当按照《1983 年商事公司法》第 2 节的规定设立。除该法对设立另有要求外，公司章程必须声明其是公共利益公司。

第 2.05 条　形态选择

（a）公司可依据本法的规定成为公共利益公司，该公司需修改其公司章程并作出该公司为公共利益公司的声明。公司章程的修改应满足最低表决要求。

（b）如果一个实体是合并或股权置换中的一方，且合并或股权置换中存续、新设或留存的实体将成为公共利益公司，那么此合并或股权置换的计划应满足最低

consolidation, or share exchange is intended to be a benefit corporation, such plan of merger, consolidation, or share exchange must be adopted by at least the minimum status vote in order to be effective.

Section 2.10. Termination of status.

(a) A benefit corporation may terminate its status as such and cease to be subject to this Act by amending its articles of incorporation to remove the statement that the corporation is a benefit corporation. In order to be effective, the amendment must be adopted by at least the minimum status vote.

(b) If a plan of merger, conversion, or share exchange would have the effect of terminating the status of a corporation as a benefit corporation, in order to be effective, the plan must be adopted by at least the minimum status vote.

(c) A sale, lease, exchange or other disposition of all or substantially all of the assets of a benefit corporation, unless the transaction is in the usual and ordinary course of business, shall not be effective unless the transaction is adopted by at least the minimum status vote.

Article 3. Corporate Purposes

Section 3.01. Corporate purposes.

(a) A benefit corporation shall have a purpose of creating general public benefit. This purpose is in addition to its purposes under Section 3.05 of the Business Corporation Act of and any specific purpose set forth in its articles of incorporation in accordance with subsection (b).

(b) The articles of incorporation of a benefit corporation may identify one or more specific public benefits the creation of which is a purpose of the benefit corporation in addition to its purposes under Section 3.05 of the Business Corporation Act of 1983 and subsection (a). The identification of a specific public benefit under this subsection does not limit the obligation of a benefit corporation under subsection (a).

(c) The creation of general public benefit and specific public benefit under subsections (a) and (b) is in the best interests of the benefit corporation.

(d) A benefit corporation may amend its articles of incorporation to add, change, or remove a specific public benefit. In order to be effective, the amendment must be adopted by at least the minimum status vote.

(e) A professional corporation that is a benefit corporation does not violate Sections 3.4 or 6 of the Professional Service Corporation Act by having the purpose to create general public benefit or a specific public benefit.

表决要求。

第 2.10 条　形态的终止

（a）公共利益公司可以通过删除公司章程中作为公共利益公司的声明来终止其公共利益公司的形态并不再受本法规定的调整。公司章程的修改应满足最低表决要求。

（b）如果兼并、财产转让或股权置换的计划会产生终止商事公司作为公共利益公司的效力，该计划应满足最低表决要求。

（c）除正常商业往来外，公共利益公司出售、出租、交换或者其他处置全部或主要财产的行为，须满足最低表决要求。

第 3 节　公司目的

第 3.01 条　公司目的

（a）公共利益公司应有服务于一般公共利益的目的。此目的在《商事公司法》第 3.05 条规定的目的和依据第（b）款的规定列明于公司章程中的特定目的之外。

（b）公共利益公司的章程可以在《1983 年商事公司法》第 3.05 条和第（a）款的规定之外确定一项或者多项特定的公共利益目的。依据本款规定设定的特定公共利益目的并不限制公共利益公司依据本款规定设定的义务。

（c）依据第（a）款和第（b）款的规定创设的一般和特定公共利益目的应为公共利益公司的最佳利益。

（d）公共利益公司可以通过修改公司章程增加、修改或删除一项特定公共利益目的。公司章程的修改需满足最低表决要求。

（e）选择公共利益形态的专业公司并不因其有创设一般或特定公共利益的目的而违反专业服务公司法第 3.4 条或第 6 条的规定。

Article 4. Accountability

Section 4.01. Standard of Conduct for Directors.

(a) Without regard to whether the benefit corporation is subject to Section 8.85 of the Business Corporation Act of 1983, in discharging the duties of their respective positions, the board of directors, committees of the board, and individual directors of a benefit corporation in considering the best interests of the benefit corporation:

(1) shall consider the effects of any action upon:

(A) the shareholders of the benefit corporation;

(B) the employees and work force of the benefit corporation, its subsidiaries, and its suppliers;

(C) the interests of customers as beneficiaries of the general public benefit or specific public benefit purposes of the benefit corporation;

(D) community and societal considerations, including those of each community in which offices or facilities of the benefit corporation, its subsidiaries or its suppliers are located;

(E) the local and global environment;

(F) the short-term and long-term interests of the benefit corporation, including benefits that may accrue to the benefit corporation from its long-term plans and the possibility that these interests may be best served by the continued independence of the benefit corporation; and

(G) the ability of the benefit corporation to accomplish its general public benefit purpose and any specific public benefit purpose; and

(2) may consider:

(A) considerations listed in Section 8.85 of the Business Corporation Act of 1983; and

(B) any other pertinent factors or the interests of any other group that they deem appropriate; but

(3) need not give priority to the interests of a particular person or group referred to in paragraphs (1) or (2) over the interests of another person or group unless the benefit corporation has stated in its articles of incorporation its intention to give priority to certain interests related to its accomplishment of its general public benefit purpose or a specific public benefit purpose identified in its articles of incorporation.

(b) The consideration of interests and factors in the manner required by subsection (a) is in addition to the ability of directors to consider interests and factors as provided in Section 8.85 of the Business Corporation Act of 1983.

(c) A director is not personally liable for monetary damages for:

(1) any action taken as a director if the director performed the duties of office in compliance with Article 8 of the Business Corporation Act of 1983 and this Section; or

第4节 责任

第4.01条 董事行为标准

（a）与公共利益公司是否受《1983年商事公司法》第8.85条调整无关，在履行各自职责时，公共利益公司的董事会、董事委员会和董事应考虑公共利益公司的最佳利益：

（1）应当考虑行为对以下对象的影响：

（A）公共利益公司的股东；

（B）公共利益公司的雇员、其子公司和其供应商；

（C）作为公共利益公司一般或特定公共利益受益者的消费者的利益；

（D）社区和社会因素，包括公共利益公司、其子公司或其供应商的办公地或设施所在地的社区；

（E）当地和全球环境；

（F）公共利益公司的短期和长期利益，包括从其长期计划中产生的利益以及公共利益公司继续保持独立可能产生的最佳利益；以及

（G）公共利益公司实现其一般和特定公共利益目的的能力；以及

（2）可以考虑的其他因素：

（A）在《1983年商事公司法》第8.85条中列出的考虑因素；以及

（B）他们认为合适的其他相关因素或其他群体的利益；但是

（3）除在公司章程中规定公司应优先考虑与实现公司章程中确定的一般或特定公共利益目的相关的某些利益，不需优先考虑第（1）项或第（2）项中某个利益或因素超过其他个人或组织的利益。

（b）对第（a）款中规定的利益和相关因素的考虑是对《1983年商事公司法》第8.85条规定的董事考虑利益和相关因素能力的补充。

（c）董事不对以下行为承担损害赔偿责任：

（1）如果该董事依据《1983年商事公司法》第8节的规定履行职责的行为；或者

(2) a failure of the benefit corporation to pursue or create general public benefit or a specific public benefit.

(d) A director does not have a duty to a person that is a beneficiary of the general public benefit purpose or a specific public benefit purpose of a benefit corporation arising from the status of the person as a beneficiary.

Section 4.05. Benefit director.

(a) The board of directors of a benefit corporation shall include a director, who:

(1) is designated as the benefit director; and

(2) has, in addition to the powers, duties, rights, and immunities of the other directors of the benefit corporation, the powers, duties, rights, and immunities provided in this Section.

(b) The benefit director shall be elected, and may be removed, in the manner provided by Article 8 of the Business Corporation Act of 1983 and shall be an individual who is independent, as defined in Section 1.10. The benefit director may serve as the benefit officer at the same time as serving as the benefit director. The articles of incorporation or bylaws of a benefit corporation may prescribe additional qualifications of the benefit director not inconsistent with this Section.

(c) The benefit director shall prepare, and the benefit corporation shall include in the annual benefit report to shareholders required by Section 5.01 of this Act, the opinion of the benefit director on:

(1) whether the benefit corporation acted in accordance with its general public benefit purpose and any specific public benefit purpose in all material respects during the period covered by the report; and

(2) whether the directors and officers complied with subsection (a) of Section 4.01 and subsection (a) of Section 4.10, respectively, and if, in the opinion of the benefit director, the directors and officers did not so comply, a description of the failure to comply.

(d) The acts of an individual in the capacity of a benefit director shall constitute, for all purposes, acts of that individual in the capacity of a director of the benefit corporation.

(e) If the bylaws of a benefit corporation provide that the powers and duties conferred or imposed upon the board of directors shall be exercised or performed by a person or persons other than the directors, in contrast to subsection (a) of Section 8.05 of the Business Corporation Act of 1983, or if the bylaws of a close corporation that is a benefit corporation provide that the business and affairs of the corporation shall be managed by or under the director of the shareholders, then the bylaws of the benefit corporation must provide that the person, persons, or shareholders who perform the duties of a board of directors shall include a person with the powers, duties, rights, and immunities of a benefit director.

A person who exercises one or more of the powers, duties, or rights of a benefit director pursuant to this subsection:

（2）公共利益公司未能追求或实现一般或特定公共利益。

（d）董事不对公共利益公司一般或特定社会目的的受益人负责。

第 4.05 条　公共利益董事

（a）公共利益公司的董事会，应包括满足以下要求的董事：

（1）被任命为公共利益董事；并且

（2）除有公共利益公司其他董事的权力、义务、权利和豁免权外，还有本条规定的权力、义务、权利和豁免权。

（b）公共利益董事应当依据《1983 年商事公司法》第 8 节的规定任免。正如第 1.10 条规定的定义，公共利益董事应当是独立个体。公共利益董事可以同时担任公共利益高管。公共利益公司的章程或章程细则可以对公共利益董事的资格作出与本条不一致的规定。

（c）公共利益董事应编写其对以下事项的意见，公共利益公司应根据本法第 5.01 条的规定将其附于年度公共利益报告中供股东查阅：

（1）在报告所述期间内，公共利益公司是否在所有重要事项上依其一般和特定公共利益目的行事；以及

（2）董事和高管是否分别依第 4.01 条第（a）款和第 4.10 条第（a）款的规定行事，尤其是公共利益董事、董事和高管是否遵守了规定。如果公共利益董事认为公共利益董事或高管未遵守规定，应陈述其未遵守规定的情况。

（d）公共利益董事在职权范围内的个人行为应视为公共利益公司董事的行为。

（e）如果公共利益公司章程细则规定，授予或施加给董事会的权力和义务应当由董事以外的人执行或履行，这与《1983 年商事公司法》第 8.05 条第（a）款的规定相反；或者如果作为公共利益公司的封闭公司的章程细则规定，公司的业务和内部事务应当由股东的董事管理，则公共利益公司的章程细则必须规定履行董事会职责的人和股东应包括有公共利益董事权力、义务、权利和豁免的人员。

依据本款规定执行一种或多种公共利益董事的权力、义务或权利的人员：

(i) does not need to be independent of the benefit corporation;

(ii) shall have the immunities of a benefit director;

(iii) may share the powers, duties, and rights of a benefit director with one or more other persons; and

(iv) shall not be subject to the procedures for election or removal of directors in Article 8 of the Business Corporation Act of 1983 unless the person is also a director of the benefit corporation or the bylaws make those procedures applicable.

(f) Regardless of whether the bylaws of a benefit corporation include a provision eliminating or limiting the personal liability of directors authorized by paragraph (3) of subsection (b) of Section 2.10 of the Business Corporation Act of 1983, a benefit director shall not be personally liable for an act or omission in the capacity of a benefit director unless the act or omission constitutes self–dealing, willful misconduct, or a knowing violation of law.

Section 4.10. Standard of conduct for officers.

(a) Each officer of a benefit corporation shall consider the interests and factors described in subsection (a) of Section 4.01 in the manner provided in that subsection if:

(1) the officer has discretion to act with respect to a matter; and

(2) it reasonably appears to the officer that the matter may have a material effect on the creation by the benefit corporation of general public benefit or a specific public benefit identified in the articles of incorporation by the benefit corporation.

(b) Exoneration from personal liability. An officer is not personally liable for monetary damages for:

(1) action taken as an officer if the officer performed the duties of the position in compliance with this Section; or

(2) failure of the benefit corporation to pursue or create general public benefit or specific public benefit.

(c) Limitation on standing. An officer does not have a duty to a person that is a beneficiary of the general public benefit purpose or a specific public benefit purpose of a benefit corporation arising from the status of the person as a beneficiary.

Section 4.15. Benefit officer.

(a) A benefit corporation may have an officer designated as the benefit officer.

(b) A benefit officer shall have:

(1) powers and duties relating to the purpose of the benefit corporation to create general public benefit or specific public benefit provided:

(A) by the bylaws of the benefit corporation; or

(B) absent controlling provisions in the bylaws, by resolutions or orders of the board of directors; and

（i）不需要独立于公共利益公司；

（ii）应当有公共利益董事的豁免权；

（iii）可以与一个或更多的其他人员分享公共利益董事的权力、义务和权利；以及

（iv）无须受《1983年商事公司法》第8节规定的董事任免程序的调整，除非此人也是公共利益公司董事或者公司章程细则规定这些程序可以适用。

（f）无论公共利益公司章程细则是否依据《1983年商事公司法》第2.10条中第（b）款第（3）项的规定删除或限制董事的个人责任，公共利益董事在履行公共利益董事职责时不对其任何作为或不作为行为承担个人责任，但自我交易或故意违法行为除外。

第4.10条　高管行为标准

（a）公共利益公司的高管应当以本款规定的行为标准考虑第4.01条第（a）款中规定的利益和因素，如果：

（1）高管对该行为有自由裁量权；以及

（2）高管有合理理由认为该行为对公共利益公司在公司章程中创设一般或特定公共利益有实质性的影响。

（b）个人责任的免除。高管不对以下行为承担损害赔偿责任：

（1）高管依据本条的规定履行职责的行为；或者

（2）公共利益公司未能追求或实现一般或特定公共利益。

（c）高管责任限制。高管不对公共利益公司一般或特定社会目的的受益人负责。

第4.15条　公共利益高管

（a）公共利益公司可以将高管任命为公共利益高管。

（b）公共利益高管应有：

（1）规定于以下文件中的与公共利益公司创造一般或特定公共利益的目的有关的权力和义务：

（A）公共利益公司的章程细则；或者

（B）在公司章程细则中没有规定时，董事会决议或者命令；以及

(2) the duty to prepare the benefit report required by Section 5.01 of this Act.

Section 4.20. Right of action; benefit enforcement proceeding.

(a) No person may bring an action or assert a claim against a benefit corporation or its directors or officers with respect to failure to pursue or create general public benefit or a specific public benefit set forth in its articles of incorporation or violation of a duty or standard of conduct under this Act except in a benefit enforcement proceeding.

(b) A benefit enforcement proceeding may be commenced or maintained only:

(1) directly by the benefit corporation; or

(2) derivatively by:

(A) a shareholder;

(B) a director;

(C) a person or group of persons that owns beneficially or of record 5% or more of the equity interests in an entity of which the benefit corporation is a subsidiary; or

(D) other persons as specified in the articles of incorporation or bylaws of the benefit corporation.

(c) A benefit corporation shall not be liable for monetary damages under this Act for any failure of the benefit corporation to pursue or create general public benefit or a specific public benefit.

Article 5. Transparency

Section 5.01. Annual benefit report.

(a) A benefit corporation shall prepare an annual benefit report including all of the following:

(1) A narrative description of:

(A) the process and rationale for selecting the third party standard used to prepare the benefit report;

(B) the ways in which the benefit corporation pursued general public benefit during the year and the extent to which general public benefit was created;

(C) the ways in which the benefit corporation pursued a specific public benefit that the articles state it is the purpose of the benefit corporation to create and the extent to which that specific public benefit was created; and

(D) any circumstances that have hindered the pursuit by the benefit corporation of its general public benefit purpose and any specific public benefit purpose or the creation by the benefit corporation of general public benefit and any specific public benefit.

(2) An assessment of the overall social and environmental performance of the benefit corporation against a third-party standard:

(A) applied consistently with any application of that standard in prior benefit reports; or

（2）本法第 5.01 条规定的编写公共利益报告的义务。

第 4.20 条　诉讼权利；公共利益实施程序

（a）非经公共利益实施程序，任何人不得因未能追求或实现在公司章程中声明的一般或特定公共利益或者违反本法规定的责任、义务或行为标准，向公共利益公司或其董事、高管提起诉讼或主张。

（b）下列情形中，可由以下主体提起公共利益实施程序：

（1）由公共利益公司直接提起；或者

（2）被以下主体派生提起：

（A）股东；

（B）董事；

（C）拥有公共利益公司母公司 5% 或以上已发行股票的登记股东或实际受益股人；或者

（D）公共利益公司章程或章程细则中列明的其他人员。

（c）公共利益公司不对本法规定下任何未能追求或创造一般或特定公共利益的行为承担损害赔偿责任。

第 5 节　透明度

第 5.01 条　年度公共利益报告

（a）公共利益公司的年度公共利益报告应包括以下内容：

（1）对以下事项的说明：

（A）编写公共利益报告时选择或更换第三方标准的程序和原因；

（B）公共利益公司本年度追求一般公共利益的方法和一般公共利益实现的情况；

（C）公共利益公司追求公司章程中规定的特定公共利益的方法以及该特定公共利益实现的情况；以及

（D）阻碍公共利益公司追求一般公共利益和特定公共利益或者实现一般公共利益和任何特定公共利益的情形。

（2）依据第三方标准对公共利益公司的社会和环境表现的整体评价：

（A）沿用先前公共利益报告中使用的标准；或者

(B) accompanied by an explanation of the reasons for any inconsistent application.

(3) The name of the benefit director and the benefit officer, if any, and the address to which correspondence to each of them may be directed.

(4) The compensation paid by the benefit corporation during the year to each director in the capacity of a director.

(5) The name of each person that owns 5% or more of the outstanding shares of the benefit corporation either:

(A) beneficially, to the extent known to the benefit corporation without independent investigation; or

(B) of record.

(6) The statement of the benefit director required by subsection (c) of Section 4.05.

(7) A statement of any connection between the organization that established the third-party standard, or its directors, officers, or material owners, and the benefit corporation or its directors, officers or material owners, including any financial or governance relationship that might materially affect the credibility of the use of the third-party standard.

(8) If the benefit corporation has dispensed with, or restricted the discretion or powers of, the board of directors, its annual benefit report must describe the persons who exercise the powers, duties, and rights, and have the immunities of the board of directors and the benefit director as required by subsection (e) of Section 4.05.

(b) The benefit corporation shall send a benefit report annually to each shareholder:

(1) within 120 days following the end of the fiscal year of the benefit corporation; or

(2) at the same time that the benefit corporation delivers any other annual report to its shareholders.

(c) A benefit corporation shall post all of its benefit reports on the public portion of its Internet website, if any, but the compensation paid to directors and financial or proprietary information included in the benefit reports may be omitted from the benefit reports as posted.

(d) If a benefit corporation does not have an Internet website, the benefit corporation shall provide a copy of its most recent benefit report, without charge, to any person that requests a copy.

（B）附一份说明以解释使用标准不一致的原因。

（3）公共利益董事和公共利益高管的姓名和联系地址。

（4）公共利益公司在上一年度支付给每位董事的薪酬。

（5）拥有公共利益公司5%以上已发行股份的持股人的姓名：

（A）实益所有，无须单独调查即被公共利益公司所知；或者

（B）名义上所有。

（6）公共利益董事依第4.05条第（c）款的规定应编写的陈述报告。

（7）建立第三方标准的机构或其董事、高管或实际控制人与公共利益公司或其董事、高管或实际控制人之间的关系，包括任何可能实质性影响第三方标准可信度的财务或管理关系。

（8）如果公共利益公司已经免除或限制董事会的自由裁量权或其他权力，其年度公共利益报告必须包括行使这些权力、履行权利和义务的人员和第4.05条第（e）款规定的对董事会和公共利益董事的豁免。

（b）公共利益公司每年应当将公共利益报告送交各股东：

（1）公共利益公司会计年度结束后120天内；或者

（2）公共利益公司向其股东送交其他年度报告的同一时间。

（c）若条件允许，公共利益公司应当将其所有公共利益报告发布于其网站的公共部分，但是可以将公共利益报告中的董事薪酬和财务、所有权信息删除。

（d）如果公共利益公司没有网站，应向所有索取报告的个人免费提供最新公共利益报告的副本。

THE STATE OF INDIANA

HOUSE BILL No. 1015

A BILL FOR AN ACT to amend the Indiana Code concerning business and other associations.

Be it enacted by the General Assembly of the State of Indiana:

SECTION 2. IC 23-1.3 IS ADDED TO THE INDIANA CODE AS A NEW ARTICLE TO READ AS FOLLOWS [EFFECTIVE JULY 1, 2015]:

ARTICLE 1.3. BENEFIT CORPORATIONS

Chapter 1. Application

Sec. 1. This article is applicable to all benefit corporations.

Sec. 2. This article does not of itself create an implication that a contrary or different rule of law is applicable to a corporation that is not a benefit corporation.

Sec. 3. This article does not affect a statute or rule of law that is applicable to a corporation that is not a benefit corporation.

Sec. 4. Except as otherwise provided in this article, IC 23-1 is generally applicable to all benefit corporations.

Sec. 5. The articles of incorporation or bylaws of a benefit corporation may not limit, be inconsistent with, or supersede this article.

Chapter 2. Definitions

Sec. 1. The definitions in IC 23-1-20 apply throughout this article.

Sec. 2. The definitions in this chapter apply throughout this article.

印第安纳州

1015 号参议院法案

修订印第安纳州法典关于企业与其他组织法的法案

由印第安纳州议会颁布：

第 2 部分　将《印第安纳州法典》第 23–1.3 章加入法典作为新的一条，内容如下［2015 年 7 月 1 日生效］：

第 1.3 章　公共利益公司

第 1 节　适用

第 1 条　本章适用于所有的公共利益公司。

第 2 条　本章未为非公共利益公司设定相反或不同的规则。

第 3 条　本条不影响非公共利益公司的有关条文或规则的适用。

第 4 条　除本章另有规定外，《印第安纳州法典》第 23–1 章应适用于所有的公共利益公司。

第 5 条　公共利益公司的公司章程或章程细则不得限制、违背或取代本章规定。

第 2 节　定义

第 1 条　《印第安纳州法典》第 23–1–20 节中的定义适用于本条。

第 2 条　本节中的定义适用于本章。

Sec. 3. "Benefit corporation"means a corporation to which both the following apply:

(1) The corporation has elected to become subject to this article.

(2) The status of the corporation as a benefit corporation has not been terminated.

Sec. 4. "Benefit director" refers to an individual designated as the benefit director of a benefit corporation under IC 23–1.3–6.

Sec. 5. "Benefit enforcement proceeding" means any claim, action, or proceeding for:

(1) the failure of a benefit corporation to pursue or create:

(A) general public benefit; or

(B) a specific public benefit if the benefit corporation identified a specific public benefit purpose in its articles of incorporation; or

(2) a violation of any obligation, duty, or standard of conduct under this article.

Sec. 6. "Benefit officer" means an individual designated as the benefit officer of a benefit corporation under IC 23–1.3–8.

Sec. 7. "General public benefit" means a material positive impact on society and the environment, taken as a whole, assessed against a third party standard, from the business and operations of a benefit corporation.

Sec. 8. "Independent" means a person that has no material relationship with a benefit corporation or a subsidiary of the benefit corporation.

Sec. 9. "Minimum status vote" means the following:

(1) For a corporation, in addition to any other required approval or vote, a vote in which:

(A) the shareholders of every class or series of shares are entitled to vote as a separate voting group on the corporate action regardless of a limitation stated in the articles of incorporation or bylaws on the voting rights of any class or series; and

(B) the corporate action is approved by vote of the shareholders of each class or series of shares entitled to cast at least ninety percent (90%) of the votes that all shareholders of the class or series are entitled to cast on the action.

(2) For a domestic business entity other than a corporation, in addition to any other required approval, vote, or consent, a vote in which:

(A) the holders of every class or series of equity interest in the entity that are entitled to receive a distribution of any kind from the entity are entitled to vote on or consent to the action regardless of any otherwise applicable limitation on the voting or consent rights of any class or series; and

(B) the action is approved by vote or consent of the holders described in clause (A) entitled to cast at least ninety percent (90%) of the votes or consents that all of the holders are entitled to cast on the action.

Sec. 10. (a) "Specific public benefit" means a benefit that serves:

(1) one or more public welfare, religious, charitable, scientific, literary, or educational

第 3 条 “公共利益公司”是指符合以下两项条件的公司：

（1）公司选择接受本章规定调整。

（2）公司的公共利益公司形态并未终止。

第 4 条 “公共利益董事”是指公共利益公司依据《印第安纳法典》第 23-1.3-6 节的规定任命的董事。

第 5 条 “公共利益实施程序”指因以下行为产生的任何主张、诉讼或程序：

（1）公共利益公司未能追求或实现：

（A）一般的公共利益；或者

（B）特定公共利益，在公共利益公司在公司章程中规定了特定公共利益目的的情形下；或者

（2）违反本章规定下的任何义务、责任或行为标准。

第 6 条 “公共利益高管”是指公共利益公司依据《印第安纳州法典》第 23-1.3-8 节的规定任命的高管。

第 7 条 “一般公共利益”是指依据第三方标准，公司的业务和经营在整体上对社会和环境产生的实质性积极影响。

第 8 条 “独立”是指与公共利益公司或其子公司没有实质性关系。

第 9 条 “最低表决要求”是指以下内容：

（1）对于一个公司，除任何其他要求的批准或表决外，该表决：

（A）每一类别或系列的股东应当有权作为一个独立的投票团体对公司行为进行投票，即使公司章程或章程细则对任何类别或系列的投票权作出了限制；并且

（B）公司行为获得每一类别或系列有投票权的所有股东至少 90% 的投票才能通过。

（2）在非公司的本州商业实体中，除任何其他要求的批准、表决或赞成外，该表决：

（A）该实体的每一类别或系列的任何权益分配形式下的股权持有者应当有权对公司行为进行投票，即使存在任何对该类别或系列的投票权的限制；并且

（B）公司行为获得在第（A）款中规定的有投票权的所有股权持有者至少 90% 的投票才能通过。

第 10 条 （a）“特定公共利益”是指服务于以下事项的利益：

（1）一个或更多的公共福利、宗教、慈善、科学、自由或者教育目的；或者

purposes; or

(2) other purposes or benefits beyond the strict interests of the shareholders of the benefit corporation.

(b) The term includes the following:

(1) Providing low income or underserved individuals or communities with beneficial products or services.

(2) Promoting economic opportunity for individuals or communities beyond the creation of jobs in the normal course of business.

(3) Protecting or restoring the environment.

(4) Improving human health.

(5) Promoting the arts, sciences, or advancement of knowledge.

(6) Increasing the flow of capital to entities with a purpose to benefit society or the environment.

(7) Conferring any other particular benefit on society or the environment.

Sec. 11. "Subsidiary" means, in relation to a person, a business entity in which the person owns at least fifty percent (50%) of the outstanding equity interests, calculated as if all outstanding rights to acquire equity interests in the entity had been exercised.

Sec. 12. "Third party standard" means a recognized standard for defining, reporting, and assessing corporate social and environmental performance that is:

(1) comprehensive because it assesses the effect of the benefit corporation and the benefit corporation's operations upon the interests listed in IC 23–1.3–5–1(1)(B) through IC 23–1.3–5–1(1)(E);

(2) developed by an entity that is not controlled by a benefit corporation;

(3) developed by an entity that:

(A) has access to necessary expertise to assess overall corporate social and environmental performance;

(B) uses a balanced multistakeholder approach to develop the standard, including a reasonable public comment period;

(C) was not materially financed by any of the following organizations and not more than one–third (1/3) of the members of the governing body of the entity are representatives of:

(i) associations or businesses operating in the same industry, the performance of whose members is measured by the standard; or

(ii) businesses from the same industry or an association of businesses in that industry; and

(4) transparent because all the following information is publicly available:

(A) The criteria considered when measuring the overall social and environmental performance of a business.

（2）公共利益公司股东法定利益以外的其他目的和利益。

（b）该术语包含以下内容：
（1）向低收入或者低福利人群或社区提供有益的产品或服务。

（2）在正常业务过程中向个人或社区提供创造就业之外的经济机会。

（3）保护或修复环境。
（4）改善人类健康。
（5）促进艺术、科学或知识进步。
（6）促进资本向有利于社会或环境目标的实体流动。

（7）给予社会或环境其他特别的利益。
第 11 条　“子公司”是指在所有购股权被视为已行使的情况下，该实体至少50% 的已发行股份被另一实体所拥有。

第 12 条　“第三方标准”是指用于定义、报告和评估公司社会和环境绩效的标准，应满足以下条件：
（1）综合，其在评估《印第安纳州法典》第 23–1.3–5–1（1）（B）项至《印第安纳州法典》第 23–1.3–5–1（1）（E）项中所列利益的基础上评价公共利益公司业务和经营绩效；
（2）其非由公共利益公司控制的第三方实体制定；
（3）制定其的实体：
（A）拥有评估公司社会和环境综合绩效所需的专业知识；

（B）使用平衡多方相关者利益的方法制定标准，包括设定合理期间以听取公众意见；
（C）并非由以下任何组织实质资助且组织的管理层中不多于 1/3 的成员是以下组织的代表：
（i）同行业的协会或企业，其成员的绩效由此标准评测；或者

（ii）同行业或者该行业的企业协会中的企业；以及

（4）透明，以下信息可公开获取：
（A）衡量整体社会和环境绩效时所考虑的标准。

(B) The relative weightings, if any, of the criteria described in clause (A).

(C) The identity of the directors, officers, material owners, and governing body of the entity that developed and controls revisions to the standard.

(D) The process by which revisions to the standard and changes to the membership of the governing body are made.

(E) An accounting of the revenue and sources of financial support for the entity, with sufficient detail to disclose any relationships that could reasonably be considered to present a potential conflict of interest.

Chapter 3. Benefit Corporation Status

Sec. 1. A benefit corporation shall be incorporated in accordance with IC 23–1–21, except that its articles of incorporation must state that it is a benefit corporation.

Sec. 2. (a) Subject to subsection (b), an existing corporation may become a benefit corporation under this article by amending its articles of incorporation to contain, in addition to any content requirements for articles of incorporation under IC 23–1, the following:

(1) A statement that the corporation is a benefit corporation.

(2) A statement reading "By enacting this article, the State of Indiana does not endorse any particular benefit corporation, or approve or disapprove any of the purposes of a benefit corporation or any claimed general public benefit or specific public benefit, and no inference should be drawn from the acceptance of any filings with respect to a benefit corporation under IC 23–1.3, that the benefit corporation has or will in fact provide any general public benefit or specific public benefit".

(b) An amendment to the articles of incorporation under subsection (a) is not effective unless the amendment is adopted by at least a minimum status vote.

Sec. 3. (a) This section does not apply to a corporation that is a party to a merger if the shareholders of the corporation are not entitled to vote on the merger under IC 23–1–40.

(b) If:

(1) a domestic entity that is not a benefit corporation is a party to:

(A) a merger, consolidation, or conversion; or

(B) the exchanging entity in a share exchange; and

(2) the surviving entity in the merger, consolidation, conversion, or share exchange is to be a benefit corporation; the plan of merger, consolidation, conversion, or share exchange must be adopted by the domestic entity by at least the minimum status vote.

Sec. 4. (a) Subject to subsection (b), a benefit corporation may terminate its status as a benefit corporation and cease to be subject to this article by amending its articles of incorporation to delete the statement in its articles of incorporation required under sections 1 and 2 of this chapter.

（B）第（A）款中所述的这些标准的相关权重。

（C）制定和控制修改标准的董事、经理、主要股东和该实体的控制人员的身份。

（D）标准修改和控制人员变动的程序。

（E）收入和资金来源的核算，包括充分披露合理认知下存在利益冲突的所有细节。

第3节　公共利益公司形态

第1条　公共利益公司应当按照《印第安纳州法典》第23–1–21节的规定设立，但其公司章程必须声明其是公共利益公司。

第2条　（a）依据第（b）款的规定，已成立的商事公司可依据本章规定成为公共利益公司，除满足《印第安纳州法典》第23–1章规定下有关公司章程的内容要求外，其修改后的公司章程应包含以下内容：

（1）本公司为公共利益公司的声明。

（2）内容为"通过公布本公司章程，印第安纳州并未认可任何特定的公共利益公司，或批准或不批准公共利益公司的任何目的或任何声称的一般或者特定公共利益，并且不应从根据《印第安纳州法典》第23–1.3章规定接受有关公共利益公司的任何备案推断出已经或将要提供一般或者特定公共利益的公共利益公司的登记不应受到干涉"的声明。

（b）依据第（a）款的规定修改的公司章程满足最低表决要求才能生效。

第3条　（a）如果合并一方的股东依据《印第安纳州法典》第23–1–40节的规定无权投票，则该条规定不适用于该公司。

（b）如果：

（1）一个非公共利益公司的本州实体是：

（A）合并或财产转换中的一方；或者

（B）股权置换中的一方；以及

（2）在该合并、财产转换或股权置换中存续的一方将成为公共利益公司；合并、财产转让或股权置换的计划必须满足本州公司的最低表决要求。

第4条　（a）依据第（b）款的规定，公共利益公司可以通过删除本节第1条和第2条规定的公司章程中的声明来终止其公共利益公司形态并不再受本节规定调整。

(b) An amendment to the articles of incorporation under subsection (a) is not effective unless the amendment is adopted by at least a minimum status vote.

Sec. 5. (a) This section does not apply to a corporation that is a party to a merger if the shareholders of the corporation are not entitled to vote on the merger under IC 23-1-40.

(b) If a plan of merger, consolidation, conversion, or share exchange would have the effect of terminating the status of a corporation as a benefit corporation, the plan must be adopted by at least a minimum status vote in order to be effective.

Sec. 6. Any sale, lease, exchange, or other disposition of all or substantially all of the assets of a benefit corporation is not effective unless one (1) or more of the following apply:

(1) The transaction is in the usual and regular course of business.

(2) The transaction is approved by at least a minimum status vote.

Chapter 4. Purpose of a Benefit Corporation

Sec. 1. A benefit corporation shall have a purpose of creating general public benefit. The purpose under this section is in addition to a benefit corporation's purpose under IC 23-1-21-2.

Sec. 2. (a) A benefit corporation may identify in its articles of incorporation one (1) or more specific public benefits that it is the purpose of the benefit corporation to create in addition to the benefit corporation's purposes under IC 23-1-21-2 and section 1 of this chapter.

(b) The identification of a specific public benefit under subsection (a) does not limit the purpose of a benefit corporation to create general public benefit under section 1 of this chapter.

Sec. 3. The creation of general public benefit and a specific public benefit under sections 1 and 2 of this chapter is in the best interests of a benefit corporation.

Sec. 4. (a) Subject to subsection (b), a benefit corporation may amend its articles of incorporation to add, amend, or delete the identification of a specific public benefit described in section 2 of this chapter.

(b) An amendment to the articles of incorporation under subsection (a) is not effective unless the amendment is adopted by a vote of the shareholders of each class or series of shares entitled to cast at least two-thirds (2/3) of the votes that all shareholders of the class or series are entitled to cast on the amendment.

Sec. 5. A professional corporation that is a benefit corporation does not violate IC 23-1.5-2-3 by having the purpose to create general public benefit or a specific public benefit.

Chapter 5. Standard of Conduct for Directors

Sec. 1.The following apply to the board of directors, committees of the board of

（b）依据第（a）款的规定，对公司章程的修改应满足最低表决要求。

第 5 条　（a）如果合并一方的股东依据《印第安纳州法典》第 23–1–40 节的规定无权投票，则该条规定不适用于该公司。

（b）如果合并、财产转换或股权置换的计划会产生终止商事公司作为公共利益公司的效力，该计划应满足最低表决要求。

第 6 条　公共利益公司的任何出售、出租、交换或者其他处置全部或者主要财产的行为无效，除非其符合以下一项或多项条件：

（1）该交易为正常商业往来。

（2）该交易满足最低表决要求。

第 4 节　公共利益公司的目的

第 1 条　公共利益公司应有服务于一般公共利益的目的。本条规定中的目的在《印第安纳州法典》第 23–1–21–2 条的规定之外。

第 2 条　（a）公共利益公司可以在章程中确定一项或者多项《印第安纳州法典》第 23–1–21–2 条和本节第 1 条规定的公共利益公司目的之外的特定公共利益目的。

（b）依据第（a）款的规定设定的特定公共利益目的并不限制公共利益公司在本节第 1 条规定下设定的一般公共利益目的。

第 3 条　依据本节第 1 条和第 2 条的规定创设的一般和特定公共利益目的为公共利益公司的最佳利益。

第 4 条　（a）依据第（b）款的规定，公共利益公司可通过修改章程增加、修改或删除本节第 2 条规定的特定公共利益目的。

（b）依据第（a）款的规定对章程的修改获得每一类别或系列有投票权的所有股东至少 2/3 的投票才能生效。

第 5 条　选择公共利益形态的专业公司并不因其创设一般或特定公共利益的目的而违反《印第安纳州法典》第 23–1.5–2–3 条的规定。

第 5 节　董事行为标准

第 1 条　董事会、董事委员会和董事，在履行各自职责和考虑公共利益公司的

directors, and individual directors of a benefit corporation in discharging the duties of their respective positions and in considering the best interests of the benefit corporation:

(1) The board of directors, committees of the board of directors, and individual directors shall consider the effects of any action or inaction upon all the following:

(A) The shareholders of the benefit corporation.

(B) The employees and workforce of the:

(i) benefit corporation;

(ii) subsidiaries of the benefit corporation; and

(iii) suppliers of the benefit corporation.

(C) The interests of customers as beneficiaries of the general public benefit or specific public benefit purposes of the benefit corporation.

(D) Community and societal factors, including the factors of each community in which:

(i) offices or facilities;

(ii) subsidiaries; or

(iii) suppliers; of the benefit corporation are located.

(E) The local and global environment.

(F) The short term and long term interests of the benefit corporation, including benefits that may accrue to the benefit corporation from its long term plans and the possibility that the interests may be best served by the continued independence of the benefit corporation.

(G) The ability of the benefit corporation to accomplish its general public benefit purpose and any specific public benefit purpose.

(2) The board of directors, committees of the board of directors, and individual directors may consider other pertinent factors or the interests of any other group that the board of directors, committees of the board of directors, or individual directors consider appropriate.

(3) The board of directors, committees of the board of directors, and individual directors are not required to give priority to a particular interest or factor listed in subdivision (1) or (2) over any other interest or factor unless the benefit corporation has stated in its articles of incorporation its intention to give priority to certain interests or factors related to its accomplishment of its general public benefit purpose or of a specific public benefit purpose identified in its articles of incorporation.

Sec. 2. The consideration of interests and factors provided in section 1 of this chapter:

(1) does not constitute a violation of IC 23-1-35; and

(2) is in addition to the ability of directors to consider interests and factors under IC 23-1-35-1.

Sec. 3. Except as otherwise provided in the bylaws of a benefit corporation, a director is not personally liable for monetary damages for:

(1) any action or inaction in the course of performing the duties of a director under

最佳利益时，应符合以下要求：

（1）董事会、董事委员会和董事应当考虑作为或不作为对以下对象的影响：

（A）公共利益公司的股东。
（B）以下主体的雇员：
（i）公共利益公司；
（ii）公共利益公司的子公司；以及
（iii）公共利益公司的供应商。
（C）作为公共利益公司一般或特定公共利益受益者的消费者的利益。

（D）社区和社会因素，包括以下主体所在地的社区：
（i）办公地或设施；
（ii）子公司；或者
（iii）供应商。
（E）当地和全球环境。
（F）公共利益公司的短期和长期利益，包括从其长期计划中产生的利益以及公共利益公司继续保持独立可能产生的最佳利益。

（G）公共利益公司实现其一般和特定公共利益目的的能力。

（2）董事会、董事委员会和董事可以考虑其他相关因素或者董事会，董事委员会和董事认为适当的其他团体的任何利益。

（3）除公司章程中要求优先考虑的特定的利益或因素优先权外，董事会、董事委员会和董事无须优先考虑第（1）款或第（2）款规定中的某个利益或因素。

第2条　对本节第1条规定的利益和因素的考虑：
（1）不违反《印第安纳州法典》第23-1-35节的规定；并且
（2）是在董事考虑《印第安纳州法典》第23-1-35-1节规定的利益和相关因素的能力之外。
第3条　除章程细则另有明确规定外，董事不对以下行为承担损害赔偿责任：

（1）在依据本节第1条的规定履行董事责任过程中的任何作为或者不作为，

section 1 of this chapter if the director performed the duties in compliance with IC 23–1–35 and this chapter; or

(2) the failure of the benefit corporation to pursue or create general public benefit or a specific public benefit.

Sec. 4. A director does not have a duty to a person that is a beneficiary of the general public benefit purpose or a specific public benefit purpose of a benefit corporation arising from the status of the person as a beneficiary.

Chapter 6. Benefit Director

Sec. 1. The board of directors of a benefit corporation must include a director who:

(1) is designated the benefit director; and

(2) has, in addition to the powers, duties, rights, and immunities of the other directors of the benefit corporation, the powers, duties, rights, and immunities provided in this chapter.

Sec. 2. (a) A benefit director shall be elected, and may be removed, in the manner provided under IC 23–1–33.

(b) Except as provided in section 6 or 7 of this chapter, a benefit director shall be an individual who is independent. An individual is conclusively presumed not independent under this subsection if any of the following apply:

(1) The individual:

(A) is; or

(B) has been within the past three (3) years; an employee, other than a benefit officer, of the benefit corporation or a subsidiary of the benefit corporation.

(2) An immediate family member of the individual:

(A) is; or

(B) has been within the past three (3) years; an executive officer, other than a benefit officer, of the benefit corporation or a subsidiary of the benefit corporation.

(3) There is ownership of at least five percent (5%) of the outstanding shares of the benefit corporation, calculated as if all outstanding rights to acquire equity interests in the benefit corporation had been exercised, by:

(A) the individual; or

(B) an entity:

(i) of which the individual is a director, an officer, or a manager; or

(ii) in which the individual owns at least five percent (5%) of the outstanding equity interests, calculated as if all outstanding rights to acquire equity interests in the business entity had been exercised.

(c) An individual serving as a benefit director or benefit officer does not in itself make the individual not independent.

在该行为符合《印第安纳州法典》第23-1-35节以及本节的规定；或者

（2）公共利益公司未能追求或实现一般或特定公共利益。

第4条　董事不对公共利益公司一般或特定社会目的的受益人负责。

第6节　公共利益董事

第1条　公共利益公司的董事会，应包括满足以下要求的董事：

（1）被任命为公共利益董事；并且

（2）有公共利益公司的其他董事的权力、义务、权利和豁免权以外，还有本节规定的权力、义务、权利和豁免权。

第2条　（a）公共利益董事应当依据《印第安纳州法典》第23-1-33节规定的方式任免。

（b）除本节第6条或第7条的规定外，公共利益董事应当是独立个体。如果符合以下任意一项，则依据本款该个体被推定为不具有独立性：

（1）该个体：

（A）是；或者

（B）在过去的3年内是；公共利益公司或其子公司的雇员，而非公共利益高管。

（2）该个体的直系亲属：

（A）是；或者

（B）在过去的3年内是；公共利益公司或者公共利益公司的子公司的执行高管，但不是公共利益高管。

（3）在所有购股权都被视为已行使的情况下，持有该公共利益公司至少5%已发行股份的以下个体：

（A）个人；或者

（B）实体：

（i）该个人是该实体的董事、高管或经理；或者

（ii）该个人在所有购股权都被视为已行使的情况下，持有该公共利益公司至少5%的已发行股份。

（c）个体担任公共利益董事或者公共利益高管并不使其丧失独立性。

(d) A benefit director may serve as the benefit officer at the same time as serving as the benefit director.

(e) A benefit corporation may prescribe in its articles of incorporation or bylaws additional qualification requirements for the benefit director if the additional qualification requirements are not inconsistent with this section.

Sec. 3. A benefit director shall prepare, and the benefit corporation shall include in the annual benefit report to shareholders required under IC 23–1.3–10, a report of the benefit director on all the following:

(1) Whether the benefit corporation acted in accordance with its general public benefit purpose and any specific public benefit purpose in all material respects during the period covered by the annual benefit report.

(2) Whether the:

(A) directors complied with IC 23–1.3–5–1; and

(B) officers complied with IC 23–1.3–7–1.

(3) If, in the opinion of the benefit director, the benefit corporation or its directors or officers failed to act or comply in the manner described in subdivision(1) or (2), a description of the ways in which the benefit corporation or its directors or officers failed to act or comply.

Sec. 4. The act or inaction of an individual in the individual's capacity as a benefit director shall constitute for all purposes an act or inaction of that individual in the capacity of a director of the benefit corporation.

Sec. 5. Regardless of whether the articles of incorporation or bylaws of a benefit corporation include a provision eliminating or limiting the personal liability of directors authorized byIC23–1–37, a benefit director is not personally liable for an act or omission in the capacity of a benefit director unless the act or omission constitutes self–dealing (other than a conflict of interest transaction described in IC 23–1–35–2(a)), willful misconduct, recklessness, or a knowing violation of law.

Sec. 6. The benefit director of a professional corporation is not required to be independent.

Sec. 7. (a) The articles of incorporation or bylaws of a benefit corporation must provide that the persons or shareholders who perform the duties of the board of directors include a person with the powers, duties, rights, and immunities of a benefit director if the articles of in corporation of the benefit corporation provide that the powers and duties conferred or imposed upon the board of directors shall be exercised or performed by a person other than the directors under IC 23–1–33–1(c).

(b) A person that exercises one (1) or more of the powers, duties, or rights of a benefit director under this section:

(1) does not need to be independent of the benefit corporation;

（d）公共利益董事可以同时担任公共利益高管。

（e）公共利益公司可以在章程或章程细则中规定其他的公共利益董事资格，如果该资格要求符合本条的规定。

第 3 条　公共利益董事应当编写其对以下事项的意见，公共利益公司应当依据《印第安纳州法典》第 23–1.3–10 节的规定将其附于年度公共利益报告中供股东查阅：

（1）在报告所述期间内，公共利益公司是否在所有重要事项上依其一般和特定公共利益目的行事。

（2）是否：
（A）董事依《印第安纳州法典》第 23–1.3–5–1 条的规定行事；以及
（B）高管依《印第安纳州法典》第 23–1.3–7–1 条的规定行事。
（3）如果公共利益董事认为公共利益公司或其董事、高管未能依第（1）款或第（2）款的规定行事，应在报告中说明公共利益公司、其董事或其高管未履行责任的情况。
第 4 条　公共利益董事在职权范围内的个人作为或不作为行为应视为该公共利益公司董事行为。

第 5 条　不论公共利益公司的公司章程或者章程细则是否依据《印第安纳州法典》第 23–1–37 节的规定删除或限制董事的个人责任，公共利益董事在履行公共利益董事职责时不对其任何作为或不作为承担个人责任，但自我交易［除了《印第安纳州法典》第 23–1–35–2（a）款中描述的利益冲突交易］或故意违法行为除外。

第 6 条　专业公司的公共利益董事不需要是独立的。

第 7 条　（a）如果公共利益公司的公司章程规定，授予或施加给董事会的权力和义务应当由《印第安纳州法典》第 23–1–33–1（c）款规定下董事以外的人执行或履行，公共利益公司的章程或章程细则必须规定履行董事会义务的人或股东，包括有公共利益董事的权力、义务、权利和豁免的人员。

（b）依据本条的规定有一项或更多公共利益董事的权力、义务或权利的人：

（1）不需要独立于公共利益公司；

(2) has the immunities of a benefit director; and

(3) may share the powers, duties, and rights of a benefit director with one (1) or more persons.

Chapter 7. Standard of Conduct for Officers

Sec. 1. Each officer of a benefit corporation shall consider the interests and factors of the persons listed in IC 23–1.3–5–1 in the manner provided under IC 23–1.3–5–1 if:

(1) the officer has discretion to act with respect to a matter; and

(2) it reasonably appears to the officer that the matter may have a material effect on the creation by the benefit corporation of general public benefit or a specific public benefit identified in the articles of incorporation of the benefit corporation.

Sec. 2. The consideration of interests and factors in the manner described in section 1 of this chapter does not constitute a violation of any duties of an officer.

Sec. 3. Except as provided in the bylaws of the benefit corporation, an officer is not personally liable for monetary damages for:

(1) an action or inaction as an officer in the course of performing the duties of an officer under section 1 of this chapter if the officer performed the duties of the position in compliance with IC 23–1 and this chapter; or

(2) failure of the benefit corporation to pursue or create general public benefit or a specific public benefit.

Sec. 4. An officer does not have a duty to a person that is a beneficiary of the general public benefit purpose or a specific public benefit purpose of a benefit corporation arising from the status of the person as a beneficiary.

Chapter 8. Benefit Officer

Sec. 1. A benefit corporation may have an officer designated as the benefit officer.

Sec. 2. A benefit officer shall have:

(1) the powers and duties relating to the purpose of the benefit corporation to create general public benefit or a specific public benefit provided:

(A) by the bylaws; or

(B) absent controlling provisions in the bylaws, by resolutions or orders of the board of directors; and

(2) the duty to prepare the benefit report required under IC 23–1.3–10.

Chapter 9. Right of Action

Sec. 1. A person may not, except in a benefit enforcement proceeding, bring an action or assert a claim against a benefit corporation or its directors or officers with respect to either

（2）拥有公共利益董事的豁免权；并且

（3）可以分享公共利益董事的权力、义务和权利给一个或更多人。

第7节　高管的行为标准

第1条　公共利益公司的高管应当以《印第安纳州法典》第23–1.3–5–1条中规定的行为标准考虑《印第安纳州法典》第23–1.3–5–1条中规定的利益和因素，如果：

（1）高管就该行为有自由裁量权；并且

（2）高管有合理理由认为该行为对公共利益公司在公司章程中创设的一般或特定公共利益有实质性影响。

第2条　对第1条中利益和相关因素的考虑不违反高管的任何义务。

第3条　除公司章程细则中另有明确规定外，高管不对以下行为承担损害赔偿责任：

（1）在依据本节第1条的规定履行高管责任过程中的任何作为或者不作为，遵守了《印第安纳州法典》第23–1章和本节规定的情形下；或者

（2）公共利益公司未能追求或实现一般或特定公共利益。

第4条　高管不对公共利益公司一般或特定社会目的的受益人负责。

第8节　公共利益高管

第1条　公共利益公司可以将高管任命为公共利益高管。

第2条　公共利益高管应有：

（1）规定于以下文件中的创设一般或特定公共利益的目的的权力和义务：

（A）公司章程细则；或者

（B）在公司章程细则中没有规定时，董事会的决议或者命令；并且

（2）《印第安纳州法典》第23–1.3–10节规定的编写公共利益报告的义务。

第9节　诉讼权利

第1条　非经公共利益实施程序，任何人不得因以下事项向公共利益公司或者其董事或高管提起诉讼或主张：

of the following:

(1) The failure to pursue or create:

(A) general public benefit; or

(B) a specific public benefit identified in the benefit corporation's articles of incorporation.

(2) A violation of an obligation, duty, or standard of conduct under this article.

Sec. 2. A benefit corporation is not liable for monetary damages under this article for any failure of the benefit corporation to pursue or create general public benefit or a specific public benefit.

Sec. 3. A benefit enforcement proceeding may be commenced or maintained only:

(1) directly by the benefit corporation; or

(2) derivatively in accordance with IC 23–1–32 by:

(A) a person or group of persons that owned at least two percent (2%) of the total number of shares of a class or series outstanding at the time of the act or omission complained of;

(B) a director;

(C) a person or group of persons that owned at least five percent (5%) of the outstanding equity interests in an entity of which the benefit corporation is a subsidiary at the time of the act or omission complained of; or

(D) other persons as specified in the benefit corporation's articles of incorporation or bylaws.

Chapter 10. Annual Benefit Report

Sec. 1. A benefit corporation shall prepare an annual benefit report that includes all the following:

(1) A narrative description of:

(A) the ways in which the benefit corporation pursued general public benefit during the year and the extent to which general public benefit was created;

(B) both the:

(i) ways in which the benefit corporation pursued a specific public benefit that the articles of incorporation state is the purpose of the benefit corporation to create;and

(ii) extent to which that specific public benefit was created;

(C) any circumstances that have hindered the creation by the benefit corporation of general public benefit or a specific public benefit; and

(D) the process and rationale for selecting or changing the third party standard used to prepare the benefit report.

(2) An assessment of the overall social and environmental performance of the benefit corporation against a third party standard:

（1）未能追求或实现：

（A）一般公共利益；或者

（B）在公共利益公司章程中确定的特定公共利益。

（2）违反本章规定下的责任、义务或行为标准。

第 2 条　公共利益公司不对本章规定下任何未能追求或实现一般或特定公共利益承担损害赔偿责任。

第 3 条　下列情形中，可由以下主体提起公共利益实施程序：

（1）由公共利益公司直接提起；或者

（2）依据《印第安纳州法典》第 23–1–32 节的规定被以下主体派生提起：

（A）在被诉的作为或不作为行为发生时，拥有公共利益公司至少 2% 某类别或系列已发行的所有股份的个人或群体；

（B）董事；

（C）在被诉作为或不作为行为发生时，拥有公共利益公司母公司至少 5% 已发行股份的登记股东或实际受益人；或者

（D）公共利益公司章程或章程细则中列明的其他人员。

第 10 节　年度公共利益报告

第 1 条　公共利益公司的年度公共利益报告应包括以下内容：

（1）对以下事项的说明：

（A）公共利益公司本年度追求一般公共利益的方法和一般公共利益实现的情况；

（B）同时包括：

（i）公共利益公司追求公司章程中规定的特定公共利益的方法；以及

（ii）该特定公共利益实现的情况。

（C）阻碍公共利益公司实现一般和特定公共利益的情形；以及

（D）编写公共利益报告时选择或更换第三方标准的程序和原因。

（2）依据第三方标准对公共利益公司的社会和环境表现作出的整体评价：

(A) applied consistently with any application of that standard in prior benefit reports; or

(B) accompanied by an explanation of the reasons for:

(i) any inconsistent application; or

(ii) the change to that standard from the standard used in the immediate prior report.

(3) The name of the benefit director and the benefit officer, if any, and the address to which correspondence to each of them may be directed.

(4) The compensation paid by the benefit corporation during the year to each director in the capacity of a director.

(5) The report of the benefit director described in IC 23–1.3–6–3.

(6) A statement regarding any connection between the organization that established the third party standard, or its directors, officers, or any holder of at least five percent (5%) of the governance interests in the organization, and the benefit corporation or its directors, officers, or any holder of at least five percent (5%) of the outstanding shares of the benefit corporation, including any financial or governance relationship that might materially affect the credibility of the use of the third party standard.

Sec. 2. If, during the year covered by a benefit report:

(1) a benefit director:

(A) resigned from or refused to stand for reelection to the position of benefit director; or

(B) was removed from the position of benefit director; and

(2) the benefit director furnished the benefit corporation with any written correspondence concerning the circumstances surrounding the resignation, refusal, or removal;the benefit report must include the correspondence described in subdivision (2) as an exhibit.

Sec. 3. The following are not required to be audited or certified by a third party:

(1) The benefit report.

(2) The assessment of the performance of the benefit corporation in the benefit report described in section 1(2) of this chapter.

Sec. 4. A benefit corporation shall send its annual benefit report to each shareholder on the earlier of:

(1) one hundred twenty (120) days following the end of the fiscal year of the benefit corporation; or

(2) the same date that the benefit corporation delivers any other annual report to its shareholders.

Sec. 5. If a benefit corporation has an Internet web site, a benefit corporation shall post all of its benefit reports on the public part of its Internet web site. However, the compensation paid to directors and financial or proprietary information included in the benefit reports may be omitted from the benefit reports posted on the Internet web site.

（A）沿用先前公共利益报告中使用的标准；或者

（B）附一份说明以解释：

（i）适用上的差异；或者

（ii）与上一份报告相比，标准的变化。

（3）公共利益董事和公共利益高管的姓名和联系地址。

（4）公共利益公司在上一年度支付给每位董事的薪酬。

（5）公共利益董事依《印第安纳州法典》第23-1.3-6-3条的规定应编写的报告。

（6）设立第三方标准的机构或其董事、高管、或该机构至少5%管理权利的持有者与公共利益公司或其董事、高管或公共利益公司至少5%已发行股份的持有者之间关系的声明，包括任何有可能实质性影响第三方标准可信度的财务或管理关系。

第2条　如果在公共利益报告所述年度期间内：

（1）公共利益董事：

（A）辞职或者拒绝连任公共利益董事；或者

（B）被免职；以及

（2）该公共利益董事与公司有任何书面的涉及辞职、拒绝连任或免职的书信往来，公共利益报告应当将第（2）款中规定的书信往来作为附件。

第3条　以下事项无须经第三方审计或证明：

（1）公共利益报告。

（2）本节第1（2）款中规定的公共利益报告中的公共利益公司绩效评估。

第4条　公共利益公司应当在以下日期将公共利益报告尽早地送交各股东：

（1）公共利益公司会计年度结束后120天内；或者

（2）公共利益公司向其股东送交其他年度报告的同一时间。

第5条　如果公共利益公司有网站，公共利益公司应当将其所有公共利益报告发布于其网站的公共部分。但是，公司可以将发布于其网站的公共利益报告中的董事薪酬和财务、所有权信息删除。

Sec. 6. (a) The benefit corporation shall deliver, concurrently with the delivery of the benefit report to shareholders under section 4 of this chapter, a copy of the benefit report to the secretary of state for filing. However, the compensation paid to directors and financial or proprietary information included in the benefit report may be omitted from the benefit report as delivered to the secretary of state.

(b) The fee established in IC 23–1–18–3(a)(27) applies to an annual benefit report delivered for filing under this section.

第 6 条 （a）在依本节第 4 条的规定将公共利益报告提交股东的同时，公共利益公司应当将该公共利益报告提交州务卿备案。但是，公司可以将公共利益报告中的董事薪酬和财务、所有权信息在提交州务卿的报告中删除。

（b）在《印第安纳州法典》第 23-1-18-3（a）（27）项中规定的费用适用于依据本条规定提交备案的年度公共利益报告。

THE STATE OF LOUISIANA

Regular Session, 2012 ACT No. 442

HOUSE BILL NO. 1178

AN ACT

To enact Chapter 27 of Title 12 of the Louisiana Revised Statutes of 1950, to be comprised of R.S. 12:1801 through 1832, relative to benefit corporations; to enact the "Benefit Corporations Law"; to provide for applicability; to provide for definitions; to provide for formation of benefit corporations; to provide for election and termination of benefit corporation status; to provide for corporate purposes; to provide for a standard of conduct for directors and officers; to provide for a benefit director; to provide for a benefit officer; to provide for a right of action; to require an annual benefits report; to provide for stock certificates; and to provide for related matters.

Be it enacted by the Legislature of Louisiana:

Section 1. Chapter 27 of Title 12 of the Louisiana Revised Statutes of 1950, comprised of R.S. 12:1801 through 1832, is hereby enacted to read as follows:

CHAPTER 27. BENEFIT CORPORATIONS

Chapter 27. Benefit Corporations

Part 1. PRELIMINARY PROVISIONS

§ 12:1801. Short title.

This Chapter shall be known and may be cited as the "Benefit Corporations Law".

§ 12:1802. Application and effect of Chapter.

A. This Chapter shall apply to all benefit corporations.

路易斯安那州

常规会议，2012 年第 442 号法案

众议院法案第 1178 号

该法案

颁布与公共利益公司有关的 1950 年《路易斯安那州修订法》第 12 编第 27 章，其由《路易斯安那州修订法》第 12 编第 1801 条至第 1832 条组成；颁布了《公共利益公司法》；规定了适用规则；规定了定义；规定了公共利益公司设立；规定了公共利益公司形态的选择和终止；规定了公司目的；规定了董事和高管的行为标准；规定了公共利益董事；规定了公共利益高管；规定了诉讼权利；要求提供年度公共利益报告；规定了股票凭证；并且规定了相关事项。

本法案由路易斯安那州立法机关颁布：

第 1 部分　1950 年《路易斯安那州修订法》第 12 编第 27 章由《路易斯安那州修订法》第 12 编第 1801 条至第 1832 条组成，称为：

第 27 章　公共利益公司

第 27 章　公共利益公司

第 1 节　初步规定

第 12:1801 条　简称

本章应当被称为并被引用为《公共利益公司法》。

第 12:1802 条　本章的适用和效力

A. 本章规定适用于所有的公共利益公司。

B. The existence of a provision of this Chapter shall not of itself create an implication that a contrary or different rule of law is applicable to a business corporation that is not a benefit corporation. This Chapter shall not affect a statute or rule of law that is applicable to a business corporation that is not a benefit corporation.

C. Except as otherwise provided in this Chapter, the Business Corporation Law, R.S. 12:1 et seq., shall be generally applicable to all benefit corporations. The specific provisions of this Chapter shall control over the general provisions of the Business Corporation Law. A benefit corporation may be simultaneously subject to this Chapter and one or more other Chapters within this Title.

D. A provision of the articles or bylaws of a benefit corporation shall not relax, be inconsistent with, or supersede a provision of this Chapter.

§ 12:1803. Definitions.

A. As used in this Chapter, the following terms and phrases shall have the meaning ascribed to them in this Section, unless the context clearly indicates otherwise:

(1) "Affiliate" means, in relation to a person, a subsidiary of the person or an entity which owns beneficially or of record a majority of the outstanding equity interests of the person.

(2) "Benefit corporation" means a business corporation which has elected to become subject to this Chapter and whose status as a benefit corporation has not been terminated.

(3) "Benefit director" means the director designated as the benefit director of a benefit corporation pursuant to R.S. 12:1822.

(4) "Benefit enforcement proceeding" means any claim or action for one or both of the following:

(a) Failure of a benefit corporation to pursue or create general public benefit or a specific public benefit set forth in its articles.

(b) Violation of any obligation, duty, or standard of conduct pursuant to this Chapter.

(5) "Benefit officer" means the individual designated as the benefit officer of a benefit corporation pursuant to R.S. 12:1824.

(6) "General public benefit" means a material positive impact on society and the environment, taken as a whole, assessed against a third–party standard, from the business and operations of a benefit corporation.

(7) "Independent" means having no material relationship with a benefit corporation or a subsidiary of the benefit corporation.

(8) "Material relationship" means the relationship between a person and a benefit corporation or any of its subsidiaries if any of the following apply:

(a) The person is, or has been within the last three years, an employee, other than a benefit officer, of the benefit corporation, or an affiliate of the benefit corporation.

B. 本章条款不为非公共利益公司设定相反或不同的规则。本章的规定不影响非公共利益公司的有关条文和规则的适用。

C. 除本章另有规定外，《商事公司法》，《路易斯安那州修订法》第 12 编第 1 章及以下各章应适用于公共利益公司。本章特定条款的效力应优于《商事公司法》的一般条款。公共利益公司可同时接受本章和本编中的一个或多个章节的调整。

D. 公共利益公司章程或者章程细则的规定不得放宽、违背或取代本章的规定。

第 12:1803 条　定义

A. 除语境明确另有意指外，本章中下列词语或短语的含义如下：

（1）“关联方”是指，作为子公司的实体或者实质或名义上拥有某实体大部分已发行股份的实体。

（2）“公共利益公司”是指，选择接受本章规定的调整且公共利益公司形态没有终止的商事公司。

（3）“公共利益董事”是指，依据《路易斯安那州修订法》第 12:1822 条的规定被任命为公共利益公司的公共利益董事的董事。

（4）“公共利益实施程序”是指，因以下一种或两种行为产生的任何主张或诉讼：

（a）未能追求或实现公司章程中规定的一般公共利益或特定公共利益；

（b）违反本章规定下的任何义务、责任或行为标准。

（5）“公共利益高管”是指，依据《路易斯安那州修订法》第 12:1824 条的规定被任命为公共利益公司的公共利益高管的个体。

（6）“一般公共利益”是指，根据第三方标准，公司的业务和经营在整体上对社会和环境产生的实质性积极影响。

（7）“独立”是指，与公共利益公司或其子公司没有实质性的关系。

（8）“实质关系”是指，个人与公共利益公司或其子公司之间存在的下列关系：

（a）此人，是或者在过去 3 年内是，公共利益公司的雇员，公共利益高管或者公共利益公司的关联方除外。

(b) An immediate family member of the person is, or has been within the last three years, an employee, officer, or director of the benefit corporation, or an affiliate of the benefit corporation.

(c) There is beneficial or record ownership of five percent or more of the outstanding shares of the benefit corporation by either the person or an entity of which the person is a director, an officer, or a manager, or in which the person owns beneficially or of record five percent or more of the outstanding equity interests.

(9) "Minimum vote" means:

(a) In the case of a business corporation, the approval by holders of two–thirds of the shares present and voting of each class or series and any other approval or vote required under the Business Corporation Law or the articles.

(b) In the case of a domestic entity other than a business corporation, the approval by holders of two–thirds of each class or series of equity interests entitled to vote on any issue and any other approval or vote required under the law governing the internal affairs of the entity or its constituent documents.

(10) "Specific public benefit" means any of the following:

(a) Serving low–income or underserved individuals or communities.

(b) Promoting economic opportunity for low–income or underserved individuals or communities.

(c) Preserving the environment, promoting positive impacts on the environment, or reducing negative impacts on the environment.

(d) Improving human health.

(e) Promoting the arts, sciences, or advancement of knowledge.

(f) Increasing the flow of capital to entities with a purpose listed in this Paragraph.

(g) Historic preservation.

(h) Urban beautification.

(11) "Subsidiary" means, in relation to a person, an entity in which the person owns beneficially or of record fifty percent or more of the outstanding equity interests.

(12) "Third–party standard" means a recognized standard for defining, reporting, and assessing the performance of corporations in producing general public benefit and specific public benefits which is all of the following:

(a) Comprehensive in that it assesses the effect of the corporation and its operations in producing general public benefit and any specific public benefit specified in the articles.

(b) Transparent because the following information about the standard is publicly available:

(i) The criteria considered when measuring the overall social and environmental performance of a business.

（b）此人的直系亲属是，或者在过去 3 年内是，公共利益公司的雇员、高管或董事，或者是公共利益公司的关联方。

（c）下述持有公共利益公司 5% 以上已发行股份的登记股东或实际受益人：个人或实体，其中个人是该实体的董事、高管或经理，或是持有公共利益公司 5% 以上已发行股份的登记股东或实际受益人。

（9）“最低表决要求”是指：

（a）在商事公司中，由持有每一类别或系列 2/3 现有股份的股东投票或按照商事公司法或者公司章程要求的方式投票批准公司行为。

（b）在非商事公司的本州实体中，由每一类别或系列有投票权的股东的 2/3 投票批准以及按照调整实体内部事务的法律或者章程文件要求的任何其他的批准和表决方式进行表决。

（10）“特定公共利益”是指以下任意一项：

（a）向低收入或者低福利人群或社区提供服务。

（b）向低收入或者低福利人群或社区提供经济机会。

（c）保护环境，促进对环境的积极影响，或者减少对环境的负面影响。

（d）改善人类健康。

（e）促进艺术、科学或知识进步。

（f）促进资本向有本项列出的目的的实体流动。

（g）文物保护。

（h）城市美化。

（11）“子公司”是指，该实体 50% 以上已发行的股份的受益所有权或登记所有权被另一实体所拥有。

（12）“第三方标准”是指用于定义、报告和评估创造一般公共利益和特定公共利益的公司社会和环境绩效的标准，其应满足以下条件：

（a）全面，其在创造一般公共利益和公司章程中特定公共利益的角度上评价公司业务和经营绩效。

（b）透明，关于标准的以下信息可以公开获取：

（i）衡量企业整体社会和环境绩效时所考虑的标准。

(ii) The relative weightings, if any, of those criteria.

(iii) The identity of the directors, officers, material owners, and the governing body of the organization that developed and controls revisions to the standard.

(iv) The process by which revisions to the standard and changes to the membership of the governing body are made.

(v) An accounting of the sources of financial support for the organization, with sufficient detail to disclose any relationships that could reasonably be considered to present a potential conflict of interest.

B. Terms not otherwise defined in Subsection A of this Section shall have the meanings given to them in the Business Corporation Law.

C. For purposes of the definitions in this Section, a percentage of ownership in an entity shall be calculated as if all outstanding rights to acquire equity interests in the association have been exercised.

§ 12:1804. Election of status; corporate name.

A. A business corporation incorporated in accordance with R.S. 12:21 et seq. may elect to be a benefit corporation under this Chapter by stating in its articles that it is a benefit corporation subject to this Chapter.

B. Any amendment to the articles of an existing business corporation to add a statement that it is a benefit corporation subject to this Chapter shall be adopted by at least the minimum vote. The notice of the meeting of shareholders to approve the amendment shall state the specific public benefits, if any, to be included in the purposes of the benefit corporation and shall explain the anticipated impact on shareholders of becoming a benefit corporation.

C. If an entity that is not a benefit corporation is a party to a merger or consolidation, and the surviving or new entity in the merger or consolidation is to be a benefit corporation, then the plan of merger or consolidation shall be adopted by at least the minimum vote.

D. The corporate name of a benefit corporation shall end with the following phrase, which may be in parentheses, "A Benefit Corporation".

§ 12:1805. Termination of status.

A. A benefit corporation may terminate its status as such and cease to be subject to this Chapter by amending its articles to delete the provision required by R.S. 12:1804 to be stated in the articles of a benefit corporation. In order to be effective, the amendment shall be adopted by at least the minimum vote.

B. If a merger or consolidation of a benefit corporation would have the effect of terminating the status of a business corporation as a benefit corporation, in order to be effective, the plan of merger or consolidation shall be adopted by at least the minimum vote of the benefit corporation. Any sale, lease, exchange, or other disposition of all or

（ii）这些标准的相关权重，如有。

（iii）制定和控制修改标准的董事、高管、主要股东和该实体的管理层人员的身份。

（iv）标准修改和管理层人员变动的程序。

（v）资金来源的核算，包括充分披露合理认知下存在利益冲突的所有细节。

B. 在本条的第 A 款中未另行定义的用语，其含义遵照《商事公司法》中规定的含义。

C. 在本条的定义中，实体中的股权比例应当在所有购股权被视为已行使的情况下计算。

第 12:1804 条　状态的选择；公司名称

A. 依据《路易斯安那州修订法》第 12:21 条等规定成立的商事公司可以依据本章规定转变为公共利益公司，在公司章程中声明其是受本章规定调整的公共利益公司。

B. 任何在已成立商事公司的章程中增加其是受本章规定调整的公共利益公司声明的修改，必须至少满足最低表决要求。股东大会批准修改的通知应当载明公共利益公司的目的中包括的特定公共利益（如有），并应解释成为一个公共利益公司对股东可能产生的影响。

C. 如果一个非公共利益公司的实体是合并或兼并的一方，并且在该合并或兼并中存续的实体或者新的实体是公共利益公司，那么该合并或兼并方案至少应满足最低表决要求。

D. 公共利益公司的公司名称应当以短语“公共利益公司”结尾，其可以在括号内。

第 12:1805 条　形态终止

A. 公共利益公司可通过删除《路易斯安那州修订法》第 12:1804 条规定的公司章程中其作为公共利益公司的声明来终止其公共利益公司的形态并不再受本章规定调整。公司章程的修改应满足最低表决要求。

B. 如果公共利益公司的合并将产生终止商事公司作为公共利益公司的效力，该合并计划应满足公共利益公司的最低表决要求。除该行为属正常商业往来外，公共利益公司的任何出售、出租、置换或者其他处置全部或者主要财产的行为，需满足最低表决要求。

substantially all of the assets of a benefit corporation, unless the transaction is in the usual and regular course of business, shall not be effective unless the transaction is approved by at least the minimum vote.

§§ 12:1806-1810. [Reserved.]

Part 2. Corporate Purposes

§ 12:1811. Corporate purposes.

A. A benefit corporation shall have a purpose of creating a general public benefit. This purpose is in addition to its purpose under R.S. 12:21 et seq.

B. The articles of a benefit corporation may identify one or more specific public benefits that it is the purpose of the benefit corporation to create in addition to its purposes under R.S. 12:21 et seq. and Subsection A of this Section. The identification of a specific public benefit under this Subsection shall not limit the obligation of a benefit corporation under Subsection A of this Section.

C. The creation of a general public benefit and specific public benefit under Subsections A and B of this Section is in the best interests of the benefit corporation.

D. A benefit corporation may amend its articles to add, amend, or delete the identification of a specific public benefit that it is the purpose of the benefit corporation to create. In order to be effective, the amendment shall be adopted by at least the minimum vote.

E. A professional corporation that is a benefit corporation shall not be deemed in violation of R.S. 12:804, 904, 984, 1054, 1074, 1089, 1113, 1133, 1154, 1193, or 1403 by having the purpose to create general public benefit or a specific public benefit.

§§ 12:1812-1820. [Reserved.]

Part 3. ACCOUNTABILITY

§ 12:1821. Standard of conduct for directors.

A. In discharging the duties of their respective positions and in considering the best interests of the benefit corporation, the board of directors, committees of the board, and individual directors of a benefit corporation:

(1) Shall consider the effects of any action or inaction upon all of the following:

(a) The shareholders of the benefit corporation.

(b) The employees and work force of the benefit corporation, its subsidiaries, and its suppliers.

(c) The interests of customers as beneficiaries of the general public benefit or specific public benefit purposes of the benefit corporation.

(d) Community and societal factors, including those of each community in which offices

第 12:1806—1810 条［保留］

第 2 节　公司目的

第 12:1811 条　公司目的

A. 公共利益公司应有服务于一般公共利益的目的。此目的是在《路易斯安那州修订法》第 12:21 条等规定之外。

B. 公共利益公司的章程可以在《路易斯安那州修订法》第 12:21 条等规定和本条的第 A 款规定之外确定一项或者多项特定公共利益目的。依据本款设定的特定公共利益目的并不限制公共利益公司在本条的第 A 款规定下的义务。

C. 依据本条中第 A 款和第 B 款的规定创设的一般和特定公共利益目的为公共利益公司的最佳利益。

D. 公共利益公司可以增加、修改或删除公司章程里设定的特定公共利益目的。公司章程的修改需满足最低表决要求。

E. 选择公共利益形态的专业公司并不因其有创设一般或特定公共利益的目的而违反《路易斯安那州修订法》第 12:804、904、984、1054、1074、1089、1113、1133、1154、1193、1403 条的规定。

第 12:1812—1820 条［保留］

第 3 节　公司责任

第 12:1821 条　董事行为标准

A. 在履行各自职责和考虑公共利益公司的最佳利益时，公共利益公司的董事会、董事委员会和董事：

（1）应当考虑作为或不作为对以下对象的影响：

（a）公共利益公司的股东。

（b）公共利益公司、其子公司和其供应商的雇员。

（c）作为公共利益公司一般或特定公共利益受益者的消费者的利益。

（d）社区和社会因素，包括公共利益公司、其子公司或其供应商的办公地或

or facilities of the benefit corporation, its subsidiaries, or its suppliers are located.

(e) The local and global environment.

(f) The short-term and long-term interests of the benefit corporation, including benefits that may accrue to the benefit corporation from its long-term plans and the possibility that these interests may be best served by the continued independence of the benefit corporation.

(g) The ability of the benefit corporation to accomplish its general public benefit purpose and any specific public benefit purpose.

(2) May consider other pertinent factors or the interests of any other group that they deem appropriate.

(3) Shall not be required to give priority to the interests of a particular person or group referred to in Paragraph (1) or (2) of this Subsection over the interests of any other person or group unless the benefit corporation has stated in its articles the intention to give priority to certain interests related to the accomplishment of its general public benefit purpose or of a specific public benefit purpose identified in the articles.

B. The consideration of interests and factors in the manner required by Subsection A of this Section shall not constitute a violation of R.S. 12:91.

C. A director shall not be personally liable for monetary damages for any of the following:

(1) Any act or omission covered by a provision in the articles of incorporation that eliminates or limits the liability of the director as authorized in R.S. 12:24(C)(4).

(2) Any act or omission as a director if the director performed the duties of office pursuant to R.S. 12:91.

(3) Failure of the benefit corporation to pursue or create a general public benefit or specific public benefit.

D. A director shall not have a duty to a person that is a beneficiary of the general public benefit purpose or a specific public benefit purpose of a benefit corporation arising from the status of the person as a beneficiary.

§ 12:1822. Benefit director.

A. The board of directors of a benefit corporation shall include a director who shall be designated the benefit director and who shall have, in addition to the powers, duties, rights, and immunities of the other directors of the benefit corporation, the powers, duties, rights, and immunities provided for in this Part.

B. The benefit director shall be elected, and may be removed, pursuant to R.S. 12:81, and shall be an individual who is independent. The benefit director may serve as the benefit officer at the same time as serving as the benefit director. The articles or bylaws of a benefit corporation may prescribe additional qualifications or duties of the benefit director not inconsistent with this Subsection.

设施所在地的社区。

（e）当地和全球环境。

（f）公共利益公司的短期和长期利益，包括从其长期计划中产生的利益以及公共利益公司继续保持独立可能产生的最佳利益。

（g）公共利益公司实现其一般和特定公共利益目的的能力。

（2）可以考虑董事认为合适的其他相关因素或其他群体的利益。

（3）除公司章程中要求的优先考虑特定的利益或因素外，不应被要求优先考虑本款第（1）项或第（2）项的规定中某个特定人或组织的利益。

B. 对本条第 A 款中要求的利益和相关因素的考虑不违反《路易斯安那州修订法》第 12:91 条的规定。

C. 董事不对以下行为承担损害赔偿责任：

（1）公司章程中消除或限制《路易斯安那州修订法》第 12:24（C）（4）项规定的董事责任的任何作为或者不作为行为。

（2）董事依据《路易斯安那州修订法》第 12:91 条的规定履行职务的任何作为或者不作为行为。

（3）公共利益公司未能追求或创造一般或特定公共利益。

D. 董事不对公共利益公司一般或特定社会目的的受益人负责。

第 12:1822 条　公共利益董事

A. 公共利益公司的董事会应当包括被任命为公共利益董事的董事，并且公共利益董事除有公共利益公司的其他董事的权力、义务、权利和豁免权外，还有本节规定的权力、义务、权利和豁免权。

B. 公共利益董事应当依据《路易斯安那州修订法》第 12:81 条的规定任免，并且应当是独立个体。公共利益董事可以同时担任公共利益高管。公共利益公司的章程或章程细则可以规定与本款不一致的公共利益董事资格或义务。

C. The benefit director shall be responsible for the preparation of an annual benefit report submitted to shareholders as required by R.S. 12:1831. The benefit director may retain an independent third party to audit the annual benefit report or conduct any other assessment of the corporation's pursuit of its general public benefit purpose and any specific public benefit purpose. The annual benefit report shall include a statement of the benefit director, in the opinion of the benefit director, on all of the following:

(1) Whether the benefit corporation acted in accordance with its general public benefit purpose and any specific public benefit purpose in all material respects during the period covered by the report.

(2) Whether the directors and officers complied with R.S. 12:1821(A) and 1823(A), respectively.

(3) If, in the opinion of the benefit director, the benefit corporation or its directors or officers failed to comply with R.S. 12:1821(A) and 1823(A), a description of the ways in which the benefit corporation or its directors or officers failed to comply.

D. The act or inaction of an individual in the capacity of a benefit director shall constitute for all purposes an act or inaction of that individual in the capacity of a director of the benefit corporation.

E. Regardless of whether the bylaws of a benefit corporation include a provision eliminating or limiting the personal liability of directors authorized by R.S. 12:24(C)(4), a benefit director shall not be personally liable for an act or omission in the capacity of a benefit director unless the act or omission constitutes self-dealing, willful misconduct, or a knowing violation of law.

F. The benefit director of a professional corporation shall not be required to be independent.

§ 12:1823. Standard of conduct for officers.

A. Each officer of a benefit corporation shall consider the interests and factors described in R.S. 12:1821 in the manner provided in that Section if all of the following applies:

(1) The officer has discretion to act with respect to the matter.

(2) It reasonably appears to the officer that the matter may have a material effect on the creation by the benefit corporation of a general public benefit or a specific public benefit identified in the articles of the benefit corporation.

B. The consideration of interests and factors pursuant to Subsection A of this Section shall not constitute a violation of R.S. 12:91.

C. An officer shall not be personally liable for monetary damages for either of the following:

(1) An action or omission as an officer if the officer performed the duties of the position

C. 公共利益董事应当有义务编写《路易斯安那州修订法》第 12:1831 条规定的供股东查阅的年度公共利益报告。公共利益董事可以雇佣一个独立第三方去审计年度公共利益报告或者对公司追求一般和特定公共利益目的的情况进行评估。年度公共利益报告的公共董事意见中应包括关于以下所有事项的公共利益董事声明：

（1）在报告所述期间内，公共利益公司是否在所有重要事项上依其一般和特定公共利益目的行事。

（2）董事和高管是否分别依《路易斯安那州修订法》第 12:1821（A）款和第 1823（A）款的规定行事。

（3）如果公共利益董事认为公共利益公司、其董事或高管未能依《路易斯安那州修订法》第 12:1821（A） 款和第 1823（A）款规定的要求行事，应在报告中陈述公共利益公司、董事或高管未能遵守规定的情况。

D. 公共利益董事在职权范围内的个人作为或不作为应被视为该公共利益公司董事的行为。

E. 无论公共利益公司的公司章程细则是否依据《路易斯安那州修订法》第 12:24（C）（4）项的规定删除或限制董事的个人责任，公共利益董事在行使公共利益董事职责时不对其任何行为承担个人责任，但自我交易或故意违法行为除外。

F. 专业公司的公共利益董事不需要是独立的。

第 12:1823 条　高管责任

A. 公共利益公司的高管应当以本条中规定的行为标准考虑《路易斯安那州修订法》第 12:1821 条中规定的利益和因素，如果出现以下情况：

（1）高管对该行为有自由裁量权。

（2）高管有合理理由认为该行为对公共利益公司在公司章程中创设的一般或特定公共利益有实质性影响。

B. 本条中第 A 款规定下的利益和因素的考虑不违反《路易斯安那州修订法》第 12:91 条的规定。

C. 高管不对以下行为承担损害赔偿责任：

（1）高管的作为或不作为，如果该高管依据《路易斯安那州修订法》第 12:91

pursuant to R.S. 12:91.

(2) Failure of the benefit corporation to pursue or create general public benefit or specific public benefit.

D. An officer shall not have a duty to a person that is a beneficiary of the general public benefit purpose or a specific public benefit purpose of a benefit corporation arising from the status of the person as a beneficiary.

§ 12:1824. Benefit officer.

A. A benefit corporation may have an officer designated as the benefit officer.

B. A benefit officer shall have all of the following:

(1) The powers and duties relating to the purpose of the corporation to create a general public benefit or specific public benefit provided by the bylaws or, absent controlling provisions in the bylaws, by resolutions or orders of the board of directors.

(2) The duty to prepare the benefit report required by R.S. 12:1831.

C. An officer shall not be personally liable for monetary damages for any of the following:

(1) Any act or omission covered by a provision in the articles of incorporation that eliminates or limits the liability of the officer as authorized in R.S. 12:24(C)(4).

(2) Any act or omission as an officer if the officer performed the duties of office pursuant to R.S. 12:91.

(3) Failure of the benefit corporation to pursue or create general public benefit or a specific public benefit.

§ 12:1825. Right of action.

A. The duties of directors and officers under this Chapter and the general public benefit purpose and any specific public benefit purpose of a benefit corporation may be enforced only in accordance with this Section in a benefit enforcement proceeding, and no person shall bring an action or assert a claim against a benefit corporation.

B. A benefit enforcement proceeding shall be commenced or maintained only directly by the benefit corporation or derivatively by one of the following parties:

(1) A shareholder.

(2) A benefit director.

(3) Other persons as specified in the articles or bylaws of the benefit corporation.

Part 4. Transparency

§ 12:1831. Annual benefit report.

A. A benefit corporation shall prepare an annual benefit report including all of the following:

(1) A narrative description of all of the following:

条的规定履行了其职责。

（2）公共利益公司未能追求或实现一般或特定公共利益。

D. 高管不对公共利益公司一般或特定社会目的的受益人负责。

第 12:1824 条　公共利益高管

A. 公共利益公司可以将高管任命为公共利益高管。

B. 公共利益高管应有：

（1）规定于章程细则或者在章程细则没有规定时由董事会决议或命令规定的，与公司创设一般或特定公共利益的公司目的相关的权力和义务。

（2）《路易斯安那州修订法》第 12:1831 条规定的编写公共利益报告的义务。

C. 高管不应当对以下行为承担损害赔偿责任：

（1）公司章程中免除或限制《路易斯安那州修订法》第 12:24（C）（4）项规定的高管责任的条款下的作为或不作为。

（2）高管依据《路易斯安那州修订法》第 12:91 条的规定履行其职务中的作为或不作为。

（3）公共利益公司未能追求或实现一般或者特定公共利益。

第 12:1825 条　诉讼权利

A. 本章规定下董事及高管的义务和公共利益公司的一般和特定公共利益目的可以依据本条规定通过公共利益实施程序实施，并且任何人不得向公共利益公司提起诉讼或主张。

B. 公共利益实施程序应只由公共利益公司直接提起或者由以下主体派生提起：

（1）股东。

（2）公共利益董事。

（3）公共管理公司章程或章程细则中规定的其他人。

第 4 节　透明度

第 12:1831 条　年度公共利益报告

A. 公共利益公司的年度公共利益报告应包括以下内容：

（1）对以下事项的说明：

(a) The ways in which the benefit corporation pursued a general public benefit during the year and the extent to which the general public benefit was created.

(b) The ways in which the benefit corporation pursued a specific public benefit that the articles state it is the purpose of the benefit corporation to create and the extent to which that specific public benefit was created.

(c) Any circumstances that have hindered the creation by the benefit corporation of a general public benefit or specific public benefit.

(d) The process and rationale for selecting or changing the third-party standard used to prepare the benefit report.

(2) An assessment of the performance of the benefit corporation in pursuing the creation of general public benefit against a third-party standard which is either applied consistently with any application of that standard in prior benefit reports or accompanied by an explanation of the reasons for any inconsistent application. The assessment shall not be required to be performed, audited, or certified by a third-party standards provider.

(3) The name of the benefit director and the benefit officer, if any, and the address to which correspondence to each of them may be directed.

(4) The compensation paid by the benefit corporation during the year to each director in the capacity of a director.

(5) The name of each person that owns five percent or more of the outstanding shares of the benefit corporation.

(6) The statement of the benefit director pursuant to R.S. 12:1822(C).

(7) A statement of any connection between the organization that established the third-party standard, or its directors, officers, or any holder of five percent or more of the governance interests in the organization, and the benefit corporation or its directors, officers, or any holder of five percent or more of the outstanding shares of the benefit corporation, including any financial or governance relationship which might materially affect the credibility of the use of the third-party standard.

B. A benefit corporation shall annually send a benefit report to each shareholder either:

(1) Within one hundred twenty days following the end of the fiscal year of the benefit corporation.

(2) At the same time that the benefit corporation delivers any other annual report to its shareholders.

C. A benefit corporation shall post all of its benefit reports on the public portion of its Internet website, if any. The compensation paid to directors and financial or proprietary information included in the benefit reports may be omitted from the benefit reports as posted.

D. If a benefit corporation does not have an Internet website, the benefit corporation shall provide a copy of its most recent benefit report, without charge, to any person that

（a）公共利益公司本年度追求一般公共利益的方法和一般公共利益实现的情况。

（b）公共利益公司追求公司章程中规定的特定公共利益的方法以及该特定公共利益实现的情况。

（c）阻碍公共利益公司实现一般公共利益和特定公共利益的情形。

（d）编写公共利益报告时选择或更换第三方标准的程序和原因。

（2）依据第三方标准对公共利益公司创造一般公共利益的表现作出的评价，其沿用先前公共利益报告中使用的标准或者附一份说明以解释使用与先前不一致的标准的原因。该评价不应被要求由第三方标准提供者执行、审计或者认证。

（3）公共利益董事和公共利益高管的姓名和联系地址。

（4）公共利益公司在上一年度支付给每位董事的薪酬。

（5）拥有公共利益公司已发行股票的5%以上的人员的姓名。

（6）《路易斯安那州修订法》第12:1822（C）款规定要求的公共利益董事陈述意见。

（7）设立第三方标准的机构或其董事、高管、或该机构5%以上管理权利的持有者与公共利益公司或其董事、高管或公共利益公司5%以上已发行股票的持有者之间关系的声明，包括任何有可能实质性影响第三方标准可信度的财务或管理关系。

B. 公共利益公司每年应将公共利益报告送交各股东：

（1）公共利益公司会计年度结束后120天之内。

（2）公共利益公司向其股东送交其他年度报告的同一时间。

C. 若条件允许，公共利益公司应当将其所有公共利益报告发布于其网站的公共部分。公司可以将公共利益报告中的董事薪酬和财务或所有权信息删除。

D. 如果公共利益公司没有网站，应向所有索取报告的个人免费提供最新公共利益报告的副本，但是可以将公共利益报告副本中的董事薪酬和财务、所有权信息

requests a copy, but the compensation paid to directors and financial or proprietary information included in the benefit report may be omitted from the copy of the benefit report provided.

§ 12:1832. Stock certificates.

All certificates representing shares in a benefit corporation shall contain, in addition to any other statements required by the Business Corporation Law, the following conspicuous language on the face of the certificate: "This corporation is a benefit corporation subject to the Benefit Corporations Law, R.S. 12:1801 et seq."

删除。

第 12:1832 条　股票证书

除《商事公司法》要求的声明外，所有代表公共利益公司股份的证书应当在证书表面载明如下明确语句:“公司是受《路易斯安那州修订法》中的《公共利益公司法》第 12:1801 条等规定调整的公共利益公司。”

THE STATE OF MARYLAND

SENATE BILL 690

Effective Date: October 1, 2010

Effect of Amendments: June 1, 2012

AN ACT concerning Corporations

–Benefit Corporation

FOR the purpose of authorizing a corporation to elect to be a certain benefit corporation by amending or including in the charter of the corporation a statement that the corporation is a benefit corporation; providing for the application of this Act; requiring the election to be approved by the stockholders in a certain manner; authorizing a corporation to terminate status as a benefit corporation in a certain manner; requiring that clear reference to the fact that a corporation is a benefit corporation appear prominently in a certain charter document; establishing that every benefit corporation shall have the purpose of creating a certain general public benefit; authorizing the charter of a benefit corporation to identify as one of the purposes of the benefit corporation the creation of certain specific public benefits; establishing that the creation of a certain public benefit as provided in this Act is in the best interests of the benefit corporation; requiring a director of a benefit corporation, in performing the duties of director, in determining what the director reasonably believes to be in the best interests of the benefit corporation, to consider the effects of any action or decision not to act on certain factors; establishing that a certain director shall not have any duty to a certain person; providing that a certain director shall have a certain immunity from liability under certain circumstances; requiring a benefit corporation to deliver to each stockholder a certain annual report; requiring a benefit corporation to post a certain report on its website or provide a copy of the report under certain circumstances; defining certain terms; and generally relating to benefit corporations.

马里兰州

参议院法案　第 690 号

生效日期：2010 年 10 月 1 日

修正案生效日期：2012 年 6 月 1 日

一个关于公司的法案

——公共利益公司

为许可公司通过修改公司章程或者在章程中增加其是公共利益公司的声明转变为公共利益公司制定本法；规定了本法的适用；要求公司行为的选择应由利益相关者以某种方式批准；要求在章程性文件中明确提及该公司是公共利益公司；规定了每个公共利益公司应当有创造某种一般公共利益的目的；授权公共利益公司的章程创设某种特定的公共利益作为公共利益公司的目的；规定了创设的本法规定的公共利益属于公共利益公司的最佳利益；要求公共利益公司的董事，在履行董事义务，考虑什么是董事认为的公共利益公司的最佳利益时，考虑任何行为和决定不要对某些要素产生不利影响；规定了某些董事不应对个人承担任何义务；规定了某些董事在某些情况下应享有豁免权；要求公共利益公司提交给利益相关者一份年度报告；要求公共利益公司将报告公布于其网站或在某些情况下提供报告的副本；界定某些用语的含义；一般与公共利益公司有关。

SECTION 1. BE IT ENACTED BY THE GENERAL ASSEMBLY OF MARYLAND, That the Laws of Maryland read as follows:

Article – Corporations and Associations

SUBTITLE 6C. BENEFIT CORPORATIONS.

§ 5-6C-01. Definitions

(a) In general. -- In this subtitle the following words have the meanings indicated.

(b) Benefit corporation. -- "Benefit corporation" means a Maryland corporation that elects to be a benefit corporation in accordance with § 5–6C–03 of this subtitle and has not ceased to be a benefit corporation through the operation of § 5–6C–04 of this subtitle.

(c) General public benefit. -- "General public benefit" means a material, positive impact on society and the environment, as measured by a third–party standard, through activities that promote a combination of specific public benefits.

(d) Specific public benefit. -- "Specific public benefit" includes:

(1) Providing individuals or communities with beneficial products or services;

(2) Promoting economic opportunity for individuals or communities beyond the creation of jobs in the normal course of business;

(3) Preserving the environment;

(4) Improving human health;

(5) Promoting the arts, sciences, or advancement of knowledge;

(6) Increasing the flow of capital to entities with a public benefit purpose; or

(7) The accomplishment of any other particular benefit for society or the environment.

(e) Third–party standard. -- "Third–party standard" means a standard for defining, reporting, and assessing best practices in corporate social and environmental performance that:

(1) Is developed by a person or entity that is independent of the benefit corporation; and

(2) Is transparent because the following information about the standard is publicly available or accessible:

(i) The factors considered when measuring the performance of a business;

(ii) The relative weightings of those factors; and

(iii) The identity of the persons who developed and control changes to the standard and the process by which those changes were made.

§ 5-6C-02. Applicability of provisions

(a) Maryland General Corporation Law. -- The provisions of the Maryland General

第 1 部分　本法案由马里兰州议会颁布。本法称为：

条例——公司与协会

第 6C 章　公共利益公司

第 5-6C-01 条　定义

（a）一般规定。——本章规定中的用语含义如下。

（b）公共利益公司。——“公共利益公司”是指选择依据本章第 5-6C-03 条的规定成为公共利益公司并且未依据本章第 5-6C-04 条的规定终止公共利益公司形态的马里兰州公司。

（c）一般公共利益。——“一般公共利益”是指根据第三方标准，公司的业务和经营在整体上对社会和环境产生的实质性积极影响。

（d）特定公共利益。——“特定公共利益”包括：

（1）向个人或社区提供有益的产品或服务；

（2）在正常的业务过程中向个人或社区提供创造就业之外的经济机会；

（3）保护环境；

（4）改善人类健康；

（5）促进艺术、科学或知识进步；

（6）促进资本向有公共利益目的的实体流动；或者

（7）给予社会或环境其他特别的利益。

（e）第三方标准。——“第三方标准”是指用于定义、报告和评估公司社会和环境绩效的最佳实践的标准，其应满足以下条件：

（1）由独立于公共利益公司的个人或实体制定；并且

（2）透明，关于标准的以下信息可以公开获取：

（i）衡量企业绩效时所考虑的因素；

（ii）这些标准的相关权重；以及

（iii）制定及控制修改标准和修改程序的人员的身份。

第 5-6C-02 条　规则适用

（a）《马里兰州普通公司法》。——《马里兰州普通公司法》适用于公共利益公司，

Corporation Law apply to benefit corporations except to the extent that:

(1) The context of a provision clearly requires otherwise; or

(2) A specific provision of this subtitle or another provision of law governing specific classes of corporations provides otherwise.

(b) Applicability of subtitle. -- This subtitle applies only to benefit corporations.

(c) Effect of subtitle on other provisions. --

(1) The existence of a provision of this subtitle does not of itself create any implication that a contrary or different rule of law is or would be applicable to a corporation that is not a benefit corporation.

(2) This subtitle does not affect any statute or rule of law as it applies to a corporation that is not a benefit corporation.

(d) Inconsistent provisions of charter or bylaws prohibited. -- A provision of the charter or bylaws of a benefit corporation may not be inconsistent with any provision of this subtitle.

§ 5-6C-03. Election by corporation to become benefit corporation

(a) In general. -- A corporation may elect to be a benefit corporation under this subtitle by amending or including in the charter of the corporation a statement that the corporation is a benefit corporation.

(b) Approval of amendment. -- An amendment described in subsection (a) of this section shall be approved in accordance with Title 2, Subtitle 6 of this article.

(c) Corporate name. -- The name of a domestic benefit corporation or a foreign benefit corporation authorized to transact business in the State must comply with Title 1, Subtitle 5 of this article.

§ 5-6C-04. Termination of status as benefit corporation

(a) In general. -- A corporation may terminate status as a benefit corporation and cease to be subject to this subtitle by amending the charter of the corporation to delete the statement that the corporation is a benefit corporation.

(b) Approval of amendment. -- An amendment terminating a corporation's status as a benefit corporation shall be approved by the stockholders of the corporation in accordance with Title 2, Subtitle 6 of this article.

§ 5-6C-05. Reference to fact of benefit corporation status

Clear reference to the fact that a corporation is a benefit corporation shall appear prominently:

(1) At the head of the charter document in which the election to be a benefit corporation is made;

(2) At the head of each subsequent charter document of the benefit corporation; and

(3) On each certificate representing outstanding stock of the benefit corporation.

除非：

（1）其他条款的内容明确另有规定；或者

（2）该章有特别规定或者调整特别种类公司的其他法律另有规定。

（b）本章规则的适用。——本章规定只适用于公共利益公司。

（c）本章对其他规定的效力。——

（1）本章不应为非公共利益公司设定相反或不同的规则。

（2）本章不影响非公共利益公司有关条文和规则的适用。

（d）禁止公司章程或章程细则中有不一致的规定。——公共利益公司的章程和章程细则的规定不得与本章中的任何规定不一致。

第 5-6C-03 条　公司选择成为公共利益公司

（a）一般规定。——公司可依据本章的规定通过修改公司章程或在章程中增加公司是公共利益公司的声明而成为公共利益公司。

（b）修改的批准。——本条第（a）款中规定的修改应当依据本条例的第 2 编中第 6 章的规定进行批准。

（c）公司名称。——本州公共利益公司或有权在本州经营业务的外州公共利益公司的名称必须遵守本条例第 1 编第 5 章的规定。

第 5-6C-04 条　公共利益公司形态的终止

（a）一般规定。——公司可以通过删除公司章程中本公司为公共利益公司的声明以终止其公共利益公司形态并不再受本章规定的调整。

（b）修改的审批。——终止公司作为公共利益公司形态应当依据本条例第 2 编第 6 章的规定由公司的利益相关者批准。

第 5-6C-05 条　提及公共利益公司形态的事实

明确提及公司是公共利益公司的事实应显著地出现在：

（1）选择成为公共利益公司的章程性文件的最前面；

（2）成为公共利益公司之后的每个章程性文件中；以及

（3）代表公共利益公司已发行股份的证书上。

§ 5-6C-06. Purpose

(a) General public benefit. –

(1) Each benefit corporation shall have the purpose of creating a general public benefit.

(2) The purpose described in paragraph (1) of this subsection is in addition to, and may be a limitation on, the purposes of the corporation under § 2–101 of this article.

(b) Specific public benefit. –

(1) In addition to its purposes under § 2–101 of this article and subsection (a) of this section, the charter of a benefit corporation may identify as one of the purposes of the benefit corporation the creation of one or more specific public benefits.

(2) The identification in its charter of a specific public benefit purpose under paragraph (1) of this subsection does not limit the obligation of a benefit corporation to create a general public benefit.

(c) Creation of benefits are in best interest. -- The creation of a general public benefit or specific public benefit as provided in subsections (a) and (b) of this section is in the best interests of the benefit corporation.

§ 5-6C-07. Duties of director

(a) Consideration of effects on decision making. -- A director of a benefit corporation, in performing the duties of a director, including the director's duties as a member of a committee and in addition to the duties described in § 2–405.1 of this article:

(1) In determining what the director reasonably believes to be in the best interests of the benefit corporation, shall consider the effects of any action, or decision not to act, on:

(i) The stockholders of the benefit corporation;

(ii) The employees and workforce of the benefit corporation and the subsidiaries and suppliers of the benefit corporation;

(iii) The interests of customers as beneficiaries of the general or specific public benefit purposes of the benefit corporation;

(iv) Community and societal considerations, including those of any community in which offices or facilities of the benefit corporation or the subsidiaries or suppliers of the benefit corporation are located; and

(v) The local and global environment; and

(2) May consider any other pertinent factors or the interests of any other group that the director determines are appropriate to consider.

(b) No duty to beneficiary of a public benefit purpose. -- A director of a benefit corporation, in the performance of duties in that capacity, does not have any duty to a person that is a beneficiary of the public benefit purposes of the benefit corporation.

(c) Immunity from liability. -- A director of a benefit corporation, in the reasonable performance of duties in accordance with the standard provided in this subtitle, shall have

第 5-6C-06 条　目的

（a）一般公共利益。——

（1）公共利益公司应有服务于一般公共利益的目的。

（2）本款第（1）项规定的目的是对第 2-101 条规定的公司目的的补充和限制。

（b）特定公共利益。——

（1）在本条例第 2-101 条和本条第（a）款规定的目的之外，公共利益公司的章程可以创设一个或更多的特定公共利益。

（2）依据本款第（1）项的规定在章程中设定的特定公共利益目的并不限制公共利益公司创设一般公共利益的义务。

（c）公共利益的实现是最佳利益。——依据本条第（a）款和第（b）款的规定创设的一般或者特定公共利益是公共利益公司的最佳利益。

第 5-6C-07 条　董事义务

（a）决策效果的考虑。——公共利益公司董事在履行董事义务，包括委员会中董事的义务和本条例第 2-405.1 条规定之外的义务时：

（1）在决定公共利益公司合理的最佳利益时，应当考虑任何作为或不作为行为对以下对象的影响：

（i）公共利益公司的股东；

（ii）公共利益公司、其子公司和其供应商的雇员；

（iii）作为公共利益公司一般或特定公共利益受益者的消费者的利益；

（iv）社区和社会因素，包括公共利益公司、其子公司或其供应商的办公地或设施所在地的社区；

（v）当地和全球环境；以及

（2）可以考虑董事认为合适的其他相关因素或其他群体的利益。

（b）不对公共利益目的的受益人负责。——公共利益公司董事在履行义务时不对公共利益公司的公共利益目的的受益人负责。

（c）责任豁免。——公共利益公司董事依据本章规定的标准合理履行义务应免于承担法院条例第 5-417 条规定的责任。

the immunity from liability described in § 5–417 of the Courts Article.

§ 5-6C-08. Benefit report

(a) Contents. -- A benefit corporation shall deliver to each stockholder an annual benefit report including:

(1) A description of:

(i) The ways in which the benefit corporation pursued a general public benefit during the year and the extent to which the general public benefit was created;

(ii) The ways in which the benefit corporation pursued any specific public benefit that its charter states is the purpose of the benefit corporation to create and the extent to which that specific public benefit was created; and

(iii) Any circumstances that have hindered the creation by the benefit corporation of the public benefit; and

(2) An assessment of the societal and environmental performance of the benefit corporation prepared in accordance with a third–party standard applied consistently with the prior year's benefit report or accompanied by an explanation of the reasons for any inconsistent application.

(b) Timing of delivery. -- The benefit report shall be delivered to each stockholder within 120 days following the end of each fiscal year of the benefit corporation.

(c) Posting on Web site. --

(1) A benefit corporation shall post its most recent benefit report on the public portion of its Web site, if any.

(2) If a benefit corporation does not have a public Web site, the benefit corporation shall provide a copy of its most recent benefit report on demand and without charge to any person who requests a copy.

SECTION 2. AND BE IT FURTHER ENACTED, That this Act shall take effect October 1, 2010.

第 5-6C-08 条　公共利益报告

（a）内容。——公共利益公司应当给每个利益相关者提交年度公共利益报告，包括：

（1）对以下事项的说明：

（i)公共利益公司本年度追求一般公共利益的方法和一般公共利益实现的情况;

（ii）公共利益公司追求公司章程中规定的特定公共利益的方法以及该特定公共利益实现的情况；以及

（iii）阻碍公共利益公司创造公共利益的情形；以及

（2）依据第三方标准对公共利益公司的社会和环境表现作出的评价，沿用先前公共利益报告中使用的标准或者附一份说明以解释使用了与先前不一致的标准的原因。

（b）提交的时间。——公共利益报告应当在公共利益公司会计年度结束后 120 天内提交给每个利益相关者。

（c）发布在网站上。——

（1）公共利益公司应当将其最新的公共利益报告发布于网站的公共部分。

（2）如果公共利益公司没有公开网站，应向所有索取报告的个人免费提供其需要的最新公共利益报告的副本。

第 2 部分　本法案将进一步实施，于 2010 年 10 月 1 日生效。

THE STATE OF MASSACHUSETTS

HOUSE BILL No. 4352

Chapter 156E Benefit Corporations

§ 1. Short Title.

This chapter shall be known and may be cited as the Massachusetts Benefit Corporation Act.

§ 2. Definitions.

As used in this chapter, the following words shall, unless the context otherwise requires, have the following meanings:--

"Benefit corporation", a corporation incorporated under chapter 156A or chapter 156D that has elected to be a benefit corporation under section 4 or 5 and has not ceased to be a benefit corporation by terminating its benefit corporation status under of section 6.

"Benefit director", either: (i) the director designated as the benefit director of a benefit corporation under subsection (a) of section 11; or (ii) a person with any of the powers, duties or rights of a benefit director to the extent provided in the bylaws under to subsection (e) of section 11.

"Benefit enforcement proceeding", a claim or action brought directly by a benefit corporation, or derivatively as authorized by this chapter on behalf of a benefit corporation, against a director or officer for: (i) failure to pursue the general public benefit purpose of the benefit corporation or a specific public benefit purpose set forth in its articles; or (ii) a violation of any obligation, duty or standard of conduct under this chapter.

"Benefit officer", the individual designated as the benefit officer of a benefit corporation under section 13.

"General public benefit", a material, positive impact on society and the environment, taken as a whole, as measured by a third-party standard, from the business and operations of

马萨诸塞州

众议院法案　第 4352 号

第 156E 章　公共利益公司

第 1 条　简称

本章应当被称为或引用为《马萨诸塞州公共利益公司法》。

第 2 条　定义

除非上下文另有规定外，本章中的用语含义如下：——

“公共利益公司”，是指依据第 156A 章或第 156D 章的规定成立的选择成为第 4 条或第 5 条规定的公共利益公司并且未依据第 6 条的规定终止公共利益公司形态的公司。

“公共利益董事”，是指：（i）依据第 11 条第（a）款的规定被任命为公共利益公司的公共利益董事的董事；或者（ii）第 11 条第（e）款规定的拥有公共利益董事的权力、义务或权利的人。

“公共利益实施程序”，是指公共利益公司因以下事项针对董事或高管提起的或者为了公共利益公司由本章授权的主体派生提起的主张或诉讼：（i）未能追求公共利益公司的一般公共利益目的或者公司章程中规定的特定公共利益目的；或者（ii）违反本章规定下的任何义务、责任或行为标准。

“公共利益高管”，是指依据第 13 条的规定被任命为公共利益公司的公共利益高管的人员。

“一般公共利益”，是指根据第三方标准，公司的业务和经营在整体上对社会和环境产生的实质性积极影响。

a benefit corporation.

"Independent", having no material relationship with a benefit corporation or a subsidiary of the benefit corporation; provided, however, that serving as a benefit director or benefit officer shall not preclude a person from being independent; provided further that a material relationship between a person and a benefit corporation or any of its subsidiaries shall be presumed to exist if 1 or more of the following apply:

(1) the person is, or has been within the last year, an employee other than a benefit officer of the benefit corporation or a subsidiary of the benefit corporation;

(2) an immediate family member of the person is, or has been within the last year, an executive officer other than a benefit officer of the benefit corporation or its subsidiary;

(3) there is beneficial or record ownership of 5 percent or more of the outstanding shares of the benefit corporation by: (i) the person; or (ii) an association of which the person is a director, an officer or a manager or in which the person owns beneficially or of record 5 per cent or more of the outstanding equity interests.

"Minimum status vote", (1) in the case of a business corporation, in addition to any other required approval or vote, the satisfaction of the following conditions:

(i) the holders of every class or series shall be entitled to vote on the corporate action regardless of a limitation stated in the articles of organization or bylaws on the voting rights of any class or series; and (ii) the corporate action shall be approved by the affirmative vote of the shareholders of each class or series entitled to cast at least two-thirds of the votes that all shareholders of the class or series are entitled to cast on the action;

(4) in the case of a domestic entity other than a business corporation, in addition to any other required approval, vote or consent, the satisfaction of the following conditions:

(i) the holders of every class or series of equity interest in the entity that are entitled to receive a distribution of any kind from the entity shall be entitled to vote on or consent to the action regardless of any otherwise applicable limitation on the voting or consent rights of any class or series; and

(ii) the action shall be approved by the affirmative vote or consent of the holders described in clause (1) entitled to cast at least two-thirds of the votes or consents that all of those holders are entitled to cast on the action.

"Specific public benefit", any of the following: (1) providing low-income or underserved individuals or communities with beneficial products or services; (2) promoting economic opportunity for individuals or communities beyond the creation of jobs in the normal course of business; (3) promoting the preservation and conservation of the environment; (4) improving human health; (5) promoting the arts, sciences, access to and advancement of knowledge; (6) increasing or facilitating the flow of capital and assets to entities with a general public benefit purpose; or (7) conferring any other particular benefit on society or the

“独立”，是指与公共利益公司或其子公司没有实质性的关系；但是，担任公共利益董事或者公共利益高管不影响其独立性；若出现下列情形，则认为该个体与公共利益公司或其子公司之间存在实质性关系：

（1）该个体是，或过去 1 年内是，公共利益公司或其子公司的除公共利益高管外的雇员；

（2）该个体的直系亲属是，或过去的 1 年内是，公共利益公司或其子公司的除公共利益高管外的执行高管；

（3）下述持有公共利益公司 5% 以上已发行股份的登记股东或实际受益人：（i）个人；或（ii）实体中的个人，是董事、高管或经理或持有公共利益公司 5% 以上已发行股份的登记股东或实际受益人。

“最低表决要求”，（1）在商事公司中，除任何其他对批准或表决的要求外，还应满足以下条件：

（i）每一类别或系列的股东应当有权对公司行为进行投票，即使公司章程或公司章程细则对该类别或系列股东的投票权作出了限制；并且（ii）公司行为必须获得每一类别或系列有投票权的所有股东至少 2/3 的赞成票才能通过；

（4）在非商事公司的本州实体中，除任何其他对批准、表决或赞成的要求外，还应满足以下条件：

（i）该实体的每个类别或系列的任何权益分配形式下的股权持有者应当有权对公司行为进行投票，即使存在任何对该类别或系列的投票权的限制。

（ii）公司行为必须获得在第（i）分项中规定的有投票权的所有股权持有者至少 2/3 的赞成票才能通过。

“特定公共利益”，是指以下内容：（1）向低收入或者低福利人群或社区提供有益的产品或服务；（2）在正常业务过程中向个人或社区提供创造就业之外的经济机会；（3）促进环境的保护或修复；（4）改善人类健康；（5）促进艺术、科学或知识的获取与提高；（6）促进资本和资产向有一般公共利益目的的实体流动；或者（7）给予社会或环境其他特别利益。

environment.

"Third–party standard", a standard for defining, reporting and assessing overall corporate social and environmental performance which is: (1) comprehensive in that it assesses the effect of the business and its operations upon the interests listed in subclauses (ii), (iii), (iv) and (v) of clause (1) of subsection (a) of section 10; (2) developed or performed by a person or organization independent of the benefit corporation and not more than one–third of the members of the governing body of the organization are representatives of any of the following: (i) an association of businesses operating in a specific industry the performance of whose members is measured by the standard; (ii) a business from a specific industry or an association of businesses in that industry; or (iii) a business whose performance is assessed against the standard; (3) not materially financed by an association of business described in clause (2); (4) credible because the standard is developed by a person that: (i) has access to necessary expertise to assess overall corporate social and environmental performance; and (ii) uses a balanced multi–stakeholder approach, including a public comment period of at least 30 days to develop the standard; (5) transparent, because the following information is publicly available about the standard: (i) the criteria considered when measuring the overall social and environmental performance of a business; (ii) the relative weighting of those criteria; (iii) the identity of the directors, officers, material owners and governing body of the organization that developed and control revisions to the standard; and (iv) an accounting of the sources of financial support for the organization, with sufficient detail to disclose any relationship that could reasonably be considered to present a potential conflict of interest.

§ 3. Relation to Other Laws.

(a) Except as otherwise provided in this chapter, a benefit corporation doing business in the commonwealth shall comply with all applicable laws regarding corporations, including chapters 156A and 156D. Chapter 156D shall apply to benefit corporations and they shall enjoy the powers and privileges and be subject to the duties, restrictions and liabilities of corporations organized under said chapter 156D except where inconsistent with this chapter. The existence of this chapter shall not excuse or exempt any business organized under the laws of the commonwealth from complying with all relevant laws and regulations in the commonwealth, except to the extent they are inconsistent with this chapter.

(b) The articles of organization, bylaws or shareholder agreement of a benefit corporation may not relax, be inconsistent with or supersede this chapter. A benefit corporation's articles of organization, bylaws or shareholder agreement that is inconsistent with this chapter shall be void and unenforceable under this subsection and shall not render the entirety or remaining provisions of the articles of organization, bylaws or shareholder agreement void or unenforceable.

“第三方标准”，是指用于定义、报告和评估公司的总体社会和环境绩效的标准，其应满足以下条件：（1）全面，其在评估第10条第（a）款第（1）项的第（ii）、（iii）、（iv）、（v）分项所列利益的基础上评价公司业务和经营绩效；（2）由独立于公共利益公司的个人或组织制定和完成，并且组织的管理层中不多于1/3的成员是以下组织的代表：（i）其成员的绩效由该标准衡量的特定行业的企业协会；（ii）特定行业或者该行业的企业协会中的组织；或者（iii）其绩效由该标准评估的企业；（3）未由第（2）项规定的企业协会提供资金；（4）可信，该标准由此类主体制定：（i）有必要的专业知识以评估公司总体的社会和环境绩效；并且（ii）使用平衡多方相关者利益的方法，包括设定至少30天听取公众意见的期间；（5）透明，关于标准的以下信息可以公开获取：（i）衡量企业整体社会和环境绩效时所考虑的标准；（ii）这些标准的相关权重；（iii）制定和控制修改程序的董事、高管、主要股东和该实体的管理层人员的身份；以及（iv）资金来源的核算，包括充分披露合理认知下存在利益冲突的所有细节。

第3条　与其他法律的关系

（a）除本章另有规定外，在联邦中经营商业的公共利益公司应遵守所有关于公司的可适用法律，包括第156A章和第156D章的规定。第156D章应适用于公共利益公司并且公共利益公司享有第156D章规定的权力和权利，遵守依据第156D章的规定成立的公司的义务、限制和责任，除非本章另有规定。本章不应使依据联邦法成立的企业免于遵守所有相关的联邦法律和规定或拥有豁免权，除非本章另有规定。

（b）公共利益公司的章程、章程细则或股东协议不得放宽、违背或者取代本章规定。与本章不符的公司章程、章程细则或者股东协议依据本款规定应为无效且不可强制执行但不应导致公司章程、章程细则或者股东协议全部或剩余的条款无效或不可强制执行。

§4. Incorporation.

A benefit corporation shall be organized under either chapter 156A or chapter 156D, as applicable, except that a benefit corporation's articles of organization shall make clear reference that it is a benefit corporation.

§ 5. Election of Status.

An existing corporation organized under chapter 156A or chapter 156D may elect to become a benefit corporation by amending its articles of organization to include a statement that the corporation is a benefit corporation. In order to be effective, the amendment shall be adopted by at least the minimum status vote. Such amendment shall be treated as an amendment of the articles under clause (4) of subsection (a) of section 13.02 of said chapter 156D and the shareholders of the corporation shall be entitled to appraisal rights under sections 13.01 to 13.31, inclusive, of said chapter 156D.

§ 6. Termination of Status.

A benefit corporation may terminate its status as a benefit corporation and cease to be subject to this chapter by amending its articles of organization to delete the statement required by sections 4 and 5 that the corporation is a benefit corporation. In order to be effective, the amendment shall be adopted by at least the minimum status vote.

§ 7. Reference to Benefit Corporation Status.

A business corporation organized under the laws of the commonwealth shall not hold itself out as, advertise itself as, or indicate in any way that it is a benefit corporation unless it was organized under and in full compliance with this chapter.

§ 8. Merger and Share Exchange.

(a) An entity that is not a benefit corporation shall become a benefit corporation and shall be subject to this chapter if:

(1) the entity that is not a benefit corporation is a party to a merger or conversion or the entity that is not a benefit corporation is the exchanging corporation in a share exchange; and

(2) the surviving corporation in the merger, share exchange or conversion is to be a benefit Corporation.

(b) In order to be effective, a plan of merger or share exchange subject to this section, shall be adopted by the minimum status vote.

(c) If a corporation that is not a benefit corporation is a party to a merger, share exchange or conversion in which the surviving or resulting corporation is a benefit corporation, the transaction shall be treated as if it were a conversion to nonprofit status for purposes of section 13.02 of chapter 156D and the shareholders of the corporation shall be entitled to appraisal rights under sections 13.01 to 13.31, inclusive, of said chapter 156D.

§ 9. Corporate Purpose.

(a) In addition to its purposes under chapter 156D as a business corporation, a benefit

第 4 条　设立

公共利益公司应当按照第 156A 章或者第 156D 章的规定设立，但其公司章程必须明确声明其是公共利益公司。

第 5 条　形态的选择

已成立的公司可依据第 156A 章或第 156D 章的规定转变为公共利益公司，公司需修改其公司章程以增加公司是公共利益公司的声明。公司章程的修改应满足最低表决要求。此种修改应当属于第 156D 章的第 13.02 条的第（a）款第（4）项规定的对公司章程的修改并且公司股东应当依据第 156D 章中第 13.01 条至第 13.31 条的规定享有股份回购请求权。

第 6 条　形态的终止

公共利益公司可以通过删除第 4 条和第 5 条规定的公司章程中作为公共利益公司的声明来终止其公共利益公司形态并不再受本章规定调整。公司章程的修改应满足最低表决要求。

第 7 条　提及公共利益公司形态

依据联邦法成立的商事公司不应当主张、宣传或者用任何方法表明自己是公共利益公司，除非它依据本章规定成立并完全遵守本章规定。

第 8 条　合并和股票置换

（a）如果满足以下条件，非公共利益公司实体将成为公共利益公司并且接受本章规定的调整：

（1）非公共利益公司的实体是合并或财产转换的一方或者非公共利益公司的实体是股权置换中的置换公司；并且

（2）合并、股权置换或者财产转换中的存续公司将成为公共利益公司。

（b）本条规定下的合并或者股权置换计划应当满足最低表决要求。

（c）如果非公共利益公司是合并、股票置换或者财产转换中的一方，其中存续或新设的公司为公共利益公司，该交易应视为该公司根据第 156D 章第 13.02 条的规定转为非营利状态，公司股东应当依据第 156D 章中第 13.01 条至第 13.31 条的规定享有回购请求权。

第 9 条　公司目的

（a）在第 156D 章规定的商事公司目的之外，公共利益公司应有服务于一般公

corporation shall have the purpose of creating general public benefit.

(b) The articles of organization of a benefit corporation may identify 1 or more specific public benefits that it is the purpose of the benefit corporation to create in addition to its purpose as a business corporation and under subsection (a). The identification of a specific public benefit under this subsection shall not limit the obligation of a benefit corporation under subsection (a).

(c) The creation of a general public benefit and a specific public benefit under subsections (a) and (b) shall be in the best interest of the benefit corporation.

(d) A benefit corporation may amend its articles of organization to add, amend or delete the identification of a specific public benefit under chapter 156D; provided, however, that the elimination of an optional specific public benefit shall not significantly diminish or eliminate the general public benefit required in this subsection.

(e) A professional corporation that is a benefit corporation shall not be in violation of section 3 of chapter 156A by having the purpose to create a general public benefit or a specific public benefit.

§ 10. Standard of Conduct for Directors.

(a) In discharging the duties of their respective positions and in considering the best interests of the benefit corporation, the board of directors, committees of the board and individual directors of a benefit corporation:

(1) shall consider the effects of any action upon:

(i) the shareholders of the benefit corporation;

(ii) the employees and workforce of the benefit corporation, its subsidiaries and its suppliers;

(iii) the interest of customers or clients as beneficiaries of the general public benefit or specific public benefit purposes of the benefit corporation;

(iv) community and societal factors, including those of each community in which offices or facilities of the benefit corporation, its subsidiaries or its suppliers are located;

(v) the local, regional and global environment;

(vi) the short–term and long–term interests of the benefit corporation, including benefits that may accrue to the benefit corporation from its long–term plans and the possibility that these interests may be best served by the continued independence of the benefit corporation; and

(vii) the ability of the benefit corporation to accomplish its general public benefit purpose and any specific public benefit purpose; and

(2) may consider:

(i) the interests of the economy of the state, the region and the country under clause (3) of subsection (a) of section 8.30 of chapter 156D; or

共利益的目的。

（b）公共利益公司的章程可以在第（a）款的规定之外确定一项或者多项公共利益公司要实现的而且在商事公司目的之外的特定公共利益。依据本款规定设定的特定的公共利益目的并不限制公共利益公司在本条第（a）款下的义务。

（c）依据第（a）款和第（b）款的规定创设的一般和特定公共利益为公共利益公司的最佳利益。

（d）公共利益公司可以修订公司章程增加、修改或删除第156D章规定下的特定公共利益；但是，删去一项特定公共利益不应当明显地减少或消除本款规定的一般公共利益。

（e）选择公共利益形态的专业公司并不因其有创设一般或特定公共利益的目的而违反第156A章第3条的规定。

第10条　董事行为标准

（a）在履行各自职责和考虑公共利益公司的最佳利益时，公共利益公司的董事会、董事委员会和董事：

（1）应当考虑作为或不作为对以下对象的影响：

（i）公共利益公司的股东；

（ii）公共利益公司、其子公司和其供应商的雇员；

（iii）作为公共利益公司一般或特定公共利益受益者的消费者的利益；

（iv）社区和社会因素，包括公共利益公司、其子公司或其供应商的办公地或设施所在地的社区；

（v）当地、地区和全球环境；

（vi）公共利益公司的短期和长期利益，包括从其长期计划中产生的利益以及公共利益公司继续保持独立可能产生的最佳利益；以及

（vii）公共利益公司实现其一般公共利益目的和特定公共利益目的的能力；并且

（2）可以考虑：

（i）第156D章的第8.30条第（a）款第（3）项中规定的州、地区和乡村的经济利益；或者

(ii) other pertinent factors or the interests of any other group that they consider deem appropriate.

(b) Directors shall consider the factors in clause (1) of subsection (a) using sound and reasonable judgment in determining corporate actions and the best interests of the benefit corporation. Directors shall not be required to give priority to the interests of a particular person or group referred to in clauses (1) or (2) of said subsection (a) over the interests of any other person or group unless the benefit corporation has stated in its articles its intention to give priority to certain interests related to its accomplishment of its general public benefit purpose or of a specific public benefit purpose identified in its articles.

(c) The consideration of interests and factors in the manner required by subsection (a) shall not constitute a violation of section 8.01 of Chapter 156D.

(d) A director shall not be personally liable for monetary damages for:

(1) any action or inaction as a director if the director performed the duties of office in compliance with section 8.30 of chapter 156D and this section; or

(2) failure of the benefit corporation to pursue or create general public benefit or a specific public benefit.

(e) A director shall not have a fiduciary duty to a person that is a beneficiary of the general or specific public benefit purposes of a benefit corporation arising from the status of the person as a beneficiary.

§ 11. Benefit Director.

(a) The board of directors of a benefit corporation shall include 1 director who shall:

(1) be designated the benefit director; and

(2) have, in addition to the powers, duties, rights and immunities of the other directors of the benefit corporation, the powers, duties, rights and immunities provided in this chapter.

(b) The benefit director shall be elected, and may be removed, in the manner provided under chapter 156D and shall be an individual who is independent. The benefit director may serve as the benefit officer at the same time as serving as the benefit director. The articles of organization, bylaws or shareholder agreement of a benefit corporation may prescribe additional qualifications of the benefit director consistent with this section.

(c) The benefit director shall prepare and the benefit corporation shall include in the annual shareholder's report the opinion of the benefit director on the following:

(1) whether the benefit corporation acted in accordance with its general public benefit and any specific public benefit purpose in all material respects during the period covered by the report;

(2) whether the directors and officers complied with subsection (a) of section 10 and subsection (a) of section 12;

(3) whether, in the opinion of the benefit director, the benefit corporation or its directors

（ii）董事认为合适的其他相关因素或其他群体的利益。

（b）董事在对公司行为和公司的最佳利益进行充分理性的判断时应当考虑第（a）款第（1）项规定的因素。除公司章程中要求优先考虑的利益或因素外，相对于其他人或组织的利益，董事不应被要求优先考虑第（a）款第（1）项或第（2）项规定中某个特定人或组织的利益。

（c）对第（a）款中规定的利益和相关因素的考虑不违反第156D章第8.01条的规定。

（d）董事不对以下行为承担损害赔偿责任：

（1）董事依据第156D章第8.30条和本条的规定履行职务的任何作为或者不作为；或者

（2）公共利益公司未能追求或创造一般或特定公共利益。

（e）董事不对公共利益公司一般或特定社会目的的受益人负信义义务。

第11条　公共利益董事

（a）公共利益公司的董事会应当包括满足以下条件的董事：

（1）被任命为公共利益董事；并且

（2）有公共利益公司的其他董事的权力、义务、权利和豁免权以外，还有本章规定的权力、义务、权利和豁免权。

（b）公共利益董事应当依据第156D章的规定任免，并且应当是独立个体。公共利益董事可以同时担任公共利益高管。公共利益公司的章程、章程细则或股东协议可以对公共利益董事的资格作出与本条不一致的规定。

（c）公共利益董事应当编写其对以下事项的意见并将其收入年度股东报告：

（1）在报告所述期间内，公共利益公司是否在所有重要事项上依其一般和特定公共利益目的行事；

（2）董事和高管是否分别依第10条第（a）款和第12条第（a）款的规定行事；

（3）如果公共利益董事认为公共利益公司、董事或高管未能依第（b）款的规

or officers failed to comply with subsection (b) and, if so, a description of the ways in which the benefit corporation or its directors or officers failed to comply; and

(4) what impact the corporation's status as a benefit corporation is having on its business, including client or consumer opinion, return on investment, impact on shareholders and impact on employees.

(d) The action or inaction of an individual in the capacity of a benefit director shall constitute, for all purposes, an action or inaction of that individual in the capacity of a director of the benefit corporation.

(e) (1) A shareholder agreement of a benefit corporation adopted under subsection (a) of section 7.32 of chapter 156D shall provide that the persons or shareholders who perform the duties of the board of directors shall include a person with the powers, duties, rights and immunities of a benefit director specified under subsection (d) of section 10.

(2) A person that exercises 1 or more of the powers, duties or rights of a benefit director under this subsection shall:

(i) not be required to be independent of the benefit corporation;

(ii) have the immunities of a benefit director;

(iii) not be subject to the procedures for election or removal of directors in chapter 156D unless the person is also a director of the benefit corporation or the shareholder agreement makes those procedures applicable; and

(iv) may share the powers, duties and rights of a benefit director with 1 or more other persons.

(f) The benefit director of a professional corporation shall not be required to be independent.

(g) Regardless of whether the bylaws of a benefit corporation include a provision eliminating or limiting the personal liability of directors authorized by chapter 156D, a benefit director shall not be personally liable for an act or omission in the capacity of a benefit director unless the act or omission constitutes self-dealing, willful and intentional misconduct or a knowing violation of the law.

§ 12. Standard of Conduct for Officers.

(a) Each officer of a benefit corporation shall consider the interests and factors described in clause (1) of subsection (a) of section 10 in the manner provided in said subsection (a) if:

(1) the officer has discretion to act with respect to a matter; and

(2) it reasonably appears to the officer that the matter may have a material effect on the creation of a general public benefit or a specific public benefit by the benefit corporation:

(b) The consideration of interests and factors in the manner described in clause (1) of subsection (a) shall not constitute a violation of section 8.41 of chapter 156D.

定行事，应在意见中陈述公共利益公司、董事或高管未能履行职责的情况；以及

（4）在业务上影响公共利益公司的公司形态的事项，包括客户或消费者意见、投资回报、对股东和雇员的影响。

（d）公共利益董事在职权范围内个人的作为或不作为应视为该公共利益公司董事的行为。

（e）（1）依据第156D章第7.32条第（a）款规定制定的公共利益公司的股东协议应当规定履行董事会义务的人或股东包括拥有第10条第（d）款规定的公共利益董事的权力、义务、权利或者豁免权的人。

（2）依据本款规定有公共利益董事的一项或更多权力、义务、权利或者豁免权的人应当：

（i）不被要求独立于公共利益公司；

（ii）有公共利益董事的豁免权；

（iii）不受第156D章规定的董事任免程序的调整，除非此人也是公共利益公司的董事或者股东协议要求适用该程序；以及

（iv）可以与一个或更多的其他人分享公共利益董事的权力、义务和权利。

（f）不要求专业公司的公共利益董事具有独立性。

（g）无论公共利益公司的章程细则是否依据第156D章的规定删除或限制董事的个人责任，公共利益董事在行使公共利益董事职责时，不对其任何作为或不作为承担个人责任，但自我交易或故意违法行为除外。

第12条　高管的行为标准

（a）公共利益公司的高管应当以第（a）款中规定的行为标准考虑第10条第（a）款第（1）项中规定的利益和因素，如果：

（1）高管对该行为有自由裁量权；并且

（2）高管有合理理由认为该行为对公共利益公司在公司章程中创设的一般或特定公共利益有实质性影响。

（b）对第（a）款第（1）项中规定的利益和相关因素的考虑不违反第156D章第8.41条的规定。

(c) An officer shall not be personally liable for monetary damages for:

(1) any action or inaction as an officer if the officer performed the duties of the position in compliance with chapter 156D and this section; or

(2) failure of the benefit corporation to pursue or create a general public benefit or a specific public benefit.

(d) An officer shall not have a fiduciary duty to a person that is a beneficiary of the general or specific public benefit purposes of a benefit corporation arising from the status of the person as a beneficiary.

§ 13. Benefit Officer.

A benefit corporation may have an officer designated as the benefit officer. A benefit officer shall have:

(1) the powers and duties relating to the purpose of the corporation to create a general public benefit or a specific public benefit provided:

(i) by the bylaws; or

(ii) absent controlling provisions in the bylaws, by resolutions or orders of the board of directors; and

(2) the duty to oversee and prepare the annual benefit report required by subsection (a) of section 15.

§ 14. Benefit Enforcement Proceeding.

(a) (1) The duties under this chapter and the general public benefit purpose and any specific public benefit purpose of a benefit corporation may be enforced only in a benefit enforcement proceeding.

(2) Except in a benefit enforcement proceeding, no person shall bring an action or assert a claim against a benefit corporation or its directors or officers with respect to:

(i) failure to pursue or create general or specific public benefits set forth in its articles; or

(ii) a violation of a duty or standard of conduct under this chapter.

(3) A benefit corporation shall not be liable for monetary damages under this chapter for any failure of the benefit corporation to pursue or create a general public benefit or a specific public benefit.

(b) A benefit enforcement proceeding shall be commenced or maintained only:

(1) directly by the benefit corporation; or

(2) derivatively by:

(i) a shareholder;

(ii) a director;

(iii) a person or group of persons that owns beneficially or of record 5 per cent or more of the equity interests in an association of which the benefit corporation is a subsidiary; or

（c）高管不对以下行为承担损害赔偿责任：

（1）高管的任何作为或者不作为，如果该高管依据第 156D 章以及本条的规定已履行高管职责；或者

（2）公共利益公司未能追求或创造一般或特定公共利益。

（d）高管不应对公共利益公司一般或特定社会目的的受益人负信义义务。

第 13 条　公共利益董事

公共利益公司可以将高管任命为公共利益高管。公共利益高管应当拥有：

（1）规定于以下文件的创设一般或特定公共利益目的的权力和义务：

（i）公司章程细则；或者

（ii）在公司章程细则中没有规定时，董事会的决议或者命令。

（2）按第 15 条第（a）款的要求监督和编写公共利益报告的义务。

第 14 条　公共利益实施程序

（a）（1）本章规定下的义务和公共利益公司的一般和特定公共利益目的可以通过公共利益实施程序实施。

（2）非经公共利益实施程序，任何人不得因以下事项向公共利益公司或者其董事或高管提起诉讼或主张：

（i）未能追求或实现在其公司章程中陈述的一般或特定公共利益；或者

（ii）违反本章规定下的义务或行为标准。

（3）公共利益公司不对本章规定下任何未能追求或实现一般或特定公共利益的行为承担损害赔偿责任。

（b）公共利益实施程序只能由以下主体提起：

（1）由公共利益公司直接提起；或者

（2）被以下主体派生提起：

（i）股东；

（ii）董事；

（iii）拥有公共利益公司母公司 5% 以上股份的登记股东或实际受益人；或者

a person or group of persons that owned beneficially or of record 5% or more of the outstanding equity interests in an entity of which the benefit corporation is a subsidiary at the time of the act or omission complained of; or

(iv) other persons as specified in the articles of organization, bylaws or shareholder agreement of the benefit corporation.

§ 15. Annual Benefit Report -- Contents.

(a) A benefit corporation shall prepare an annual benefit report, including all of the following information:

(1) a narrative description of:

(i) the ways in which the benefit corporation pursued a general public benefit during the year and the extent to which general public benefit was created;

(ii) the ways in which the benefit corporation pursued a specific public benefit that the articles of organization state it is the purpose of the benefit corporation to create and the extent to which that specific public benefit was created;

(iii) any circumstances that have hindered the creation by the benefit corporation of general public benefit or specific public benefit; and

(iv) the process and rationale for selecting or changing the third–party standard used to prepare the benefit report;

(2) an assessment of the overall social and environmental performance of the benefit corporation against a third–party standard:

(i) applied consistently with any application of that standard in prior benefit reports; or

(ii) accompanied by an explanation of the reasons for any inconsistent application;

(3) the name of the benefit director and the benefit officer, if any, and the address to which correspondence to each of them may be directed;

(4) the compensation paid by the benefit corporation during the year to each director in the capacity of a director;

(5) the name of each person that owns 5 per cent or more of the outstanding shares of the benefit corporation either: (i) of record; or (ii) beneficially, to the extent known to the benefit corporation without investigation;

(6) the statement of the benefit director described in subsection (c) of section 11;

(7) a statement of any connection between the organization that established the third–party standard, or its directors, officers or any holder of 5 per cent or more of the governance interests in the organization, and the benefit corporation or its directors, officers or any holder of 5 per cent or more of the outstanding shares of the benefit corporation, including any financial or governance relationship which might materially affect the credibility of the use of the third–party standard; and

(8) if the benefit corporation has dispensed with, or restricted the discretion or powers

（iv）公共利益公司章程、章程细则或股东协议中列明的其他人员。

第 15 条　年度公共利益报告——内容

（a）公共利益公司的年度公共利益报告应包括以下内容：

（1）对以下事项的说明：

（i）公共利益公司本年度追求一般公共利益的方法和实现的情况；

（ii）公共利益公司追求公司章程中规定的特定公共利益的方法和实现的情况；

（iii）阻碍公共利益公司创造一般和特定公共利益的情形；以及

（iv）编写公共利益报告时选择或更换第三方标准的程序和原因；

（2）依据第三方标准对公共利益公司的社会和环境表现作出的整体评价：

（i）沿用先前公共利益报告中使用的标准；或者

（ii）附一份说明以解释使用与先前不一致的标准的原因；

（3）公共利益董事和公共利益高管的姓名和联系地址（如有）；

（4）公共利益公司在上一年度支付给每位董事的薪酬。

（5）拥有 5% 以上的公共利益公司已发行股份的人员的姓名：（i）名义上的；或者（ii）实质上的，公共利益公司无需调查即知晓的；

（6）第 11 条第（c）款规定的公共利益董事的陈述意见；

（7）设立第三方标准的机构或其董事、高管、或该机构 5% 以上管理权利的持有者与公共利益公司、其董事、高管或公共利益公司 5% 以上已发行股份的持有者之间关系的声明，包括任何有可能实质性影响第三方标准可信度的财务或管理关系。

（8）如果公共利益公司免除或者限制董事会的自由裁量权，需说明：

of the board of directors, a description of:

(i) the persons that exercise the powers, duties and rights and who have the immunities of the board of directors; and

(ii) the benefit director, as required by subsection (d) of section 11.

(b) Nothing in this chapter shall require the benefit report or the assessment of the performance of the benefit corporation in the benefit report required by clause (2) of subsection (a) to be audited or certified by a third party standards provider.

§ 16. Annual Benefit Report -- Distribution.

(a) The annual benefit report shall be sent to each shareholder at the same time that the benefit corporation delivers any other annual report to its shareholders, or within 120 days following the end of the fiscal year of the benefit corporation.

(b) A benefit corporation shall post its most recent annual benefit report on the public portion of its website, if any, but the compensation paid to directors and financial, confidential or proprietary information included in the benefit report may be omitted from the benefit report as posted.

(c) If a benefit corporation does not have a website, the benefit corporation shall provide a copy of its most recent benefit report, without charge to any person that requests a copy, but the compensation paid to directors and financial or proprietary information included in the benefit report may be omitted from the copy of the benefit report provided.

(d) The benefit corporation shall deliver a copy of the benefit report to the state secretary, with its annual report required by section 16.22 of chapter 156D, but the compensation paid to directors and financial, confidential or proprietary information included in the benefit report may be omitted from the benefit report as filed. The state secretary shall charge a fee of $ 75 for filing a benefit report in addition to the fee required for the annual report.

（i）行使权力、履行权利和义务并享有董事会豁免权的人；以及

（ii）第 11 条第（d）款要求的公共利益董事。

（b）本章没有要求公共利益报告或者第（a）款第（2）项中要求的公共利益报告中对公共利益公司表现的评估需经第三方标准的提供者审计或认证。

第 16 条　年度公共利益报告——分发

（a）公共利益公司应当在公共利益公司向其股东送交其他年度报告的同一时间，或者公共利益公司会计年度结束后 120 天内将公共利益报告送交各股东。

（b）如果条件允许，公共利益公司应当将其所有公共利益报告发布于其网站的公共部分；但是可以将公共利益报告中的董事薪酬和财务、所有权信息删除。

（c）如果公共利益公司没有网站，其应在任何个人索取副本时向其免费提供最新公共利益报告的副本，但是可以将公共利益报告副本中的董事薪酬和财务、所有权信息删除。

（d）公共利益公司应当将该公共利益报告的副本，和第 156D 章第 16.22 条要求的年度报告提交给州务卿，但是可以将公共利益报告中的董事薪酬和财务、所有权信息在备案的公共利益报告中删除。州务卿应当在年报要求的费用之外收取 75 美元的公共利益报告备案费。

THE STATE OF MINNESOTA

State of Minnesota

HOUSE OF REPRESENTATIVES

EIGHTY-EIGHTH SESSION

H.F.No. 2582

A bill for an act relating to corporations; providing for the organization and operation of public benefit corporations; proposing coding for new law as Minnesota Statutes, chapter 304A.

BE IT ENACTED BY THE LEGISLATURE OF THE STATE OF MINNESOTA:

Section 1. 304A.001 CITATION

This chapter may be cited as the "Minnesota Public Benefit Corporation Act."

APPLICATION

Sec.2. 304A.011 APPLICATION AND EFFECT OF CHAPTER

Subdivision 1. General rule.

This chapter applies to all public benefit corporations.

Subd. 2. Laws applicable.

Chapter 302A applies to all public benefit corporations and all statutes and rules of law that apply to a corporation formed under chapter 302A also apply to a public benefit corporation. If chapter 302A conflicts with sections 304A.001 to 304A.301, sections 304A.001 to 304A.301 govern. The chapter does not affect a statute or rule of law that applies to a corporation formed under chapter 302A that is not a public benefit corporation.

明尼苏达州

明尼苏达州

众议院

第八十八次会议

H.F. 第 2582 号

关于公司的法案；规定了公共利益公司的组织和经营；提议制定新法作为《明尼苏达州法典》的第 304A 章。

本法案由明尼苏达州立法机构颁布：

第 304A.001 条　引用

本章可被引用为《明尼苏达公共利益公司法》。

适用

第 304A.011 条　本章的适用与效力

第 1 款　一般规则

本章适用于所有公共利益公司。

第 2 款　适用的法律

第 302A 章的规定适用于所有公共利益公司，依据第 302A 章的规定成立的公司所适用的所有法律和规则也适用于公共利益公司。如果第 302A 章的规定与第 304A.001 条至第 304A.301 条的规定相冲突，适用第 304A.001 条至第 304A.301 条的规定。该章不影响依据第 302A 章的规定成立的非公共利益公司的有关条文和规则的适用。

Subd. 3. Articles;bylaws.

A provision of the articles, shareholder control agreement, or bylaws of a public benefit corporation may not limit, be inconsistent with, or supersede a provision of this chapter.

304A.021 DEFINITIONS

Subdivision 1. Terms.

For the purposes of this chapter, unless the language or context clearly indicates that a different meaning is intended, the words, terms, and phrases defined in this section have the meanings given them.

Subd. 2. General benefit corporation.

"General benefit corporation" means a public benefit corporation that elects in its articles to pursue general public benefit and that may state in its articles a specific public benefit purpose it elects to pursue.

Subd. 3. General public benefit.

"General public benefit" means a net material positive impact from the business and operations of a general benefit corporation on society, the environment, and the well–being of present and future generations.

Subd. 4. Independent.

"Independent" means having no material relationship with a public benefit corporation or a parent, a subsidiary, or other affiliate of a public benefit corporation.

Subd. 5. Minimum status vote.

"Minimum status vote" means that the shareholders shall take action by the affirmative vote of the holders of at least two–thirds of all of the issued and outstanding shares.

Subd. 6. Organization.

"Organization" means a domestic or foreign business or nonprofit corporation, limited liability company, whether domestic or foreign, partnership, limited partnership, joint venture, association, trust, estate, enterprise, or other legal or commercial entity.

Subd. 7. Public benefit corporation.

"Public benefit corporation" means a corporation formed under chapter 302A:

(1) that has elected to become subject to this chapter; and

(2) whose status as a public benefit corporation has not been terminated or revoked.

Subd. 8. Specific benefit corporation.

"Specific benefit corporation" means a public benefit corporation that states in its articles a specific public benefit purpose it elects to pursue, but does not include a general benefit corporation that states in its articles a specific public benefit purpose it elects to pursue.

第 3 款　公司章程；章程细则

公共利益公司的章程，股东控制协议或者章程细则的条款不得限制、违背或取代本章的规定。

第 304A.021 条　定义

第 1 款　用语

除本章中的语言或者上下文明确另有规定外，本节中的词语、用语和短语的含义如下。

第 2 款　一般公共利益公司

"一般公共利益公司"指在其公司章程中规定追求的一般公共利益和在其公司章程中规定追求的特定公共利益目的的公共利益公司。

第 3 款　一般公共利益

"一般公共利益"是指，公共利益公司的业务和经营活动对社会、环境和现代及后代福祉产生的实质性积极影响。

第 4 款　独立

"独立"是指，与公共利益公司或公共利益公司的母公司，子公司或者其他关联机构没有实质性的关系。

第 5 款　最低表决要求

"最低表决要求"是指，股东采取行动应获得所有已发行股份至少 2/3 的赞成票才能通过。

第 6 款　组织

"组织"是指，本州或外州的商业或非营利公司、有限责任公司（无论本州还是外州），合伙、有限合伙、合资企业、协会、信托、不动产、企业，或者其他法律或商业实体。

第 7 款　公共利益公司

"公共利益公司"是指，一家依据第 302A 章的规定成立的公司：

（1）选择接受本章规定调整；并且

（2）公共利益公司形态并未终止或被撤销。

第 8 款　特定公共利益公司

"特定公共利益公司"是指，在公司章程中规定其追求的特定公共利益目的的公共利益公司，但不包括在公司章程中规定追求特定公共利益目的的一般公共利益公司。

Subd. 9. Specific public benefit.

"Specific public benefit" means one or more positive impacts, or reduction of a negative impact, on specified categories of natural persons, entities, communities, or interests, other than shareholders in their capacity as shareholders, as enumerated in the articles of a public benefit corporation.

Subd. 10. Third-party standard.

"Third–party standard" means:

(1) a publicly available standard or guideline for defining, reporting, and assessing the performance of a business enterprise as a social or benefit corporation;

(2) promulgated by a natural person or an organization; and

(3) that is independent of the public benefit corporation.

304A.101 INCORPORATION OF A PUBLIC BENEFIT CORPORATION

Subdivision 1. Incorporation.

A public benefit corporation must be incorporated in accordance with chapter 302A, and its articles must also state that the public benefit corporation is a:

(1) general benefit corporation;

(2) general benefit corporation that also elects to pursue a specific public benefit purpose as stated in its articles; or

(3) a specific benefit corporation that elects to pursue a specific public benefit purpose as stated in its articles.

Subd. 2. Name requirements.

A public benefit corporation name must comply with the requirements of section 302A.115 other than subdivision 1, paragraph (b), and with respect to:

(1) a general benefit corporation, contain the words "general benefit corporation," or the abbreviation "GBC;" and

(2) a specific benefit corporation, contain the words "specific benefit corporation," or the abbreviation "SBC."

304A.102 ELECTION OF PUBLIC BENEFIT CORPORATION STATUS

Subdivision 1. By amendment.

In accordance with the procedures stated in chapter 302A and with approval by the minimum status vote, an existing corporation formed under chapter 302A may elect to become a public benefit corporation under this chapter by amending its articles to meet the requirements of section 304A.101.

第 9 款　特定公共利益

“特定公共利益”是指，除股东外，对公共利益公司章程中列举的特定种类的自然人、实体、社区或利益的一种或多种积极影响，或负面影响的减少。

第 10 款　第三方标准

“第三方标准”是指：

（1）用于定义、报告和评估作为社会或公共利益公司的商事企业绩效的公开标准或指引；

（2）由自然人或者组织公布；以及

（3）独立于公共利益公司。

第 304A.101 条　公共利益公司的设立

第 1 款　设立

公共利益公司应当按照第 302A 章的规定设立，但其公司章程必须声明公共利益公司是：

（1）一般公共利益公司；

（2）选择追求章程中声明的特定公共利益的一般公共利益公司；或者

（3）选择追求章程中声明的特定公共利益的特定公共利益公司。

第 2 款　名称要求

公共利益公司的名称必须遵守第 302A.115 条中第 1 款第（b）项外的规定：

（1）一般公共利益公司，包含“一般公共利益公司”字样，或者“GBC”的缩写；并且

（2）特定公共利益公司，包含“特定公共利益公司”字样，或者“SBC”的缩写。

第 304A.102 条　公共利益公司状态的选择

第 1 款　通过修改

依据第 302A 章规定的程序并在满足最低表决要求的情况下，依据第 302A 章规定成立的公司可依据本章规定选择成为公共利益公司，公司需修改章程以满足第 304A.101 条的要求。

Subd. 2. By merger, exchange, conversion, or transfer.

(a) This subdivision applies if:

(1) an organization, other than a nonprofit corporation, that is not a public benefit corporation is a party to a merger, exchange, or conversion, or a transfer in accordance with section 302A.601; and

(2) the surviving organization in the merger, the acquiring organization in an exchange, the converted organization in the conversion, or the transferee is to be a public benefit corporation.

(b) If this subdivision applies, the transfer or the plan of merger, exchange, or conversion, must be adopted in accordance with the procedures stated in chapter 302A and with approval by the minimum status vote.

Subd. 3. Rights of dissenting shareholders.

A shareholder of a corporation or the member of a limited liability company may dissent from, and obtain payment for the fair value of the shareholder's shares or the member's membership interests pursuant to sections 302A.471 and 302A.473, or section 322B.383 or 322B.386, in the event of an election of public benefit corporation status pursuant to this section.

304A.103 TERMINATION OF PUBLIC BENEFIT CORPORATION STATUS

Subdivision 1. By amendment.

In accordance with the procedures stated in chapter 302A and with approval by the minimum status vote, a public benefit corporation may terminate its status as a public benefit corporation and cease to be subject to this chapter by amending its articles to delete the requirements of section 304A.101, subdivision 1, and change its name to remove the information required by section 304A.101, subdivision 2.

Subd. 2. Merger, exchange, conversion, or transfer.

If a merger, exchange, conversion, or transfer would have the effect of terminating the status of a public benefit corporation under this chapter, the transfer or the plan of merger, exchange, or conversion must be approved by the minimum status vote.

Subd. 3. Rights of dissenting shareholders.

A shareholder of a public benefit corporation may dissent from, and obtain payment for the fair value of the shareholder's shares pursuant to sections 302A.471 and 302A.473 in the event of a termination of public benefit corporation status pursuant to this section.

Subd. 4. Effects of termination.

A public benefit corporation that terminates its status, or has its status revoked more than once pursuant to section 304A.301, subdivision 5, may not elect to become a public

第 2 款　通过合并，置换，转换或转让

（a）如有以下情形，适用本款规定：

（1）非营利公司以外的非公共利益公司，是依据第 302A.601 条的规定进行合并、置换、转换或转让的一方；以及

（2）合并中的存续组织，置换中的收购组织，转换中的转换组织或者受让人是公共利益公司；

（b）若适用本款规定，转让、合并、置换或转换的计划应当依据第 302A 章规定的程序获得批准并满足最低表决要求。

第 3 款　异议股东的权利

公司股东或者有限责任公司的成员可反对依据本条规定选择公共利益公司形态，并且可以依据第 302A.471 条和第 302A.473 条，或者第 322B.383 条或第 322B.386 条的规定，获得公司对股份或者成员权的公允价格偿付。

第 304A.103 条　公共利益公司形态的终止

第 1 款　通过修改

依据第 302A 章规定的程序和在满足最低表决要求的情况下，公共利益公司可通过修改公司章程删除第 304A.101 条中第 1 款的要求并通过改变名称移除第 304A.101 条第 2 款要求的信息，来终止其公共利益公司的形态并不再受本章规定调整。

第 2 款　合并，置换，转换或转让

如果依据本章规定，合并，置换，转换或转让有终止公共利益公司形态的效力，转让或者合并、置换、转换的计划必须满足最低表决要求。

第 3 款　异议股东的权利

公共利益公司的股东可以反对依据本条规定终止公共利益公司形态并且依据第 302A.471 条和第 302A.473 条的规定获得对其股份的公允价格偿付。

第 4 款　终止的效力

不止一次依据第 304A.301 条第 5 款的规定终止或者撤销其形态的公共利益公司不得再依据本章规定选择成为公共利益公司，直到其终止或撤销行为生效之后经过

benefit corporation under this chapter until three years have passed since the effective date of termination or revocation.

304A.104 PUBLIC BENEFIT CORPORATION PURPOSES

Subdivision 1. General benefit corporation purpose.

A general benefit corporation has a purpose of pursuing general public benefit. A general benefit corporation may also state in its articles one or more specific public benefit purposes the general benefit corporation elects to pursue. Purposes under these subdivisions are in addition to the purposes under section 302A.101.

Subd. 2. Specific benefit corporation purpose.

A specific benefit corporation shall have a purpose of pursuing one or more specific public benefit purposes stated in its articles. Purposes under this subdivision are in addition to the purposes under section 302A.101. The election to pursue a specific public benefit purpose under this subdivision does not require a specific benefit corporation to pursue general public benefit under subdivision 1.

Subd. 3. Effect of purposes.

The pursuit of general public benefit or a specific public benefit purpose under subdivision 1, or a specific public benefit purpose under subdivision 2, is in the best interests of a public benefit corporation.

Subd. 4. Amendment of a specific public benefit purpose.

In accordance with the procedures stated in chapter 302A and with approval by the minimum status vote, a general benefit corporation or a specific benefit corporation may amend its articles to add, amend, or delete a specific public benefit purpose unless the amendment would cause a termination of public benefit corporation status under section 304A.103.

ACCOUNTABILITY

304A.201 STANDARD OF CONDUCT FOR DIRECTORS

Subdivision 1. Considerations for a general benefit corporation.

In discharging the duties of the position of director of a general benefit corporation, a director:

(1) shall consider the effects of any proposed, contemplated, or actual conduct on:

(i) the general benefit corporation's ability to pursue general public benefit;

(ii) if the articles also state a specific public benefit purpose, the general benefit corporation's ability to pursue its specific public benefit; and

3年。

第 304A.104 条　公共利益公司的目的

第 1 款　一般公共利益公司目的

一般公共利益公司有服务于一般公共利益的目的。一般公共利益公司也可以在公司章程中声明一项或更多的特定公共利益目的。这些目的在第 302A.101 条规定的目的之外。

第 2 款　特定公共利益公司目的

特定公共利益公司应当追求章程中陈述的一项或多项特定公共利益目的。本款规定下的目的在第 302A.101 条规定的目的之外。选择追求本款规定的特定公共利益目的不要求特定公共利益公司追求第 1 款规定下的一般公共利益目的。

第 3 款　目的效力

第 1 款规定的一般或者特定公共利益目的，或者第 2 款规定的特定公共利益目的，为公共利益公司的最佳利益。

第 4 款　特定公共利益目的的修改

依据第 302A 章规定的程序并在满足最低表决要求的情况下，一般或者特定公共利益公司可通过修改其章程增加、修改或者删除其特定公共利益目的，除非修改将导致第 304A.103 条规定的公共利益公司形态的终止。

公司责任

第 304A.201 条　董事行为标准

第 1 款　一般公共利益公司的考虑因素

公共利益公司的董事在履行职责时，董事：

（1）应当考虑提议、计划中的或实施的行为对以下因素的影响：

（i）一般公共利益公司追求一般公共利益的能力；

（ii）一般公共利益公司追求特定公共利益的能力，如果章程中规定了特定公共利益目的；以及

(iii) the interests of the constituencies stated in section 302A.251, subdivision 5, including the pecuniary interests of its shareholders; and

(2) may not give regular, presumptive, or permanent priority to:

(i) the pecuniary interests of the shareholders; or

(ii) any other interest or consideration unless the articles identify the interest or consideration as having priority.

Subd. 2. Considerations for a specific benefit corporation.

In discharging the duties of the position of director of a specific benefit corporation, a director:

(1) shall consider the effects of any proposed, contemplated, or actual conduct on:

(i) the pecuniary interest of its shareholders; and

(ii) the specific benefit corporation's ability to pursue its specific public benefit purpose;

(2) may consider the interests of the constituencies stated in section 302A.251, subdivision 5; and

(3) may not give regular, presumptive, or permanent priority to:

(i) the pecuniary interests of the shareholders; or

(ii) any other interest or consideration unless the articles identify the interest or consideration as having priority.

Subd. 3. Liability.

A director who performs the duties of a director stated in subdivisions 1 and 2 is not liable by reason of being or having been a director of a public benefit corporation.

Subd. 4. Other applicable law.

The conduct and liability of a director of a public benefit corporation is subject to section 302A.251, subdivisions 1, 2, 3, and 4.

Subd. 5. Duty of loyalty.

The articles of a public benefit corporation may include a provision that any disinterested failure to satisfy subdivision 1 or 2 of this section shall not, for purposes of this section or section 302A.251, subdivision 4, constitute a breach of the duty of loyalty.

304A.202 RIGHT OF ACTION

Subdivision 1. Standing and grounds for claims.

(a) No person other than a shareholder may assert a claim under this chapter or chapter 302A against a public benefit corporation, its directors, or its officers on account of the public benefit corporation's director's or officer's failure to pursue or create general public benefit or a specific public benefit.

(b) A public benefit corporation is not liable for monetary damages under this chapter

（iii）第 302A.251 条第 5 款规定的利益相关者的利益，包括股东的金钱利益；以及

（2）可以不给予以下利益或因素通常的、推定的或者永久的优先权：

（i）股东的金钱利益；或者

（ii）任何其他利益或者公司章程中明确规定拥有优先权的利益或因素。

第 2 款　特定公共利益公司的考虑因素

特定公共利益公司的董事在履行职责时，董事：

（1）应当考虑提议、计划的或实施的行为对以下因素的影响：

（i）股东的金钱利益；以及

（ii）特定公共利益公司追求特定公共利益目的的能力；

（2）可以考虑第 302A.251 条第 5 款规定利益相关者的利益；以及

（3）不得给予以下利益或因素常规的、推定的或者永久的优先权：

（i）股东的金钱利益；或者

（ii）任何其他利益或因素，除非公司章程中明确规定其拥有优先权。

第 3 款　责任

履行第 1 款和第 2 款中规定的董事义务的董事不会因成为公共利益公司的董事而承担责任。

第 4 款　其他适用的法律

公共利益公司董事的行为和责任受第 302A.251 条第 1 款、第 2 款、第 3 款、第 4 款的规定调整。

第 5 款　　忠诚义务

公共利益公司的章程可以包含一个条款，即就本条或第 302A.251 条第 4 款中规定而言，未满足本条第 1 款或第 2 款中规定的行为不违反忠实义务。

第 304A.202 条　诉讼权利

第 1 款　主张的资格和理由

（a）除股东外任何人不得依据本章或者第 302A 章的规定以公共利益公司的董事或高管没能追求或实现一般或者特定公共利益为由，向公共利益公司其董事或高管提出主张。

（b）公共利益公司不对本章规定下任何未能追求或实现一般或特定公共利益

for any failure of the public benefit corporation to pursue or create general public benefit or a specific public benefit.

Subd. 2. Grounds for relief.

In addition to the grounds for relief stated in section 302A.751, subdivision 1, paragraph (b), a court may grant relief under this chapter when:

(1) directors or those in control of a public benefit corporation have breached the duties stated in section 304A.201 to a substantial extent and in a sustained manner; or

(2) the public benefit corporation has for an unreasonably long period of time failed to pursue:

(i) in the case of a general benefit corporation:

(A) general public benefit; or

(B) any specific public benefit purpose stated in its articles; and

(ii) in the case of a specific benefit corporation, any specific public benefit purpose stated in its articles.

Subd. 3. Particular relief available.

(a) In an action under this chapter, in addition to granting any other equitable relief the court deems just and reasonable in the circumstances, the court may:

(1) order the public benefit corporation to terminate its status as a public benefit corporation pursuant to section 304A.103, subdivision 1;

(2) remove one or more directors from the public benefit corporation's board of directors and determine whether the vacancy will be filled:

(i) as provided in section 302A.225; or

(ii) by court appointment, with the appointee to serve only until a qualified successor is elected by the shareholders at the next regular or special meeting of the shareholders;

(3) appoint a receiver of the public benefit corporation to:

(i) wind up and liquidate the activities and business of the public benefit corporation; or

(ii) carry on the business and activities of the public benefit corporation in a manner consistent with this chapter.

(b) Paragraph (a) does not imply any limitations on the relief available in a proceeding brought under section 302A.751 without reference to this chapter.

TRANSPARENCY

304A.301 ANNUAL BENEFIT REPORT

Subdivision 1. Report required.

No later than 90 days after the conclusion of each calendar year, a public benefit corporation must deliver to the secretary of state for filing an annual benefit report covering

的行为承担损害赔偿责任。

第 2 款　救济的理由

除第 302A.751 条第 1 款第（b）项规定的救济理由外，法院可以依据本章规定提供救济，当：

（1）董事或者控制公共利益公司的人本质上持续违反第 304A.201 条规定的义务；或者

（2）公共利益公司没有正当理由长期未能追求：

（i）一般公共利益公司的：

（A）一般公共利益；或者

（B）公司章程中规定的任何特定公共利益目的；以及

（ii）特定公共利益公司的任何章程中规定的任何特定公共利益目的。

第 3 款　可用的特别救济

（a）在本章规定的诉讼中，除给予法院认为在该情况下公正合理的平等救济外，法院可以：

（1）依据第 304A.103 条第 1 款的规定命令公共利益公司终止其公共利益公司形态；

（2）解雇一个或多个公共利益公司董事会中的董事并决定是否填充空缺：

（i）按照第 302A.225 条的规定；或者

（ii）被法院任命的人履职至一个适格的继任者在下一次常规或特别股东会中被股东选出；

（3）任命一个公共利益公司的接收人：

（i）结束和清算公共利益公司的活动和业务；或者

（ii）依据本章规定经营公共利益公司的业务和活动。

（b）第（a）项的规定不意味着对在非本章的第 302A.751 条规定的程序中的可用救济进行限制。

透明度

第 304A.301 条　年度公共利益报告

第 1 款　要求的报告

在每年结束后的 90 天内，公共利益公司必须向州务卿提交一份期间为 12 个月并在该年 12 月 31 日结束的年度公共利益报告以进行备案，并且向州务卿支付 35 美

the 12–month period ending on December 31 of that year and pay a fee of $ 35 to the secretary of state. The annual benefit report must state the name of the public benefit corporation, be signed by the public benefit corporation's chief executive officer not more than 30 days before the report is delivered to the secretary of state for filing, and must be current when signed.

Subd. 2. Annual benefit report for a specific benefit corporation.

For a specific benefit corporation, the annual benefit report must contain:

(1) with regard to the period covered by the report, a narrative description of:

(i) the ways in which the corporation pursued and created the specific public benefit stated in its articles;

(ii) the extent to which that specific public benefit purpose was pursued and created; and

(iii) any circumstances that hindered efforts to pursue or create the specific public benefit; and

(2) a certification that its board of directors has reviewed and approved the report.

Subd. 3. Annual benefit report for a general benefit corporation.

The annual benefit report of a general benefit corporation must:

(1) certify that its board of directors has:

(i) chosen the third–party standard designated pursuant to clause (2), item (i);

(ii) determined that the organization that promulgated the third–party standard is independent; and

(iii) approved the report;

(2) with regard to the period covered by the report:

(i) identify a third–party standard determined by the board; and

(ii) with reference to that third–party standard, describe:

(A) how the corporation has pursued general public benefit;

(B) the extent to which and the ways in which the corporation has created general public benefit; and

(C) any circumstances that hindered efforts to pursue or create general public benefit;

(3) if the report is the first delivered for filing by the general benefit corporation, explain how and why the board chose the third–party standard identified under clause (2), item (i);

(4) if the third–party standard identified under clause (2), item (i), is the same third–party standard identified in the immediately prior report:

(i) state whether the third–party standard is being applied in a manner consistent with the third–party standard's application in the prior reports; and

(ii) if the third–party standard is not being so applied in a consistent manner, explain why;

元的费用。

第 2 款　特定公共利益公司的年度公共利益报告

对于特定公共利益公司，其年度公共利益报告必须包含：

（1）报告所述期间内对以下事项的说明：

（i）公共利益公司追求和实现公司章程中规定的特定公共利益的方法；

（ii）追求和创造特定公共利益的范围；以及

（iii）阻碍追求或实现特定公共利益的情形；以及

（2）董事会已经收到并批准这份报告的证明。

第 3 款　一般公共利益公司的年度公共利益报告

一般公共利益公司的年度公共利益报告必须：

（1）证明董事会已经：

（i）选择按第（2）项第（i）目要求指定的第三方标准；

（ii）认定发布第三方标准的组织是独立的；

（iii）批准报告；

（2）关于报告所涉期间：

（i）确定董事会决定的第三方标准；以及

（ii）提及的第三方标准，要说明：

（A）公司如何追求一般公共利益；

（B）公司实现一般公共利益的范围和方法；以及

（C）阻碍追求或实现一般公共利益的情形；

（3）如果该一般公共利益公司第一次送交报告进行备案，应解释说明董事会选用第（2）项第（i）目规定要求的第三方标准的程序和原因；

（4）如果依据第（2）项第（i）目的规定确定的第三方标准是在之前报告中确定的第三方标准：

（i）说明该第三方标准是否与之前报告的第三方标准以同样的方式适用；以及

（ii）如果该第三方标准没有被以同样的方式适用，解释原因；

(5) if the third–party standard identified under clause (2), item (i), is not the same as the third–party standard identified in the immediately prior report, explain how and why the board chose a different third–party standard; and

(6) if the general benefit corporation has also stated a specific public benefit purpose in its articles, the information required in subdivision 2, clause (1).

Subd. 4. Audit not required.

A public benefit corporation is not required to have its annual benefit report audited, certified, or otherwise evaluated by a third party.

Subd. 5. Failure to file an annual benefit report.

If a public benefit corporation fails to file an annual benefit report in accordance with this section within 90 days of the date on which an annual benefit report is due, the secretary of state shall revoke the corporation's status as a public benefit corporation under this chapter and must notify the public benefit corporation of the revocation using the information provided by the corporation pursuant to section 5.002 or 5.34 or provided in the articles.

Subd. 6. Effects of revocation; reinstatement.

(a) A public benefit corporation that has lost its public benefit corporation status for failure to timely file an annual benefit report is not entitled to the benefits afforded to a public benefit corporation under this chapter as of the date of revocation.

(b) Within 30 days of issuance of revocation of public benefit corporation status by the secretary of state, filing a renewal complying with this section and a $ 500 fee with the secretary of state will reinstate the corporation as a public benefit corporation under this chapter as of the date of revocation.

Subd. 7. Intentional failure to file an annual benefit report.

A shareholder of the public benefit corporation may obtain payment for the fair value of the shareholder's shares pursuant to section 302A.473 as a result of revocation of public benefit corporation status pursuant to this section caused by the intentional failure to file an annual benefit report.

（5）如果依据第（2）项第（i）目的规定确定的第三方标准不同于之前报告中的第三方标准，应解释董事会选择一个不同的标准的程序和原因；以及

（6）第2款第（1）项中要求的信息，如果一般公共利益公司也已经在公司章程中规定了一个特定公共利益。

第4款　无须审计

不要求公共利益公司的年度公共利益报告要经第三人审计、认证或者以其他方式评价。

第5款　未能备案年度公共利益报告

如果公共利益公司未能依据本条规定在年度公共利益报告到期后90天内备案，州务卿应当依据本章规定撤销公司的公共利益公司形态，且必须使用公司依据第5.002条或第5.34条或公司章程规定的信息向公共利益公司作出通知。

第6款　撤销的效果；恢复

（a）未能及时备案年度公共利益报告而失去公共利益公司形态的公共利益公司自被撤销之日起无权获得依据本章规定提供给公共利益公司的利益。

（b）在州务卿公布撤销公共利益公司状态后的30天内，依据本条规定申请恢复并向州务卿缴纳500美元的公司将依据本章规定自撤销之日起恢复为公共利益公司。

第7款　故意不备案年度公共利益报告

公共利益公司故意不备案年度公共利益报告导致其公共利益公司形态依据本条规定被撤销的，公共利益公司股东可以依据第302A.473条的规定获得对股东股份的公允价格偿付。

THE STATE OF MONTANA

HOUSE BILL NO. 258

AN ACT CREATING THE MONTANA BENEFIT CORPORATION ACT; AUTHORIZING AND REGULATING THE FORMATION AND GOVERNANCE OF BENEFIT CORPORATIONS; ALLOWING AN EXISTING CORPORATION TO BECOME A BENEFIT CORPORATION; PROVIDING THAT A BENEFIT CORPORATION MAY BE FORMED FOR THE PURPOSE OF CREATING GENERAL PUBLIC BENEFIT OR SPECIFIC PUBLIC BENEFITS; REQUIRING DIRECTORS TO CONSIDER THE IMPACTS OF ANY ACTION OR PROPOSED ACTION ON SPECIFIED CONSTITUENCIES; REQUIRING THE BOARD OF DIRECTORS TO PREPARE A STATEMENT RELATING TO THE PUBLIC BENEFIT PURPOSES OF THE CORPORATION; REQUIRING THE BENEFIT CORPORATION TO ANNUALLY PREPARE AND DISSEMINATE A BENEFIT REPORT; DESCRIBING THE LIMITED FIDUCIARY DUTY AND LIABILITY OF A DIRECTOR OR OFFICER OF A BENEFIT CORPORATION; AND PROVIDING THAT THE DUTIES OF A DIRECTOR OR OFFICER AND THE PUBLIC BENEFIT PURPOSE OF A BENEFIT CORPORATION MAY BE ENFORCED ONLY IN A BENEFIT ENFORCEMENT PROCEEDING.

BE IT ENACTED BY THE LEGISLATURE OF THE STATE OF MONTANA:

Section 1. Short title.

[Sections 1 through 12] may be known and may be cited as the "Montana Benefit Corporation Act".

Section 2. Definitions.

As used in [sections 1 through 12], the following definitions apply:

(1) "Benefit corporation" means a corporation organized in this state that has elected to become subject to [sections 1 through 12] and whose status as a benefit corporation has not

蒙大拿州

参议院议案　第 258 号

本法案创设了《蒙大拿州公共利益公司法》；批准和规制公共利益公司的成立和治理；允许一个已成立的公司成为公共利益公司；规定一个公共利益公司可为一般或者特定公共利益而成立；要求董事考虑任何行为或计划中的行为对特定利益相关者的影响；要求董事会编制关于公司公共利益目的的声明；要求公共利益公司每年编制并公布公共利益报告；规定公共利益公司董事或高管的有限信义义务和责任；并且规定董事或高管的义务和公共利益公司的公共利益目的只能通过公共利益实施程序执行。

本法案由蒙大拿州立法机构颁布：

第 1 条　简称

［第 1–12 条］可以被称为和引用为《蒙大拿州公共利益公司法》。

第 2 条　定义

在［第 1–12 条］中适用以下含义：

（1）“公共利益公司”是指在本州成立、选择接受［第 1–12 条］规定的调整且公共利益公司形态并未依［第 8 条］的规定终止的公司。

been terminated as provided in [section 8].

(2) "Benefit enforcement proceeding" means a claim or action relating to:

(a) failure to pursue the general public benefit purpose of the benefit corporation or any specific public benefit purpose set forth in its articles of incorporation;

(b) violation of a duty or standard of conduct imposed on a director or officer pursuant to [sections 1 through 12]; or

(c) failure of the benefit corporation to deliver, provide, or post an annual benefit report as required in [section 10].

(3) "Director" means an individual elected to or otherwise serving on the board of directors of a benefit corporation.

(4) "General public benefit" means a material, positive impact on society and the environment, taken as a whole, as assessed against a third-party standard, from the business and operations of a benefit corporation.

(5) "Independent" means having no material relationship with a benefit corporation or a subsidiary of a benefit corporation.

(6) "Minimum status vote" means:

(a) in the case of a corporation, that in addition to any other approval or vote required by law or by the articles of incorporation:

(i) the shareholders of every class or series are entitled to vote on the corporate action regardless of any limitation stated in the articles of incorporation; and

(ii) the corporate action must be approved by the outstanding shares of each class or series by at least two-thirds of the votes that all shareholders of the class or series are entitled to cast on that action or by a greater vote if required in the articles of incorporation; or

(b) in the case of a domestic business entity other than a corporation and in addition to any other approval, vote, or consent required by law that principally governs the internal affairs of the domestic business entity or any provision of the publicly filed record or document required to form the domestic business entity, if any, or of any agreement binding some or all of the holders of equity interests in the entity:

(i) the holders of every class or series of interest in the entity that are entitled to receive a distribution of any kind from the entity are entitled to vote on the action regardless of any otherwise applicable limitation on the voting rights of the interest; and

(ii) the action must be approved by the vote or consent of the holders described in subsection (6)(b)(i) by at least two-thirds of the votes of the holders or by a greater vote if required in the publicly filed record, document, or agreement binding holders of equity interests.

(7) "Specific public benefit" means:

（2）“公共利益实施程序”是指因以下行为产生的主张或诉讼：

（a）未能追求公共利益公司的一般公共利益目的或公司章程中规定的任何特定公共利益目的；

（b）违反［第 1–12 条］规定的董事或高管的任何义务或行为标准。

（c）公共利益公司未能提交、提供或公布［第 10 条］中要求的年度公共利益报告。

（3）“董事”是指被选为或以其他方式担任公共利益公司董事的人。

（4）“一般公共利益”是指根据第三方标准，公司的业务和经营在整体上对社会和环境产生的实质性积极影响。

（5）“独立”是指与公共利益公司或其子公司没有实质性关系。

（6）“最低表决要求”是指：

（a）在公司中，除任何其他法律或公司章程对批准或表决的要求外：

（i）每一类别或系列的股东应当有权对公司行为进行投票，即使公司章程作出了限制；并且

（ii）公司行为必须获得每一类别或系列有投票权的所有股东的至少 2/3 投票才能通过或者遵循公司章程中规定的更严格的表决要求。

（b）在非商事公司的本州实体中，除主要调整本州商业实体内部事务或本州商业实体成立要求公开登记记录或文件的法律，或约束实体中部分或全部股东权益持有者的任何协议中规定的任何其他批准、表决或赞成要求外：

（i）该实体的每一类别或系列的任何权益分配形式下的股权持有者应有权对公司行为进行投票，即使存在投票权的限制；并且

（ii）公司行为必须获得第（6）（b）（i）目中规定的股权持有者至少 2/3 的投票或者更严格的投票才能通过，如果在公开登记的记录、文件或者约束股东权益的持有者协议中有所要求。

（7）“特定公共利益”是指：

(a) providing low–income or underserved individuals or communities with beneficial products or services;

(b) promoting economic opportunity for individuals or communities beyond the creation of jobs in the ordinary course of business;

(c) preserving the environment;

(d) improving human health;

(e) promoting the arts, sciences, or advancement of knowledge;

(f) increasing the flow of capital to entities with a public benefit purpose; or

(g) the accomplishment of any other particular benefit for society or the environment.

(8) "Subsidiary" means an entity in which a parent entity owns beneficially or of record 50% or more of the outstanding equity interests of the subsidiary. For the purposes of this definition, the percentage of ownership held by a parent entity in a subsidiary must be calculated as if all outstanding rights to acquire equity interests in the subsidiary have been exercised.

(9) "Third–party standard" means a standard for defining, reporting, and assessing overall corporate social and environmental performance to which all of the following apply:

(a) the standard is a comprehensive assessment of the impact of the business and the business's operations on the considerations listed in [section 6(2)(a)];

(b) the standard is developed by an entity that has no material financial relationship with the benefit corporation or any of its subsidiaries and:

(i) not more than one–third of the members of the governing body of the entity are representatives of:

(A) associations of businesses operating in a specific industry for which the performance is measured by the standard;

(B) businesses from a specific industry or an association of businesses in that industry; or

(C) businesses whose performance is assessed against the standard; and

(ii) the entity is not materially financed by an association or business described in subsection (9)(b)(i);

(c) the standard is developed by an entity that:

(i) accesses necessary and appropriate expertise to assess overall corporate social and environmental performance; and

(ii) uses a balanced multistakeholder approach, including a public comment period of at least 30 days, to develop the standard; and

(d) the following information regarding the standard is publicly available:

(i) the criteria considered when measuring the overall social and environmental performance of a business;

（a）向低收入或者低福利人群或社区提供有益的产品或服务；

（b）在正常业务过程中，向个人或社区提供创造就业之外的经济机会；

（c）保护环境；
（d）改善人类健康；
（e）促进艺术、科学进步或知识传播；
（f）促进资本向有公共利益目的的实体流动；或者
（g）给予社会或环境其他特别利益。
（8）“子公司”是指母公司拥有其50%以上已发行的股份的受益所有权或登记所有权的实体。在本定义中，母公司在子公司中所拥有的股权比例必须在所有购股权被视为已行使的情况下计算。

（9）“第三方标准”是指用于定义、报告和评估公司总体社会和环境绩效的标准，其应满足以下条件：
（a）该标准是对企业和企业经营对［第6（2）（a）项］所列因素产生的影响的全面综合评价；
（b）该标准是由与公共利益公司或者其子公司没有实质关系的实体制定并且：

（i）该实体管理层中的不多于1/3的成员是以下组织的代表：

（A）在由该标准衡量的特定行业的企业协会；

（B）特定行业或者该行业的企业协会中的组织；或者

（C）其绩效由该标准评估的企业；以及
（ii）该实体实质上并非由第（9）（b）（i）目规定的协会或企业提供经费；

（c）制定该标准的实体：
（i）有必要和适当的专业知识去评价公司整体的社会和环境效益；以及

（ii）使用平衡多方相关者利益的方法制定标准，包括设定至少30天的公开听取意见期间；并且
（d）与标准相关的以下信息可以公开获取：
（i）当衡量整体社会和环境效益时考虑的标准；

(ii) the relative weightings assigned to the criteria described in subsection (9)(d)(i);

(iii) the identity of the directors, the officers, any material owners, and the governing body of the entity that developed and controls revisions to the standard;

(iv) the process by which revisions to the standard and changes to the membership of the governing body of the entity described in subsection (9)(d)(iii) are made; and

(v) an accounting of the sources of financial support for the entity with sufficient detail to disclose any relationships that could reasonably be considered to present a potential conflict of interest.

Section 3. Purpose.

(1) The purpose of a benefit corporation is to create general public benefit. This purpose is in addition to and may be a limitation on the corporation's purpose under 35–1–114 and any specific public benefit purpose set forth in the corporation's articles of incorporation in accordance with subsection (2).

(2) In addition to the applicable provisions required under 35–1–216, the articles of incorporation of a benefit corporation must contain the following statement: "This corporation is a benefit corporation." The articles of incorporation of a benefit corporation may identify one or more specific public benefits as the purpose or purposes of the benefit corporation. The identification of a specific public benefit under this subsection does not limit the obligation of a benefit corporation to create general public benefit.

(3) The creation of general public benefit and one or more specific public benefits as provided in subsections (1) and (2) is considered to be in the best interests of the benefit corporation.

(4) A benefit corporation may amend its articles of incorporation to add, amend, or delete the identification of a specific public benefit as a purpose of the benefit corporation to create. The amendment is effective only if the amendment is adopted by at least the minimum status vote.

Section 4. Applicability.

(1) Unless otherwise provided in [sections 1 through 12], the provisions of Title 35, chapter 1, apply to all benefit corporations.

(2) The provisions of [sections 1 through 12] do not:

(a) imply that a contrary or different rule of law does or would apply to a business corporation that is not a benefit corporation; or

(b) affect any provision of [sections 1 through 12] that does or would apply to a corporation that is not a benefit corporation.

Section 5. Benefit corporation -- formation.

A benefit corporation may be formed in accordance with [sections 1 through 12]. The articles of incorporation must:

（ii）第（9）（d）（i）目规定的标准的相关权重；

（iii）制定和控制修改程序的董事、高管、主要股东和该实体控制人员的身份；

（iv）标准修改和第（9）（d）（iii）目规定的实体管理层人员变动的程序；以及

（v）实体资金来源的核算，包括充分披露合理认知下存在利益冲突的所有细节。

第3条　目的

（1）公共利益公司的目的是创造一般公共利益。该目的在第35–1–114条规定的公司目的和依据第（2）款的规定在公司章程中规定的目的之外，并可能对上述目的构成限制。

（2）在第35–1–216条规定的适用条款外，公共利益公司的章程必须包含下列声明："公司是公共利益公司。"公共利益公司的章程可设定一项或多项特定公共利益作为公共利益公司的目的。依据本款规定设定的特定公共利益不限制公共利益公司实现一般公共利益的义务。

（3）创造第（1）款和第（2）款规定的一般公共利益和一项或多项特定公共利益为公共利益公司的最佳利益。

（4）公共利益公司可以通过修改公司章程增加、修改或删除作为公共利益公司目的的特定公共利益。公司章程的修改满足最低表决要求才能生效。

第4条　适用

（1）除［第1–12条］另有规定外，第35编第1章的规定适用于所有公共利益公司。

（2）［第1–12条］的规定并未：

（a）给非公共利益公司设定相反或不同的规则；或者

（b）影响非公共利益公司有关条文或规则的适用。

第5条　公共利益公司——成立

公共利益公司可依据［第1–12条］的规定成立。公司章程必须：

(1) state that the corporation is a benefit corporation; and

(2) identify any specific public benefits adopted pursuant to [section 3].

Section 6. Benefit corporation governance -- liability.

(1) A director of a public benefit corporation shall:

(a) perform the duties of a director in good faith and in a manner the director believes to be in the best interests of the benefit corporation; and

(b) conduct reasonable inquiry in the manner that a prudent person in a similar position would conduct under similar circumstances.

(2) In discharging their respective duties and in considering the best interests of the benefit corporation, the board of directors, committees of the board, and individual directors of a benefit corporation:

(a) shall consider the impacts of every action or proposed action on:

(i) the shareholders of the benefit corporation;

(ii) the employees and workforce of the benefit corporation and its subsidiaries and suppliers;

(iii) the interests of customers of the benefit corporation as beneficiaries of the general public benefit purpose or any specific public benefit purpose of the benefit corporation;

(iv) community and societal considerations, including those of a community in which offices or facilities of the benefit corporation or its subsidiaries or suppliers are located;

(v) the local and global environment;

(vi) the short–term and long–term interests of the benefit corporation, including benefits that may accrue to the benefit corporation from its long–term plans and the possibility that the interests may be best served by retaining control of the benefit corporation rather than selling or transferring control to another person; and

(vii) the ability of the benefit corporation to accomplish its general public benefit purpose and any specific public benefit purpose;

(b) may consider:

(i) the resources, intent, and conduct, including past, stated, and potential conduct, of any person seeking to acquire control of the benefit corporation; and

(ii) any other pertinent factors or the interests of any other person or group; and

(c) are not required to give priority to any particular factor or the interests of any particular person or group referred to in this subsection (2) over any other factor or the interests of any other person or group unless the benefit corporation has stated its intention to give priority to a specific public benefit purpose identified in the articles of incorporation.

(3) In performing the duties of a director, a director may rely on information, opinions, reports, or statements, including financial statements and other financial data, in each case prepared or presented by:

（1）声明公司是公共利益公司；并且

（2）明确依据［第3条］的规定设定的特定公共利益。

第6条 公共利益公司治理——责任

（1）公共利益公司董事应当：

（a）善意地并以董事认为符合公共利益公司最佳利益的方式履行董事义务；以及

（b）以谨慎之人在相似情况下将采取的方式进行合理的调查。

（2）在履行义务和考虑公共利益公司最佳利益时，公共利益公司的董事会、董事会委员会和董事：

（a）应当考虑每一行为或者提议的行为对以下对象的影响：

（i）公共利益公司的股东；

（ii）公共利益公司、其子公司和其供应商的雇员；

（iii）作为公共利益公司一般或特定公共利益受益者的消费者的利益；

（iv）社区和社会因素，包括公共利益公司、其子公司或其供应商的办公地或设施所在地的社区；

（v）当地和全球环境；

（vi）公共利益公司的短期和长期利益，包括从其长期计划中产生的利益以及保留公共利益公司的控制权而不是将控制权出售或转让给其他人可能产生的最佳利益；以及

（vii）公共利益公司实现其一般和特定公共利益目的的能力；

（b）可以考虑：

（i）寻求获取公共利益公司控制权的人的财力、意图和行为，包括过去、现在和潜在的行为；以及

（ii）任何其他人或组织的任何其他相关因素或其利益；以及

（c）除公共利益公司在公司章程中声明要优先考虑特定的利益或因素外，相较于其他人和组织的利益，无须优先考虑第（2）款中规定的人或组织的特定利益。

（3）在履行董事义务时，董事可以在不同情况下信赖由以下主体准备或提供的信息、意见、报告或报表，包括财报表和其他财务数据：

(a) one or more officers or employees of the benefit corporation whom the director believes to be reliable and competent in the matters presented;

(b) counsel, independent accountants, or other persons as to matters that the director believes to be within those persons' professional or expert competence; or

(c) a committee of the board on which the director does not serve if the director believes the committee merits confidence and if the director acts in good faith and without knowledge that would cause the director's confidence in the committee to be unwarranted.

(4) A person who performs the duties of a director in accordance with [sections 1 through 12] is not liable for monetary damages for any alleged failure:

(a) to discharge the person's obligations as a director; or

(b) of the benefit corporation to pursue or create general public benefit or a specific public benefit.

(5) In addition to the limitations provided in subsection (4), the liability of a director for monetary damages may be eliminated or limited in a benefit corporation's articles of incorporation to the extent provided for in 35–1–216(2)(d).

(6) A director does not have a duty to a person who is a beneficiary of the general public benefit purpose or a specific public benefit purpose of a benefit corporation arising from the status of the person as a beneficiary.

Section 7. Conversion to benefit corporation.

(1) A corporation may become a benefit corporation under [sections 1 through 12] by amending the corporation's articles of incorporation to include a statement that the corporation is a benefit corporation. The amendment is effective only if it is adopted by at least the minimum status vote. If the amendment is adopted, a shareholder of the corporation may require the corporation to purchase at fair market value the shares owned by the shareholder as provided for in 35–1–827.

(2) If a corporation or other entity that is not a benefit corporation is a constituent corporation or entity in a merger reorganization or is the acquired corporation or entity in an exchange reorganization and the surviving corporation in the merger or exchange reorganization is to be a benefit corporation or the articles of incorporation of the acquired corporation or entity are to be amended in the merger or exchange reorganization to provide that the newly formed corporation will be a benefit corporation, the reorganization is effective only if it is approved by the newly formed corporation or other entity by at least the minimum status vote.

(3) If any other entity is a party to a merger reorganization and the surviving corporation in the reorganization is to be a benefit corporation, the reorganization is effective only if the reorganization is approved by the other entity by at least the minimum status vote.

(4) If another entity is the converting entity in a conversion in which the converted

（a）公共利益公司中的一个或多个董事认为可靠并且能够胜任的高管或雇员；

（b）董事认为此事在其专业能力范围之内的顾问、独立会计或者其他人；或者

（c）该董事没有参加的董事委员会，如果董事认为该委员会值得信任以及董事善意行事且不知道其对委员会的信任可能没有根据。

（4）依据［第1–12条］规定履行董事义务的人不因未实施以下行为而承担损害赔偿责任：

（a）履行此人作为董事的义务；或者

（b）公共利益公司追求或创造一般或者特定公共利益。

（5）除第（4）款规定的限制外，董事损害赔偿责任可以在第35–1–216（2）（d）项规定的范围内被免除或限制。

（6）董事不对公共利益公司一般或特定社会目的的受益人负责。

第7条　转变为公共利益公司

（1）公司可以依据［第1–12条］的规定通过修改公司章程使章程包含公司为公共利益公司的声明而转变为公共利益公司。公司章程的修改只有满足最低表决要求才能生效。如果修改被批准，公司股东可依据第35–1–827条的规定要求公司以公允价格购买股东拥有的股份。

（2）如果非公共利益公司的公司或者其他实体是合并重组中的被合并公司或者置换重组中的被收购公司，并且合并或置换重组中的存续公司是公共利益公司，或者被收购公司或实体的公司章程在合并或置换重组中将要修改以规定新成立的公司是公共利益公司，该重组只有在满足最低表决要求而获得新设公司或实体批准才能生效。

（3）如果任何其他实体是合并重组的一方并且重组中的存续公司是公共利益公司，重组只有在满足最低表决要求后被其他实体批准才能生效。

（4）如果其他实体是转换中的转换实体且转换后的公司是公共利益公司，该

corporation is a benefit corporation, the conversion is effective only if the conversion is approved by the other entity by at least the minimum status vote.

Section 8. Termination -- reorganization -- other actions affecting benefit corporation.

(1) A benefit corporation may terminate its status as a benefit corporation and cease to be subject to [sections 1 through 12] by deleting from the benefit corporation's articles of incorporation the statement and identification of public benefits required under [section 5]. The amendment is effective only if the amendment is adopted by at least the minimum status vote. If the amendment is adopted, a shareholder of the corporation may require the corporation to purchase at fair market value the shares owned by the shareholder as provided for in 35–1–827.

(2) If a reorganization of a benefit corporation would terminate the status of the corporation as a benefit corporation, the reorganization is effective only if the reorganization is approved by at least the minimum status vote.

(3) If a benefit corporation is the converting corporation in a conversion, the conversion is effective only if the conversion is approved by at least the minimum status vote.

(4) A sale, lease, conveyance, exchange, transfer, or other disposition of all or substantially all of the assets of a benefit corporation, unless the transaction is in the usual and ordinary course of business of the benefit corporation, is effective only if the transaction is approved by at least the minimum status vote. If a transaction described in this subsection is not in the usual and ordinary course of business and is approved, a shareholder of the corporation may require the corporation to purchase at fair market value the shares owned by the shareholder as provided in 35–1–827.

Section 9. Officers -- duty -- limits.

(1) Each officer of a benefit corporation shall consider the interests and factors described in [section 6] in the manner provided in [section 6] whenever the officer:

(a) has discretion to act with respect to a matter; and

(b) reasonably believes that the matter may have a material effect on:

(i) the creation of general public benefit or a specific public benefit by the benefit corporation; or

(ii) any of the interests or factors referred to in [section 6(2)].

(2) The consideration by an officer of interests and factors in the manner described in subsection (1) does not constitute a violation of the duties of the officer.

(3) An officer is not liable for monetary damages under [sections 1 through 12] for:

(a) any action taken as an officer if the officer performed the duties of the position in compliance with this section; or

(b) any failure of the benefit corporation to create general public benefit or a specific

转换只有在满足最低表决要求被其他实体批准后才能生效。

第 8 条　终止——重组——其他影响公共利益公司的行为

（1）公共利益公司可以通过删除［第 5 条］要求的公司章程中的声明或公共利益的认定以终止其公共利益公司形态并不再受［第 1–12 条］规定的调整。公司章程的修改应满足最低表决要求才能生效。如果修改被批准，公司股东可以依据第 35–1–827 条的规定要求公司以公允价格购买其拥有的股份。

（2）如果公共利益公司的重组将终止公司的公共利益公司形态，该重组应满足最低表决要求。

（3）如果公共利益公司是转换中的转换公司，该转换应满足最低表决要求。

（4）买卖、租赁、让与、置换、转让或者其他处分全部或主要公共利益公司财产，交易应满足最低表决要求，交易属于公共利益公司正常商业往来的除外。若本款规定的交易不属于正常商业往来并且被批准，公司股东可以依据第 35–1–827 条的规定要求公司以公允价格购买其拥有的股份。

第 9 条　高管——义务——限制

（1）公共利益公司的高管应当以［第 6 条］规定的行为标准考虑［第 6 条］中规定的利益和因素，当高管：

（a）有对该行为的自由裁量权；以及

（b）有合理理由认为该行为对以下事项有实质性影响：

（i）公共利益公司一般或特定公共利益的实现；或者

（ii）［第 6（2）款］提到的任何利益或因素。

（2）对第（1）款中规定的利益和相关因素的考虑不违反董事的义务。

（3）依据［第 1–12 条］的规定高管不对以下行为承担损害赔偿责任：

（a）作为高管采取的行为，如果高管依据本条的规定履行职责；或者

（b）公共利益公司未能追求或实现一般或特定公共利益。

public benefit.

(4) An officer does not have a fiduciary duty to a person who is a beneficiary of the general public benefit purpose or a specific public benefit purpose of a benefit corporation arising from the status of the person as a beneficiary.

Section 10. Report.

(1) Each year, the board of directors of a benefit corporation shall have prepared and delivered to each shareholder an annual benefit report that must include:

(a) a narrative description of:

(i) the process used and rationale for selecting the third–party standard used to prepare the benefit report;

(ii) the ways in which the benefit corporation pursued general public benefit during the applicable year and the extent to which general public benefit was created;

(iii) the ways in which the benefit corporation pursued any specific public benefit that the articles of incorporation state it is the purpose of the benefit corporation to create and the extent to which the specific public benefit was created; and

(iv) any circumstances that may have hindered the creation by the benefit corporation of general public benefit or any specific public benefit;

(b) an assessment of the overall social and environmental performance of the benefit corporation prepared in accordance with a third–party standard applied consistently with any application of that standard in prior benefit reports or accompanied by an explanation of the reasons for any inconsistent application;

(c) a statement indicating whether the benefit corporation failed to pursue its general public benefit purpose or any specific public benefit purpose in all material respects during the period covered by the report;

(d) the same statement required by [section 11] to be printed on ownership certificates; and

(e) a statement of any connection between the entity that established the third–party standard or the entity's directors, officers, or material owners and the benefit corporation or the benefit corporation's directors, officers, and material owners, including any financial or governance relationship that might materially affect the credibility of the objective assessment reached by using the third–party standard.

(2) If the statement required under subsection (1)(c) indicates that the benefit corporation failed to pursue its general public benefit purpose or any specific public benefit purpose, the annual benefit report must include a description of the ways in which the benefit corporation failed to pursue the general public benefit purpose or specific public benefit purpose.

(3) The report must be provided to each shareholder within 120 days following the

（4）高管并不对公共利益公司一般或特定社会目的的受益人负信义义务。

第 10 条　报告

（1）每年，公共利益公司的董事会应当编写并提交给每一个股东包括以下内容的年度公共利益报告：

（a）对以下事项的说明：

（i）编写公共利益报告时选择或更换第三方标准的程序和原因；

（ii）公共利益公司本年度追求一般公共利益的方法和一般公共利益实现的情况；

（iii）公共利益公司追求公司章程中规定的特定公共利益的方法以及该特定公共利益实现的情况；以及

（iv）阻碍公共利益公司实现一般和特定公共利益的情形；

（b）依据第三方标准对公共利益公司的社会和环境表现作出的整体评价，其沿用先前公共利益报告中使用的标准或者附一份说明以解释使用了不一致的标准的原因；

（c）在报告所述期间公共利益公司是否在某些方面未能追求一般或者特定公共利益目的。

（d）［第 11 条］要求的与印在所有权证书上的相同声明；

（e）设立第三方标准的机构或其董事、高管、或实际拥有者与公共利益公司或其董事、高管实际拥有者之间关系的声明，包括任何有可能实质性影响使用第三方标准进行客观评价的可信度的财务或管理关系。

（2）如果第（1）（c）项要求的陈述意见表明公共利益公司未能追求一般或特定公共利益目的，年度公共利益报告必须包括公共利益公司未能追求一般或特定公共利益目的的情况。

（3）报告必须在公共利益公司会计年度结束后 120 天内或者公共利益公司向

end of each fiscal year of the benefit corporation or at the same time that the benefit corporation delivers any other annual report to its shareholders. The report may be provided electronically or by other means.

(4) (a) Subject to the provisions of subsection (4)(c), a benefit corporation shall post all of its benefit reports on the public portion of its internet website, if any.

(b) If a benefit corporation does not have an internet website, the benefit corporation shall provide, without charge, a copy of its most recent benefit report to any person who requests a copy.

(c) The benefit corporation may omit the compensation paid to directors or any proprietary or financial information from the copy of a benefit report posted pursuant to subsection (4)(a) or provided pursuant to subsection (4)(b).

Section 11. Ownership certificates.

In addition to all other legal requirements, each certificate representing shares of a benefit corporation must have conspicuously printed on the face of the certificate: "This entity is a benefit corporation organized under [section 1] through [section 12] of the Montana Code Annotated."

Section 12. Enforcement.

(1) A person may bring an action or assert a claim against a benefit corporation or its directors or officers only through a benefit enforcement proceeding under this section.

(2) A benefit enforcement proceeding may be commenced or maintained:

(a) directly by the benefit corporation; or

(b) derivatively by:

(i) a shareholder;

(ii) a director;

(iii) a person or group of persons that owns beneficially or of record 5% or more of the equity interests in an entity of which the benefit corporation is a subsidiary; or

(iv) any other person who may be specified in the articles of incorporation of the benefit corporation.

(3) A benefit corporation is not liable for monetary damages for any failure of the benefit corporation to create general public benefit or a specific public benefit.

(4) If the court in a benefit enforcement proceeding finds that a failure to comply with [sections 1 through 12] was without justification, the court may award an amount sufficient to reimburse the plaintiff for the reasonable expenses incurred by the plaintiff, including attorney fees and expenses, in connection with the benefit enforcement proceeding.

Section 13.Saving clause.

[This act] does not affect rights and duties that matured, penalties that were incurred, or proceedings that were begun before [the effective date of this act].

其股东送交其他年度报告的同一时间送交给股东。报告可以以电子或其他方式提供。

（4）（a）根据第（4）（c）项的规定，公共利益公司应当将公共利益报告中所有的内容发布于其网站的公开位置。

（b）如果公共利益公司没有网站，应向所有索取报告的个人免费提供最新公共利益报告的副本。

（c）公共利益公司可以将公共利益报告中的董事薪酬和财务、所有权信息在第（4）（a）项 或第（4）（b）项规定的公共利益报告的副本中删除。

第 11 条　所有权证书

除所有其他法律要求外，每一代表公共利益公司的股份证书必须在证书表面明确印上："该实体是依据蒙大拿法典的［第 1 条］至［第 12 条］成立的公共利益公司。"

第 12 条　实施

（1）任何人只能依据本条规定通过公共利益实施程序向公共利益公司或其董事或高管提起诉讼或者提出主张。

（2）公共利益实施程序可以被以下主体提起：

（a）直接被公共利益公司提起；或者

（b）派生地被：

（i）股东；

（ii）董事；

（iii）拥有公共利益公司的母公司 5% 以上股份的商事公司；或者

（iv）公共利益公司章程细则中列明的其他人员。

（3）公共利益公司不对任何未能实现一般或特定公共利益的行为承担损害赔偿责任。

（4）如果公共利益实施程序中的法院发现没有正当理由违反［第 1–12 条］的规定，法院可以判决被告对原告的合理费用进行充分赔偿，包括律师费和与公共利益实施程序的相关费用。

第 13 条　保留条款

［本法案］不影响［本法案］生效前产生的权利和义务，作出的惩罚，或已开始的程序。

Section 14. Codification instruction.

[Sections 1 through 12] are intended to be codified as an integral part of Title 35, chapter 1, and the provisions of Title 35, chapter 1, apply to [sections 1 through 12].

第 14 条　法典汇编指引

［第 1–12 条］被编为第 35 编第 1 章的一个完整部分，并且第 35 编第 1 章的条款适用于［第 1–12 条］。

THE STATE OF NEBRASKA

LEGISLATURE OF NEBRASKA

ONE HUNDRED THIRD LEGISLATURE

SECOND SESSION

LEGISLATIVE BILL 751

Final Reading

Read first time January 09, 2014

Committee: Banking, Commerce and Insurance

FOR AN ACT relating to corporations; to amend section 84–511, Revised Statutes Supplement, 2013; to adopt the Nebraska Benefit Corporation Act; to harmonize provisions; and to repeal the original section.

Be it enacted by the people of the State of Nebraska,

Section 1. Sections 1 to 14 of this act shall be known and may be cited as the Nebraska Benefit Corporation Act.

Sec. 2. (1) The Nebraska Benefit Corporation Act applies to all benefit corporations.

(2) The existence of a provision of the Nebraska Benefit Corporation Act does not of itself create an implication that a contrary or different rule of law is applicable to a business corporation that is not a benefit corporation. The act does not affect a statute or rule of law that is applicable to a business corporation that is not a benefit corporation.

(3) Except as otherwise provided in the Nebraska Benefit Corporation Act, the Business Corporation Act is generally applicable to all benefit corporations. The specific provisions of the Nebraska Benefit Corporation Act control over the general provisions of the Business Corporation Act. A benefit corporation may be subject simultaneously to the Nebraska Benefit Corporation Act and one or more other statutes that provide for the incorporation of a

内布拉斯加州

内布拉斯加州 103 号立法

立法案编号 751

第二会期

立法案编号 751

最终版本

一读时间为 2014 年 1 月 9 日

委员会：银行、商事和保险

本法与公司有关，修改公司法第 84–511 节，增加《内布拉斯加州公共利益公司法》，同时废除原有的规定。

该法在内布拉斯加州范围内生效。

第 1 条　本法第 1 条至第 14 条为内布拉斯加州对公共利益公司的规定。

第 2 条　（1）《内布拉斯加州公共利益公司法》（以下简称本法）适用于公共利益公司。

（2）本法不应为非公共利益公司设定相反或不同的规则。本法不影响非公共利益公司有关条文和规则的适用。

（3）除本法另有规定外，本法应适用于所有公共利益公司。本法特别条款优先于本法的一般条款适用。公共利益公司同时受本法和特定类型商事公司法的规制。

specific type of business corporation.

(4) A provision of the articles of incorporation or bylaws of a benefit corporation may not limit, be inconsistent with, or supersede a provision of the Nebraska Benefit Corporation Act.

Sec. 3. The following words and phrases when used in the Nebraska Benefit Corporation Act have the meanings given to them in this section unless the context clearly indicates otherwise:

(1)Benefit corporation means a business corporation:

(a) Which has elected to become subject to the act; and

(b) The status of which as a benefit corporation has not been terminated;

(2) Benefit director means the director designated as the benefit director of a benefit corporation under section 9 of this act;

(3) Benefit enforcement proceeding means any claim or action or proceeding for:

(a) Failure of a benefit corporation to pursue or create general public benefit or a specific public benefit purpose set forth in its articles of incorporation; or

(b) Violation of any obligation, duty, or standard of conduct under the act;

(4) Benefit officer means the officer designated as the benefit officer of a benefit corporation under section 11 of this act;

(5) Business corporation means a domestic corporation as defined in section 21–2014;

(6) General public benefit means a material positive impact on society and the environment, taken as a whole, assessed against a third–party standard, from the business and operations of a benefit corporation;

(7) Independent means having no material relationship with a benefit corporation or a subsidiary of the benefit corporation. Serving as benefit director or benefit officer does not make an individual not independent. A material relationship between an individual and a benefit corporation or any of its subsidiaries will be conclusively presumed to exist if:

(a) The individual is, or has been within the last three years, an employee other than a benefit officer of the benefit corporation or a subsidiary;

(b) An immediate family member of the individual is, or has been within the last three years, an executive officer other than a benefit officer of the benefit corporation or a subsidiary; or

(c) There is beneficial or record ownership of five percent or more of the outstanding shares of the benefit corporation, calculated as if all outstanding rights to acquire equity interests in the benefit corporation had been exercised, by:

(i) The individual; or

(ii) An entity:

(A) Of which the individual is a director, an officer, or a manager; or

(B) In which the individual owns beneficially or of record five percent or more of the

（4）公共利益公司的公司章程或公司章程细则不能限制、违背或取代本法。

第3条　除另有规定外，本条下列用语的含义如下：

（1）公共利益公司是指一个商事公司：
（a）选择接受本法的规定的调整；
（b）公共利益公司形态并未终止。
（2）公共利益董事是指公共利益公司依第302条的规定任命的董事。

（3）公共利益实施程序是指因以下行为产生的任何主张、诉讼或程序：
（a）公共利益公司未追求或实现公司章程规定的一般或特定公共利益目的；或者
（b）公共利益公司违反本法规定的任何义务、责任或行为标准；
（4）公共利益高管是指公司依据本法第11条的规定任命的公共利益高管。

（5）商事公司是指由第21-2014条定义的本州公司；
（6）一般公共利益是指根据第三方标准，公司的业务和经营在整体上对社会和环境产生的实质性积极影响；

（7）独立是指与公共利益公司或其子公司没有实质性关系。个体担任公共利益董事或公共利益高管并不当然丧失独立性。符合下列情形，则认为个体与公共利益公司或其子公司之间存在实质性的关系：

（a）该个体是，或在过去3年内是，公共利益公司或其子公司除公共利益高管以外的雇员；
（b）该个体的直系亲属是，或在过去的3年内是，公共利益公司或其子公司的执行高管；或者

（c）在所有购股权都被视为已行使的情况下，下述持有公共利益公司5%以上已发行股份的登记股东或实际受益人：

（i）个人；或者
（ii）满足以下任一条件的实体：
（A）该个人是该实体的董事、高管或经理；或者
（B）在所有购股权都被视为已行使的情况下，该实体中的个人为持有公共利

outstanding equity interests, calculated as if all outstanding rights to acquire equity interests in the entity had been exercised;

(8) Minimum status vote means:

(a) In the case of a business corporation, in addition to any other required approval or vote, the satisfaction of the following conditions:

(i) The shareholders of every class or series are entitled to vote separately on a corporate action regardless of a limitation stated in the articles of incorporation or bylaws on the voting rights of any class or series; and

(ii) The corporate action must be approved by a vote of the shareholders of each class or series entitled to cast at least two-thirds of the votes that all shareholders of the class or series are entitled to cast on the action; and

(b) In the case of a domestic entity other than a business corporation, in addition to any other required approval, vote, or consent, the satisfaction of the following conditions:

(i) The holders of every class or series of equity interests in the entity that are entitled to receive a distribution of any kind from the entity are entitled to vote separately on or consent to the action regardless of any otherwise applicable limitation on the voting or consent rights of any class or series; and

(ii) The action must be approved by a vote or consent of the holders described in subdivision (i) of this subdivision entitled to cast at least two-thirds of the votes or consents that all of those holders are entitled to cast on the action;

(9) Publicly traded corporation means a business corporation that has shares listed on a national securities exchange or traded in a market maintained by one or more members of a national securities association;

(10) Specific public benefit includes:

(a) Providing low-income or underserved individuals or communities with beneficial products or services;

(b) Promoting economic opportunity for individuals or communities beyond the creation of jobs in the normal course of business;

(c) Protecting or restoring the environment;

(d) Improving human health;

(e) Promoting the arts, sciences, or advancement of knowledge;

(f) Increasing the flow of capital to entities with a purpose to benefit society or the environment; and

(g) Conferring any other particular benefit on society or the environment;

(11) Subsidiary means in relation to a person, an entity in which the person owns beneficially or of record fifty percent or more of the outstanding equity interests; and

(12) Third-party standard means a recognized standard for defining, reporting, and

益公司 5% 以上已发行股份的登记股东或实际受益人。

（8）最低表决要求是指：

（a）在商事公司中，除其他批准或表决的要求外，还应满足以下条件：

（i）每一类别或系列的股东有权作为一个独立的投票团体对公司行为进行投票，即使公司章程或章程细则对某一类别或系列投票权作出了限制；而且

（ii）公司行为必须获得每个类别或系列有投票权的所有股东至少 2/3 的赞成票才能通过；以及

（b）在非商事公司的本州实体中，除其他批准、表决或赞成的要求外，还应满足以下条件：

（i）该实体的每一类别或系列任何权益分配形式下的股权持有者有权对公司行为进行投票，即使存在任何对该类别或系列投票权的限制；而且

（ii）公司行为必须获得第（i）分项规定的有投票权的所有股东至少 2/3 的赞成票才能通过；

（9）上市公司是指在美国证券交易所或美国证券协会中一个或几个成员形成的市场上进行交易的商事公司；

（10）特定的公共利益包括：

（a）向低收入、低福利人群或社区提供有益的产品或服务；

（b）在正常的业务过程中向个人或社区提供创造就业之外的经济机会；

（c）保护或修复环境；

（d）改善人类健康；

（e）促进艺术、科学或知识进步；

（f）促进资本向拥有有利于社会或环境目标的实体流动；以及

（g）实现其他有利于社会或环境的特别利益；

（11）子公司是指在所有购股权被视为已行使的情况下，该实体 50% 以上已发行股份的受益所有权或登记所有权被另一实体所拥有。

（12）第三方标准是指用于定义、报告和评估公司社会和环境绩效的标准，其

assessing corporate social and environmental performance that is:

(a) Comprehensive because it assesses the effect of the business and its operations upon the interests listed in subdivisions (1)(a)(ii), (iii), (iv), and (v) of section 8 of this act;

(b) Developed by an entity that is not controlled by the benefit corporation;

(c) Credible because it is developed by an entity that both:

(i) Has access to necessary expertise to assess overall corporate social and environmental performance; and

(ii) Uses a balanced multistakeholder approach to develop the standard, including a reasonable public comment period; and

(d) Transparent because the following information is publicly available:

(i) About the standard:

(A) The criteria considered when measuring the overall social and environmental performance of a business; and

(B) The relative weightings, if any, of those criteria; and

(ii) About the development and revision of the standard:

(A) The identity of the directors, officers, material owners, and governing body of the entity that developed and controls revisions to the standard;

(B) The process by which revisions to the standard and changes to the membership of the governing body are made; and

(C) An accounting of the revenue and sources of financial support for the entity, with sufficient detail to disclose any relationships that could reasonably be considered to present a potential conflict of interest.

Sec. 4. A benefit corporation shall be incorporated in accordance with the Business Corporation Act, but its articles of incorporation must also state that it is a benefit corporation.

Sec. 5. (1) An existing business corporation may become a benefit corporation under the Nebraska Benefit Corporation Act by amending its articles of incorporation so that they contain, in addition to the requirements of section 21-2018, a statement that the corporation is a benefit corporation. In order to be effective, the amendment must be adopted by at least the minimum status vote.

(2) An entity that is not a benefit corporation may become a benefit corporation pursuant to subsection (1) of this section if the entity is (a) a party to a merger or conversion or (b) an exchanging entity in a share exchange, and the surviving, new, or resulting entity in the merger, conversion, or share exchange is to be a benefit corporation. In order to be effective, a plan of merger, conversion, or share exchange subject to this subsection must be adopted by at least the minimum status vote.

Sec. 6. (1) A benefit corporation may terminate its status as such and cease to be

应满足以下条件：

（a）综合，根据本法第8条第（1）（a）（ii）、（iii）、（iv）和（v）分项规定所列明的利益评估公司业务和经营绩效；

（b）独立，经非由公共利益公司控制的第三方实体制定；

（c）可信，该标准由满足以下两项标准的实体制定：

（i）拥有评估公司社会和环境综合绩效所需的专业知识；以及

（ii）使用平衡多方相关者利益的方法制定标准，包括设定合理期间以听取公众意见。

（d）透明，以下信息可公开获取：

（i）关于标准本身：

（A）衡量企业整体社会和环境绩效时所考虑的指标；以及

（B）这些指标的相关权重；以及

（ii）标准的制定及修改：

（A）制定和控制修改标准的董事、高管、实际控制人等相关人员的身份；

（B）标准修改的程序；

（C）该实体收入和资金来源的核算，包括充分披露合理认知下存在利益冲突的所有细节。

第4条　公共利益公司应当按照《商事公司法》关于公司设立的条款设立，但公司章程必须声明该公司是公共利益公司。

第5条　（1）已成立的商事公司可依据本法的规定成为公共利益公司，除满足第21-2018条的规定外，还应在公司章程中声明其为公共利益公司。公司章程的修改应满足最低表决要求才能生效。

（2）如果一家本州非公共利益公司是（a）兼并合并或财产转换的一方，或者是（b）股权置换中的一方，并且在该兼并合并、财产转换或股权置换中存续新设或留存的实体属公共利益公司，那么该公司可以依据本条第（1）款的规定成为公共利益公司。兼并合并、财产转换或股权置换的计划须满足最低表决要求才能生效。

第6条　（1）公共利益公司可根据《内布拉斯加州公共利益公司法》第4条

subject to the Nebraska Benefit Corporation Act by amending its articles of incorporation to delete the provision required by section 4 or 5 of this act to be stated in the articles of a benefit corporation. In order to be effective, the amendment must be adopted by at least the minimum status vote.

(2) If a plan of merger, conversion, or share exchange would have the effect of terminating the status of a business corporation as a benefit corporation, the plan must be adopted by at least the minimum status vote in order to be effective. Any sale, lease, exchange, or other disposition of all or substantially all of the assets of a benefit corporation, unless the transaction is in the usual and regular course of business, is not effective unless the transaction is approved by at least the minimum status vote.

Sec. 7. (1) A benefit corporation shall have a purpose of creating general public benefit. This purpose is in addition to its purpose under section 21–2024.

(2) The articles of incorporation of a benefit corporation may identify one or more specific public benefits that it is the purpose of the benefit corporation to create in addition to its purposes under section 21–2024 and subsection (1) of this section. The identification of a specific public benefit under this subsection does not limit the purpose of a benefit corporation to create general public benefit under subsection (1) of this section.

(3) The creation of general public benefit and specific public benefit under subsections (1) and (2) of this section is in the best interests of the benefit corporation.

(4) A benefit corporation may amend its articles of incorporation to add, amend, or delete the identification of a specific public benefit that it is the purpose of the benefit corporation to create. In order to be effective, the amendment must be adopted by at least the minimum status vote.

Sec. 8. (1) In discharging the duties of their respective positions and in considering the best interests of the benefit corporation, the board of directors, committees of the board, and individual directors of a benefit corporation:

(a) Shall consider the effects of any action or inaction upon:

(i) The shareholders of the benefit corporation;

(ii) The employees and work force of the benefit corporation, its subsidiaries, and its suppliers;

(iii) The interests of customers as beneficiaries of the general public benefit or specific public benefit purposes of the benefit corporation;

(iv) Community and societal factors, including those of each community in which offices or facilities of the benefit corporation, its subsidiaries, or its suppliers are located;

(v) The local and global environment;

(vi) The short–term and long–term interests of the benefit corporation, including benefits that may accrue to the benefit corporation from its long–term plans and the

或第 5 条的规定，通过修改公司章程，删除章程中公司性质为公共利益公司的声明以表示其不再受本法的调整。公司章程的修改应满足最低表决要求才能生效。

（2）如果兼并合并、财产转换或股权置换计划将产生终止商事公司作为公共利益公司的效力，该交易计划应满足最低表决要求。除该交易属于正常商事往来外，公共利益公司的任何出售、出租、交换或者其他处置全部或主要财产的行为，须满足最低表决要求。

第 7 条　（1）除第 21–2024 条规定的公司目的外，公共利益公司应当有服务于一般公共利益的目的。

（2）公共利益公司的章程可以在第 21–2024 条和本条第（1）款的规定外确定一项或者多项特定公共利益目的。依据本款规定设定的特定公共利益目的并不限制公共利益公司依据本条第（1）款规定设定的一般公共利益目的。

（3）依据本条第（1）款和第（2）款的规定创设的一般和特定公共利益目的为公共利益公司的最佳利益。

（4）公共利益公司可以增加、修改或删除公司章程里设定的特定公共利益目的。公共利益公司对章程的修改需满足最低表决要求才能生效。

第 8 条　（1）在履行各自职责和考虑公共利益公司最佳利益时，公共利益公司的董事会、董事委员会和独立董事：

（a）应当考虑其行为对以下主体的影响：

（i）公共利益公司的股东；

（ii）公共利益公司、其子公司和其供应商的雇员；

（iii）作为公共利益公司一般或特定公共利益受益者的消费者的利益；

（iv）社区和社会因素，包括公共利益公司、其子公司或其供应商的办公地或设施所在地的社区；

（v）当地和全球环境；

（vi）公司的短期和长期利益，包括可能从其长期计划中产生的利益，以及公共利益公司继续保持独立可能产生的最佳利益；以及

possibility that these interests may be best served by the continued independence of the benefit corporation; and

(vii) The ability of the benefit corporation to accomplish its general public benefit purpose and any specific public benefit purpose;

(b) May consider other pertinent factors or the interests of any other group that they deem appropriate; and

(c) Need not give priority to the interests of a particular person or group referred to in subdivision (a) or (b) of this subsection over the interests of any other person or group unless the benefit corporation has stated in its articles of incorporation its intention to give priority to certain interests related to its accomplishment of its general public benefit purpose or of a specific public benefit purpose identified in its articles of incorporation.

(2) The consideration of interests and factors in the manner required by subsection (1) of this section does not constitute a violation of section 21–2095.

(3) Except as provided in the articles of incorporation or bylaws, a director is not personally liable for monetary damages for:

(a) Any action or inaction in the course of performing the duties of a director under subsection (1) of this section if the director performed the duties of office in compliance with section 21–2095 and this section; or

(b) Failure of the benefit corporation to pursue or create general public benefit or specific public benefit.

(4) A director does not have a duty to a person that is a beneficiary of the general public benefit purpose or a specific public benefit purpose of a benefit corporation arising from the status of the person as a beneficiary.

(5) A director who makes a business judgment in good faith fulfills the duty under this section if the director:

(a) Is not interested in the subject of the business judgment;

(b) Is informed with respect to the subject of the business judgment to the extent the director reasonably believes to be appropriate under the circumstances; and

(c) Rationally believes that the business judgment is in the best interests of the benefit corporation.

Sec. 9. (1) The board of directors of a benefit corporation that is a publicly traded corporation shall, and the board of any other benefit corporation may, include a director, who:

(a) Shall be designated the benefit director; and

(b) Shall have, in addition to the powers, duties, rights, and immunities of the other directors of the benefit corporation, the powers, duties, rights, and immunities provided in this section.

（vii）公共利益公司实现其一般公共利益目的和特定公共利益目的的能力；

（b）还可以考虑董事认为合适的其他相关因素或其他群体的利益；以及

（c）无须给予第（a）项或第（b）项中某个利益或因素优先权，除非公共利益公司在其公司章程中表明为了实现其一般公共利益或特定公共利益而给予特定的利益或因素优先权。

（2）本条第（1）款规定的利益和因素并不构成对第 21-2095 条规定的违反。

（3）除非公司章程或章程细则另有规定，董事个人不对以下行为承担损害赔偿责任：

（a）根据本条第（1）款的规定履行董事义务时，任何符合第 21-2095 条和本条规定的作为和不作为；或者

（b）公共利益公司未能实现其一般或特定公共利益。

（4）除非公司章程或章程细则另有规定，董事不对公共利益公司的一般或特定公共利益目的的法定受益人负信义义务。

（5）如果该董事满足以下条件，则认为善意作出商业判断的董事履行了本条规定的义务：

（a）在商业判断中不涉及个人利益；

（b）对商业判断知情，并在该情形下认为该商事判断是合理的；以及

（c）有合理理由认为该商业判断符合公共利益公司的最佳利益。

第 9 条　（1）上市的公共利益公司以及其他形式的公共利益公司的董事会，需包含满足以下要求的董事：

（a）被任命为公共利益董事；并且

（b）除有公共利益公司其他董事的权力、义务、权利和豁免权外，还有本条规定的权力、义务、权利和豁免权。

(2) The benefit director shall be elected and may be removed in the manner provided by the Business Corporation Act. The benefit director shall be an individual who is independent. The benefit director may serve as the benefit officer at the same time as serving as the benefit director. The articles of incorporation or bylaws of a benefit corporation may prescribe additional qualifications of the benefit director not inconsistent with this subsection.

(3) The benefit director shall prepare, and the benefit corporation shall include in the annual benefit report to shareholders required by section 13 of this act, the opinion of the benefit director on all of the following:

(a) Whether the benefit corporation acted in accordance with its general public benefit purpose and any specific public benefit purpose in all material respects during the period covered by the benefit report;

(b) Whether the directors and officers complied with subsection (1) of section 8 of this act and subsection (1) of section 10 of this act, respectively; and

(c) If, in the opinion of the benefit director, the benefit corporation or its directors or officers failed to act or comply in the manner described in subdivisions (3)(a) and (b) of this subsection, a description of the ways in which the benefit corporation or its directors or officers failed to act or comply.

(4) The action or inaction of an individual in the capacity of a benefit director constitutes for all purposes an action or inaction of that individual in the capacity of a director of the benefit corporation.

(5) Regardless of whether the articles of incorporation or bylaws of a benefit corporation include a provision eliminating or limiting the personal liability of directors authorized by section 21–2018, a benefit director is not personally liable for an act or omission in the capacity of a benefit director unless the act or omission constitutes self–dealing, willful misconduct, or a knowing violation of law.

Sec. 10. (1) Each officer of a benefit corporation shall consider the interests and factors described in subsection (1) of section 8 of this act in the manner provided in that subsection if:

(a) The officer has discretion to act with respect to a matter; and

(b) It reasonably appears to the officer that the matter may have a material effect on the creation by the benefit corporation of general public benefit or a specific public benefit identified in the articles of incorporation of the benefit corporation.

(2) The consideration of interests and factors in the manner described in subsection (1) of this section does not constitute a violation of section 21–2099.

(3) Except as provided in the articles of incorporation or bylaws, an officer is not personally liable for monetary damages for:

(a) An action or inaction as an officer in the course of performing the duties of an officer

（2）公共利益董事应当依据商事公司法董事选任条款选任，并可根据商事公司法董事解除条款免职。公共利益董事应当是独立的个体。公共利益董事可以同时担任公共利益高管。公共利益公司的公司章程或公司章程细则可对公共利益董事的资格作出与本款不一致的规定。

（3）公共利益董事应当编写其对以下事项的意见，公共利益公司应当根据第13条的规定将其附于年度公共利益报告中供股东查阅：

（a）公共利益公司是否在报告所述期间，在所有重要事项上依其一般公共利益目的和特定公共利益目的行事；

（b）董事和高管是否分别依本法第8条第（1）款和第10条第（1）款的规定行事；

（c）如果公共利益董事认为公共利益公司或其董事、高管未能依本款第（3）（a）项和第（b）项的要求行事，其应陈述公共利益公司或其董事、高管未能履行责任的情形。

（4）公共利益董事在职权范围内的个人的作为或不作为应视为公共利益公司董事的行为。

（5）无论公共利益公司的公司章程或者公司章程细则是否依第21-2010条规定的董事责任免除条款删除或限制董事的个人责任，公共利益董事在行使职责时不对其任何作为或不作为行为承担个人责任，但自我交易或故意违法行为除外。

第10条 （1）公共利益公司的每一位高管应当以本法第8条第（1）款中规定的行为标准考虑该条规定的利益和因素，如果：

（a）高管就该行为有自由裁量权；以及

（b）高管有合理理由认为该行为对公共利益公司在章程中创设的一般或特定公共利益有实质性影响。

（2）对本条第（1）款中利益和相关因素的考虑不构成对第21-2099条规定的违反。

（3）除非在公司章程及章程细则中明确表明，高管不对以下行为承担损害赔偿责任：

（a）依据本条第（1）款规定履行职责过程中的任何作为或者不作为，如该行

under subsection (1) of this section if the officer performed the duties of the position in compliance with section 21–2099 and this section; or

(b) Failure of the benefit corporation to pursue or create general public benefit or specific public benefit.

(4) An officer does not have a duty to a person that is a beneficiary of the general public benefit purpose or a specific public benefit purpose of a benefit corporation arising from the status of the person as a beneficiary.

(5) An officer who makes a business judgment in good faith fulfills the duty under this section if the officer:

(a) Is not interested in the subject of the business judgment;

(b) Is informed with respect to the subject of the business judgment to the extent the officer reasonably believes to be appropriate under the circumstances; and

(c) Rationally believes that the business judgment is in the best interests of the benefit corporation.

Sec. 11. (1) A benefit corporation may have an officer designated the benefit officer.

(2) A benefit officer shall have:

(a) The powers and duties relating to the purpose of the corporation to create general public benefit or specific public benefit provided:

(i) By the bylaws; or

(ii) Absent controlling provisions in the bylaws, by resolutions or orders of the board of directors; and

(b) The duty to prepare the annual benefit report required by section 13 of this act.

Sec. 12.(1)(a) Except in a benefit enforcement proceeding, no person may bring an action or assert a claim against a benefit corporation or its directors or officers with respect to:

(i) Failure to pursue or create general public benefit or a specific public benefit set forth in its articles of incorporation; or

(ii) Violation of an obligation, duty, or standard of conduct under the Nebraska Benefit Corporation Act.

(b) A benefit corporation is not liable for monetary damages under the act for any failure of the benefit corporation to pursue or create general public benefit or a specific public benefit.

(2) A benefit enforcement proceeding may be commenced or maintained only:

(a) Directly by the benefit corporation; or

(b) Derivatively in accordance with the Business Corporation Act by:

(i) A person or group of persons that owned beneficially or of record at least two percent of the total number of shares of a class or series outstanding at the time of the act or omission

为符合本条和第 21–2099 条的规定；或者

（b）公共利益公司未能追求或实现一般或特定公共利益。

（4）高管不对任何一般公共利益或特定公共利益的法定受益人负信义义务。

（5）如果高管满足以下条件，则认为善意作出商业判断的董事履行了本条规定的义务：

（a）在商业判断过程中不涉及个人利益；

（b）拥有使其在该情形下做出合理商业判断的充分信息；以及

（c）有合理理由认为该商业判断符合公共利益公司的最佳利益。

第 11 条 （1）公共利益公司可以将高管任命为公共利益高管。

（2）公共利益高管应当有：

（a）规定于以下文件中的创设一般或特定公共利益目的的权力和义务：

（i）公司章程细则；或者

（ii）在公司章程细则中没有规定时，董事会作出的有关决议或者命令；以及

（b）本法第 14 条规定的公共利益报告的编写义务。

第 12 条 （1）（a）非经公共利益实施程序，任何人不得因以下事项向公共利益公司或者其董事、高管提起诉讼或主张：

（i）未能追求或实现其在公司章程中陈述的一般或特定公共利益；或者

（ii）违反本法规定下的责任、义务或行为标准。

（b）公共利益公司不对本法规定下的任何未能追求或实现一般或特定公共利益的行为承担损害赔偿责任。

（2）可以由下列主体提起公共利益实施程序：

（a）由公共利益公司直接提起；或者

（b）依据商业公司法由以下主体派生提起：

（i）在被诉作为或不作为行为发生时，拥有公共利益公司 2% 以上已发行的某类别或系列股份的个人或群体；

complained of;

(ii) A director;

(iii) A person or group of persons that owned beneficially or of record five percent or more of the outstanding equity interests in an entity of which the benefit corporation is a subsidiary at the time of the act or omission complained of; or

(iv) Other persons as specified in the articles of incorporation or bylaws of the benefit corporation.

(3) For purposes of this section, a person is the beneficial owner of shares or equity interests if the shares or equity interests are held in a voting trust or by a nominee on behalf of the beneficial owner.

Sec. 13. (1) A benefit corporation shall prepare an annual benefit report including all of the following:

(a) A narrative description of:

(i) The ways in which the benefit corporation pursued general public benefit during the year and the extent to which general public benefit was created;

(ii) Both:

(A) The ways in which the benefit corporation pursued a specific public benefit that the articles of incorporation state it is the purpose of the benefit corporation to create; and

(B) The extent to which that specific public benefit was created;

(iii) Any circumstances that have hindered the creation by the benefit corporation of general public benefit or specific public benefit; and

(iv) The process and rationale for selecting or changing the third–party standard used to prepare the benefit report;

(b) An assessment of the overall social and environmental performance of the benefit corporation against a third–party standard:

(i) Applied consistently with any application of that standard in prior benefit reports; or

(ii) Accompanied by an explanation of the reasons for:

(A) Any inconsistent application; or

(B) The change to that standard from the one used in the immediately prior benefit report;

(c) The name of the benefit director and the benefit officer, if any, and the address to which correspondence to each of them may be directed;

(d) The compensation paid by the benefit corporation during the year to each director in the capacity of a director;

(e) The statement of the benefit director described in subsection (3) of section 9 of this act; and

(f) A statement of any connection between the organization that established the

（ii）董事；

（iii）持有公共利益公司母公司 5% 以上已发行股份的登记股东或实际受益人；或者

（iv）在公共利益公司章程或章程细则中列明的其他人员。

（3）就本条规定而言，若股份或股利由表决权信托或指定第三人代持，则将此人视为该股份或股利的实益所有权人。

第 13 条　（1）年度公共利益报告应包含以下内容：

（a）对以下事项的说明：

（i）公共利益公司本年度追求一般公共利益的方法及其实现的情况。

（ii）同时包括：

（A）公共利益公司实现公司章程中列明的特定公共利益的方法；以及

（B）该特定公共利益实现的情况；

（iii）阻碍公共利益公司实现一般和特定公共利益的情形；

（iv）为编写公共利益报告而选择或更换第三方标准的程序和原因；

（b）依据第三方标准对公共利益公司整体社会和环境表现作出的评价：

（i）沿用先前公共利益报告中使用的标准；或者

（ii）附一份说明以解释：

（A）适用中的差异；或者

（B）与上一份报告相比所使用的标准的变化；

（c）公共利益董事和公共利益高管的姓名和联系地址（如有）；

（d）公共利益公司在上一年度支付给每位董事的薪酬；

（e）公共利益董事依第 9 条第（3）款规定编写的陈述意见；以及

（f）设立第三方标准的机构或其董事、高管或 5% 以上管理权利的持有者与公

third–party standard, or its directors, officers, or any holder of five percent or more of the governance interests in the organization, and the benefit corporation or its directors, officers, or any holder of five percent or more of the outstanding shares of the benefit corporation, including any financial or governance relationship which might materially affect the credibility of the use of the third–party standard.

(2) If, during the year covered by a benefit report, a benefit director resigned from or refused to stand for reelection to the position of benefit director, or was removed from the position of benefit director, and the benefit director furnished the benefit corporation with any written correspondence concerning the circumstances surrounding the resignation, refusal, or removal, the benefit report shall include that correspondence as an exhibit.

(3) Neither the benefit report nor the assessment of the performance of the benefit corporation in the benefit report required by subdivision (1)(b) of this section needs to be audited or certified by a third–party standards provider.

Sec. 14. (1) A benefit corporation shall send its annual benefit report to each shareholder:

(a) Within one hundred twenty days following the end of the fiscal year of the benefit corporation; or

(b) At the same time that the benefit corporation delivers any other annual report to its shareholders.

(2) A benefit corporation shall post all of its benefit reports on the public portion of its Internet web site, if any, except that the compensation paid to directors and financial or proprietary information included in the benefit reports may be omitted from the benefit reports as posted.

(3) If a benefit corporation does not have an Internet web site, the benefit corporation shall provide a copy of its most recent benefit report, without charge, to any person that requests a copy, except that the compensation paid to directors and financial or proprietary information included in the benefit report may be omitted from the copy of the benefit report provided.

(4)(a) Concurrently with the delivery of the benefit report to shareholders under subsection (1) of this section, the benefit corporation shall deliver a copy of the benefit report to the Secretary of State for filing, except that the compensation paid to directors and financial or proprietary information included in the benefit report may be omitted from the benefit report as delivered to the Secretary of State.

(b) The Secretary of State shall charge a fee in the amount prescribed in subdivision (1)(y) of section 21–2005 for filing a benefit report. The fee shall be remitted to the State Treasurer for credit to the Corporation Cash Fund.

共利益公司或其董事、高管或公共利益公司 5% 以上已发行股份持有者之间关系的声明，包括任何可能实质性影响第三方标准可信度的财务或管理关系。

（2）在公共利益报告年度内，如果公共利益董事辞职、拒绝连任或被免职，且该公共利益董事与公司有任何书面的涉及辞职、拒绝连任或免职的书信往来，公共利益公司应当将该书信往来作为公共利益报告的附件。

（3）公共利益报告和依据本条第（1）（b）项的规定编写的公共利益报告中的公共利益公司表现评价书都无须经审计或第三方证明。

第 14 条　（1）公共利益公司应根据以下要求向每位股东提交公共利益报告：

（a）公共利益公司财政年度结束后 120 天内；或者

（b）公共利益公司向其股东送交其他年度报告的同一时间。

（2）若条件允许，公共利益公司应当将其所有公共利益报告发布于其网站的公共部分；但公司可将公共利益报告中的董事薪酬和财务、所有权信息删除。

（3）如果公共利益公司没有网站，其应向所有索取报告的个人免费提供最新公共利益报告的副本，但可将公共利益报告副本中的董事薪酬和财务、所有权信息删除。

（4）（a）在依本条第（1）款的规定将公共利益报告提交给股东的同时，公共利益公司应当将该公共利益报告提交州务卿备案，但可将公共利益报告中的董事薪酬、财务或所有权信息在提交州务卿的报告中删除。

（b）州务卿应根据第 21-2005（1）（y）项的规定收取备案费用，该费用应纳入本州公司现金储备基金。

THE STATE OF NEVADA

Assembly Bill No. 89

AN ACT relating to business entities; authorizing the formation of benefit corporations; providing for the operation and governance of benefit corporations; and providing other matters properly relating thereto.

THE PEOPLE OF THE STATE OF NEVADA, REPRESENTED IN SENATE AND ASSEMBLY, DO ENACT AS FOLLOWS:

Section 1.Title 7 of NRS is hereby amended by adding thereto a new chapter to consist of the provisions set forth as sections 2 to 20, inclusive, of this act.

Sec.2.As used in this chapter, unless the context otherwise requires, the words and terms defined in sections 3 to 9, inclusive, of this act have the meanings ascribed to them in those sections.

Sec.3. "Benefit corporation "means a corporation organized under chapter 78 or 78A of NRS, NRS 81.010 to 81.160, inclusive, or chapter 89 of NRS that has elected to become subject to this chapter and whose status as a benefit corporation has not been terminated pursuant to this chapter.

Sec.4."Benefit enforcement proceeding" means a claim or action for:

1. Failure of a benefit corporation to pursue the general public benefit purpose of the benefit corporation or any specific public benefit purpose set forth in its articles of incorporation;

2. Violation of a duty or standard of conduct imposed on a director or officer of a benefit corporation pursuant to this chapter; or

3. Failure of a benefit corporation to deliver or post on its Internet website an annual benefit report as required by section 19 of this act.

Sec.5."General public benefit" means a material positive impact on society and the environment, taken as a whole, as assessed against a third–party standard, from the business and operations of a benefit corporation.

内华达州

议会法案第 89 号

本法与商事实体有关，授权设立公共利益公司；为公共利益公司的管理及与此相关的其他问题提供规则。

内华达州议会颁布如下法令：

第 1 条 《内华达州修订法》第 7 编新的一章，由本法第 2 条至第 20 条组成。

第 2 条 除非另有规定，在本章第 3 条至第 9 条中出现的名词的含义如下：

第 3 条 “公共利益公司”是指根据《内华达州修订法》第 78 章或第 78A 章、《内华达州修订法》第 81.010 条至第 81.160 条或《内华达州修订法》第 89 章的规定，选择接受本章规定调整且不存在本章规定的“终止情形”的公司。

第 4 条 “公共利益实施程序”是指因以下事项提起的诉讼或请求：
1. 公共利益公司未能追求或实现公司章程规定的一般或特定公共利益目的；

2. 公共利益公司违反本章规定下的任何义务、责任或行为标准；或者

3. 公共利益公司未依照本法第 19 条的规定在其网站上公布其年度公共利益报告。

第 5 条 “一般公共利益”是指根据第三方标准，公司的业务和经营整体上对社会和环境产生的实质性积极影响。

Sec.6. "Minimum status vote" means:

1. In the case of a corporation, in addition to any other approval or vote required by chapter 78 or 78A of NRS, NRS to 81.160, inclusive, or chapter 89 of NRS, whichever is applicable, by chapter 92A of NRS or by the articles of incorporation, satisfaction of both of the following conditions:

(a) The shareholders of every class or series are entitled to vote on the corporate action regardless of any limitation on the voting rights of any class or series stated in the articles of incorporation or bylaws.

(b) The corporate action must be approved by the outstanding shares of each class or series by at least two-thirds of the votes, or the greater vote if required by the articles of incorporation, that all shareholders of the class or series are entitled to cast on that action.

2. In the case of a business entity organized and existing under the laws of this State other than a corporation, in addition to any other approval, vote or consent required by the laws of this State that govern the internal affairs of the entity, by any provision of the publicly filed record or document required to form the entity, or by any agreement binding some or all of the holders of the equity interests in the entity, satisfaction of both of the following conditions:

(a) The holders of every class or series of interest in the entity that are entitled to receive a distribution of any kind from the entity or partnership are entitled to vote on or consent to the action regardless of any otherwise applicable limitation on the voting or consent rights of any class or series.

(b) The action must be approved by the vote or consent of the holders described in paragraph (a) by at least two-thirds of the votes or consent of those holders, or the greater vote or consent if required by the publicly filed record or document required to form the entity or partnership or by any agreement binding those holders.

Sec.7. "Specific public benefit" includes, without limitation:

1. Providing low-income or underserved individuals or communities with beneficial products or services;

2. Promoting economic opportunity for individuals or communities beyond the creation of jobs in the normal course of business;

3. Protecting, preserving or restoring the environment;

4. Improving human health;

5. Promoting the arts, sciences or advancement of knowledge;

6. Increasing the flow of capital to entities with a general public benefit purpose; and

7. The accomplishment of any other particular benefit for society or the environment.

Sec.8. "Subsidiary" means an entity in which a person owns beneficially or of record 50 percent or more of the outstanding equity interests.

第 6 条　“最低表决要求”是指：

1. 在商事公司中，除《内华达州修订法》第 78 章或《内华达州修订法》第 78A 章、《内华达州修订法》第 81.010 条至第 81.160 条或《内华达州修订法》第 89 章的规定或公司章程规定的表决要求外，还应满足以下条件：

（a）每一类别或系列的股东应当有权作为一个独立的投票团体对公司行为进行投票，即使公司章程或公司章程细则对某一类别或系列的投票权作出了限制。

（b）公司行为必须获得每个类别或系列有投票权的所有股东的至少 2/3 的赞成票才能通过。

2. 非商事公司的本州实体，除本州公司内部治理相关法律，约束部分或所有股权持有者协议的规定或设立其他形式的实体所需要的公开登记记录或文件中规定的其他批准、表决或赞成的要求外，还应满足以下两个条件：

（a）该实体的每一类别或系列享有任何权益分配形式的股权持有者有权对公司行为进行投票，即使存在任何对该类别或系列的投票权限制；

（b）公司行为必须获得第（a）项规定的有投票权的所有股东至少 2/3 的赞成票才能通过。

第 7 条　“特定的公共利益”包括但不限于：

1. 向低收入、低福利人群或社区提供有益的产品或服务；

2. 在正常的业务过程中向个人或社区提供创造就业之外的经济机会；

3. 保护或修复环境；

4. 改善人类健康；

5. 促进艺术、科学或知识进步；

6. 促进资本向拥有有利于社会或环境目标的实体流动；以及

7. 实现其他有利于社会或环境的特定利益。

第 8 条　“子公司”是指在所有购股权都被视为已行使的情况下，该公司 50% 以上已发行的股份的受益所有权或登记所有权被另一实体所拥有。

Sec.9."Third-party standard" means a standard for defining, reporting and assessing overall corporate social and environmental performance:

1. That provides for a comprehensive assessment of the impact of the benefit corporation and its operations upon the considerations listed in paragraphs (b) to (e), inclusive, of subsection 1 of section 15 of this act; and

2. That is developed by an entity that:

(a) Has no material financial relationship with the benefit corporation or a subsidiary of the benefit corporation;

(b) Is governed by a governing body of which not more than one-third of the members are representatives of:

(1) Associations of businesses operating in a specific industry whose members' performances are measured by the standard;

(2) Businesses from a specific industry or an association of businesses in that industry; or

(3) Businesses whose performance is assessed against that standard;

(c) Is not materially financed by an association or business described in paragraph (b);

(d) Accesses necessary and appropriate expertise to assess overall corporate social and environmental performance; and

(e) Uses a balanced, multi stakeholder approach to develop the standard, including, without limitation, a public comment period of at least 30 days; and

3. About which the following information is available to the public:

(a)The criteria considered when measuring the overall social and environmental performance of a business;

(b) The relative weightings assigned to the criteria described in paragraph (a);

(c) The identity of the directors, officers, material owners and the governing body of the entity that developed, and controls revisions to, the standard;

(d) The process for revising the standard and changing the membership of the governing body that developed, and controls revisions to, the standard; and

(e) An accounting of the sources of financial support for the entity that developed, and controls revisions to, the standard which provides sufficient detail to disclose any relationships that could reasonably be considered to present a potential conflict of interest.

Sec.10.1.This chapter is applicable to all benefit corporations.

2. The provisions of this chapter do not create any implication that a contrary or different rule of law is or would be applicable to a corporation that is not a benefit corporation. The provisions of this chapter do not affect any statute or rule of law that is or would be applicable to a corporation that is not a benefit corporation.

3. The provisions of chapters 78 and 78A of NRS, NRS 81.010 to 81.160, inclusive,

第9条　“第三方标准”是指用于定义、报告和评估公司社会和环境绩效的标准，其应满足以下条件：

1. 根据本法第15条第1款第（b）项至第（e）项所列明的考虑因素综合性地评估公共利益公司的影响及其运营活动；以及

2. 该标准由以下实体制定：

（a）与公共利益公司及其子公司没有重大经济关系；

（b）制定或实际控制标准制定的实体不少于1/3的成员是以下群体的代表：

（1）在特定行业经营的企业协会，其成员的绩效由该标准衡量；

（2）特定行业或该行业的企业协会中的企业；

（3）绩效由该标准评价的企业；

（c）实体并非由第（b）项规定的协会或企业资助；或者

（d）拥有评估公司社会和环境综合绩效所需的专业知识；以及

（e）使用平衡多方相关者利益的方法制定标准，包括但不限于设定至少30日的期间以听取公众意见；以及

3. 该标准的以下信息可以公开获取：

（a）衡量企业整体和环境综合绩效时所考虑的指标；

（b）第（a）项中所述的指标的相关权重；

（c）制定和控制修改标准的实体的董事、高管、实际控制人等相关人员的身份；

（d）标准的修改以及制定、控制或修改标准的主体成员变更的程序；以及

（e）该实体的收入和资金来源的核算，包括充分披露合理认知下存在利益冲突的所有细节。

第10条　1. 本章适用于所有公共利益公司。

2. 本法不应为非公共利益公司设定相反或不同的规则。本法不影响其他适用于非公共利益公司的公司法规或规则的效力。

3. 除《内华达州修订法》第78章或第78A章、《内华达州修订法》第81.010

and chapters 89 and 92A of NRS apply to benefit corporations except where those provisions conflict or are inconsistent with the provisions of this chapter. A benefit corporation may be subject simultaneously to this chapter and chapter 78 or 78A of NRS, NRS 81.010 to 81.160, inclusive, or chapter 89 of NRS, as applicable.

4. A provision of the articles of incorporation or bylaws of a benefit corporation may not limit, be inconsistent with or supersede a provision of this chapter.

Sec.11. A benefit corporation must be formed in accordance with NRS 78.030 to 78.055, inclusive, except that the articles of incorporation must:

1. State that the corporation is a benefit corporation; and

2. Identify any specific public benefit adopted by the corporation pursuant to section 14 of this act.

Sec.12.1.A domestic corporation may become a benefit corporation under this chapter by amending its articles of incorporation so that the articles of incorporation contain a statement that the domestic corporation is a benefit corporation. The amendment must be adopted by at least the minimum status vote. If the amendment is adopted, a shareholder of the corporation may, by complying with the provisions of NRS 92A.300 to 92A.500, inclusive, require the corporation to purchase at their market value the shares owned by the shareholder which are dissenting shares in accordance with the procedures set forth in NRS 92A.300 to 92A.500, inclusive, as if the adoption of the amendment were an action to which those provisions were applicable.

2. If a corporation that is not a benefit corporation is a constituent entity in a merger or is acquired in an exchange, and the surviving entity in the merger is to be a benefit corporation or the articles of incorporation of the acquired corporation are to be amended in the exchange to provide that the acquired corporation will be a benefit corporation, the merger or exchange, whichever is applicable, is not effective unless the plan of merger or exchange, whichever is applicable, is approved by the corporation by the minimum status vote.

3. If a domestic other business entity is a constituent entity in a merger and the surviving entity in the merger is to be a benefit corporation, the merger is not effective unless the plan of merger is approved by the domestic other business entity by at least the minimum status vote.

4. If a domestic other business entity is the constituent entity in a conversion in which the resulting entity will be a benefit corporation, the plan of conversion is not effective unless the conversion is approved by the converting entity by at least the minimum status vote.

5. As used in this section:

(a) "Constituent entity" has the meaning ascribed to it in NRS 92A.015.

(b) "Domestic corporation" means a corporation organized and existing under chapter

条至第 81.160 条以及《内华达州修订法》第 89 章、第 92A 章与本章存在冲突外，上述条款适用于公共利益公司。公共利益公司同时受本章和《内华达州修订法》第 78 章或第 78A 章、《内华达州修订法》第 81.010 条至第 81.160 条以及《内华达州修订法》第 89 章、第 92A 章的规制。

4. 公共利益公司的公司章程或章程细则不能限制、违背或取代本章的规定。

第 11 条　公共利益公司必须根据《内华达州修订法》第 78.030 条至第 78.055 条的规定设立，除此之外，公司章程还必须：

1. 声明其为公共利益公司；并且

2. 根据本法第 14 条的规定确定其特定的公共利益。

第 12 条　1. 本州已成立的商业公司可依据本章的规定转变为公共利益公司，除满足《商业公司法》有关公司章程的要求外，还需修改公司章程，作出该公司为公共利益公司的声明。公司章程的修改应满足最低表决要求。如果公司章程的修改获得通过，该公司的股东可根据《内华达州修订法》第 92A.300 条至第 92A.500 条的规定，要求公司根据《内华达州修订法》第 92A.300 条至第 92A.500 条的规定，以公允价值收购异议股东的股份，就像修改章程的通过是适用这些规定的行为。

2. 如果一家本州非公共利益公司是合并或财产转换的一方，或者是股权置换中的一方，并且该合并、财产转换或股权置换中存续、新设或留存的实体属公共利益公司，那么合并、财产转换或股权置换的计划须满足最低表决要求才能生效。

3. 如果一家本州的其他商事实体是被兼并的一方，兼并后新设实体为公共利益公司，那么该兼并计划须满足最低表决要求才能生效。

4. 如果本州一家不具有公共利益公司形态的商事公司将其股份转换为公共利益公司股份，那么该转换计划须满足最低表决要求才能生效。

5. 本条所使用的名词：

（a）“被吸收实体”的含义由《内华达州修订法》第 92A.015 条规定。

（b）“本州公司”是指根据《内华达州修订法》第 78 章、第 78A 章、第 89

78, 78A or 89 of NRS, or a nonprofit cooperative corporation organized pursuant to NRS 81.010 to 81.160, inclusive.

(c) "Domestic other business entity" means a limited–liability company organized and existing under chapter 86 of NRS, a limited partnership organized and existing under chapter 87A or 88 of NRS or a business trust organized and existing under chapter 88A of NRS.

(d) "Exchange" has the meaning ascribed to it in NRS 92A.050.

(e) "Resulting entity" has the meaning ascribed to it in NRS 92A.090.

Sec.13.1.A benefit corporation may terminate its status as a benefit corporation and cease to be subject to this chapter by amending its articles of incorporation to delete the statement in the articles of incorporation that the corporation is a benefit corporation as required by section 11 or 12 of this act. To be effective, the amendment must be adopted by at least the minimum status vote.

2. If a benefit corporation is a constituent entity in a merger, conversion or exchange and the effect of the merger, conversion or exchange will terminate the status of the benefit corporation as a benefit corporation, the plan or merger, conversion or exchange, whichever is applicable, is not effective unless it is approved by at least the minimum status vote.

3. If not made in the usual and regular course of business, a sale, lease, exchange or other disposition of all or substantially all of the property of a benefit corporation is not effective unless it is approved by at least the minimum status vote.

4. As used in this section:

(a) "Constituent entity" has the meaning ascribed to it in NRS 92A.015.

(b)"Exchange" has the meaning ascribed to it in NRS 92A.050.

Sec.14.1.A benefit corporation shall have the purpose of creating general public benefit. This purpose is in addition to, and may be a limitation on, the corporation's purpose under NRS78.030 and any specific purpose set forth in its articles of incorporation pursuant to NRS 78.037.

2. In addition to the provisions required to be stated in the articles of incorporation pursuant to NRS 78.035, the articles of incorporation of a benefit corporation must contain a statement that the corporation is a benefit corporation. The articles of incorporation may identify the creation of one or more specific public benefits as a purpose or as purposes of the benefit corporation. The identification of any specific public benefit pursuant to this subsection does not limit the obligation of the benefit corporation to create general public benefit.

3. The creation of general and specific public benefits as provided in subsections 1 and 2 is in the best interests of the benefit corporation.

4. A professional corporation that is a benefit corporation does not violate NRS 89.050 by providing the professional services for which it was incorporated for the purpose of

章的规定设立的公司或根据《内华达州修订法》第81.010条至第81.160条的规定设立的非营利性公司。

（c）“本州其他商事实体是指”根据《内华达州修订法》第86章的规定设立的有限责任公司，根据《内华达州修订法》第87A章或第88章设立的有限合伙或根据《内华达州修订法》第88A章设立的商事信托。

（d）“交易”的含义由《内华达州修订法》第92A.050条规定。

（e）“新设实体”的含义由《内华达州修订法》第92A.090条规定。

第13条　1. 公共利益公司可通过删除本法第11条或第12条规定的公司章程中作为公共利益公司的声明来终止其公共利益公司的形态并不再受本章规定的调整。公司章程的修改应满足最低表决要求才能生效。

2. 如果公共利益公司是兼并合并、财产转换或是股权置换中的被吸收的实体，合并、财产转换或股权置换将终止其作为公共利益公司的形态，则合并、财产转换或股权置换等计划须满足最低表决要求才能生效。

3. 除正常商业往来外，公共利益公司的任何出售、出租、交换或者其他处置全部或主要财产的行为，须满足最低表决要求。

4. 本条使用的名词的含义如下：

（a）“被吸收实体”的含义由《内华达州修订法》第92A.015条规定。

（b）“交易”的含义由《内华达州修订法》第92A.050条规定。

第14条　1. 公共利益公司应当有服务于一般公共利益的目的。该目的可能在《内华达州修订法》第78.030条所规定的公司目的或公司根据《内华达州修订法》第78.037条在其公司章程中所设特定目的之外，或对上述目的产生限制。

2. 公司章程除满足《内华达州修订法》第78.035条的规定外，公共利益公司还应在章程中声明其为公共利益公司。公司章程可以确定一个或多个特定公共利益作为公司目的。根据本款的规定设定的特定公共利益并不限制公共利益公司创造一般公共利益的义务。

3. 依据第1款和第2款规定创设的一般和特定公共利益目的为公共利益公司的最佳利益。

4. 专业公共利益公司通过提供专业服务实现一般和任何特定公共利益并不构成对《内华达州修订法》第89.050条规定的违反。

creating general public benefit or any specific public benefit.

5. A benefit corporation may amend its articles of incorporation to add, amend or delete the identification of any specific public benefit that must be the purpose of the benefit corporation to create. To be effective, the amendment must be adopted by at least the minimum status vote.

Sec.15.1.In discharging the duties of their respective positions, and in considering the best interests of the benefit corporation, the board of directors, committees of the board of directors and individual directors of a benefit corporation must consider the impacts of any action or inaction upon:

(a) The shareholders of the benefit corporation.

(b) The employees and workforce of the benefit corporation and its subsidiaries and suppliers.

(c) The interests of customers of the benefit corporation as beneficiaries of the general public benefit purpose or any specific public benefit purpose of the benefit corporation.

(d) Community and societal factors, including, without limitation, factors in the community in which offices or facilities of the benefit corporation or its subsidiaries or suppliers are located.

(e) The local and global environment.

(f) The short–term and long–term interests of the benefit corporation, including, without limitation, benefits that may accrue to the benefit corporation from its long–term plans and the possibility that those interests may be best served by control of the benefit corporation remaining unchanged.

(g) The ability of the benefit corporation to accomplish its general public benefit purpose and any specific public benefit purpose.

2. In discharging their respective duties, the board of directors, committees of the board of directors and individual directors of a benefit corporation may consider:

(a) The resources, intent and conduct, including, without limitation, the past, stated and potential conduct, of any person seeking to acquire control of the benefit corporation.

(b) Any other pertinent factors or the interests of any other person or group.

3. In discharging their respective duties, the board of directors, committees of the board of directors and individual directors of a benefit corporation are not required to give priority to any particular factor or the interests of any particular person or group referred to in subsection 1 or 2 over any other factor or the interests of any other person or group, unless the benefit corporation has stated its intention to give priority to a specific public benefit purpose identified in the articles of incorporation of the benefit corporation.

4. In performing his or her duties, a director of a benefit corporation is entitled to rely on information, opinions, reports, books of account or statements, including financial

5. 公共利益公司可以通过修改公司章程增加、修改或删除其设定的特定公共利益目标。公司对章程的修改须满足最低表决要求才能生效。

第 15 条　1. 在履行各自职责和考虑公共利益公司最佳利益时，公共利益公司的董事会、董事委员会和独立董事应当考虑其行为对以下主体的影响：

（a）公共利益公司的股东。

（b）公共利益公司、其子公司和供应商的雇员。

（c）作为公共利益公司一般或特定公共利益受益者的消费者的利益。

（d）社区和社会因素，包括但不限于公共利益公司、其子公司或其供应商的办公地或设施所在地的社区。

（e）当地和全球环境。

（f）公司的短期和长期利益，包括可能从其长期计划中产生的利益，以及公共利益公司继续保持独立可能产生的最佳利益。

（g）公共利益公司实现其一般公共利益目的和特定公共利益目的的能力。

2. 在履行各自职责时，公共利益公司的董事会、董事委员会和独立董事可以考虑：

（a）试图获取公司控制权的人的资源、意图和行为，包括过去、现在和未来的行为；

（b）董事认为合适的其他相关因素或其他群体的利益。

3. 除非公共利益公司在其公司章程中明确规定，公共利益公司的董事、董事委员会和独立董事在履行职责过程中无须给予第 1 款或第 2 款中某个利益或因素优先权。

4. 为履行其职责，公共利益公司的董事有权获得以下主体提供的信息、意见、报表或报告以及金融报表和其他财政数据：

statements and other financial data, that are prepared or presented by:

(a) One or more directors, officers or employees of the benefit corporation reasonably believed to be reliable and competent in the matters prepared or presented;

(b) Counsel, public accountants, financial advisers, valuation advisers, investment bankers or other persons as to matters reasonably believed to be within the preparer's or presenter's professional or expert competence; or

(c) A committee on which the director does not serve, established in accordance with NRS 78.125, as to matters within the committee's designated authority and matters on which the committee is reasonably believed to merit confidence, but a director is not entitled to rely on such information, opinions, reports, books of account or statements if the director has knowledge concerning the matter in question that would cause reliance thereon to be unwarranted.

5. The consideration of interests and factors in the manner required by this section does not constitute a violation of NRS 78.138 or 78.139 and is in addition to the ability of directors to consider the interests and factors set forth in NRS 78.138 and 78.139.

6. A director of a benefit corporation is not liable for monetary damages for:

(a) Any action or inaction in the course of performing the duties of a director under this section if the director performed the duties of a director in compliance with this section and NRS 78.138 and 78.139.

(b) Failure of the benefit corporation to pursue or create general public benefit or any specific public benefit identified in the articles of incorporation of the benefit corporation pursuant to section 14 of this act.

7. A director does not have a duty to a person who is a beneficiary of the general public benefit purpose or any specific public benefit purpose identified in the articles of incorporation of the benefit corporation pursuant to section 14 of this act arising from the status of the person as a beneficiary.

8. In performing his or her duties, a director of a benefit corporation has the benefit of the presumptions established by subsection 3 of NRS 78.138.

Sec.16.1.The board of directors of a benefit corporation shall prepare and include in the annual benefit report to shareholders required by section 19 of this act a statement indicating whether, in the opinion of the board of directors, the benefit corporation failed in any material respect to pursue its general public benefit purpose and any specific public benefit purpose identified in the articles of incorporation pursuant to section 14 of this act during the period covered by the report.

2. If, in the opinion of the board of directors, the benefit corporation failed to pursue its general public benefit purpose or any specific public benefit purpose identified in the articles of incorporation pursuant to section 14 of this act, the statement required by

（a）董事认为相关事项中可靠并能够胜任的一个或多个公共利益公司的董事、高管或其雇员；

（b）公司顾问、公共会计和金融咨询师、估值评估师、投资银行或其他具备专业资质或专家水平的人员；或者

（c）根据《内华达州修订法》第 78.125 条的规定设立的非由董事组成的委员会，在该委员会被授权范围内，根据合理判断确信的事项。但是如果董事知道有关事项会导致该确信无根据，则董事不能信赖此类信息、意见、报告、账簿或报表。

5. 对本条规定的利益和因素的考量并不构成对《内华达州修订法》第 78.138 条或《内华达州修订法》第 78.139 条的规定的违反。

6. 董事不对以下行为承担个人损害赔偿责任：

（a）根据本条和《内华达州修订法》第 78.138 条和第 78.139 条的规定履行本条规定的董事义务的作为和不作为。

（b）公共利益公司未能实现根据本法第 14 条的规定在公司章程中设定的一般或特定公共利益。

7. 除非公司章程或章程细则根据本法第 14 条的规定另有规定，董事对公共利益公司的一般或特定公共利益目标的法定受益人不负有信义义务。

8. 为履行其义务，公共利益董事享有《内华达州修订法》第 78.138 条第 3 款所规定的权利。

第 16 条　1. 公共利益董事应当编写其对以下事项的意见，公共利益公司应当根据本法第 19 条的规定将其附于年度公共利益报告中供股东查阅，报告内容应包括在报告所述时间内，公共利益公司未能实现根据本法第 14 条规定在公司章程中的一般或特定公共利益的情况。

2. 如果公共利益董事认为公共利益公司或其董事、高管未能实现公司章程中根据本法第 14 条的规定设定的一般或特定利益，则必须根据第 1 款的规定陈述公共利益公司或其董事、高管未能履行责任的情况。

subsection 1 must include a description of the ways in which the benefit corporation failed to pursue its general public benefit purpose or any specific public benefit purpose.

Sec.17.1.Each officer of a benefit corporation shall consider the interests and factors described in section 15 of this act if:

(a) The officer has discretion to act with respect to a matter; and

(b) It reasonably appears to the officer that the matter may have a material effect on:

(1) The creation of general public benefit or any specific public benefit identified in the articles of incorporation of the benefit corporation pursuant to section 14 of this act; or

(2) Any of the interests or factors described in subsections 2 and 3 of section 15 of this act.

2. The consideration by an officer of a benefit corporation of interests and factors in the manner described in subsection 1 does not constitute a violation of the duties of the officer.

3. An officer is not liable for monetary damages for:

(a) Any action or inaction as an officer in the course of performing the duties of an officer under subsection 1 if the officer performed the duties of his or her position in compliance with this section.

(b) Failure of the benefit corporation to pursue or create general public benefit or any specific public benefit identified in the articles of incorporation pursuant to section 14 of this act.

4. An officer does not have a duty to a person who is a beneficiary of the general public benefit purpose or any specific public benefit purpose identified in the articles of incorporation of the benefit corporation pursuant to section 14 of this act arising from the status of the person as a beneficiary.

5. In performing his or her duties, an officer of a benefit corporation has the benefit of the presumptions established by subsection 3 of NRS 78.138.

Sec. 18.1.Except in a benefit enforcement proceeding, no person may bring an action or assert a claim against a benefit corporation or its directors or officers with respect to:

(a) Failure to pursue or create general public benefit or any specific public benefit identified in the articles of incorporation of a benefit corporation pursuant to section 14 of this act; or

(b) A violation of an obligation, duty or standard of conduct under this chapter.

2. A benefit enforcement proceeding may be commenced or maintained only:

(a) Directly by the benefit corporation; or

(b) Derivatively by:

(1) A shareholder who owned beneficially or of record at least 2 percent of the total number of shares of a class or series outstanding at the time of the act or omission complained of;

第 17 条　1. 如果出现以下情况，公共利益高管应考虑本法第 15 条所述的利益和因素：

（a）该高管拥有就某一事项采取行动的自由裁量权；以及

（b）该高管有合理理由认为该事项可能对以下方面产生重大影响：

（1）根据本法第 14 条的规定，实现公共利益公司的公司章程中确定的一般或任何特定公共利益；或者

（2）本法第 15 条第 2 款和第 3 款中所述的任何利益或因素。

2. 公共利益公司的高管以第 1 款所述的方式考虑利益和因素，不构成对高管职责的违反。

3. 公共利益高管不对以下行为承担损害赔偿责任：

（a）依据第 1 款的规定履行高管责任过程中的任何作为或者不作为，若该行为符合商业公司法高管责任条款及本条的规定。

（b）公共利益公司未能追求或实现公司章程中设定的一般或特定公共利益。

4. 高管不对公共利益公司一般目的或特定社会目的的受益人负信义义务。

5. 公共利益高管在履行职责时，推定其享有《内华达州修订法》第 78.138 条第 3 款规定的利益。

第 18 条　1. 非经公共利益实施程序，任何人不得因以下事项向公共利益公司或者其董事、高管提起诉讼或主张：

（a）未能追求或实现其根据本法第 14 条的规定在公司章程中陈述的一般或特定公共利益；

（b）违反本章规定下的责任、义务或行为标准。

2. 公共利益实施程序只能由以下主体提起：

（a）由公共利益公司直接提起；或者

（b）由以下主体提派生提起：

（1）在被诉作为或不作为发生行为时，拥有公共利益公司 2% 以上已发行的某类别或系列股份的个人或群体；

(2) A director;

(3) A person or group of persons that owns beneficially or of record 5 percent or more of the equity interests in an entity of which the benefit corporation is a subsidiary at the time of the act or omission complained of; or

(4) Any other person authorized in the articles of incorporation or bylaws of the benefit corporation to commence and maintain a benefit enforcement proceeding.

3. A benefit corporation is not liable for monetary damages under this chapter for any failure of the benefit corporation to create general public benefit or any specific public benefit identified in the articles of incorporation of the benefit corporation pursuant to section 14 of this act.

4. If the court in a benefit enforcement proceeding finds that a failure to comply with this chapter was without justification, the court may award an amount sufficient to reimburse the plaintiff for the reasonable expenses incurred by the plaintiff, including attorney's fees and expenses, in connection with the benefit enforcement proceeding.

Sec.19.1.A benefit corporation shall deliver to each shareholder an annual benefit report which includes the following:

(a) A narrative description of:

(1) The process and rationale for selecting the third–party standard used to prepare the benefit report;

(2) The ways in which the benefit corporation pursued general public benefit during the applicable year and the extent to which that general public benefit was created;

(3) The ways in which the benefit corporation pursued any specific public benefit identified in the articles of incorporation of the benefit corporation pursuant to section 14 of this act and the extent to which that specific public benefit was created; and

(4) Any circumstances that have hindered the creation by the benefit corporation of general public benefit or any specific public benefit identified in the articles of incorporation of the benefit corporation pursuant to section 14 of this act.

(b) An assessment of the overall social and environmental performance of the benefit corporation, prepared in accordance with a third–party standard applied consistently with any application of that standard in prior benefit reports or accompanied by an explanation of the reasons for any inconsistent application. The assessment is not required to be audited or certified by a third party.

(c) The statement required by section 16 of this act.

(d) A statement of any connection between the entity that established the third–party standard, or its directors, officers or material owners, and the benefit corporation, or its directors, officers and material owners, including, without limitation, any financial or governance relationship that might materially affect the credibility of the objective

（2）董事；

（3）在被诉作为或不作为行为发生时，持有公共利益公司母公司 5% 以上已发行股份的登记股东或实际受益人；或者

（4）公共利益公司章程或章程细则中列明的其他人员。

3. 公共利益公司在本章规定下不对任何未能实现一般公共利益或特定公共利益的行为承担损害赔偿。

4. 如果法院在公共利益执行程序中发现公共利益公司无正当理由不遵守本章规定，可判决公共利益公司承担原告因此受到的损失，包括律师费和因公共利益实施程序而产生的其他费用。

第 19 条　1. 年度公共利益报告应包含以下内容：

（a）对以下事项的说明：

（1）为编写公共利益报告而选择的第三方标准的程序和合理性；

（2）本年度公共利益公司追求一般公共利益的方法及其实现的程度；

（3）本年度公共利益公司根据本法第 14 条追求特定或一般公共利益的方法及其实现的程度；以及

（4）阻碍公共利益公司创造一般和特定公共利益的情形。

（b）依据第三方标准对公共利益公司整体社会和环境表现作出的评估，并说明该标准是否与先前公共利益报告中使用的标准一致，或附一份说明解释适用不同标准的原因。该评估无须经第三方机构审计或认证。

（c）评估的具体要求由本法第 16 条规定。

（d）陈述设立第三方标准的机构或其董事、经理、实际控制人与公共利益公司或其董事、经理、实际控制人之间的关系，包括但不限于任何经济或控制关系等可能实质性影响标准可信度的经济或管理关系。

assessment of the third–party standard.

2. The annual benefit report required by subsection 1 must be sent annually to each shareholder within 120 days following the end of the fiscal year of the benefit corporation or at the same time that the benefit corporation delivers any other annual report to its shareholders.

3. A benefit corporation shall post all of its annual benefit reports on the public portion of its Internet website, if any, except that the compensation paid to directors and any financial or proprietary information included in the annual benefit report may be omitted from the annual benefit report posted on the Internet website.

4. If a benefit corporation does not have an Internet website, the benefit corporation must provide a copy of its most recent annual benefit report, without charge, to any person requesting a copy. The benefit corporation may omit any proprietary or financial information, including, without limitation, the compensation paid to directors, from the copy of an annual benefit report that the corporation provides pursuant to this subsection.

Sec.20.In addition to any other statement required by chapter 78 or 78A of NRS, NRS 81.010 to 81.160, inclusive, or chapter 89 of NRS, each certificate representing a share of a benefit corporation shall contain conspicuously on the face of the certificate the following statement:

This entity is a benefit corporation.

2. 公共利益公司应当在公共利益公司财政年度结束后 120 天内或公共利益公司向其股东送交其他年度报告的同一时间将公共利益报告送交各股东。

3. 公共利益公司应当将其所有公共利益报告在其网站上公开发布，但可将公共利益报告中的董事薪酬和财务或所有权信息删除。

4. 如果公共利益公司没有网站，应向所有索取报告的个人免费提供最新公共利益报告的副本，但可将公共利益报告副本中的董事薪酬和财务、所有权信息删除。

第 20 条　除《内华达州修订法》第 78 章、第 78A 章，《内华达州修订法》第 81.010 条至第 81.160 条或第 89 章所要求的申明外，代表公共利益公司股份的每份证书都应在证书的显著位置申明：

本实体是公共利益公司。

THE STATE OF NEW HAMPSHIRE

STATE OF NEW HAMPSHIRE

In the Year of Our Lord Two Thousand Fourteen

AN ACT authorizing benefit corporations.

Be it Enacted by the Senate and House of Representatives in General Court convened:

216:1 New Chapter; Benefit Corporations. Amend RSA by inserting after chapter 293–B the following new chapter:

CHAPTER 293–C
BENEFIT CORPORATIONS

Preliminary Provisions

293-C:1 Short Title, Application, and Effect of Chapter.

I. This chapter shall be known and may be cited as the "New Hampshire Benefit Corporation Act."

II. This chapter shall be applicable to all benefit corporations.

III. The existence of a provision of this chapter shall not itself create an implication that a contrary or different rule of law is applicable to a business corporation that is not a benefit corporation. This chapter shall not affect a statute or rule of law that is applicable to a business corporation that is not a benefit corporation.

IV. Except as otherwise provided in this chapter, RSA 293–A shall be generally

新罕布什尔州

新罕布什尔州

2014 年

法案授权设立公共利益公司

由参议院以及众议院一般法庭颁布：

216:1 新章节；公共利益公司。在《修订法》第 293–B 章后增加以下新章节：

第 293–C 章
公共利益公司

初步条款

293–C:1 简称、适用及法律效果

Ⅰ. 本章被称为《新罕布什尔州公共利益公司法》。

Ⅱ. 本章的规定适用于所有公共利益公司。

Ⅲ. 本章条款不应为非公共利益公司设定相反或不同的规则。本章不影响非公共利益公司有关条文和规则的适用。

Ⅳ. 除本章另有规定外，《修订法》第 293–A 章应适用于所有公共利益公司。

applicable to all benefit corporations. A benefit corporation may be subject simultaneously to this chapter and one or more other chapters of this title, including RSA 294-A. The provisions of this chapter shall control over the provisions of RSA 293-A and RSA 294-A.

V. A provision of the articles of incorporation or bylaws of a benefit corporation may not limit, be inconsistent with, or supersede a provision of this chapter.

293-C:2 Definitions.

In this chapter:

I. "Benefit corporation" means a business corporation:

(a) That has elected to become subject to this chapter; and

(b) The status of which as a benefit corporation has not been terminated.

II. "Benefit director" means either:

(a) The director designated as the benefit director of a benefit corporation under 26 RSA 293-C:8; or

(b) A person with one or more of the powers, duties, or rights of a benefit director to the extent provided in the bylaws under RSA 293-C:8, VI.

III. "Benefit enforcement proceeding" means any claim or action or proceeding for:

(a) Failure of a benefit corporation to pursue or create general public benefit or a specific public benefit purpose set forth in its articles; or

(b) Violation of any obligation, duty, or standard of conduct under this chapter.

IV. "Benefit officer" means the individual designated as the benefit officer of a benefit corporation under RSA 293-C:10.

V. "General public benefit" means a material positive effect on society and the environment, taken as a whole, assessed against a third-party standard, from the business and operations of a benefit corporation.

VI. "Independent" means having no material relationship with a benefit corporation or a subsidiary of the benefit corporation. Serving as benefit director or benefit officer does not make an individual not independent. A material relationship between an individual and a benefit corporation or any of its subsidiaries shall be conclusively presumed to exist if any of the following apply:

(a) The individual is, or has been within the last 3 years, an employee, other than a benefit officer, of the benefit corporation or a subsidiary.

(b) An immediate family member of the individual is, or has been within the last 3 years, an executive officer, other than a benefit officer, of the benefit corporation or a subsidiary.

(c) There is beneficial or record ownership of 5 percent or more of the outstanding shares of the benefit corporation, calculated as if all outstanding rights to acquire equity interests in the benefit corporation had been exercised, by:

公共利益公司同时受本章和其他包括《修订法》第 294–A 章在内的特殊类型商事公司法规的约束。本章条款应优先于《修订法》第 293–A 章和《修订法》第 294–A 章的规定适用。

Ⅴ. 公共利益公司的公司章程或章程细则不得限制、违背或取代本章的条款。

293–C:2　定义

本章中：

Ⅰ. “公共利益公司”是指：

（a）选择接受本章规定调整；并且

（b）公共利益公司形态并未终止。

Ⅱ. “公共利益董事”是指满足以下情形之一的董事：

（a）依《修订法》第 293–C:8 条的规定任命的董事为公共利益董事；或者

（b）拥有公司章程或《修订法》第 293–C:8 Ⅵ款所规定的，与公共利益董事相关的一项或多项权力、义务或权利的人员。

Ⅲ. “公共利益实施程序”是指因以下行为产生的任何主张、诉讼或程序：

（a）公共利益公司未追求或实现公司章程规定的一般或特定公共利益目的；或者

（b）公共利益公司违反本章规定下的任何义务、责任或行为标准。

Ⅳ. “公共利益高管”是指公共利益公司依《修订法》第 293–C:10 条的规定任命的公共利益高管。

Ⅴ. “一般公共利益”是指根据第三方标准，公司的业务和经营在整体上对社会和环境产生的实质性积极影响。

Ⅵ. “独立”是指与公共利益公司或其子公司没有实质性关系。担任公共利益董事或公共利益高管并不当然丧失独立性。若符合下列情形，则认为该个体与公共利益公司或其子公司存在实质性关系：

（a）该个体是，或在过去的 3 年内是，公共利益公司或其子公司除公共利益高管外的雇员。

（b）该个体的直系亲属是，或在过去的 3 年内是，公共利益公司或其子公司除公共利益高管外的执行高管。

（c）在所有购股权都被视为已行使的情况下，下述持有公共利益公司 5% 以上已发行股份的登记股东或实际受益人：

(1) The individual; or

(2) An entity:

(A) Of which the individual is a director, an officer, or a manager; or

(B) In which the individual owns beneficially or of record 5 percent or more of the outstanding equity interests, calculated as if all outstanding rights to acquire equity interests in the entity had been exercised.

VII. "Minimum status vote" means:

(a) In the case of a business corporation, in addition to any other required approval or vote, the satisfaction of the following conditions:

(1) The shareholders of every class or series shall be entitled to vote as a separate voting group on the corporate action regardless of a limitation stated in the articles of incorporation or bylaws on the voting rights of any class or series.

(2) The corporate action shall be approved by vote of the shareholders of each class or series entitled to cast at least 2/3 of the votes that all shareholders of the class or series are entitled to cast on the action.

(b) In the case of a domestic entity other than a business corporation, in addition to any other required approval, vote, or consent, the satisfaction of the following conditions:

(1) The holders of every class or series of equity interest in the entity that are entitled to receive a distribution of any kind from the entity shall be entitled to vote on or consent to the action regardless of any otherwise applicable limitation on the voting or consent rights of any class or series.

(2) The action shall be approved by vote or consent of the holders described in subparagraph (b)(1) entitled to cast at least 2/3 of the votes or consents that all of those holders are entitled to cast on the action.

VIII. "Publicly-traded corporation" means a business corporation that has shares listed on a national securities exchange or traded in a market maintained by one or more members of a national securities association.

IX. "Specific public benefit" includes:

(a) Providing low-income or underserved individuals or communities with beneficial products or services;

(b) Promoting economic opportunity for individuals or communities beyond the creation of jobs in the normal course of business;

(c) Protecting or restoring the environment;

(d) Improving human health;

(e) Promoting the arts, sciences, or advancement of knowledge;

(f) Increasing the flow of capital to entities with a purpose to benefit society or the environment; and

（1）个人；或者

（2）满足以下任一条件的实体：

（A）该个人是该实体的董事、高管或管理人员；或者

（B）该个人在所有购股权都被视为已行使的情况下，拥有 5% 以上该公共利益公司已发行股票的受益所有权或登记所有权。

Ⅶ．“最低表决要求”是指：

（a）在商事公司中，除任何其他对批准或表决的要求外，还应满足以下条件：

（1）每一类别或系列的股东应当有权作为一个独立的投票团体对公司行为进行投票，即使公司章程或章程细则对某一类别或系列投票权作出了限制。

（2）公司行为必须获得每个类别或系列有投票权的所有股东至少 2/3 的赞成票才能通过。

（b）在非商事公司的本州实体中，除其他批准、表决或赞成的要求外，还应满足以下条件：

（1）该实体的每一类别或系列任何权益分配形式下的股权持有者有权对公司行为进行投票，即使存在任何对该类别或系列投票权的限制。

（2）公司行为须经第（b）（1）分项规定的有投票权的所有股东至少 2/3 赞成票才能通过。

Ⅷ．“上市公司”是指在美国证券交易所或美国证券协会中一个或几个成员形成的市场上进行交易的商业公司。

Ⅸ．“特定公共利益”包括：

（a）向低收入、低福利人群或社区提供有益的产品或服务；

（b）在正常的业务过程中向个人或社区提供创造就业之外的经济机会；

（c）保护或修复环境；

（d）改善人类健康；

（e）促进艺术、科学或传播知识；

（f）促进资本向拥有有利于社会或环境目的的实体流动；以及

(g) Conferring any other particular benefit on society or the environment.

X. "Subsidiary" means, in relation to a person, an entity in which the person owns beneficially or of record 50 percent or more of the outstanding equity interests, calculated as if all outstanding rights to acquire equity interests in the entity had been exercised.

XI. "Third–party standard" means a recognized standard for defining, reporting, and assessing corporate social and environmental performance that is:

(a) Comprehensive because it assesses the effect of the business and its operations upon the interests listed in RSA 293–C:7, I(a).

(b) Developed by an entity that is not controlled by the benefit corporation.

(c) Credible because it is developed by an entity that both:

(1) Has access to necessary expertise to assess overall corporate social and environmental performance; and

(2) Uses a balanced approach to develop the standard, including a reasonable public comment period.

(d) Transparent because the following information is publicly available:

(1) About the standard:

(A) The criteria considered when measuring the overall social and environmental performance of a business.

(B) The relative weightings, if any, of those criteria.

(2) About the development and revision of the standard:

(A) The identity of the directors, officers, material owners, and the governing body of the entity that developed and controls revisions to the standard.

(B) The process by which revisions to the standard and changes to the membership of the governing body are made.

(C) An accounting of the revenue and sources of financial support for the entity, with sufficient detail to disclose any relationships that could reasonably be considered to present a potential conflict of interest.

293-C:3 Incorporation of Benefit Corporation.

A benefit corporation shall be incorporated in accordance with RSA 293–A:2.01 through RSA 293–A:2.07, but its articles of incorporation shall also state that it is a benefit corporation.

293-C:4 Election of Benefit Corporation Status.

I. An existing business corporation may become a benefit corporation under this chapter by amending its articles of incorporation so that they contain, in addition to the requirements of RSA 293–A:2.02, a statement that the corporation is a benefit corporation. In order to be effective, the amendment shall be adopted by at least the minimum status vote. II. The following rules apply to a merger, interest exchange, or conversion:

（g）给予社会或环境其他特别的利益。

Ⅹ．“子公司”是指在所有购股权都被视为已行使的情况下，50% 以上已发行的股份的受益所有权或登记所有权被另一实体所拥有。

Ⅺ．“第三方标准”是指用于定义、报告和评估公司社会和环境绩效的标准：

（a）综合，根据《修订法》第 293–C:7I（a）项中所列的利益评估公司业务和经营绩效。

（b）独立，经非由公共利益公司控制的第三方实体制定；

（c）可信，该标准由满足以下所有条件的第三方实体制定：

（1）拥有评估公司社会和环境综合绩效所需的专业知识；并且

（2）使用平衡多方相关者利益的方法制定标准，包括设定合理期间以听取公众意见。

（d）透明，以下信息可公开获取：

（1）标准的内容：

（A）衡量整体社会和环境绩效时所考虑的指标。

（B）这些指标的相关权重。

（2）关于标准的制定和修改：

（A）制定和控制修改程序的董事、高管、主要股东和该实体的控制人员的身份。

（B）标准修改和控制人员变动的程序。

（C）收入和资金来源的核算，包括充分披露合理认知下存在利益冲突的所有关系。

293–C:3　公共利益公司的设立

公共利益公司应当按照《修订法》第 293–A:2.07 条的规定设立且须符合《修订法》第 293–A:2.01 条的规定，此外，其公司章程应当声明其是公共利益公司。

293–C:4　公共利益公司形态的选择

Ⅰ. 已成立的商事公司可依据本章规定修改公司章程，修改后的章程除包含《修订法》第 293–A:2.02 条规定的内容外，还应在章程中作出该公司为公共利益公司的声明。公共利益公司修改的公司章程应满足最低表决要求才能生效。

(a) Except as provided in subparagraph (b), if a domestic entity that is not a benefit corporation is a party to a merger or conversion or is the exchanging entity in a share exchange and the surviving, new, or resulting entity in the merger, conversion, or share exchange is to be a benefit corporation, the plan of merger, conversion, or share exchange shall be approved by the domestic entity by at least the minimum status vote.

(b) Subparagraph (a) shall not apply in the case of a corporation that is a party to a merger if the shareholders of the corporation are not entitled to vote on the merger pursuant to RSA 27 293–A:11.05.

293-C:5 Termination of Benefit Corporation Status.

I. A benefit corporation may terminate its status as such and cease to be subject to this

chapter by amending its articles of incorporation to delete the provision required by RSA 293–C:3 or RSA 293–C:4, I to be stated in the articles of a benefit corporation. In order to be effective, the amendment shall be adopted by at least the minimum status vote.

II. The following rules apply to a merger, interest exchange, or conversion:

(a) Except as provided in subparagraph (b), if a plan of merger, conversion, or share exchange would have the effect of terminating the status of a business corporation as a benefit corporation, the plan shall be adopted by at least the minimum status vote in order to be effective.

(b) Subparagraph (a) shall not apply in the case of a corporation that is a party to a merger if the shareholders of the corporation are not entitled to vote on the merger pursuant to RSA 293–A:11.05.

III. Any sale, lease, exchange, or other disposition of all or substantially all of the assets of a benefit corporation, unless the transaction is in the usual and regular course of business, shall not be effective unless the transaction is approved by at least the minimum status vote.

Corporate Purposes

293-C:6 Corporate Purposes.

I. A benefit corporation shall have a purpose of creating general public benefit. This purpose is in addition to its purpose under RSA 293–A:7.

II. The articles of incorporation of a benefit corporation may identify one or more specific public benefits that it is the purpose of the benefit corporation to create in addition to its purposes under paragraph I and RSA 293–A:7. The identification of a specific public benefit under is paragraph shall not limit the purpose of a benefit corporation to create general public benefit under paragraph I.

III. The creation of general public benefit and specific public benefit under paragraphs I and II is in the best interests of the benefit corporation.

IV. A benefit corporation may amend its articles of incorporation to add, amend, or

（a）除第（b）项的规定外，如果一家本州非公共利益公司是兼并合并或财产转换的一方，或者是股权置换中的一方，并且在该兼并合并、财产转换或股权置换中存续新设或留存的实体属于公共利益公司，那么兼并合并、财产转换或股权置换的计划须满足最低表决要求才能获准。

（b）若兼并一方的股东根据《修订法》第 27 293–A:11.05 条的规定无权投票，则第（a）项的规定不适用于此种情形。

293–C:5　公司公共利益形态的终止

Ⅰ. 公共利益公司可以通过删除《修订法》第 293–C:3 条或《修订法》第 293–C:4 条规定的公司章程中的公共利益公司的声明来终止其公共利益公司的形态并不再受本章规定的调整。公司章程的修改应满足最低表决要求才能生效。

Ⅱ. 以下规则适用于兼并合并、财产转让或股权置换：

（a）除第（b）款的规定外，若兼并合并、财产转让或股权置换计划有终止商事公司作为公共利益公司的效力，该交易应满足最低表决要求才能生效。

（b）如果兼并一方的股东根据《修订法》第 293–A:11.05 条商事公司法的“简易合并”条款无权投票，则第（a）项的规定不适用于此种情形。

Ⅲ. 除正常商业往来外，公共利益公司的任何出售、出租、交换或者其他处置全部或主要财产的行为，须满足最低表决要求。

公司目的

293–C:6　公司目的

Ⅰ. 公共利益公司应当拥有创造一般公共利益的目的。此目的在《修订法》第 293–A:7 条所规定的目的之外。

Ⅱ. 公共利益公司的章程可根据第 I 款和《修订法》第 293–A:7 条的规定确定一项或者多项特定公共利益目的。依据本款规定设定的特定公共利益目的并不限制公共利益公司根据第 I 款的规定设定的一般公共利益目的。

Ⅲ. 依据第 I 款和第 Ⅱ 款的规定设定的一般和特定公共利益目的为公共利益公司的最佳利益。

Ⅳ. 公共利益公司可以通过修改公司章程增加、修改或删除公司章程中设定的

delete the identification of a specific public benefit that it is the purpose of the benefit corporation to create. In order to be effective, the amendment shall be adopted by at least the minimum status vote.

V. A professional corporation that is a benefit corporation does not violate RSA 294–A:2 by having the purpose to create general public benefit or a specific public benefit.

Accountability

293-C:7 Standard of Conduct for Directors.

I. In discharging the duties of their respective positions and in considering the best interests of the benefit corporation, the board of directors, committees of the board, and individual directors of a benefit corporation:

(a) Shall consider the effects of any action or inaction upon:

(1) The shareholders of the benefit corporation;

(2) The employees and work force of the benefit corporation, its subsidiaries, and its suppliers;

(3) The interests of customers as beneficiaries of the general public benefit or specific public benefit purposes of the benefit corporation;

(4) Community and societal factors, including those of each community in which offices or facilities of the benefit corporation, its subsidiaries, or its suppliers are located;

(5) The local and global environment;

(6) The short–term and long–term interests of the benefit corporation, including benefits that may accrue to the benefit corporation from its long–term plans and the possibility that these interests may be best served by the continued independence of the benefit corporation; and

(7) The ability of the benefit corporation to accomplish its general public benefit purpose and any specific public benefit purpose; and

(b) May consider other pertinent factors or the interests of any other group that they deem appropriate; but

(c) Need not give priority to a particular interest or factor referred to in subparagraph (a) or (b) over any other interest or factor unless the benefit corporation has stated in its articles of incorporation its intention to give priority to certain interests or factors related to its accomplishment of its general public benefit purpose or of a specific public benefit purpose identified in its articles.

II. The consideration of interests and factors in the manner required by paragraph I shall not constitute a violation of RSA 293–A:8.30.

III. Except as provided in the articles of incorporation or bylaws, a director is not personally liable for monetary damages for:

特定公共利益目的。公司对章程的修改需满足最低表决要求才能生效。

Ⅴ. 公共利益公司并不因其创设一般或特定公共利益目的而违反《修订法》第294-A:2 条的规定。

公司责任

293-C:7 董事行为标准

Ⅰ. 在履行各自职责和考虑公共利益公司最佳利益时，公共利益公司的董事会、董事委员会和董事：

（a）应当考虑其作为或不作为对以下主体的影响：

（1）公共利益公司的股东；

（2）公共利益公司、其子公司和其供应商的雇员；

（3）作为公共利益公司一般或特定公共利益受益者的消费者的利益；

（4）社区和社会影响，包括公共利益公司、其子公司或其供应商的办公地或设施所在地的社区；

（5）当地和全球环境；

（6）公司的短期和长期利益，包括可能从其长期计划中产生的利益，以及公共利益公司继续保持独立可能产生的最佳利益；以及

（7）公共利益公司实现其一般和特定公共利益目的的能力；以及

（b）还可以考虑董事认为合适的其他相关因素或其他群体的利益；但是

（c）除公司章程中赋予特定利益或因素优先权外，无须给予第（a）项或第（b）项中规定的某个利益或因素优先权。

Ⅱ. 对第Ⅰ款中规定的相关利益和因素的考虑不构成对《修订法》第 293-A:8.30 条的规定违反。

Ⅲ. 除非在公司章程或章程细则中有明确规定，董事不对以下行为承担损害赔偿责任：

(a) Any action or inaction in the course of performing the duties of a director under this chapter if the director performed the duties of office in compliance with RSA 293-A:8.30 and this section; or

(b) Failure of the benefit corporation to pursue or create general public benefit or specific public benefit.

IV. A director shall not have a duty to a person that is a beneficiary of the general public benefit purpose or a specific public benefit purpose of a benefit corporation arising from the status of the person as a beneficiary.

V. A director who makes a business judgment in good faith fulfills the duty under this section if the director:

(a) Is not interested in the subject of the business judgment;

(b) Is informed with respect to the subject of the business judgment to the extent the director reasonably believes to be appropriate under the circumstances; and

(c) Rationally believes that the business judgment is in the best interests of the benefit corporation.

293-C:8 Benefit Director.

I. The board of directors of a benefit corporation that is a publicly traded corporation shall, and the board of any other benefit corporation may, include a director, who:

(a) Shall be designated the benefit director; and

(b) Shall have, in addition to the powers, duties, rights, and immunities of the other directors of the benefit corporation, the powers, duties, rights, and immunities provided in this chapter.

II. The benefit director shall be elected, and may be removed, in the manner provided by RSA 293-A:8.01 through RSA 293-A:8.11. Except as provided in paragraphs VI and VII, the benefit director shall be an individual who is independent. The benefit director may serve as the benefit officer at the same time as serving as the benefit director. The articles of incorporation or bylaws of a benefit corporation may prescribe additional qualifications of the benefit director not inconsistent with this paragraph.

III. The benefit director shall prepare, and the benefit corporation shall include in the annual benefit report to shareholders required by section RSA 293-C:12, the opinion of the benefit director on all of the following:

(a) Whether the benefit corporation acted in accordance with its general public benefit purpose and any specific public benefit purpose in all material respects during the period covered by the report.

(b) Whether the directors and officers complied with RSA 293-C:7 and RSA 293-C:9.

(c) If, in the opinion of the benefit director, the benefit corporation or its directors or

（a）根据《修订法》第 293–A:8.30 条和本条的规定履行董事责任过程中的任何作为或不作为；或者

（b）公共利益公司未能追求或实现一般公共利益或特定公共利益。

Ⅳ. 董事对公共利益公司一般或特定公益目的的受益人不负有信义义务。

Ⅴ. 如董事行为满足以下要求，善意进行商业判断的董事则视为已履行本条所规定的义务：

（a）在商业判断过程中不涉及个人利益；

（b）拥有使其在该情形下作出合理商业判断的充分信息；以及

（c）有合理理由认为该商事判断符合公共利益公司的最佳利益。

293–C:8　公共利益董事

Ⅰ. 上市的公共利益公司以及其他形式的公共利益公司的董事会，需包含满足以下要求的董事：

（a）被任命公共利益董事；并且

（b）除有公共利益公司其他董事的权力、义务、权利和豁免权外，还有本章规定的权力、义务、权利和豁免权。

Ⅱ. 公共利益董事应根据《修订法》第 293–A:8.01 条至《修订法》第 293–A:8.11 条的规定任免。除第Ⅵ款和第Ⅶ款的规定外，公共利益董事应当是独立个体。公共利益董事可以同时担任公共利益高管。公共利益公司的章程或章程细则可对公共利益董事的资格作出与本款不一致的规定。

Ⅲ. 公共利益董事应编写其对以下事项的意见，公共利益公司应当根据《修订法》第 293–C:12 条的规定将其附于年度公共利益报告中供股东查阅：

（a）在报告所述时间内，公共利益公司是否在所有重要事项上依一般和特定公共利益目的行事。

（b）董事和经理是否分别依《修订法》第 293–C:7 条和《修订法》第 293–C:9 条的规定行事。

（c）如果公共利益董事认为公共利益公司或其董事、高管未能依第Ⅰ款和第Ⅱ

officers failed to act or comply in the manner described in paragraphs I and II, a description of the ways in which the benefit corporation or its directors or officers failed to act or comply.

IV. The act or inaction of an individual in the capacity of a benefit director shall constitute for all purposes an act or inaction of that individual in the capacity of a director of the benefit corporation.

V. Regardless of whether the articles of incorporation or bylaws of a benefit corporation include a provision eliminating or limiting the personal liability of directors authorized by RSA 293–A:2.02(b)(4), a benefit director shall not be personally liable for an act or omission in the capacity of a benefit director unless the act or omission constitutes self–dealing, willful misconduct, or a knowing violation of law.

VI. The articles of incorporation or bylaws of a benefit corporation shall provide that the persons or shareholders who perform the duties of the board of directors include a person with the powers, duties, rights, and immunities of a benefit director if the articles of incorporation or bylaws of the benefit corporation or a shareholder agreement provide that the powers and duties conferred or imposed upon the board of directors shall be exercised or performed by a person other than the directors under RSA 293–A:7.32. A person that exercises one or more of the powers, duties, or rights of a benefit director under this paragraph:

(a) Does not need to be independent of the benefit corporation;

(b) Shall have the immunities of a benefit director;

(c) May share the powers, duties, and rights of a benefit director with persons; and

(d) Shall not be subject to the procedures for election or removal of directors in RSA 293–A:8.01 through RSA 293–A:8.11 unless:

(1) The person is also a director of the benefit corporation; or

(2) The articles, bylaws, or shareholder agreement make those procedures applicable.

VII. The benefit director of a professional corporation does not need to be independent.

293-C:9 Standard of Conduct for Officers.

I. Each officer of a benefit corporation shall consider the interests and factors described in RSA 293–C:7 in the manner provided in that section if:

(a) The officer has discretion to act with respect to a matter; and

(b) It reasonably appears to the officer that the matter may have a material effect on the creation by the benefit corporation of general public benefit or a specific public benefit identified in the articles of incorporation of the benefit corporation.

II. The consideration of interests and factors in the manner required by paragraph I shall not constitute a violation of RSA 293–A:8.42.

III. Except as provided in the articles of incorporation or bylaws, an officer shall not be personally liable for monetary damages for:

款的要求行事，应陈述公共利益公司或其董事、高管未能履行责任的情况。

Ⅳ. 公共利益董事在职权范围内的个人作为或不作为应视为公共利益公司董事的行为。

Ⅴ. 不论公共利益公司章程或章程细则是否依据商业公司法董事责任免除条款删除或限制董事《修订法》第 293-A:2.02（b）（4）目规定的个人责任，公共利益董事在行使职责时不对其任何作为或不作为承担个人责任，但自我交易或故意违法行为除外。

Ⅵ. 公共利益公司章程或章程细则应赋予个人或股东履行董事义务所应有的权力、义务和权利，如果公共利益公司章程或股东协议规定由不受《修订法》第 293-A:7.32 条规制的主体控制董事会的运营或由闭锁公共利益公司章程（在此情形下，公司运营受股东的影响）授予该主体运营公司的权利，则公司章程必须规定董事会成员应包含可以行使权力、履行职责与拥有豁免权的公共利益董事。该个人有以下一项或多项权力、义务或权利：

（a）无须独立于公共利益公司；

（b）拥有公共利益董事的豁免权；

（c）可以与其他主体分享公共利益董事的权力、义务和权利；并且

（d）除下述情况外，不受《修订法》第 293-A:8.01 条至第 293-A:8.11 条规定的董事任免程序的约束：

（1）该个人同时是公共利益公司的董事；或者

（2）公司章程、章程细则或股东协议约定了上述程序。

Ⅶ. 专业公司的公共利益董事的独立性不作要求。

293-C:9　高管行为标准

Ⅰ. 公共利益公司高管应当根据《修订法》第 293-C:7 条规定的行为标准考虑该条规定的利益和因素，如果：

（a）高管享有依据该行为标准行事的自由裁量权；并且

（b）高管有合理理由认为该行为对一般公共利益或章程规定的特定公共利益的实现有实质性影响。

Ⅱ. 以第Ⅰ款要求的方式考虑利益和因素，不应构成对《修订法》第 293-A:8.42 条规定的违反。

Ⅲ. 除公司章程或章程细则的规定外，高管不应对以下情况承担损害赔偿责任：

(a) An action or inaction as an officer in the course of performing the duties of an officer under this section if the officer performed the duties of the position in compliance with RSA 293–A:8.42 and this section; or

(b) Failure of the benefit corporation to pursue or create general public benefit or specific public benefit.

IV. An officer shall not have a duty to a person that is a beneficiary of the general public benefit purpose or a specific public benefit purpose of a benefit corporation arising from the status of the person as a beneficiary.

V. An officer who makes a business judgment in good faith fulfills the duty under this section if the officer:

(a) Is not interested in the subject of the business judgment;

(b) Is informed with respect to the subject of the business judgment to the extent the officer reasonably believes to be appropriate under the circumstances; and

(c) Rationally believes that the business judgment is in the best interests of the benefit corporation.

293-C:10 Designation of Benefit Officer.

I. A benefit corporation may have an officer designated the benefit officer.

II. A benefit officer shall have:

(a) The powers and duties relating to the purpose of the corporation to create general public benefit or specific public benefit provided:

(1) By the bylaws; or

(2) Absent controlling provisions in the bylaws, by resolutions or orders of the board of director.

(b) The duty to prepare the benefit report required by RSA 293–C:12.

293-C:11 Right of Action.

I. Except in a benefit enforcement proceeding, no person shall bring an action or assert a claim against a benefit corporation or its directors or officers with respect to:

(a) Failure to pursue or create general public benefit or a specific public benefit set forth in its articles of incorporation; or

(b) Violation of an obligation, duty, or standard of conduct under this chapter.

II. A benefit corporation shall not be liable for monetary damages under this chapter for any failure of the benefit corporation to pursue or create general public benefit or a specific public benefit.

III. A benefit enforcement proceeding shall be commenced or maintained only:

(a) Directly by the benefit corporation; or

(b) Derivatively in accordance with RSA 293–A:7.40 through RSA 293–A:7.48 by:

（a）高管在履行本条规定的职责过程中的作为或不作为，如果该高管在履行职责时符合《修订法》第 293-A:8.42 条和本条的规定；或者

（b）公共利益公司未能追求或实现一般或特定公共利益。

Ⅳ. 高管并不对公共利益公司一般或特定社会目的的受益人承担责任。

Ⅴ. 如高管行为满足以下要求，善意进行商业判断的高管则视为已履行本条所规定的义务：

（a）在商业判断过程中不涉及个人利益；

（b）拥有使其在该情形下作出合理商业判断的充分信息；以及

（c）有合理理由认为该商业判断符合公共利益公司的最佳利益。

293-C:10 公共利益高管的任命

Ⅰ. 公共利益公司可以任命公共利益高管。

Ⅱ. 公共利益高管应当有：

（a）关于创造一般或特定公共利益的权力和职责，规定于：

（1）公司章程细则；或者

（2）在公司章程细则中没有规定时，董事会作出的有关决议或者命令。

（b）编写《修订法》第 293-C:12 条要求的公共利益报告的义务。

293-C:11 诉讼权利

Ⅰ. 非经公共利益实施程序，任何人不得因以下事项向公共利益公司或者其董事、高管提起诉讼或主张：

（a）未能追求或实现其在公司章程中设定的一般或特定公共利益；或者

（b）违反本章规定下的责任、义务或行为标准。

Ⅱ. 公共利益公司不对本章规定下任何未能追求或创造一般或特定公共利益的行为承担损害赔偿责任。

Ⅲ. 公共利益实施程序只能由以下主体提起：

（a）由公共利益公司直接提起；或者

（b）依据《修订法》第 293-A:7.40 条（《商事公司法》）至《修订法》第 293-A:7.48 条的规定，派生诉讼由以下主体派生提起：

(1) A person or group of persons that owned beneficially or of record at least 2 percent of the total number of shares of a class or series outstanding at the time of the act or omission complained of;

(2) A director;

(3) A person or group of persons that owned beneficially or of record 5 percent or more of the outstanding equity interests in an entity of which the benefit corporation is a subsidiary at the time of the act or omission complained of; or

(4) Other persons as specified in the articles of incorporation or bylaws of the benefit corporation.

IV. For purposes of this section, a person is the beneficial owner of shares or equity interests if the shares or equity interests are held in a voting trust or by a nominee on behalf of the beneficial owner.

V. In an action commenced under this section, if it is determined that a corporation established pursuant to this chapter has failed to pursue a general public benefit or a specific public benefit set forth in its articles of incorporation, the secretary of state may revoke the corporation's status as a benefit corporation under this chapter.

Transparency

293-C:12 Preparation of Annual Benefit Report.

I. A benefit corporation shall prepare an annual benefit report including all of the following:

(a) A narrative description of:

(1) The ways in which the benefit corporation pursued general public benefit during the year and the extent to which general public benefit was created.

(2) Both:

(A) The ways in which the benefit corporation pursued a specific public benefit that the articles of incorporation state it is the purpose of the benefit corporation to create; and

(B) The extent to which that specific public benefit was created.

(3) Any circumstances that have hindered the creation by the benefit corporation of general public benefit or specific public benefit.

(4) The process and rationale for selecting or changing the third-party standard used to prepare the benefit report.

(b) An assessment of the overall social and environmental performance of the benefit corporation against a third-party standard:

(1) Applied consistently with any application of that standard in prior benefit reports; or

(2) Accompanied by an explanation of the reasons for:

(A) Any inconsistent application; or

（1）在被诉作为或不作为行为发生时，拥有公共利益公司 2% 以上已发行的某类别或系列股份的个人或群体；

（2）董事；

（3）在被诉作为或不作为行为发生时，持有公共利益公司母公司 5% 以上已发行股份的登记股东或实际受益股人；或者

（4）公共利益公司章程或章程细则中列明的其他人员。

Ⅳ. 为实现本条目的，若股份或者股利由表决权信托或指定第三人代持，则将此人视为该股份和股利的实益所有权人。

Ⅴ. 根据本条规定所提起的诉讼，如果法院判定该公司没有实现一般公共利益或公司章程规定的特定公共利益，州务卿可根据本章规定撤销其公共利益公司的地位。

透明度

293-C:12　年度公共利益报告的编写

Ⅰ. 公共利益公司的年度公共利益报告中应包括以下内容：

（a）对以下事项的说明：

（1）公共利益公司本年度追求一般公共利益的方法及其实现的程度。

（2）同时包括：

（A）公共利益公司实现公司章程中列明的特定公共利益的方法；以及

（B）该特定公共利益实现的程度。

（3）阻碍公共利益公司实现一般和特定公共利益的情形。

（4）为编写公共利益报告而选择或更换第三方标准的程序和原因。

（b）依据第三方标准对公共利益公司整体社会和环境表现作出的整体评价：

（1）沿用先前公共利益报告中使用的标准；或者

（2）附一份说明以解释：

（A）适用中的差异；或者

(B) The change to that standard from the one used in the immediately prior report.

(c) The name of the benefit director and the benefit officer, if any, and the address to which correspondence to each of them may be directed.

(d) The compensation paid by the benefit corporation during the year to each director in the capacity of a director.

(e) The statement of the benefit director described in RSA 293–C:8, III.

(f) A statement of any connection between the organization that established the third–party standard, or its directors, officers, or any holder of 5 percent or more of the governance interests in the organization, and the benefit corporation or its directors, officers, or any holder of 5 percent or more of the outstanding shares of the benefit corporation, including any financial or governance relationship which might materially affect the credibility of the use of the third–party standard.

(g) If the benefit corporation has dispensed with, or restricted the discretion or powers of, the board of directors, a description of:

(1) The persons that exercise the powers, duties, and rights and who have the immunities of the board of directors; and

(2) The benefit director, as required by RSA 293–C:8, VI.

II. If, during the year covered by a benefit report, a benefit director resigned from or refused to stand for reelection to the position of benefit director, or was removed from the position of benefit director, and the benefit director furnished the benefit corporation with any written correspondence concerning the circumstances surrounding the resignation, refusal, or removal, the benefit report shall include that correspondence as an exhibit.

III. Neither the benefit report nor the assessment of the performance of the benefit corporation required by subparagraph I(b) shall be audited or certified by a third party.

293-C:13 Availability of Annual Benefit Report.

I. A benefit corporation shall send its annual benefit report to each shareholder on the earlier of:

(a) 120 days following the end of the fiscal year of the benefit corporation; or

(b) The same time that the benefit corporation delivers any other annual report to its shareholders.

II. A benefit corporation shall post all of its benefit reports on the public portion of its Internet website, if any; but the compensation paid to directors and financial or proprietary information included in the benefit reports may be omitted from the benefit reports as posted.

III. If a benefit corporation does not have an Internet website, the benefit corporation shall provide a copy of its most recent benefit report, without charge, to any person that requests a copy, but the compensation paid to directors and financial or proprietary information included in the benefit report may be omitted from the copy of the benefit report

（B）与上一份报告相比，该标准不一致之处。

（c）公共利益董事和公共利益高管的姓名和联系地址（如有）。

（d）公共利益公司在上一年度支付给每位董事的薪酬。

（e）公共利益董事依《修订法》第293-C:8条第Ⅲ款的规定编写的陈述报告。

（f）设立第三方标准的组织或其董事、高管或5%以上管理权利的持有者与公共利益公司或其董事、高管或公共利益公司5%以上已发行股份持有者之间关系的声明，包括所有可能影响第三方标准可信度的财务或管理关系。

（g）如果公共利益公司剥夺或限制董事会的权力，需说明：

（1）行使该权利的权力、权利或履行义务的主体以及豁免董事会的主体；以及

（2）《修订法》第293-C:8条第Ⅵ款规定的公共利益董事。

Ⅱ. 如果在公共利益报告年度期间，公共利益董事辞职、拒绝连任或被免职，且该公共利益董事与公司有任何书面的涉及辞职、拒绝连任或免职的书信往来，应当将该书信往来作为公共利益报告附件。

Ⅲ. 公共利益报告和依据第Ⅰ（b）项的规定编写的公共利益报告中对公共利益公司表现的评价都无须经审计或第三方证明。

293-C:13　年度公共利益报告的提供

Ⅰ. 公共利益公司应当在以下日期内较早地将公共利益报告送交各股东：

（a）公共利益公司财政年度结束后120天内；或者

（b）公共利益公司向其股东送交其他年度报告的同一时间。

Ⅱ. 若条件允许，公共利益公司应当将其所有公共利益报告发布于其网站的公共部分；但可将公共利益报告中的董事薪酬和财务、所有权信息删除。

Ⅲ. 如果公共利益公司没有网站，应在任何个人索取副本时向其免费提供最新公共利益报告的副本，但是可以将公共利益报告副本中的董事薪酬和财务、所有权信息删除。

provided.

IV. Concurrently with the delivery of the benefit report to shareholders under paragraph I, the benefit corporation shall deliver a copy of the benefit report to the secretary of state for filing, but the compensation paid to directors and financial or proprietary information included in the benefit report may be omitted from the benefit report as delivered to the secretary of state. The secretary of state shall charge a fee of $35 for filing a benefit report.

V. If the secretary of state determines that a benefit corporation established pursuant to this chapter fails to make available its annual benefit report pursuant to RSA 293–C:12 and RSA 293–C:13, the secretary of state shall administratively dissolve the corporation in accordance with the procedures in RSA 293–A:14.21.

216:2 Effective Date.

This act shall take effect January 1, 2015.

Approved: July 11, 2014

Effective Date: January 1, 2015

Ⅳ. 在依第 I 款的规定将公共利益报告提交给股东的同时，公共利益公司应当将该公共利益报告提交州务卿备案，但可将公共利益报告中的董事薪酬、财务或所有权信息在提交州务卿的报告中删除。州务卿应收取 35 美元作为备案费用。

Ⅴ. 如果公共利益公司未根据《修订法》第 293-C:12 条和《修订法》第 293-C:1 条的规定向州务卿提交报告，州务卿可根据《修订法》第 293-A:14.21 条规定颁发一份申明，终止该公司的公共利益形态。

216:2　生效日期

本法案自 2015 年 1 月 1 日起生效。

通过日：2014 年 7 月 11 日

生效日：2015 年 1 月 1 日

THE STATE OF NEW JERSEY

ASSEMBLY, No. 3595

STATE OF NEW JERSEY

214th LEGISLATURE

AN ACT concerning benefit corporations and supplementing Title 14A of the New Jersey Statutes.

BE IT ENACTED by the Senate and General Assembly of the State of New Jersey:

1. For purposes of this act:

"Benefit corporation" means a corporation organized under provisions of the "New Jersey Business corporation Act," N.J.S.14A:1–1 et seq., that has elected to become subject to this act and whose status as a benefit corporation has not been terminated as provided in this act.

"Benefit director" means the director designated as the benefit director of a benefit corporation as provided in section 7 of this act.

"Benefit enforcement proceeding" means a claim or action brought directly by a benefit corporation, or derivatively on behalf of a benefit corporation, against a director or officer for:

(1) Failure to pursue the general public benefit purpose of the benefit corporation or any specific public benefit purpose set forth in its certificate of incorporation; or

(2) Violation of a duty or standard of conduct under this act.

"Benefit officer" means the officer of a benefit corporation, if any, designated as the benefit officer as provided in section 9 of this act.

"General public benefit" means a material positive impact on society and the environment by the operations of a benefit corporation through activities that promote some combination of specific public benefits.

"Independent" means that a person has no material relationship with a benefit corporation or any of its subsidiaries (other than the relationship of serving as the benefit director or benefit officer), either directly or as a shareholder, partner, member or other

新泽西州

新泽西州议会第 3959 号法案

第 214 项立法

2010 年 12 月 6 日提交

关于公共利益公司的有关规定，作为《新泽西州成文法》第 14A 节 新增内容。

由新泽西州议会制定。

1. 就本法而言，以下词语的定义如下：

“公共利益公司”是指，根据《新泽西州商事公司法》第 14A:1–1 条等规定设立，同时选择接受本法规定调整，且其公共利益公司形态并未终止的公司。

“公共利益董事”是指，公共利益公司依本法第 7 条规定被任命的董事。

“公共利益实施程序”是指，因以下行为，由公共利益公司直接提起或由公共利益公司代表派生提起的对董事或高管的诉讼，理由是：

（1）公共利益公司未追求或实现公司章程规定的一般或特定公共利益目的；或者

（2）公共利益公司违反本法规定下的任何义务、责任或行为标准。

“公共利益高管”是指，公共利益公司依本法第 9 条的规定任命的高管。

“一般公共利益”是指，根据第三方标准，公司的业务和经营在整体上对社会和环境产生的实质性积极影响。

“独立”是指，一个人与公共利益公司或其子公司没有实质性关系（不包含担任公共利益董事或者公共利益高管的关系），无论是直接关系还是作为与公共利益公司或其子公司有实质性关系的实体的股东、合伙人、其他所有权人、董事、高管

owner or a director, officer or other manager of an entity that has a material relationship with the benefit corporation or any of its subsidiaries. A material relationship between an individual and a benefit corporation or any of its subsidiaries will be conclusively presumed to exist if:

(1) The person is, or has been within the last three years, an employee of the benefit corporation or any of its subsidiaries, other than as a benefit officer;

(2) An immediate family member of the person is, or has been within the last three years, an executive officer, other than a benefit officer, of the benefit corporation or any of its subsidiaries; or

(3) The person, or an entity of which the person is a director, officer or other manager or in which the person owns beneficially or of record 5% or more of the outstanding equity interests, owns beneficially or of record 5% or more of the outstanding shares of the benefit corporation.

A percentage of ownership in an entity shall be calculated as if all outstanding rights to acquire equity interests in the entity had been exercised.

"Minimum status vote" means that, in addition to any other approval or vote required by Title 14A of the New Jersey Statutes or the certificate of incorporation:

(1) The holders of shares of every class or series shall be entitled to vote on the corporate action regardless of any limitation stated in the certificate of incorporation on the voting rights of any class or series; and

(2) The corporate action must be approved by vote of the shareholders of each class or series entitled to cast at least two– thirds of the votes that all shareholders of the class or series are entitled to cast on the action.

"Specific public benefit" includes:

(1) Providing low–income individuals or communities with beneficial products or services;

(2) Promoting economic opportunity for individuals or communities beyond the creation of jobs in the normal course of business;

(3) Preserving the environment;

(4) Improving human health;

(5) Promoting the arts, sciences or advancement of knowledge;

(6) Increasing the flow of capital to entities with a public benefit purpose; and

(7) The accomplishment of any other particular benefit for society or the environment.

"Subsidiary" of a person means an entity in which the person owns beneficially or of record 50% or more of the outstanding equity interests. A percentage of ownership in an entity shall be calculated as if all outstanding rights to acquire equity interests in the entity had been exercised.

或其他管理者。若出现以下情形，则认为该个体与公共利益公司或其子公司存在实质性的关系：

（1）该个体是，或在过去的3年内是，公共利益公司或其子公司的除公共利益高管外的雇员；

（2）该个体的直系亲属是，或在过去的3年内是，公共利益公司或其子公司的除公共利益高管外的执行高管；或者

（3）该个人为某一实体的董事或高管，或为持有公共利益公司5%以上已发行股份的登记股东或实际受益人。

在该实体所有购股权已被行使的情况下，应计算股权的比例。

"最低表决要求"，是指除满足《新泽西州成文法》第14A节或公司章程对投票的授权和要求外，还应满足以下条件：

（1）每个类别或系列的股东应当有权作为一个独立的投票团体对公司行为进行投票，即使公司章程或章程细则对某一类别或系列投票权作出了限制。

（2）公司行为必须获得每个类别或系列有投票权的所有股东的至少2/3的赞成票才能通过。

"特定公共利益"包括：

（1）向低收入、低福利人群或社区提供有益的产品或服务；

（2）在正常的业务过程中向个人或社区提供创造就业之外的经济机会；

（3）保护或修复环境；

（4）改善人类健康；

（5）促进艺术、科学或知识进步；

（6）促进资本向拥有有利于社会或环境目的的实体流动；以及

（7）给予社会或环境其他特别的利益。

"子公司"是指，在所有购股权都被视为已行使的情况下，该实体50%以上已发行的股票的受益所有权或登记所有权被另一实体所拥有。

"Third-party standard" means a recognized standard for defining, reporting and assessing corporate social and environmental performance that is:

(1) Developed by a person that is independent of the benefit corporation; and

(2) Transparent because the following information about the standard is publicly available:

(a) the factors considered when measuring the performance of a business;

(b) the relative weightings of those factors; and

(c) the identity of the persons who developed and control changes to the standard and the process by which those changes are made.

2. A benefit corporation shall be formed in accordance with chapter 2 of Title 14A of the New Jersey Statutes, except that its certificate of incorporation shall also state that it is a benefit corporation.

3. a. A corporation organized under the provisions of the "New Jersey Business Corporation Act," N.J.S.14A:1-1 et seq., may become a benefit corporation under this act by amending its certificate of incorporation so that it contains a statement that the corporation is a benefit corporation. The amendment shall not be effective unless it is adopted by at least the minimum status vote.

b. If a corporation that is not a benefit corporation is a party to a merger or consolidation or is the exchanging corporation in a share exchange, and the surviving or new corporation in the merger, consolidation, or share exchange is to be a benefit corporation, then the plan of merger, consolidation, or share exchange shall not be effective unless it is adopted by the corporation by at least the minimum status vote.

4. a. A benefit corporation may terminate its status as a benefit corporation and cease to be subject to this act by amending its certificate of incorporation to delete the provision required by section 2 or subsection a. of section 3 of this act. The amendment shall not be effective unless it is adopted by at least the minimum status vote.

b. If a plan of merger, consolidation or exchange would have the effect of terminating the status of a corporation as a benefit corporation, the plan shall not be effective unless it is adopted by at least the minimum status vote.

5. a. Every benefit corporation shall have the purpose of creating a general public benefit. This purpose is in addition to, and may be a limitation on, its purpose under its certificate of incorporation and any specific purpose set forth in its certificate of incorporation.

b. The certificate of incorporation of a benefit corporation may identify one or more specific public benefits that is the purpose of the benefit corporation to create in addition to its purposes under its certificate of incorporation and subsection a. of this section. The identification of a specific public benefit under this subsection does not limit the obligation

“第三方标准”是指，用于定义、报告和评估公司社会和环境绩效的标准：

（1）经非由公共利益公司控制的第三方实体制定；并且
（2）透明，以下信息可公开获取：

（a）衡量整体社会和环境绩效时所考虑的具体指标；
（b）这些指标的相关权重；以及
（c）制定和控制修改程序的人员的身份。

2. 公共利益公司应该根据《新泽西州成文法》第 2 章第 14A 节的规定设立，此外，应在公司章程中声明其为公共利益公司。

3. a. 根据《新泽西州商事公司法》《新泽西州成文法》第 14A:1–1 条等条款设立的公司可以根据本法的规定，在其公司注册证上增加公共利益性质的声明，从而转变为公共利益公司。公司章程的修改应满足最低表决要求方能生效。

b. 如果一家本州非公共利益公司是兼并合并或财产转换的一方，或者是股权置换中的一方，并且在该兼并合并、财产转换或股权置换中存续新设或留存的实体属于公共利益公司，那么该兼并合并、财产转换或股权置换的计划须满足最低表决要求才能获准。

4.a. 公共利益公司可以通过删除本法第 2 条或第 3 条第 a 款规定的在公司章程中的其作为公共利益公司的声明来终止其公共利益公司形态并不再受本法规定调整。公司章程的修改应满足最低表决要求才能生效。

b. 如兼并合并、财产转换或股权置换计划有终止商业公司作为公共利益公司的效力，该交易计划应满足最低表决要求才能生效。

5. a. 公共利益公司应当有创造一般公共利益的目的，此目的可能会对公司章程中设定的目的和任一特定目的构成限制。

b. 公共利益公司的章程可在商事公司法公司目的条款和本条第 a 款之外确定一项或者多项特定的公共利益目的。依据本款规定设定的特定公共利益目的并不限制公共利益公司在本条第 a 款规定下设定的一般公共利益目的。

of a benefit corporation to create general public benefit.

c. The creation of general and specific public benefits, as provided in subsections a. and b. of this section, shall be in the best interests of the benefit corporation.

d. A benefit corporation may amend its certificate of incorporation to add, amend or delete a specific public benefit that is the purpose of the benefit corporation to create. The amendment shall not be effective unless it is adopted by at least the minimum status vote.

6. a. The board of directors, committees of the board and individual directors of a benefit corporation, in considering the best interests of the benefit corporation shall consider the effects of any action upon:

(1) the shareholders of the benefit corporation;

(2) the employees and workforce of the benefit corporation and its subsidiaries and suppliers;

(3) the interests of customers as beneficiaries of the general or specific public benefit purposes of the benefit corporation;

(4) community and societal considerations, including those of any community in which offices or facilities of the benefit corporation or its subsidiaries or suppliers are located;

(5) the local and global environment; and

(6) the short–term and long–term interests of the benefit corporation, including benefits that may accrue to the benefit corporation from its long–term plans and the possibility that these interests may be best served by the continued independence of the benefit corporation;

b. The board of directors, committees of the board and individual directors of a benefit corporation, in considering the best interests of the benefit corporation may consider: (1) matters listed in subsection (2) of N.J.S.14A:6–1; and

(2) any other pertinent factors or the interests of any other group that they deem appropriate; and

c. The board of directors, committees of the board and individual directors of a benefit corporation shall not be required to give priority to the interests of any particular person or group referred to in subsection a. or subsection b. of this section over the interests of any other person or group unless the benefit corporation has stated its intention to give priority to interests related to a specific public benefit purpose identified in its certificate of incorporation.

d. A director is not personally liable for monetary damages for failure of the benefit corporation to create general or specific public benefits.

7. a. The board of directors of a benefit corporation shall include one director who shall be designated the "benefit director" and shall have, in addition to all of the powers, duties, rights and immunities of the other directors of the benefit corporation, the powers, duties, rights and immunities provided in this act.

c. 依据本条第 a 款和第 b 款的规定设定的一般和特定公共利益目的为公共利益公司的最佳利益。

d. 公共利益公司可以修改公司章程以增加、修改或删除设定的特定公共利益目的。公共利益公司对章程的修改须满足最低表决要求才能生效。

6. a. 在履行各自职责和考虑公共利益公司最佳利益时，公共利益公司的董事会、董事委员会和董事应当考虑其行为对以下主体的影响：

（1）公共利益公司的股东；

（2）公共利益公司、其子公司和其供应商的雇员；

（3）作为公共利益公司一般或特定公共利益受益者的消费者的利益；

（4）社区和社会影响，包括公共利益公司、其子公司或其供应商的办公地或设施所在地的社区；

（5）当地和全球环境；以及

（6）公共利益公司的短期和长期利益，包括可能从其长期计划中产生的利益，以及公共利益公司继续保持独立可能产生的最佳利益。

b. 在履行各自职责和考虑公共利益公司最佳利益时，公共利益公司的董事会、董事委员会和董事可以考虑：（1）《新泽西州成文法》第 14A:6–1 款第（2）项中所列因素；以及

（2）董事认为合适的其他相关因素或其他群体的利益；以及

c. 董事会、董事委员会和董事无须给予本条第 a 款或第 b 款中某个利益或因素优先权，除非公共利益公司在其公司章程中表明为实现其一般公共利益或特定公共利益而给予特定的利益或因素优先权。

d. 董事不对未能实现一般公共利益或特定公共利益承担损害赔偿责任。

7. a. 公共利益公司的董事会应至少包含一名公益董事，该董事除拥有公共利益公司与其他董事相同的权力、义务、权利和豁免权外，还应当享有本法规定的权力、权利和豁免权并承担相应义务。

b. The benefit director shall be elected, and may be removed, in the manner provided by chapter 6 of Title 14A of the New Jersey Statutes, and shall be an individual who is independent. The benefit director may serve as the benefit officer, designated pursuant to section 9 of this act, at the same time as serving as the benefit director. The certificate of incorporation or bylaws of a benefit corporation may prescribe additional qualifications of the benefit director not inconsistent with this subsection.

c. The benefit director shall prepare, and the benefit corporation shall include in the annual benefit report to shareholders required by section 11 of this act, a statement whether, in the opinion of the benefit director, the benefit corporation acted in accordance with its general, and any specific, public benefit purpose in all material respects during the period covered by the report and whether the directors and officers complied with subsection a. of section 6 of this act and subsection a. of section 8 of this act. If in the opinion of the benefit director the benefit corporation or its directors or officers failed to act in accordance with its public benefit purpose, then the statement of the benefit director shall include a description of the ways in which the benefit corporation or its directors or officers failed to act.

d. If the by–laws of a benefit corporation provide that the powers and duties conferred or imposed upon the board of directors shall be exercised or performed by a person other than the directors pursuant to N.J.S.14A:6–1, then the bylaws of the benefit corporation must provide that the person or shareholders who perform the duties of a board of directors shall include a person with the powers, duties, rights and immunities of a benefit director.

e. Regardless of whether the certificate of incorporation of a benefit corporation includes a provision eliminating or limiting the personal liability of directors authorized by subsection (3) of N.J.S.14A:2–7, a benefit director shall not be personally liable for any act or omission in the capacity of a benefit director unless the act or omission constitutes self–dealing, willful misconduct or a knowing violation of law.

8. a. Each officer of a benefit corporation shall consider the interests and factors described in subsection a. of section 6 of this act when:

(1) The officer has discretion to act with respect to a matter; and

(2) It reasonably appears to the officer that the matter may have a material effect on:

(a) the creation of general or specific public benefits by the benefit corporation; or

(b) any of the interests or factors referred to in subsection a. of section 6 of this act.

b. The consideration of interests and factors in the manner described in subsection c. of section 6 of this act.

c. An officer is not personally liable for monetary damages for failure of the benefit corporation to create general or specific public benefit.

9. A benefit corporation may have an officer designated the "benefit officer" who shall have authority and shall perform duties in the management of the benefit corporation relating

b. 公共利益董事的任免应依据《新泽西州成文法》第 6 章第 14A 节的有关规定。公共利益董事应当是独立个体。根据本法第 9 条的规定，公共利益董事可以同时担任公共利益高管。公共利益公司的公司章程或公司章程细则可以明确本款未规定的公共利益董事资格。

c. 公共利益公司应当根据本法第 11 条的规定向股东提交年度公共利益报告，公共利益董事负责报告的准备并就下列事项出具董事意见：在报告所述期间内，公共利益公司是否在所有重要事项上依其一般和特定公共利益目的行事；董事和经理是否分别依本法第 6 条第 a 款和第 8 条第 a 款的规定行事。如果公共利益董事认为公共利益公司或其董事、高管不符合一般公共利益的要求，则需陈述公共利益公司或其董事、高管未能履行责任的情况。

d. 如果公共利益公司的章程规定，由董事以外的人行使或履行根据《新泽西州成文法》第 14A:6–1 条的规定赋予董事会的权力和职责，那么公共利益公司的章程必须规定，履行董事会职责的人或股东应包括具有公共利益董事的权力、职责、权利和豁免权的人员。

e. 无论公司章程或者章程细则是否依据《新泽西州成文法》第 14A:2–7 条第（3）款的规定删除或限制董事个人责任，公共利益董事在行使职责时不对其任何作为或不作为承担个人责任，但自我交易或故意违法行为除外。

8. a 公共利益公司的每个高管应当依本法第 6 条第 a 款规定的行为标准考虑该款规定的利益和因素，如果：

（1）高管有依据该行为标准行事的自由裁量权；并且

（2）高管有合理理由相信该行为对以下事项有实质性影响：

（a）一般公共利益或特定公共利益的实现；或者

（b）本法第 6 条第 a 款规定的利益或因素。

b. 对利益和相关因素的考虑不能被认为构成对本法第 6 条第 c 款规定的违反。

c. 高管不对未能实现一般公共利益或特定公共利益承担个人责任。

9. 公共利益公司可以任命“公共利益高管”，该高管有权履行法律或公司章程规定的与一般或特定公共利益创设有关的职责；或者在公司章程细则中没有规定时，

to the purpose of the corporation to create general or specific public benefits as may be provided by or pursuant to the by–laws or, in the absence of controlling provisions in the by–laws, as may be determined by or pursuant to resolutions or orders of the board of directors. If a benefit corporation has a benefit officer, the duties of the benefit officer shall include preparing the benefit report required by section 11 of this act.

10. a. The duties of directors and officers under this act, and the general and any specific public benefit purpose of a benefit corporation, may be enforced only in a benefit enforcement proceeding. No person may bring an action or assert a claim against a benefit corporation or its directors or officers with respect to the duties of directors and officers under this act and the general and any specific public benefit purpose of the benefit corporation except in a benefit enforcement proceeding.

b. A benefit enforcement proceeding may be commenced or maintained only:

(1) Directly by the benefit corporation; or

(2) Derivatively by:

(a) a shareholder;

(b) a director;

(c) a person or group of persons that owns beneficially or of record 10% or more of the equity interests in an entity of which the benefit corporation is a subsidiary; or

(d) such other persons as may be specified in the certificate of incorporation or by–laws of the benefit corporation.

11. a. A benefit corporation shall deliver to each shareholder an annual benefit report including:

(1) A narrative description of:

(a) The ways in which the benefit corporation pursued a general public benefit during the year and the extent to which the general public benefit was created;

(b) The ways in which the benefit corporation pursued any specific public benefit that the certificate of incorporation states is the purpose of the benefit corporation to create and the extent to which that specific public benefit was created; and

(c) Any circumstances that have hindered the creation by the benefit corporation of general or specific public benefits;

(2) An assessment of the social and environmental performance of the benefit corporation, prepared in accordance with a third–party standard applied consistently with any application of that standard in prior benefit reports or accompanied by an explanation of the reasons for any inconsistent application;

(3) The name of the benefit director and the benefit officer, if any, and the address to which correspondence to each of them may be directed;

(4) The compensation paid by the benefit corporation during the year to each director in

执行董事会作出的有关决议或者命令。若公司设有公共利益高管，其职责还包括根据本法第 11 条的规定编写公共利益报告。

10. a. 本法规定的公共利益董事和高管的义务以及公共利益公司的任何一般和特定公共利益目的的执行应通过公共利益实施程序进行。非经公共利益实施程序，任何人不得向公共利益公司或者其董事、高管提起诉讼或提起主张。

b. 公共利益实施程序只能由下列主体提起：

（1）直接由公共利益公司提起；或者

（2）由以下主体派生提起：

（a）股东；

（b）董事；

（c）拥有公共利益公司母公司 10% 或以上已发行股票的收益所有权或登记所有权的个人或群体；或者

（d）公共利益公司章程或章程细则中列明的其他人员。

11. a. 公共利益公司在年度公共利益报告中应包括以下内容：

（1）对以下事项的说明：

（a）公共利益公司本年度追求一般公共利益的方法及其实现程度；

（b）公共利益公司实现公司章程中列明的特定公共利益的方法及其实现程度；以及

（c）阻碍公共利益公司设定一般和特定公共利益的情形；

（2）根据第三方标准对公共利益公司的整体社会和环境表现作出的评价，并说明该标准是否沿用了先前公共利益报告中使用的标准；或者附一份说明以解释使用不一致标准的原因并载明与上一份报告相比标准的变化之处；

（3）公共利益董事和公共利益高管的姓名和联系地址（如有）。

（4）公共利益公司在上一年度支付给每位董事的薪酬。

that capacity;

(5) The name of each person that owns 5% or more of the outstanding shares of the benefit corporation either beneficially, to the extent known to the benefit corporation without independent investigation, or of record; and

(6) The statement of the benefit director described in section 7 of this act.

b. The benefit report must be sent annually to each shareholder within 120 days following the end of the fiscal year of the benefit corporation or at the same time that the benefit corporation delivers any other annual report to its shareholders.

c. A benefit corporation must post its most recent benefit report on the public portion of its website, if any, except that the compensation paid to directors and any financial or proprietary information included in the benefit report may be omitted from the benefit report as posted.

d. (1) With the delivery of the benefit report to shareholders pursuant to subsection b. of this section, the benefit corporation must deliver a copy of the benefit report to the Department of Treasury for filing, except that the compensation paid to directors and any financial or proprietary information included in the benefit report may be omitted from the benefit report as filed under this section. The State Treasurer shall charge a fee of $70 for filing a benefit report.

(2) If a benefit corporation has not delivered a benefit report to the department for a period of two years, the department may prepare and file a statement that the corporation has forfeited its status as a benefit corporation and is no longer subject to this act. If the corporation subsequently delivers a benefit report to the department for filing, the status of the corporation as a benefit corporation shall be automatically reinstated upon the filing of the benefit report by the department and the corporation shall again be subject to this act.

12. This act shall take effect immediately.

STATEMENT

This bill provides for the creation of a benefit corporation. The purpose of a benefit corporation is to create a general public benefit, defined as a material positive impact on society and the environment, through activities that promote some combination of specific public benefits.

The bill states that a benefit corporation may identify one or more specific public benefits in addition to its stated purpose of creating a general public benefit. A specific public benefit includes:

(1) Providing low-income or underserved individuals or communities with beneficial products or services;

(2) Promoting economic opportunity for individuals or communities beyond the creation

（5）拥有公共利益公司 5% 以上已发行股票实际或名义股东的姓名，无论是实益所有，无须单独调查即被公共利益公司所知，还是有记录的；以及

（6）本法第 7 条规定的公共利益董事年度合规申明。

b. 公共利益公司应当在公共利益公司财政年度结束后 120 天内或公共利益公司向其股东送交其他年度报告的同一时间将公共利益报告送交各股东。

c. 若条件允许，公共利益公司应当将其所有公共利益报告发布于其网站的公共部分；但可将公共利益报告中的董事薪酬和财务、所有权信息删除。

d.（1）在依本条第 b 款的规定将公共利益报告提交给股东的同时，公共利益公司应当将该公共利益报告提交州务卿备案，但可将公共利益报告中的董事薪酬、财务或所有权信息在提交州务卿的报告中删除。州务卿应收取 70 美元作为备案费用。

（2）如果公共利益公司连续 2 年未向州务卿提交报告，则州务卿可颁发一份申明，终止该公司公共利益形态，公司不再受本法规定的调整。如果该公司此后又向州务卿递交了公共利益报告，则其公共利益形态将自行恢复，公司将重新接受本法规定的调整。

12. 本法立即生效。

声明

本法为公共利益公司的创设提供了相关规定。公共利益公司的目的在于实现一般公共利益，其定义为对社会和环境的实质性积极影响，并通过运营活动促进其与特定利益的结合。

本法认为，一个公共利益公司除声明其追求实现一般公共利益外，还可以规定一个或多个特定公共利益，特定公共利益可以包括：

（1）向低收入、低福利人群或社区提供有益的产品或服务；

（2）在正常的业务过程中向个人或社区提供创造就业之外的经济机会；

of jobs in the normal course of business;

(3) Preserving the environment;

(4) Improving human health;

(5) Promoting the arts, sciences or advancement of knowledge;

(6) Increasing the flow of capital to entities with a public benefit purpose; and

(7) The accomplishment of any other particular benefit for society or the environment.

The bill provides for a benefit corporation to be formed in accordance with all corporations subject to Title 14A of the New Jersey Statutes. An existing corporation may become a benefit corporation by amending its certificate of incorporation to state that the corporation is a benefit corporation.

The bill also provides for a benefit corporation to terminate its status as a benefit corporation by amending its certificate of incorporation to delete the statement that the corporation is a benefit corporation.

At least the minimum status vote is needed in order for a corporation to amend its certificate of incorporation to either become a benefit corporation or terminate its status as a benefit corporation. Minimum status vote means that, in addition to any other approval or vote required by the "New Jersey Business Corporation Act," N.J.S.14A:1–1 et seq...or the certificate of incorporation:

(1) The holders of shares of every class or series shall be entitled to vote on the corporate action regardless of any limitation stated in the certificate of incorporation on the voting rights of any class or series;

(2) The corporate action must be approved by vote of the shareholders of each class or series entitled to cast at least two– thirds of the votes that all shareholders of the class or series are entitled to cast thereon.

The bill provides for a standard of conduct for a benefit corporation's board of directors and officers. The bill also provides for a benefit corporation to designate a "benefit director" and a "benefit officer." It is the duty of the benefit director to determine whether or not the benefit corporation has acted in accordance with its general, and any specific, public benefit purpose. The benefit officer will perform any duties in the management of the benefit corporation relating to the purpose of the corporation to create a general or specific public benefit.

A benefit corporation must deliver an annual benefit report including the following information:

(1) The ways in which the corporation pursued any general and specific public benefit during the year, the extent to which the public benefit was created, and any circumstances that hindered the creation of a public benefit;

(2) An assessment of the social and environmental performance of the corporation;

（3）保护或修复环境；
（4）改善人类健康；
（5）促进艺术、科学或传播知识；
（6）促进资本向以公共利益为目的的企业流动；以及
（7）实现其他有利于社会或环境的特定利益。

本法适用于所有依据《新泽西州成文法》第 14A 节的规定创设的公共利益公司。已经成立的公司可通过修改其公司章程声明其转换为公共利益公司。

本法还规定，公共利益公司可以通过修改公司章程，删除章程中公司性质为公共利益公司的声明来终止其公共利益公司形态。

公司章程中有关选择或终止公共利益公司状态的修改应满足最低表决要求才能生效。最低表决形态是指，《新泽西州商事公司法》《新泽西州成文法》第 14A:1-1 条等条款或公司章程中规定的其他授权或投票要求。

（1）无论公司章程是否对任一类别的投票权进行了限制，每个类别或系列的股票持有人都有权对公司行为进行投票；

（2）公司行为必须获得有投票权的每个类别的股权持有者的至少 2/3 的赞成票才能通过。

本法为公共利益公司董事会的行为提供了标准。本法同时提供了任命“公共利益董事”“公共利益高管”的规则。公共利益董事的职责是判断公共利益公司的行为是否符合一般公共利益或某一特定公共利益。公共利益高管将具体履行公共利益公司与实现一般或特定公共利益有关的管理职责。

公共利益公司的年度公共利益报告中必须包含以下信息：

（1）公共利益公司本年度追求一般和特定公共利益的方法及其实现的程度；

（2）对公共利益公司整体社会和环境表现作出的评估；

(3) The name of the benefit director and the benefit officer;

(4) The compensation paid by the corporation during the year to the benefit director;

(5) The name of each person that owns 5% or more of the outstanding shares of the benefit corporation; and

(6) A statement detailing whether, in the opinion of the benefit director, the benefit corporation acted in accordance with its general, and any specific, public benefit purpose.

Finally, the annual benefit report must be sent to each shareholder within 120 days following the end of the fiscal year of the benefit corporation. The benefit corporation must also post its most recent benefit report on the public portion of its website, except that any proprietary information and the compensation paid to directors may be omitted from the report. Benefit corporations are also required to deliver a copy of the benefit report to the Department of Treasury, and the State Treasurer will charge a fee of $70 for filing the benefit report.

（3）公共利益董事和公共利益高管的姓名和联系地址；

（4）公共利益公司在上一年度支付给每位董事的薪酬；

（5）拥有公共利益公司 5% 以上已发行股票的股东的姓名；以及

（6）公共利益董事就公共利益公司的行为是否符合一般或特定公共利益目的的详细陈述意见。

最后，公共利益公司应当在公共利益公司财政年度结束后 120 天内将公共利益报告送交各股东。公共利益公司应当将最近的公共利益报告发布于其网站的公共部分；但是可将公共利益报告中的董事薪酬和财务或所有权信息删除。该公共利益报告应同时提交州务卿备案，州务卿应收取 70 美元作为备案费用。

THE STATE OF NEW YORK

4692--A

2011-2012 Regular Sessions IN ASSEMBLY

February 4, 2011

THE PEOPLE OF THE STATE OF NEW YORK, REPRESENTED IN SENATE AND ASSEM- BLY, DO ENACT AS FOLLOWS:

AN ACT to amend the general construction law and the business corporation law, in relation to authorizing the incorporation of benefit corporations, providing for the public benefit to be created by benefit corporations, for the election and termination of the status of a benefit corporation, for the standards of conduct for directors of a benefit corporation, and for the preparation and distribution of an annual benefit report by a benefit corporation.

§ 1701. Application and effect of article.

(a) This article shall be applicable to all benefit corporations.

(b) The existence of a provision of this article shall not of itself create any implication that a contrary or different rule of law is or would be applicable to a business corporation that is not a benefit corporation. This article shall not affect any statute or rule of law that is or would be applicable to a business corporation that is not a benefit corporation.

(c) Except as otherwise provided in this article, this chapter shall be applicable to all benefit corporations. The specific provisions of this article shall control over the general provisions of this chapter.

(d) A provision of the certificate of incorporation or bylaws of a benefit corporation may not relax, be inconsistent with or supersede any provision of this article.

§ 1702. Definitions.

As used in this article, unless the context otherwise requires, the term:

(a) "Benefit corporation" means a business corporation incorporated under this article and whose status as a benefit corporation has not been terminated as provided in this article.

(b) "General public benefit" means a material positive impact on society and the

纽约州

4692——A

2011-2012 常规会议

2011 年 2 月 4 日

纽约州议会参众两院颁布以下成文法：

本法是对《普通建筑法》和《商事公司法》的修订，以授权设立、选择、终止公共利益的公司形态，为公共利益公司的董事行为设立标准，同时规定了年度公共利益报告的标准。

第 1701 条　法律的适用与效果

（a）本法适用于所有的公共利益公司。

（b）本法不应为非公共利益公司设定相反或不同的规则。本法不影响非公共利益公司法的效力。

（c）除本法另有规定外，本章规定适用于所有公共利益公司。本法的特别规定优先于本章的普通规定。

（d）公共利益公司的公司章程或章程细则不得放宽或排除本法规定的标准，不得与本法相抵触。

第 1702 条　定义

除另有规定外，本法出现的词语的含义如下：

（a）“公共利益公司”是指根据本法的规定设立，作为公共利益公司的状态并未终止的公司。

（b）“一般公共利益”是指经第三方标准评估，公共利益公司的运营在总体

environment, taken as a whole, assessed against a third-party standard, from the business and operations of a benefit corporation.

(c) "Independent" means that a person has no material relationship with a benefit corporation or any of its subsidiaries. A material relationship between a person and a benefit corporation or any of its subsidiaries will be conclusively presumed to exist if:

(1) the person is, or has been within the last three years, an employee of the benefit corporation or any of its subsidiaries;

(2) an immediate family member of the person is, or has been within the last three years, an executive officer of the benefit corporation or any of its subsidiaries; or

(3) the person, or an entity of which the person is a director, officer or other manager or in which the person owns beneficially or of record five percent or more of the equity interests, owns beneficially or of record five percent or more of the shares of the benefit corporation. A percentage of ownership in an entity shall be calculated as if all outstanding rights to acquire equity interests in the entity had been exercised.

(d) "Minimum status vote" means that, in addition to any other approval or vote required by this chapter, the certificate of incorporation or a bylaw adopted by the shareholders:

(1) The holders of shares of every class or series that are entitled to vote on the corporate action shall be entitled to vote as a class on the corporate action; and

(2) The corporate action must be approved by vote of the shareholders of each class or series entitled to cast at least three-quarters of the votes that all shareholders of the class or series are entitled to cast thereon.

(e) "Specific public benefit," includes:

(1) providing low-income or underserved individuals or communities with beneficial products or services;

(2) promoting economic opportunity for individuals or communities beyond the creation of jobs in the normal course of business;

(3) preserving the environment;

(4) improving human health;

(5) promoting the arts, sciences or advancement of knowledge;

(6) increasing the flow of capital to entities with a public benefit purpose; and

(7) the accomplishment of any other particular benefit for society or the environment.

(f) "Subsidiary" means an entity in which a person owns beneficially or of record fifty percent or more of the equity interests. A percentage of ownership in an entity shall be calculated as if all outstanding rights to acquire equity interests in the entity had been exercised.

(g) "Third-party standard" means a recognized standard for defining, reporting and assessing general public benefit that is:

上对社会和环境产生的实质性积极影响。

（c）“独立”是指与公共利益公司或其子公司没有实质性关系的个体。若出现以下情形，则认为该个体与公共利益公司或其子公司存在实质性关系：

（1）该个体是，或在过去的3年内是，公共利益公司或其子公司的除公共利益高管外的雇员。

（2）该个体的直系亲属是，或在过去的3年内是，公共利益公司或其子公司的除公共利益高管外的执行高管；或者

（3）持有公共利益公司5%以上已发行股份的登记股东或实际受益人，或该个人为某一实体的董事或高管。在该实体所有购股权被视为已行使的情况下，应计算股权的比例。

（d）“最低表决要求”是指，在商事公司中，除本章对批准或表决规定的要求外，公司章程或章程细则还应规定以下条件：

（1）每个类别或系列的股东应当有权作为一个独立的投票团体对公司行为进行投票；并且

（2）公司行为须获得每个类别或系列有投票权的所有股东的至少3/4的赞成票才能通过。

（e）“特定的公共利益”包括：

（1）向低收入、低福利人群或社区提供有益的产品或服务；

（2）在正常业务过程中向个人或社区提供创造就业之外的经济机会；

（3）保护或修复环境；

（4）改善人类健康；

（5）促进艺术、科学或传播知识；

（6）促进资本向以公共利益为目的的企业流动；以及

（7）实现其他有利于社会或环境的特定利益。

（f）“子公司”是指在所有购股权都被视为已行使的情况下，该实体50%以上已发行的股票的受益所有权或登记所有权被另一实体所拥有。

（g）“第三方标准”是指对一般公共利益进行定义、报告和评估的公认标准，其满足以下条件：

(1) developed by a person that is independent of the benefit corporation; and

(2) transparent because the following information about the standard is publicly available:

(A) the factors considered when measuring the performance of a business;

(B) the relative weightings of those factors; and

(C) the identity of the persons who developed and control changes to the standard and the process by which those changes are made.

§ 1703. Formation of benefit corporations.

A benefit corporation shall be formed in accordance with this chapter except that its certificate of incorporation shall also state that it is a benefit corporation.

§ 1704. Election of an existing business corporation to become a benefit corporation.

(a) A business corporation may become a benefit corporation under this article by amending its certificate of incorporation so that it contains a statement that the corporation is a benefit corporation. The amendment shall not be effective unless it is adopted by at least the minimum status vote.

(b) Any corporation that is not a benefit corporation that is a party to a merger or consolidation in which the surviving or consolidated corporation will be a benefit corporation must approve the plan of merger or consolidation by at least the minimum status vote in addition to any other vote required by this chapter, the certificate of incorporation or the bylaws.

(c) Any corporation that is not a benefit corporation that is party to a merger or consolidation in which shares of stock of such corporation will be converted into a right to receive shares of stock of a benefit corporation must approve the plan of merger or consolidation by at least the minimum status vote in addition to any other vote required by this chapter, the certificate of incorporation or the bylaws.

§ 1705. Termination of benefit corporation status.

(a) A benefit corporation may terminate its status as such and cease to be subject to this article by amending its certificate of incorporation to delete the statement that the corporation is a benefit corporation. The amendment shall not be effective unless it is adopted by at least the minimum status vote.

(b) If a benefit corporation is a party to a merger or consolidation in which the surviving or new corporation will not be a benefit corporation, the plan of merger or consolidation shall not be effective unless it is adopted by at least the minimum status vote in addition to any other vote required by this chapter, the certificate of incorporation or the bylaws.

(c) Any benefit corporation that is party to a merger or consolidation in which shares of stock of such benefit corporation will be converted into a right to receive shares of stock of a

（1）独立，由独立于公共利益公司的个体制定；
（2）透明，该标准的以下信息可被公众获取：

（A）衡量企业整体社会和环境绩效时所考虑的指标；
（B）这些指标的相关权重；以及
（C）标准制定者的身份以及修改标准的程序。

第 1703 条　公共利益公司的设立

公共利益公司应根据本章的规定设立，此外，公司章程必须声明其为公共利益公司。

第 1704 条　已有商事公司转变为公共利益公司

（a）成立的商业公司可依据本法规定转变为公共利益公司，修改后的公司章程上载明“公共利益公司”字样。公司章程的修改必须满足最低表决要求。

（b）如果一家不具有公共利益公司形态的实体是兼并或合并的一方，并且在该兼并、合并中存续或新设的一方为公共利益公司，那么该兼并或合并计划须获得后者以不低于本章或公司章程（章程细则）规定的最低表决票数才能通过。

（c）如果一家不具有公共利益公司形态的商事公司将其股份转换为公共利益公司股份，则该商事公司须以不低于本章或公司章程（章程细则）规定的最低表决票数通过该兼并或合并的计划。

第 1705 条　公司公共利益形态的终止

（a）公共利益公司可以通过修改公司章程，删除章程中公司性质为公共利益公司的声明以表示其不再受本法规定的调整。公司章程的修改须满足最低表决要求才能生效。

（b）如果兼并或合并的一方主体为公共利益公司，合并或新设的公司将转变为非公共利益公司，则该兼并或合并计划须经公共利益公司以不低于本章或公司章程规定的最低票数通过。

（c）如果兼并或合并的一方主体为公共利益公司，其股份将被转化为商事公司的股份，该兼并或合并计划需经公共利益公司以不低于本章或公司章程规定的最低

corporation that is not a benefit corporation must approve the plan of merger or consolidation by at least the minimum status vote in addition to any other vote required by this chapter, the certificate of incorporation or the bylaws.

(d) A sale, lease, conveyance, exchange, transfer, or other disposition of all or substantially all of the assets of a benefit corporation, unless the transaction is in the usual and regular course of business of the benefit corporation, shall not be effective unless the transaction is approved by at least the minimum status vote in addition to any other vote required by this chapter, the certificate of incorporation or the bylaws.

§ 1706. Corporate purposes.

(a) Every benefit corporation shall have a purpose of creating general public benefit. This purpose is in addition to its purposes under section two hundred one of this chapter and any specific purpose set forth in its certificate of incorporation under paragraph (b) of this section. The purpose to create general public benefit shall be a limitation on the other purposes of the benefit corporation, and shall control over any inconsistent purpose of the benefit corporation.

(b) The certificate of incorporation of a benefit corporation may identify one or more specific public benefits that it is the purpose of the benefit corporation to create in addition to its purposes under section two hundred one of this chapter and paragraph (a) of this section. The identification of a specific public benefit under this paragraph does not limit the obligation of a benefit corporation to create general public benefit.

(c) The creation of general and specific public benefits as provided in paragraphs (a) and (b) of this section is in the best interests of the benefit corporation.

(d) A benefit corporation may amend its certificate of incorporation to add, amend or delete the identification of a specific public benefit that it is the purpose of the benefit corporation to create. The amendment shall not be effective unless it is adopted by at least the minimum status vote.

§ 1707. Standard of conduct for directors and officers.

(a) In discharging the duties of their respective positions, the board of directors, committees of the board and individual directors and officers of a benefit corporation:

(1) shall consider the effects of any action upon:

(A) the ability for the benefit corporation to accomplish its general and any specific public benefit purpose;

(B) the shareholders of the benefit corporation;

(C) the employees and workforce of the benefit corporation and its subsidiaries and suppliers;

(D) the interests of customers as beneficiaries of the general or specific public benefit purposes of the benefit corporation;

票数通过。

（d）公共利益公司任何出售、出租、置换或者其他处置全部或者大部分财产的行为，除非该行为属于正常商事往来，否则须满足最低表决要求才能生效。

第 1706 条　公司目的

（a）每个公共利益公司都应当有实现一般公共利益的目的。此目的在本章第 201 条和本条第（b）款规定的公司章程之外。规定一般公共利益的目的是限制公共利益公司的其他特定目的，防止某一特定目的与一般公共利益目的相冲突。

（b）除本章第 201 条和本条第（a）款的规定外，公共利益公司的章程可以规定一个或多个特定的公共利益目的。根据本款规定对特定公共利益的界定并不对公共利益公司的一般公共利益目的构成限制。

（c）根据本条第（a）款和第（b）款规定设定的一般和特定公共利益目的为公共利益公司的最佳利益。

（d）公共利益公司可以增加、修改或删除公司章程里设定的特定公共利益目的。公共利益公司对章程的修改须满足最低表决要求才能生效。

第 1707 条　公司董事及其高管的行为标准

（a）在履行各自职责和考虑公共利益公司最佳利益时，公共利益公司的董事会、董事会委员会、董事和公司高管：

（1）应该考虑以下行为的影响：

（A）公司实现其一般和特定公共利益目的的能力；

（B）公共利益公司的股东；

（C）公共利益公司的雇员及其子公司和供应商；

（D）作为公共利益公司一般或特定公共利益目的的受益人的消费者的利益；

(E) community and societal considerations, including those of any community in which offices or facilities of the benefit corporation or its subsidiaries or suppliers are located;

(F) the local and global environment; and

(G) the short–term and long–term interests of the benefit corporation, including benefits that may accrue to the benefit corporation from its long–term plans and the possibility that these interests may be best served by the continued independence of the benefit corporation;

(2) may consider:

(A) the resources, intent and conduct (past, stated and potential) of any person seeking to acquire control of the corporation; and

(B) any other pertinent factors or the interests of any other group that they deem appropriate; and

(3) shall not be required to give priority to the interests of any particular person or group referred to in subparagraphs one and two of this paragraph over the interests of any other person or group unless the benefit corporation has stated its intention to give priority to interests related to a specific public benefit purpose identified in its certificate of incorporation.

(b) The consideration of interests and factors in the manner required by paragraph (a) of this section: (1) shall not constitute a violation of the provisions of sections seven hundred fifteen or seven hundred seventeen of this chapter; and

(2) is in addition to the ability of directors to consider interests and factors as provided in section seven hundred seventeen of this chapter.

(c) A director does not have a fiduciary duty to a person that is a beneficiary of the general or specific public benefit purposes of a benefit corporation arising from the status of the person as a beneficiary, unless otherwise stated in the certificate of incorporation or the bylaws of the benefit corporation.

§ 1708. Annual benefit report.

(a) A benefit corporation must deliver to each shareholder an annual benefit report including:

(1) a narrative description of:

(A) the process and rationale for selecting the third party standard used to prepare the benefit report;

(B) the ways in which the benefit corporation pursued general public benefit during the year and the extent to which general public benefit was created;

(C) the ways in which the benefit corporation pursued any specific public benefit that the certificate of incorporation states it is the purpose of the benefit corporation to create and the extent to which that specific public benefit was created; and

(D) any circumstances that have hindered the creation by the benefit corporation of

（E）社区和社会影响，包括公共利益公司及其子公司或其供应商的办公地或设施所在地的社区；

（F）当地和全球环境；以及

（G）公共利益公司的短期和长期利益，包括可能从其长期计划中产生的利益，以及公共利益公司继续保持独立可能产生的最佳利益。

（2）还可以考虑以下因素：

（A）试图获得公司控制权的人员所使用的资源意图和行为（过去、现在和将来）；以及

（B）董事认为合理的其他相关因素或其他群体的利益；以及

（3）除非公共利益公司在其公司章程中表明为实现其一般或特定公共利益而给予特定的利益或因素优先权，否则公司并不会被要求给予上述两项规定中某个利益或因素优先权。

（b）对本条第（a）款中相关利益和因素的考虑：（1）不构成对本章第 715 条或第 717 条规定的违反；

（2）是对本章第 717 条规定的董事考虑利益和相关因素的能力的补充。

（c）除非公司章程或章程细则另有规定，董事对公共利益公司的一般或特定公共利益目的的法定受益人不负信义义务。

第 1708 条　年度公益报告

（a）公共利益公司每年必须向每位股东呈交的公益报告应包含以下内容：

（1）对以下事项的说明：

（A）为编写年度公益报告而选择的第三方标准的程序和原因；

（B）公共利益公司本年度实现一般公共利益的方式及其实现程度；

（C）公共利益公司实现公司章程中列明的特定公共利益的方法及其实现程度；以及

（D）阻碍公共利益公司实现一般和特定公共利益的情形；

general or specific public benefit;

(2) an assessment of the performance of the benefit corporation, relative to its general public benefit purpose assessed against a third-party standard applied consistently with any application of that standard in prior benefit reports or accompanied by an explanation of the reasons for any inconsistent application and, if applicable, assessment of the performance of the benefit corporation, relative to its specific public benefit purpose or purposes;

(3) the compensation paid by the benefit corporation during the year to each director in that capacity; and

(4) the name of each person that owns beneficially or of record five percent or more of the outstanding shares of the benefit corporation.

(b) The benefit report must be sent annually to each shareholder within one hundred twenty days following the end of the fiscal year of the benefit corporation. Delivery of a benefit report to shareholders is in addition to any other requirement to deliver an annual report to shareholders.

(c) A benefit corporation must post its most recent benefit report on the public portion of its website, if any, except that the compensation paid to directors and any financial or proprietary information included in the benefit report may be omitted from the benefit report as posted.

(d) Concurrently with the delivery of the benefit report to shareholders pursuant to paragraph (b) of this section, the benefit corporation must deliver a copy of the benefit report to the department for filing, except that the compensation paid to directors and any financial or proprietary information included in the benefit report may be omitted from the benefit report as filed under this section.

(e) The annual benefit report shall be in addition to all other reporting requirements under this chapter.

§ 1709. Conspicuous language on the face of certificates.

All certificates representing shares of a benefit corporation shall contain, in addition to any other statements required by the business corporation law, the following conspicuous language on the face of the certificate: "This entity is a benefit corporation organized under article seventeen of the New York business corporation law."

S4 Subparagraph 1 of paragraph (a) of section 720 of the business corporation law is amended by adding a new clause (C) to read as follows:

(C) In the case of directors or officers of a benefit corporation organized under article seventeen of this chapter: (I) the failure to pursue the general public benefit purpose of a benefit corporation or any specific public benefit set forth in its certificate of incorporation; (II) the failure by a benefit corporation to deliver or post an seventeen of this chapter; or

（2）依据第三方标准对公共利益公司整体社会和环境表现作出的评价，并说明该标准是否沿用先前公共利益报告中使用的标准；或附一份说明以解释使用不一致标准的原因并载明与上一份报告相比标准的变化；

（3）公共利益公司在上一年度支付给每位董事的薪酬；以及

（4）公共利益公司的实际所有权人或拥有 5% 以上已发行股票的股东的姓名。

（b）公共利益年度报告必须在公司财政年度结束后 120 天内呈交给股东；此外，还可以根据其他约定的时间向股东提交年度报告。

（c）公共利益公司应当将所有公共利益报告发布于其网站的公共部分；但可将公共利益报告中的董事薪酬和财务、所有权信息删除。

（d）在依本条第（b）款的规定将公共利益报告提交给股东的同时，公司应当将该公共利益报告提交州务卿备案，但可将报告中的董事薪酬、财务或所有权信息在提交的报告中删除。

（e）年度公共利益报告还应满足本章的其他要求。

第 1709 条　公司章程中应载明的内容

所有含有公共利益股份的公司还应根据商事公司法的规定，在公司章程中载明以下内容："本实体是根据《纽约州商事公司法》第 17 条设立的公共利益公司。"

S 4《商事公司法》第 720 条第 1 款第（a）项增加的第（C）目如下：

（C）根据本章第 17 条的规定，设立公共利益公司的董事或公司高管如果：（Ⅰ）未能追求公共利益公司章程中规定一般或特定的公共利益目的；（Ⅱ）不能按本章第 17 条的规定提交公共利益公司的年度报告；或（Ⅲ）其存在过失、渎职或其他违反本章第 17 条规定的行为。

(III) the neglect of, or failure to perform, or other violation of this or her duties or standard of conduct under article seventeen of this chapter.

S5 This act shall take effect on the sixtieth day after it shall have become a law.

S 5 本法在其生效后的第 16 日成为法律。

THE STATE OF OREGON

77th OREGON LEGISLATIVE ASSEMBLY--2013 Regular Session

Enrolled

House Bill 2296

AN ACT

Relating to benefit companies.

SECTION 1. As used in sections 1 to 11 of this 2013 Act:

(1) "Benefit company" means a corporation or a limited liability company that is incorporated, organized, formed or created under section 3 of this 2013 Act.

(2) "Benefit governor" means an individual who is designated as the benefit governor of a benefit company under section 7 of this 2013 Act.

(3) "General public benefit" means a material positive impact on society and the environment, taken as a whole, from the business and operations of a benefit company.

(4) "Governor" means a director of a corporation that is a benefit company, a member in a member–managed limited liability company that is a benefit company or a manager in a manager–managed limited liability company that is a benefit company.

(5) "Minimum status vote" means a decision that an entity makes in accordance with section 4 of this 2013 Act.

(6) "Third–party standard" means a recognized standard for defining, reporting and assessing an entity's social and environmental performance that:

(a) Establishes criteria that apply to all of the interests described in section 6 (1)(b), (c), (d), (e) and (f) of this 2013 Act;

(b) Is developed by an organization that is not under the control of the benefit company or any of the benefit company's affiliates; and

(c) Has information publicly available concerning:

(A) The criteria the standard uses to measure an entity's overall social and

俄勒冈州

2013年俄勒冈州第77次立法议会——2013年立法季

颁布

2296号议会法案

本法

与公共利益公司有关。

第1条　本法第1条至第13条使用的词语的含义如下：

（1）“公共利益公司”是指根据本法第3条的规定组织、设立、形成或创设的公司或有限责任公司。

（2）“公共利益执行官”是指公共利益公司根据本法第7条的规定任命的董事为公共利益董事。

（3）“一般公共利益”是指公司的业务和经营在整体上对社会和环境产生的实质性积极影响。

（4）“执行官”是指公共利益公司的董事，作为公共利益公司的成员管理有限责任公司或作为公共利益公司的经理。

（5）“最低表决要求”是指实体根据本法第4条的规定作出的决定。

（6）“第三方标准”是指用于定义、报告和评估公司社会和环境绩效的标准，其应满足以下条件：

（a）根据本法第6条第（1）（b）项、第（c）项、第（d）项、第（e）项和第（f）项中所列利益评估公司业务和经营绩效。

（b）经非由公共利益公司或其子公司控制的第三方实体制定；

（c）以下信息可公开获取：

（A）衡量企业整体社会和环境绩效时所考虑的指标及其权重；

environmental performance and the relative weight the standard gives to each criterion;

(B) The process by which the standard is developed and revised; and

(C) The organization that developed the standard that is sufficient in detail to disclose any relationships that might compromise the organization's independence, including:

(i) The material owners and members of the organization's governing body;

(ii) How the organization selects members of the organization's governing body; and

(iii) The organization's sources of financial support.

SECTION 2. (1) Except as otherwise provided in sections 1 to 11 of this 2013 Act, sections 1 to 11 of this 2013 Act apply to:

(a) A corporation that states in the corporation's articles of incorporation or articles of conversion that the corporation is subject to sections 1 to 11 of this 2013 Act;

(b) A limited liability company that states in the limited liability company's articles of organization or articles of conversion that the limited liability company is subject to sections 1 to 11 of this 2013 Act; or

(c) A corporation or limited liability company that elects to become a benefit company under section 3 of this 2013 Act.

(2)(a) Except as provided in paragraph (c) of this subsection, a benefit company that is a corporation incorporated under ORS chapter 60 is subject to ORS chapter 60 and to sections 1 to 11 of this 2013 Act.

(b) Except as provided in paragraph (c) of this subsection, a benefit company that is a limited liability company organized under ORS chapter 63 is subject to ORS chapter 63 and to sections 1 to 11 of this 2013 Act.

(c) To the extent that a provision of sections 1 to 11 of this 2013 Act conflicts with a provision of ORS chapter 60 or 63, a specific provision of sections 1 to 11 of this 2013 Act controls over a general provision of ORS chapter 60 or 63.

(3) Sections 1 to 11 of this 2013 Act do not apply to a corporation that is not a benefit company or to a limited liability company that is not a benefit company.

SECTION 3. (1)(a) Notwithstanding ORS 60.074 (2), a corporation incorporated under ORS chapter 60 is a benefit company under sections 1 to 11 of this 2013 Act if the corporation's articles of incorporation state that the corporation is a benefit company subject to sections 1 to 11 of this 2013 Act.

(b) Notwithstanding ORS 63.074 (3), a limited liability company organized under ORS chapter 63 is a benefit company under sections 1 to 11 of this 2013 Act if the limited liability company's articles of organization state that the limited liability company is a benefit company subject to sections 1 to 11 of this 2013 Act.

(2)(a) A corporation that is incorporated under ORS chapter 60 may become a benefit company by amending the corporation's articles of incorporation to state, in addition to the

（B）标准制定和修改的程序；以及

（C）充分披露影响标准制定机构独立性的详细信息，包括：

（i）实际所有人以及公共利益执行机构；

（ii）该组织选择公共利益执行机构成员的方式；以及

（iii）该机构的经济来源。

第 2 条　（1）除本法第 1 条至第 11 条另有规定外，第 1 条至第 11 条适用于：

（a）在公司章程或公司形态转换文件中声明其接受本法第 1 条至第 11 条规定调整的公司；

（b）在公司章程或公司形态转换文件中声明其接受本法第 1 条至第 11 条规定调整的有限责任公司；或者

（c）根据本法第 3 条转换成公共利益公司的公司或有限责任公司。

（2）（a）除本款第（c）项另有规定外，根据《俄勒冈州修订法》第 60 章的规定设立的公司同时受《俄勒冈州修订法》第 60 章和本法第 1 条至第 11 条规定的调整。

（b）（a）除本款第（c）项另有规定外，根据《俄勒冈州修订法》第 63 章的规定设立的有限责任公司同时受《俄勒冈州修订法》第 63 章和本法第 1 条至第 11 条规定的调整。

（c）如果本法第 1 条至第 11 条与《俄勒冈州修订法》第 60 章或第 63 章的规定存在冲突，前者作为特别条款优先于后者适用。

（3）本法第 1 条至第 11 条的规定不适用于非公共利益公司或非公共利益有限责任公司。

第 3 条　（1）（a）尽管公司根据《俄勒冈州修订法》第 60.074（2）款的规定设立，但如果公司在其章程中申明受本法第 1 条至第 11 条规定的调整，其仍为本法规定的公共利益公司。

（b）尽管有限责任公司根据《俄勒冈州修订法》第 63.074（3）款的规定设立，但如果公司在其章程中申明受本法第 1 条至第 11 条规定的调整，其仍为本法规定的公共利益有限责任公司。

（2）（a）根据《俄勒冈州修订法》第 60 章的规定设立的有限公司可以通过修改公司章程成为公共利益公司，公司须在章程中声明除接受《俄勒冈州修订法》第

requirements set forth in ORS 60.047, that the corporation is a benefit company subject to sections 1 to 11 of this 2013 Act. The amendment to the articles of incorporation must be approved by a minimum status vote.

(b) A limited liability company that is organized under ORS chapter 63 may become a benefit company by amending the limited liability company's articles of organization to state, in addition to the requirements set forth in ORS 63.047, that the limited liability company is a benefit company subject to sections 1 to 11 of this 2013 Act. The amendment to the articles of organization must be approved by a minimum status vote.

(3) A benefit company may be formed by means of a conversion if articles of conversion that state that the converted entity will be a benefit company that is subject to sections 1 to 11 of this 2013 Act are approved by a minimum status vote.

(4) An entity that is not a benefit company may become a benefit company by merging or exchanging equity interests with a benefit company if the shareholders or holders of equity interests of the entity that is not the benefit company approve, by a minimum status vote, a plan of merger or a plan for exchanging equity interests with a benefit company under which the surviving entity will be a benefit company.

(5) A benefit company may become an entity other than a benefit company only if an action to remove from the articles of incorporation, articles of organization or articles of conversion the provision that states that the entity is a benefit company subject to sections 1 to 11 of this 2013 Act is approved by a minimum status vote.

(6)(a) A plan for a benefit company must be approved by a minimum status vote if the plan would:

(A) Merge the benefit company with an entity that is not a benefit company, if the surviving entity would not be a benefit company;

(B) Provide for exchanging equity interests with an entity that is not a benefit company, if the exchange would create an entity that is not a benefit company and that would hold substantially all of the benefit company's assets;

(C) Convert the benefit company to an entity that is not a benefit company; or

(D) Otherwise cause sections 1 to 11 of this 2013 Act not to apply to the benefit company.

(b) A sale, lease, exchange or other disposition of all or substantially all of a benefit company's assets must be approved by a minimum status vote unless the benefit company conducts the sale, lease, exchange or other disposition in the ordinary course of the benefit company's business.

(7) A provision of a benefit company's articles of incorporation, articles of organization, articles of conversion or plan described in subsection (6) of this section may be inconsistent with or supersede a provision of sections 1 to 11 of this 2013 Act only to the extent that

60.047条的规定调整外，还接受本法第1条至第11条的规定调整。公司章程的修改必须满足最低表决要求才能通过。

（b）根据《俄勒冈州修订法》第63章的规定设立的有限责任公司可以通过修改公司章程成为公共利益公司，公司须在章程中声明除接受《俄勒冈州修订法》第60.047条的规定调整外，还接受本法第1条至第11条规定的调整。公司章程的修改须满足最低表决要求才能通过。

（3）公共利益公司可以通过在公司转换文件中声明其接受本法第1条至第11条规定的调整，公司形态的转换须满足最低表决要求才能通过。

（4）如果非公共利益公司获得其股东或收益所有人最低表决要求通过，则该公司可通过与公共利益公司兼并或股权置换的方式成为公共利益公司。在此情形下，存续的实体将成为公共利益公司。

（5）公共利益公司可通过删除公司章程中其作为公共利益公司的声明来终止其公共利益公司的形态，并不再受本法第1条至第11条规定的调整。公司章程的修改须满足最低表决要求才能通过。

（6）（a）公共利益公司的以下决议须满足最低表决要求才能通过：

（A）公共利益公司与非公共利益公司合并，且存续的实体为非公共利益公司；

（B）与非公共利益公司进行股权置换时，股权置换后新设一个非公共利益公司且该公司持有公共利益公司的主要资产；

（C）将公共利益公司转换为非公共利益公司；或者
（D）导致公共利益公司无法适用本法第1条至第11条某些规定的其他情形；

（b）除正常商业往来外，公共利益公司的任何出售、出租、置换或者其他处置全部或主要财产的行为，须满足最低表决要求。

（7）为确保本法第1条至第11条目标的实现，本条第（6）款所规定的公共利益公司的章程、组织性文件、形态转换文件或计划只有在比本法第1条至第11条的规定更严格时，才优先于后者适用。

the provision in the articles of incorporation, articles of organization, articles of conversion or plan imposes a more stringent requirement on the benefit company, in keeping with the purposes set forth in sections 1 to 11 of this 2013 Act, than a provision of sections 1 to 11 of this 2013 Act imposes.

SECTION 4. (1) Except as provided in subsections (2) and (3) of this section, an approval of an action described in section 3 (2) to (6) of this 2013 Act is effective only if, in addition to any other applicable requirements, a majority of the interests that are entitled to vote on the action are voted to approve the action.

(2) If an entity's governing documents or the provisions of ORS chapter 60 or 63, as applicable, require more than a majority vote or require each class or series to vote separately, approval of the action is effective only if the requirement for the greater vote or for separate class or series voting is met.

(3) If, as of the effective date of this 2013 Act, an entity has shares that are listed on a national securities exchange or are regularly traded in a market that a member of a national or affiliated securities association maintains, each class or series of the entity's shares must separately meet the requirement to approve the action by two–thirds of the shares that are entitled to vote.

SECTION 5. (1) In addition to any purpose set forth in or adopted in accordance with ORS 60.047 (2)(c)(A), 60.074, 63.047 or 63.074, a benefit company has the purpose of providing a general public benefit.

(2)(a) The articles of incorporation or articles of organization for a benefit company may identify a specific public benefit for the benefit company in addition to the purposes described in subsection (1) of this section. A benefit company's identification of a specific public benefit does not limit the benefit company's obligation to fulfill the purposes described in subsection (1) of this section.

(b) A benefit company may amend the articles of incorporation or articles of organization to add, amend or remove a specific public benefit in the manner otherwise provided for amending the benefit company's purpose in the articles of incorporation or articles of organization.

(3) Notwithstanding the requirement in ORS 58.076 that a professional corporation have rendering professional service as the professional corporation's sole purpose, a professional corporation that is a benefit company shall have the purposes set forth in ORS 58.076 and the purpose of providing a general public benefit. The professional corporation may identify a specific public benefit in addition to the purposes described in this subsection.

SECTION 6. (1) A governor of a benefit company shall act in the best interests of the benefit company and shall discharge the governor's duties as provided for a director of a corporation in ORS 60.357, or as provided for a member or manager of a limited liability

第4条 （1）除本条第（2）款和第（3）款另有规定外，公司对本法第3条第（2）至第（6）款规定的行为的批准除满足其他要求外，还须获得对行为有投票权的主要利益人的通过。

（2）如果公共利益实施文件、《俄勒冈州修订法》第60章或第63章要求多数票、每个类别或系列股东分别同意公司行为，公司内部文件只有在要求更严格时才能优先适用。

（3）如果本法生效前，该实体的股份在全国性的股票交易所上市或交易，公司行为必须分别获得每个类别或系列有投票权的所有股东至少2/3的赞成票才能通过。

第5条 （1）公共利益公司除根据《俄勒冈州修订法》第60.047（2）（c）（A）目，第60.074条，第63.047条或者第63.074条的规定设定公司利益外，还须设立一般公共利益。

（2）（a）公共利益公司的章程可以在商业公司法公司目的条款和本条第（1）款的规定外确定一项或多项特定公共利益目的。依据本条第（1）款的规定设定的特定公共利益目的并不限制公共利益公司在本条第（1）款下设定一般公共利益目的的义务。

（b）公共利益公司可以增加、修改或删除公司章程中设定的特定公共利益目的。

（3）尽管《俄勒冈州修订法》第58.076条规定专业公司提供专业性服务是公司的唯一目的，但专业性公共利益公司应根据《俄勒冈州修订法》第58.076条和一般公共利益目的条款所规定的目的。除本款规定的目的外，公共利益公司应确定一项特定公共利益。

第6条 （1）公共利益公司的执行官应以公共利益公司的最佳利益为出发点，并应根据公共利益公司的组织形式，履行《俄勒冈州修订法》第60.357条中对公司董事的规定或《俄勒冈州修订法》第63.155条中对有限责任公司成员或经理的规定，

company under ORS 63.155, as appropriate for the benefit company's form of organization. In determining the best interests of the benefit company, the governor shall consider how an action of the governor or of the benefit company, or a decision not to act, will affect:

(a) The shareholders or members of the benefit company;

(b) The employees and work force of the benefit company and the employees and work force of the benefit company's subsidiaries and suppliers;

(c) The benefit company's subsidiaries and suppliers;

(d) The interests the benefit company's customers have in receiving a portion of the general public benefit or specific public benefit that the benefit company provides;

(e) The communities that the benefit company's activities affect including, but not limited to, the communities in which the benefit company is located, operates or has offices or other facilities and in which the benefit company's subsidiaries and suppliers are located, operate or have offices or other facilities;

(f) The local and global environment;

(g) The short–term and long–term interests of the benefit company, including an interest in benefits that might accrue from the benefit company's long–term plans and the possibility that the interests of the benefit company are best served by keeping the benefit company independent; and

(h) The benefit company's ability to fulfill the benefit company's general public benefit purpose and any specific public benefit identified in the benefit company's articles of incorporation or articles of organization.

(2) A governor of a benefit company may consider how an action of the governor or of the benefit company, or decision not to act, will affect other interests the governor deems pertinent.

(3) A governor of a benefit company need not give a particular interest identified in subsection (1) or (2) of this section priority over another interest identified in subsection (1) or (2) of this section unless the benefit company's articles of incorporation or articles of organization identify an interest to which the governor must give priority.

(4) A governor's consideration under this section of the effects of an action, or a decision not to act, is in accordance with ORS 60.357 or 63.155 as ORS 60.357 or 63.155 applies to the governor.

(5)(a) A governor of a benefit company is not personally liable for money damages as a consequence of taking an action or deciding not to act if the governor discharged the governor's duties in accordance with this section and with ORS 60.357 or 63.155, as appropriate for the benefit company's form of organization.

(b) A governor of a benefit company is not personally liable for money damages for the benefit company's failure to provide a general public benefit or a specific public benefit.

履行执行官的职责。在确定公共利益公司的最佳利益时，执行官应考虑执行官或公共利益公司的行动，或不采取行动的决定，将如何影响：

（a）公共利益公司的股东；

（b）公共利益公司、其子公司和供应商的雇员；

（c）公共利益公司的子公司及其供应商；

（d）作为公共利益公司一般或特定公共利益受益者的消费者的利益；

（e）社区和社会因素，包括公共利益公司及其子公司或供应商办公地或设施所在地的社区；

（f）当地和全球环境；

（g）公共利益公司的短期和长期利益，包括从其长期计划中产生的利益以及通过保持公共利益公司独立而尽可能地促进其利益；以及

（h）公共利益公司实现公司章程或章程细则规定的一般和特定公共利益目的的能力。

（2）执行官认为合适的其他相关因素或其他群体的利益。

（3）除公司章程或章程细则中赋予特定利益或因素优先权外，执行官无须给予本条第（1）款或第（2）款中某个利益或因素优先权。

（4）执行官对本条所规定的作为或不作为的影响的考虑不构成对《俄勒冈州修订法》第60.357条、第63.155条规定的董事责任条款的违反，正如俄勒冈州修订法第60.357条或第63.155条对管理者的适用。

（5）（a）公共利益公司执行官在依据本条和《俄勒冈州修订法》第60.357条或第63.155条的规定行使职责时，不对其任何作为或不作为承担个人损害赔偿责任。

（b）公共利益公司未能实现一般公共利益或特定公共利益时，公共利益公司执行官不承担个人损害赔偿责任。

(c) A governor of a benefit company does not have a duty to a person as a consequence of the person's status as a beneficiary of the general public benefit or a specific public benefit that the benefit company provides.

SECTION 7. (1)(a) A benefit company must have a board of governors and may designate at least one member of the board as a benefit governor. A benefit governor, in addition to the powers, duties, rights, privileges and immunities that other governors of the benefit company have, has the powers, duties, rights, privileges and immunities set forth in this section.

(b) The articles of incorporation, articles of organization, bylaws or other organizational documents of the benefit company may set forth additional qualifications for a benefit governor that are consistent with this section.

(2) The benefit company's governors shall elect or appoint and may remove a benefit governor in accordance with procedures set forth in the benefit company's articles of incorporation or articles of organization or in accordance with procedures the governors adopt if the articles of incorporation or articles of organization do not specify a procedure.

(3) The benefit governor shall provide information or statements to other governors of the benefit company concerning the other governors' obligations under section 6 of this 2013 Act.

(4) An individual's action or decision not to act made in the capacity of benefit governor is for all purposes the individual's action or decision not to act in the individual's capacity as a governor of the benefit company.

(5) A benefit governor is not personally liable for an action or omission the benefit governor makes in the benefit governor's capacity as a benefit governor unless the action or omission constitutes self-dealing, willful misconduct or a knowing violation of law.

SECTION 8. (1) A member that has management duties with respect to a benefit company, or an officer or a manager of a benefit company, shall act in the best interests of the benefit company and shall discharge the member's, officer's or manager's duties as provided in ORS 60.374 and 60.377 or in ORS 63.155, as appropriate for the benefit company's form of organization. In addition, the member, officer or manager shall consider the effects of an action of the member, officer or manager or of the benefit company, or of a decision not to act:

(a) To the extent the member, officer or manager has the discretion to take the action or to decide not to act;

(b) If, in the member's, officer's or manager's reasonable judgment, the action or decision not to act may have a material effect on the general public benefit or a specific public benefit the benefit company provides; and

(c) In accordance with the provisions of section 6 (1) to (3) of this 2013 Act for a

（c）公共利益公司执行官不对公共利益公司一般或特定社会目的的受益人负责。

第 7 条 （1）（a）公共利益公司必须设立执行官委员会并至少任命一位董事会成员作为公共利益执行官。公共利执行官除有其他执行官的权力、义务、权利和豁免权外，还有本条规定的权力、义务、权利和豁免权。

（b）公共利益公司章程、章程细则或其他组织性文件与本条规定不存在冲突时，还可以设定公共利益执行官的其他任职资格。

（2）公共利益公司执行官应根据公共利益公司章程或组织性文件设定的程序选任或解除。若公司章程或章程细则未规定有关程序，可按照执行官同意的程序进行。

（3）公共利益执行官应根据本法第 6 条的规定提供公共利益公司其他执行官履行职责的信息和陈述意见。

（4）公共利益执行官在职权范围内的个人作为或不作为应视为公共利益公司执行官的行为。

（5）公共利益执行官在行使职责时不对其任何作为或不作为承担个人责任，但自我交易或故意违法行为除外。

第 8 条 （1）承担公共利益公司管理职责的成员、公共利益公司高管或经理应以公司利益最大化的原则履行《俄勒冈州修订法》第 60.374 条、第 60.377 条或《俄勒冈州修订法》第 63.155 条规定的职责。此外，上述人员还应考虑其作为或不作为的影响：

（a）成员、公司高管或经理行使自由裁量权的范围；

（b）如果根据董事会成员、公司高管或经理的合理判断，该行为会对公共利益公司设定的一般或特定公共利益产生实质性影响；以及

（c）符合本法第 6 条第（1）款至第（3）款对执行官行为影响的规定。

governor's consideration of the effects of the action or the decision not to act.

(2) A member's, officer's or manager's consideration under this section of the effects of an action, or a decision not to act, is in accordance with ORS 60.374 and 60.377 or with ORS 63.155, as appropriate for the benefit company's form of organization, as those provisions apply to a member, officer or manager of a benefit company.

(3)(a) A member, officer or manager of a benefit company is not personally liable for money damages as a consequence of taking an action or deciding not to act if the member, officer or manager discharged the member's, officer's or manager's duties in accordance with this section and with ORS 60.374 and 60.377 or with ORS 63.155, as appropriate for the benefit company's form of organization.

(b) A member, officer or manager of a benefit company is not personally liable for money damages for the benefit company's failure to provide a general public benefit or a specific public benefit.

(c) A member, officer or manager of a benefit company does not have a duty to a person as a consequence of the person's status as a beneficiary of the general public benefit or a specific public benefit that the benefit company provides.

SECTION 9. (1) Except as provided in subsection (2) of this section, a person may not commence a proceeding against a benefit company, or against the governors, members, officers or managers of a benefit company, to assert a claim that the benefit company, governors, members, officers or managers:

(a) Failed to pursue, create or provide a general public benefit or a specific public benefit identified in the benefit company's articles of incorporation or articles of organization; or

(b) Violated a duty or a standard of conduct prescribed under sections 1 to 11 of this 2013 Act.

(2) A person may commence a direct or derivative proceeding, as appropriate, to compel a benefit company to provide a general public benefit or a specific public benefit or to require a governor, member, officer or manager to act in accordance with a duty or a standard of conduct set forth in the benefit company's articles of incorporation or articles of organization, or prescribed under sections 1 to 11 of this 2013 Act, only if the person is:

(a) The benefit company;

(b) A governor;

(c) A shareholder or member; or

(d) Another person identified in the benefit company's bylaws, articles of incorporation or articles of organization as having a right to commence a proceeding under this section.

(3) A benefit company is not liable for money damages as a consequence of failing to provide a general public benefit or a specific public benefit.

（2）成员、公司高管或经理依据本条规定对某一作为或不作为的决定的影响进行考虑时，应符合俄勒冈州修订法第60.374条、第60.377条或《俄勒冈州修订法》第63.155条（视公共利益公司的组织形式而定），因为这些规定适用于利益公司的成员、高管或经理。

（3）（a）如果公共利益公司的董事、公司高管或经理根据《俄勒冈州修订法》第60.374条、第60.377条或《俄勒冈州修订法》第63.155条的规定履行职责，则上述人员在履行职责时不对其任何作为或不作为承担个人损害赔偿责任。

（b）如果公共利益公司未能提供一般公共利益或特定公共利益，成员、公司高管或经理不对此承担个人损害赔偿责任。

（c）公共利益公司的成员、公司高管或经理不对公共利益公司一般或特定社会目的的受益人负责。

第9条 （1）除本条第（2）款另有规定外，任何人不得因以下事项向公共利益公司或者其执行官、成员、高管提起诉讼或主张：

（a）未能追求或创造其在公司章程中陈述的一般或特定公共利益；或者

（b）违反本法第1条至第11条规定的责任、义务或行为标准。

（2）以下主体可以提起直接诉讼或派生诉讼以强制公共利益公司或其执行官、成员、高管或经理根据公司章程、组织性文件或本法第1条至第11条的规定提供一般或特定公共利益：

（a）公共利益公司；
（b）公共利益执行官；
（c）股东或公司董事会成员；或者
（d）公共利益公司章程、章程细则或组织性文件中规定的其他人员。

（3）公共利益公司在未能提供一般或特定公共利益时不承担损害赔偿责任。

SECTION 10. (1) A benefit company each year shall prepare a benefit report.

(2)(a) The benefit report shall give a narrative description of:

(A) The extent to which the benefit company provided a general public benefit and the actions and methods the benefit company used to provide the general public benefit.

(B) The extent to which the benefit company provided a specific public benefit identified in the benefit company's articles of incorporation or articles of organization, and the actions and methods the benefit company used to provide the specific public benefit.

(C) Any circumstances that hindered or prevented the benefit company from providing a general public benefit or a specific public benefit.

(b) In addition to the narrative descriptions required under paragraph (a) of this subsection, the benefit report shall:

(A) Assess the extent to which the benefit company met or exceeded a third–party standard that the benefit company selected and identified in the benefit report. The benefit company shall conduct the assessment and evaluate the benefit company's performance with respect to the third–party standard in a manner that is consistent with assessments and evaluations conducted in previous benefit reports or shall explain the reasons for an inconsistent assessment or evaluation.

(B) Describe the process and rationale the benefit company used to select or to change the third–party standard described in subparagraph (A) of this paragraph.

(C) A benefit report prepared under this section does not need to be audited or certified by a third party.

(3) The benefit company each year shall deliver a copy of the benefit report to each holder of an equity interest within 120 days after the end of the benefit company's fiscal year or at the same time the benefit company delivers any other annual report to a holder of an equity interest.

(4) A benefit company shall post on the publicly accessible pages of the benefit company's website all of the benefit company's benefit reports or shall provide without charge a copy of the most recent benefit report to a person that requests a copy unless providing the copy would violate a provision of applicable law.

SECTION 11. The benefit company shall assess the extent to which the benefit company provides a general public benefit and any specific public benefit identified in the benefit company's articles of incorporation or articles of organization against a third–party standard.

Passed by House April 18, 2013

第 10 条　（1）公共利益公司应编写年度公共利益报告。

（2）（a）年度公共利益报告应包括对以下内容的说明：

（A）公共利益公司本年度提供一般公共利益的方法和一般公共利益实现的情况。

（B）公共利益公司提供公司章程中规定的特定公共利益的方法以及该特定公共利益实现的情况。

（C）阻碍公共利益公司提供一般和特定公共利益的情形。

（b）除描述本款第（a）项规定的内容外，公共利益报告还应包括：

（A）依据第三方标准对公共利益公司的社会和环境表现作出的整体评价，并且在报告中说明其是否沿用先前公共利益报告中的标准，并解释标准不同于上一份报告或评估的原因。

（B）为编写公共利益报告而选择或更换本项第（A）目中所述第三方标准的程序和原因。

（C）本条所规定的公共利益报告并不要求经第三方审计或认证。

（3）公共利益公司应在公共利益公司财政年度结束后 120 天内或公共利益公司向其股东送交其他年度报告的同一时间向股东提交公共利益报告的副本。

（4）公共利益公司应当将其所有公共利益报告发布于其网站的公共部分或向所有索取报告的个人免费提供最新公共利益报告的副本，除非提供副本的行为违法现行法律规定。

第 11 条　公共利益公司应根据第三方标准评估其公司章程或组织性文件中规定的一般或特定公共利益的实现程度。

本法于 2013 年 4 月 18 日由议会通过

THE STATE OF PFNNSYLVANIA

THE GENERAL ASSEMBLY OF PENNSYLVANIA

HOUSE BILL

No. 1616 Session of 2011

AN ACT

Amending Title 15 (Corporations and Unincorporated Associations) of the Pennsylvania Consolidated Statutes, further providing for benefit corporations.

The General Assembly of the Commonwealth of Pennsylvania hereby enacts as follows:

Section 1. Article C of Subpart B of Title 15 of the Pennsylvania Consolidated Statutes is amended by adding a chapter to read:

CHAPTER 33
BENEFIT CORPORATIONS

Subchapter

A. Preliminary Provisions

B. Corporate Purposes

C. Accountability

D. Transparency

SUBCHAPTER A.
PRELIMINARY PROVISIONS

Sec.

3301. Application and effect of chapter.

宾夕法尼亚州

宾夕法尼亚州议会

众议院法案

2011 年第 1616 次会议

该法案

修改《宾夕法尼亚州合并成文法》第 15 编（法人和非法人组织），对法律条文进行合并，规定公共利益公司。

宾夕法尼亚州众议员颁布决议如下：

第 1 部分　《宾夕法尼亚州合并成文法》第 15 编的第 B 分编第 C 条款增加以下章节：

第 33 章
公共利益公司

分章

A. 初步条款

B. 公司目的

C. 公司责任

D. 透明度

第 A 分章　初步条款

条款

第 3301 条 本章的适用及效力

3302. Definitions.
3303. Formation of benefit corporations.
3304. Election of an existing business corporation to become a benefit corporation.
3305. Termination of benefit corporation status.

§ 3301. Application and effect of chapter.

(a) General rule.--This chapter shall apply to all benefit corporations.

(b) Application of business corporation law generally.—The existence of a provision of this chapter shall not of itself create any implication that a contrary or different rule of law is or would be applicable to a business corporation that is not a benefit corporation. This chapter shall not affect any statute or rule of law that is or would be applicable to a business corporation that is not a benefit corporation.

(c) Laws applicable to benefit corporations.--Except as otherwise provided in this chapter, this subpart shall apply generally to benefit corporations. The specific provisions of this chapter shall control over the general provisions of this subpart. A benefit corporation may be simultaneously subject to this chapter and one or more other chapters of this article.

(d) Organic records may not be inconsistent.--A provision of the articles or bylaws of a benefit corporation may not relax, be inconsistent with or supersede any provision of this chapter.

§ 3302. Definitions.

The following words and phrases when used in this chapter shall have the meanings given to them in this section unless the context clearly indicates otherwise:

"Benefit corporation." A business corporation that has elected to become subject to this chapter and whose status as a benefit corporation has not been terminated as provided in this chapter.

"Benefit director." The director designated as the benefit director of a benefit corporation as provided in section 3322 (relating to benefit director).

"Benefit enforcement proceeding." A claim or action brought directly by a benefit corporation, or derivatively on behalf of a benefit corporation, against a director or officer for:

(1) failure to pursue the general public benefit purpose of the benefit corporation or any specific public benefit purpose set forth in its articles;

(2) violation of a duty or standard of conduct under this chapter.

"Benefit officer." The officer of a benefit corporation, if any, designated as the benefit officer as provided in section 3324 (relating to benefit officer).

"General public benefit." A material positive impact on society and the environment by the operations of a benefit corporation taken as a whole, as measured by a third-party standard, through activities that promote some combination of specific public benefits.

"Independent." When a person has no material relationship with a benefit corporation

第 3302 条　定义
第 3303 条　公共利益公司的设立
第 3304 条　已有商事公司转换为公共利益公司
第 3305 条　公共利益公司形态的终止

第 3301 条　本章的适用及效力

（a）一般规则。——本章适用于所有公共利益公司。

（b）普通商事公司法的适用。——本章条款不应为非公共利益公司设定相反或不同的规则。本章条款不应为非公共利益公司设定相反或不同的规则。本章不影响非公共利益公司有关条文和规则的适用。

（c）适用于公共利益公司的法律。——除本章另有规定外，本分编的规定应适用于所有的公共利益公司。本章特别条款优先适用于本分编的一般条款。公共利益公司同时受本章和本法其他章节的调整。

（d）公司内部文件不能与本章规定相抵触。——公共利益公司的公司章程或章程细则不得放宽、违背或取代本章的规定。

第 3302 条　定义

除另有规定外，本章出现的词语的含义如下：

“公共利益公司”选择接受本章规定调整的商事公司，并且其不存在本章规定的终止情形。

“公共利益董事”依第 3322 条（公共利益董事条款）的规定被任命的董事为公共利益董事。

“公共利益实施程序”董事、公司高管存在以下行为，可由公共利益公司提起直接之诉或为公司利益代表公共利益公司提起派生之诉：

（1）公共利益公司未能追求公司章程中规定的一般的公共利益目的或某项公共利益目的；或者

（2）公共利益公司违反本章规定下的任何义务、责任或行为标准。

“公共利益高管”公共利益公司依据第 3324 条（公共利益高管条款）的规定任命的高管为公共利益高管。

“一般公共利益”是指经第三方标准评估，公共利益公司的运营在总体上对社会和环境产生的实质性积极影响。

“独立”是指与公共利益公司或其附属机构没有实质性关系的个体，直接作为

or any of its subsidiaries, other than the relationship of serving as the benefit director or benefit officer, either directly or as a shareholder, partner, member or other owner or a director, officer or other manager of an association that has a material relationship with the benefit corporation or any of its subsidiaries. A material relationship between an individual and a benefit corporation or any of its subsidiaries will be conclusively presumed to exist if:

(1) the person is, or has been within the last three years, an employee of the benefit corporation or any of its subsidiaries, other than as a benefit officer;

(2) an immediate family member of the person is, or has been within the last three years, an executive officer, other than a benefit officer, of the benefit corporation or any of its subsidiaries; or

(3) the person, or an association of which the person is a director, officer or other manager or in which the person owns beneficially or of record 5% or more of the outstanding equity interests, owns beneficially or of record 5% or more of the outstanding shares of the benefit corporation. The percentage of ownership in an association shall be calculated as if all outstanding rights to acquire equity interests in the association had been exercised.

"Minimum status vote." When in addition to any other approval or vote required by this subpart or a bylaw adopted by the shareholders:

(1) The holders of shares of every class or series shall be entitled to vote on the corporate action regardless of any limitation stated in the articles of incorporation or bylaws on the voting rights of any class or series.

(2) The corporate action must be approved by vote of the shareholders of each class or series entitled to cast at least two-thirds of the votes that all shareholders of the class or series are entitled to cast on the corporate action.

"Specific public benefit." Includes the following:

(1) providing low-income or under served individuals or communities with beneficial products or services;

(2) promoting economic opportunity for individuals or communities beyond the creation of jobs in the normal course of business;

(3) preserving the environment;

(4) improving human health;

(5) promoting the arts, sciences or advancement of knowledge;

(6) increasing the flow of capital to entities with a public benefit purpose; and

(7) the accomplishment of any other particular benefit for society or the environment.

"Subsidiary." An association in which a person owns beneficially or of record 50% or more of the outstanding equity interests. The percentage of ownership in an association shall be calculated as if all outstanding rights to acquire equity interests in the association had been exercised.

股东、合伙人、董事会成员、其他与公共利益公司或其附属机构存在实质性关系的高管、经理除外。若出现以下情形，则认为该个体与公共利益公司或其子公司存在实质性的关系：

（1）该个体是，或在过去 3 年内是，公共利益公司或其子公司除公共利益高管以外的雇员；

（2）该个体的直系亲属是，或在过去的 3 年内是，公共利益公司或其子公司除公共利益高管以外的执行高管；或者

（3）该个体是某一实体的董事或高管，或者由该个体担任董事或高管的机构在所有购股权都被视为已行使的情况下，是持有公共利益公司 5% 以上已发行股份的登记股东或实际受益人。

“最低表决要求”在商事公司中，除本分编对批准或表决的要求外，公司章程、章程细则还应规定以下条件：

（1）每个类别或系列的股东应当有权作为一个独立的投票团体对公司行为进行投票，无论公司章程是否对每个类别或系列的投票权作出了限制；并且

（2）公司行为必须获得每个类别或系列有投票权的所有股东至少 2/3 的赞成票才能通过。

“特定公共利益”包括：

（1）向低收入、低福利人群或社区提供有益的产品或服务；

（2）在正常业务过程中向个人或社区提供创造就业之外的经济机会；

（3）保护或修复环境；

（4）改善人类健康；

（5）促进艺术、科学或知识传播；

（6）促进资本向有公共利益目的的实体流动；以及

（7）实现其他有利于社会或环境的特定利益。

“子公司”是指在所有购股权都被视为已行使的情况下，该实体 50% 以上已发行的股票的受益所有权或登记所有权被另一实体所拥有。

"Third–party standard." A recognized standard for defining, reporting and assessing corporate social and environmental performance that is:

(1) developed by a person that is independent of the benefit corporation; and

(2) transparent because the following information about the standard is publicly available:

(i) the factors considered when measuring the performance of a business;

(ii) the relative weightings of those factors; and

(iii) the identity of the persons who developed and control changes to the standard and the process by which those changes are made.

§ 3303. Formation of benefit corporations.

A benefit corporation shall be formed in accordance with Article B (relating to domestic business corporations generally) except that its articles shall also state that it is a benefit corporation.

§ 3304. Election of an existing business corporation to become a benefit corporation.

(a) Amendment.––A business corporation may become a benefit corporation by amending its articles so that they contain, in addition to the requirements of section 1911(b) (relating to amendment of articles authorized), a statement that the corporation is a benefit corporation. The amendment shall not be effective unless it is adopted by at least the minimum status vote.

(b) Fundamental transactions.––If a corporation that is not a benefit corporation is a party to a merger, consolidation or division or is the exchanging corporation in a share exchange, and the surviving, new or any resulting corporation in the merger, consolidation, division or share exchange is to be a benefit corporation, then the plan of merger, consolidation, division or share exchange shall not be effective unless it is adopted by the corporation by at least the minimum status vote.

§ 3305. Termination of benefit corporation status.

(a) Amendment.––A benefit corporation may terminate its status as a benefit corporation and cease to be subject to this chapter by amending its articles to delete the provision required under section 3304 (relating to election of an existing business corporation to become a benefit corporation) to be stated in the articles of a benefit corporation. The amendment shall not be effective unless it is adopted by at least the

(b) Fundamental transactions.––If a plan would have the effect of terminating the status of a business corporation as a benefit corporation, the plan shall not be effective unless it is adopted by at least the minimum status vote.

(c) Involuntary termination.––The status of a corporation as a benefit corporation may be terminated involuntarily under section 3331(e) (relating to annual benefit report) if it fails to file an annual benefit report.

“第三方标准”是指用于定义、报告和评估公司社会和环境绩效的标准，其应满足以下条件：

（1）由独立于公共利益公司的个体制定；以及

（2）透明性，该标准的以下信息可被公众获取：

（i）衡量企业整体社会和环境绩效时考虑的指标；

（ii）这些指标的相关权重；以及

（iii）标准制定者的身份以及修改标准的程序。

第 3303 条　公共利益公司的设立

公共利益公司应根据 B 条款（本州普通商事公司条款）的规定设立，且公司章程须同时声明其为公共利益公司。

第 3304 条　已有商事公司转换为公共利益公司

（a）修改公司章程。——已成立的商业公司可依据本章规定转换为公共利益公司，除满足 第 1911 条第（b）款（已生效章程的修改条款）的规定外，其还应在公司章程中声明其为公共利益公司。修改后的公司章程应满足最低表决要求才能生效。

（b）重大交易。——如果一家本州非公共利益公司是兼并合并或财产转换的一方，或者是股权置换中的一方，并且在该兼并合并、财产转换或股权置换中存续新设或留存的实体属于公共利益公司，那么此等兼并合并、财产转换或股权置换的计划须满足最低表决要求才能获准。

第 3305 条　公共利益公司形态的终止

（a）修改公司章程。——公共利益公司可以通过修改公司章程，删除章程中第 3304 条（已成立的商事公司转换为公共利益公司条款）规定的公司性质为公共利益公司的声明以表示其不再受本章规定的规制。修改后的公司章程应满足最低表决要求才能生效。

（b）重大交易。——如果一项计划将对公共利益公司形态的终止产生实质性影响，则该计划需满足最低表决要求才能生效。

（c）非自愿终止。——如果公共利益公司违反第 3331 条第（e）款的规定（年度公共利益报告条款），未能提交年度报告，则其公共利益形态将被迫终止。

SUBCHAPTER B CORPORATE PURPOSES

§ 3311. Corporate purposes.

(a) General public benefit purpose.--A benefit corporation shall have the purpose of creating general public benefit. This purpose is in addition to, and may be a limitation on, its purpose under section 1301 (relating to purposes) and any specific purpose set forth in its articles under subsection (b).

(b) Optional specific public benefit purpose.--The articles of a benefit corporation may identify one or more specific public benefits that it is the purpose of the benefit corporation to create in addition to its purposes under section 1301 and subsection (a). The identification of a specific public benefit does not limit the obligation of a benefit corporation to create general public benefit.

(c) Effect of purposes.--The creation of general and specific public benefit as provided in subsections (a) and (b) is in the best interests of the benefit corporation.

(d) Amendment.--A benefit corporation may amend its articles to add, amend or delete the identification of a specific public benefit that it is the purpose of the benefit corporation to create. The amendment shall not be effective unless it is adopted by at least the minimum status vote.

SUBCHAPTER C ACCOUNTABILITY

Sec.

3321. Standard of conduct for directors.

3322. Benefit director.

3323. Standard of conduct for officers.

3324. Benefit officer.

3325. Right of action.

§ 3321. Standard of conduct for directors.

(a) Required considerations.--Without regard to whether the benefit corporation is subject to section 1715 (relating to exercise of powers generally) or 1716 (relating to alternative standard), in discharging the duties of their respective positions, the board of directors, committees of the board and individual directors of a benefit corporation, in considering the best interest of the benefit corporation:

(1) shall consider the effects of any action upon:

(i) the shareholders of the benefit corporation;

(ii) the employees and work force of the benefit corporation and its subsidiaries and suppliers;

(iii) the interests of customers as beneficiaries of the general or specific public benefit

第B分章　公司目的

第3311条　公司目的

（a）一般公共利益目的。——公共利益公司应当有创造一般公共利益的目的。该目的在第1301条规定的商事目的以及根据第（b）款规定在公司章程中设定的其他特定目的之外，且可能对上述目的构成限制。

（b）任意特定公共利益目的。——公共利益公司的章程可以在第1301条和第（a）款规定外确定一项或者多项特定公共利益目的。依据本款设定的特定公共利益目的并不限制公共利益公司设定一般公共利益目的的义务。

（c）目的效力。——依据第（a）款和第（b）款规定设定的一般和特定公共利益目的为公共利益公司的最佳利益。

（d）公司章程的修改。——公共利益公司可以增加、修改或删除公司章程中里设定的特定公共利益目的。对章程的修改需通过最低形态表决才能生效。

第C分章　公司责任

条款

第3321条　董事行为标准
第3322条　公共利益董事
第3323条　高管的行为标准
第3324条　公共利益高管
第3325条　诉讼权利

第3321条　董事行为标准

（a）利益的考虑。——不管公共利益公司是否受第1715条（权力行使条款）或第1716条（可选择的标准条款）规定的调整，在履行各自职责和考虑公共利益公司最佳利益时，公共利益公司的董事会、董事委员会和董事：

（1）应当考虑其行为对以下主体的影响：

（i）公共利益公司的股东；

（ii）公共利益公司、其子公司和其供应商的雇员；

（iii）作为公共利益公司一般或特定公共利益受益者的消费者的利益；

purposes of the benefit corporation;

(iv) community and societal considerations, including those of any community in which offices or facilities of the benefit corporation or its subsidiaries or suppliers are located;

(v) the local and global environment; and

(vi) the short–term and long–term interests of the benefit corporation, including benefits that may accrue to the benefit corporation from its long–term plans and the possibility that these interests may be best served by the continued independence of the benefit corporation.

(2) may consider:

(i) the resources, intent and conduct, whether past, stated or potential, of any person seeking to acquire control of the corporation; and

(ii) any other pertinent factors or the interests of any other group that they deem appropriate; and

(3) shall not be required to give priority to the interests of any person or group referred to in paragraphs (1) and (2) over the interests of any other person or group unless the benefit corporation has stated its intention to give priority to interests related to a specific public benefit purpose identified in its articles.

(b) Coordination with other provisions of law.––The consideration of interests and factors in the manner required under subsection (a):

(1) shall not constitute a violation of section 1712 (relating to standard of care and justifiable reliance); and

(2) is in addition to the ability of directors to consider interests and factors as provided in section 1715 or 1716.

(c) Personal liability of directors.––A director shall not be personally liable, as such, for monetary damages for any action taken as a director if the director performed the duties of his or her office in compliance with section 1712 and this section.

§ 3322. Benefit director.

(a) General rule.––The board of directors of a benefit corporation shall include one director who shall be designated as the benefit director and shall have, in addition to all of the powers, duties, rights and immunities of the other directors of the benefit corporation, the powers, duties, rights and immunities provided in this subchapter.

(b) Election, removal and qualifications.––The benefit director shall be elected, and may be removed, in the manner provided under Subchapter C of Chapter 17 (relating to directors and officers), and shall be an individual who is independent. The benefit director may serve as the benefit officer at the same time as serving as the benefit director. The articles or bylaws of a benefit corporation may prescribe additional qualifications of the benefit director not inconsistent with this subsection.

(c) Annual compliance statement.––The benefit director shall prepare, and the benefit

（iv）社区和社会影响，包括公共利益公司、其子公司或其供应商的办公地或设施所在地的社区；

（v）当地和全球环境；以及

（vi）公共利益公司的短期和长期利益，包括从其长期计划中产生的利益，以及公共利益公司继续保持独立可能最好地满足这些利益的可能性；以及

（2）还可以考虑以下因素：

（i）试图对公司行使控制权的人员所使用的资源、意图和行为（过去、现在和将来的）；以及

（ii）董事认为合理的其他相关因素或其他群体的利益；以及

（3）除公司章程中赋予特定利益或因素以优先权外，无须给予第（1）项或第（2）项中某个利益或因素优先权。

（b）与法律的其他规定相一致——对本条第（a）款规定中相关利益和因素的考虑：

（1）不构成对第 1712 条规定（谨慎标准和合理信赖条款）的违反；以及

（2）对董事考虑利益和相关因素的要求需同时满足第 1715 条或第 1716 条的规定。

（c）董事个人责任。——除公司章程或章程细则另有规定外，董事如果按照本条和第 1712 条的规定履行职责，则其对公共利益公司的一般或特定公共利益目的的法定受益人不负有信义义务。

第 3322 条　公共利益董事

（a）一般规则。——公共利益公司的董事会应至少包含一名公共利益董事，并且该董事除有公共利益公司其他董事的权力、义务、权利和豁免权外，还应有本分章规定的权力、义务、权利和豁免权。

（b）选任、解除和资格。——公共利益董事应根据董事选任条款选任，并可根据 第 17 章第 C 分章（商业公司法董事解除条款）的规定解除。公共利益董事应当是独立的个体。公共利益董事可同时担任公共利益高管。公共利益公司的公司章程或章程细则可以明确本款未规定的公共利益董事的资格。

（c）年度合规声明。——公共利益董事应编写其对以下事项的意见，公共利益

corporation shall include in the annual benefit report to shareholders required under section 3331 (relating to annual benefit report), a statement whether, in the opinion of the benefit director, the benefit corporation acted in accordance with its general and any specific public benefit purpose in all material respects during the period covered by the report and whether the directors and officers complied with sections 3321(a) (relating to standard of conduct for directors) and 3323(a) (relating to standard of conduct for officers), respectively. If, in the opinion of the benefit director, the benefit corporation or its directors or officers failed so to act.

(d) Status of actions.--The acts of an individual in the capacity of a benefit director shall constitute for all purposes acts of that individual in the capacity of a director of the benefit corporation.

(e) Alternative governance arrangements.--If the bylaws of a benefit corporation provide that the powers and duties conferred or imposed upon the board of directors shall be exercised or performed by a person or persons other than the directors pursuant to section 1721(a) (relating to board of directors) or the bylaws of a statutory close corporation that is a benefit corporation provide that the business and affairs of the corporation shall be managed by or under the direction of the shareholders, then the bylaws of the benefit corporation must provide that the person or persons or shareholders who perform the duties of a board of directors shall include a person with the powers, duties, rights and immunities of a benefit director.

(f) Personal liability of directors.--Regardless of whether the bylaws of a benefit corporation include a provision eliminating or limiting the personal liability of directors authorized under section 1713 (relating to personal liability of directors), a benefit director shall not be personally liable for any act or omission in the capacity of a benefit director unless the act or omission constitutes self-dealing, willful misconduct or a knowing violation of law.

§ 3323. Standard of conduct for officers.

(a) General rule.--Each officer of a benefit corporation shall consider the interests and factors described in section 3321(a) (relating to standard of conduct for directors) in the manner provided in that subsection when:

(1) the officer has discretion to act with respect to a matter; and

(2) it reasonably appears to the officer that the matter may have a material effect on:

(i) the creation of general or specific public benefit by the benefit corporation; or

(ii) any of the interests or factors referred to in section 3321(a).

(b) Coordination with other provisions of law.--The consideration of interests and factors in the manner described in subsection (a) shall not constitute a violation of section 1712(c) (relating to standard of care and justifiable reliance).

公司应根据第 3331 条（年度公共利益报告条款）的规定将其附于年度公共利益报告中供股东查阅，陈述公共利益公司在报告所述时间内是否在所有重要事项上依其一般和特定公共利益目的行事；董事和高管是否分别依第 3321 条第（a）款（董事行为标准条款）和第 3323 条第（a）款（高管行为标准条款）的规定行事；如果公共利益董事认为公共利益公司或其董事、高管未能按要求行事，应陈述公共利益公司或其董事、高管未能履行责任的情况。

（d）行为效力归属。——公共利益董事在职权范围内个人的作为或不作为应视为公共利益公司董事的行为。

（e）其他治理协议。——如果公共利益公司章程规定由不受第 1721 条第（a）款（董事会条款）规定的主体控制董事会运营或由闭锁公共利益公司章程（在此情形下，公司运营受股东的影响）授予该主体运营公司的权利，则公司章程必须规定董事会成员应包含可以行使权力、职责与豁免权的公共利益董事。

（f）董事的个人责任。——无论公共利益公司的公司章程或者章程细则是否依据第 1713 条（董事责任免除条款）的规定删除或限制董事的个人责任，公共利益董事在行使其职务时不应对其任何作为或不作为承担个人责任，但自我交易或故意违法行为除外。

第 3323 条　高管的行为标准

（a）一般规则。——公共利益公司的每一位高管应当以第 3321 条第（a）款（董事行为标准条款）规定的行为标准考虑该款规定的利益和因素，如果：

（1）高管就该行为有自由裁量权；并且

（2）高管有合理理由认为该行为对以下事项有实质性影响：

（i）一般或特定公共利益的实现；

（ii）第 3321 条第（a）款规定的利益或因素。

（b）与其他法律条款的协调。——对第（a）款中利益和相关因素的考虑不构成对第 1712 条第（c）款（注意标准与合理信赖条款）的违反。

(c) Personal liability of officers.--An officer shall not be personally liable, as such, for monetary damages for any action taken as an officer if the officer performed the duties of the position in compliance with section 1712(c) and this section.

§ 3324. Benefit officer.

A benefit corporation may have an officer designated as the benefits officer who shall have such authority and shall perform such duties in the management of the benefit corporation relating to the purpose of the corporation to create general or specific public benefit as may be provided by or pursuant to the bylaws or, in the absence of controlling provisions in the bylaws, as may be determined by or pursuant to resolutions or orders of the board of directors. If a benefit corporation has a benefit officer, the duties of the benefit officer shall include preparing the benefit report required under section 3331 (relating to annual benefit report).

§ 3325. Right of action.

(a) General rule.--The duties of directors and officers under this chapter, and the general and any specific public benefit purpose of a benefit corporation, may be enforced only in a benefit enforcement proceeding. No person may bring an action or assert a claim against a benefit corporation or its directors or officers with respect to the duties of directors and officers under this chapter, and the general and any specific public benefit purpose of the benefit corporation, except in a benefit enforcement proceeding.

(b) Parties with standing.--A benefit enforcement proceeding may be commenced or maintained only:

(1) directly by the benefit corporation; or

(2) derivatively by:

(i) a shareholder;

(ii) a director;

(iii) a person or group of persons that owns beneficially or of record 10% or more of the equity interests in an association of which the benefit corporation is a subsidiary; or

(iv) such other persons as may be specified in the articles or bylaws of the benefit corporation.

(c) Cross reference.--The provisions of Subchapter F of Chapter 17 (relating to derivative actions) shall apply to derivative actions under this section.

SUBCHAPTER D TRANSPARENCY

§ 3331. Annual benefit report.

(a) General rule.--A benefit corporation must deliver to each shareholder an annual benefit report including:

(1) a narrative description of:

（c）高管的个人责任。——如果高管行为符合本条和第 1712 条第（c）款的规定，则其不会因履行高管职责而承担个人赔偿责任。

第 3324 条　公共利益高管

公共利益公司可以将高管任命为公共利益高管，该高管有权履行法律或公司章程规定的与一般或特定公共利益的实现有关的职责；如果在公司章程细则中没有规定，则依据董事会作出的有关决议或者命令。若公司设有公共利益高管，其职责还包括根据第 3331 条（年度公共利益报告条款）的规定编写公共利益报告。

第 3325 条　诉讼权利

（a）一般规则。——本章规定的公共利益董事及高管的职责以及公共利益公司的任何一般和特定公共利益目的的执行，只能通过公共利益执行程序进行。除本章规定的公共利益实施程序外，任何人不得以非本章规定的程序向公共利益公司的董事或高管提起违反本章规定的义务的诉讼或主张。

（b）诉讼资格。——公共利益实施程序只能由下列主体提起：

（1）由公共利益公司直接提起；或者

（2）由以下主体派生提起：

（i）股东；

（ii）董事；

（iii）拥有公共利益公司母公司 10% 以上已发行股票的收益所有权或登记所有权的个人或群体；或者

（iv）公共利益公司章程或章程细则中列明的其他人员。

（c）交叉引用。——第 17 章第 F 分章（派生诉讼条款）的规定可适用于本条派生诉讼。

第 D 分章　透明度

第 3331 条　年度公共利益报告

（a）一般规则。——公共利益公司的年度公共利益报告中应包括以下内容：

（1）对以下事项的说明：

(i) the ways in which the benefit corporation pursued general public benefit during the year and the extent to which general public benefit was created;

(ii) the ways in which the benefit corporation pursued any specific public benefit that the articles state is the purpose of the benefit corporation to create and the extent to which that specific public benefit was created; and

(iii) any circumstances that have hindered the creation by the benefit corporation of general or specific public benefit.

(2) an assessment of the social and environmental performance of the benefit corporation, prepared in accordance with a third-party standard applied consistently with any application of that standard in prior benefit reports or accompanied by an explanation of the reasons for any inconsistent application;

(3) the name of the benefit director and the benefit officer, if any, and the address to which correspondence to each of them may be directed;

(4) the compensation paid by the benefit corporation during the year to each director in that capacity;

(5) the name of each person that owns 5% or more of the outstanding shares of the benefit corporation either beneficially, to the extent known to the benefit corporation without independent investigation, or of record; and

(6) the statement of the benefit director described in section 3322(c) (relating to benefit director).

(b) Timing of report.--The benefit report must be sent annually to each shareholder within 120 days following the end of the fiscal year of the benefit corporation or at the same time that the benefit corporation delivers any other annual report to its shareholders.

(c) Internet website posting.--A benefit corporation must post its most recent benefit report on the public portion of its Internet website, if any, except that the compensation paid to directors and any financial or proprietary information included in the benefit report may be omitted from the benefit report as posted.

(d) Filing of report.--Concurrently with the delivery of the benefit report to shareholders pursuant to subsection (b), the benefit corporation must deliver a copy of the benefit report to the Department of State for filing, except that the compensation paid to directors and any financial or proprietary information included in the benefit report may be omitted from the benefit report as filed under this section. The department shall charge a fee of $70 for filing a benefit report.

(e) Failure to file report.--If a benefit corporation has not delivered a benefit report to the department for a period of two years, the department may prepare and file a statement that the corporation has forfeited its status as a benefit corporation and is no longer subject to this chapter. If the corporation subsequently delivers a benefit report to the department for

（i）公共利益公司本年度追求一般公共利益的方法及其实现的程度；

（ii）公共利益公司追求公司章程中列明的特定公共利益的方法；以及

（iii）阻碍公共利益公司实现一般公共利益和特定公共利益的情形；

（2）依据第三方标准对公共利益公司整体社会和环境表现作出的评价，并说明该报告是否沿用先前公共利益报告中使用的标准，或附一份说明以解释使用不一致标准的原因并载明与上一份报告相比标准的变化；

（3）公共利益董事和公共利益高管的姓名和联系地址；

（4）公共利益公司在上一年度支付给每位董事的薪酬；

（5）拥有公共利益公司 5% 以上已发行股票的实际或名义股东的姓名；以及

（6）第 3322 条第（c）款（公共利益董事条款）规定的公益董事年度合规申明。

（b）报告的日期。——公共利益公司应当在公共利益公司财政年度结束后 120 天内或公共利益公司向其股东送交其他年度报告的同一时间将公共利益报告送交各股东。

（c）网站发布。——若条件允许，公共利益公司应当将其最近的公共利益报告发布于其网站上的公共部分；但是可将公共利益报告中的董事薪酬和财务或所有权信息删除。

（d）报告的备案。——在依第（b）款的规定将公共利益报告提交给股东的同时，公共利益公司应当将该公共利益报告提交州务卿备案，但可将公共利益报告中的董事薪酬、财务或所有权信息在提交州务卿的报告中删除。州务卿应收取 70 美元作为备案费用。

（e）未能提交报告。——如果公共利益公司连续 2 年未向州务卿提交报告，州务卿可颁发一份申明，终止该公司的公共利益形态，公司不再受本章规定的约束。如果公司此后又向州务卿递交了公共利益报告，那么公司自动恢复其公共利益公司的形态，公司将重新适用本章的规定。

filing, the status of the corporation as a benefit corporation shall be automatically reinstated upon the filing of the benefit report by the department, and the corporation shall again be subject to this chapter.

Section 2. This act shall take effect in 60 days.

第 2 部分　本法将于 60 天后生效。

THE STATE OF RHODE ISLAND

STATE OF RHODE IS LAND

IN GENERAL ASSEMBLY

JANUARY SESSION, A.D. 2013

AN ACT RELATING TO CORPORATIONS, ASSOCIATIONS AND PARTNERSHIPS

Introduced By: Representatives Tanzi, Blazejewski, Ajello, O`Grady, and Valencia

Date Introduced: February 28, 2013

Referred To: House Corporations

It is enacted by the General Assembly as follows:

SECTION 1. Title 7 of the General Laws entitled "CORPORATIONS, ASSOCIATIONS, AND PARTNERSHIPS" is hereby amended by adding thereto the following chapter:

CHAPTER 5.3 BENEFIT CORPORATIONS

7-5.3-1. Application and effect of chapter.

(a) This chapter shall be applicable to all benefit corporations.

(b) The existence of a provision of this chapter shall not of itself create an implication that a contrary or different rule of law is applicable to a corporation that is not a benefit corporation. This chapter shall not affect a statute or rule of law that is applicable to a corporation that is not a benefit corporation.

(c) Except as otherwise provided in this chapter, chapter 7–1.2 (The Rhode Island Business Corporation Act), shall be generally applicable to all benefit corporations. A benefit corporation may be subject simultaneously to this chapter and chapters 5.1, 6.1 or 8 of this

罗得岛州

罗得岛州

州议会

公元 2013 年 1 月议会期

与公司、协会、合伙有关的法案

由众议院议员 Tanzi，Blazejewski，Ajello，O`Grady 和 Valencia 提起

提案日：2013 年 2 月 28 日

涉及：公司组织

州议会立法通过以下条文：

第 1 部分《普通法》第 7 编“公司、协会、合伙”章节下增加以下章节：

第 5.3 章　公共利益公司

第 7–5.3–1 条　本章的应用及效力

（a）本章适用于所有的公共利益公司。

（b）本章条款不应为非公共利益公司设定相反或不同的规则。本章不影响适用于非公共利益公司的公司法规或规则的效力。

（c）除本章另有规定外，第 7–1.2 章（《罗得岛州商业公司法》）的规定应适用于公共利益公司。公共利益公司会同时受本章和本编第 5.1 章、第 6.1 章、第 8 章所设定的法规约束。本章条款应制约商业公司法条款和规制专业公司和合作公司的

title. The provisions of this chapter shall control over the provisions of any other chapter to this title to which a benefit corporation is subject.

(d) A provision of the articles of incorporation or bylaws of a benefit corporation may not limit, be inconsistent with, or supersede a provision of this chapter.

7-5.3-2. Definitions.

As used in this chapter:

(1) "Benefit corporation" means a corporation that is subject to this chapter.

(2) "Benefit director" means either:

(i) The director designated as the benefit director of a benefit corporation under section 7–5.3–8; or

(ii) A person with one or more of the powers, duties or rights of a benefit director to the extent provided in the bylaws under subsection 7–5.3–8(f).

(3) "Benefit enforcement proceeding" means any claim or action or proceeding for:

(i) Failure of a benefit corporation to pursue or create general public benefit or a specific public benefit purpose set forth in its articles; or

(ii) Violation of any obligation, duty, or standard of conduct under this chapter.

(4) "Benefit officer" means the individual, if any, designated as the benefit officer of a benefit corporation under section 7–5.3–10.

(5) "General public benefit" means a material positive impact on society and the environment, taken as a whole, assessed against a third–party standard, from the business and operations of a benefit corporation.

(6) "Independent" means having no material relationship with a benefit corporation or a subsidiary of the benefit corporation. Serving as benefit director or benefit officer does not make an individual not independent. A material relationship between an individual and a benefit corporation or any of its subsidiaries will be conclusively presumed to exist if any of the following apply:

(i) The individual is, or has been within the last three (3) years, an employee other than a benefit officer of the benefit corporation or a subsidiary.

(ii) An immediate family member of the individual is, or has been within the last three (3) years, an executive officer other than a benefit officer of the benefit corporation or a subsidiary.

(iii) There is beneficial or record ownership of five percent (5%) or more of the outstanding shares of the benefit corporation, calculated as if all outstanding rights to acquire equity interests in the benefit corporation had been exercised, by:

(A) The individual; or

(B) An entity:

(I) Of which the individual is a director, an officer, or a manager; or

相关法规的条款。

（d）公共利益公司的公司章程或公司章程细则不能限制、违背或取代本章的规定。

第 7–5.3–2 章　定义

本章所使用的词语的含义如下：

（1）“公共利益公司”是指选择接受本章规定调整的商业公司。

（2）“公共利益董事”是指：

（i）依第 7–5.3–8 条之规定被任命的董事；或者

（ii）根据第 7–5.3–8（f）款的规定在公司章程中规定的有公共利益董事权力、义务或权利之人。

（3）“公共利益实施程序”是指因以下事项而提出请求或诉讼时使用的程序：

（i）公共利益公司未能追求或实现公司章程中规定的一般的公共利益或某项特定公共利益目的；或者

（ii）公共利益公司违反本章规定下的任何义务、责任或行为标准。

（4）“公共利益高管”是指公共利益公司依据第 7–5.3–10 条之规定任命的公共利益经理。

（5）“一般公共利益”是指经第三方标准评估，公共利益公司的业务、经营在整体上对社会和环境产生的实质性积极影响。

（6）“独立”是指与公共利益公司或其子公司没有实质性的关系。担任公共利益董事或者公共利益高管并不当然丧失独立性。若出现以下情形，则认为该个体与公共利益公司或其子公司存在实质性的关系：

（i）该个体是，或在过去的 3 年内是，公共利益公司或其子公司的除公共利益高管外的雇员。

（ii）该个体的直系亲属是，或在过去的 3 年内是，公共利益公司或其子公司的除公共利益高管外的执行高管。

（iii）在所有购股权都被视为已行使的情况下，持有 5% 或以上的该公共利益公司已发行股票的受益所有权或登记所有权的以下个体：

（A）个人；或者

（B）满足以下任一条件的实体：

（I）该个人是该实体的董事、经理或管理人员；或者

(II) In which the individual owns beneficially or of record five percent (5%) or more of the outstanding equity interests, calculated as if all outstanding rights to acquire equity interests in the entity had been exercised.

(7) "Minimum status vote" means:

(i) In the case of a corporation, in addition to any other required approval or vote, the satisfaction of the following conditions:

(A) The shareholders of every class or series shall be entitled to vote as a class on the corporate action regardless of a limitation stated in the articles of incorporation or bylaws on the voting rights of any class or series.

(B) The corporate action must be approved by vote of the shareholders of each class or series entitled to cast at least two–thirds (2/3) of the votes that all shareholders of the class or series are entitled to cast on the action.

(ii) In the case of a domestic entity other than a corporation, in addition to any other required approval, vote, or consent, the satisfaction of the following conditions:

(A) The holders of every class or series of equity interest in the entity that are entitled to receive a distribution of any kind from the entity shall be entitled to vote on or consent to the action regardless of any otherwise applicable limitation on the voting or consent rights of any class or series.

(B) The action must be approved by vote or consent of the holders described in subparagraph (A) entitled to cast at least two–thirds (2/3) of the votes or consents that all of those holders are entitled to cast on the action.

(8) "Publicly traded corporation" means a corporation that has shares listed on a national securities exchange or traded in a market maintained by one or more members of a national securities association.

(9) "Specific public benefit" includes:

(i) Providing low–income or underserved individuals or communities with beneficial products or services;

(ii) Promoting economic opportunity for individuals or communities beyond the creation of jobs in the normal course of business;

(iii) Protecting or restoring the environment;

(iv) Improving human health;

(v) Promoting the arts, sciences, or advancement of knowledge;

(vi) Increasing the flow of capital to entities with a purpose to benefit society or the environment; and

(vii) Conferring any other particular benefit on society or the environment.

(10) "Subsidiary" means, in relation to a person, an entity in which the person owns beneficially or of record fifty percent (50%) or more of the outstanding equity interests,

（Ⅱ）该个人在所有购股权都被视为已行使的情况下，持有 5% 以上的该公共利益公司已发行股票的受益所有权或登记所有权。

（7）“最低表决要求”是指：
（i）在商业公司中，除任何其他对批准或表决的要求外，满足以下条件的行为：

（A）每个类别或系列的股东应当有权作为一个独立的投票团体对公司行为进行投票，即使公司章程或公司章程细则对任何类别或系列的投票权作出了限制。

（B）公司行为必须获得每个类别或系列有投票权的所有股东的至少 2/3 的赞成票才能通过。

（ii）在非商业公司的本州实体中，除任何其他对批准、表决或赞成的要求外，还应满足以下条件：
（A）持有该实体的每个类别或系列的任何权益分配形式的股权的主体应当有权对公司行为进行投票，即使存在任何对该类别或系列的投票权的限制。

（B）公司行为必须获得在第（A）款中规定的有投票权的所有股权持有者至少 2/3 的赞成票才能通过。

（8）“上市公司”是指在美国的证券交易所或者在由美国的证券协会中一个或几个成员形成的市场上进行交易的商业公司。

（9）“特定公共利益”包括：
（i）向低收入或者低福利人群或社区提供有益的产品或服务；

（ii）在正常的业务过程中向个人或社区提供创造就业之外的经济机会；

（iii）保护或修复环境；
（iv）改善人类健康；
（v）促进艺术、科学或知识传播；
（vi）促进资金向拥有有利于社会或环境的目的实体流动；以及

（vii）给予社会或环境其他特别的利益。
（10）“子公司”，是指在所有购股权都被视为已行使的情况下，该实体 50% 或以上已发行的股票的受益所有权或登记所有权被另一实体所拥有。

calculated as if all outstanding rights to acquire equity interests in the entity had been exercised.

(11) "Third–party standard" means a recognized standard for defining, reporting, and assessing corporate social and environmental performance that is:

(i) Comprehensive because it assesses the effect of the business and its operations upon the interests listed in paragraphs 7–5.3–7(a)(1)(ii), (iii), (iv) and (v).

(ii) Developed by an entity that is not controlled by the benefit corporation.

(iii) Credible because it is developed by an entity that both:

(A) Has access to necessary expertise to assess overall corporate social and environmental performance; and

(B) Uses a balanced multi–stakeholder approach to develop the standard, including a reasonable public comment period.

(iv) Transparent because the following information is publicly available:

(A) About the standard:

(I) The criteria considered when measuring the overall social and environmental performance of a business.

(II) The relative weightings, if any, of those criteria.

(B) About the development and revision of the standard:

(I) The identity of the directors, officers, material owners, and the governing body of the entity that developed and controls revisions to the standard.

(II) The process by which revisions to the standard and changes to the membership of the governing body are made.

(III) An accounting of the revenue and sources of financial support for the entity, with sufficient detail to disclose any relationships that could reasonably be considered to present a potential conflict of interest.

7-5.3-3. Incorporation of benefit corporation.

-- A benefit corporation shall be incorporated in accordance with section 7–1.2–202, but its articles of incorporation must also state that it is a benefit corporation.

7-5.3-4. Election of benefit corporation status.

(a) An existing corporation may become a benefit corporation under this chapter by amending its articles of incorporation so that they contain, in addition to the requirements of section 7–1.2–202, a statement that the corporation is a benefit corporation. In order to be effective, the amendment must be adopted by at least the minimum status vote.

(b) If an entity that is not a benefit corporation is a party to a merger or conversion and the surviving or resulting entity in the merger or consolidation is to be a benefit corporation, the merger or conversion must be approved by the entity by at least the minimum status vote.

（11）“第三方标准”是指用于定义、报告和评估公司社会和环境绩效的标准：

（i）全面，因为其在评估第 7–5.3–7（a）（1）（ii）目、（iii）目、（iv）目和（v）目中所列利益的基础上评价公司业务和经营绩效。

（ii）独立，其经非由公共利益公司控制的第三方实体制定；

（iii）可信，因为制定其的第三方实体同时具备以下条件：

（A）拥有评估公司社会和环境综合绩效所需的专业知识；并且

（B）使用平衡多方利益相关者的方法制定标准，包括设定合理的听取公众意见的期间；

（iv）透明，因为以下信息可以公开获取：

（A）关于标准：

（Ⅰ）衡量整体社会和环境绩效时所考虑的指标。

（Ⅱ）这些指标的相关权重。

（B）关于标准的制定和修改：

（Ⅰ）制定和控制修改程序的董事、高管、主要股东和该实体的控制人员的身份。

（Ⅱ）标准修改和控制人员变动的程序。

（Ⅲ）收入和资金来源的计量，包括充分披露合理认知下存在利益冲突的所有关系。

第 7–5.3–3 条　公共利益公司的设立

公共利益公司应当按照第 7–1.2–202 条的规定成立，但公司章程必须声明其是公共利益公司。

第 7–5.3–4 条　公共利益公司形态的选择

（a）已成立的商业公司可依据本章规定成为公共利益公司，除了满足第 7–1.2–202 条有关公司章程所需内容的要求外，还需修改其公司章程，作出该公司为公共利益公司的声明。公司章程的修改应满足最低表决要求才能生效。

（b）如果一家不具有公共利益公司形态的本州实体是兼并合并或财产转换的一方，或者是股权置换中的一方，并且在该兼并合并、财产转换或股权置换中存续新设或留存的一方为公共利益公司，那么此等兼并合并、财产转让或股权置换的计划应满足公司最低表决要求才能采用获准。

7-5.3-5. Termination of benefit corporation status.

(a) A benefit corporation may terminate its status as such and cease to be subject to this chapter by amending its articles of incorporation to delete the provision required by section 7–5.3–3 or section 7–5.3–4 to be stated in the articles of a benefit corporation. In order to be effective, the amendment must be adopted by at least the minimum status vote.

(b) If a merger or conversion would have the effect of terminating the status of a business corporation as a benefit corporation, the merger or conversion must be adopted by at least the minimum status vote in order to be effective. Any sale, lease, exchange, or other disposition of all or substantially all of the assets of a benefit corporation, unless the transaction is in the usual and regular course of business, shall not be effective unless the transaction is approved by at least the minimum status vote.

7-5.3-6. Corporate purposes.

(a) A benefit corporation shall have a purpose of creating general public benefit. This purpose is in addition to its purpose under section 7–1.2–301.

(b) The articles of incorporation of a benefit corporation may identify one or more specific public benefits that it is the purpose of the benefit corporation to create in addition to its purposes under section 7–1.2–301 and subsection (a). The identification of a specific public benefit under this subsection does not limit the purpose of a benefit corporation to create general public benefit under subsection (a).

(c) The creation of general public benefit and specific public benefit under subsections (a) and (b) is in the best interests of the benefit corporation.

(d) A benefit corporation may amend its articles of incorporation to add, amend, or delete the identification of a specific public benefit that it is the purpose of the benefit corporation to create. In order to be effective, the amendment must be adopted by at least the minimum status vote.

7-5.3-7. Standard of conduct for directors.

(a) In discharging the duties of their respective positions and in considering the best interests of the benefit corporation, the board of directors, committees of the board, and individual directors of a benefit corporation:

(1) Shall consider the effects of any action or inaction upon:

(i) The shareholders of the benefit corporation;

(ii) The employees and work force of the benefit corporation, its subsidiaries, and its suppliers;

(iii) The interests of customers as beneficiaries of the general public benefit or specific public benefit purposes of the benefit corporation;

(iv) Community and societal factors, including those of each community in which offices or facilities of the benefit corporation, its subsidiaries, or its suppliers are located;

第 7–5.3–5 条　公司公共利益形态的终止

（a）公共利益公司可以通过删除第 7–5.3–3 条或第 7–5.3–4 条要求的公司章程中作为公共利益公司的声明来终止其公共利益公司的形态并不再受本章规制。修改的公司章程应满足最低表决要求才能生效。

（b）如果兼并合并、财产转让或股权置换的计划有终止商业公司作为公共利益公司的效力。任何计划交易应满足最低表决要求才能生效。

第 7–5.3–6 条　公司目的

（a）公共利益公司应当有创造一般公共利益的目的。此目的在第 7–1.2–301 条规定的目的之外。

（b）公共利益公司的章程可以根据第 7–1.2–301 条和第（a）款的规定确定一项或者多项特定的公共利益目的。依据本款规定设定的特定公共利益目的并不限制公共利益公司在本条第（a）款规定下设定的一般公共利益目的。

（c）依据第（a）款和第（b）款规定设定的一般公共利益目的和特定公共利益目的应当符合公共利益公司的最佳利益。

（d）公共利益公司可以通过修改公司章程增加、修改或删除公司章程里设定的特定公共利益目的。公共利益公司对章程的修改须满足最低表决要求才能生效。

第 7–5.3–7 条　董事行为标准

（a）在履行各自职责和考虑公共利益公司最佳利益时，公共利益公司的董事会、董事委员会和独立董事：

（1）应当考虑其作为或不作为对以下主体的影响：

（i）公共利益公司的股东；

（ii）公共利益公司、其子公司及其供应商的雇员；

（iii）作为公共利益公司一般或特定公共利益受益人的消费者的利益；

（iv）社区和社会影响，包括公共利益公司、其子公司或其供应商的办公地或设施所在地的社区；

(v) The local and global environment;

(vi) The short-term and long-term interests of the benefit corporation, including benefits that may accrue to the benefit corporation from its long-term plans and the possibility that these interests may be best served by the continued independence of the benefit corporation; and

(vii) The ability of the benefit corporation to accomplish its general public benefit purpose and any specific public benefit purpose; and

(2) May consider other pertinent factors or the interests of any other group that they deem appropriate; but

(3) Need not give priority to the interests of a particular person or group referred to in subdivision (1) or (2) over the interests of any other person or group unless the benefit corporation has stated in its articles of incorporation its intention to give priority to certain interests related to its accomplishment of its general public benefit purpose or of a specific public benefit purpose identified in its articles.

(b) The consideration of interests and factors in the manner required by subsection (a) does not constitute a violation of section 7-1.2-801.

(c) Except as provided in the articles of incorporation, a director is not personally liable for monetary damages for:

(1) Any action or inaction in the course of performing the duties of a director under subsection (a) if the director performed the duties of office in compliance with section 7-1.2-801 and this section; or

(2) Failure of the benefit corporation to pursue or create a general public benefit or a specific public benefit.

(d) A director does not have a duty to a person that is a beneficiary of the general public benefit purpose or a specific public benefit purpose of a benefit corporation arising from the status of the person as a beneficiary.

(e) A director who makes a business judgment in good faith fulfills the duty under this section if the director:

(1) Is not interested in the subject of the business judgment;

(2) Is informed with respect to the subject of the business judgment to the extent the director reasonably believes to be appropriate under the circumstances; and

(3) Rationally believes that the business judgment is in the best interests of the benefit corporation.

7-5.3-8. Benefit director.

(a) The board of directors of a benefit corporation that is a publicly traded corporation shall, and the board of any other benefit corporation may, include a director, who:

(1) Shall be designated the benefit director; and

（v）当地和全球环境；

（vi）公司的短期和长期利益，包括从其长期计划中产生的利益以及公共利益公司继续保持独立可能产生的最佳利益；以及

（vii）公共利益公司实现其一般公共利益目的和特定公共利益目的的能力；

（2）还可以考虑董事认为合适的其他群体的有关因素和利益；但是

（3）不需给予第（1）项或第（2）项中某个利益或因素优先权，除非公共利益公司在其公司章程中表明为实现其一般公共利益或特定公共利益而给予特定的利益或因素优先权。

（b）对第（a）款中相关利益和因素的考虑不构成对第7–1.2–801条规定的违反。

（c）除非在公司章程和公司章程细则中有明确规定，董事不对以下行为承担损害赔偿责任：

（1）在依据第（a）款规定履行董事责任过程中的任何作为或者不作为，如果该董事依据本条及第7–1.2–801条的规定履行了董事职责；或者

（2）公共利益公司未能追求或实现一般公共利益或特定公共利益。

（d）董事对公共利益公司一般公共利益目的或特定社会目的的受益人不负有个人责任。

（e）善意地进行了商业判断的董事被认为满足了本条对董事责任的要求，如果该董事：

（1）在商业判断过程中不涉及个人利益；

（2）拥有使其在该情形下作出合理商业判断的充分信息；并且

（3）有合理理由认为该商业判断符合公共利益公司的最佳利益。

第7–5.3–8条　公共利益董事

（a）上市的公共利益公司以及其他形式的公共利益公司的董事会，包括满足以下条件的董事：

（1）被任命为公共利益董事的董事；并且

(2) Shall have, in addition to the powers, duties, rights, and immunities of the other directors of the benefit corporation, the powers, duties, rights, and immunities provided in this chapter.

(b) The benefit director shall be elected, and may be removed, in the manner provided by chapter 7–1.2. Except as provided in subsections (f) and (g), the benefit director shall be an individual who is independent. The benefit director may serve as the benefit officer at the same time as serving as the benefit director. The articles of incorporation or bylaws of a benefit corporation may prescribe additional qualifications of the benefit director not inconsistent with this subsection.

(c) The benefit director shall prepare, and the benefit corporation shall include in the annual benefit report to shareholders required by section 7–5.3–12, the opinion of the benefit director on all of the following:

(1) Whether the benefit corporation acted in accordance with its general public benefit purpose and any specific public benefit purpose in all material respects during the period covered by the report.

(2) Whether the directors and officers complied with subsection 7–5.3–7(a) and 7–5.3–9(a), respectively.

(3) If, in the opinion of the benefit director, the benefit corporation or its directors or officers failed to act or comply in the manner described in subdivisions (1) and (2), a description of the ways in which the benefit corporation or its directors or officers failed to act or comply.

(d) The act or inaction of an individual in the capacity of a benefit director shall constitute for all purposes an act or inaction of that individual in the capacity of a director of the benefit corporation.

(e) Regardless of whether the articles of incorporation of a benefit corporation include a provision eliminating or limiting the personal liability of directors authorized by subdivision 7– 1.2–202(b)(3), a benefit director shall not be personally liable for an act or omission in the capacity of a benefit director unless the act or omission constitutes self–dealing, willful misconduct, or a knowing violation of law.

(f) If the articles of incorporation of a benefit corporation provide that the powers and duties conferred or imposed upon the board of directors shall be exercised or performed by a person other than the directors as permitted by subsection 7–1.2–801(a), the articles must provide that the persons or shareholders who perform the duties of the board of directors include a person with the powers, duties, rights and immunities of a benefit director. A person that exercises one or more of the powers, duties or rights of a benefit director under this subsection:

(1) Does not need to be independent of the benefit corporation;

（2）除有公共利益公司的其他董事的权力、义务、权利和豁免权外，应有本章规定的权力、义务、权利和豁免权。

（b）公共利益董事应当依据第 7-1.2. 章的规定任免。除第（f）款和第（g）的规定外，公共利益董事应当是独立的个体。公共利益董事可以同时担任公共利益高管。公共利益公司的公司章程或公司章程细则可以明确本款未规定的公共利益董事的资格。

（c）公共利益董事应当编写其对以下事项的意见，公共利益公司应当根据第 7-5.3-12 条的规定将其附于年度公共利益报告中供股东查阅：

（1）公共利益公司在报告所述时间内是否在所有重要事项上依其一般公共利益目的和特定公共利益目的行事。

（2）董事和高管是否分别依第 7-5.3-7（a）款的规定和第 7-5.3- 9（a）款的规定行事。

（3）如果公共利益董事认为公共利益公司或其董事或高管未能依第（1）项和第（2）项的要求行事，则应陈述公共利益公司或其董事或公司未能履行责任的情况。

（d）公共利益董事的个人的作为或不作为应被视为该公共利益公司的董事的个人行为。

（e）无论公共利益公司的公司章程或者公司章程细则是否依据第 7-1.2-202（b）（3）项的规定删除或限制董事的个人责任，公共利益董事在行使其职责时不应对其任何行为或过失承担个人责任，除非该行为或过失属于自我交易、故意不法行为或故意违法行为。

（f）如果公共利益公司章程规定，由不受第 7-1.2-801（a）款规制的主体控制董事会的运营，或由闭锁公共利益公司章程（在此情形下，公司运营受股东的影响）授予该主体运营公司的权利，那么公司章程必须规定董事会成员应包含能行使权力、履行职责、有豁免权的公共利益董事。该个人可以根据以下规定行使其作为公共利益董事的一项或多项职权并履行相关义务：

（1）无须独立于公共利益公司；

(2) Shall have the immunities of a benefit director; and

(3) May share the powers, duties, and rights of a benefit director with one or more other persons.

(g) The benefit director of a professional corporation or consumer cooperative does not need to be independent.

7-5.3-9. Standard of conduct for officers.

(a) Each officer of a benefit corporation shall consider the interests and factors described in subsection 7–5.3–7(a) in the manner provided in that subsection if:

(1) The officer has discretion to act with respect to a matter; and

(2) It reasonably appears to the officer that the matter may have a material effect on the creation by the benefit corporation of general public benefit or a specific public benefit identified in the articles of incorporation of the benefit corporation.

(b) The consideration by an officer of interests and factors in the manner described in subsection (a) shall not constitute a violation of the duties of the officer.

(c) Except as provided in the articles of incorporation, an officer is not personally liable for monetary damages for:

(1) An action or inaction as an officer in the course of performing the duties of an officer under subsection (a) if the officer performed the duties of the position in compliance with subsection 7–1.2–812(b) and this section; or

(2) Failure of the benefit corporation to pursue or create a general public benefit or a specific public benefit.

(d) An officer does not have a duty to a person that is a beneficiary of the general public benefit purpose or a specific public benefit purpose of a benefit corporation arising from the status of the person as a beneficiary.

(e) An officer who makes a business judgment in good faith fulfills the duty under this section if the officer:

(1) Is not interested in the subject of the business judgment;

(2) Is informed with respect to the subject of the business judgment to the extent the officer reasonably believes to be appropriate under the circumstances; and

(3) Rationally believes that the business judgment is in the best interests of the benefit corporation.

7-5.3-10. Benefit officer.

(a) A benefit corporation may have an officer designated as the benefit officer.

(b) A benefit officer shall have:

(1) The powers and duties relating to the purpose of the corporation to create general public benefit or specific public benefit provided:

(i) By the bylaws; or

（2）享有公共利益董事的豁免权；以及
（3）可与其他人分享相关职权和义务。

（g）专业公司的公共利益董事并不需要独立。

第 7–5.3–9 条　高管行为标准

（a）公共利益公司的每一位高管应当以第 7–5.3–7（a）款中规定的行为标准考虑该款规定的利益和因素，如果：
（1）高管有依据该行为标准行事的自由裁量权；并且
（2）高管有合理理由认为该行为对公共利益公司实现公司章程中设定的一般公共利益或特定公共利益有实质性的影响。

（b）对第（a）款中利益和相关因素的考虑构成对高管职责的违反。

（c）除非在公司章程中明确表明，高管不对以下行为承担损害赔偿责任：

（1）在依据第（a）款规定履行经理职责过程中的任何作为或者不作为，如果该高管的行为符合本条或第 7–1.2–812（b）款的规定；或者

（2）公共利益公司未能追求或实现一般公共利益或特定公共利益。

（d）高管并不对公共利益公司一般公共利益目的或特定社会目的的受益人承担个人责任。

（e）善意地进行了商业判断的高管被认为满足了本条对高管责任的要求，如果该高管：
（1）在商业判断过程中不涉及个人利益；
（2）拥有使其在该情形下作出合理商业判断的充分信息；以及

（3）有合理理由认为该商业判断符合公共利益公司的最佳利益。

第 7–5.3–10 条　公共利益高管

（a）公共利益公司可以任命公共利益高管。
（b）公共利益高管应当拥有：
（1）关于实现一般公共利益或特定公共利益的公司目的的权力和权利，规定于：

（i）公司章程细则；或者

(ii) Absent controlling provisions in the bylaws, by resolutions or orders of the board of directors.

(2) The duty to prepare the benefit report required by section 7–5.3–12.

7-5.3-11. Right of action.

(a) Except in a benefit enforcement proceeding, no person may bring an action or assert a claim against a benefit corporation or its directors or officers with respect to:

(1) Failure to pursue or create general public benefit or a specific public benefit set forth in its articles of incorporation; or

(2) Violation of an obligation, duty, or standard of conduct under this chapter.

(b) A benefit corporation shall not be liable for monetary damages under this chapter for any failure of the benefit corporation to pursue or create general public benefit or a specific public benefit.

(c) A benefit enforcement proceeding may be commenced or maintained only:

(1) Directly by the benefit corporation; or

(2) Derivatively in accordance with the procedures in section 7–1.2–711 by:

(i) A person or group of persons that owned beneficially or of record at least two percent (2%) of the total number of shares of a class or series outstanding at the time of the act or omission complained of;

(ii) A director;

(iii) A person or group of persons that owned beneficially or of record five percent (5%) or more of the outstanding equity interests in an entity of which the benefit corporation is a subsidiary at the time of the act or omission complained of; or

(iv) Other persons as specified in the articles of incorporation or bylaws of the benefit corporation.

(d) For purposes of this section, a person is the beneficial owner of shares or equity interests if the shares or equity interests are held in a voting trust or by a nominee on behalf of the beneficial owner.

7-5.3-12. Preparation of annual benefit report.

(a) A benefit corporation shall prepare an annual benefit report including all of the following:

(1) A narrative description of:

(i) The ways in which the benefit corporation pursued general public benefit during the year and the extent to which general public benefit was created.

(ii) Both:

(A) The ways in which the benefit corporation pursued a specific public benefit that the articles of incorporation state it is the purpose of the benefit corporation to create; and

(B) The extent to which that specific public benefit was created.

（ii）在公司章程细则中没有规定时，董事会作出的有关决议或者命令。

（2）编写第 7–5.3–12 条要求的公共利益报告的义务。

第 7–5.3–11 条 诉讼权利

（a）非经公共利益实施程序，任何人不得因以下事项向公共利益公司或者其董事、高管提起诉讼或主张：

（1）未能追求或创造在其公司章程中陈述的一般公共利益或特定公共利益；

（2）违反本章规定下的责任、义务或行为标准。

（b）公共利益公司在本章规定下不对任何未能遵循或设立一般公共利益或特定公共利益的行为承担损害赔偿责任。

（c）公共利益实施程序仅可由以下主体提起：

（1）由公共利益公司直接提起；或者

（2）由以下主体依据第 7–1.2–711 条的规定提起派生之诉：

（i）在被诉行为或过失行为发生时，拥有公共利益公司 2% 或以上某类别或系列已发行的所有股票的个人或群体；

（ii）董事；

（iii）在被诉行为或过失行为发生时，拥有公共利益公司母公司的 5% 或以上已发行股票的收益所有权或登记所有权的个人或群体；或者

（iv）公共利益公司章程或章程细则中列明的其他人员。

（d）为实现本条的目的，若股份或股权由表决权信托或指定第三人代持时，将此人视为该股份和股权的实益所有权人。

第 7–5.3–12 条 年度公共利益报告的编写

（a）公共利益公司的年度公共利益报告中应包括以下内容：

（1）对以下事项的说明：

（i）公共利益公司本年度追求一般公共利益的方法及其实现的程度。

（ii）同时包括：

（A）公共利益公司实现公司章程中列明的特定公共利益的方法；以及

（B）该特定公共利益实现的程度。

(iii) Any circumstances that have hindered the creation by the benefit corporation of general public benefit or specific public benefit.

(iv) The process and rationale for selecting or changing the third–party standard used to prepare the benefit report.

(2) An assessment of the overall social and environmental performance of the benefit corporation against a third–party standard:

(i) Applied consistently with any application of that standard in prior benefit reports; or

(ii) Accompanied by an explanation of the reasons for:

(A) Any inconsistent application; or

(B) The change to that standard from the one used in the immediately prior report.

(3) The name of the benefit director and the benefit officer, if any, and the address to which correspondence to each of them may be directed.

(4) The compensation paid by the benefit corporation during the year to each director in the capacity of a director.

(5) The statement of the benefit director described in subsection 7–5.3–8(c).

(6) A statement of any connection between the organization that established the third–party standard, or its directors, officers or any holder of five percent (5%) or more of the governance interests in the organization, and the benefit corporation or its directors, officers or any holder of five percent (5%) or more of the outstanding shares of the benefit corporation, including any financial or governance relationship which might materially affect the credibility of the use of the third–party standard.

(7) If the benefit corporation has dispensed with, or restricted the discretion or powers of, the board of directors, a description of:

(i) The persons that exercise the powers, duties, and rights and who have the immunities of the board of directors; and

(ii) The benefit director, as required by subsection 7–5.3–8(f).

(b) If, during the year covered by a benefit report, a benefit director resigned from or refused to stand for reelection to the position of benefit director, or was removed from the position of benefit director, and the benefit director furnished the benefit corporation with an written correspondence concerning the circumstances surrounding the resignation, refusal, or removal, the benefit report shall include that correspondence as an exhibit.

(c) Neither the benefit report nor the assessment of the performance of the benefit corporation in the benefit report required by subdivision (a)(2) needs to be audited or certified by a third party.

7-5.3-13. Availability of annual benefit report.

(a) A benefit corporation shall send its annual benefit report to each shareholder on the earlier of:

（iii）阻碍公共利益公司实现一般公共利益和特定公共利益的情形；

（iv）为编写公共利益报告而选择或更换第三方标准的程序和原因。

（2）依据第三方标准对公共利益公司整体社会和环境表现作出的评价：

（i）沿用先前公共利益报告中使用的标准；或者
（ii）附一份说明以解释：
（A）使用的不一致的标准；或者
（B）与上一份报告相比使用的标准的变化。
（3）公共利益董事和公共利益高管的姓名和联系地址（如有）。

（4）公共利益公司在上一年度支付给每位董事的薪酬。

（5）公共利益董事依第 7–5.3–8（c）款规定应编写的陈述意见。
（6）设立第三方标准的机构及其董事、高管，或该机构 5% 以上管理权利的持有者与公共利益公司及其董事、高管或公共利益公司 5% 以上已发行股票的持有者之间关系的声明，包括任何有可能实质性影响第三方标准可信度的财务或管理关系。

（7）如果公共利益公司剥夺或限制董事会的权力，需说明：

（i）行使该权力、权利或履行义务的主体以及获得董事会豁免权的主体；以及

（ii）第 7–5.3–8（f）款规定的公共利益董事。
（b）如果在公共利益报告年度期间，公共利益董事辞职、拒绝连任或被免职，且该公共利益董事与公司有任何书面的涉及辞职、拒绝连任或免职的书信往来，公共利益公司应当将该书信往来作为公共利益报告的附件。

（c）公共利益报告和依据第（a）（2）项编写的公共利益报告中的公共利益公司表现评价书都无须经审计或者第三方证明。

第 7–5.3–13 条　年度公共利益报告的提供
（a）公共利益公司应当在以下日期内尽早地将公共利益报告送交各股东：

(1) One hundred twenty (120) days following the end of the fiscal year of the benefit corporation; or

(2) The same time that the benefit corporation delivers any other annual report to its shareholders.

(b) A benefit corporation shall post all of its benefit reports on the public portion of it Internet website, if any, but the compensation paid to directors and financial or proprietary information included in the benefit reports may be omitted from the benefit reports as posted.

(c) If a benefit corporation does not have an Internet website, the benefit corporation shall provide a copy of its most recent benefit report, without charge, to any person that requests copy, but the compensation paid to directors and financial or proprietary information included in the benefit report may be omitted from the copy of the benefit report provided.

(d) Concurrently with the delivery of the benefit report to shareholders under subsection (c), the benefit corporation shall deliver a copy of the benefit report to the secretary of state for filing, but the compensation paid to directors and financial or proprietary information included in the benefit report may be omitted from the benefit report as delivered to the secretary of state. The secretary of state shall charge a fee of ten dollars ($10.00) for filing a benefit report.

SECTION 2. This act shall take effect upon passage.

（1）公共利益公司财政年度结束后 120 天内；或者

（2）公共利益公司向其股东送交其他年度报告的同一时间。

（b）若条件允许，公共利益公司应当将其所有公共利益发布于其网站的公共部分；但是可以将公共利益报告中的董事薪酬和财务或所有权信息删除。

（c）如果公共利益公司没有网站，应在任何个人索取报告副本时向其免费提供最新公共利益报告的副本，但是可以将公共利益报告副本中的董事薪酬、财务或所有权信息删除。

（d）在依第（c）款的规定将公共利益报告提交给股东的同时，公共利益公司应当将该公共利益报告提交州务卿备案，但是可以将公共利益报告中的董事薪酬、财务或所有权信息在提交州务卿的报告中删除。州务卿应收取 10 美元作为备案费用。

第 2 部分　本法一经通过即生效。

THE STATE OF SOUTH CAROLINA

South Carolina General Assembly

119th Session, 2011-2012

A277, R306, H4766
STATUS INFORMATION

General Bill
Sponsors: Reps. Stringer, Weeks and Funderburk
Companion/Similar bill(s): 1405

Introduced in the House on February 9, 2012
Introduced in the Senate on May 1, 2012
Last Amended on May 31, 2012
Passed by the General Assembly on June 7, 2012
Governor's Action: June 14, 2012, Signed

AN ACT TO AMEND THE CODE OF LAWS OF SOUTH CAROLINA, 1976, BY ADDING CHAPTER 38 TO TITLE 33 SO AS TO ENACT THE "SOUTH CAROLINA BENEFIT CORPORATION ACT" WHICH PERMITS A CORPORATION TO ELECT AS A CORPORATE PURPOSE THE PROVIDING OF CERTAIN PUBLIC BENEFITS WITHOUT SUBJECTING THE CORPORATION OR ITS DIRECTORS TO LIABILITY OR DERIVATIVE SUIT EXCEPT FOR SPECIFIED REASONS.

SECTION 1. Title 33 of the 1976 Code is amended by adding:

"CHAPTER 38

South Carolina Benefit Corporation Act"

南卡罗来纳州

南卡罗来纳州大会

2011-2012 第 119 届

第 4766 号法案
法令信息

一般法案
支持者代表：斯特林格，威克斯及芬德伯克
文件样本号：1405

众议院备案日：2012 年 2 月 9 日
参议院备案日：2012 年 5 月 1 日
最后修正日：2012 年 5 月 31 日
大会通过日：2012 年 6 月 7 日
州长签署日：2012 年 6 月 14 日

本法案修正了 1976 年《南卡罗来纳州法典》，在该法典第 33 编中加入第 38 章《南卡罗来纳州公共利益公司法》，允许商事公司成为实现特定公共利益的公司，除法律另有规定外，公共利益公司不受一般商事公司或股东责任或派生诉讼的限制。

第 1 部分 修改 1976 年法典第 33 编，增加
第 38 章
《南卡罗来纳州公共利益公司法》

Article 1 Preliminary Provisions

Section 33-38-110. This chapter may be referred to and cited as the"South Carolina Benefit Corporation Act".

Section 33-38-120.

(A) This chapter applies to all benefit corporations.

(B) The provisions contained in Chapters 1–19 of this title apply to benefit corporations except where those provisions conflict with provisions contained in this chapter, in which case the provisions contained in this chapter control.

(C) Other than as provided in Section 33–38–210, corporations that are not benefit corporations are not subject to this chapter, and this chapter does not otherwise affect a statute or rule of law that is applicable to a corporation that is not a benefit corporation. A benefit corporation may be simultaneously subject to this chapter and one or more other statutes that provide for the incorporation of a specific type of business corporation, including, but not limited to, a statutory close corporation or a professional corporation.

(D) A provision of the articles of incorporation or bylaws of a benefit corporation may not be inconsistent with a provision of this chapter.

(E) The formation of a business entity pursuant to provisions other than Title 33, Chapter 38 does not prohibit the business entity from including in its general powers consideration or donations for the public welfare, or for charitable, scientific, or educational purposes, as provided in the South Carolina Business Corporation Act.

Section 33-38-130.

(A) The following definitions apply to this chapter:

(1)"Benefit corporation" means a domestic corporation that has elected to become subject to this chapter and that has not terminated its status as a benefit corporation pursuant to Section 33–38–220.

(2)"Benefit director" means either:

(a) the director of the benefit corporation as designated pursuant to Section 33–38–410; or

(b) a person with one or more powers, duties, or rights of a benefit director to the extent provided in the articles of incorporation pursuant to Section 33–38–410(D).

(3)"Benefit enforcement proceeding" means any claim or action for any of the following:

(a) failing to pursue or create the general public benefit or a specific public benefit purpose pursuant to its articles of incorporation; or

(b) violating a duty or standard of conduct under this chapter.

(4)"Benefit officer" means the officer of the benefit corporation designated as such pursuant to Section 33–38–420.

第一节　初步条款

第 33–38–110 条

本章被称为《南卡罗来纳州公共利益公司法》。

第 33–38–120 条

（A）本章适用于所有公共利益公司。

（B）本编第 1 至 19 章的规定适用于公共利益公司，本章另有规定的除外。

（C）除第 33–38–210 条有规定外，非公共利益公司不受本章规定的调整，本章不影响非公共利益公司有关条文和规则的适用。公共利益公司可能同时受到本章和其他特定类型商事公司法的规制，包括但不限于商事公司法和专业公司的相关法规。

（D）公共利益公司章程或章程细则不得违背本章的规定。

（E）除依第 33 编的规定设立的商事主体外，第 38 章不禁止商事主体从事主营业务范围内的事项、实现向公共捐款、追求慈善、科学或教育等《南卡罗来纳州商事公司法》规定的目的。

第 33–38–130 条

（A）本章采用的词语的定义如下：

（1）“公共利益公司”是指一家本州商事公司，选择接受本章规定调整，且未依据第 33–38–220 条的规定终止其公共利益公司形态。

（2）“公共利益董事”是指：

（a）按照第 33–38–410 条的规定任命的公共利益公司董事；或者

（b）按照第 33–38–410（D）款的规定和公司章程，享有公共利益董事的权力、权利或履行义务的人。

（3）“公共利益实施程序”是指因以下行为产生的任何主张和诉求：

（a）公共利益公司未能追求或实现公司章程所规定的一般或特定公共利益目的；或者

（b）公共利益公司违反本章项下的任何义务、责任或行为标准。

（4）“公共利益高管”是指公共利益公司依据第 33–38–420 条规定任命的高管。

(5)"General public benefit" means a material positive impact on society and the environment taken as a whole, as assessed against a third-party standard, from the business and operations of a benefit corporation.

(6)"Independent person" means, with respect to a benefit corporation, a person who does not have any material relationship with the benefit corporation or a subsidiary of the benefit corporation, either directly as a shareholder of the benefit corporation or as a partner, a member, or an owner of a subsidiary of the benefit corporation or indirectly as a director, an officer, a general partner, or a manager of an entity that has a material relationship with the benefit corporation or a subsidiary of the benefit corporation. A person does not have a material relationship solely by virtue of serving as the benefit director or the benefit officer of the benefit corporation or of any subsidiary of the benefit corporation that is itself a benefit corporation. A material relationship between a person and the benefit corporation or any of its subsidiaries is presumed to exist if any of the following apply:

(a) the person is, or has been within the last three years, an employee, other than the benefit officer, of the benefit corporation or a subsidiary of the benefit corporation;

(b) an immediate family member of the person is, or has been within the last three years, an officer, other than the benefit officer, of the benefit corporation or a subsidiary of the benefit corporation; or

(c) the person, or an entity in which the person is a director, an officer, a general partner, or a manager or owns, directly or indirectly, five percent or more of the outstanding equity interests, or owns, directly or indirectly, five percent or more of the outstanding shares of any series or class of stock of the benefit corporation.

(7)"Specific public benefit purpose" means a benefit that serves one or more public welfare, religious, charitable, scientific, literary, or educational purposes, or other purposes or benefits beyond the strict interest of the shareholders of the benefit corporation, including:

(a) providing low-income or underserved individuals, families, or communities with beneficial products, services, or educational opportunities;

(b) promoting economic opportunity for individuals or communities beyond the creation of jobs in the normal course of business;

(c) preserving or improving the environment;

(d) improving human health;

(e) promoting the arts, sciences, or advancement of knowledge;

(f) increasing the flow of capital to entities with a public benefit purpose;or

(g) conferring any other particular benefit on society and the environment.

(8)"Subsidiary of a person" means an entity in which the person owns, beneficially or of record, fifty percent or more of the outstanding equity interests.

(9)"Third-party standard" means a standard for defining, reporting, and assessing

（5）“一般公共利益”是指根据第三方标准，公司的业务和经营在整体上对社会和环境产生的实质性积极影响。

（6）“独立主体”是指与公共利益公司或其子公司没有实质关系的个体，实质关系既包括与公共利益公司及其子公司有直接关系的公共利益公司的股东或合伙人、成员或子公司的所有人，也包括与之有间接关系的公共利益公司或其子公司的董事、高管、一般合伙人和经理。个人在公共利益公司或其子公司担任公共利益董事或高管并不意味着必然存在实质关系。若出现以下情形，则认为个人与公共利益公司及其子公司存在实质性关系：

（a）该个人是，或在过去的3年内是，公共利益公司或其子公司的公共利益高管以外的雇员；

（b）该个体的直系亲属是，或在过去的3年内是，公共利益公司或其子公司的非公共利益高管的执行高管；或者

（c）个人或实体中个人是董事、高管、一般合伙人、经理，直接或间接持有5%以上该公共利益公司已发行股份的登记股东或实际受益人。

（7）“特定公共利益”是指一项或多项有益于公共福利、宗教、慈善、科学社会、文化或教育的利益，或是公共利益公司股东直接利益之外的其他利益，包括：

（a）向低收入、低福利个体、家庭或社区提供有益的产品、服务或受教育机会；

（b）在正常的业务过程中向个人或社区提供创造就业之外的经济机会；

（c）保护或改善环境；

（d）改善人类健康；

（e）促进艺术、科学或知识进步；

（f）促进资本流向具有公共利益目的的实体；以及

（g）给予社会或环境其他特别的利益。

（8）“子公司”是指该实体50%以上已发行的股份的受益所有权或登记所有权被另一实体所拥有。

（9）“第三方标准”是指用于定义、报告和评估公司社会和环境绩效的标准，

corporate, social, and environmental performance that meets all of the following requirements:

(a) the standard assesses the effect of the business and its operations upon the interests listed in items (2) through (5) of Section 33–38–400(A);

(b) the standard is developed by an entity that is independent of the benefit corporation and satisfies the following:

(i) not more than one–third of the members of the governing body of the entity are representatives of an association of businesses operating in a specific industry the performance of whose members is measured by the standard, businesses from a specific industry or an association of businesses in that industry, or businesses whose performance is assessed against the standard; or

(ii) the entity is not materially financed by an association or business described in subitem (i) of this item;

(c) the standard is developed by a person that satisfies the following:

(i) has access to necessary expertise to assess overall corporate, social, and environmental performance; and

(ii) uses a balanced multistakeholder approach including a public comment period of at least thirty days to develop the standard;

(d) the standard is transparent because the following information about the standard is publicly available:

(i) the criteria considered when measuring the overall social and environmental performance of a business, as well as the relative weightings of those criteria; and

(ii) the process for the development and revision of the standard, including:

(A) the identity of the directors, officers, any material owners, and the governing body of the entity that developed and controls revisions to the standard;

(B) the process by which revisions to the standard and changes to the membership of the governing body are made; and

(C) an accounting of the sources of financial support for the entity, with sufficient detail to disclose any relationships that could reasonably be considered to present a potential conflict of interest.

(B) For purposes of the definitions of "independent person" and "subsidiary of a person" in subsection (A) of this section, a percentage of ownership in an entity must be calculated as if all outstanding rights to acquire equity interests in the entity had been exercised.

Section 33-38-140.

A benefit corporation is not entitled to claim an exemption from any property tax imposed by law.

其应满足以下条件：

（a）在第 33-38-400（A）款所列第 2 至 5 项利益的基础上评价公司业务和经营绩效；

（b）由独立于公共利益公司的实体制定，且满足以下条件：

（i）该实体管理机构中不超过 1/3 的成员属以下情形：属于特定行业的协会的组成人员，且该协会成员的绩效评价采用该标准，属于该特定行业或该协会内的人员，属于其他依据该标准评价商业绩效的企业；或者

（ii）第（i）目所述的行会和公司和该实体没有实质的经济关系；

（c）制定标准的主体应满足以下要件：

（i）拥有评估公司社会和环境综合绩效所需的专业知识；并且

（ii）使用平衡多方相关者利益的方法制定标准，包括设定至少 30 天听取公众意见的期间以制定标准；

（d）有关标准的以下信息可公开获得：

（i）整体衡量企业的社会、环境绩效时所考虑的指标以及这些指标的相关权重；以及

（ii）标准的制定和修改过程，包括：

（A）制定和控制修改过程的董事、高管、主要股东和该实体的控制人员的身份；

（B）标准修改和控制人员变动的程序；以及

（C）资金来源的计量，包括充分披露合理认知下存在利益冲突的所有细节。

（B）本条第（A）款中的“独立个体”和“子公司个体”必须在所有购股权都被视为已行使的情况下，计算持有的已发行股份受益所有权或登记所有权的份额。

第 33-38-140 条

公共利益公司不得主张任何财产税务法律方面的豁免。

Article 2 Adoption and Change of Status

Section 33-38-200.

A domestic corporation, including a domestic corporation incorporated upon a conversion, may be incorporated as a benefit corporation by including in its original articles of incorporation a provision stating that the corporation is a benefit corporation governed by this chapter. The articles of incorporation also must include an identification of a specific public benefit purpose as required by Section 33–38–300.

Section 33-38-210.

(A) An existing domestic corporation shall become a benefit corporation on the effective date of the amendment to its articles of incorporation to include a provision providing that the corporation is a benefit corporation governed by this chapter. As amended, the articles of incorporation also must include an identification of any specific public benefit purpose as required by Section 33–38–300. An amendment under this section must be approved in the manner required by Section 33–38–230.

(B) If a corporation or other entity that is not a benefit corporation is a party to a merger, conversion, or share exchange, and the surviving or resulting entity in the merger, conversion, or share exchange is, or is to be as a result of such transaction, a benefit corporation, the plan of merger, conversion, or share exchange must be approved in the manner required by Section 33–38–230. Upon the completion of the transaction, in order for the surviving or resulting entity to be a benefit corporation it must include a provision in its articles of incorporation providing that the corporation is a benefit corporation governed by this chapter and identify any specific public benefit purpose as required by Section 33–38–300.

Section 33-38-220.

(A) A benefit corporation may terminate its status and cease to be subject to this chapter by amending its articles of incorporation to remove the provision that the corporation is a benefit corporation governed by this chapter. The amendment must be approved in the manner required by Section 33–38–230. Any sale, lease, exchange, or other disposition of all, or substantially all, of the property of a benefit corporation, unless the transaction is in the usual and regular course of business, shall not be effective unless it is approved in the manner required by Section 33–38–20.

(B) If a plan of merger, conversion, or share exchange would have the effect of terminating the status of a benefit corporation as a benefit corporation, the plan must be approved in the manner required by Section 33–38–230.

Section 33-38-230.

In addition to any other requirements of applicable law, where specified in this chapter

第二节　公司的设立和变更

第 33–38–200 条

包括转换公司形态成为公共利益公司在内的本州公司可按本章规定，在公司章程中声明其为公共利益公司。公司章程条款同时应按第 33–38–300 条的要求规定其特定的公共利益目的。

第 33–38–210 条

（A）本州公司修改其公司章程，声明其为受本章调整的公共利益公司的，自章程修正案生效之日起转换为公共利益公司。修改后的公司章程应满足第 33–38–300 条关于特定公共利益目的的要求。本条的修改方式应满足第 33–38–230 条关于表决的要求。

（B）如果本州非公共利益公司或其他实体是兼并、财产转换或股权置换的一方，并且在该兼并、财产转换或股权置换中存续的实体属于公共利益公司，则此等兼并、财产转换或股权置换计划应当满足第 33–38–230 条的要求方可通过。完成交易后，公共利益公司需在公司章程中载明其为接受本章调整的公共利益公司，并按照第 33–38–300 条的要求设定特定公共利益目的。

第 33–38–220 条

（A）公共利益公司可通过删除公司章程中关于其为公共利益公司的声明终止其公共利益公司形态，表明其不再受本章规定调整。公司章程的修改应符合第 33–38–230 条的要求。除正常商业往来外，公共利益公司的任何出售、出租、交换或其他处置全部或主要财产的行为，满足第 33–38–20 条的要求才能生效。

（B）如果兼并、财产转换或股权置换的计划会导致公共利益公司形态终止，则该计划或交易应满足第 33–38–230 条的要求。

第 33–38–230 条

除满足法律的其他要求外，本章明确规定须依照本条规定进行批准的事项，其

that approval of a matter must be in the manner required by this section, the following requirements apply:

(1) With respect to a corporation, including a benefit corporation, the matter must be approved by the affirmative vote of sixty–six and two–thirds percent of the outstanding shares of each class and series of stock of the corporation, voting as separate voting groups, regardless of any limitation in the corporation's articles of incorporation or bylaws of the voting rights of such class or series.

(2) With respect to any entity incorporated as a nonprofit corporation, the matter must be approved by the affirmative vote of sixty–six and two–thirds percent of the votes cast by the members entitled to vote.

(3) With respect to an entity organized as a limited liability corporation or partnership, the matter must be approved in the same manner as would be required for the approval of a merger of the entity, unless otherwise provided in the entity's organizational documents, operating agreement, or partnership agreement of the entity.

Article 3 Corporate Purposes

Section 33-38-300.

(A) In addition to corporate purposes provided in Section 33–3–101, a benefit corporation shall have as one of its corporate purposes the creation of a general public benefit.

(B) A benefit corporation may include as a corporate purpose in its articles of incorporation one or more specific public benefit purposes in addition to its purposes under subsection (A) of this section. The identification of a specific public benefit purpose pursuant to this subsection does not limit the obligation of a benefit corporation pursuant to subsection (A).

(C) A benefit corporation may amend its articles of incorporation to add, amend, or remove the identification of a specific public benefit purpose. The amendment must be approved by the shareholders of the benefit corporation in the manner required by Section 33–38–230.

(D) The creation of general public benefit and specific public benefit pursuant to subsections (A) and (B) is in the best interests of a benefit corporation.

(E) A professional corporation that is a benefit corporation does not violate Section 33–19–110.

Article 4 Accountability

Section 33-38-400.

(A) In discharging the duties of their respective positions and in considering the

要求如下：

（1）包括公共利益公司在内的公司事项，每个类别或系列的股东应当有权作为一个独立的投票团体对公司行为进行投票，且有关批准事项应经每一团体中持有公司已发行股权 66% 或者 2/3 以上的人表决通过，即使公司章程或章程细则对该类别或系列的表决权作出了限制。

（2）涉及非营利性公司实体，有关事项的批准须经公司 66% 或 2/3 以上有投票权的人通过。

（3）涉及有限责任公司或合伙企业的事项，有关事项的批准与实体兼并计划的批准要求相同，该实体的组织文件、经营协议或合伙协议另有规定的除外。

第三节　公司目的

第 33–38–300 条

（A）除第 33–3–101 条规定的公司目的外，公共利益公司还应创设一般公共利益目的。

（B）公共利益公司章程可在本条第（A）款的规定之外确定一项或多项特定公共利益目的。依本款设定的特定公共利益目的不限制公共利益公司在本条第（A）款规定下设定一般公共利益目的义务。

（C）公共利益公司可增加、修改或删除公司章程中设定的特定公共利益目的。公司章程的修改应符合第 33–38–230 条的要求。

（D）依第（A）款和第（B）款的规定设定的一般和特定公共利益目的为公共利益公司的最佳利益。

（E）具备公共利益形态的专业公司不违反第 33–19–110 条的规定。

第四节　公司责任

第 33–38–400 条

（A）在履行职责和考虑公共利益公司最佳利益时，公共利益公司的董事会、

best interests of the benefit corporation, the board of directors, committees of the board of directors, and individual directors of a benefit corporation, shall consider the effects of any action or decision not to act upon the following:

(1) the shareholders of the benefit corporation;

(2) the employees and workforce of the benefit corporation, its subsidiaries, and suppliers;

(3) the interests of customers to the extent they are beneficiaries of the general or specific public benefit purposes of the benefit corporation;

(4) community and societal factors, including the interests of each community in which offices or facilities of the benefit corporation, its subsidiaries, or suppliers are located;

(5) the local and global environment;

(6) the short–term and long–term interests of the benefit corporation, including benefits that may accrue to the benefit corporation from its long–term plans and the possibility that these interests may be best served by the continued independence of the benefit corporation; and

(7) the ability of the benefit corporation to accomplish its general and any specific public benefit purpose.

(B) In addition to the required considerations in subsection (A), a director of a benefit corporation may consider the following:

(1) the resources, intent, and past, stated, and potential conduct of any person seeking to acquire control of the benefit corporation; and

(2) other pertinent factors or the interests of any other group that the director in good faith considers to be appropriate.

(C) A director of a benefit corporation need not give priority to the interests of a particular person or group referred to in subsections (A) and (B) of this section over the interests of any other person or group unless the benefit corporation's articles of incorporation explicitly specify its intention to give priority to certain interests related to its accomplishment of its general public benefit purpose or of a specific public benefit purpose.

(D) The consideration of interests and factors in the manner required by this section is not considered to be inconsistent with the requirements of Section 33–38–300.

(E) A director is not personally liable for monetary damages for:

(1) any act taken as a director, or any omission to act as a director, if the director performed the duties of office in compliance with Sections 33–8–300, 33–8–310, 33–8–320, or 33–8–330; or

(2) the failure of the benefit corporation to pursue or create a general or specific public benefit.

(F) A director does not have a duty to a person that is a beneficiary of the general public

董事委员会和董事应当考虑其任何行为或决定对下列主体的影响：

（1）公共利益公司的股东；

（2）公共利益公司、其子公司和其供应商的雇员；

（3）作为公共利益公司一般公共利益或特定公共利益受益者的消费者的利益；

（4）社区和社会因素，包括公共利益公司及其子公司或其供应商的办公地或设施所在地的社区；

（5）当地和全球环境；

（6）公共利益公司的短期和长期利益，包括从其长期计划中产生的利益以及公共利益公司继续保持独立可能产生的最佳利益；以及

（7）公共利益公司实现其一般和特定公共利益目的的能力。

（B）除第（A）款规定的考量因素外，公共利益公司的董事还可以考虑：

（1）试图控制公共利益公司的人员的资源和目的，包括过去、现在及未来可能的行为；以及

（2）董事应以审慎态度考量的其他合理的因素或其他任何团体的利益。

（C）除公司章程为实现一般或特定公共利益而明确赋予特定利益或因素优先权外，公共利益公司的董事不需给予第（A）款或第（B）款中某个特定人或群体的利益优先权。

（D）对本条规定的利益和因素的考量不构成对第33–38–300条规定的违反。

（E）在以下情形中，董事不承担个人损害赔偿责任：

（1）董事履行职责过程中的作为或不作为，如果董事履行职责的行为符合第33–8–300条、第33–8–310条、第3–8–320条或第33–8–330条的规定；

（2）公共利益公司未能追求或实现一般或特定公共利益。

（F）董事不对公共利益公司一般或特定公共利益目的的受益人负责。

benefit purpose or a specific public benefit purpose of a benefit corporation arising from the status of the person as a beneficiary.

Section 33-38-410.

(A) The board of directors of a benefit corporation shall designate one director who is an independent person to be the benefit director. The benefit director, in addition to the powers, duties, rights, and immunities of the other directors of the benefit corporation, shall have the powers, duties, rights, and immunities provided in this section. The benefit director shall be elected, and may be removed, in the manner provided in Article 1, Chapter 8, Title 33.

(B) The benefit director may serve as the benefit officer at the same time as serving as the benefit director. The articles of incorporation or bylaws of a benefit corporation may prescribe additional qualifications of the benefit director not inconsistent with this section.

(C)(1) The benefit director shall prepare, and the benefit corporation shall include in the annual benefit report to shareholders required by Section 33–38–500, the opinion of the benefit director concerning the following matters:

(a) whether the benefit corporation acted in accordance with its general and any specific public benefit purpose in all material respects during the period covered by the report;

(b) whether the benefit corporation conferred a general public benefit and any specific public benefit during the period covered by the report; and

(c) whether the directors complied with Section 33–38–400.

(2) If the benefit director finds a failure under item (a), (b), or (c) of this subsection, the benefit director shall include in the annual benefit report a description, to the extent relevant, of the ways in which the benefit corporation or its directors failed to act or comply.

(D) If a benefit corporation dispenses with a board of directors as provided by law, the articles of incorporation of the benefit corporation must provide that a person who exercises one or more of the powers, duties, rights, or obligations of a benefit director under this subsection shall have the powers, duties, rights, and obligations of a benefit director or may share the powers, duties, rights, and obligations of a benefit director with one or more other persons. A person who has the powers, duties, rights, and obligations of a benefit director pursuant to this subsection:

(1) does not need to be independent of the benefit corporation;

(2) shall have the immunities of a benefit director; and

(3) shall not be subject to the procedures for election or removal of directors pursuant to Article 1, Chapter 8, Title 33 unless the bylaws make those procedures applicable.

(E) The benefit director of a professional corporation does not need to be independent.

(F) Regardless of whether the articles of incorporation or the bylaws of a benefit corporation include a provision limiting or eliminating the personal liability of directors, a benefit director is not personally liable for monetary damages for any act or omission taken

第 33–38–410 条

（A）公共利益公司的董事会应当任命一名董事为公共利益董事。除了公共利益公司的其他董事的权力、义务、权利和豁免权，公共利益董事还有本条规定的权力、义务、权利和豁免权。公共利益董事应当按照第 33 编第 8 章第 1 节的规定进行任免。

（B）公共利益董事可兼任公共利益高管。除本条的规定外，公共利益公司章程或章程细则还可明确公共利益董事的其他任职要求。

（C）（1）公共利益董事应当编写其对以下事项的意见，公共利益公司应当根据第 33–38–500 条的要求将其附于年度公共利益报告中供股东查阅：

（a）在报告所述时间内，公共利益公司是否在所有重要事项上依一般和特定公共利益目的行事；

（b）在报告所述时间内，公共利益公司是否实现了一般和特定公共利益目的；以及

（c）董事是否遵守了第 33–38–400 条的规定；

（2）如果公共利益董事认为公共利益公司或其董事、高管未能依第（a）目、第（b）目或第（c）目的要求行事，则应陈述公共利益公司或董事未能履行责任的情况。

（D）如果公共利益公司根据法律规定未设董事会，该公司的章程必须规定有本款规定的公共利益董事权力、责任、义务和权利的个人。公共利益董事可以和其他人分享本款规定的权力、责任、义务和权利。根据本款规定行使公共利益董事权力、责任、义务和权利的个人：

（1）无须独立于公共利益公司；

（2）应有公共利益董事的豁免权；以及

（3）除公司章程另有规定外，不受第 33 编第 8 章第 1 节规定的董事任免程序的约束。

（E）专业公司的公共利益董事不需要具有独立性。

（F）无论公共利益公司的章程或章程细则是否限制或消除董事的个人责任，公共利益董事不对其作为或不作为承担赔偿责任，该作为或不作为属于董事获取不正当个人利益、故意不当行为或故意违法行为的除外。

in that capacity unless the act or omission constitutes a transaction from which the director derived an improper personal benefit, wilful misconduct, or a knowing violation of law.

Section 33-38-420.

(A) Each officer of a benefit corporation shall consider the interests and factors described in Section 33–38–400 in the manner provided in that section if:

(1) the officer has discretion to act with respect to a matter; and

(2) it reasonably appears to the officer that the matter may have a material effect on the creation by the benefit corporation of a general public benefit or a specific public benefit identified in the public benefit corporation's articles of incorporation.

(B) The consideration of interests and factors in the manner described in subsection (A) shall not constitute a violation of Section 33–8–420.

(C) An officer is not personally liable for monetary damages for:

(1) any act taken as an officer, or any omission to act as an officer, if the officer performed the duties of office in compliance with Section 33–8–410; or

(2) failure of the benefit corporation to pursue or create a general public benefit or a specific public benefit.

(D) An officer does not have a duty to any specific person that is a beneficiary of the general public benefit purpose or a specific public benefit purpose of a public benefit corporation arising from the status of the person as a beneficiary.

Section 33-38-430.

(A) A benefit corporation may have an officer designated as the benefit officer.

(B) The duties of the benefit officer include the following:

(1) monitoring the benefit corporation's pursuit of the general and any specific public benefits purpose of the benefit corporation and the general and any specific public benefit created by the benefit corporation;

(2) performing such other duties to the extent provided in either the bylaws of the benefit corporation or a resolution adopted by the board of directors of the benefit corporation that is not in conflict with the bylaws; and

(3) preparing the annual benefit report required by Section 33–38–500.

Section 33-38-440.

(A) The duties of directors under this chapter may be enforced only in a benefit enforcement proceeding. A person may not bring an action or assert a claim against a benefit corporation or its directors or officers with respect to:

(1) failure to pursue or create general public benefit or a specific public benefit set forth in its articles of incorporation; or

(2) violation of a duty or standard of conduct under this chapter.

(B) A benefit corporation shall not be liable for monetary damages under this chapter for

第 33–38–420 条

（A）公共利益公司高管应以本条规定的行为标准考虑第 33–38–400 条中规定的利益和因素，如果：

（1）高管就该行为有自由裁量权；并且

（2）高管有合理理由认为该行为对实现公共利益公司在章程中创设的一般或特定公共利益有实质性影响。

（B）对第（A）款中规定利益和相关因素的考虑不构成对第 33–8–420 条规定的违反。

（C）在以下情形中，公共利益高管不承担个人损害赔偿责任：

（1）高管履行职责中的任何作为或不作为，如果高管履行职责的行为符合第 33–8–410 条的规定；或者

（2）公共利益公司未能追求或实现一般和特定公共利益目的。

（D）高管不对公共利益公司一般或特定公共利益目的的受益人负责。

第 33–38–430 条

（A）公共利益公司可以任命公共利益高管。

（B）公共利益高管的职责包括：

（1）监督公共利益公司追求和实现一般和任何特定公共利益目的的情况；

（2）行使由公共利益公司章程或董事会决议所要求的不违背法律规定的其他职责；以及

（3）按照第 33–38–500 条的要求编写年度公共利益报告。

第 33–38–440 条

（A）针对本章规定下的董事义务，只能提起公共利益实施程序。任何人不得因以下事由对公共利益公司或其董事、高管提起诉讼或主张：

（1）未能追求或实现在其公司章程中设定的一般或特定公共利益；

（2）违反本章规定下的责任、义务或行为标准。

（B）公共利益公司未能追求或创造一般或特定公共利益的，不承担本章规定

any failure of the benefit corporation to pursue or create general public benefit or a specific public benefit.

(C) A benefit enforcement proceeding may be commenced or maintained by only the following:

(1) directly, by the benefit corporation; or

(2) derivatively, by any of the following:

(a) a shareholder;

(b) a director;

(c) a person or group of persons that owns, beneficially or of record, five percent or more of the outstanding equity interests in an entity of which the benefit corporation is a subsidiary; or

(d) other persons specified in the articles of incorporation or bylaws of the benefit corporation.

(D) A benefit enforcement proceeding commenced or maintained derivatively under item (2) of subsection (C) of this section as provided by law is subject to the requirements applicable to derivative proceedings, except that such requirements may be interpreted to reflect that a benefit enforcement proceeding may be commenced and maintained by those persons listed in item (2) of subsection (B) of this section.

Article 5 Annual Reporting

Section 33-38-500.

(A) A benefit corporation shall prepare an annual benefit report that includes all of the following:

(1) a narrative description:

(a) the manner in which the benefit corporation has pursued its general public benefit purposes during the year and the extent to which a general public benefit was created;

(b) the manner in which the benefit corporation has pursued any specific public benefit purposes during the year and the extent to which a specific public benefit was created;

(c) circumstances that have hindered the creation by the benefit corporation of a general or specific public benefit; and

(d) the process and rationale for selecting or changing the third–party standard used to prepare the benefit report;

(2) an assessment of the overall social or environmental, or social and environmental, performance of the benefit corporation against a third–party standard applied consistently with any application of that standard in prior benefit reports or accompanied by an explanation of the reasons for any inconsistent application. The assessment does not need to be performed, audited, or certified by a third–party standards provider;

下的损害赔偿责任。

（C）在下列情形中，以下主体可提起公共利益实施程序：

（1）由公共利益公司直接提起；或者
（2）由以下主体派生提起：
（a）股东；
（b）董事；
（c）拥有公共利益公司的母公司5%以上已发行股份的登记股东或实际受益人，包括个人和团体；或者

（d）公共利益公司章程或章程细则中规定的其他人员。

（D）派生诉讼的有关规定适用于根据本条第（C）（2）项提起派生之诉的公共利益实施程序，派生诉讼规定由本条第（B）（2）项所列的人员提起的除外。

第五节　年度报告

第33-38-500条

（A）公共利益公司的年度公共利益报告应包括以下内容：

（1）对以下事项的说明：
（a）公共利益公司本年度追求一般公共利益的方法和一般公共利益的实现情况；
（b）公共利益公司追求公司章程中规定的特定公共利益的方法以及该特定公共利益的实现情况；
（c）阻碍公共利益公司实现一般或特定公共利益的情形；

（d）为编写公共利益报告而选择或更换第三方标准的程序和原因；

（2）依据第三方标准，对公共利益公司的整体社会和环境绩效作出评价时，一般应沿用此前公共利益报告所使用的标准，采用新标准的，应说明原因。该评价无须经第三方标准提供方实施、审计或证明。

(3) the name of the benefit director and the benefit officer and the address to which correspondence to each of them may be directed;

(4) the compensation paid by the benefit corporation during the year to each director in their capacity as a director;

(5) the name of each person that owns five percent or more of the outstanding shares of the benefit corporation either beneficially to the extent known to the benefit corporation without independent investigation, or of record;

(6) the statement of the benefit director described in Section 33–38–410(C);

(7) a statement of any connection between the organization that established the third–party standard, or its directors, officers, or any holder of five percent or more of the governance interests in the organization, and the benefit corporation or its directors, officers, or any holder of five percent or more of the outstanding shares of the benefit corporation, including any financial or governance relationship which might materially affect the credibility of the use of the third–party standard; and

(8) if the benefit corporation has dispensed with, or restricted the discretion or powers of, the board of directors, a description of:

(a) the persons that exercise the powers, duties, and rights and who have the immunities of the board of directors; and

(b) the benefit director, as required by Section 33–38–410(D).

(B) The benefit report must be sent annually to each shareholder within one hundred twenty days following the end of the fiscal year of the benefit corporation or at the same time that the benefit corporation delivers any other annual report to its shareholders.

(C) A benefit corporation shall post all of its annual benefit reports on the publicly accessible portion of its Internet website, if it maintains a website. The compensation paid to directors and any financial or proprietary information included in the benefit reports may be omitted from the benefit reports as posted.

(D) If a benefit corporation does not have an Internet website, the benefit corporation shall provide a copy of its most recent annual benefit report, without charge, to any person that requests a copy, but the compensation paid to directors and financial or proprietary information included in the benefit report may be omitted from the copy of the benefit report provided.

(E) The annual report that a benefit corporation is required to deliver to the Secretary of State must include the most recent benefit report delivered to shareholders pursuant to subsection (B), except that the compensation paid to directors and any financial or proprietary information included in the benefit report may be omitted from the benefit report delivered to the Secretary of State under this section.

（3）公共利益董事、高管的姓名及联系地址；

（4）公共利益公司在上一年度支付给每位董事的薪酬；

（5）持有公共利益公司 5% 以上已发行股份的登记股东或实际受益人的姓名；

（6）公共利益董事依第 33–38–410（C）款规定编写的陈述报告；

（7）设立第三方标准的组织或其董事、高管或持股 5% 以上的股东与公共利益公司或其董事、高管或拥有公共利益公司 5% 以上已发行股份的股东之间关系的声明，包括任何有可能实质性影响第三方标准可信度的财务或管理关系。

（8）公共利益公司解除或限制董事会自由裁量权或权力的，应当在报告中说明：

（a）行使董事会权力、权利和履行义务及拥有董事会豁免权的人员；以及

（b）第 33–38–410（D）款规定的公共利益董事。

（B）公共利益公司应当在每年公共利益公司会计年度结束后 120 天内，或向其股东送交其他年度报告的同一时间将公共利益报告送交各股东。

（C）若条件允许，公共利益公司应当将其所有公共利益报告发布于其网站的公共部分，但可将公共利益报告中的董事薪酬、财务或所有权信息删除。

（D）如果公共利益公司没有网站，则其应向任何索取报告的个人免费提供最新公共利益报告的副本，但可将公共利益报告副本中的董事薪酬、财务或所有权信息删除。

（E）公共利益公司提交州务卿备案的年度报告中，应包括第（B）款规定的送交股东的最新版公共利益报告，但可将公共利益报告中的董事薪酬、财务或所有权信息在该报告中删除。

Article 6 Shareholder Dissent

Section 33-38-600.

In addition to any other rights granted by law, a shareholder is entitled to dissent from and obtain payment of the fair value of his shares in the event of the consummation of a designation of a corporation as a benefit corporation pursuant to Section 33–38–210(A).

Time effective

SECTION 2. This act takes effect upon approval by the Governor.

Ratified the 12th day of June, 2012.

Approved the 14th day of June, 2012.

第六节　异议股东

第 33-38-600 条

除法律赋予的权利外，股东有权依第 33-38-210（A）款的规定，在公司转变为公共利益公司时提起异议，并有权要求公司以合理价格回购其股权。

生效时间

第 2 部分　本法经州长同意后生效。

修改日为 2012 年 6 月 12 日。

批准日为 2012 年 6 月 14 日。

THE STATE OF TENNESSEE

HOUSE BILL 767

By Powell

AN ACT to amend Tennessee Code Annotated,
Title 48, relative to for–profit benefit corporations.

BE IT ENACTED BY THE GENERAL ASSEMBLY OF THE STATE OF TENNESSEE:

SECTION 1. Tennessee Code Annotated, Title 48, is amended by adding the following language as a new chapter:

48-28-101.

This chapter shall be known and may be cited as the "For–Profit Benefit Corporation Act."

48-28-102.

(a) This chapter shall be applicable to all for–profit benefit corporations.

(b) The existence of a provision of this chapter shall not of itself create an implication that a contrary or different rule of law is applicable to a business corporation that is not a for–profit benefit corporation. This chapter shall not affect a statute or rule of law that is applicable to a business corporation that is not a for–profit benefit corporation.

(c) Except as otherwise provided in this chapter, the Tennessee Business Corporation Act, compiled in chapters 11—27 of this title, shall be generally applicable to all for–profit benefit corporations. A for–profit benefit corporation may be subject simultaneously to this chapter and the Tennessee Professional Corporation Act, compiled in chapter 101, part 6 of this title. This chapter shall control over the Tennessee Business Corporation Act and the Tennessee Professional Corporation Act.

(d) A provision of the articles of incorporation or bylaws of a for–profit benefit corporation may not limit, be inconsistent with, or supersede a provision of this chapter.

田纳西州

767 号众议院法案

提案人：鲍威尔

《田纳西州法典》第 48 编中涉及营利性公共利益公司的修正案

本法案由田纳西州议会制定：

第 1 部分　《田纳西州法典》原第 48 编新增以下内容：

第 48–28–101 条
本章被称为《营利性公共利益公司法》。

第 48–28–102 条
（a）本章适用于所有的营利性公共利益公司。
（b）本章条款不应为非营利性公共利益公司设定相反或不同的规则。本章条款不影响非公共利益公司有关条文和规则的适用。

（c）除本章另有规定外，《田纳西州商事公司法》本编第 11 至 27 章的内容适用于所有的营利性公共利益公司。营利性公共利益公司可同时适用本章和《田纳西州专业公司法》第 6 部分第 101 章的规定。本章的效力优先于《田纳西州商事公司法》和《田纳西州专业公司法》。

（d）营利性公共利益公司章程或章程细则不应限制、违背或取代本章的规定。

48-28-103.

As used in this chapter:

(1) "Benefit director" means the director designated as the benefit director of a for-profit benefit corporation under § 48–28–302;

(2) "Benefit enforcement proceeding" means any claim, action, or proceeding for:

(A) Failure of a for-profit benefit corporation to pursue or create general public benefit or a specific public benefit purpose set forth in its articles of incorporation; or

(B) Violation of any obligation, duty, or standard of conduct under this chapter;

(3) "Benefit officer" means the individual designated as the benefit officer of a for-profit benefit corporation under § 48–28–304;

(4) "For-profit benefit corporation" means a business corporation:

(A) That has elected to become subject to this chapter; and

(B) The status of which as a for-profit benefit corporation has not been terminated;

(5) "General public benefit" means a material positive impact on society and the environment, taken as a whole, assessed against a third-party standard, from the business and operations of a for-profit benefit corporation;

(6) "Independent" means having no material relationship with a for-profit benefit corporation or a subsidiary of the for-profit benefit corporation. Serving as benefit director or benefit officer does not make an individual not independent. A material relationship between an individual and a for-profit benefit corporation or any of its subsidiaries shall be conclusively presumed to exist if any of the following apply:

(A) The individual is, or has been within the last three (3) years, an employee other than a benefit officer of the for-profit benefit corporation or a subsidiary of the for-profit benefit corporation;

(B) An immediate family member of the individual is, or has been within the last three (3) years, an executive officer other than a benefit officer of the for-profit benefit corporation or a subsidiary of the for-profit benefit corporation; or

(C) There is beneficial or record ownership of five percent (5%) or more of the outstanding shares of the for-profit benefit corporation, calculated as if all outstanding rights to acquire equity interests in the for-profit benefit corporation had been exercised, by:

(i) The individual; or

(ii) An entity:

(a) Of which the individual is a director, an officer, or a manager; or

(b) In which the individual owns beneficially or of record five percent (5%) or more of the outstanding equity interests, calculated as if all outstanding rights to acquire equity interests in the entity had been exercised;

(7) "Minimum status vote" means:

第 48–28–103 条

本章所用词语的含义如下：

（1）“公共利益董事”是指公共利益公司依第 48–28–302 条规定任命的营利性公共利益公司的董事；

（2）“公共利益实施程序”是指因以下事由产生的任何主张、诉讼或法律程序：

（A）营利性公共利益公司未能追求或实现公司章程规定的一般或特定公共利益目的；或者

（B）营利性公共利益公司违反本章规定的任何义务、责任或行为标准；

（3）“公共利益高管”是指营利性公共利益公司依第 48–28–304 条规定任命的高管；

（4）“营利性公共利益公司”是指符合以下条件的商事公司：

（A）选择接受本章规定调整；以及

（B）营利性公共利益公司形态并未终止；

（5）“一般公共利益”是指根据第三方标准，营利性公共利益公司的业务和经营在整体上对社会和环境产生的实质性积极影响；

（6）“独立”是指与营利性公共利益公司或其子公司没有实质性的关系。担任公共利益董事或公共利益高管并不当然丧失独立性。在以下情形中，认为该个体与公共利益公司或其子公司存在实质性的关系：

（A）该个体是，或在过去的 3 年内是，营利性公共利益公司或其子公司公共利益高管以外的雇员；

（B）该个体的直系亲属是，或在过去的 3 年内是，营利性公共利益公司或其子公司公共利益高管以外的执行高管；或者

（C）在所有购股权都被视为已行使的情况下，下述持有 5% 以上该营利性公共利益公司已发行股份的登记股东或实际受益人：

（i）个人；或者

（ii）实体：

（a）该个人是该实体的董事、高管或经理；或者

（b）在所有购股权都被视为已行使的情况下，持有 5% 以上该营利性公共利益公司已发行股份的登记股东或实际受益人；

（7）“最低表决要求”：

(A) In the case of a business corporation, in addition to any other required approval or vote, the satisfaction of the following conditions:

(i) The shareholders of every class or series being entitled to vote as a separate voting group on the corporate action regardless of a limitation stated in the articles of incorporation or bylaws on the voting rights of any class or series; and

(ii) The corporate action being approved by the affirmative vote of the shareholders of each class or series entitled to cast at least two–thirds (2/3) of the votes that all shareholders of the class or series are entitled to cast on the action; and

(B) In the case of a domestic entity other than a business corporation, in addition to any other required approval, vote, or consent, the satisfaction of the following conditions:

(i) The holders of every class or series of equity interest in the entity that are entitled to receive a distribution of any kind from the entity being entitled to vote on or consent to the action regardless of any otherwise applicable limitation on the voting or consent rights of any class or series; and

(ii) The action being approved by the affirmative vote or consent of the holders described in subdivision (7)(B)(i) entitled to cast at least two–thirds (2/3) of the votes or consents that all of those holders are entitled to cast on the action;

(8) "Publicly traded corporation" means a business corporation that has shares listed on a national securities exchange or traded in a market maintained by one (1) or more members of a national securities association;

(9) "Specific public benefit" includes:

(A) Providing low–income or underserved individuals or communities with beneficial products or services;

(B) Promoting economic opportunity for individuals or communities beyond the creation of jobs in the normal course of business;

(C) Protecting or restoring the environment;

(D) Improving human health;

(E) Promoting the arts, sciences, or advancement of knowledge;

(F) Increasing the flow of capital to entities with a purpose to benefit society or the environment; and

(G) Conferring any other particular benefit on society or the environment;

(10) "Subsidiary" means in relation to a person, an entity in which the person owns beneficially or of record fifty percent (50%) or more of the outstanding equity interests, calculated as if all outstanding rights to acquire equity interests in the entity had been exercised; and

(11) "Third–party standard" means a recognized standard for defining, reporting, and assessing corporate social and environmental performance that is:

（A）在商事公司中，除其他批准或表决的要求外，还应满足以下条件：

（i)每一类别或系列的股东有权作为一个独立的投票团体对公司行为进行投票，即使公司章程或公司章程细则对某一类别或系列的投票权作出了限制；

（ii）公司行为必须获得每个类别或系列有投票权的所有股东的至少2/3的赞成票才能通过；以及

（B）针对本州非商事公司实体，除任何其他要求的批准、表决或赞成外，还应满足以下条件：

（i）该实体的每一类别或系列任何权益分配形式下的股权持有者有权对公司行为进行投票，即使存在任何对该类别或系列的投票权的限制；以及

（ii）公司行为必须获得第（7）（B）（i）目规定的有投票权的所有股东至少2/3的赞成票才能通过；

（8）“上市公司”指在美国的证券交易所或美国证券协会中一个或几个成员形成的市场上进行交易的商事公司；

（9）“特定公共利益”包括：

（A）向低收入或者低福利人群或社区提供有益的产品或服务；

（B）在正常的业务过程中向个人或社区提供创造就业之外的经济机会；

（C）保护或修复环境；

（D）改善人类健康；

（E）促进艺术、科学或知识进步；

（F）促进资本流向拥有有利于社会和环境目标的实体；以及

（G）给予社会或环境其他特别的利益。

（10）“子公司”是指在所有购股权被视为已行使的情况下，该实体50%以上已发行的股份的受益所有权或登记所有权被另一实体所拥有；以及

（11）“第三方标准”是指用于定义、报告和评估公司社会和环境绩效的标准，其应满足以下条件：

(A) Comprehensive because the standard assesses the effects of the business and its operations upon the interests listed in § 48–28–301(a)(1)(B), (C), (D), and (E);

(B) Developed by an entity that is not controlled by the for–profit benefit corporation;

(C) Credible because it is developed by an entity that both:

(i) Has access to necessary expertise to assess overall corporate social and environmental performance; and

(ii) Uses a balanced, multi–stakeholder approach to develop the standard, including a reasonable public comment period; and

(D) Transparent because the following information is publicly available:

(i) About the standard:

(a) The criteria considered when measuring the overall social and environmental performance of a business; and

(b) The relative weightings, if any, of those criteria; and

(ii) About the development and revision of the standard:

(a) The identity of the directors, officers, material owners, and governing body of the entity that developed and controls revisions to the standard;

(b) The process by which revisions to the standard and changes to the membership of the governing body are made; and

(c) An accounting of the revenue and sources of financial support for the entity, with sufficient detail to disclose any relationships that could reasonably be considered to present a potential conflict of interest.

48-28-104.

A for–profit benefit corporation shall be incorporated in accordance with the Tennessee Business Corporation Act, compiled in chapters 11—27 of this title, but the for–profit benefit corporation's articles of incorporation shall also state that it is a for–profit benefit corporation.

48-28-105.

(a) An existing business corporation may become a for–profit benefit corporation under this chapter by amending its articles of incorporation so that the articles of incorporation contain, in addition to the requirements of § 48–12–102, a statement that the corporation is a for–profit benefit corporation. In order to be effective, the amendment shall be adopted by at least the minimum status vote.

(b) (1) Except as provided in subdivision (b)(2), if a domestic entity that is not a for–profit benefit corporation is a party to a merger or conversion or is the exchanging entity in a share exchange, and the surviving, new, or resulting entity in the merger, conversion, or share exchange is to be a for–profit benefit corporation, the plan of merger, conversion, or share exchange shall be approved by the domestic entity by at least the minimum status vote.

（A）综合，根据第 48-28-301（a）（1）（B）、（C）、（D）和（E）目中所列利益评估公司业务和经营绩效；

（B）独立，非由营利性公共利益公司控制的第三方实体制定；

（C）可信，该标准由满足以下条件的第三方实体制定：

（i）拥有评估公司社会和环境综合绩效所需的专业知识；并且

（ii）使用平衡的多方利益相关者的方法制定标准，包括设定合理期间以听取公众意见；以及

（D）透明，以下信息可公开获取：

（i）关于标准：

（a）衡量企业整体社会和环境绩效时所考虑的指标；以及

（b）这些指标的相关权重；以及

（ii）关于标准的制定和修改：

（a）制定、控制修改程序的董事、高管、主要股东和该实体的控制人员的身份；

（b）标准修改和控制人员变动的程序；以及

（c）收入和资金来源的计量，包括充分披露合理认知下存在利益冲突的所有细节。

第 48-28-104 条

营利性公共利益公司的章程应符合《田纳西州商事公司法》本编第 11 至 27 章的规定，章程条款应声明其为营利性公共利益公司。

第 48-28-105 条

（a）按照本章的规定，已设立的商事公司可通过修改公司章程转换为营利性公共利益公司。除满足第 48-12-102 条的规定外，公司章程应声明其为营利性公共利益公司。公司章程的修改应满足最低表决要求才能生效。

（b）（1）除第（b）（2）项另有规定外，如果本州非营利性公共利益公司是兼并、财产转换或股份置换中的一方，并且在该兼并、财产转换或股权置换中存续的实体属于营利性公共利益公司，则此等兼并、财产转换或股权置换计划的通过须满足最低表决要求。

(2) Subdivision (b)(1) does not apply in the case of a corporation that is a party to a merger if the shareholders of the corporation are not entitled to vote on the merger pursuant to § 48–21–105.

48-28-106.

(a) A for–profit benefit corporation may terminate its for–profit benefit corporation status and cease to be subject to this chapter by amending its articles of incorporation to delete the provision required by § 48–28–104 or § 48–28–105 to be stated in the articles of incorporation of a for–profit benefit corporation. In order to be effective, the amendment shall be adopted by at least the minimum status vote.

(b) (1) Except as provided in subdivision (b)(2), if a plan of merger, conversion, or share exchange would have the effect of terminating the status of a business corporation as a for–profit benefit corporation, the plan shall be adopted by at least the minimum status vote in order to be effective.

(2) Subdivision (b)(1) does not apply in the case of a corporation that is a party to a merger if the shareholders of the corporation are not entitled to vote on the merger pursuant to § 48–21–105.

(3) Any sale, lease, exchange, or other disposition of all or substantially all of the assets of a for–profit benefit corporation, unless the transaction is in the usual and regular course of business, shall not be effective unless the transaction is approved by at least the minimum status vote.

48-28-201.

(a) A for–profit benefit corporation shall have a purpose of creating general public benefit. This purpose is in addition to its purpose under § 48–13–101.

(b) The articles of incorporation of a for–profit benefit corporation may identify one (1) or more specific public benefits that it is the purpose of the for–profit benefit corporation to create in addition to its purposes under § 48–13–101 and subsection (a). The identification of a specific public benefit under this subsection (b) does not limit the purpose of a for–profit benefit corporation to create general public benefit under subsection (a).

(c) The creation of general public benefit and any specific public benefits under subsections (a) and (b) are in the best interests of the for–profit benefit corporation.

(d) A for–profit benefit corporation may amend its articles of incorporation to add, amend, or delete the identification of any specific public benefit that it is the purpose of the for–profit benefit corporation to create. In order to be effective, the amendment shall be adopted by at least the minimum status vote.

(e) A professional corporation that is a for–profit benefit corporation does not violate § 48–101–608 by having the purpose to create general public benefit or any specific public benefit.

（2）第（b）（1）项的规定不适用于并购一方公司的股东按第 48-21-105 条规定无权对并购表决的情形。

第 48-28-106 条

（a）营利性公共利益公司可通过修改公司章程和删除章程中依第 48-28-104 条和第 48-28-105 条所规定的内容终止营利性公共利益公司的形态，不再受本章规定调整。公司章程的修改应满足最低表决要求才能生效。

（b）（1）除第（b）（2）项另有规定外，如果兼并、财产转换或股权置换计划会导致营利性公共利益公司形态的终止，该计划应满足最低表决要求才能生效。

（2）第（b）（1）项的规定不适用于并购一方公司的股东按第 48-21-105 条的规定无权对并购表决的情形。

（3）除正常商业往来外，营利性公共利益公司资产的任何出售、租赁、交换或其他处分全部或主要财产的行为必须经满足最低表决要求的表决通过。

第 48-28-201 条

（a）除满足第 48-13-101 条规定的目的外，营利性公共利益公司应设立一般公共利益的目的。

（b）除符合第 48-13-101 条和第（a）款的规定外，营利性公共利益公司章程可以设定一项或多项特定公共利益目的。第（b）款规定的特定公共利益目的并不限制营利性公共利益公司依照第（a）款规定设立的一般公共利益目的。

（c）一般公共利益目的和按照第（a）款和第（b）款设定的特定公共利益为营利性公共利益公司的最佳利益。

（d）营利性公共利益公司可通过修订公司章程增加、修改或删除特定公共利益的目的。公司章程的修订应满足最低表决要求才能生效。

（e）营利性公共利益公司形态的专业公司并不因其有创设一般和特定公共利益的目的而违反第 48-101-608 条的规定。

48-28-301.

(a) In discharging the duties of their respective positions and in considering the best interests of the for–profit benefit corporation, the board of directors, committees of the board, and individual directors of a for–profit benefit corporation:

(1) Shall consider the effects of any action or inaction upon:

(A) The shareholders of the for–profit benefit corporation;

(B) The employees and work force of the for–profit benefit corporation, its subsidiaries, and its suppliers;

(C) The interests of customers as beneficiaries of the general public benefit or specific public benefit purposes of the for–profit benefit corporation;

(D) Community and societal factors, including those of each community in which offices or facilities of the for–profit benefit corporation, its subsidiaries, or its suppliers are located;

(E) The local and global environment;

(F) The short–term and long–term interests of the for–profit benefit corporation, including benefits that may accrue to the for–profit benefit corporation from its long–term plans and the possibility that these interests may be best served by the continued independence of the for–profit benefit corporation; and

(G) The ability of the for–profit benefit corporation to accomplish its general public benefit purpose and any specific public benefit purpose;

(2) May consider other pertinent factors or the interests of any other group that they deem appropriate; and

(3) Need not give priority to a particular interest or factor referred to in subdivision (a)(1) or (a)(2) over any other interest or factor unless the for–profit benefit corporation has stated in its articles of incorporation its intention to give priority to certain interests or factors related to the accomplishment of its general public benefit purpose or of any specific public benefit purpose identified in its articles of incorporation.

(b) The consideration of interests and factors in the manner provided by subsection (a) does not constitute a violation of § 48–18–301.

(c) Except as provided in the articles of incorporation, a director is not personally liable for monetary damages for:

(1) Any action or inaction in the course of performing the duties of a director under subsection (a), if the director performed the duties of office in compliance with § 48–18–301 and this section; or

(2) Failure of the for–profit benefit corporation to pursue or create general public benefit or any specific public benefit.

(d) A director does not have a duty to a person that is a beneficiary of the general public benefit purpose or any specific public benefit purpose of a for–profit benefit corporation

第 48-28-301 条

（a）董事会、董事会委员会和董事行使其职责和考虑营利性公共利益公司最佳利益时，应考虑到：

（1）其任何作为或不作为对以下主体的影响：

（A）营利性公共利益公司的股东；

（B）营利性公共利益公司及其子公司和供应商的雇员；

（C）作为营利性公共利益公司一般或特定公共利益受益人的消费者的利益；

（D）社区和社会因素，包括营利性公共利益公司及其子公司和供应商办公地或设施所在地的社区；

（E）当地和全球环境；

（F）营利性公共利益公司短期和长期利益，包括可能从其长期计划中产生的利益，以及公共利益公司继续保持独立可能产生的最佳利益；

（G）营利性公共利益公司实现其一般和特定公共利益目的的能力；

（2）可以考虑董事认为合适的其他相关因素或其他群体的利益；

（3）除营利性公共利益公司为实现其一般或特定公共利益而在公司章程中赋予特定利益或因素优先权外，无须给予第（a）（1）项或第（a）（2）项中某个利益或因素优先权。

（b）考虑第（a）款所列的利益和因素不构成对第 48-18-301 条规定的违反。

（c）除公司章程另有规定外，董事不对以下行为承担损害赔偿责任：

（1）依据第（a）款的规定履行董事责任的任何作为或不作为，若该行为符合第 48-18-301 条及本条的规定；或者

（2）营利性公共利益公司未能追求或实现一般或特定公共利益目的。

（d）董事不对营利性公共利益公司一般或特定公共利益的受益人负责。

arising from the status of the person as a beneficiary.

(e) A director who makes a business judgment in good faith fulfills the duty under this section if the director:

(1) Is not interested in the subject of the business judgment;

(2) Is informed with respect to the subject of the business judgment to the extent the director reasonably believes to be appropriate under the circumstances; and

(3) Rationally believes that the business judgment is in the best interests of the for-profit benefit corporation.

48-28-302.

(a) The board of directors of a for-profit benefit corporation that is a publicly traded corporation shall, and the board of any other for-profit benefit corporation may, include a director, who:

(1) Shall be designated the benefit director; and

(2) Shall have, in addition to the powers, duties, rights, and immunities of the other directors of the for-profit benefit corporation, the powers, duties, rights, and immunities provided in this chapter.

(b) The benefit director shall be elected, and may be removed, in the manner provided by chapter 18, part 1 of this title. Except as provided in subsection (f), the benefit director shall be an individual who is independent. The benefit director may serve as the benefit officer at the same time as serving as the benefit director. The articles of incorporation or bylaws of a for-profit benefit corporation may prescribe additional qualifications of the benefit director not inconsistent with this subsection (b).

(c) The benefit director shall prepare, and the for-profit benefit corporation shall include in the annual benefit report to shareholders required by § 48-28-401, the opinion of the benefit director on the following:

(1) Whether the for-profit benefit corporation acted in accordance with its general public benefit purpose and any specific public benefit purpose in all material respects during the period covered by the report;

(2) Whether the directors and officers complied with §§ 48-28-301(a) and 48-28-303(a), respectively; and

(3) If, in the opinion of the benefit director, the for-profit benefit corporation, its directors, or its officers failed to act or comply in the manner described in subdivisions (c)(1) and (2), a description of the ways in which the for-profit benefit corporation, its directors, or its officers failed to act or comply.

(d) The action or inaction of an individual in the capacity of a benefit director shall constitute for all purposes an action or inaction of that individual in the capacity of a director of the for-profit benefit corporation.

（e）若董事行为满足以下要求，善意进行商业判断的董事可被视为已履行本条所规定的义务：

（1）在商业判断过程中不涉及个人利益；

（2）拥有使其在该情形下作出合理商业判断的充分信息；

（3）有合理理由认为该商业判断符合公共利益公司的最佳利益。

第 48-28-302 条

（a）上市的营利性公共利益公司以及其他营利性公共利益公司的董事会，需包含满足以下要求的董事：

（1）被任命为公共利益董事；并且

（2）除有公共利益公司的其他董事的权力、义务、权利和豁免权外，还有本章规定的权力、义务、权利和豁免权。

（b）公共利益董事应当依据第 18 章第 1 部分的规定任免。除第（f）款另有规定外，公共利益董事应为独立个体。公共利益董事可同时担任公共利益高管。营利性公共利益公司章程或章程细则可明确本款未规定的公共利益董事的资格。

（c）公共利益董事应当编写其对以下事项的意见，公共利益公司应当根据第 48-28-401 条的规定将其附于年度公共利益报告中供股东查阅：

（1）在报告所述时间内，公共利益公司是否在所有重要事项上依一般和特定公共利益目的行事；

（2）董事和高管是否分别依第 48-28-301（a）款和第 48-28-303（a）款的规定行事；

（3）如果公共利益董事认为营利性公共利益公司或其董事、高管未能依第（c）（1）项和第（2）项的要求行事，应陈述营利性公共利益公司或其董事、高管未能履行责任的情况。

（d）公共利益董事在职权范围内的个人作为或不作为应视为公共利益公司董事的行为。

(e) Regardless of whether the articles of incorporation or bylaws of a for–profit benefit corporation include a provision eliminating or limiting the personal liability of directors authorized by § 48–12–102(b)(3), a benefit director shall not be personally liable for an act or omission in the capacity of a benefit director unless the act or omission constitutes self–dealing, willful misconduct, or a knowing violation of law.

(f) The benefit director of a professional corporation, as defined in § 48–101–603, does not need to be independent.

48-28-303.

(a) Each officer of a for–profit benefit corporation shall consider the interests and factors described in § 48–28–301(a)(1) in the manner provided in § 48–28–301(a)(3), if:

(1) The officer has discretion to act with respect to a matter; and

(2) It reasonably appears to the officer that the matter may have a material effect on the creation by the for–profit benefit corporation of general public benefit or any specific public benefit identified in the articles of incorporation of the for–profit benefit corporation.

(b) The consideration of interests and factors in the manner provided in subsection (a) shall not constitute a violation of § 48–18–403.

(c) Except as provided in the articles of incorporation, an officer is not personally liable for monetary damages for:

(1) An action or inaction as an officer in the course of performing the duties of an officer under subsection (a), if the officer performed the duties of the position in compliance with § 48–18–403 and this section; or

(2) Failure of the for–profit benefit corporation to pursue or create general public benefit or any specific public benefit.

(d) An officer does not have a duty to a person that is a beneficiary of the general public benefit purpose or any specific public benefit purpose of a for–profit benefit corporation arising from the status of the person as a beneficiary.

(e) An officer who makes a business judgment in good faith fulfills the duty under this section if the officer:

(1) Is not interested in the subject of the business judgment;

(2) Is informed with respect to the subject of the business judgment to the extent the officer reasonably believes to be appropriate under the circumstances; and

(3) Rationally believes that the business judgment is in the best interests of the for–profit benefit corporation.

48-28-304.

(a) A for–profit benefit corporation may have an officer designated the benefit officer.

(b) A benefit officer shall have:

(1) The powers and duties relating to the purpose of the corporation to create general

（e）无论营利性公共利益公司章程或章程细则是否依据第 48-12-102（b）（3）项的规定豁免或限制董事的个人责任，公共利益董事在行使职责时不对其任何作为或不作为承担个人责任，但自我交易、故意不当行为或故意违法行为除外。

（f）根据第 48-101-603 条的规定，对专业公司的公共利益董事的独立性不作要求。

第 48-28-303 条

（a）公共利益公司高管应以第 48-28-301（a）（1）项中规定的行为标准考虑第 48-28-301（a）（3）项中规定的利益和因素，如果：

（1）高管就该行为有自由裁量权；以及

（2）高管有合理理由认为该行为对公共利益公司在章程中创设的一般或特定公共利益有实质性影响。

（b）对第（a）款中利益和相关因素的考虑不违反第 48-18-403 条的规定。

（c）除公司章程或章程细则另有规定外，高管一般不对以下行为承担损害赔偿责任：

（1）依据第（a）款规定履行高管责任过程中的任何作为或不作为，若该行为符合第 48-18-403 条及本条的规定；或者

（2）营利性公共利益公司未能追求或实现一般或特定公共利益。

（d）高管不对营利性公共利益公司一般或特定公共利益的受益人负责。

（e）若高管行为满足以下要求，善意进行商业判断的高管可被视为已履行本条所规定的义务：

（1）在商业判断过程中不涉及个人利益；

（2）拥有使其在该情形下做出合理商业判断的充分信息；以及

（3）有合理理由认为该商业判断符合营利性公共利益公司的最佳利益。

第 48-28-304 条

（a）营利性公共利益公司可以将高管任命为公共利益高管。

（b）公共利益高管应当有：

（1）规定于以下文件中的创造一般或特定公共利益目的的权力和义务：

public benefit or any specific public benefit provided:

(i) By the bylaws; or

(ii) Absent controlling provisions in the bylaws, by resolution or order of the board of directors.

(2) The duty to prepare the annual benefit report required by § 48–28–401.

48-28-305.

(a) Except in a benefit enforcement proceeding, no person may bring an action or assert a claim against a for–profit benefit corporation, its directors, or its officers with respect to:

(1) Failure to pursue or create general public benefit or any specific public benefit set forth in its articles of incorporation; or

(2) Violation of an obligation, duty, or standard of conduct under this chapter.

(b) A for–profit benefit corporation shall not be liable for monetary damages under this chapter for any failure of the for–profit benefit corporation to pursue or create general public benefit or any specific public benefit.

(c) A benefit enforcement proceeding may be commenced or maintained only:

(1) Directly by the for–profit benefit corporation; or

(2) Derivatively by:

(i) A person or group of persons that owned beneficially or of record at least two percent (2%) of the total number of shares of a class or series outstanding at the time of the act or omission complained of;

(ii) A director;

(iii) A person or group of persons that owned beneficially or of record five percent (5%) or more of the outstanding equity interests in an entity of which the for–profit benefit corporation is a subsidiary at the time of the act or omission complained of; or

(iv) Other persons as specified in the articles of incorporation or bylaws of the for–profit benefit corporation.

(d) For purposes of this section, a person is the beneficial owner of shares or equity interests if the shares or equity interests are held in a voting trust or by a nominee on behalf of the beneficial owner.

48-28-401.

(a) A for–profit benefit corporation shall prepare an annual benefit report including the following:

(1) A narrative description of:

(A) The ways in which the for–profit benefit corporation pursued general public benefit during the year and the extent to which general public benefit was created;

(B) (i) The ways in which the for–profit benefit corporation pursued a specific public benefit that the articles of incorporation state it is the purpose of the for–profit benefit

（i）公司章程细则；或者

（ii）在公司章程细则中没有规定时，董事会的决议或者命令。

（2）按照第 48-28-401 条的要求编写年度公共利益报告的义务。

第 48-28-305 条

（a）非经公共利益实施程序，任何人不得因以下事项向营利性公共利益公司或其董事、高管提起诉讼或主张：

（1）未能追求或创造在公司章程中设定的一般或特定公共利益；或者

（2）违反本章规定下的责任、义务或行为标准。

（b）营利性公共利益公司不对本章规定下任何未能追求或实现一般或特定公共利益承担损害赔偿责任。

（c）下列情形中，以下主体可提起公共利益实施程序：

（1）由公共利益公司直接提起；或者

（2）由以下主体派生提起：

（i）在被诉作为或不作为行为发生时，持有营利性公共利益公司 2% 以上已发行的某类别或系列股份的个人或群体；

（ii）董事；

（iii）在被诉作为或不作为行为发生时，持有营利性公共利益公司母公司 5% 以上已发行股份的登记股东或实际受益人；或者

（iv）营利性公共利益公司章程或章程细则中规定的其他人员。

（d）为实现本条目的，若股份或者股利由表决权信托或指定第三人代持，则将此人视为该股份和股利的实益所有权人。

第 48-28-401 条

（a）营利性公共利益公司的年度公共利益报告中应包括以下内容：

（1）对以下事项的说明：

（A）营利性公共利益公司本年度追求一般公共利益的方法和一般公共利益实现的情况；

（B）同时包括：

（i）营利性公共利益公司追求章程中规定的特定公共利益的方法；以及

corporation to create; and

(ii) The extent to which that specific public benefit was created;

(C) Any circumstances that have hindered the creation by the for–profit benefit corporation of general public benefit or any specific public benefit; and

(D) The process and rationale for selecting or changing the third–party standard used to prepare the benefit report;

(2) An assessment of the overall social and environmental performance of the for–profit benefit corporation against a third–party standard:

(A) Applied consistently with any application of that standard in prior benefit reports; or

(B) Accompanied by an explanation of the reasons for:

(i) Any inconsistent application; or

(ii) The change to that standard from the standard used in the immediately prior annual benefit report;

(3) The name of the benefit director and the benefit officer, if any, and the address to which correspondence to each may be directed;

(4) The compensation paid by the for–profit benefit corporation during the year to each director in the capacity of a director;

(5) The opinion of the benefit director described in § 48–28–302(c); and

(6) A statement of any connection between the organization that established the third–party standard, or its directors, its officers, or any holder of five percent (5%) or more of the governance interests in the organization, and the for–profit benefit corporation or its directors, its officers, or any holder of five percent (5%) or more of the outstanding shares of the for–profit benefit corporation, including any financial or governance relationship that might materially affect the credibility of the use of the third–party standard.

(b) If, during the year covered by a benefit report, a benefit director resigned from or refused to stand for reelection to the position of benefit director, or was removed from the position of benefit director, and the benefit director furnished the for–profit benefit corporation with any written correspondence concerning the circumstances surrounding the resignation, refusal, or removal, the annual benefit report shall include that correspondence as an exhibit.

(c) Neither the benefit report nor the assessment of the performance of the for–profit benefit corporation in the benefit report required by subdivision (a)(2) needs to be audited or certified by a third party.

48-28-402.

(a) A for–profit benefit corporation shall send its annual benefit report to each shareholder on the earlier of:

（ii）该特定公共利益实现的情况；
（C）阻碍营利性公共利益公司实现一般和特定公共利益的情形；

（D）为编写公共利益报告而选择或更换第三方标准的程序和原因；

（2）依据第三方标准对公共利益公司的社会和环境表现作出的整体评价：

（A）应沿用先前公共利益报告中使用的标准；或者

（B）附一份说明以解释：
（i）适用中的差异；或者
（ii）与上一份报告相比标准的变化；

（3）公共利益董事和公共利益高管的姓名及联系地址；

（4）营利性公共利益公司在上一年度支付给每位董事的薪酬；

（5）公共利益董事按照第 48-28-302（c）款的规定应编写的陈述报告；以及
（6）设立第三方标准的组织或其董事、高管或 5% 以上管理权利的持有者与公共利益公司或其董事、高管或公共利益公司 5% 以上已发行股份持有者之间关系的声明，包括任何可能影响第三方标准可信度的财务或管理关系。

（b）在公共利益报告年度内，如果公共利益董事辞职、拒绝连任或被免职，且该公共利益董事与公司有任何书面的涉及辞职、拒绝连任或免职的书信往来，公共利益公司应当将该书信往来作为公共利益报告的附件。

（c）公共利益报告和依据第（a）（2）项编写的公共利益报告中的公共利益公司表现评价书都无须经审计或第三方证明。

第 48-28-402 条
（a）营利性公共利益公司应当在以下日期内将公共利益报告尽早地送交各股东：

(1) One hundred twenty (120) days following the end of the fiscal year of the for–profit benefit corporation; or

(2) The same time that the for–profit benefit corporation delivers any other annual report to its shareholders.

(b) A for–profit benefit corporation shall post all of its annual benefit reports on the public portion of its web site, if any, but the compensation paid to directors and financial or proprietary information included in the annual benefit reports may be omitted from the annual benefit reports as posted.

(c) If a for–profit benefit corporation does not have a web site, the for–profit benefit corporation shall provide a copy of its most recent annual benefit report, without charge, to any person that requests a copy, but the compensation paid to directors and financial or proprietary information included in the annual benefit report may be omitted from the copy of the annual benefit report provided.

(d) Concurrently with the delivery of the annual benefit report to shareholders under subsection (a), the for–profit benefit corporation shall deliver a copy of the annual benefit report to the secretary of state for filing, but the compensation paid to directors and financial or proprietary information included in the annual benefit report may be omitted from the annual benefit report delivered to the secretary of state. The secretary of state may charge a fee for filing an annual benefit report.

SECTION 2. This act shall take effect upon becoming a law, the public welfare requiring it.

（1）营利性公共利益公司财政年度结束后 120 天内；或者

（2）营利性公共利益公司向其股东送交其他年度报告的同一时间。

（b）若条件允许，营利性公共利益公司应当将其所有公共利益报告发布于其网站的公共部分；但可将公共利益报告中的董事薪酬和财务、所有权信息删除。

（c）如果营利性公共利益公司没有网站，则其应向所有索取报告的个人免费提供最新公共利益报告的副本，但可将报告副本中的董事薪酬和财务、所有权信息删除。

（d）在依第（a）款规定将公共利益报告提交给股东的同时，营利性公共利益公司应当将该公共利益报告提交州务卿备案，但可将公共利益报告中的董事薪酬和财务、所有权信息在提交州务卿的报告中删除。州务卿可收取一定的备案费用。

第 2 部分　基于公共利益需求，本法将以法律的形式生效。

THE STATE OF UTAH

S.B. 133 Enrolled

BENEFIT CORPORATION AMENDMENTS

2014 GENERAL SESSION

STATE OF UTAH

Chief Sponsor: John L. Valentine

House Sponsor: Keven J. Stratton

Cosponsor: Patricia W. Jones

General Description:

This bill modifies corporate provisions to enact the Benefit Corporation Act.

Highlighted Provisions:

This bill: enacts the Benefit Corporation Act, including: providing for the application and effect of chapter; defining terms; providing for incorporation as a benefit corporation; providing for election to become a benefit corporation; allowing for termination of benefit corporation status; addressing establishment of corporate purposes; imposing standards of conduct for directors; providing for a benefit director; imposing standards of conduct for officers; providing for a benefit officer; establishing a right of action; requiring an annual benefit report; and addressing availability of an annual benefit report; and makes technical and conforming changes.

Money Appropriated in this Bill: None

Other Special Clauses: None

Be it enacted by the Legislature of the state of Utah.

犹他州

登记为 S. B. 133

犹他州公共利益公司法修正案

2014 年犹他州大会

法案主要支持者：约翰 L. 瓦伦丁

众议院支持者：凯文 J. 斯特拉顿

支持者：帕特里夏 W. 琼斯

一般说明：本法案对公司法进行修正以制定《公共利益公司法》。

重要条款：本法案为《公共利益公司法》，具体条款包括：本章的使用和生效、界定用语、公共利益公司的设立、公共利益公司的形态转换、公共利益公司形态的终止、设立公司的目的、董事行为标准、公共利益董事行为标准、高管行为标准、公共利益高管行为标准、诉讼权利、年度公共利益报告、年度公共利益报告的内容标准以及技术和变化。

本法案无财务条款。
本法案无其他特别条款。
本法案由犹他州立法机构制定。

CHAPTER 10b. BENEFIT CORPORATION ACT

16-10b-101. Title.

This chapter is known as the "Benefit Corporation Act."

16-10b-102. Application and effect of chapter.

(1) This chapter applies to a benefit corporation organized under this chapter.

(2) The existence of a provision of this chapter does not of itself create an implication that a contrary or different rule of law is applicable to a business corporation that is not a benefit corporation. This chapter does not affect a statute or rule of law that is applicable to a business corporation that is not a benefit corporation.

(3) (a) Except as otherwise provided in this chapter, Chapter 10a, Utah Revised Business Corporation Act, is applicable to a benefit corporation.

(b) A benefit corporation may be subject simultaneously to this chapter and other chapters of this title, including Chapter 11, Professional Corporation Act.

(c) This chapter controls over Chapter 10a, Utah Revised Business Corporation Act, and Chapter 11, Professional Corporation Act, or other laws.

(4) The articles of incorporation or bylaws of a benefit corporation may not limit, be inconsistent with, or supersede a provision of this chapter.

16-10b-103. Definitions.

As used in this chapter:

(1) "Annual benefit report" means a report required under Section 16–10b–401.

(2) "Benefit corporation" means a business corporation:

(a) that elects to become subject to this chapter; and

(b) the status of which as a benefit corporation has not been terminated.

(3) "Benefit director" means the director designated as the benefit director of a benefit corporation under Section 16–10b–302.

(4) "Benefit enforcement proceeding" means a proceeding in a court of competent jurisdiction for:

(a) failure of a benefit corporation to pursue or create general public benefit or a specific public benefit purpose set forth in its articles of incorporation; or

(b) a violation of an obligation, duty, or standard of conduct under this chapter.

(5) "Benefit officer" means the individual designated as the benefit officer of a benefit corporation under Section 16–10b–304.

(6) "Business corporation" means a corporation formed under Chapter 10a, Utah Revised Business Corporation Act, or Chapter 11, Professional Corporation Act.

(7) "Division" means the Division of Corporations and Commercial Code.

第 10b 章　公共利益公司法

第 16–10b–101 条　标题

本章为《公共利益公司法》。

第 16–10b–102 条　本章的适用范围和效力

（1）本章适用于依本章规定设立的公共利益公司。

（2）本章条款不应为非公共利益公司设定相反或不同的规则。本章不影响非公共利益公司有关条文和规则的适用。

（3）（a）除本章另有规定外，《犹他州商事公司法修正案》第 10a 章适用于所有公共利益公司。

（b）公共利益公司可同时适用本章和本编的其他章节，包括第 11 章中的专业公司法。

（c）在适用上，本章效力优先于《犹他州商事公司法修正案》第 10a 章以及第 11 章专业公司法或其他法律。

（4）公共利益公司章程或章程细则规定不能限制、违背或取代本章的规定。

第 16–10b–103 条　定义

本章使用词语的定义如下：

（1）"年度公共利益报告"是指第 16–10b–401 条要求的报告；

（2）"公共利益公司"指满足下列条件的商事公司：

（a）选择接受本章调整；并且

（b）公共利益公司形态并未终止；

（3）"公共利益董事"是指公共利益公司依第 16–10b–302 条规定任命的董事。

（4）"公共利益实施程序"是指因下列事项而向有管辖权法院提起的法律程序：

（a）公共利益公司未能追求或实现公司章程规定的一般或特定公共利益目的；或者

（b）公共利益公司违反本章规定下的任何义务、责任或行为标准。

（5）"公共利益高管"是指公共利益公司依第 16–10b–304 条规定任命的高管。

（6）"商事公司"是指依《犹他州商事公司法修正案》第 10a 章或《专业公司法》第 11 章的规定设立的公司。

（7）"条"是指公司和商事法典的条文。

(8) "Executive officer" means:

(a) a benefit corporation's president;

(b) a vice president of the benefit corporation in charge of a principal business unit, division, or function; or

(c) any other officer who performs a policy-making function for the benefit corporation.

(9) "General public benefit" means a material positive impact on society and the environment:

(a) taken as a whole;

(b) assessed against a third-party standard; and

(c) from the business of a benefit corporation.

(10) "Immediate family" means a parent, spouse, surviving spouse, child, or sibling of a person.

(11) (a) "Independent" means having no material relationship with a benefit corporation or a subsidiary of the benefit corporation.

(b) Serving as a benefit director or benefit officer does not make an individual not independent.

(c) A material relationship between an individual and a benefit corporation or any of its subsidiaries will be conclusively presumed to exist if one or more of the following apply:

(i) the individual is, or has been within the last three years, an employee other than a benefit officer of the benefit corporation or a subsidiary of the benefit corporation;

(ii) an immediate family member of the individual is, or has been within the last three years, an executive officer other than a benefit officer of the benefit corporation or a subsidiary of the benefit corporation; or

(iii) there is beneficial or record ownership of 5% or more of the outstanding shares of the benefit corporation, calculated as if all outstanding rights to acquire equity interests in the benefit corporation had been exercised, by:

(A) the individual; or

(B) an entity of which the individual is a director, an officer, or a manager, or in which the individual owns beneficially or of record 5% or more of the outstanding equity interests, calculated as if all outstanding rights to acquire equity interests in the entity had been exercised.

(12) "Minimum status vote" means:

(a) in the case of a business corporation, in addition to any other required approval or vote, the satisfaction of the following conditions:

(i) the shareholders of every class or series may vote as a separate voting group on the corporate action regardless of a limitation stated in the articles of incorporation or bylaws on the voting rights of a class or series; and

（8）“执行高管”是指：

（a）公共利益公司的董事长；

（b）公共利益公司中负责主要商业机构、部门或核心业务运行的副董事长；或者

（c）任何在公共利益公司从事决策制定的其他高管。

（9）“一般公共利益”是指对社会和环境产生的实质和积极的影响，一般公共利益应：

（a）整体考虑；

（b）用第三方标准评价；以及

（c）从公共利益公司的商事活动角度考量。

（10）“直系亲属”是指父母、配偶、子女和兄弟姐妹。

（11）（a）“独立”是指与公共利益公司或其子公司无实质性关系。

（b）担任公共利益董事或高管并不当然丧失独立性。

（c）若符合下列情形，则认为该个体与公共利益公司或其子公司存在实质性关系：

（i）该个体是，或在过去的3年内是，公共利益公司或其子公司公共利益高管以外的雇员；

（ii）该个体的直系亲属是，或在过去的3年内是，公共利益公司或其子公司公共利益高管以外的执行高管；或者

（iii）在所有购股权被视为已行使的情况下，下述持有公共利益公司5%以上已发行股份的登记股东或实际受益人：

（A）个人；或者

（B）实体。该个人是该实体的董事、高管或经理；或在所有购股权被视为已行使的情况下，该实体中的个人为持有公共利益公司5%以上已发行股份的登记股东或实际受益人。

（12）“最低表决要求”：

（a）在商事公司中，除其他批准或表决的要求外，还应满足以下条件：

（i）每一类别或系列的股东有权作为一个独立的投票团体对公司行为进行投票，即使公司章程或章程细则对某一类别或系列投票权作出了限制；以及

(ii) the corporate action is required to be approved by vote of the shareholders of each class or series entitled to cast at least two–thirds of the votes that all shareholders of the class or series are entitled to cast on the action; or

(b) in the case of a domestic entity other than a business corporation, in addition to any other required approval, vote, or consent, the satisfaction of the following conditions:

(i) the holders of every class or series of equity interest in the entity that are entitled to receive a distribution of any kind from the entity may vote on or consent to the action regardless of any otherwise applicable limitation on the voting or consent rights of a class or series; and

(ii) the action must be approved by vote or consent of the holders described in Subsection (12)(b)(i) entitled to cast at least two–thirds of the votes or consents that all of those holders are entitled to cast on the action.

(13) "Publicly traded corporation" means a business corporation that has shares listed on a national securities exchange or traded in a market maintained by one or more members of a national securities association.

(14) "Specific public benefit" includes:

(a) providing low–income or underserved individuals or communities with beneficial products or services;

(b) promoting economic opportunity for individuals or communities beyond the creation of jobs in the normal course of business;

(c) protecting or restoring the environment;

(d) improving human health;

(e) promoting the arts, sciences, or advancement of knowledge;

(f) increasing the flow of capital to entities with a purpose to benefit society or the environment; and

(g) conferring any other particular benefit on society or the environment.

(15) "Subsidiary" means, in relation to a person, an entity in which the person owns beneficially or of record 50% or more of the outstanding equity interests, calculated as if all outstanding rights to acquire equity interests in the entity had been exercised.

(16) "Third–party standard" means a recognized standard for defining, reporting, and assessing corporate social and environmental performance that:

(a) assesses the effect of the business and its operations upon the interests listed in Subsections 16–10b–301(1)(a)(ii), (iii), (iv), and (v);

(b) is developed by an entity that is not controlled by the benefit corporation;

(c) is developed by an entity that both:

(i) has access to necessary expertise to assess overall corporate social and environmental performance; and

（ii）公司行为必须获得每个类别或系列有投票权的所有股东至少 2/3 的赞成票才能通过。

（b）在本州非商事公司实体中，除其他批准、表决或赞成的要求外，还应满足以下条件：

（i）该实体的每一类别或系列任何权益分配形式下的股权持有者有权对公司行为进行投票，即使存在任何对该类别或系列投票权的限制；以及

（ii）公司行为必须获得第（12）（b）（i）目规定的有投票权的所有股东至少 2/3 的赞成票才能通过。

（13）"上市公司"是指在美国的证券交易所或由美国的证券协会中一个或几个成员形成的市场上进行交易的商事公司。

（14）"特定公共利益"是指：

（a）向低收入、低福利人群或社区提供有益的产品或服务；

（b）在正常的业务过程中向个人或社区提供创造就业之外的经济机会；

（c）保护或修复环境；

（d）改善人类健康；

（e）促进艺术、科学或知识进步；

（f）促进资本流向拥有有利于社会或环境目标的实体；以及

（g）给予社会或环境其他特别的利益。

（15）"子公司"是指在所有购股权被视为已行使的情况下，该实体 50% 以上已发行的股份的受益所有权或登记所有权被另一实体所拥有。

（16）"第三方标准"是指用于定义、报告和评估公司社会和环境绩效的标准，其应满足以下条件：

（a）根据第 16-10b-301（1）（a）（ii）目、第（iii）目、第（iv）目和第（v）目中所列利益评估公司业务和经营绩效；

（b）其经非由公共利益公司控制的第三方实体制定；

（c）制定标准的第三方实体应同时符合下列条件：

（i）拥有评估公司社会和环境综合绩效所需的专业知识；并且

(ii) uses a balanced multistakeholder approach to develop the standard, including a reasonable public comment period; or

(d) makes the following information publicly available:

(i) about the standard:

(A) the criteria considered when measuring the overall social and environmental performance of a business; and

(B) the relative weightings, if any, of those criteria; and

(ii) about the development and revision of the standard:

(A) the identity of the directors, officers, material owners, and the governing body of the entity that developed and controls revisions to the standard;

(B) the process by which revisions to the standard and changes to the membership of the governing body are made; or

(C) an accounting of the revenue and sources of financial support for the entity, with sufficient detail to disclose a relationship that could reasonably be considered to present a potential conflict of interest.

16-10b-104. Incorporation of benefit corporation.

A person shall incorporate a benefit corporation in accordance with Chapter 10a, Part 2, Incorporation, but its articles of incorporation shall also state that it is a benefit corporation.

16-10b-105. Election of benefit corporation status.

(1) A business corporation may become a benefit corporation under this chapter by amending its articles of incorporation so that the articles of incorporation contain, in addition to the requirements of Section 16–10a–202, a statement that the corporation is a benefit corporation. To be effective, the amendment must be adopted by at least the minimum status vote.

(2) (a) Except as provided in Subsection (2)(b), if a domestic entity that is not a benefit corporation is a party to a merger or the exchanging entity in a share exchange and the surviving entity in the merger or share exchange is to be a benefit corporation, the plan of merger or share exchange must be approved by the domestic entity by at least the minimum status vote.

(b) Subsection (2)(a) does not apply in the case of a corporation that is a party to a merger if the shareholders of the corporation are not entitled to vote on the merger pursuant to Section 16–10a–1104.

16-10b-106. Termination of benefit corporation status.

(1) A benefit corporation may terminate its status as a benefit corporation and cease to be subject to this chapter by amending its articles of incorporation to delete the provision required by Section 16–10b–104 or 16–10b–105 to be stated in the articles of incorporation of a benefit corporation. To be effective, the amendment must be adopted by at least the

（ii）使用平衡多方利益相关者的方法制定标准，包括设定合理期间听取公众意见；或者

（d）以下信息可公开获取：

（i）关于标准：

（A）衡量企业整体社会和环境绩效时所考虑的指标；以及

（B）这些指标的相关权重；以及

（ii）关于标准的制定和修改：

（A）制定和控制修改程序的董事、高管、主要股东和该实体的控制人员的身份；

（B）标准修改和控制人员变动的程序；或者

（C）收入和资金来源的计量，包括充分披露合理认知下存在利益冲突的所有细节。

第 16-10b-104 条　公共利益公司的设立

公共利益公司应当按照第 10a 章第 2 节的规定设立，但公司章程必须声明其为公共利益公司。

第 16-10b-105 条　公共利益公司形态的选择

（1）已设立的商事公司可依本章规定转换为公共利益公司，除了满足第 16-10a-202 条的要求外，还需修改公司章程，作出该公司为公共利益公司的声明。公司章程的修改应当满足最低表决要求才能生效。

（2）（a）除了第（2）（b）项另有规定外，如果一家本州非公共利益公司是兼并或股权置换的一方，并且在该兼并或股权置换中存续的实体属于公共利益公司，那么此等兼并或股权置换的计划须满足最低表决要求才能获准。

（b）如果兼并一方的股东根据第 16-10a-1104 条的规定无权投票，则第（2）（a）项的规定不适用于此情形。

第 16-10b-106 条　公共利益公司形态的终止

（1）公共利益公司可通过删除第 16-10b-104 条或第 16-10b-105 条规定的公司章程中其作为公共利益公司的声明来终止公共利益公司形态，并不再受本章规定调整。公司章程的修改应满足最低表决要求才能生效。

minimum status vote.

(2) (a) Except as provided in Subsection (2)(b), if a plan of merger or share exchange would have the effect of terminating the status of a business corporation as a benefit corporation, the plan must be adopted by at least the minimum status vote to be effective.

(b) Subsection (2)(a) does not apply in the case of a corporation that is a party to a merger if the shareholders of the corporation are not entitled to vote on the merger pursuant to Section 16–10a–1104.

(3) A sale, lease, exchange, or other disposition of all or substantially all of the assets of a benefit corporation, unless the transaction is in the usual and regular course of business, is not effective unless the transaction is approved by at least the minimum status vote.

16-10b-201. Corporate purposes.

(1) A benefit corporation shall have a purpose of creating general public benefit. This purpose is in addition to its purpose under Section 16–10a–301.

(2) The articles of incorporation of a benefit corporation may identify one or more specific public benefits that it is the purpose of the benefit corporation to create in addition to its purposes under Section 16–10a–301 and Subsection (1). The identification of a specific public benefit under this Subsection (2) does not limit the purpose of a benefit corporation to create general public benefit under Subsection (1).

(3) The creation of general public benefit and a specific public benefit under Subsections (1) and (2) is considered in the best interests of the benefit corporation.

(4) A benefit corporation may amend its articles of incorporation to add, amend, or delete the identification of a specific public benefit that it is the purpose of the benefit corporation to create. To be effective, the amendment must be adopted by at least the minimum status vote.

(5) A professional corporation that is a benefit corporation does not violate Section 16–11–6 by having the purpose to create general public benefit or a specific public benefit.

16-10b-301. Standard of conduct for directors.

(1) Subject to Subsection (2), the board of directors, committees of the board of directors, and individual directors of a benefit corporation, in discharging the duties of their respective positions and in considering the best interests of the benefit corporation:

(a) shall consider the effects of an action or inaction upon:

(i) the shareholders of the benefit corporation;

(ii) the employees and workforce of the benefit corporation, its subsidiaries, and its suppliers;

(iii) the interests of customers as beneficiaries of the general public benefit or specific public benefit purposes of the benefit corporation;

(iv) community and societal factors, including those of each community in which offices

（2）（a）除第（2）（b）项另有规定外，如果兼并或股权置换的计划会导致公共利益公司形态终止，则该计划应满足最低表决要求才能生效。

（b）如果兼并一方的股东根据第16-10a-1104条的规定无权投票，则第（2）（a）项的规定不适用于此情形。

（3）除正常商业往来外，公共利益公司的任何出售、出租、交换或者其他处置全部或主要财产的行为，须满足最低表决要求才能生效。

第16-10b-201条　公司目的

（1）公共利益公司应当有服务于一般公共利益的目的。此目的是在第16-10a-301条的规定之外。

（2）公共利益公司的章程可以在第16-10a-301条和本条第（1）款规定外确定一项或多项特定公共利益目的。依据第（2）款规定设定的特定公共利益目的并不限制公共利益公司在本条第（1）款规定下设定一般公共利益目的。

（3）依据第（1）款和第（2）款规定设定的一般和特定公共利益目的为公共利益公司的最佳利益。

（4）公共利益公司可以增加、修改或删除章程所设定的特定公共利益目的。公司章程的修改须满足最低表决要求才能生效。

（5）公共利益形态的专业公司创设一般和特定公共利益的目的，并不构成对第16-11-6条规定的违反。

第16-10b-301条　董事行为标准

（1）在履行各自职责和考虑公共利益公司最佳利益时，公共利益公司董事会、董事委员会和董事，应受第（2）款规定的调整。

（a）其作为或不作为应当考虑对以下主体的影响：

（i）公共利益公司的股东；

（ii）公共利益公司、其子公司和其供应商的雇员；

（iii）作为公共利益公司一般或特定公共利益受益者的消费者的利益；

（iv）社区和社会因素，包括公共利益公司、其子公司或其供应商的办公地或

or facilities of the benefit corporation, its subsidiaries, or its suppliers are located;

(v) the local and global environment;

(vi) the short-term and long-term interests of the benefit corporation, including benefits that may accrue to the benefit corporation from its long-term plans and the possibility that these interests may be best served by the continued independence of the benefit corporation; and

(vii) the ability of the benefit corporation to accomplish its general public benefit purpose and a specific public benefit purpose; and

(b) may consider other pertinent factors or the interests of any other group that they consider appropriate.

(2) (a) Subject to Subsection (2)(b), in discharging the duties of their respective positions and in considering the best interests of the benefit corporation, the board of directors, committees of the board of directors, and individual directors of a benefit corporation need not give priority to a particular interest or factor referred to in Subsection (1) over any other interest or factor.

(b) Subsection (2)(a) does not apply if the benefit corporation has stated in its articles of incorporation its intention to give priority to certain interests or factors related to its accomplishment of its general public benefit purpose or of a specific public benefit purpose identified in its articles of incorporation.

(3) The consideration of interests and factors in the manner required by Subsections (1) and (2) does not constitute a violation of Section 16-10a-840.

(4) Except as provided in the articles of incorporation or bylaws, a director is not personally liable for monetary damages for:

(a) an action or inaction in the course of performing the duties of a director under Subsections (1) and (2) if the director performed the duties of office in compliance with Section 16-10a-840 and this section; or

(b) failure of the benefit corporation to pursue or create general public benefit or specific public benefit.

(5) A director does not have a duty to a person that is a beneficiary of the general public benefit purpose or a specific public benefit purpose of a benefit corporation arising from the status of the person as a beneficiary.

16-10b-302. Benefit director.

(1) The board of directors of a benefit corporation that is a publicly traded corporation shall, and the board of directors of any other benefit corporation may, include a director, who:

(a) is designated the benefit director; and

(b) shall have, in addition to the powers, duties, rights, and immunities of the other

设施所在地的社区；

（v）当地和全球环境；

（vi）公共利益公司的短期和长期利益，包括可能从其长期计划中产生的利益，以及公共利益公司继续保持独立可能产生的最佳利益；以及

（vii）公共利益公司实现其一般和特定公共利益目的的能力；并且

（b）可以考虑董事认为合适的其他相关因素或其他群体利益：

（2）（a）公共利益公司董事会、董事委员会和董事在履行职务和考虑公司最佳利益时应按照第（2）（b）项的相关规定，无须优先考虑第（1）款中所列的利益或因素。

（b）若公共利益公司章程或章程细则明确规定对一般或特定公共利益目的相关的利益或因素优先考虑，那么不再适用第（2）（a）项的规定。

（3）对第（1）款和第（2）款中利益和相关因素的考虑不构成对第16-10a-840条规定的违反。

（4）董事不对以下行为承担损害赔偿责任，公司章程或章程细则中另有明确规定的除外：

（a）依据第（1）和（2）款规定履行董事责任过程中的任何作为或者不作为，如果该董事行为符合第16-10a-840条以及本条的规定；或者

（b）公共利益公司未能追求或实现一般或特定公共利益。

（5）董事不对公共利益公司一般或特定社会目的的受益人负责。

第16-10b-302条　公共利益董事

（1）上市的公共利益公司的董事会，应包含一名满足以下条件的董事，其他形式的公共利益公司的董事会亦可包含该类型的董事：

（a）被任命为公共利益董事；并且

（b）在公共利益公司董事的权力、义务、权利和豁免权外，拥有本章规定的权力、

directors of the benefit corporation, the powers, duties, rights, and immunities provided in this chapter.

(2) (a) A benefit director shall be elected, and may be removed, in the manner provided by Sections 16–10a–801 through 16–10a–810.

(b) Except as provided in Subsection (6), the benefit director shall be an individual who is independent.

(c) The benefit director may serve as the benefit officer at the same time as serving as the benefit director.

(d) The articles of incorporation or bylaws of a benefit corporation may prescribe additional qualifications of the benefit director not inconsistent with this Subsection (2).

(3) The benefit director shall prepare, and the benefit corporation shall include in the annual benefit report to shareholders required by Section 16–10b–401, the opinion of the benefit director on all of the following:

(a) whether the benefit corporation acted in accordance with its general public benefit purpose and any specific public benefit purpose in all material respects during the period covered by the report;

(b) whether the directors and officers complied with Subsections 16–10b–301(1) and 16–10b–303(1), respectively; and

(c) if, in the opinion of the benefit director, the benefit corporation or its directors or officers failed to act or comply in the manner described in Subsections (3)(a) and (b), a description of the ways in which the benefit corporation or its directors or officers failed to act or comply.

(4) The act or inaction of an individual in the capacity of a benefit director shall constitute for all purposes an act or inaction of that individual in the capacity of a director of the benefit corporation.

(5) Regardless of whether the articles of incorporation or bylaws of a benefit corporation include a provision eliminating or limiting the personal liability of directors authorized by Section 16–10a–841, a benefit director may not be personally liable for an act or omission in the capacity of a benefit director unless the act or omission constitutes self–dealing, willful misconduct, or a knowing violation of law.

(6) The benefit director of a professional corporation does not need to be independent.

16-10b-303. Standard of conduct for officers.

(1) An officer of a benefit corporation shall consider the interests and factors described in Subsection 16–10b–301(1) in the manner provided in Subsections 16–10b–301(1) and (2) if:

(a) the officer has discretion to act with respect to a matter; and

(b) it reasonably appears to the officer that the matter may have a material effect on

义务、权利和豁免权。

（2）（a）公共利益董事应当依据第 16–10a–801 条至第 16–10a–810 条的规定任免。

（b）除第（6）款的规定外，公共利益董事应当是独立的个体。

（c）公共利益董事可以同时担任公共利益高管。

（d）公共利益公司可在章程或章程细则中对本款未规定的公共利益董事的资格予以明确。

（3）公共利益董事应当编写其对以下事项的意见，公共利益公司应当根据第 16–10b–401 条的规定将其附于年度公共利益报告中供股东查阅：

（a）在报告所述时间内，公共利益公司是否在所有重要事项上依其一般和特定公共利益目的行事；

（b）董事和高管是否依第 16–10b–301（1）款和第 16–10b–303（1）款的规定行事；以及

（c）如果公共利益董事认为公共利益公司或其董事、高管未能依第（3）（a）项和（b）项的要求行事，则其应陈述公共利益公司或其董事、高管未能履行责任的情况。

（4）公共利益董事的个人作为或不作为应当被视为该公共利益公司董事的行为。

（5）无论公共利益公司章程或者章程细则是否依据第 16–10a–841 条的规定免除或限制董事的个人责任，公共利益董事在行使公共利益董事职责时不对其任何作为或不作为承担个人责任，但该作为或不作为属于自我交易、故意不当行为或故意违法行为的除外。

（6）对专业公司的公共利益董事的独立性不作要求。

第 16–10b–303 条　高管行为标准

（1）公共利益公司高管应当以第 16–10b–301（1）款和第（2）款中规定的行为标准考虑第 16–10b–301（1）款中规定的利益和因素，如果：

（a）高管有依据该行为标准行事的自由裁量权；并且

（b）高管有合理理由认为该行为对公共利益公司实现在公司章程中创设的一

the creation by the benefit corporation of general public benefit or a specific public benefit identified in the articles of incorporation of the benefit corporation.

(2) The consideration of interests and factors in the manner described in Subsection (1) may not constitute a violation of Section 16–10a–831 or 16–10a–840.

(3) Except as provided in the articles of incorporation or bylaws of a benefit corporation, an officer is not personally liable for monetary damages for:

(a) an action or inaction as an officer in the course of performing the duties of an officer under Subsection (1) if the officer performed the duties of the position in compliance with Section 16–10a–831 or 16–10a–840 and this section; or

(b) failure of the benefit corporation to pursue or create general public benefit or specific public benefit.

(4) An officer does not have a duty to a person that is a beneficiary of the general public benefit purpose or a specific public benefit purpose of a benefit corporation arising from the status of the person as a beneficiary.

16-10b-304. Benefit officer.

(1) A benefit corporation may have an officer designated as the benefit officer.

(2) A benefit officer has:

(a) the powers and duties relating to the purpose of the corporation to create general public benefit or specific public benefit provided:

(i) by the bylaws; or

(ii) absent controlling provisions in the bylaws, by resolutions or orders of the board of directors; and

(b) the duty to prepare the benefit report required by Section 16–10b–401.

16-10b-305. Right of action.

(1) Except in a benefit enforcement proceeding, a person may not bring an action or assert a claim against a benefit corporation or its directors or officers with respect to:

(a) failure to pursue or create general public benefit or a specific public benefit set forth in its articles of incorporation; or

(b) violation of an obligation, duty, or standard of conduct under this chapter.

(2) A benefit corporation may not be liable for monetary damages under this chapter for a failure of the benefit corporation to pursue or create general public benefit or a specific public benefit.

(3) (a) A benefit enforcement proceeding may be commenced or maintained only:

(i) directly by the benefit corporation; or

(ii) derivatively by:

(A) a person or group of persons that owns beneficially or of record at least 2% of the total number of shares of a class or series outstanding at the time of the act or omission

般或特定公共利益有实质性的影响。

（2）对第（1）款中利益和相关因素的考虑不构成对第 16–10a–831 条或 16–10a–840 条规定的违反。

（3）除公司章程或公司章程细则另有明确规定外，高管不对以下行为承担损害赔偿责任：

（a）在依据第（1）款履行高管职责过程中的任何作为或者不作为，如果该高管依据第 16–10a–831 条或第 16–10a–840 条以及本条的规定履行高管责任；或者

（b）公共利益公司未能追求或实现一般或特定公共利益。

（4）高管不对公共利益公司一般或特定公共利益目的的受益人负责。

第 16–10b–304 条　公共利益高管

（1）公共利益公司可以将高管任命为公共利益高管。

（2）公共利益高管应当有：

（a）规定于以下文件的创造一般或特定公共利益的公司目的的权力和义务：

（i）公司章程细则；或者

（ii）在公司章程细则中没有规定时，董事会决议或者命令。

（b）编写第 16–10b–401 条要求的公共利益报告的义务。

第 16–10b–305 条　诉讼权利

（1）非经公共利益实施程序，任何人不得因以下事项向公共利益公司或者其董事、高管提起诉讼或主张：

（a）未能追求或实现在其公司章程中设定的一般或特定公共利益；或者

（b）违反本章规定下的责任、义务或行为标准。

（2）公共利益公司在本章规定下不对任何未能追求或实现一般或特定公共利益的行为承担损害赔偿。

（3）（a）在以下情形中，只能由以下主体提起公共利益实施程序：

（i）由公共利益公司直接提起；或者

（ii）由以下主体派生提起：

（A）在被诉作为或不作为行为发生时，拥有公共利益公司 2% 以上已发行的某类别或系列股份的个人或群体；

complained of;

(B) a director;

(C) a person or group of persons that own beneficially or of record 5% or more of the outstanding equity interests in an entity of which the benefit corporation is a subsidiary at the time of the act or omission complained of; or

(D) other persons as specified in the articles of incorporation or bylaws of the benefit corporation.

(b) A benefit corporation may provide in its articles of incorporation a greater degree of ownership by a person or group of persons than those listed under Subsection (3)(a) to bring a derivative action.

(4) For purposes of this section, a person is the beneficial owner of shares or equity interests if the shares or equity interests are held in a voting trust or by a nominee on behalf of the beneficial owner.

16-10b-401. Preparation of annual benefit report.

(1) A benefit corporation shall prepare an annual benefit report that includes all of the following:

(a) a narrative description of:

(i) the ways in which the benefit corporation pursued general public benefit during the year and the extent to which general public benefit was created;

(ii) (A) the ways in which the benefit corporation pursued a specific public benefit that the articles of incorporation state it is the purpose of the benefit corporation to create; and

(B) the extent to which that specific public benefit was created; and

(iii) circumstances that have hindered the creation by the benefit corporation of general public benefit or specific public benefit;

(b) an assessment of the overall social and environmental performance of the benefit corporation against a third-party standard:

(i) applied consistently with the application of that third-party standard in prior benefit reports; or

(ii) accompanied by an explanation of the reasons for an inconsistent application;

(c) the name of the benefit director and the benefit officer, if any, and the address to which correspondence to each of them may be directed;

(d) the statement of the benefit director described in Subsection 16-10b-302(3);

(e) an identification of the third-party standard that will be used to prepare the next benefit report of the benefit corporation and a discussion of:

(i) the process and rationale for selecting that third-party standard and, if it is different from the previous third-party standard used by the benefit corporation, the reasons for the change; and

（B）董事；

（C）在被诉作为或不作为行为发生时，持有公共利益公司母公司 5% 以上已发行股份的登记股东或实际受益股人；或者

（D）在公共利益公司章程或章程细则中列明的其他人员。

（b）公共利益公司可以在章程中规定可由股权持有比例高于第（3）（a）项要求的个人或集体提起派生诉讼。

（4）为实现本条目的，股份或者股利由表决权信托或者指定的人代为持有的，将此人视为该股份和股利的实益所有权人。

第 16-10b-401 条　年度公益报告的编写

（1）公共利益公司的年度公共利益报告应包括以下内容：

（a）对以下事项的说明：

（i)公共利益公司本年度追求一般公共利益的方法和一般公共利益的实现情况;

（ii）（A）公共利益公司追求章程中所列的特定公共利益的方法；以及

（B）该特定公共利益的实现情况；以及

（iii）阻碍公共利益公司实现一般或特定公共利益的情形；

（b）依据第三方标准，对公共利益公司整体社会和环境表现作出的评价：

（i）沿用先前公共利益报告中使用的标准；或者

（ii）使用标准发生变化的，附一份说明以解释原因；

（c）公共利益董事和公共利益高管的姓名及联系地址（如有）；

（d）公共利益董事依第 16-10b-302（3）项的规定应编写的陈述意见。

（e）准备用来编制公共利益公司下一年公共利益报告的第三方标准以及对下列情况的说明：

（i）选择第三方标准的程序和理由，与先前使用的第三方标准不同的，还需说明更换的理由；

(ii) any connection between the organization that established the third–party standard, or its directors, officers, or a holder of 5% or more of the governance interests in the organization, and the benefit corporation or its directors, officers, or a holder of 5% or more of the outstanding shares of the benefit corporation, including a financial or governance relationship that might materially affect the credibility of the use of the third–party standard; and

(f) if the benefit corporation has dispensed with, or restricted the discretion or powers of, the board of directors, a description of the persons that exercise the powers, duties, and rights and who have the immunities of the board of directors.

(2) If, during the year covered by a benefit report, a benefit director resigns, refuses to stand for reelection to the position of benefit director, or is removed from the position of benefit director, and the benefit director furnishes the benefit corporation with written correspondence concerning the circumstances surrounding the resignation, refusal, or removal, the benefit report shall include that correspondence as an exhibit.

(3) Neither the benefit report nor the assessment of the performance of the benefit corporation in the benefit report required by Subsection (1)(b) needs to be audited or certified by a third party.

16-10b-402. Availability of annual benefit report.

(1) A benefit corporation shall send its annual benefit report required by Section 16–10b–401 to each shareholder on the earlier of:

(a) 120 days following the end of the fiscal year of the benefit corporation; or

(b) the same time that the benefit corporation delivers another annual report to its shareholders.

(2) A benefit corporation shall post all of its annual benefit reports on the public portion of its Internet website, if any, but financial or proprietary information included in the annual benefit reports may be omitted from the annual benefit reports as posted.

(3) If a benefit corporation does not have an Internet website, the benefit corporation shall provide a copy of its most recent annual benefit report, without charge, to a person that requests a copy, but financial or proprietary information included in the annual benefit report may be omitted from the copy of the benefit report provided.

(4) (a) At the same time that the benefit corporation files its annual report with the division in accordance with Section 16–10a–1607, the benefit corporation shall deliver the most recent copy of the annual benefit report to the division for filing, but financial or proprietary information included in the annual benefit report may be omitted from the annual benefit report as delivered to the division.

(b) The division shall charge a fee established by the division in accordance with Section 63J–1–504 for filing an annual benefit report.

（ii）设立第三方标准的组织或其董事、高管或持股 5% 以上的权利人与公共利益公司或其董事、高管或拥有公共利益公司 5% 以上已发行股份的持有者之间关系的声明，包括任何可能影响第三方标准可信度的财务或管理关系；以及

（f）公共利益公司免除或限制董事会权力和自由裁量权的，需说明董事会中拥有相应权力、责任、权利和豁免权的董事的情况。

（2）在公共利益报告年度内，如果公共利益董事辞职、拒绝连任或被免职，且该公共利益董事与公司有任何书面的涉及辞职、拒绝连任或免职的书信往来，公共利益公司应当将该书信往来作为公共利益报告的附件。

（3）公共利益报告和依据第（1）（b）项规定编写的公共利益报告中的公共利益公司表现评价书不需要经审计或者第三方证明。

第 16–10b–402 条　年度公共利益报告的提供

（1）公共利益公司应当按照第 16–10b–401 条的要求将年度公共利益报告送交各股东：

（a）公共利益公司财政年度结束后 120 天；或者

（b）公共利益公司向其股东送交其他年度报告的同一时间。

（2）若条件允许，公共利益公司应当将其所有年度公共利益报告发布于其网站的公共部分；但可将公共利益报告中的董事财务和所有权信息删除。

（3）如果公共利益公司没有网站，其应在任何个人索取副本时向其免费提供最新报告的副本，但可将年度公共利益报告副本中的董事财务和所有权信息删除。

（4）（a）在依第（2）款规定将公共利益报告提交给股东的同时，公司应当将该公共利益报告的副本提交相关机构备案，但可将报告中的董事财务和所有权信息在提交的报告中删除。

（b）相关机构应按照第 63J–1–504 条的规定收取一定的费用。

(c) The benefit corporation shall file the annual benefit report in addition to the annual report required by Section 16–10a–1607.

（c）除第 16-10a-1607 条规定的年度报告外，公共利益公司还应按照规定提交年度公共利益报告备案。

THE STATE OF VERMONT

No. 113. An act relating to the Vermont Benefit Corporations Act.

(S.263)

It is hereby enacted by the General Assembly of the State of Vermont:

Sec. 1. 11A V.S.A. chapter 21 is added to read:

CHAPTER 21. BENEFIT CORPORATIONS

§ 21.01. SHORT TITLE

§ 21.02. LAW APPLICABLE

§ 21.03. DEFINITIONS

§ 21.04. INCORPORATION OF A BENEFIT CORPORATION

§ 21.05. ELECTION OF EXISTING CORPORATION TO BECOME A BENEFIT CORPORATION

§ 21.06. MERGER AND SHARE EXCHANGE

§ 21.07. TERMINATION OF BENEFIT CORPORATION STATUS BY AMENDMENT OF ARTICLES OF INCORPORATION; VOTE REQUIRED

§ 21.08. CORPORATE PURPOSE

§ 21.09. STANDARD OF CONDUCT FOR DIRECTORS

§ 21.10. BENEFIT DIRECTOR

§ 21.11. STANDARD OF CONDUCT FOR OFFICERS

§ 21.12. BENEFIT OFFICER

§ 21.13. RIGHT OF ACTION

§ 21.14. ANNUAL BENEFIT REPORT

§ 21.01. SHORT TITLE

This chapter shall be known and may be cited as the "Vermont Benefit Corporations Act."

佛蒙特州

第 113 号法案：有关佛蒙特州公共利益公司法的法案

（S.263）

本法由佛蒙特州大会制定：
第一部分 《佛蒙特州修订法》第 11A 编中增加如下第 21 章的内容：

第 21 章 公共利益公司
第 21.01 条 简称
第 21.02 条 法律的适用
第 21.03 条 定义
第 21.04 条 公共利益公司的设立
第 21.05 条 已设立公司向公共利益公司的转变

第 21.06 条 合并和股权置换
第 21.07 条 修改章程终止公共利益公司形态；表决要求

第 21.08 条 公司目的
第 21.09 条 董事行为标准
第 21.10 条 公共利益董事
第 21.11 条 高管行为标准
第 21.12 条 公共利益高管
第 21.13 条 诉讼权利
第 21. 14 条 年度公共利益报告

第 21.01 条 简称
本章简称为《佛蒙特州公共利益公司法》。

§ 21.02. LAW APPLICABLE

(a) This chapter shall apply only to a domestic corporation meeting the definition of a benefit corporation in subdivision 21.03(a)(1) of this title. The provisions of this title other than those set forth in this chapter shall apply to a benefit corporation in the absence of a contrary or inconsistent provision in this chapter. A corporation whose status as a benefit corporation terminates shall immediately become subject to the obligations and rights of a general corporation as provided in this title.

(b) The existence of a provision of this chapter does not of itself create any implication that a contrary or different rule of law is or would be applicable to a corporation that is not a benefit corporation. This chapter does not affect any statute or rule of law as it applies to a corporation that is not a benefit Corporation.

(c) A provision of the articles of incorporation or bylaws of a benefit corporation may not be inconsistent with any provision of this chapter.

(d) Terms that are defined in other chapters of this title shall have the same meaning when used in this chapter, except that in this chapter, "corporation" shall have the meaning set forth in section 1.40 of this title.

§ 21.03. DEFINITIONS

(a) As used in this chapter:

(1) "Benefit corporation" means a corporation as defined in section 1.40 of this title whose articles of incorporation include the statement "This corporation is a benefit corporation."

(2) "Benefit director" means a director designated as a benefit director of a benefit corporation as provided in section 21.10 of this title.

(3) "Benefit officer" means the officer of a benefit corporation, if any, designated as the benefit officer as provided in section 21.12 of this title.

(4) "General public benefit" means a material positive impact on society and the environment, as measured by a third–party standard, through activities that promote some combination of specific public benefits.

(5) "Independent" means that a person has no material relationship with a benefit corporation or any of its subsidiaries (other than the relationship of serving as the benefit director or benefit officer), either directly or as an owner or manager of an entity that has a material relationship with the benefit corporation or any of its subsidiaries. A material relationship between a person and the benefit corporation or any of its subsidiaries will be conclusively presumed to exist if:

(A) the person is, or has been within the last three years, an employee of the benefit corporation or any of its subsidiaries, other than as a benefit officer;

(B) an immediate family member of the person is, or has been within the last three

第 21.02 条　法律的适用

（a）本章只适用于本编第 21.03（a）（1）项规定的满足公共利益公司定义的本州公司。除本章另有规定外，本编的条款也适用于不与本章规定相冲突的公共利益公司。终止公共利益公司形态的公司享有和履行一般公司的权利和义务。

（b）本章条款不为非公共利益公司设定相反或不同的规则。本章不影响非公共利益公司有关条文和规则的适用。

（c）公共利益公司的章程或章程细则不得违背本章的规定。

（d）本章的用语含义与本编下其他章所使用的用语保持一致，本章另有规定的除外，“公司”一词和本编第 1.40 条中规定的含义相同。

第 21.03 条　定义

（a）本章用语的含义如下：

（1）“公共利益公司”为本编第 1.40 条所定义的公司，其公司章程须载明“本公司为公共利益公司”。

（2）“公共利益董事”为公共利益公司依据第 21.10 条规定任命的董事。

（3）“公共利益高管”为公共利益公司依据第 21.12 条规定任命的高管。

（4）“一般公共利益”是指根据第三方标准，公司一系列促进特定公共利益的活动对社会和环境产生的实质性积极影响。

（5）“独立”是指与公共利益公司或其子公司没有实质性的关系的个体（除非个人为公共利益董事或高管），其与公共利益公司没有直接关联，且不是有实质性关系的实体的所有人和管理人。以下情形中，认为该个体与公共利益公司及其子公司存在实质性关系：

（A）该个体是，或在过去的 3 年间是，公共利益公司或其子公司的公共利益高管以外的雇员；

（B）该个体的直系亲属是，或在过去的 3 年间是，公共利益公司或其子公司

years, an executive officer, other than a benefit officer, of the benefit corporation or any of its subsidiaries; or

(C) the person, or an entity of which the person is a manager or in which the person owns beneficially or of record five percent or more of the equity interests, owns beneficially or of record five percent or more of the shares of the benefit corporation.

(6) "Specific public benefit" includes:

(A) providing low income or underserved individuals or communities with beneficial products or services;

(B) promoting economic opportunity for individuals or communities beyond the creation of jobs in the normal course of business;

(C) preserving or improving the environment;

(D) improving human health;

(E) promoting the arts or sciences or the advancement of knowledge;

(F) increasing the flow of capital to entities with a public benefit purpose; and

(G) the accomplishment of any other identifiable benefit for society or the environment.

(7) "Subsidiary" of a person means an entity in which the person owns beneficially or of record 50 percent or more of the equity interests.

(8) "Third–party standard" means a recognized standard for defining, reporting, and assessing corporate social and environmental performance that:

(A) is developed by a person that is independent of the benefit corporation; and

(B) is transparent because the following information about the standard is publicly available:

(i) the factors considered when measuring the performance of a business;

(ii) the relative weightings of those factors; and

(iii) the identity of the persons who developed and control changes to the standard and the process by which those changes are made.

(b) For purposes of subdivisions (a)(5)(C) and (7), a percentage of ownership in an entity shall be calculated as if all outstanding rights to acquire equity interests in the entity had been exercised.

§ 21.04. INCORPORATION OF A BENEFIT CORPORATION

A benefit corporation shall be formed in accordance with sections 2.01, 2.02, 2.03, and 2.05 of this title, except that its articles of incorporation shall also contain the provision required by subdivision 21.03(a)(1) of this title to meet the definition of a benefit corporation.

§ 21.05. ELECTION OF EXISTING CORPORATION TO BECOME A BENEFIT CORPORATION

Any corporation organized under this title may become a benefit corporation by amending its articles of incorporation to add the statement required by subdivision 21.03(a)(1)

的非公共利益高管以外的执行高管；

（C）持有公共利益公司 5% 以上股份的登记股东或实际受益人，包括个人，该个人担任经理的实体，该个人作为持有公共利益公司 5% 以上股份的登记股东或实际受益人的实体。

（6）“特定公共利益”包括：

（A）向低收入或者低福利人群或社区提供有益的产品或服务；

（B）在正常的业务过程中向个人或社区提供创造就业之外的经济机会；

（C）保护或改善环境；

（D）改善人类健康；

（E）促进艺术、科学或知识进步；

（F）促进资本流向具有公共利益目的的实体；以及

（G）实现社会或环境其他可见的利益。

（7）“子公司”指该实体 50% 以上股份的受益所有权或登记所有权被另一实体所拥有。

（8）“第三方标准”是指用于定义、报告和评估公司社会和环境绩效的标准，其应满足以下条件：

（A）独立，由独立于公共利益公司的个体制定；并且

（B）透明，有关该标准的以下信息可公开获取：

（i）衡量企业绩效考虑的指标；

（ii）这些指标的相关权重；以及

（iii）制定、控制修改标准和程序的人员的身份。

（b）为实现第（a）（5）（c）目和第（7）项的目的，在计算实体中所有者权益的比例时，所有购股权都应视为已行使。

第 21.04 条　公共利益公司的设立

公共利益公司应当按照第 2.01 条、第 2.02 条、第 2.03 条和第 2.05 条的要求设立，其公司章程也应包含第 21.03（a）（1）项有关公共利益公司要求的条款。

第 21.05 条　已设立公司向公共利益公司的转换

本编规定下任何已设立的商业公司，均可通过修改公司章程转换为公共利益公司。其应按照第 21.03（a）（1）项的要求，在章程中作出该公司为公共利益公司的

of this title to meet the definition of a benefit corporation. The amendment shall be adopted and shall become effective in accordance with sections 10.01 through 10.09 of this title, except that:

(1) the notice of the meeting of shareholders that will approve the amendment shall include a statement from the board of directors of the reasons why the board is proposing the amendment and the anticipated effect on shareholders of becoming a benefit corporation; and

(2) the amendment shall be approved by the higher of:

(A) the vote required by the articles of incorporation; or

(B) two–thirds of the votes entitled to be cast by the outstanding shares of the corporation, provided that if any class of shares is entitled to vote as a group, approval shall also require the affirmative vote of the holders of at least two–thirds of the votes entitled to be cast by the outstanding shares of each voting group.

§ 21.06. MERGER AND SHARE EXCHANGE

(a) A plan of merger or share exchange that if effected would terminate the benefit corporation status of a corporation shall be adopted and shall become effective in accordance with chapter 11 of this title, except that:

(1) the notice of the meeting of shareholders that will approve the plan shall include a statement from the board of directors of the reasons why the board is proposing that the surviving corporation should not be a benefit corporation and the anticipated effect on the shareholders of the surviving corporation ceasing to be a benefit corporation; and

(2) the plan shall be approved by the higher of:

(A) the vote required by the articles of incorporation; or

(B) two–thirds of the votes entitled to be cast by the outstanding shares of the corporation, provided that if any class of shares is entitled to vote as a group, approval shall also require the affirmative vote of the holders of at least two–thirds of the votes entitled to be cast by the outstanding shares of each voting group.

(b) If a corporation that is not a benefit corporation is a party to a plan of merger or share exchange in which the surviving corporation is a benefit corporation, the plan of merger shall be adopted and shall become effective in accordance with chapter 11 of this title, except that:

(1) the notice of the meeting of shareholders that will approve the plan shall include a statement from the board of directors of the reasons why the board is proposing that the surviving corporation should become a benefit corporation and the effect on the shareholders of the surviving corporation becoming a benefit corporation; and

(2) the plan shall be approved in the case of the corporation that is not a benefit corporation by the higher of:

(A) the vote required by the articles of incorporation; or

声明。公司章程修改的通过和生效应满足第 10.01 至 10.09 条的要求，此外：

（1）召开股东会通过上述修正案时，董事会应在召开股东会的通知中说明修订理由以及该转换对公共利益公司股东的预期影响；并且

（2）修订的通过应达到：
（A）公司章程的表决要求；或者
（B）公司 2/3 股权表决通过。若按照团体表决的方式，须经各个团体至少占 2/3 股权的股东表决通过。

第 21.06 条　合并和股权置换

（a）进行合并或股权置换会终止公共利益公司状态的，该交易计划的通过和生效除须满足本编第 11 章的要求外，

（1）召开股东会通过上述计划时，董事会应在股东会召开通知中说明公司不再作为公共利益公司存续的原因，以及该转换对公共利益公司股东的预期影响；并且

（2）上述计划的通过应达到：
（A）公司章程的表决要求；或者
（B）公司 2/3 股权表决通过。若按照团体表决的方式，须经各个团体至少占 2/3 股权的股东表决通过。

（b）如果一家非公共利益公司是合并或股权置换的一方，并且在该合并或股权置换中存续的实体属于公共利益公司，那么此等合并计划的通过和生效，除应满足本编第 11 章的相关要求外：

（1）召开股东会通过上述计划时，董事会应在股东会召开通知中说明公司合并后作为公共利益公司存续的理由以及该转换对公共利益公司股东的预期影响；并且

（2）上述计划的通过应达到：

（A）公司章程的表决要求；或者

(B) two-thirds of the votes entitled to be cast by the outstanding shares of the corporation, provided that if any class of shares is entitled to vote as a group, approval shall also require the affirmative vote of the holders of at least two-thirds of the votes entitled to be cast by the outstanding shares of each voting group.

§ 21.07. TERMINATION OF BENEFIT CORPORATION STATUS BY AMENDMENT OF ARTICLES OF INCORPORATION; VOTE REQUIRED

A corporation may terminate its status as a benefit corporation and cease to be subject to this chapter by amending its articles of incorporation to delete the provision required by subdivision 21.03(a)(1) of this title to meet the definition of a benefit corporation, in addition to the provisions required by section 2.02 of this title to be stated in the articles of incorporation of a benefit corporation. The amendment shall be adopted and shall become effective in accordance with sections 10.01 through 10.09 of this title, except that:

(1) the notice of the meeting of shareholders that will approve the plan shall include a statement from the board of directors of the reasons why the board is proposing the amendment and the effect of terminating the status of the corporation as a benefit corporation; and

(2) the amendment shall be approved by the higher of:

(A) the vote required by the articles of incorporation; or

(B) two-thirds of the votes entitled to be cast by the outstanding shares of the corporation, provided that if any class of shares is entitled to vote as a group, approval shall also require the affirmative vote of the holders of at least two-thirds of the votes entitled to be cast by the outstanding shares of each voting group.

§ 21.08. CORPORATE PURPOSE

(a) A benefit corporation shall have the purpose of creating general public benefit. This purpose is in addition to, and may be a limitation on, the purposes of the benefit corporation under subsection 3.01(a) of this title.

(b) The articles of incorporation of a benefit corporation may identify one or more specific public benefits that are the purpose of the benefit corporation to create in addition to its purposes under subsection 3.01(a) of this title and subsection (a) of this section. The adoption of a specific public benefit purpose under this subsection does not limit the obligation of a benefit corporation to create general public benefit.

(c) The creation of general and specific public benefit as provided in subsections (a) and (b) of this section is in the best interests of the benefit corporation.

(d) A benefit corporation may amend its articles of incorporation to add, amend, or delete a specific public benefit. The amendment shall be adopted and shall become effective in accordance with sections 10.01 through 10.09 of this title and shall be approved by the higher of the vote required by the articles of incorporation or by subsection (e) of this section.

（B）公司 2/3 股权表决通过。若按照团体表决的方式，须经各个团体至少占 2/3 股权的股东表决通过。

第 21.07 条　修改章程终止公共利益公司形态；表决要求

公共利益公司可通过删除第 21.03（a）（1）项规定的条款以及第 2.02 条要求的公司章程中其为公共利益公司的声明来终止公共利益公司形态，并不再接受本章规定调整。公司章程修改的通过和生效除应满足第 10.01 至 10.09 条的要求外：

（1）召开股东会通过上述计划时，董事会应在股东会召开通知中说明提出章程修订案的原因以及终止公共利益公司形态的影响；并且

（2）上述计划的通过应达到：

（A）公司章程的表决要求；或者

（B）公司 2/3 股权表决通过。若按照团体表决的方式，须经各个团体至少占 2/3 股权的股东表决通过。

第 21.08 条　公司目的

（a）公共利益公司应当拥有创造一般公共利益的目的。此目标应在本编第 3.01（a）款规定的基础上设立，但不限于该条规定。

（b）公共利益公司的章程可在本编第 3.01（a）款和本条第（a）款基础之上确定一项或多项特定公共利益目标。依本款规定设定的特定公共利益目标并不限制公共利益公司设定一般公共利益目标的义务。

（c）依据本条第（a）款和第（b）款规定设定的一般和特定公共利益目标属公共利益公司的最佳利益。

（d）公共利益公司可以增加、修改或删除公司章程中设定的特定公共利益目标。公司章程修改的通过和生效应当满足第 10.01 至 10.09 条的要求，且章程修改的通过表决应按照章程的要求或本条第（e）款规定中表决要求较高的方式。

(e) An amendment of the articles of incorporation of a benefit corporation to add, amend, or delete a specific public benefit in the articles of incorporation shall be adopted by a vote of at least two–thirds of the votes entitled to be cast by the outstanding shares of the corporation, provided that if any class of shares is entitled to vote as a group, approval shall also require the affirmative vote of the holders of at least two–thirds of the votes entitled to be cast by the outstanding shares of each voting group.

§ 21.09. STANDARD OF CONDUCT FOR DIRECTORS

(a) Each director of a benefit corporation, in discharging his or her duties as a director, including the director's duties as a member of a committee:

(1) shall, in determining what the director reasonably believes to be in the best interests of the benefit corporation, consider the effects of any action or inaction upon:

(A) the shareholders of the benefit corporation;

(B) the employees and workforce of the benefit corporation and its subsidiaries and suppliers;

(C) the interests of customers to the extent they are beneficiaries of the general or specific public benefit purposes of the benefit corporation;

(D) community and societal considerations, including those of any community in which offices or facilities of the benefit corporation or its subsidiaries or suppliers are located;

(E) the local and global environment; and

(F) the long–term and short–term interests of the benefit corporation, including the possibility that those interests may be best served by the continued independence of the benefit corporation;

(2) may consider any other pertinent factors or the interests of any other group that the director determines are appropriate to consider;

(3) shall not be required to give priority to the interests of any particular person or group referred to in subdivisions (1) or (2) of this subsection over the interests of any other person or group unless the benefit corporation has stated its intention to give priority to interests related to its specific public benefit purpose in its articles of incorporation; and

(4) shall not be subject to a different or higher standard of care when an action or inaction might affect control of the benefit corporation.

(b) The consideration of interests and factors in the manner described in subsection (a) of this section shall not constitute a violation of section 8.30 of this title.

(c) A director is not liable for the failure of a benefit corporation to create general or specific public benefit.

(d) A director is not liable to the benefit corporation or any person entitled to bring a benefit enforcement proceeding under section 21.13 of this title for any action or failure to take action in his or her official capacity if the director performed the duties of his or her

（e）公共利益公司可增加、修改或删除公司章程中设定的特定公共利益目标的条款，公司章程的修订须经拥有 2/3 以上公司已发行股份的股东表决通过。若按照团体表决的方式，须经各个团体至少占 2/3 股权的股东表决通过。

第 21.09 条　董事行为标准

（a）在履行董事职责和董事委员会成员职责的过程中，公共利益公司的董事：

（1）应考虑公共利益公司的最佳利益，其行为应考虑对以下主体的影响：

（A）公共利益公司的股东；

（B）公共利益公司、其子公司和其供应商的雇员；

（C）作为公共利益公司一般或特定公共利益受益者的消费者的利益；

（D）社区和社会因素，包括公共利益公司、其子公司或其供应商的办公地或设施所在地的社区；

（E）当地和全球环境；

（F）公共利益公司的短期和长期利益，包括可能从其长期计划中产生的利益，以及公共利益公司继续保持独立可能产生的最佳利益；

（2）可以考虑董事认为合适的其他相关因素或其他群体的利益；

（3）除公司章程中规定为实现一般或特定公共利益而赋予特定利益或因素优先权外，无须给予本款第（1）项或第（2）项中某个利益或因素优先权；并且

（4）作为或不作为可能影响公共利益公司的控制权时，不适用不同的或更高标准的注意义务。

（b）对本条第（a）款中所列的利益和因素的考量不违反本编第 8.30 条的规定。

（c）董事不对公共利益公司未能实现一般或特定公共利益承担个人责任。

（d）若董事履行义务的行为符合第 8.30 条的要求，则其不因职责范围内的任何作为或不作为，对公共利益公司或按照本编第 21.13 条的规定提起公共利益实施程序的主体承担个人责任。

office in compliance with section 8.30 of this title and with this section.

(e) A director of a benefit corporation shall have a fiduciary duty only to those persons entitled to bring a benefit enforcement proceeding against the benefit corporation under section 21.13 of this title. A director of a benefit corporation shall not have any fiduciary duty to a person who is a beneficiary of the general or specific public benefit purposes of the benefit corporation arising only from the person's status as a beneficiary.

§ 21.10. BENEFIT DIRECTOR

(a) The board of directors of a benefit corporation shall include at least one director who shall be designated a "benefit director" and shall have, in addition to all of the powers, duties, rights, and immunities of the other directors of the benefit corporation, the powers, duties, rights, and immunities provided in this section.

(b) A benefit director shall be elected and may be removed in the manner provided by subchapter 1 of chapter 8 of this title and shall be an individual who is independent of the benefit corporation. A benefit director may serve as the benefit officer at the same time as serving as a benefit director. The articles of incorporation or bylaws of a benefit corporation may prescribe additional qualifications of a benefit director not inconsistent with this subsection.

(c)(1) A benefit director shall be responsible for the preparation of the annual benefit report required under section 21.14 of this title.

(2) A benefit director may retain an independent third party to audit the annual benefit report or conduct any other assessment of the benefit corporation's social and environmental performance.

(3) A benefit director shall prepare and shall include in the annual benefit report a statement whether, in the opinion of the benefit director:

(A) the benefit corporation acted in accordance with its general public benefit purpose and any specific public benefit purpose in all material respects during the period covered by the report; and

(B) the directors and officers acted in accordance with the requirements of subsection 21.09(a) and section 21.11 of this title, respectively.

(4) If in the opinion of the benefit director the benefit corporation failed to act in accordance with its general and any specific public benefit purposes or if its directors or officers failed to act in accordance with the requirements of subsection 21.09(a) and section 21.11 of this title, respectively, then the statement of the benefit director shall include a description of the ways in which the benefit corporation or its directors or officers failed to so act.

(d) The acts and omissions of an individual in the capacity of a benefit director shall constitute for all purposes acts and omissions of that individual in the capacity of a director

（e）公共利益公司的董事只对依照第 21.13 条的规定提出公共利益实施程序的主体负有信义义务，不对公共利益公司一般或特定公共利益目的受益人负信义义务。

第 21.10 条　公共利益董事

（a）公共利益公司应设至少一名公共利益董事，该董事除了拥有其他类型董事的权力、义务、权利和豁免权外，还拥有本条所规定的权力、义务、权利和豁免权。

（b）公共利益董事应当依据第 8 章第 1 节的规定任免。公共利益董事应当是独立的个体，其可同时担任公共利益高管。公共利益公司章程或章程细则可对本款未规定的公共利益董事的资格予以明确。

（c）（1）公共利益董事应该按照第 21.14 条的规定编写年度公共利益报告。

（2）公共利益董事可委派独立第三方对年度公共利益报告进行审计或对公共利益公司的社会、环境绩效进行评价。

（3）公共利益董事在编制年度公共利益报告中应就以下事项提出自己的意见：

（A）在报告所述时间内，公共利益公司是否在所有重要事项上依照一般和特定公共利益目标行事；并且

（B）董事和高管是否分别按照第 21.09（a）款和第 21.11 条的规定行事。

（4）如果公共利益董事认为公共利益公司或其董事、高管未能依第 21.09（a）款和第 21.11 条的要求行事，应陈述公共利益公司或其董事未能履行责任的情况。

（d）公共利益董事的个人作为或不作为应当被视为该公共利益公司董事的行为。

of the benefit corporation.

(e) If the articles of incorporation of a benefit corporation that is a close corporation dispense with a board of directors pursuant to sections 20.08 and 20.09 of this title, then the articles of incorporation shall provide that the persons who perform the duties of a board of directors shall include at least one person with the powers, duties, rights, and immunities of a benefit director.

(f) Regardless of whether the articles of incorporation of a benefit corporation include a provision eliminating or limiting the personal liability of directors authorized by subdivision 2.02(b)(4) of this title, a benefit director shall not be personally liable for any act or omission taken in his or her official capacity as a benefit director unless the act or omission is not in good faith, involves intentional misconduct or a knowing violation of law, or involves a transaction from which the director directly or indirectly derived an improper personal benefit.

§ 21.11. STANDARD OF CONDUCT FOR OFFICERS

(a) An officer of a benefit corporation shall consider the interests and factors described in subsection 21.09(a) of this title in the manner provided in that subsection when:

(1) the officer has discretion in how to act or not act with respect to a matter; and

(2) it reasonably appears to the officer that the matter may have a material effect on:

(A) the creation of general or specific public benefit by the benefit corporation; or

(B) any of the interests or factors referred to in section 21.09(a)(1) of this title.

(b) The consideration of interests and factors in the manner described in subsection (a) of this section shall not constitute a violation of the fiduciary duty of an officer to the benefit corporation.

(c) An officer is not liable to the benefit corporation or any person entitled to bring a benefit enforcement proceeding under section 21.13 of this title for any action or failure to take action in his or her official capacity if the officer performed the duties of the position in compliance with section 8.41 of this title and with this section.

(d) An officer is not liable for the failure of a benefit corporation to create general or specific public benefit.

(e) An officer of a benefit corporation shall have a fiduciary duty only to those persons entitled to bring a benefit enforcement proceeding against the benefit corporation under section 21.13 of this title. An officer of a benefit corporation shall not have any fiduciary duty to a person that is a beneficiary of the general or specific public benefit purposes of the benefit corporation arising only from the person's status as a beneficiary.

§ 21.12. BENEFIT OFFICER

A benefit corporation may have an officer designated the "benefit officer" who shall have the authority and shall perform the duties in the management of the benefit corporation

（e）若公共利益公司属于封闭性公司，其章程按照第 20.08 条和第 20.09 条的要求不设立董事会，那么公司章程必须载明至少一名拥有公共利益董事的权力、义务、权利和豁免权的主体。

（f）无论公共利益公司章程是否依据第 2.02（b）（4）项的规定免除或限制董事的个人责任，公共利益董事在行使公共利益董事职权时不应对其任何作为或不作为承担个人责任，该作为或不作为属不诚信、故意不当行为、故意违法行为或通过交易获取直接或间接不正当个人利益行为的除外。

第 21.11 条　高管行为标准

（a）公共利益公司的高管应当以本款所规定的标准，考虑第 21.09（a）款中规定的利益和因素，如果：

（1）高管有依据该行为标准行事的自由裁量权；并且

（2）高管有合理理由认为其下列行为可能产生实质性影响：

（A）公共利益公司实现一般或特定公共利益；或者

（B）本编第 21.09（a）（1）项规定的任何利益或因素。

（b）对本条第（a）款中利益和相关因素的考虑，不违反公共利益公司法的高管信义义务条款的规定。

（c）若高管履行义务的行为符合第 8.41 条和本条的要求，则其不因职责范围内的任何作为或不作为，对公共利益公司或按照本编第 21.13 条的规定提出公共利益实施程序的主体承担个人责任。

（d）高管不对公共利益公司未能实现一般或特定公共利益负责。

（e）公共利益公司的董事只对依照第 21.13 条规定提出公共利益实施程序的主体负有信义义务，不对公共利益公司一般或特定公共利益目的受益人负信义义务。

第 21.12 条　公共利益高管

公共利益公司可以将高管任命为“公共利益高管”。公共利益高管拥有创设公共利益目标的权力，履行管理公共利益公司章程规定有关公共利益的义务，或者

relating to the purpose of the corporation to create public benefit as set forth with respect to the office in the bylaws or, to the extent not inconsistent with the bylaws, prescribed with respect to the office by the board of directors or by direction of an officer authorized by the board of directors to prescribe the duties of the office.

§ 21.13. RIGHT OF ACTION

(a) The duties of directors and officers under this chapter and the general and specific public benefit purposes of a benefit corporation may be enforced only in a benefit enforcement proceeding, and no person may bring such an action or claim against a benefit corporation or its directors or officers except as provided in this section.

(b) A benefit enforcement proceeding may be commenced or maintained only by:

(1) a shareholder that would otherwise be entitled to commence or maintain a proceeding in the right of the benefit corporation on any basis;

(2) a director of the corporation;

(3) a person or group of persons that owns beneficially or of record 10 percent or more of the equity interests in an entity of which the benefit corporation is a subsidiary; or

(4) such other persons as may be specified in the articles of incorporation of the benefit corporation.

(c) As used in this chapter, "benefit enforcement proceeding" means a claim or action against a director or officer for:

(1) failure to pursue the general public benefit purpose of the benefit corporation or any specific public benefit purpose set forth in its articles of incorporation; or

(2) violation of a duty or standard of conduct under this chapter.

§ 21.14. ANNUAL BENEFIT REPORT

(a) A benefit corporation shall deliver to each shareholder, in a format approved by the directors, an annual benefit report, which shall include:

(1)(A) a statement of the specific goals or outcomes identified by the benefit corporation for creating general public benefit and any specific public benefit for the period of the benefit report;

(B) a description of the actions taken by the benefit corporation to attain the identified goals or outcomes and the extent to which the goals or outcomes were attained;

(C) a description of any circumstances that hindered the attainment of the identified goals or outcomes and the creation of general public benefit or any specific public benefit; and

(D) specific actions the benefit corporation can take to improve its social and environmental performance and attain the goals or outcomes identified for creating general public benefit and any specific public benefit.

(2) an assessment of the social and environmental performance of the benefit corporation

在公司章程没有规定时，公共利益高管行使董事会授权的权力，履行董事会要求的义务。

第 21.13 条　诉讼权利

（a）公共利益公司的董事和高管未按照本章规定履行职责，或公共利益有限公司未能实现一般和特定公共利益目的的，可提起公共利益实施程序。除本章特别规定外，任何人不得对公共利益公司或其董事、高管提起诉讼或主张。

（b）公共利益实施程序只能由下列人员提起：

（1）基于维护公共利益公司权益目的的股东；

（2）公司董事；

（3）持有公共利益公司子公司 10% 以上股份的登记股东或实际受益人，包括个人或团体；或者

（4）公共利益公司章程规定的其他人员。

（c）本章所指的“公共利益实施程序”为因下列事项向董事、高管提起的诉讼或主张：

（1）未能追求公共利益公司章程设定的一般或任何特定公共利益目标；或者

（2）违反本章规定下的责任或行为标准。

第 21.14 条　年度公共利益报告

（a）公共利益公司应向股东送交经董事认可的年度报告，报告内容应包括：

（1）（A）公共利益公司本年度实现一般或特定公共利益目标的情况或成果；

（B）公共利益公司为实现确定的目标或成果所采取的行动以及该目标和成果的实现程度；

（C）阻碍实现上述目标和创造一般或特定公共利益目标的情形，以及；

（D）公共利益公司为了改善社会和环境绩效以及达成一般或特定公共利益目标所能够采取的特别行动。

（2）沿用上年度第三方标准对公共利益公司的社会和环境表现进行评价，适

prepared in accordance with a third-party standard that has been applied consistently with prior benefit reports or accompanied by an explanation of the reasons for any inconsistent application;

(3) a statement of specific goals or outcomes identified by the benefit corporation and approved by the shareholders for creating general public benefit and any specific public benefit for the period of the next benefit report;

(4) the name of each benefit director and the benefit officer, if any, and the address to which correspondence to each of them may be directed;

(5) the compensation paid by the benefit corporation during the year to each director in that capacity;

(6) the name of each person that owns beneficially or of record five percent or more of the shares of the benefit corporation; and

(7) the statement of a benefit director described in subsection 21.10(c) of this title.

(b) A benefit corporation shall annually deliver the benefit report to each shareholder within 120 days following the end of the fiscal year of the benefit corporation or at the same time that the benefit corporation delivers any other annual report to its shareholders.

(c) After reasonable opportunity for review, the shareholders of the benefit corporation shall approve or reject the annual benefit report by majority vote at the annual meeting of shareholders or at a special meeting held for that purpose.

(d) A benefit corporation shall post its most recent benefit report endorsed by its shareholders on the public portion of its website, if any, except that the compensation paid to directors and any financial or proprietary information included in the benefit report may be omitted from the benefit report as posted. If a benefit corporation does not have a public website, it shall deliver a copy of its most recent benefit report on demand and without charge to any person who requests a copy.

Sec. 2. EFFECTIVE DATE

This act shall take effect on July 1, 2011.

Approved: May 19, 2010

用标准与上年度不一致的，应附一份解释说明原因；

（3）陈述下一年度公共利益报告中创造一般或特定公共利益的目标或要取得的成果，该声明应由公共利益公司确认并经股东同意；

（4）公共利益董事和公共利益高管的姓名及联系地址（如有）；

（5）公共利益公司在上一年度支付给每位董事的薪酬；

（6）拥有公共利益公司 5% 及以上股权的登记股东或实际受益人的姓名；以及

（7）第 21.10（c）款要求的公共利益董事的声明。

（b）公共利益公司应当在公共利益公司财政年度结束后 120 天内，或在向其股东送交其他年度报告的同一时间将公共利益报告送交各股东。

（c）经过合理的审查后，公共利益公司的股东可以同意也可以否决年度公共利益报告，表决应在股东年度大会或者特别会议上通过多数决的方式作出。

（d）公共利益公司应当将最新的经股东审查通过的公共利益报告发布于其网站的公共部分；但可将公共利益报告中的董事薪酬、财务及所有权信息删除。如果公共利益公司没有网站，则其应在任何个人索取副本时向其免费提供最新报告的副本。

第 2 部分　生效日期

本法于 2011 年 7 月 1 日生效。

获得批准：2010 年 5 月 19 日

THE STATE OF VIRGINIA

VIRGINIA ACTS OF ASSEMBLY -- 2011 SESSION

CHAPTER 698

An Act to amend the Code of Virginia by adding in Chapter 9 of Title 13.1 an article numbered 22, consisting of sections numbered 13.1–782 through 13.1–791, relating to benefit corporations.

Approved March 26, 2011

Be it enacted by the General Assembly of Virginia:

1. That the Code of Virginia is amended by adding in Chapter 9 of Title 13.1 an article numbered 22, consisting of sections numbered 13.1–782 through 13.1–791, as follows:

Article 22. Benefit Corporations.

§ 13.1-782. Definitions.

As used in this article:

"Benefit corporation" means a corporation organized pursuant to the provisions of this chapter:

1. That has elected to become subject to this article; and

2. The status of which as a benefit corporation has not been terminated under § 13.1–786.

"Benefit enforcement proceeding" means any claim or action brought directly by a benefit corporation, or derivatively on behalf of a benefit corporation, against a director or officer for

(i) failure to pursue the general public benefit purpose of the benefit corporation or any specific public benefit purpose set forth in its articles of incorporation or bylaws or otherwise adopted by its board of directors; or

弗吉尼亚州

弗吉尼亚州议会法案——2011 立法会议

第 698 章

本法案对《弗吉尼亚法典》进行了修订，在第 13.1 编的第 9 章中增加第 22 节，包括的第 13.1–782 条至 13.1–791 条，与公共利益公司有关。

2011 年 3 月 26 日

由弗吉尼亚议会通过：

1.《弗吉尼亚法典》修订，在第 13.1 编的第 9 章中增加了第 22 节，包括第 13.1–782 条至第 13.1–791 条，修订内容如下：

第 22 节　公共利益公司

第 13.1–782 条　定义

在本节中：

“公共利益公司”是指依据本章规定设立，符合以下条件的公司：

1. 受本章规定的调整；以及
2. 公共利益公司形态并未依第 13.1–786 条的规定终止。

“公共利益实施程序”是指基于以下事由，由公共利益公司直接提起或由代表公司利益的主体派生提起的针对董事、高管的主张或诉求：

（i）公共利益公司未追求其章程中规定的或董事会通过的一般或特定公共利益目标；或者

(ii) a violation of a duty or standard of conduct under this article.

"General public benefit" means a material positive impact on society and the environment taken as a whole, as measured by a third–party standard, from the business and operations of a benefit corporation.

"Independent" means having no material relationship with a benefit corporation or a subsidiary of the benefit corporation, either directly as a shareholder of the benefit corporation or as a partner, a member, or an owner of a subsidiary of the benefit corporation or indirectly as a director, an officer, an owner, or a manager of an entity that has a material relationship with the benefit corporation or a subsidiary of the benefit corporation. A material relationship between a person and a benefit corporation or any of its subsidiaries will be conclusively presumed to exist if:

1. The person is, or has been within the last three years, an employee of the benefit corporation or a subsidiary of the benefit corporation;

2. An immediate family member of the person is, or has been within the last three years, an executive officer of the benefit corporation or its subsidiary; or

3. There is beneficial ownership of five percent or more of the outstanding shares of the benefit corporation by:

a. The person; or

b. An entity:

(1) Of which the person is a director, an officer, or a manager; or

(2) In which the person owns beneficially five percent or more of the outstanding equity interests, which percentage shall be calculated as if all outstanding rights to acquire equity interests in the entity had been exercised.

"Specific public benefit" means a benefit that serves one or more public welfare, religious, charitable, scientific, literary, or educational purposes, or other purpose or benefit beyond the strict interest of the shareholders of the benefit corporation, including:

1. Providing low–income or underserved individuals or communities with beneficial products or services;

2. Promoting economic opportunity for individuals or communities beyond the creation of jobs in the normal course of business;

3. Preserving or improving the environment;

4. Improving human health;

5. Promoting the arts, sciences, or advancement of knowledge;

6. Increasing the flow of capital to entities with a public benefit purpose; and

7. Conferring any other particular benefit on society or the environment.

"Subsidiary" means, in relation to an individual, an entity in which the individual either (i) owns directly or indirectly equity interests entitled to cast a majority of the votes

（ii）违反本节规定下的任何职责或行为标准。

“一般公共利益”是指根据第三方标准，公司的业务和经营在整体上对社会和环境产生的实质性积极影响。

“独立”是指与公共利益公司或其子公司没有实质关系，该实质关系的主体既包括与公共利益公司及其子公司有直接关系的公共利益公司的股东或合伙人、成员或子公司的所有人，也包括与之有间接关系的公共利益公司或其子公司的董事、高管、一般合伙人和经理。存在以下情形的，认为该个体与公共利益公司及其子公司存在实质性关系：

1. 该个体是，或在过去的 3 年间是，公共利益公司或其子公司的公共利益高管以外的雇员；

2. 该个体的直系亲属是，或在过去的 3 年间是，公共利益公司或其子公司的公共利益高管以外的执行高管；或者

3. 下述持有公共利益公司 5% 以上已发行股份的登记股东或实际受益人：

a. 个人；或者

b. 实体：

（1）该个人是该实体的董事、高管或经理；或者

（2）在所有购股权被视为已行使的情况下，该实体中的个人为持有公共利益公司 5% 以上已发行股份的登记股东或实际受益人。

“特定公共利益”指一项或多项有益于公共福利、宗教、慈善、科学、文化或教育目的的利益，或公共利益公司股东直接利益之外的其他利益，包括：

1. 向低收入或者低福利人群或社区提供有益的产品或服务；

2. 在正常的业务过程中向个人或社区提供创造就业之外的经济机会；

3. 保护或改善环境；

4. 改善人类健康；

5. 促进艺术、科学或知识进步；

6. 促进资本流向拥有有利于社会或环境目标的实体；以及

7. 给予社会或环境其他特别的利益。

“子公司”是指符合下列条件的个人或实体：

（i）直接或间接拥有可以使其在该法人董事或管理层选举中享有多数投票权的

entitled to be cast generally in an election of directors or members of the governing body of the entity; or

(ii) otherwise owns or controls voting or contractual power to exercise effective governing control of the entity. The percentage of ownership of equity interests or ownership or control of power to exercise control shall be calculated as if all outstanding rights to acquire equity interests in the entity had been exercised.

"Third-party standard" means a recognized standard for defining, reporting, and assessing corporate social and environmental performance that:

1. Is developed by a person that is independent of the benefit corporation; and

2. Is transparent because the following information about the standard is publicly available:

a. The factors considered when measuring the performance of a business;

b. The relative weightings of those factors; and

c. The identity of the persons that develop and control changes to the standard and the process by which those changes are made.

§ 13.1-783. Application and effect of article.

A. This article shall apply to all benefit corporations.

B. The existence of a provision of this article shall not of itself create an implication that a contrary or different rule of law applies to a corporation organized pursuant to the provisions of this chapter that is not a benefit corporation. This article shall not affect a statute or rule of law that applies to a corporation that is not a benefit corporation.

C. The specific provisions of this article shall control over the general provisions of other articles of this chapter.

§ 13.1-784. Formation of benefit corporations.

A benefit corporation shall be formed in accordance with Article 3 (§ 13.1-618 et seq.), and its articles, as initially filed with the Commission or as amended, shall state that it is a benefit corporation.

§ 13.1-785. Election of status after formation.

A corporation that was not formed as a benefit corporation may become a benefit corporation by amending its articles so that they contain, in addition to matters required by § 13.1-619, a statement that the corporation is a benefit corporation. Any such amendment to the articles of incorporation shall be adopted in accordance with the procedures set forth in § 13.1-707; however, the amendment shall be approved by all shareholders entitled to vote on the amendment, or if no shares have yet been issued, in accordance with § 13.1-709.

§ 13.1-786. Termination of status

A benefit corporation may terminate its status as such and cease to be subject to this article by amending its articles to delete the provision required by § 13.1-784 to be set forth

股权；或者

（ii）在所有购股权被视为已行使的情况下，拥有或控制投票权或订立合同的权力，实质控制该实体。

“第三方标准”是指的是用以定义、描述和评估公司的社会与环境绩效的标准，其应符合下列条件：

1. 由独立于公共利益公司的第三方制定；

2. 透明，以下关于该标准的信息可公开获取：

a. 衡量一项商业行为时所考虑的指标；

b. 这些指标的相关权重；以及

c. 制定、控制标准修改及其程序的人员的身份。

第 13.1–783 条　适用及效力

A. 本节条款适用于所有公共利益公司。

B. 该节条款不应为非公共利益公司设定相反或不同的规则，也不影响非公共利益公司有关条文和规则的适用。

C. 本节条款中特别条款的效力优于本章其他节的一般条款。

第 13.1–784 条　公共利益公司的设立

公共利益公司依第 3 节（第 13.1–618 条等）的规定设立，其公司章程拟定或修改时，应载明其为公共利益公司。

第 13.1–785 条　公共利益公司形态的选择

已设立的非公共利益公司可通过修改公司章程的方式转换为公共利益公司，公司章程的修改除符合第 13.1–619 条的要求外，还需载明其为公共利益公司。任何上述修改都应符合第 13.1–707 条的规定；并且，该修改还应经具有投票权的所有股东表决通过，若该公司的股票尚未发行，则表决应符合第 13.1–709 条的规定。

第 13.1–786 条　公共利益公司形态的终止

公共利益公司可以通过修改其章程以删除第 13.1–784 条要求的在公司章程中规定的条款来终止其形态，并不再受本章的约束，该修改应根据第 13.1–707 条规定的

in the articles of incorporation, which amendment shall be adopted in accordance with the procedures set forth in § 13.1–707, or if no shares have yet been issued, in accordance with § 13.1–709.

§ 13.1-787. Corporate purposes.

A.A benefit corporation shall have as one of its purposes the purpose of creating a general public benefit. The articles of incorporation of a benefit corporation may identify one or more specific public benefits that it is the purpose of the benefit corporation to create. A specific public benefit may also be specified in the bylaws or otherwise adopted by the board of directors. This purpose is in addition to its purpose under § 13.1–626.

B.The creation of a general public benefit and one or more specific public benefits, if any, under subsection A is in the best interests of the benefit corporation.

C.A benefit corporation may amend its articles of incorporation to add, amend, or delete the identification of a specific public benefit that it is the purpose of the benefit corporation to create, which amendment shall be adopted in accordance with the procedures set forth in § 13.1–707.

§ 13.1-788. Standard of conduct for directors.

A. Subject to § 13.1–690, in discharging the duties of their respective positions and in considering the best interests of the benefit corporation, the board of directors, committees of the board, and individual directors of a benefit corporation:

1. Shall consider the effects of any corporate action upon:

a. The shareholders of the benefit corporation;

b. The employees and workforce of the benefit corporation, its subsidiaries, and suppliers;

c. The interests of customers as beneficiaries of the general or specific public benefit purposes of the benefit corporation;

d. Community and societal considerations, including those of each community in which offices or facilities of the benefit corporation, its subsidiaries, or suppliers are located;

e. The local and global environment;

f. The short–term and long–term interests of the benefit corporation, including benefits that may accrue to the benefit corporation from its long–term plans and the possibility that these interests and the general and specific public benefit purposes of the benefit corporation may be best served by the continued independence of the benefit corporation; and

g. The ability of the benefit corporation to accomplish its general and any specific public benefit purpose;

2. May consider:

a. The resources; intent; and past, stated, and potential conduct of any person seeking to acquire control of the benefit corporation; and

程序通过，或者如果还没有发行股票，则根据第 13.1–709 条规定的程序通过。

第 13.1–787 条　公司目的

A. 公共利益公司应至少设立一项一般公共利益目的。公共利益公司章程可规定一个或多个特定公共利益目的。特定公共利益目的可在公司章程中载明或由董事会拟定。该目的应在第 13.1–626 条要求的目的之外。

B. 根据第 A 款规定创设的一般或特定公共利益为公共利益公司的最佳利益。

C. 公共利益公司可通过修改章程增加、修改或删除某项其要实现的特定公共利益，章程的修改应符合第 13.1–707 条规定的程序。

第 13.1–788 条　董事行为标准

A. 在履行各自职责和考虑公共利益公司最佳利益时，公共利益公司的董事会、董事委员会和董事，应受第 13.1–690 条的约束。

1. 其任何行为，应当考虑对以下对象的影响：

a. 公共利益公司的股东；

b. 公共利益公司、其子公司和其供应商的雇员；

c. 作为公共利益公司一般公共利益或特定公共利益受益者的消费者的利益；

d. 社区和社会因素，包括公共利益公司、其子公司或其供应商的办公地或设施所在地的社区；

e. 当地和全球环境；

f. 公共利益公司的短期和长期利益，包括可能从其长期计划中产生的利益，以及公共利益公司继续保持独立可能产生的最佳利益；以及

g. 公共利益公司实现其一般和特定公共利益目标的能力；

2. 可供参考的其他因素：

a. 试图取得公共利益公司控制权的任何主体的资源、意图和行为，包括过去、现在和未来的行为。

b. Other pertinent factors or the interests of any other person that they deem appropriate; and

3. Need not give priority to the interests of a particular person referred to in subdivisions 1 and 2 over the interests of any other person unless the benefit corporation has stated its intention to give priority to interests related to a specific public benefit purpose identified in its articles.

B. The consideration of interests and factors in the manner required by subsection A shall not constitute a violation of § 13.1–690 or a director conflict of interests under § 13.1–691.

C. In any proceeding brought by or in the right of a benefit corporation or brought by or on behalf of the shareholders of a benefit corporation, a director is not personally liable for monetary damages for:

1. Any action taken as a director if the director performed the duties of office in compliance with § 13.1–690 and this section; or

2. Failure of the benefit corporation to create general public benefit or any specific public benefit specified in its articles of incorporation or bylaws or otherwise adopted by the board of directors.

§ 13.1-789. Limitation upon liability of officers.

An officer of a benefit corporation shall have no liability for actions taken that the officer believes, in his good faith business judgment, are consistent with

(i) the general public benefit or specific public benefit specified in the articles of incorporation or bylaws or otherwise adopted by the board of directors; and

(ii) the requirements of any third–party standard then in effect for the corporation.

§ 13.1-790. Right of action.

A. The duties of directors and officers under this article, the obligation of a benefit corporation to prepare and make available the annual benefit report required under § 13.1–791, and the general and any specific public benefit purpose of a benefit corporation may be enforced only in a benefit enforcement proceeding. No person may bring an action or assert a claim against a benefit corporation or its directors or officers with respect to the duties of directors and officers under this article and the general and any specific public benefit purpose of the benefit corporation except in a benefit enforcement proceeding.

B. A benefit enforcement proceeding may be commenced or maintained only:

1. Directly by the benefit corporation; or

2. Derivatively by:

a. A shareholder of the benefit corporation;

b. A director of the benefit corporation; or

c. Other persons as specified in the articles of incorporation or bylaws of the benefit

b. 董事认为合适的其他因素或其他人的利益；以及

3. 除公司章程中规定为实现特定公共利益而赋予特定利益或因素优先权外，无须给予第 1 项及第 2 项中某个利益或因素优先权。

B. 考虑第 A 款所列的利益和因素，不构成对第 13.1–690 条规定的违反，也不会被视为存在第 13.1–691 条规定的利害冲突。

C. 在任何由公共利益公司提起的或有权提起的诉讼中，或在任何由公共利益公司股东提起的或有权作为代表提起的诉讼中，董事个人不对以下行为承担损害赔偿责任：

1. 董事履行职责的行为符合第 13.1–690 条以及本条的规定；或者

2. 公共利益公司未能实现其公司章程或董事会设定的一般或特定公共利益。

第 13.1–789 条　高管的责任限制

公共利益公司高管在善意商业判断之下，对符合以下标准的行为，不承担个人责任：

（i）行为符合公司章程、章程细则或董事会设定的一般或特殊公共利益目标；

（ii）行为符合公司所采用的在高管实施行为时有效的第三方标准。

第 13.1–790 条　诉讼权利

A. 根据董事和高管在本节规定下的职责，公共利益公司有依据第 13.1–791 条的规定制作和发布年度公共利益报告的义务，而且，一般和特定公共利益目标的实施，只能通过公共利益实施程序。非经公共利益实施程序，任何人不得就公司及其董事、高管在本节规定下的责任以及公共利益目标的实施提起诉求或主张。

B. 公共利益实施程序只能由以下主体提起：

1. 由公共利益公司提起直接诉讼；或者

2. 由以下个体提起派生诉讼：

a. 公共利益公司的股东；

b. 公司董事；或者

c. 公共利益公司章程或章程细则中规定的其他人。

corporation.

§ 13.1-791. Annual benefit report.

A. A benefit corporation shall prepare an annual benefit report that includes all of the following:

1. A narrative description of:

a. The ways in which the benefit corporation pursued the general public benefit during the year and the extent to which the general public benefit was created; and

b. Both:

(1) The ways in which the benefit corporation pursued any specific public benefit that the articles of incorporation or bylaws, or other action taken by the board of directors, state it is the purpose of the benefit corporation to create; and

(2) The extent to which that specific public benefit was created; and

c. Any circumstances that have hindered the creation by the benefit corporation of the general or any specific public benefit;

2. An assessment of the social and environmental performance of the benefit corporation. The assessment shall be:

a. Prepared in accordance with a third–party standard specified in the articles of incorporation, the bylaws, or otherwise adopted by the board of directors and applied consistently with any application of that standard in prior benefit reports; or

b. Accompanied by an explanation of the reasons for any inconsistent application; and

3. Any other information or disclosures that may be required under any third–party standard adopted by the directors of the benefit corporation.

B. The benefit report shall be made available annually to each shareholder of the benefit corporation:

1. Within 120 days following the end of the fiscal year of the benefit corporation; or

2. At the same time that the benefit corporation delivers any other annual report to its shareholders.

C. A benefit corporation shall post its most recent benefit report on a publicly accessible portion of its Internet website, if any. If a benefit corporation does not have an Internet website, it shall make a written or electronic copy of its most recent benefit report available upon written request from any person. A benefit corporation shall not be required to publically disclose to persons other than its shareholders any proprietary, confidential, or individual compensation information contained in its benefit report to the extent that any third–party standard adopted by the directors of the benefit corporation permits the omission of such information from public disclosure.

第 13.1–791 条 年度公共利益报告

A. 公共利益公司应编制包含如下内容的年度公共利益报告：

1. 对以下事项的说明：
a. 公共利益公司本年度追求一般或特定公共利益的方式和实现情况；以及

b. 同时包括：
（1）实现公共利益公司章程、章程细则或董事会的决议所规定的特殊公共利益的方式；以及

（2）该特殊公共利益实现的情况；以及
c. 阻碍实现一般或特定公共利益的情形；

2. 对公共利益公司的社会和环境表现作出的评价，该评价应：

a. 沿用先前公共利益报告所使用的第三方标准，该标准依照公司章程、章程细则选定或由董事会选定；或者

b. 如果未能持续适用上述标准，还应说明原因；以及
3. 公共利益公司董事决定采用的第三方标准所要求提供或披露的其他信息。

B. 公共利益公司应当在每一年度的以下时限内将公共利益报告送交各股东：

1. 公共利益公司财政年度结束后 120 天；或者
2. 公共利益公司向其股东送交其他年度报告的同一时间。

C. 若条件允许，公共利益公司应当将其最新版的公共利益报告发布于其网站的公共部分；如果公共利益公司没有网站，其应在任何个人以书面方式索取报告副本时，向其免费提供最新报告的纸质版本或电子版本。公共利益公司可拒绝向股东以外的人披露公共利益报告中的个人薪酬、所有权和机密信息，依据第三方标准在向公众披露时可将该类信息删除。

WASHINGTON DISTRICT OF COLUMBIA

To amend Title 29 of the District of Columbia Official Code (Business Organizations)to provide for the incorporation of benefit corporations, for the rights, duties and obligations of benefit corporations and their shareholders, directors, and officers, and to impose powers and duties on the Mayor.

BE IT ENACTED BY THE COUNCIL OF THE DISTRICT OF COLUMBIA, That this act may be cited as the "Benefit Corporation Act of 2012".

Sec. 2. Title 29 of the District of Columbia Official Code is amended as follows:

(a) The table of contents is amended by adding a new chapter designation to read as follows: "13. Benefit Corporations.".

(b) A new Chapter 13 is added to read as follows:

CHAPTER 13. BENEFIT CORPORATIONS.

Subchapter I. Preliminary Provisions.

Section

29-1301.01. Short title.

29-1301.02. Definitions.

29-1301.03. Applicability; construction.

29-1301.04. Formation of benefit corporations.

29-1301.05. Election of status.

29-1301.06. Termination of status.

Subchapter II. Corporate Purposes.

29-1302.01. Corporate purposes.

Subchapter III. Accountability.

29-1303.01. Standard of conduct for directors.

华盛顿哥伦比亚特区

《哥伦比亚特区官方法典》第 29 编（商业组织）修正案，本法调整公共利益公司的设立；公共利益公司及其股东、董事和高管的权利、义务和责任；政府的权力和责任。

本法的立法机关为哥伦比亚特区行政委员会。本法可被称为《2012 年公共利益公司法》。

第 2 部分 《哥伦比亚特区官方法典》第 29 编的修改内容如下：

（a）目录处增加新的一章：“13. 公共利益公司”。

（b）正文新增第 13 章，内容如下：

第 13 章 公共利益公司法

第一节 初步条款

第 29–1301.01 条 简称
第 29–1301.02 条 定义
第 29–1301.03 条 适用和解释
第 29–1301.04 条 公共利益公司的设立
第 29–1301.05 条 公共利益公司形态的选择
第 29–1301.06 条 公共利益公司形态的终止
第二节 公司目的
第 29–1302.01 条 公司目的
第三节 公司责任
第 29–1303.01 条 董事行为标准

29–1303.02. Benefit director.
29–1303.03. Standard of conduct for officers.
29–1303.04. Benefit officer.
29–1303.05. Right of action.
Subchapter IV. Transparency.
29–1304.01. Annual benefit report.

Subchapter I. Preliminary Provisions.

§ 29-1301.01. Short title.

This chapter may be cited as the "Benefit Corporation Act of 2012".

§ 29-1301.02. Definitions.

(a) For the purposes of this chapter, the term:

(1) "Benefit corporation" means a business corporation:

(A) That has elected to become subject to this chapter; and

(B) The status of which as a benefit corporation has not been terminated under § 29–1301.06.

(2) "Benefit director" means either:

(A) The director designated as the benefit director of a benefit corporation under § 29–1303.02; or

(B) A person with one or more of the powers, duties, or rights of a benefit director to the extent provided in the bylaws under § 29–1303.02.

(3) "Benefit enforcement proceeding" means any claim or action for:

(A) Failure of a benefit corporation to pursue or create general public benefit or a specific public benefit purpose set forth in its articles of incorporation; or

(B) A violation of any obligation, duty, or standard of conduct under this Chapter.

(4) "Benefit officer" means the individual designated as the benefit officer of a benefit corporation under § 29–1303.04.

(5) "General public benefit" means the material positive impact that the business and operations of a benefit corporation has on society and the environment, taken as a whole, assessed against a third–party standard.

(6) "Independent", subject to subsection (b) of this section, means having no material relationship with a benefit corporation or a subsidiary of the benefit corporation. A person who serves as a benefit director or benefit officer is not independent by virtue of such service. A material relationship between a person and a benefit corporation or any of its subsidiaries will be conclusively presumed to exist if any of the following apply:

(A) The person is, or has been within the last 3 years, an employee other than a benefit officer of the benefit corporation or a subsidiary of the benefit corporation.

第 29–1303.02 条　公共利益董事
第 29–1303.03 条　高管行为标准
第 29–1303.04 条　公共利益高管
第 29–1303.05 条　诉讼权利
第四节　透明度
第 29–1304.01 条　年度公共利益报告

第一节　初步条款

第 29–1301.01 条　简称

本法案可被称为《2012 年公共利益公司法》。

第 29–1301.02 条　定义

（a）本章中使用的概念的含义如下：

（1）“公共利益公司”是指满足以下条件的商事公司；

（A）选择接受本章规定调整；并且

（B）依据第 29–1301.06 条的规定，公共利益公司形态并未终止。

（2）“公共利益董事”是指：

（A）公共利益公司依据第 29–1303.02 条的规定设立的董事；或者

（B）拥有依据第 29–1303.02 条的规定所设章程中规定的一项或多项公共利益董事的权力、权利或义务的董事。

（3）“公共利益实施程序”是指因以下行为产生的任何主张或诉讼：

（A）公共利益公司未追求或实现公司章程所规定的一般或特定公共利益目的；或者

（B）公共利益公司违反本章规定下的任何义务、责任或行为标准。

（4）“公共利益高管”是指公共利益公司依据第 29–1303.04 条的规定设立的高管。

（5）“一般公共利益”是指根据第三方标准，公司的业务和经营在整体上对社会和环境产生的实质性积极影响。

（6）“独立”是指依照本条第 b 款规定，与公共利益公司或其子公司没有实质性的关系。个体担任公共利益董事或公共利益高管并不当然丧失独立性。存在以下情形，则认为该个体与公共利益公司或其子公司存在实质性的关系：

（A）该个体是，或在过去的 3 年内是，公共利益公司或其子公司的除公共利益高管外的雇员。

(B) An immediate family member of the person is, or has been within the last 3 years, an executive officer other than a benefit officer of the benefit corporation or its subsidiary.

(C) There is beneficial or record ownership of 5% or more of the outstanding shares of the benefit corporation by:

(i) The person; or

(ii) An entity of which the person is a director, an officer, or a manager or in which the person owns beneficially or of record 5% or more of the outstanding equity interests.

(7) "Minimum status vote" means:

(A) In the case of a business corporation, in addition to any other required approval or vote, the satisfaction of the following conditions:

(i) The shareholders of every class or series shall be entitled to vote as a separate voting group on the corporate action regardless of a limitation stated in the articles of incorporation or bylaws on the voting rights of any class or series.

(ii) The corporate action must be approved by vote of the shareholders of each voting group entitled to cast at least 2/3 of the votes that all shareholders of the voting group are entitled to cast on the action.

(B) In the case of an entity other than a business corporation, in addition to any other required approval, vote, or consent, the satisfaction of the following conditions:

(i) The holders of each class or series of equity interest in the entity that are entitled to receive a distribution of any kind from the entity shall be entitled as a separate voting group to vote on or consent to the action regardless of any otherwise applicable limitation on the voting or consent rights of any class or series.

(ii) The action must be approved by vote or consent of each voting group described in sub–subparagraph (i) of this subparagraph entitled to cast at least 2/3 of the votes or consents that all the members of the group are entitled to cast on the action.

(8) "Specific public benefit" includes:

(A) Providing low–income or underserved individuals or communities with beneficial products or services;

(B) Promoting economic opportunity for individuals or communities beyond the creation of jobs in the normal course of business;

(C) Preserving the environment;

(D) Improving human health;

(E) Promoting the arts, sciences, or advancement of knowledge;

(F) Increasing the flow of capital to entities with a public benefit purpose;and

(G) The accomplishment of any other particular benefit on society or the environment.

(9) "Subsidiary" means, subject to subsection (b) of this section, in relation to a person, an entity in which the person owns beneficially or of record 50% or more of the outstanding

（B）该个体的直系亲属是，或在过去的 3 年内是，公共利益公司或其子公司的除公共利益高管外的执行高管。

（C）下述持有公共利益公司 5% 以上已发行股份的登记股东或实际受益人：

（i）个人；或者

（ii）实体。其中，该个人是该实体的董事、高管或经理，或是该实体中持有公共利益公司 5% 以上已发行股份的登记股东或实际受益人。

（7）"最低表决要求"是指：

（A）在商事公司中，除其他批准或表决的要求外，表决还应满足以下条件：

（i）每一类别或系列的股东应当有权作为一个独立的投票团体对公司行为进行投票，无论公司章程或章程细则是否对某一类别或系列的投票权作出了限制。

（ii）公司行为必须获得每个类别或系列有投票权的所有股东的至少 2/3 的赞成票才能通过。

（B）非商事公司的实体，除其他批准、表决或赞成的要求外，其表决还应满足以下条件：

（i）该实体的每一类别或系列的任何权益分配形式下的股权持有者有权对公司行为进行投票，即使存在对该类别或系列的投票权的限制。

（ii）公司行为必须获得第 i 目规定的每个类别有投票权的所有股权持有者的至少 2/3 的赞成票才能通过。

（8）"特定公共利益"包括：

（A）向低收入、低福利人群或社区提供有益的产品或服务；

（B）在正常的业务过程中向个人或社区提供除创造就业外的经济机会；

（C）保护环境；

（D）改善人类健康；

（E）促进艺术、科学或知识进步；

（F）促进资本流向拥有有利于社会或环境目标的实体；以及

（G）给予社会或环境其他特别的利益。

（9）"子公司"是指，受本条第 b 款规定调整的，50% 以上已发行的股份的受益所有权或登记所有权被另一实体所拥有的实体。

equity interests.

(10) "Third–party standard" means a recognized standard for defining, reporting, and assessing corporate social and environmental performance that is:

(A) Comprehensive in that it assesses the effect of the business and its operations upon the interests listed in § 29–1303.01(a)(1)(B), (C), (D), and (E);

(B) Developed by an organization that is independent of the benefit corporation and satisfies the following requirements:

(i) Not more than 1/3 of the members of the governing body of the organization are representatives of any of the following:

(I) An association of businesses operating in a specific industry the performance of whose members is measured by the third–party standard;

(II) Businesses from a specific industry or an association of businesses in that industry; or

(III) Businesses whose performance is assessed against the standard.

(ii) The organization is not materially financed by an association or business described in sub–subparagraph (i) of this subparagraph;

(C) Credible because the standard is developed by a person that both:

(i) Has access to necessary expertise to assess overall corporate social and environmental performance; and

(ii) Uses a balanced multi–stakeholder approach, including a public comment period of at least 30 days to develop the standard; and

(D) Transparent because the following information is publicly available:

(i) About the standard:

(I) The criteria considered when measuring the overall social and environmental performance of a business; and

(II) The relative weightings of those criteria; and

(ii) About the development and revision of the standard:

(I) The identity of the directors, officers, material owners, and the governing body of the organization that developed and controls revisions to the standard;

(II) The process by which revisions to the standard and changes to the membership of the governing body are made; and

(III) An accounting of the sources of financial support for the organization, with sufficient detail to disclose any relationships that could reasonably be considered to present a potential conflict of interest.

(b) For purposes of the definitions of the terms "independent" and "subsidiary" in subsection (a) of this section, a percentage of ownership in an entity shall be calculated as if all outstanding rights to acquire equity interests in the entity have been exercised.

（10）“第三方标准”是指用于定义、报告和评估公司社会和环境绩效的标准，其应满足以下条件：

（A）综合，根据第 29-1303.01 条第（a）（1）（B）、（C）、（D）和（E）分项中所列利益评估公司业务和经营绩效；

（B）独立，其经独立于公共利益公司的第三方实体制定，并满足如下条件：

（i）该实体的管理团队中不超过 1/3 的组成人员属以下情形：

（Ⅰ）特定行业经营的商业协会的组成人员，其绩效评价采用该第三方标准；

（Ⅱ）特定行业或该行业商业协会内的人员；或者

（Ⅲ）依据标准评价商业绩效。

（ii）该组织并非由本项第（i）目规定的企业或协会所实质资助。

（C）可信，该标准由满足以下条件的第三方实体制定：

（i）拥有评估公司社会和环境综合绩效所需的专业知识；并且

（ii）使用平衡的多方相关者利益的方法制定标准，包括设定至少 30 日的合理期间以听取公众意见；以及

（D）透明，以下信息可公开获取：

（i）有关标准的内容：

（Ⅰ）衡量企业整体社会和环境绩效时所考虑的指标；以及

（Ⅱ）这些指标的相关权重；以及

（ii）关于标准的制定和修改：

（Ⅰ）制定、控制修改程序的董事、高管、主要股东和该实体的控制人员的身份；

（Ⅱ）标准修改和控制人员变动的程序；以及

（Ⅲ）资金来源的核算，包括充分披露合理认知下存在利益冲突的所有细节。

（b）为实现本条第（a）款中“独立”和“子公司”所包含的目的，在计算实体中所有者权益的比例时，所有购股权都应被视为已行使。

§ 29-1301.03. Applicability; construction.

(a) This chapter shall be applicable to all benefit corporations.

(b) This chapter shall not affect a statute or rule of law that is applicable to a business corporation that is not a benefit corporation, and shall not in and of itself create an implication that a contrary or different rule is applicable to a business corporation and not a benefit corporation.

(c) Except as otherwise provided in this chapter, Chapters 1, 2, and 3 of this title shall apply to a benefit corporation organized under this chapter. A benefit corporation may simultaneously be subject to this chapter and one or more other chapters of this title.

(d) A provision of the articles of incorporation or bylaws of a benefit corporation may not relax, be inconsistent with, or supersede a provision of this chapter.

§ 29-1301.04. Formation of benefit corporations.

A benefit corporation must be formed in accordance with Chapter 3 of this title, but its articles of incorporation must also state that it is a benefit corporation.

§ 29-1301.05. Election of status.

(a) An existing business corporation may become a benefit corporation under this chapter by amending its articles of incorporation so that they contain, in addition to the requirements of § 29–308.01, a statement that the corporation is a benefit corporation. To be effective, the amendment must be adopted by at least the minimum status vote.

(b)(1) This subsection applies if all of the following apply:

(A) An entity that is not a benefit corporation is:

(i) A party to a merger or consolidation; or

(ii) The exchanging entity in a share exchange; and

(B) The surviving, new, or resulting entity in the merger, consolidation, or share exchange is to be a benefit corporation.

(2) To be effective, a plan of merger, consolidation or share exchange subject to this subsection must be adopted by at least the minimum status vote.

§ 29-1301.06. Termination of status.

(a) A benefit corporation may terminate its status as a benefit corporation and cease to be subject to this chapter by amending its articles of incorporation and deleting the provision required by § 29–1301.05. To be effective, the amendment must be adopted by at least the minimum status vote.

(b) If a plan would have the effect of terminating the status of a business corporation as a benefit corporation, to be effective, the plan must be adopted by at least the minimum

第 29–1301.03 条　适用和解释

（a）本章条款适用于公共利益公司；

（b）本章条款不影响非公共利益公司有关条文和规则的适用。本章条款不应为非公共利益公司设定相反或不同的规则。

（c）除本章另有规定外，第 1、2、3 章的规则仍适用于依本章规定设立的公共利益公司。公共利益公司同时受本章及其他章节规定的调整。

（d）公共利益公司章程及章程细则不得放宽、违背或取代本章条款的规定。

第 29–1301.04 条　公共利益公司的设立

公共利益公司须依第 3 章的规定设立，公司章程必须声明其是公共利益公司。

第 29–1301.05 条　公共利益公司形态的选择

（a）已设立的公司可通过修改章程转换为公共利益公司，除满足第 29–308.01 条的要求外，还应在章程中作出该公司为公共利益公司的声明。公司章程的修改满足最低表决要求才能生效。

（b）（1）满足以下全部条件，也可成为公共利益公司：

（A）非公共利益公司被公共利益公司：

（i）兼并或合并；或者

（ii）置换股权；并且

（B）兼并、合并、置换股权后存续的公司或新公司为公共利益公司。

（2）此等兼并、合并、股权置换的计划必须满足最低表决要求才能生效。

第 29–1301.06 条　公共利益公司形态的终止

（a）公共利益公司可以通过删除依据第 29–1301.05 条规定设立的公司章程中其作为公共利益公司的声明条款来终止其公共利益公司形态，不再受本章规定的调整。公司章程的修改应满足最低表决要求才能生效。

（b）如果计划会导致公共利益公司形态终止，该计划应当满足最低表决要求才能生效。除该交易属于正常商业往来外，公共利益公司的任何出售、出租、交换

status vote. Any sale, lease, exchange, or other disposition of all or substantially all of the assets of a benefit corporation, unless the transaction is in the usual and regular course of business, shall not be effective unless the transaction is approved by at least the minimum status vote.

Subchapter II. Corporate Purposes.

§ 29-1302.01. Corporate purposes.

(a) A benefit corporation shall have a purpose of creating general public benefit. This purpose is in addition to its purpose under § 29–303.01.

(b) The articles of incorporation of a benefit corporation may identify one or more specific public benefits that it is the purpose of the benefit corporation to create in addition to its purposes under § 29–303.01 and subsection (a) of this section. The identification of a specific public benefit under this subsection does not limit the obligation of a benefit corporation under subsection (a) of this section.

(c) The creation of general public benefit and specific public benefit under subsections(a) and (b) of this section is in the best interests of the benefit corporation.

(d) A benefit corporation may amend its articles of incorporation to add, amend, or delete the identification of a specific public benefit for that benefit corporation. To be effective, the amendment must be adopted by at least the minimum status vote.

(e) A professional corporation that is a benefit corporation does not violate § 29–505 by having its purpose be to create general public benefit or a specific public benefit.

Subchapter III. Accountability.

§ 29-1303.01. Standard of conduct for directors.

(a) In discharging the duties of their respective positions and in considering the best interests of the benefit corporation, the board of directors, committees of the board, and individual directors of a benefit corporation:

(1) Shall consider the effects of any action upon:

(A) The shareholders of the benefit corporation;

(B) The employees and work force of the benefit corporation, its subsidiaries, and its suppliers;

(C) The interests of customers as beneficiaries of the general public benefit or specific public benefit purposes of the benefit corporation;

(D) Community and societal factors, including those of each community in which offices or facilities of the benefit corporation, its subsidiaries, or its suppliers are located;

(E) The local and global environment;

(F) The short–term and long–term interests of the benefit corporation, including benefits

或者其他处置全部或主要财产的行为，须满足最低表决要求才能生效。

第二节　公司目的

第 29–1302.01 条　公司目的

（a）公共利益公司应当依据第 29–303.01 条的规定创设一般公共利益目的。该目的在第 29–303.01 条所规定的目的之外。

（b）设立公共利益公司时，除第 29–303.01 条和本条第（a）款所规定的目的外，公司章程可设定一项或多项特定公共利益目的。依据本款规定设定的特定公共利益目的并不限制公共利益公司在本条第（a）款规定下设定的义务。

（c）依据本条第（a）款和第（b）款规定设定的一般和特定公共利益目的为公共利益公司的最佳利益。

（d）公共利益公司可以增加、修改或删除公司章程中设定的特定公共利益目的。公司章程的修改须满足最低表决要求才能生效。

（e）选择公共利益形态的专业公司并不因其有创设一般和特定公共利益的目的而违反第 29–505 条的规定。

第三节　公司责任

第 29–1303.01 条　董事行为标准

（a）在履行各自职责和考虑公共利益公司最佳利益的同时，公共利益公司的董事会、董事委员会和董事：

（1）应当考虑其行为对以下对象的影响：

（A）公共利益公司的股东；

（B）公共利益公司、其子公司和其供应商的雇员；

（C）作为公共利益公司一般或特定公共利益受益者的消费者的利益；

（D）社区和社会因素，包括公共利益公司及其子公司或其供应商的办公地或设施所在地的社区；

（E）当地和全球环境；

（F）公共利益公司的短期和长期利益，包括可能从其长期计划中产生的利益，

that may accrue to the benefit corporation from its long–term plans and the possibility that these interests may be best served by the continued independence of the benefit corporation; and

(G) The ability of the benefit corporation to accomplish its general public benefit purpose and any specific public benefit purpose;

(2) May consider other pertinent factors or the interests of any other group that they deem appropriate; and

(3) Need not give priority to the interests of a particular person or group referenced in paragraph (1) or (2) of this subsection over the interests of any other person or group, unless the benefit corporation has stated in its articles of incorporation its intention to give priority to certain interests related to its accomplishment of its general public benefit purpose or of a specific public benefit purpose identified in its articles of incorporation.

(b) The consideration of interests and factors in the manner required by subsection (a) of this section does not constitute a violation of § 29–306.30.

(c) A director is not personally liable for monetary damages for:

(1) Any action taken as a director if the director performed the duties of office in compliance with § 29–306.30 and this section; or

(2) Failure of the benefit corporation to create general public benefit or specific public benefit.

(d) A director does not have a duty to a person that is a beneficiary of the general public benefit purpose or a specific public benefit purpose of a benefit corporation arising from the status of the person as a beneficiary.

§ 29-1303.02. Benefit director.

(a) The board of directors of a benefit corporation shall include one director, who:

(1) Shall be designated the benefit director; and

(2) Shall have, in addition to the powers, duties, rights, and immunities of the other directors of the benefit corporation, the powers, duties, rights, and immunities provided in this subchapter.

(b) The benefit director shall be elected, and may be removed, in the manner provided by subchapter VI of Chapter 3 of this title, and shall be an individual who is independent. The benefit director may serve as the benefit officer at the same time as serving as the benefit director.The articles of incorporation or bylaws of a benefit corporation may prescribe additional qualifications of the benefit director not inconsistent with this section.

(c) The benefit director shall prepare, and the benefit corporation shall include in the annual benefit report to shareholders required by § 29–1304.01, the opinion of the benefit director on each of the following:

(1) Whether the benefit corporation acted in accordance with its general public benefit

以及公共利益公司继续保持独立可能产生的最佳利益；以及

（G）公共利益公司实现其一般和特定公共利益目的的能力；

（2）可考虑董事认为合适的其他相关因素或其他群体利益；并且

（3）公共利益公司的董事会、董事委员会和董事履行职务时不应将特定个人或群体的利益置于本款第（1）、（2）项所设定的公共利益之上，公司章程中规定为实现一般或特定公共利益目的而赋予特定个人或群体利益优先权的除外。

（b）对本条第（a）款规定中利益和相关因素的考虑不构成对第 29-306.30 条规定的违反。

（c）除公司章程或章程细则另有明确规定外，董事不对以下行为承担损害赔偿责任：

（1）其履行职责的行为符合第 29-306.30 条 和本条的规定；或者

（2）公共利益公司未能追求或实现一般或特定公共利益。

（d）董事不对公共利益公司一般或特定社会目的的受益人负责。

第 29-1303.02 条　公共利益董事

（a）公共利益公司的董事会，需包含满足以下要求的董事：

（1）被任命为公共利益董事；并且

（2）除有公共利益公司其他董事的权力、义务、权利和豁免权外，还有本节规定的权力、义务、权利和豁免权。

（b）公共利益董事应当依据本法第 3 章第 5 节的规定进行任免。公共利益董事应当是独立的个体，其可同时担任公共利益高管。公共利益公司章程或章程细则可对本条未规定的公共利益董事的资格予以明确。

（c）公共利益董事应当编写其对以下事项的意见，公共利益公司应当根据第 29-1304.01 条的规定将其附于年度公共利益报告中供股东查阅：

（1）在报告所述时间内，公共利益公司是否在所有重要事项上依一般和特定

purpose and any specific public benefit purpose in all material respects during the period covered by the report; and

(2) Whether the directors and officers complied with §§ 29–1303.01(a) and 29–1303.03(a), respectively.

(3) If, in the opinion of the benefit director, the benefit corporation or its directors or officers failed to comply with §§ 29–1303.01(a) and 29–1303.03(a), a description of the ways in which the benefit corporation or its directors or officers failed to comply.

(d) The acts of an individual in the capacity of a benefit director shall constitute for all purposes acts of that individual in the capacity of a director of the benefit corporation.

(e)(1) If an agreement among the shareholders of a benefit corporation under § 29–305.42 provides that the powers and duties conferred or imposed upon the board of directors shall be exercised or performed by a person other than the directors, the bylaws of a benefit corporation must provide that the persons or shareholders who perform the duties of the board of directors include a person with the powers, duties, rights, and immunities of a benefit director.

(2) A person that exercises one or more of the powers, duties or rights of a benefit director under this subsection:

(A) Does not need to be independent of the benefit corporation;

(B) Shall have the immunities of a benefit director;

(C) May share the powers, duties, and rights of a benefit director with one or more other persons; and

(D) Shall not be subject to the procedures for election or removal of directors in § 29–306 unless:

(i) The person is also a director of the benefit corporation; or

(ii) The bylaws make those procedures applicable.

(f) Regardless of whether the articles of incorporation of a benefit corporation include a provision eliminating or limiting the personal liability of directors authorized by § 29–302.02(b)(4), a benefit director shall not be personally liable for any action taken, or any failure to take any action, as a director, except liability for:

(1) The amount of a financial benefit received by a director to which the director is not entitled;

(2) An intentional infliction of harm on the corporation or the shareholders;

(3) A violation of § 29–306.32; or

(4) A violation of criminal law.

§ 29-1303.03. Standard of conduct for officers.

(a) Each officer of a benefit corporation shall consider the interests and factors described and in the manner provided in § 29–1303.01(a) if:

公共利益目的行事；以及

（2）董事和高管是否分别依据第 29-1303.01（a）款和第 29-1303.03（a）款的规定行事。

（3）如果公共利益董事认为公共利益公司或其董事、高管未能依第 29-1303.01（a）款和第 29-1303.03（a）款的要求行事，应陈述公共利益公司或其董事、高管未能履行责任的情况。

（d）公共利益董事在职权范围内的个人行为应视为公共利益公司董事的行为。

（e）（1）如果股东协议依据第 29-305.42 条的规定，指定由不限于董事的特定人员拥有董事会的权利义务，则章程细则须载明有该等权力、权利、义务和豁免权的人员或股东必须包括一名公共利益董事；

（2）有本款规定的一项或多项公共利益董事权力、权利和义务的个人：

（A）不需独立于公共利益公司；

（B）应享有公共利益董事的豁免权；

（C）可与他人共同享有或负担该等权力、权利和义务；

（D）不作为依据第 29-306 条规定任免的对象，除非：

（i）其同时为公共利益公司的董事；或者

（ii）章程细则对此作出特别规定。

（f）无论公共利益公司章程或章程细则是否依据第 29-302.02（b）（4）项的规定删除或限制董事的个人责任，公共利益董事在行使公共利益董事职责时不对其任何作为或不作为承担个人责任，以下情形除外：

（1）获取经济利益的董事不具备相应资格；

（2）故意伤害公司和股东利益；

（3）构成对第 29-306.32 条规定的违反；或者

（4）违反刑事法律。

第 29-1303.03 条　高管行为标准

（a）公共利益公司的高管应考虑第 29-1303.01（a）款所规定的利益和因素，如果：

(1) The officer has discretion to act with respect to a matter; and

(2) It is reasonably apparent to the officer that the matter may have a material effect on the creation of general public benefit or a specific public benefit identified in the articles of incorporation of the benefit corporation.

(b) The consideration of interests and factors as provided by subsection (a) of this section shall not constitute a violation of § 29–306.42.

(c) An officer is not personally liable for monetary damages for:

(1) Action taken as an officer if the officer performed the duties of the position in compliance with § 29–306.42 and this section; or

(2) Failure of the benefit corporation to pursue or create general public benefit or specific public benefit.

(d) An officer does not have a duty to a beneficiary of the general public benefit purpose or a specific public benefit purpose of a benefit corporation arising from the beneficiary's status.

§ 29-1303.04. Benefit officer.

(a) A benefit corporation may designate a benefit officer.

(b) A benefit officer shall have:

(1) The powers and duties relating to the purpose of the corporation to create general public benefit or specific public benefit provided:

(A) By the bylaws; or

(B) Absent controlling provisions in the bylaws, by resolutions or orders of the board of directors; and

(2) The duty to prepare the benefit report required by § 29–1304.01.

§ 29-1303.05. Right of action.

(a) Except in a benefit enforcement proceeding, no person may bring an action or assert a claim against a benefit corporation or its directors or officers with respect to:

(1) Failure to pursue or create general public benefit or a specific public benefit set forth in its articles of incorporation; or

(2) Violation of a duty or standard of conduct under this chapter.

(b) A benefit corporation shall not be liable for monetary damages under this chapter for any failure of the benefit corporation to pursue or create general public benefit or a specific public benefit.

(c) A benefit enforcement proceeding may be commenced or maintained only:

(1) Directly by the benefit corporation; or

(2) Derivatively by:

(A) A shareholder;

(B) A director;

（1）高管就该行为有自由裁量权；并且

（2）高管有合理理由认为该行为对公共利益公司在章程中创设的一般或特定公共利益目标有实质性影响。

（b）对本条第（a）款中利益和相关因素的考虑不构成对第 29-306.42 条规定的违反。

（c）高管不对以下行为承担损害赔偿责任：

（1）高管依据第 29-306.42 条以及本条的规定履行高管责任的行为；或者

（2）公共利益公司未能追求或实现一般或特定公共利益。

（d）高管不对公共利益公司一般或特定社会公共利益目的的受益人负责。

第 29-1303.04 条　公共利益高管

（a）公共利益公司可以任命公共利益高管。

（b）公共利益高管应当拥有：

（1）规定于以下文件的实现一般或特定公共利益的公司目的的权力和义务：

（A）公司章程细则；或者

（B）在公司章程细则中没有规定时，董事会决议或者命令；以及

（2）按照第 29-1304.01 条的要求编写公共利益报告。

第 29-1303.05 条　诉讼权利

（a）非经公共利益实施程序，任何人不得因以下事项向公共利益公司或者其董事、高管提起诉讼或主张：

（1）未能追求或实现在其公司章程中设定的一般或特定公共利益；或者

（2）违反本章规定下的责任或行为标准。

（b）公共利益公司不对本章规定下任何未能追求或实现一般或特定公共利益的事项承担损害赔偿责任。

（c）下列情形中，只有以下主体可提起公共利益实施程序：

（1）由公共利益公司直接提起；或者

（2）由以下主体派生提起：

（A）股东；

（B）董事；

(C) A person or group of persons that owns beneficially or of record 5% or more of the equity interests in an entity of which the benefit corporation is a subsidiary; or

(D) Other persons as specified in the articles of incorporation or bylaws of the benefit corporation.

Subchapter IV. Transparency

§ 29-1304.01. Annual benefit report.

(a) A benefit corporation shall prepare an annual benefit report including all of the following:

(1) A narrative description of:

(A) The process and rationale for selecting the third–party standard used to prepare the benefit report;

(B) The ways in which the benefit corporation pursued general public benefit during the year and the extent to which general public benefit was created;

(C)(i) The ways in which the benefit corporation pursued a specific public benefit that the articles of incorporation state it is the purpose of the benefit corporation to create; and

(ii) The extent to which that specific public benefit was created;and

(D) Any circumstances that have hindered the pursuit or creation of the general public benefit purpose and any specific public benefit purpose.

(2) An assessment of the overall social and environmental performance of the benefit corporation against a third–party standard:

(A) Applied consistently with the application of that standard in prior benefit reports; or

(B) If the third–party standard was not applied consistently, an explanation of the reasons for any inconsistent application.

(3) The name of the benefit director and the benefit officer, if any, and the address to which correspondence to each of them may be directed.

(4) The compensation paid by the benefit corporation during the year to each director in the capacity of a director.

(5) The name of each person that owns 5% or more of the outstanding shares of the benefit corporation either:

(A) Beneficially, to the extent known to the benefit corporation without independent investigation; or

(B) Of record.

(6) The statement of the benefit director described in § 29–1303.02(c).

(7) A statement of any connection between the organization that established the third–party standard, or its directors, officers, or material owners, and the benefit corporation or its directors, officers, or material shareholders, including any financial or governance relationship

（C）作为持有公共利益公司母公司 5% 以上已发行股份的登记股东或实际受益人的个人或团体；或者

（D）公共利益公司章程或章程细则中规定的其他人员。

第四节 透明度

第 29-1304.01 条 年度公益报告

（a）公共利益公司的年度公共利益报告应包括以下内容：

（1）对以下事项的说明：

（A）选择第三方标准的程序和合理性；

（B）公共利益公司本年度追求一般公共利益的方法和一般公共利益的实现情况；

（C）（i）公共利益公司追求公司章程规定的特定公共利益的方法；以及

（ii）该特定公共利益的实现情况；以及

（D）阻碍公共利益公司实现一般或特定公共利益的情形。

（2）依据第三方标准，对公共利益公司整体社会和环境表现作出的评价：

（A）沿用先前公共利益报告中使用的标准；或者

（B）如果之前的第三方标准不再适用，附一份解释说明原因。

（3）公共利益董事和公共利益高管的姓名及联系地址（如有）。

（4）公共利益公司在上一年度支付给每位董事的薪酬。

（5）公共利益公司 5% 以上已发行股份持有人的姓名，其：

（A）未经独立审计的情况下，被公司视为实益股东；或者

（B）为登记股东。

（6）公共利益董事依第 29-1303.02（c）款的规定应编写的陈述报告。

（7）设立第三方标准的组织及其董事、高管或主要股东与公共利益公司及其董事、高管或主要股东之间关系的声明，包括任何可能影响第三方标准可信度的实质关系。

which might materially affect the credibility of the use of the third–party standard.

(8) If the benefit corporation has dispensed with or restricted the discretion or powers of the board of directors, a description of:

(A) The persons that exercise the powers, duties, and rights and have the immunities of the board of directors; and

(B) The person with the powers, duties, and rights of a benefit director if required by § 29–1303.02(e).

(b) A benefit corporation shall annually send a benefit report to each shareholder:

(1) Within 120 days following the end of the fiscal year of the benefit corporation; or

(2) At the same time that the benefit corporation delivers any other annual report to its shareholders.

(c) A benefit corporation shall post all of its benefit reports on the public portion of its website, if any, but the compensation paid to directors and financial or proprietary information included in the benefit reports may be omitted from the benefit reports as posted.

(d) If a benefit corporation does not have a website, the benefit corporation shall provide a copy of its most recent benefit report, without charge, to any person that requests a copy.

(e) The benefit corporation shall deliver a copy of the benefit report to the Mayor for filing when filing the biennial report required by § 29–102.11, but the compensation paid to directors and financial or proprietary information included in the benefit report may be omitted from the copy of the benefit report that is delivered to the Mayor.

（8）如果公共利益公司免除或限制董事会的自由裁量权，需对以下情形进行说明：

（A）行使董事会权力、权利和豁免权，履行义务的个人；

（B）依照第 29-1303.02（e）款的要求，享有和负担公共利益董事权力、权利和义务的个人。

（b）公共利益公司应当在以下时间内将公共利益报告送交各股东：

（1）公共利益公司会计年度结束后 120 天内；或者

（2）公共利益公司向其股东送交其他年度报告的同一时间。

（c）若条件允许，公共利益公司应当将其所有公共利益报告发布于其网站公共部分；但可将公共利益报告中的董事薪酬和财务、所有权信息删除。

（d）如果公共利益公司没有网站，应向所有索取报告的个人免费提供最新报告的副本。

（e）公司应当依第 29-102.11 条的要求将公共利益报告的副本提交相关机构备案，但可将报告中的董事薪酬和财务、所有权信息在提交的报告中删除。

THE STATE OF WEST VIRGINIA

Senate Bill No.202

(By Senator Unger)

[Passed March 7 ,2014;to take effect July 1,2014]

An ACT amend the Code of West Virginia, 1931, as amended, by adding thereto a new chapter, designated §31F–1–101, §31F–1–102, §31F–1–103, §31F–2–201, §31F–2–202, §31F–2–203, §31F–3–301, §31F–4–401, §31F–4–402, §31F–4–403 and §31F–5–501, all relating to authorizing a corporation to elect to be a benefit corporation ; authorizing a corporation to amend its articles of incorporation to include a statement that the corporation is a benefit corporation ; authorizing a corporation to terminate status as a benefit corporation; authorizing the articles of a benefit corporation to identify as one of the purposes of the benefit corporation the creation of specific public benefits ; establishing that a director shall not have a duty to a certain person ; providing that a director shall have immunity from liability under certain circumstances ; requiring a benefit corporation to deliver to each stockholder an annual report ; defining terms ; and generally relating to benefit corporations.

Chapter 31F West Virginia Benefit Corporation Act

ARTICLE 1. GENERAL PROVISIONS

§31F-1-101. Short title.

This chapter is and may be cited as the West Virginia Benefit Corporation Act.

§31F-1-102 Definitions.

As used in this article:

(a) "Benefit corporation" means a corporation organized pursuant to the provisions of

西弗吉尼亚州

参议院第 202 号法案

（参议员昂格尔）

［2014 年 3 月 7 日通过；2014 年 7 月 1 日生效］

经由西弗吉尼亚州立法，1931 年的《西弗吉尼亚州公司法》增加新的一章，包括第 31F–1–101 条，第 31F–1–102 条，第 31F–1–103 条，第 31F–2–201 条，第 31F–2–202 条，第 31F–2–203 条，第 31F–3–301 条，第 31F–4–401 条，第 31F–4–402 条，第 31F–4–403 条和第 31F–5–501 条等条款，其内容如下：授权公司自行选择成为公共利益公司；授权公司修改其章程，在章程中声明其为公共利益公司；授权公司终止其公共利益公司形态；授权公共利益公司在其章程内规定特定公共利益；明确公共利益公司的董事不对特定的个人负责；明确公共利益公司董事在特定条件下的法律责任豁免；规定了公共利益公司向各股东送交年度报告的义务；规定了相关用语的概念；并规定了有关公共利益公司的其他一般性事项。

第 31F 章　西弗吉尼亚州公共利益公司法

第一节　一般规定

第 31F–1–101 条　简称

本章标题为《西弗吉尼亚公共利益公司法》。

第 31F–1–102 条　定义

本法中所使用的相关用语的定义如下：

（a）依据本章的规定，“公共利益公司”是指：

this chapter:

(1) That has elected to become subject to this article; and

(2) The status of which as a benefit corporation has not been terminated under section two hundred three [31F–2–203], article two of this chapter.

(b) "Benefit enforcement proceeding" means any claim or action brought directly by a benefit corporation, or derivatively on behalf of a benefit corporation, against a director or officer for: (i) Failure to pursue the general public benefit purpose of the benefit corporation or any specific public benefit purpose set forth in its articles of incorporation or bylaws or otherwise adopted by its board of directors; or (ii) a violation of a duty or standard of conduct under this article.

(c) "General public benefit" means a material positive impact on society and the environment taken as a whole, as measured by a third–party standard, from the business and operations of a benefit corporation.

(d) "Independent" means having no material relationship with a benefit corporation or a subsidiary of the benefit corporation, either directly as a shareholder of the benefit corporation or as a partner, a member or an owner of a subsidiary of the benefit corporation or indirectly as a director, an officer, an owner, or a manager of an entity that has a material relationship with the benefit corporation or a subsidiary of the benefit corporation. A material relationship between a person and a benefit corporation or any of its subsidiaries will be conclusively presumed to exist if:

(1) The person is, or has been within the last three years, an employee of the benefit corporation or a subsidiary of the benefit corporation;

(2) An immediate family member of the person is, or has been within the last three years, an executive officer of the benefit corporation or its subsidiary; or

(3) There is beneficial ownership of five percent or more of the outstanding shares of the benefit corporation by:

(A) The person; or

(B) An entity:

(i) Of which the person is a director, an officer or a manager; or

(ii) In which the person owns beneficially five percent or more of the outstanding equity interests, which percentage shall be calculated as if all outstanding rights to acquire equity interests in the entity had been exercised.

(e) "Specific public benefit" means a benefit that serves one or more public welfare, religious, charitable, scientific, literary or educational purposes, or other purpose or benefit beyond the strict interest of the shareholders of the benefit corporation, including:

(1) Providing low–income or underserved individuals or communities with beneficial products or services;

（1）选择接受本章规定调整；并且

（2）公共利益公司形态并未依照本章第 31F-2-203 条的规定终止。

（b）“公共利益实施程序”是指基于以下事由，由公共利益公司直接提起或代表公司利益派生提起的针对董事或高管的主张或诉求：（i）未能追求公司章程、章程细则或董事会设定的一般或特定公共利益目标；或者（ii）违反本法规定下的责任或行为标准。

（c）“一般公共利益”是指根据第三方标准，公司的业务和经营在整体上对社会和环境产生的实质性积极影响。

（d）“独立”是指与公共利益公司或其子公司没有实质关系，该实质关系的主体既包括与公共利益公司及其子公司有直接关系的公共利益公司的股东、合伙人、成员或子公司的所有人，也包括与之有间接关系的公共利益公司或其子公司的董事、高管、一般合伙人和经理。个人在公共利益公司或其子公司担任公共利益董事或高管不意味必然存在实质关系。存在以下情形的，认为个人与公共利益公司及其子公司存在实质性关系：

（1）该个体是，或在过去的 3 年间是，公共利益公司或其子公司的除公共利益高管外的雇员；

（2）该个体的直系亲属是，或在过去的 3 年间是，公共利益公司或其子公司的除公共利益高管外的执行高管；或者

（3）下述持有公共利益公司 5% 以上已发行股份的登记股东或实际受益人：

（A）个人；或者

（B）实体：

（i）该个人担任该实体的董事、高管或经理；或者

（ii）在所有购股权都被视为已行使的情况下，该实体中的个人为持有公共利益公司 5% 以上已发行股份的登记股东或实际受益人。

（e）“特定公共利益”是指一项或多项有益于公共福利、宗教、慈善、科学、文化或教育目的利益，或在公共利益公司股东直接利益之外的其他利益，包括：

（1）向低收入或者低福利人群或社区提供有益的产品或服务；

(2) Promoting economic opportunity for individuals or communities beyond the creation of jobs in the normal course of business;

(3) Preserving or improving the environment;

(4) Improving human health;

(5) Promoting the arts, sciences or advancement of knowledge;

(6) Increasing the flow of capital to entities with a public benefit purpose; and

(7) Conferring any other particular benefit on society or the environment.

(f) "Subsidiary" means, in relation to an individual, an entity in which the individual either: (i) Owns directly or indirectly equity interests entitled to cast a majority of the votes entitled to be cast generally in an election of directors or members of the governing body of the entity; or (ii) otherwise owns or controls voting or contractual power to exercise effective governing control of the entity. The percentage of ownership of equity interests or ownership or control of power to exercise control shall be calculated as if all outstanding rights to acquire equity interests in the entity had been exercised.

(g) "Third–party standard" means a recognized standard for defining, reporting, and assessing corporate social and environmental performance that:

(1) Is developed by a person that is independent of the benefit corporation; and

(2) Is transparent because the following information about the standard is publicly available:

(A) The factors considered when measuring the performance of a business;

(B) The relative weightings of those factors; and

(C) The identity of the persons that develop and control changes to the standard and the process by which those changes are made.

§31F-1-103 Construction of chapter.

(a) This chapter shall apply to all benefit corporations.

(b) The existence of a provision of this chapter does not of itself create an implication that a contrary or different rule of law applies to a corporation organized pursuant to the provisions of this code that is not a benefit corporation. This chapter does not affect a statute or rule of law that applies to a corporation that is not a benefit corporation.

(c) The specific provisions of this chapter control over the general provisions of other chapters of this code.

ARTICLE 2. INCORPORATION.

§31F-2-201 Formation of benefit corporations.

A benefit corporation shall be formed in accordance with article two [Ë 31D–2–201 et seq.], chapter thirty–one–d of this code, and its articles as initially filed with the Secretary of State or as amended, shall state that it is a benefit corporation.

（2）在正常的业务过程中向个人或社区提供除创造就业外的经济机会；

（3）保护或改善环境；

（4）改善人类健康；

（5）促进艺术、科学或知识进步；

（6）促进资本流向拥有有利于社会或环境目标的实体；以及

（7）给予社会或环境其他特别的利益。

（f）“子公司”是指符合下列条件的与个人或法人有关系的实体：在该实体中，某个体（i）直接或间接拥有可以使其在该法人董事或管理层选举中享有多数投票权的股权；或者（ii）在所有购股权被视为已行使的情况下，拥有或控制投票权或有订立合同的权力，实质控制该机构。

（g）“第三方标准”指的是用以定义、描述和评估公司的社会与环境绩效的标准，其应符合下列条件：

（1）由独立于公共利益企业的第三方制定；

（2）透明，因为以下信息可公开获取：

（A）衡量一项商业行为时所考虑的指标；

（B）这些指标的相关权重；

（C）制定、控制标准修改及其程序的人员身份。

第 31F-1-103 条　本章的适用

（a）本章适用于所有公共利益公司。

（b）本章条款不应为非公共利益公司设定相反或不同的规则，也不影响非公共利益公司有关条文和规则的适用。

（c）本章中的特别条款的效力优于其他章的一般条款。

第二节　法人组织

第 31F-2-201 条　公共利益公司的设立

公共利益公司依本法第 31D 章第二节［ Ė 31D-2-201 等］的规定设立，其公司章程拟定提交备案或修改时，均应载明其为公共利益公司。

§31F-2-202 Election of status after formation.

A corporation that was not formed as a benefit corporation may become a benefit corporation by amending its articles so that they contain, in addition to matters required by section two hundred two [31D–2–202], article two, chapter thirty–one–d of this code, a statement that the corporation is a benefit corporation. Any such amendment to the articles of incorporation shall be adopted in accordance with the procedures set forth in article ten [Ë 31D–10–1001 et seq.], chapter thirty–one–d of this code.

§31F-2-203 Termination of status.

A benefit corporation may terminate its status as such and cease to be subject to this chapter by amending its articles to delete the provision required by section two hundred one [31F–2–201] of this article to be set forth in the articles of incorporation, which amendment shall be adopted in accordance with the procedures set forth in article ten [Ë 31D–10–1001 et seq.], chapter thirty–one–d of this code.

ARTICLE 3. PURPOSES.

§31F-3-301 Corporate purposes.

(a) A benefit corporation shall have as one of its purposes the purpose of creating a general public benefit. The articles of incorporation of a benefit corporation may identify one or more specific public benefits that it is the purpose of the benefit corporation to create. A specific public benefit may also be specified in the bylaws or otherwise adopted by the board of directors. This purpose is in addition to its purpose under section three hundred two [31D–3–302], article three, chapter thirty–one–d of this code.

(b) The creation of a general public benefit and one or more specific public benefits, if any, under subsection (a) of this section is in the best interests of the benefit corporation.

(c) A benefit corporation may amend its articles of incorporation to add, amend or delete the identification of a specific public benefit that it is the purpose of the benefit corporation to create, which amendment shall be adopted in accordance with the procedures set forth in article ten [Ë 31D–10–1001 et seq.], chapter thirty–one–d of this code.

ARTICLE 4. DIRECTORS AND OFFICERS.

§31F-4-401 Standard of conduct for directors.

(a) Subject to article eight [Ë 31D–8–801 et seq.], chapter thirty–one–d of this code, in discharging the duties of their respective positions and in considering the best interests of the benefit corporation, the board of directors, committees of the board and individual directors of a benefit corporation:

(1) Shall consider the effects of any corporate action upon:

(A) The shareholders of the benefit corporation;

第 31F-2-202 条　公共利益公司形态的选择

已设立的非公共利益公司可通过修改公司章程的方式转换为公共利益公司，章程的修改除了符合本法第 31D 章第 2 节第 202 条［31D-2-202］的要求外，还需载明其为公共利益公司。任何上述修改都应符合第 31D 章第 10 节［Ë 31D-10-1001 等］的规定。

第 31F-2-203 条　公共利益公司形态的终止

公共利益公司可以通过删除依照本节第 201 条的规定设立的公司章程条款终止其公共利益公司形态，不再接受本章规定调整，上述章程的修改应符合本法第 31D 章第 10 节［Ë 31D-10-1001 等］规定的表决要求。

第三节　目的

第 31F-3-301 条　公司目的

（a）公共利益公司至少应设定一项一般公共利益目标。公共利益公司章程可规定一个或多个特定公共利益目标。特定公共利益亦可由章程细则规定或董事会拟定。该目的应符合本法第 31D 章第三节第 302 条［31D-3-302］的要求。

（b）根据本条第（a）款设立的一般或特定公共利益为公共利益公司的最佳利益。

（c）公共利益公司可通过修改公司章程增加、修改或删除某项特定公共利益目标，章程的修改应符合第 31D 章第 10 节［Ë 31D-10-1001 等］所规定的表决要求。

第四节　董事及高管

第 31F-4-401 条　董事行为标准

（a）在履行职责和考虑公共利益公司最佳利益时，公共利益公司的董事会、董事委员会和董事，应受第 31D 章第 8 节［Ë 31D-8-801 等］规定的约束。

（1）其履行职责，应当考虑对以下对象的影响：

（A）公共利益公司的股东；

(B) The employees and workforce of the benefit corporation, its subsidiaries, and suppliers;

(C) The interests of customers as beneficiaries of the general or specific public benefit purposes of the benefit corporation;

(D) Community and societal considerations, including those of each community in which offices or facilities of the benefit corporation, its subsidiaries, or suppliers are located;

(E) The local and global environment;

(F) The short–term and long–term interests of the benefit corporation, including benefits that may accrue to the benefit corporation from its long–term plans and the possibility that these interests and the general and specific public benefit purposes of the benefit corporation may be best served by the continued independence of the benefit corporation; and

(G) The ability of the benefit corporation to accomplish its general and any specific public benefit purpose;

(2) May consider:

(A) The resources; intent; and past, stated and potential conduct of any person seeking to acquire control of the benefit corporation; and

(B) Other pertinent factors or the interests of any other person that they deem appropriate; and

(3) Need not give priority to the interests of a particular person referred to in subdivisions (1) and (2) of this section over the interests of any other person unless the benefit corporation has stated its intention to give priority to interests related to a specific public benefit purpose identified in its articles.

(b) The consideration of interests and factors in the manner required by subsection (a) of this section does not constitute a violation of section eight hundred thirty [31D–8–830], article eight, chapter thirty–one–d of this code or a director conflict of interests under section eight hundred sixty [31D–8–860], article eight, chapter thirty–one–d of this code.

(c) In any proceeding brought by or in the right of a benefit corporation or brought by or on behalf of the shareholders of a benefit corporation, a director is not personally liable for monetary damages for:

(1) Any action taken as a director if the director performed the duties of office in compliance with section eight hundred thirty, article eight, chapter thirty–one–d of this code and this section; or

(2) Failure of the benefit corporation to create general public benefit or any specific public benefit specified in its articles of incorporation or bylaws or otherwise adopted by the board of directors.

（B）公共利益公司、其子公司和其供应商的雇员；

（C）作为公共利益公司一般或特定公共利益受益者的消费者的利益；

（D）社区和社会因素，包括公共利益公司、其子公司或其供应商的办公地或设施所在地的社区；
（E）当地和全球环境；
（F）公共利益公司的短期和长期利益，包括可能从其长期计划中产生的利益，以及公共利益公司继续保持独立可能产生的最佳利益；以及

（G）公共利益公司实现其一般和特定公共利益目标的能力；

（2）可以参考的其他因素：
（A）试图取得公共利益公司控制权的任何主体的资源、意图和行为，包括过去、现在、将来的行为。
（B）董事认为合适的其他因素或其他人的利益；以及

（3）除公司章程中为实现特定公共利益而赋予特定利益或因素优先权外，无须给予本条第（1）目及第（2）目中某个利益或因素优先权。

（b）考虑本条第（a）款所列的因素，不构成对第31D章第8节第830条［31D-8-830］规定的违反，也不认为存在第31D章第8节第860条［31D-8-860］下的利害冲突。

（c）在任何由公共利益公司提起的或有权提起的诉讼中，或在任何由公共利益公司股东提起的或代表该股东提起的诉讼中，董事不对以下行为承担损害赔偿责任：
（1）董事履行职责的行为符合31D章第8节第830条的规定；

（2）公共利益公司未能实现其公司章程或董事会设定的一般或特定公共利益。

§31F-4-402 Limitation upon liability of officers.

An officer of a benefit corporation has no liability for actions taken that the officer believes, in his or her good faith business judgment, are consistent with: (i) The general public benefit or specific public benefit specified in the articles of incorporation or bylaws or otherwise adopted by the board of directors; and (ii) the requirements of any third–party standard then in effect for the corporation.

§31F-4-403 Right of action.

(a) The duties of directors and officers under this chapter, the obligation of a benefit corporation to prepare and make available the annual benefit report required under section five hundred one [31F–5–501], article five of this chapter and the general and any specific public benefit purpose of a benefit corporation may be enforced only in a benefit enforcement proceeding. No person may bring an action or assert a claim against a benefit corporation or its directors or officers with respect to the duties of directors and officers under this article and the general and any specific public benefit purpose of the benefit corporation except in a benefit enforcement proceeding.

(b) A benefit enforcement proceeding may be commenced or maintained only:

(1) Directly by the benefit corporation; or

(2) Derivatively by:

(A) A shareholder of the benefit corporation;

(B) A director of the benefit corporation; or

(C) Other persons as specified in the articles of incorporation or bylaws of the benefit corporation.

ARTICLE 5. REPORT.

§31F-5-501 Annual benefit report.

(a) A benefit corporation shall prepare an annual benefit report that includes all of the following:

(1) A narrative description of:

(A) The ways in which the benefit corporation pursued the general public benefit during the year and the extent to which the general public benefit was created; and

(B) Both:

(i) The ways in which the benefit corporation pursued any specific public benefit that the articles of incorporation or bylaws, or other action taken by the board of directors, state it is the purpose of the benefit corporation to create; and

(ii) The extent to which that specific public benefit was created; and

(C) Any circumstances that have hindered the creation by the benefit corporation of the general or any specific public benefit;

第 31F-4-402 条　高管的责任限制

公共利益公司的高管在善意商业判断之下，对符合以下标准的行为，不承担个人责任：（i）符合公司章程、章程细则或董事会设定的一般或特殊公共利益目标；（ii）符合公司所采用的且在高管实施行为时有效的第三方标准。

第 31F-4-403 条　诉讼权利

（a）针对董事和高管在本章下的职责，公共利益公司依据本章第 5 节第 501 条规定制作和发布年度公共利益报告的义务的履行，以及任何一般和特定公共利益目标的实施，只能通过公共利益实施程序。非经公共利益实施程序，任何人不得就公司及其董事、高管在本章规定下的责任以及公共利益目标的实施提起诉讼或主张。

（b）公共利益实施程序只能由以下主体提起：

（1）由公共利益公司直接提起；或者

（2）被以下个体派生提起：

（A）公共利益公司的股东；或者

（B）公司董事；

（C）公共利益公司章程或章程细则中规定的其他人。

第五节　报告

第 31F-5-501 条　年度公共利益报告

（a）公共利益公司应编制包含如下内容的年度公共利益报告：

（1）对以下事项的说明：

（A）公共利益公司本年度追求一般或特定公共利益的方法和实现情况；以及

（B）同时包括：

（i）实现公共利益公司章程、章程细则或董事会的决议所规定的特殊公共利益的方式；

（ii）该特殊公共利益所实现的情况；以及

（C）阻碍实现一般或特定公共利益的情形；

(2) An assessment of the social and environmental performance of the benefit corporation. The assessment shall be:

(A) Prepared in accordance with a third-party standard specified in the articles of incorporation, the bylaws, or otherwise adopted by the board of directors and applied consistently with any application of that standard in prior benefit reports; or

(B) Accompanied by an explanation of the reasons for any inconsistent application; and

(3) Any other information or disclosures that may be required under any third-party standard adopted by the directors of the benefit corporation.

(b) The benefit report shall be made available annually to each shareholder of the benefit corporation:

(1) Within one hundred twenty days following the end of the fiscal year of the benefit corporation; or

(2) At the same time that the benefit corporation delivers any other annual report to its shareholders.

(c) A benefit corporation shall post its most recent benefit report on a publicly accessible portion of its Internet website, if any. If a benefit corporation does not have an Internet website, it shall make a written or electronic copy of its most recent benefit report available upon written request from any person. A benefit corporation is not required to publically disclose to persons other than its shareholders any proprietary, confidential, or individual compensation information contained in its benefit report to the extent that any third-party standard adopted by the directors of the benefit corporation permits the omission of such information from public disclosure.

（2）对公共利益公司的社会和环境表现作出的评价，该评价应：

（A）沿用先前公共利益报告所使用的第三方标准，该标准依照公司章程或章程细则选定，或由董事会选定；或者

（B）如果未能持续适用上述标准，还应说明原因；以及

（3）任何依据公共利益公司董事的决定采用的第三方标准所要求提供或披露的其他信息。

（b）公共利益公司应当每一年度在以下时限内将公共利益报告送交各股东：

（1）公共利益公司财政年度结束后 120 天；或者

（2）公共利益公司向其股东送交其他年度报告的同一时间。

（c）若条件允许，公共利益公司应当将其最新版的公共利益报告公布于其网站的公共部分；如果公共利益公司没有网站，其应在任何个人以书面方式索取报告副本时，向其免费提供最新报告的纸质版本或电子版本。公共利益公司可拒绝向股东以外的人披露公共利益报告中的个人薪酬、所有权和机密信息，依据第三方标准向公众披露时可将该类信息删除。

LOW-PROFIT LIMITED LIABILITY COMPANY ACT

微利有限责任公司法

THE STATE OF ILLINOIS

AN ACT concerning business.

Be it enacted by the People of the State of Illinois, represented in the General Assembly:

Section 5. The Limited Liability Company Act is amended by changing Sections 1–5, 1–10, and 15–5 and adding Section 1–26 as follows:

Sec. 1-5. Definitions.

As used in this Act, unless the context otherwise requires:

...

"L3C" or "low–profit limited liability company" means a for–profit limited liability company which satisfies the requirements of Section 1–26 of this Act and does not have as a significant purpose the production of income or the appreciation of property.

...

Sec. 1-10. Limited liability company name.

(a) The name of each limited liability company as set forth in its articles of organization: (1) shall contain the terms "limited liability company", "L.L.C.", or "LLC", or, if organized as a low–profit limited liability company under Section 1–26 of this Act, shall contain the term "L3C"; ...

Sec. 1-26. Low-profit limited liability company.

(a) A low–profit limited liability company shall at all times significantly further the accomplishment of one or more charitable or educational purposes within the meaning of Section 170(c)(2)(B) of the Internal Revenue Code of 1986, 26 U.S.C. 170(c)(2)(B), or its successor, and would not have been formed but for the relationship to the accomplishment of such charitable or educational purposes.

(b) A limited liability company which intends to qualify as a low–profit limited liability company pursuant to the provisions of this Section shall so indicate in its articles of organization, and further state that: (1) no significant purpose of the company is the production of income or the appreciation of property; however, the fact that a person produces significant income or capital appreciation shall not, in the absence of other factors,

伊利诺伊州

关于商业的法案。

由议会代表伊利诺伊州人民颁布：

第 5 部分　《有限责任公司法》通过修改第 1–5 条、第 1–10 条并增加第 1–26 条进行修订：

第 1–5 条　定义

除上下文另有要求外，在本法中：

……

“L3C”或者“微利有限责任公司”是指一个满足本法第 1–26 条的要求并且未将收入增长或财产增值作为主要目标的营利有限责任公司。

……

第 1–10 条　有限责任公司名称

（a）每个有限责任公司在公司章程中设定的名称：（1）应当包含“有限责任公司”，“L.L.C.”，或者“LLC”，或者，如果是依据本法第 1–26 条组建的微利有限责任公司应当包含 “L3C”的用语；……

第 1–26 条　微利有限责任公司

（a）微利有限责任公司应当始终积极促进，美国《1986 年国内税收法典》第 170（c）（2）（B）分项或后续法律规定下的，一项或多项慈善或教育目标的实现，非为实现那些慈善或教育目标，则微利有限责任公司不能成立。

（b）依据本条规定要成为微利有限责任公司的有限责任公司应当在其公司章程中表明，并进一步声明：（1）公司主要目标不是收入增加和财产增值；但是，在没有其他因素的情况下，创造大量收入或者资本增值不应作为认定其主要目标包括收入增加和财产增值的决定性证据；并且（2）公司目标不是实现美国《1986 年国内税收法典》第 170（c）（2）（D）分项或其后续法律规定下的，一项或者多项

be conclusive evidence of a significant purpose involving the production of income or the appreciation of property; and (2) no purpose of the company is to accomplish one or more political or legislative purposes within the meaning of Section 170(c)(2)(D) of the Internal Revenue Code of 1986, 26 U.S.C. 170(c)(2)(D), or its successor.

(c) A company that no longer satisfies the requirements of this Section 1–26 continues to exist as a limited liability company and shall promptly amend its articles of organization so that its name and purpose no longer identify it as a low–profit limited liability company or L3C.

(d) Any company operating or holding itself out as a low–profit limited liability company in Illinois, any company formed as a low–profit limited liability company under this Act, and any chief operating officer, director, or manager of any such company is a "trustee" as defined in Section 3 of the Charitable Trust Act.

(e) Nothing in this Section 1–26 prevents a limited liability company that is not organized under it from electing a charitable or educational purpose in whole or in part for doing business under this Act.

Sec. 15-5. Operating agreement.

...

(b) The operating agreement may not:

...

(6.5) eliminate or reduce the obligations or purposes a low–profit limited liability company undertakes when organized under Section 1–26; or

...

政治或者法律目标。

（c）不满足第 1–26 条规定要求的公司要继续作为有限责任公司存在，应当立即修改其公司章程，使其名称和目标不再包含表明其是微利有限责任公司或者 L3C 的词语。

（d）任何作为伊利诺伊州微利有限责任公司进行经营或宣传的公司，任何依据本法成为微利有限责任公司的公司，以及这些公司的主要经营管理人员、董事或经理是《慈善信托法》第 3 条定义的“受托人”。

（e）第 1–26 条不阻止非依其成立的有限责任公司依本法规定经营业务时选择一个慈善或者教育目标。

第 15–5 条　经营协议

……

（b）经营协议不得：

……

（6.5）消除或减少依据第 1–26 条规定组建的微利有限责任公司应承担的义务或实现的目标；或者

……

THE STATE OF LOUISIANA

Regular Session, 2010

HOUSE BILL NO. 1421

ACT No. 417

Be it enacted by the Legislature of Louisiana:

1031.Definitions

...

(21) "Low–profit limited liability company" or "L3C" means a limited liability company organized for the purposes set forth in R.S. 12:1302(C).

...

1032. Purpose

...

C.(1) A limited liability company organized as a low–profit limited liability company shall set forth in its articles of organization a business purpose that satisfies and which limited liability company is at all times operated to satisfy each of the following requirements:

(a) The entity significantly furthers the accomplishment of one or more charitable or educational purposes within the meaning of Section 170(c)(2)(B) of the Internal Revenue Code and would not have been formed but for the entity's relationship to the accomplishment of charitable or educational purposes.

(b) No significant purpose of the entity is the production of income or the appreciation of property provided; however, the fact that an entity produces significant income or capital appreciation shall not, in the absence of other factors, be conclusive evidence of a significant purpose involving the production of income or the appreciation of property.

(c) No purpose of the entity is to accomplish one or more political or legislative purposes within the meaning of Section 170(c)(2)(D) of the Internal Revenue Code.

(2) If a company that is organized pursuant to the requirements of Paragraph (1) of this Subsection at its formation at any time ceases to satisfy any one of the requirements, it shall

路易斯安那州

常规会议，2010

参议院议案　第 1421 号

法案　第 417 号

由路易斯安那州议会颁布：

第 1031 条　定义

……

（21）“微利有限责任公司”或者“L3C”是指为实现《路易斯安那州修订法》第 12:1302（C）款中所列目标而组建的有限责任公司。

……

第 1032 条　目标

……

C.（1）作为微利有限责任公司的有限责任公司应当在公司章程中设定一个要实现的并且在经营中始终满足以下要求的商业目标：

（a）该实体大力推动《1986 年国内税收法典》第 170（c）（2）（B）分项或后续法规定下的，一项或多项慈善或教育目标的实现，非为实现那些慈善或教育目标，则微利有限责任公司不能成立。

（b）实体的主要目标不是收入增加和财产增值；但是，在没有其他因素的情况下，实体创造大量收入或者资本增值不应作为认定其主要目标包括收入增加和财产增值的决定性证据。

（c）公司目标不是实现《1986 年国内税收法典》第 170（c）（2）（D）分项下的一项或多项的政治或法律目标。

（2）如果依据本款的第（1）项的规定组建的公司不再满足这些要求，它应立即终止微利公共利益公司的形态，但是仍符合本章其他要求的可以继续作为有限责

immediately cease to be a low–profit limited liability company, but by continuing to meet all the other requirements of this Chapter, shall continue to exist as a limited liability company. The name of the company shall be changed to be in conformance with R.S. 12:1306.

...

1035.Articles of organization; initial report

...

B. The articles of organization shall set forth the following:

...

(3) Whether the company is a low–profit limited liability company.

...

1036.Name

A. The name of each limited liability company as set forth in its articles of organization:

(1)(a) Except for low–profit limited liability companies, shall contain the words "limited liability company", the abbreviation "L.L.C.", or the abbreviation "L.C.".

(b) For low–profit limited liability companies, shall contain the words "low– profit limited liability company", the abbreviation "L3C", or the abbreviation "l3c".

...

1039.Amendment of articles of organization

A. The articles of organization shall be amended when any of the following occurs:

...

(4) In accordance with R.S. 12:1302(C)(2), the company ceases to be a low– profit limited liability company.

...

任公司存在。公司名称应当依据《路易斯安那州修订法》第 12:1306 条的规定修改。

……

第 1035 条　公司章程；初始报告

……

B. 公司章程应记载以下内容：

……

（3）公司是否为微利有限责任公司。

……

第 1036 条　名称

A. 每个有限责任公司在公司章程中的名称：

（1）（a）除微利有限责任公司外，应当包含“有限责任公司”字样，“L.L.C.”或者“L.C.”的缩写。

（b）微利有限责任公司，应当包含“微利有限责任公司”的字样，“L3C”或者“l3c”的缩写。

……

第 1039 条　公司章程的修订

A. 公司章程应当在以下情况发生时修订：

……

（4）依据《路易斯安那州修订法》第 12:1302（C）（2）项的规定，公司不再是微利有限责任公司。

……

THE STATE OF MAINE

An Act To Replace the Maine Limited Liability Company Act
Be it enacted by the People of the State of Maine as follows:

CHAPTER 21
LIMITED LIABILITY COMPANIES

1508. Limited liability company name

1. Requirements.

A limited liability company name must contain the words “limited liability company” or “limited company” or the abbreviation “L.L.C.,” “LLC,” “L.C.” or “LC” or, in the case of a low-profit limited liability company, “L3C” or “13c.” The word “limited” may be abbreviated as “ Ltd.,” and “company” may be abbreviated as “Co.” unless the limited liability company is filing an assumed name under section 1510 or a registration of a name of a foreign limited liability company under section 1511. If the words “Limited Liability Company,” “Limited Liability Company, Chartered,” “Limited Liability Company, Professional Association,” “Limited Liability Company, P.A.” or any of the designations without commas are used, a limited liability company may also use the abbreviation “L.L.C.” or the designation “LLC” without filing an assumed name under section 1510. In the case of a low-profit limited liability company, if the words “Low-profit Limited Liability Company” are used, a limited liability company may also use the abbreviation “L3C” or the designation “l3c” without filing an assumed name under section 1510.

缅因州

代替《缅因州有限责任公司法》的法案
由缅因州人民颁布：

第 21 章
有限责任公司

第 1508 条　有限责任公司名称

1. 要求

有限责任公司的名称必须包含“有限责任公司”或“有限公司”或者缩写“L.L.C.”“LLC”“L.C.”或“LC”，或者，属于微利有限责任公司的情况下，包含“L3C”或者“l3c.”。“有限”一词可以被缩写为“Ltd.”并且“公司”可以被缩写为“Co.”，除非有限责任公司依据第 1510 条的规定备案了一个别名或者依据第 1511 条的规定登记了一个外州有限责任公司的名称。如果使用了“有限责任公司”“有限责任公司，特许””有限责任公司，专业协会”“有限责任公司，P.A.”，或者任何没有逗号的名称，有限责任公司也可以使用缩写“L.L.C.”或“LLC”而不用依据第 1510 条的规定备案一个别名。在微利有限责任公司的情况下，如果使用了“微利有限责任公司”字样，有限责任公司也可以使用“L3C”或“l3c”而不用依据第 1510 条的规定备案别名。

SUBCHAPTER 9
LOW-PROFIT LIMITED LIABILITY COMPANIES

1611. Low-profit limited liability company

1. Purpose.

A low-profit limited liability company must at all times significantly further the accomplishment of one or more charitable or educational purposes within the meaning of Section 170(c) (2)(B) of the Internal Revenue Code of 1986, as it may be amended, revised or succeeded, and will not qualify as a low-profit limited liability company but for the relationship to the accomplishment of those charitable or educational purposes.

2. Qualifications of low-profit limited liability company to be set forth in certificate of formation.

In order to qualify as a low-profit limited liability company pursuant to this section, the limited liability company's certificate of formation must state that:

A. The company intends to qualify as a low-profit limited liability company;

B. The company must at all times significantly further the accomplishment of one or more of the charitable or educational purposes within the meaning of Section 170(c)(2)(B) of the Internal Revenue Code of 1986, as it may be amended, revised or succeeded, and must list the specific charitable or educational purposes the company will further;

C. No significant purpose of the company is the production of income or the appreciation of property. The fact that a person produces significant income or capital appreciation is not, in the absence of other factors, conclusive evidence of a significant purpose involving the production of income or the appreciation of property; and

D. No purpose of the company is to accomplish one or more political or legislative purposes within the meaning of Section 170(c)(2)(D) of the Internal Revenue Code of 1986, or its successor.

The limited liability company agreement of a low-profit limited liability company must include each statement made in the limited liability company's certification of formation required by this subsection. The fact that the low-profit limited liability company has a certificate of formation filed with the office of the Secretary of State meeting the requirements of this subsection is conclusive evidence that statements set forth in the certificate of formation are included in the low-profit limited liability company's limited liability company agreement.

3. Change of status.

A company that no longer satisfies the requirements of this section continues to exist as a limited liability company and shall promptly amend its certificate of formation so that its name and purpose no longer identify it as a low-profit limited liability company, L3C or 13C.

第 9 节
微利有限责任公司法

第 1611 条　微利有限责任公司

1. 目标

微利有限责任公司必须始终大力推动在可能被修改、修订或替换的《1986 年国内税收法典》第 170（c）（2）（B）分项中规定的，一项或多项慈善或者教育目标的实现，非为实现那些慈善或教育目标，则该公司不符合微利有限责任公司的要求。

2. 微利有限责任公司的资格应记载在成立证书上

为依据本条规定成为微利有限责任公司，有限责任公司的成立证书必须声明：

A. 公司要成为微利有限责任公司；

B. 微利有限责任公司必须始终大力推动一项或多项，在可能被修改、修订或替换的《1986 年国内税收法典》第 170（c）（2）（B）分项中规定的，慈善或者教育目标的实现，并且必须列明公司追求的特定慈善或教育目标；

C. 公司的主要目标不是收入增加和财产增值。在没有其他因素的情况下，创造大量收入或者资本增值不是认定其主要目标包括收入增加和财产增值的决定性证据；以及

D. 公司目标不是实现一项或者多项，在《1986 年国内税收法典》第 170（c）（2）（D）分项或其后续立法规定的，政治或者法律目标。

微利有限责任公司的有限责任公司协议必须包含本款要求的在微利有限责任公司成立证书中需记载的所有声明。向州务卿办公室备案的微利有限责任公司成立证书符合本款要求，是认定成立证书中的声明被包含在微利有限责任公司协议中的决定性证据。

3. 形态的改变

不再满足本条要求的公司要继续作为有限责任公司存在，应当立即修订其成立证书以使公司名称和目标区别于微利有限责任公司，L3C 或者 l3C。

4. Duties of members and other persons.

Notwithstanding section 1521, subsection 3, any company formed as a low-profit limited liability company under this chapter is bound by section 1559 and no member or person may, through the limited liability company agreement or otherwise, restrict or eliminate the duties, including fiduciary duties, set forth in section 1559.

5. No limitation.

Nothing in this section prevents a limited liability company that is not organized under this section from electing a charitable or educational purpose in whole or in part for doing business under this chapter.

4. 成员和其他人的义务

尽管第 1521 条第 3 款有规定，任何依据本章规定成为微利有限责任公司的公司受第 1559 条约束并且成员或其他人不得通过有限责任公司协议或者其他方式，限制或免除此义务，包括第 1559 条规定的信义义务。

5. 无限制

本条规定不限制非依本条规定成立的有限责任公司依据本章规定，在经营业务时全部或部分地选择一项慈善或教育目标。

THE STATE OF MICHIGAN

STATE OF MICHIGAN 94TH LEGISLATURE

REGULAR SESSION OF 2008

ENROLLED SENATE BILL No. 1445

Sec. 102.

(1) Unless the context requires otherwise, the definitions in this section control the interpretation of this act.

(2) As used in this act:

...

(m) "Low-profit limited liability company" means a limited liability company that has included in its articles of organization a purpose that meets, and that at all times conducts its activities to meet, all of the following requirements:

(i) The limited liability company significantly furthers the accomplishment of 1 or more charitable or educational purposes described in section 170(c)(2)(B) of the internal revenue code, 26 USC 170, and would not have been formed except to accomplish those charitable or educational purposes.

(ii) The production of income or appreciation of property is not a significant purpose of the limited liability company. However, in the absence of other factors, the fact that a limited liability company produces significant income or capital appreciation is not conclusive evidence of a significant purpose involving the production of income or the appreciation of property.

(iii) The purposes of the limited liability company do not include accomplishing 1 or more political or legislative purposes described in section 170(c)(2)(D) of the internal revenue code, 26 USC 170.

...

密歇根州

密歇根州第 94 次立法会

2008 年常规会议

第 1445 号已登记参议院议案

第 102 条

（1）除本条另有规定外，本条对相关用语的定义适用于该法。

（2）在本法中：

……

（m）“微利有限责任公司”是指在公司组织章程中规定的公司目的及其行为满足以下所有要求的有限责任公司：

（i）有限责任公司需大力推动《1986 年国内税收法典》第 170（c）（2）（B）分项（《美国法典》第 26 卷第 170 条）规定的一项或多项慈善或教育目的的实现，若不能实现那些慈善或教育目的则该公司设立失败。

（ii）创造收入及财产增值并不是有限责任公司的主要目的。但是，在缺乏其他因素的情况下，有限责任公司创造了大量收入或者实现资本增值的事实，不能成为认定其主要目的包含创收或财产升值的决定性证据。

（iii）有限公司的目的不包括实现《1986 年国内税收法典》第 170（c）（2）（D）分项（《美国法典》第 26 卷第 170 条）规定的政治目的或法律目的。

……

THE STATE OF NORTH CAROLINA

GENERAL ASSEMBLY OF NORTH CAROLINA

SESSION 2009

SESSION LAW 2010-187

SENATE BILL 308

AN ACT TO PROVIDE FOR THE FORMATION OF A LIMITED LIABILITY COMPANY AS A LOW-PROFIT LIMITED LIABILITY COMPANY.

The General Assembly of North Carolina enacts:

§ 57C-2-01.

...

(d) L3C. – Formation and operation of a limited liability company as a low-profit limited liability company is a lawful purpose. A low-profit limited liability company is a limited liability company whose articles of organization state that the company is formed for both a business purpose and a charitable purpose that requires operation of the company in accordance with the requirements of this subsection. A company that operates in accordance with these requirements is considered a for-profit entity and not a charitable entity for all tax purposes. A company's failure to operate in accordance with these requirements does not affect its status as a limited liability company. The charitable purpose requirements are as follows:

(1)To accomplish one or more charitable or educational purposes within the meaning of section 170(c)(2)(B) of the Code, as defined in G.S. 105-228.90.

(2)To operate so that no significant purpose of the company is the production of income or the appreciation of property. The fact that a company produces significant income or capital appreciation is not, in the absence of other factors, conclusive evidence of a significant purpose to produce income or accumulate capital.

北卡罗来纳州

北卡罗来纳州议员大会

2009 年度会议

2010-187 条

议会法案 308

本法为有限责任公司设立微利有限责任公司提供规范。

北卡罗来纳州议会颁布以下规定：

第 57C-2-01 条

……

（d）L3C.——将有限责任公司作为微利有限责任公司进行设立和经营是合法的目标。微利有限责任公司是指，其公司组织章程明确规定，公司以商事和慈善为公司目的且公司运营符合本章规定的。公司运营符合本章规定的公司在税法上仍为营利性实体而非慈善实体。公司运营不符合本章规定的，不影响其作为有限责任公司的法律地位。慈善目的是指：

（1）以实现本法第 170（c）（2）（B）项（规定于《北卡罗来纳州法典》第 105-228.90 章）规定的一项或多项慈善或教育目的。

（2）公司的运营不以追求创造收入和财产增值为主要目的。但是，在缺乏其他证据的条件下，有限责任公司获得大量收入和财产增值的事实并不构成公司以此为主要目的的决定性证据。

(3)To operate so that no purpose of the company is to accomplish one or more political or legislative purposes within the meaning of section 170(c)(2)(D) of the Code, as defined in G.S. 105–228.90."

§ 57C-2-21. Articles of organization.

(a)The articles of organization must set forth all of the following:

...

(6)If the limited liability company is formed as a low–profit limited liability company, a statement that operation of the company must meet the charitable purpose requirements of G.S. 57C–2–01(d).

§ 55D-20(a)

...

(6) The name of a low–profit limited liability company must contain the words "low–profit limited liability company" or the abbreviation "L3C".

（3）有限公司的目的不包括实现《北卡罗来纳州法典》（G.S.）第 105–228.90 章第 170（c）（2）（D）项规定的政治目的或立法目的。

第 57C–2–21 条 公司章程

（a）公司章程必须记载以下事项：

……

（6）如果有限责任公司为微利有限责任公司，则公司必须声明其运营符合 G.S. 57C–2–01（d）款对慈善目的所做的规定。

第 55D–20（a）款

……

（6）微利有限责任公司的名称必须包含“微利有限责任公司”或其缩写“L3C”字样。

THE STATE OF RHODE ISLAND

2011 — H 5279

STATE OF RHODE ISLAND

IN GENERAL ASSEMBLY

JANUARY SESSION, A.D. 2011

AN ACT RELATING TO CORPORATIONS, ASSOCIATIONS AND PARTNERSHIPS — LOW PROFIT LIMITED LIABILITY COMPANIES

7-16-2. Definitions.

As used in this chapter, unless the context otherwise requires:

...

(27) "L3C" or "low-profit limited liability company" means a limited liability company that is organized and existing under the laws of this state under this chapter and which satisfies the requirements of section 7-16-76.

...

7-16-9. Name.

(a) The name of each limited liability company as set forth in its articles of organization:

Shall end with either the words "limited liability company" or the upper or lower case letters "l.l.c." with or without punctuations or, if organized as a low-profit limited liability company, shall end with either the words "low-profit limited liability company" or the abbreviation "L3C" or "13c";

...

7-16-49. Registration of foreign limited liability company.

...

(b) In order to register, a foreign limited liability company shall submit to the secretary of state, in duplicate, an application for registration as a foreign limited liability company, signed by a person with authority to do so under the laws of the state or other jurisdiction of its organization and setting forth:

...

罗得岛州

2011——H 5279 号
罗得岛州
州议会
2011 年 1 月立法季
本法案涉及公司、组织和合伙——微利有限责任公司

第 7–16–2 条　定义

除上下文另有规定外，在本章中：

……

（27）“L3C”或“微利有限责任公司”是指根据本章第 7–16–76 条的规定设立或存在的有限责任公司。

……

第 7–16–9 条　名称

（a）记载于有限责任公司章程中的名称应满足以下条件：

（1）以“有限责任公司”或其首字母的缩写“l.l.c”结尾，如果该组织为微利有限责任公司，则应以“微利有限责任公司”或其缩写“L3C”或“l3c”结尾；

……

第 7–16–49 条　外州有限责任公司的登记

……

（b）为进行登记，外州有限责任公司应向州务卿提交两份外州有限责任公司的登记申请，由本州或机构所在地获得法律授权的人签字，并记载以下事项：

……

(9) A statement indicating whether the company has been duly organized in its state of formation as a low–profit limited liability company.

7-16-76. Low-profit limited liability company.

(a) A low–profit limited liability company shall at all times significantly further the accomplishment of one or more charitable or educational purposes within the meaning of Section 170(c)(2)(B) of the Internal Revenue Code of 1986, 26 U.S.C. section 170(c)(2)(B), or its successor, and would not have been formed but for the entity's relationship to the accomplishment of charitable or educational purposes.

(b) A limited liability company which intends to qualify as a low–profit limited liability company pursuant to the provisions of section 7–16–76 shall so indicate in its articles of organization, shall organize under the provisions of section 7–16–6, and shall further state that:

(1) No significant purpose of the entity is the production of income or the appreciation of property provided; however, that the fact that an entity produces significant income or capital appreciation shall not, in the absence of other factors, be conclusive evidence of a significant purpose involving the production of income or the appreciation of property.

(2) No purpose of the entity is to accomplish one or more political or legislative purposes within the meaning of Section 170(c)(2)(D) of the Internal Revenue Code of 1986, 26 U.S.C. section 170(c)(2)(D), or its successor.

(c) If an entity that met the requirements of section 7–16–76 at its formation at any time ceases to satisfy any one of the requirements, it shall immediately cease to be a low–profit limited liability company, but by continuing to meet all the other requirements of this chapter, will continue to exist as a limited liability company. The name of the entity must be changed to be in conformance with section 7–16–9.

(d) Nothing in section 7–16–76 shall prevent a limited liability company that is not organized under it from electing charitable or educational purpose in whole or in part for doing business under this chapter.

(e) Except as otherwise provided in this subsection, all provisions of the Rhode Island Limited Liability Act, Chapter 7–16 of this title, applicable to domestic limited liability companies are applicable to low–profit limited liability companies.

（9）表明该公司在其所在州是否已经成为微利有限责任公司的陈述。

第 7–16–76 条　微利有限责任公司

（a）微利有限责任公司始终应以实现一个或多个慈善或教育目标为公司目的，这些目标被规定于《1986 年国内税收法典》第 170（c）（2）（B）分项［《美国法典》第 26 卷第 170（c）（2）（B）分项］之中，非为实现那些慈善或教育目标的微利有限责任公司不能设立。

（b）欲依据第 7–16–76 条的规定成为微利有限责任公司的有限责任公司应在公司章程中表明其依据第 7–16–76 条的规定组建并进一步载明：

（1）该实体不以盈利或资产增值为主要目的；但是，在没有其他证据的情况下，获得较多盈利和资产增值并不能认定公司以盈利或资产增值为主要目的。

（2）该实体不以追求《1986 年国内税收法典》第 170（c）（2）（D）分项［《美国法典》第 26 卷第 170（c）（2）（D）分项］所规定的政治或法律目标为目的。

（c）如果设立时满足第 7–16–76 条要求的实体在任何时候不再满足该这些要求，其应立即终止微利有限责任公司的形态，但是其仍然满足该章其他规定时，仍为有限责任公司。该实体的名称应根据第 7–16–9 条的规定进行变更。

（d）第 7–16–76 条的任何规定并不限制其他非依该规定设立的公司在其部分或全部业务中选择慈善或教育目的。

（e）除另有规定外，本法第 7–16 章和《罗得岛州有限责任公司法》的其他规定同时适用于本州有限责任公司和微利有限责任公司。

THE STATE OF UTAH

Title 48 Unincorporated Business Entity Act
Chapter 3a Revised Uniform Limited Liability Company Act
Part 13 Low–Profit Limited Liability Companies

Utah Code Ann. § 48–3a–1301 (2015)

48-3a-1301. Application of this part.

If a conflict arises between this part and another provision of this chapter, this part controls.

48-3a-1302. Requirements.

(1) To be a low–profit limited liability company, a limited liability company shall:

(a) contain in its name the abbreviation "L3C" or "l3c";

(b) state in its certificate of organization that it is a low–profit limited liability company;

(c) organize under this chapter; and

(d) be organized for a business purpose that satisfies, and at all times operates to satisfy each of the requirements under Subsection (2).

(2) A low–profit limited liability company:

(a) shall significantly further the accomplishment of one or more charitable or educational purposes within the meaning of Section 170(c)(2)(B), Internal Revenue Code;

(b) shall demonstrate that it would not be formed but for the limited liability company's relationship to the accomplishment of a charitable or educational purpose;

(c) subject to Subsection (3), may not have as a significant purpose the production of income or the appreciation of property; and

(d) may not have as a purpose to accomplish one or more political or legislative purposes within the meaning of Section 170(c)(2)(D), Internal Revenue Code.

(3) Notwithstanding Subsection (2), if a low–profit limited liability company produces significant income or capital appreciation, in the absence of other factors, the fact that the low–profit limited liability company produces significant income or capital appreciation is

犹他州

第 48 编　非公司企业法
第 3a 章　统一有限责任公司修订条例
第 13 节　微利有限责任公司

《犹他州法典》第 48–3a–1301 条（2015）

第 48–3a–1301 条　本节的适用

本节规定与本章其他条款相冲突的，优先适用本节规定。

第 48–3a–1302 条　要求

（1）有限责任公司要成为微利有限责任公司，应满足以下条件：

（a）在公司名称中加入“L3C”或“l3c”的缩写；

（b）在公司章程中声明其为微利有限责任公司；

（c）接受本章规定的调整；并且

（d）公司的商业目的满足并且在经营过程中始终满足第（2）款的要求。

（2）微利有限责任公司：

（a）应大力推动《1986 年国内税收法典》第 170（c）（2）（B）分项下规定的一个或多个慈善或教育目的的实现；

（b）应表明有限责任公司不是仅为实现慈善或教育目的而设立；

（c）依据第（3）款规定，不得以创造收入或财产增值为主要目的；并且

（d）不得将《1986 年国内税收法典》第 170（c）（2）（D）分项下的一个或多个政治或法律性目的作为公司目的。

（3）尽管根据第（2）款规定，公司不得以创造收入或财产升值为主要目的，但在没有其他证据的情况下，微利有限责任公司创造了大量收入或者实现资本升值的事实不能成为认定其以此为主要目的的决定性证据。

not conclusive evidence of a significant purpose involving the production of income or the appreciation of property.

48-3a-1303. Ceasing to be a low-profit limited liability company.

(1) If a limited liability company that is a low–profit limited liability company at its formation at any time ceases to meet a requirement to be a low–profit limited liability company under Section 48–3a–1302, the limited liability company:

(a) ceases to be a low–profit limited liability company on the day on which the limited liability company no longer meets the requirement; and

(b) if it continues to meet the requirements of this chapter to be a limited liability company, continues to exist as a limited liability company that is not a low–profit limited liability company.

(2) A low–profit limited liability company's failure to meet a requirement of Section 48–3a–1302 may be:

(a) voluntary, in order to convert to a limited liability company that is not a low–profit limited liability company; or

(b) involuntary.

(3) If a low–profit limited liability company ceases to be a low–profit limited liability company in accordance with this section, the limited liability company shall:

(a) change its name to conform with Section 48–3a–108; and

(b) amend its certificate of organization in accordance with Section 48–3a–202.

48-3a-1304. Merger, interest exchange, conversion, or domestication of a low-profit limited liability company.

A low–profit limited liability company may engage in a merger, interest exchange, conversion, or domestication under Part 10, Merger, Interest Exchange, Conversion, and Domestication, to the same extent as a limited liability company that is not a low–profit limited liability company.

第 48–3a–1303 条　微利有限责任公司形态的终止

（1）作为微利有限责任公司的有限责任公司，当其在任何时候不再符合第 48–3a–1302 条的要求时，其应：

（a）在其不符合上述要求之日起终止其微利有限责任公司形态；

（b）仍符合本章中有限责任公司的相关规定的，其可作为非微利有限责任公司的有限责任公司存续。

（2）微利有限责任公司未能符合第 48–3a–1302 条规定的，可以

（a）自愿由微利有限责任公司转化为有限责任公司；或者

（b）非自愿转化。

（3）微利有限责任公司按照本条规定终止其形态的，该有限责任公司应当：

（a）依照第 48–3a–108 条规定变更公司名称；以及

（b）依照第 48–3a–202 条规定变更其机构证书。

第 48–3a–1304 条　微利有限责任公司的合并、利益置换、财产转换和国有化

微利有限责任公司涉及第 10 节规定的合并、利益置换、财产转换和国有化等事项时，适用与有限责任公司相同的规定。

THE STATE OF WYOMING

ORIGINAL HOUSE

BILL NO. 0182

ENROLLED ACT NO. 34, HOUSE OF REPRESENTATIVES

SIXTIETH LEGISLATURE OF THE STATE OF WYOMING

2009 GENERAL SESSION

AN ACT relating to limited liability companies; providing for creation of low profit limited liability companies; providing a definition; providing for use of abbreviations; providing for administrative dissolution; and providing for an effective date.

Be It Enacted by the Legislature of the State of Wyoming:

Section 1.

W.S. 17–15–102(a) by creating a new paragraph (ix), 17–15–105(a)(intro) and (b) and 17–15–112 by creating a new subsection (e) are amended to read:

17-15-102. Definitions.

(a) As used in this act:

...

(ix) "Low profit limited liability company" means a limited liability company that has set forth in its articles of organization a business purpose that satisfies, and which limited liability company is at all times operated to satisfy, each of the following requirements:

(A) The entity significantly furthers the accomplishment of one (1) or more charitable or educational purposes within the meaning of section 170(c)(2)(B) of the Internal Revenue Code and would not have been formed but for the entity's relationship to the accomplishment of charitable or educational purposes;

(B) No significant purpose of the entity is the production of income or the appreciation of property provided, however, that the fact that an entity produces significant income or capital appreciation shall not, in the absence of other factors, be conclusive evidence of a significant purpose involving the production of income or the appreciation of property; and

(C) No purpose of the entity is to accomplish one (1) or more political or legislative

怀俄明州

原有议案

议案第 0182 号
众议院第 34 号登记法案
第 16 届怀俄明州议会
2009 年全体大会

本法涉及有限责任公司的相关规定，包括微利有限责任公司的设立；相关定义；缩写的用法；行政解散和生效期等内容。

本法由怀俄明州议会颁布：

第 1 部分

《怀俄明州法典》第 17–15–102（a）款增加了一项（ix）；第 17–15–105（a）款（简介）和第（b）款进行了修正；第 17–15–112 条增加了（e）款。具体如下：

第 17–15–102 条　定义

（a）在本法中：

……

（ix）“微利有限责任公司”是指，一家有限责任公司，其公司章程中规定的商业目的以及其从始至终的经营过程，都满足以下全部要求：

（A）该实体大力推动《1986 年国内税收法典》第 170（c）（2）（B）分项下的一个或多个慈善或教育目的的实现。该实体不仅为实现慈善或教育目的所需的关系而设立；

（B）该实体不得以创造收入或财产升值为主要目的。但是，在没有其他证据的情况下，实体创造了大量收入或者实现资本升值的事实不能成为认定该实体以此为主要目的的决定性证据；以及

（C）该实体的目的不得为《1986 年国内税收法典》第 170（c）（2）（D）分

purposes within the meaning of section 170(c)(2)(D) of the Internal Revenue Code.

...

17-15-105. Name.

(a) The words "limited liability company," or its abbreviations "LLC" or "L.L.C.," "limited company," or its abbreviations "LC" or "L.C.," "Ltd. liability company," "Ltd. liability co." or "limited liability co." shall be included in the name of every limited liability company formed under the provisions of this act and, except the name of a low profit limited liability company, as defined in W.S. 17–15–102(a)(ix) shall contain the abbreviations "L3C," "l3c," "low profit ltd. liability company," "low profit ltd. liability co." or "low profit limited liability co.". In addition, the limited liability company name may not:

(b) Omission of the words "limited liability company," or its abbreviations "LLC" or "L.L.C.," "limited company," or its abbreviations "LC" or "L.C.," "Ltd. liability company," "Ltd. liability co." or "limited liability co.," or in the case of a low profit limited liability company, as defined in W.S. 17–15–102(a)(ix), omission of the words "low profit limited liability company" or its abbreviations "L3C," "l3c," "low profit ltd. liability company," "low profit ltd. liability co." or "low profit limited liability co.," in the use of the name of the limited liability company shall render any person who participates in the omission, or knowingly acquiesces in it, liable for indebtedness, damage or liability occasioned by the omission.

17-15-112. Administrative forfeiture of authority and certificate of organization.

...

(e) In addition to the other provisions of this section, if any low profit limited liability company has ceased to meet the definition of a low profit limited liability company as provided in W.S. 17–15–102(a)(ix) and has failed for thirty (30) days after ceasing to meet the definition to file an amendment to its articles of organization with the secretary of state amending its name to conform with the requirements of W.S. 17–15–105(a), it shall be deemed to be transacting business in this state without authority and to have forfeited any franchises, rights or privileges acquired under the laws thereof and the forfeiture shall be made effective in the same manner as provided in subsection (a) of this section. The reinstatement provisions and fees provided in subsection (a) of this section shall apply.

...

Section 2. This act is effective July 1, 2009.

项下的一个或多个政治或法律目的。

……

第 17-15-105 条　名称

（a）依据本法设立的有限责任公司，其名称中应包含“有限责任公司”，或其缩写“LLC”“L.L.C.”“limited company”“LC”“L.C.”“Ltd. Liability company”“Ltd. liability co.”或“limited liability co.”。《怀俄明州法典》第 17-15-102（a）（ix）项中定义的微利有限责任公司，其名称则应包含缩写“L3C”“l3c”“low profit ltd. liability company”“low profit ltd. liability co.”或“low profit limited liability co.”。

（b）有限责任公司使用其公司名称时，不得遗漏“有限责任公司”或其缩写“LLC”“L.L.C.”“limited company”“LC”“L.C.”“Ltd. Liability company”“Ltd. liability co.”或“limited liability co.”；使用《怀俄明州法典》第 17-15-102（a）（ix）项定义的微利有限责任公司的名称时，不得遗漏“微利有限责任公司”或其缩写“L3C”“l3c”“low profit ltd. liability company”“low profit ltd. liability co.”或“low profit limited liability co.”。参与或故意默许该省略行为的个人应承担由此导致的债务、损害或责任。

第 17-15-112 条　主管部门的行政罚没和组织机构证书

……

（e）除本条另有规定外，微利有限责任公司未能满足怀俄明州法第 17-15-102（a）（ix）项中有关的微利有限责任公司的定义，且未在 30 日内依据《怀俄明州法典》第 17-15-105（a）款的规定修正其名称并向州务卿备案公司章程修正案的，公司将被视为在本州无经营授权，并没收依本法规定的所有特许经营权、权利或特权，该罚没行为按本条第（a）款规定的同一方式进行。本条第（a）款规定下的恢复条款和费用亦适用于此情形。

……

第 2 部分　本法案自 2009 年 7 月 1 日起生效。

SOCIAL PURPOSE CORPORATIONS ACT

社会目的公司法

THE STATE OF CALIFORNIA

CALIFORNIA CORPORATIONS CODE
Title 1. Corporations
Division 1.5. Social Purpose Corporations Act

§2500. Citation of division

This division shall be known and may be cited as the Social Purpose Corporations Act.

§2501. Laws applicable to corporations organized under division; References; "Social purpose corporation"

Except as otherwise expressly stated, the provisions of Division 1 (commencing with Section 100) shall apply to corporations organized under this division, and references in that division to the terms "close corporation," "constituent corporation," "corporation," "disappearing corporation," "domestic corporation," "foreign corporation," "surviving corporation," and similar terms shall be read to apply, in the same manner, to include the similar "social purpose corporation."

§ 2502. Applicability of division

This division applies only to social purpose corporations organized expressly under this division whether organized or existing under this division or amended, merged or converted into a social purpose corporation in accordance with Chapter 9 (commencing with Section 900) of Division 1, Chapter 11 (commencing with Section 1100) of Division 1 or Chapter 11.5 (commencing with Section 1150) of Division 1, including all flexible purpose corporations formed under this division prior to January 1, 2015, and now existing except as provided in paragraph (2) of subdivision (b) of Section 2601 and paragraph (3) of subdivision (b) of Section 2602.

§ 2502.01. Presumption that social purpose corporation organized under laws of state is agency of United States

Every social purpose corporation organized under the laws of this state or similar foreign social purpose corporation, all of the capital stock of which is beneficially owned by the United States, an agency or instrumentality of the United States or any social purpose

加利福尼亚州

《加利福尼亚州公司法典》
第 1 编　公司
第 1.5 分编　社会目的公司

第 2500 条　本分编的引用

本分编被称为和被引用为《社会目的公司法》。

第 2501 条　依据本分编规定组建的公司所适用的法律；参照适用；“社会目的公司法”

除了另有明确规定外，第 1 分编的条款（从第 100 条开始）应适用于依据本分编规定组建的公司，该部分提及的“封闭公司”“子公司”“公司”“消失公司”“本州公司”“外州公司”“存续公司”等类似术语应以同样的方式适用于相似的“社会目的公司”。

第 2502 条　本分编的适用

本分编只适用于明确依据本分编规定组建或存续的社会目的公司或依据第 1 分编的第 9 章（从第 900 条开始），第 11 章（从第 1100 条开始）或第 11.5 章（从第 1150 条开始）的规定改变、合并或转换的社会目的公司，包括所有在 2015 年 1 月 1 日之前依据本分编规定成立的灵活目标公司，和除了规定在第 2601 条第（b）款第（2）项和第 2602 条第（b）款第（3）项的现存公司。

第 2502.01 条　依据州法组建的社会目的公司被推定为美国的机构

全部股份由美国、美国的机构或部门实益所有的根据本州法律成立的社会目的公司或类似的外州社会目的公司，或者全部股份由美国或美国的机构或部门所有的社会目的公司或类似的外州社会目的公司，将最终被推定为美国的机构和部门，并

corporation or similar foreign social purpose corporation the whole of the capital stock of which is owned by the United States or by an agency or instrumentality of the United States, is conclusively presumed to be an agency and instrumentality of the United States and is entitled to all privileges and immunities to which the holders of all of its stock are entitled as agencies of the United States.

§ 2502.02. Construction of references to statutes

Unless otherwise expressly provided, whenever reference is made in this division to any other state or federal statute, that reference is to that statute as it may be amended from time to time, whether before or after the enactment of this division.

§ 2502.03. Amenability to suit

A social purpose corporation may be sued in the same manner as a corporation as provided in the Code of Civil Procedure.

§ 2502.04. Subject to provisions of Code of Civil Procedure authorizing the attachment of corporate property

A social purpose corporation formed under this division shall, in respect of its property, as a condition of its existence as a social purpose corporation, be subject, in the same manner as a corporation, to the provisions of the Code of Civil Procedure authorizing the attachment of corporate property.

§ 2502.05. Filing fees

The fees of the Secretary of State for filing instruments by or on behalf of social purpose corporations shall be the same fees prescribed for corporations in Article 3 (commencing with Section 12180) of Chapter 3 of Part 2 of Division 3 of Title 2 of the Government Code.

§ 2502.06. Use of facts ascertainable outside of articles or agreement

(a) Provisions of the articles described in paragraph (3) of subdivision (e) of Section 2602 and subdivisions (a) and (b) of Section 2603 may be made dependent upon facts ascertainable outside of the articles, if the manner in which those facts shall operate upon those provisions is clearly and expressly set forth in the articles. Similarly, any of the terms of an agreement of merger pursuant to Section 1101 may be made dependent upon facts ascertainable outside of that agreement, if the manner in which those facts shall operate upon the terms of the agreement is clearly and expressly set forth in the agreement of merger.

(b) Notwithstanding subdivision (a), when any provisions or terms of articles or an agreement of merger are made dependent upon facts ascertainable outside of the filed instrument through a reference to an agreement or similar document, the social purpose corporation filing that instrument shall maintain at its principal executive office a copy of that referenced agreement or document and all amendments, and shall provide to its shareholders, in the case of articles, or to shareholders of any constituent corporation or other business entity, in the case of an agreement of merger, a copy of them upon written request

且其所有股票持有者将作为美国机构享有特权和豁免权。

第 2502.02 条　引用法律的解释

除另有明确规定外，在本分编中引用任何州或联邦的法规时，引用的是最新修订的法规，无论其在本分编颁布之前或之后。

第 2502.03 条　服从诉讼

按照民事诉讼法的规定，社会目的公司得以与公司相同的方式被起诉。

第 2502.04 条　受民事诉讼法中授权扣押公司财产的条款调整

依据本分编规定成立的社会目的公司，其作为社会目的公司存在的一个条件便是，应以与其他公司相同的方式遵守民事诉讼法中授权扣押公司财产的规定。

第 2502.05 条　备案费用

州务卿对社会目的公司文件的备案费用应与《政府法典》的第 2 编第 3 分编第 2 部分的第 3 章第 3 节（从第 12180 条开始）为公司规定的费用相同。

第 2502.06 条　对章程或协议以外可确定事实的使用

（a）第 2602 条的第 (e) 款第 (3) 项和第 2603 条的第 (a) 款和第 (b) 款规定的公司章程可以章程之外可确定的事实为依据，如果这些事实对章程的作用方式在章程中明确规定。同样，根据第 1101 条成立的合并协议的任何条款可以该协议之外可确定的事实为依据，如果这些事实对该协议条款的作用方式在合并协议中有明确规定。

（b）虽有第（a）款规定，但当公司章程或合并协议中的任何条款或术语，以备案文件以外的协议或相似文件的可确定事实为依据时，备案该文件的社会目的公司应在其主要办公地点置备引用的协议或文件及所有修订的副本；在文件为公司章程的情况下，应提供给股东；在文件为合并协议的情况下，应提供给任何子公司或其他商事实体的股东；这些文件的副本经书面请求可免费提供。

and without charge.

(c) For the purposes of this section, "referenced agreement" means an agreement or contract to which the social purpose corporation is a party. An amendment or revision of a referenced agreement shall require shareholder approval, in addition to any other required approvals, upon any of the following circumstances:

(1) If the amendment or revision of the referenced agreement would result in a material change in the rights, preferences, privileges, or restrictions of a class or series of shares, the amendment or revision shall be approved by the outstanding shares, as defined in Section 152, of that class or series.

(2) If the amendment or revision of the referenced agreement would result in a material change in the rights or liabilities of any class or series of shares with respect to the subject matter of paragraph (1), (2), (3), (5), or (9) of subdivision (a) of Section 2603, the amendment or revision shall be approved by the outstanding shares, as defined in Section 152, of that class or series.

(3) If the amendment or revision of the referenced agreement would result in a material change in the restrictions on transfer or hypothecation of any class or series of shares, the amendment or revision shall be approved by the outstanding shares, as defined in Section 152, of that class or series.

(4) If the amendment or revision of the referenced agreement would result in a change of any of the principal terms of an agreement of merger, the amendment or revision shall be approved in the same manner as required by Section 3504 for a change in the principal terms of an agreement of merger.

§ 2502.07. Applicability of general provisions governing offer or sale of voting common stock

Nothing contained in this division shall be construed to modify the provisions of subdivision (h) of Section 25102, or the conditions provided there in to the availability of an exemption under that subdivision.

§ 2503. "Annual report"

"Annual report" means the report required by subdivision (a) of Section 3500, including the information specified in subdivision (b) of Section 3500.

§ 2503.1. "Close social purpose corporation"

"Close social purpose corporation" means a social purpose corporation that is also a close corporation.

§ 2504. "Constituent social purpose corporation"

"Constituent social purpose corporation" means a social purpose corporation that is merged with or into one or more corporations or one or more other business entities and includes a surviving social purpose corporation.

（c）本条所称的“参考协议”是指社会目的公司是其中一方的协议或合同。除任何其他批准的要求外，在以下情形中，参考协议的修改或修订应得到股东批准：

（1）如果参考协议的修改或修订将导致一个类别或系列股份的权利、优先权、特权或限制发生实质改变，该修改或修订应由第 152 条规定的该类别或系列已发行股份通过。

（2）如果参考协议的修改或修订将导致任何类别或系列股份关于第 2603 条第（a）款第（1）、（2）、（3）、（5）、（9）项中规定的标的的权利或责任发生实质改变，该修改或修订应由第 152 条规定的该类别或系列已发行股份通过。

（3）如果参考协议的修改或修订将导致任何类别或系列股份在交易或抵押上的限制发生实质改变，该修改或修订应由第 152 条规定的该等级或系列已发行股份通过。

（4）如果参考协议的修改或修订将导致任何合并协议的主要条款发生改变，该修改或修订应由第 3504 条规定的与改变合并协议主要条款同样的方式通过。

第 2502.07 条　规定有投票权普通股的一般条款的适用

本分编不应被解释为修改了第 25102 条第（h）款，或本款中规定的豁免条件。

第 2503 条　“年度报告”

“年度报告”是指第 3500 条的第（a）款要求的报告，包括第 3500 条第（b）款规定的信息。

第 2503.1 条　“封闭社会目的公司”

“封闭社会目的公司”是指同为封闭公司的社会目的公司。

第 2504 条　“合并社会目标公司”

“合并社会目标公司”是指一个或多个公司，或与一个或多个的商业实体合并的社会目的公司，包括存续的社会目的公司。

§ 2505. "Conversion"

"Conversion" means a conversion pursuant to Chapter 11.5 (commencing with Section 1150) of Division 1 and Chapter 9 (commencing with Section 3300) of this division.

§ 2506. "Disappearing social purpose corporation"

"Disappearing social purpose corporation" means a constituent social purpose corporation that is not the surviving entity.

§ 2507. "Domestic social purpose corporation"

"Domestic social purpose corporation" means a corporation organized under this division.

§ 2509. "Social purpose corporation"

"Social purpose corporation," unless otherwise expressly provided, refers only to a corporation organized under this division.

§ 2510. "Social purpose corporation subject to the Banking Law"

"Social purpose corporation subject to the Banking Law" means any of the following:

(a) A social purpose corporation that, with the approval of the Commissioner of Business Oversight, is incorporated for the purpose of engaging in, or that is authorized by the Commissioner of Business Oversight to engage in, the commercial banking business under the Banking Law (Division 1 (commencing with Section 99) of the Financial Code).

(b) Any social purpose corporation that, with the approval of the Commissioner of Business Oversight, is incorporated for the purpose of engaging in, or that is authorized by the Commissioner of Business Oversight to engage in, the industrial banking business under the Banking Law (Division 1 (commencing with Section 99) of the Financial Code).

(c) Any social purpose corporation, other than a social purpose corporation described in subdivision (d), that, with the approval of the Commissioner of Business Oversight, is incorporated for the purpose of engaging in, or that is authorized by the Commissioner of Business Oversight to engage in, the trust business under the Banking Law (Division 1 (commencing with Section 99) of the Financial Code).

(d) Any social purpose corporation that is authorized by the Commissioner of Business Oversight and the Commissioner of Insurance to maintain a title insurance department to engage in title insurance business and a trust department to engage in trust business.

(e) Any social purpose corporation that, with the approval of the Commissioner of Business Oversight, is incorporated for the purpose of engaging in, or that is authorized by the Commissioner of Business Oversight to engage in, business under Article 1 (commencing with Section 3500) of Chapter 19 of Division 1 of the Financial Code.

§ 2510.1. "Social purpose corporation subject to the Insurance Code as an insurer"

"Social purpose corporation subject to the Insurance Code as an insurer" means a social

第 2505 条 “转换”

“转换”是指依据第 1 分编的第 11.5 章（从第 1150 条开始）和本分编的第 9 章的规定（从第 3300 条开始）进行的一项转换。

第 2506 条 “消失社会目的公司”

“消失社会目标公司”是指不属于存续实体的合并社会目的公司。

第 2507 条 “本州社会目的公司”

“本州社会目的公司”是指依据本分编规定组建的公司。

第 2509 条 “社会目的公司”

除另有明确规定外，“社会目的公司”仅指依据本分编规定组建的公司。

第 2510 条 “受《银行法》调整的社会目的公司”

“受《银行法》调整的社会目的公司”是指以下公司：

（a）经过商业监督委员批准成立，或经过商业监督委员许可，从事《银行法》规定下的商业银行业务[《金融法》的第 1 分编（从第 99 条开始）]的社会目的公司。

（b）经过商业监督委员批准成立，或经过商业监督委员许可，从事《银行法》规定下的产业银行业务[《金融法》的第 1 分编（从第 99 条开始）]的社会目的公司。

（c）除了在第（d）款规定的社会目的公司，经过商业监督委员批准成立以从事，或经过商业监督委员许可从事，《银行法》规定下的信托业务［《金融法》的第 1 分编（从第 99 条开始）］的任何社会目的公司。

（d）经过商业监督委员和保险委员许可，设置产权保险部从事产权保险业务以及信托部从事信托业务的任何社会目的公司。

（e）经过商业监督委员批准成立以从事，或经商业监督委员许可从事，《金融法》第 1 分编的第 19 章第 1 节（从第 3500 条开始）规定下业务的任何社会目的公司。

第 2510.1 条 “受《保险法》调整的作为保险人的社会目的公司”

“受《保险法》调整的作为保险人的社会目的公司”是指满足第 201.5 条、第

purpose corporation that has met the requirements of Sections 201.5, 201.6, and 201.7.

§ 2511. "Reorganization"

"Reorganization" means a merger reorganization, an exchange reorganization, or a sale of assets reorganization.

(a) "Merger reorganization" means a merger pursuant to Chapter 11 (commencing with Section 1100) of Division 1 and Chapter 8 (commencing with Section 3200), of this division, other than a short-form merger.

(b) "Exchange reorganization" means the acquisition by one domestic social purpose corporation, foreign social purpose corporation, or other business entity in exchange, in whole or in part, for its equity securities, or the equity securities of a domestic social purpose corporation, a foreign social purpose corporation, or an other business entity that is in control of the acquiring entity, of equity securities of another domestic social purpose corporation, foreign social purpose corporation, or other business entity if, immediately after the acquisition, the acquiring entity has control of the other entity.

(c) "Sale-of-assets reorganization" means the acquisition by one domestic social purpose corporation, foreign social purpose corporation, or other business entity in exchange in whole or in part for its equity securities, or the equity securities of a domestic social purpose corporation, a foreign social purpose corporation, or an other business entity that is in control of the acquiring entity, or for its debt securities, or debt securities of a domestic social purpose corporation, foreign social purpose corporation, or other business entity that is in control of the acquiring entity, that are not adequately secured and that have a maturity date in excess of five years after the consummation of the reorganization, or both, of all or substantially all of the assets of another domestic social purpose corporation, foreign social purpose corporation, or other business entity.

§ 2512. "Share exchange tender offer"

"Share exchange tender offer" means any acquisition by one social purpose corporation in exchange in whole or in part for its equity securities, or the equity securities of a corporation or a social purpose corporation that is in control of the acquiring social purpose corporation, of shares of another corporation or social purpose corporation, other than an exchange reorganization (subdivision (b) of Section 2511).

§ 2513. "Special purpose"

"Special purpose" means the special purpose set forth in a social purpose corporation's articles pursuant to subdivision (b) of Section 2602.

§ 2514. "Special purpose current report"

"Special purpose current report" means the report required of a social purpose corporation pursuant to Section 3501.

201.6 条和第 201.7 条要求的社会目标公司。

第 2511 条　“重组”

“重组”是指合并重组、置换重组或出售资产重组。

（a）“合并重组”是指依据第 1 分编第 11 章（从第 1100 条开始）和本分编第 8 章（从第 3200 条开始）的规定进行的合并，简易合并除外。

（b）“置换重组”是指一家本州社会目的公司、外州社会目的公司或其他置换中的商业实体，为了其股票或一家本州社会目的公司、外州社会目的公司或其他控制该收购实体的商业实体的股票，收购全部或部分其他本州社会目的公司、外州社会目的公司或其他商业实体的股票，在收购后该收购实体掌握了其他实体的控制权。

（c）“出售资产重组”是指一家本州社会目的公司、外州社会目的公司或其他置换中的商业实体，为了其股票或一家本州社会目的公司、外州社会目的公司或其他控制该收购实体的商业实体的股票，或者为了其债券或一家本州社会目的公司、外州社会目标公司或其他控制该收购实体的商业实体的没有充足的担保并在重组完成后 5 年内到期的债券，又或是为了两者，收购全部或部分其他本州社会目的公司、外州社会目的公司或其他商业实体的全部或大部分资产。

第 2512 条　“股份置换要约收购”

“股份置换要约收购”是指在置换中的社会目的公司，为了其股票或控制收购中的社会目的公司的公司或社会目的公司的股票，收购全部或部分其他公司或社会目的公司的股份，在置换重组［第 2511 条第（b）款］中的情况除外。

第 2513 条　“特定目的”

“特定目的”是指依据第 2602 条第（b）款的规定在社会目的公司的公司章程中规定的特定目的。

第 2514 条　“特定目的的现况报告”

“特定目的的现况报告”是指第 3501 条要求的社会目的公司报告。

§ 2515. "Special purpose MD&A"

"Special purpose MD&A" means the management discussion and analysis required of a social purpose corporation pursuant to subdivision (b) of Section 3500.

§ 2516. "Special purpose objectives"

"Special purpose objectives" means those objectives set forth by management and the directors of a social purpose corporation for purposes of measuring the impact of the social purpose corporation's efforts relating to its special purpose in accordance with Section 3500.

§ 2517. "Surviving social purpose corporation"

"Surviving social purpose corporation" means a social purpose corporation into which one or more other corporations or one or more other business entities is merged.

§ 2600. Formation; Filing of articles of incorporation

(a) One or more natural persons, partnerships, associations, social purpose corporations, or corporations, domestic or foreign, may form a social purpose corporation under this division by executing and filing articles of incorporation.

(b) If initial directors are named in the articles, each director named in the articles shall sign and acknowledge the articles. If initial directors are not named in the articles, the articles shall be signed by one or more incorporators who shall be persons described in subdivision (a).

(c) The corporate existence begins upon the filing of the articles and continues perpetually, unless otherwise expressly provided by law or in the articles.

§ 2600.5. Incorporation of existing business association; Required documents; Succession

(a) An existing business association organized as a trust under the laws of this state or of a foreign jurisdiction may incorporate under this division upon approval by its board of trustees or similar governing body and approval by the affirmative vote of two–thirds of the outstanding voting shares of beneficial interest, or a greater proportion of the outstanding shares of beneficial interest or the vote of those other classes of shares of beneficial interest as may be specifically required by its declaration of trust or bylaws, and the filing of articles with a certificate attached pursuant to this chapter.

(b) In addition to the matters required to be set forth in the articles pursuant to Section 2602, the articles filed pursuant to this section shall state that an existing unincorporated association, stating its name, is being incorporated by the filing of the articles.

(c) The articles filed pursuant to this section shall be signed by the president, or any vice president, and the secretary, or any assistant secretary, of the existing association and shall be accompanied by a certificate signed and verified by those officers signing the articles and stating that the incorporation of the association has been approved by the trustees and by the required vote of holders of shares of beneficial interest in accordance with subdivision (a).

第 2515 条　“特定目的管理讨论及分析”

“特定目的管理讨论及分析”，是指第 3500 条第（b）款要求的社会目的公司的管理讨论及分析。

第 2516 条　“特定目的标准”

“特定目的标准”是指社会目的公司的管理人员和董事为了衡量社会目的公司实现其依据第 3500 条规定设定的特定目的的效果所规定的标准。

第 2517 条　“存续社会目的公司”

“存续社会目的公司”，是指一个或多个其他公司，一个或多个商业实体被合并后存续的社会目的公司。

第 2600 条　成立；公司章程的备案

（a）一个或多个自然人，合伙，组织，社会目的公司或公司，本州或外州，可以依据本分编规定通过执行并备案公司章程成立社会目的公司。

（b）如果初始董事在公司章程中记名，每个在公司章程中记名的董事应签署并承认章程。如果初始董事不在公司章程中记名，公司章程应由一个或多个符合第（a）款规定的人签署。

（c）公司的存在始于公司章程备案并长期持续，法律或公司章程另有明确规定的除外。

第 2600.5 条　现存商业组织成为公司；要求的文件；继受

（a）依据本州或外州法律组建的作为信托的现存商业组织可以依据本分编的规定，经受托委员会或相似的管理机构的批准，并经享有受益权的已发行有表决权股份 2/3 或更多赞成票批准，或经信托或章程细则特别要求的其他类别的享有受益权的股份投票批准而成为公司，并依据本章规定在章程备案中附上证书。

（b）除第 2602 条要求在公司章程中列明的事项外，依据本条规定备案的章程应声明一个现存的非法人组织，表明其名称，通过备案公司章程而成为公司。

（c）依据本条规定备案的章程应由现存组织的总裁或副总裁和秘书或助理秘书签署，并应包含由管理人员签署和认证的证书，声明该组织的成立已由受托人批准，并依据第（a）款的规定由受益权股份持有人经规定的投票批准。

(d) Upon the filing of articles pursuant to this section, the social purpose corporation shall succeed automatically to all of the rights and property of the association being incorporated and shall be subject to all of its debts and liabilities in the same manner as if the social purpose corporation had itself incurred them. The incumbent trustees of the association shall constitute the initial directors of the social purpose corporation and shall continue in office until the next annual meeting of the shareholders or their earlier death, resignation, or removal. All rights of creditors and all liens upon the property of the association shall be preserved unimpaired. Any action or proceeding pending by or against the association may be prosecuted to judgment, which shall bind the social purpose corporation, or the social purpose corporation may be proceeded against or substituted in its place.

(e) The filing for record in the office of the county recorder of any county in this state in which any of the real property of the association is located of a copy of the articles filed pursuant to this section, certified by the Secretary of State, shall evidence record ownership in the social purpose corporation of all interests of the association in and to the real property located in that county.

§ 2601. Filing where "bank," "trust," or "trustee" in name; Certificate of approval of Commissioner of Business Oversight; Misleading or deceptive name; Reservation

(a) The Secretary of State shall not file articles setting forth a name in which "bank" "trust" "trustee" or related words appear, unless the certificate of approval of the Commissioner of Business Oversight is attached to the articles.

This subdivision does not apply to the articles of any social purpose corporation subject to the Banking Law on which is endorsed the approval of the Commissioner of Business Oversight or to which a certificate of approval of the Commissioner of Business Oversight is attached to the articles.

(b) (1) The Secretary of State shall not file articles that set forth a name that is likely to mislead the public or that is the same as, or resembles so closely as to tend to deceive, the name of a domestic corporation, the name of a domestic social purpose corporation, or the name of a foreign corporation that is authorized to transact intrastate business or has registered its name pursuant to Section 2101, a name that a foreign corporation has assumed under subdivision (b) of Section 2106, a name that will become the record name of a corporation or social purpose corporation or a foreign corporation upon the effective date of a filed corporate instrument where there is a delayed effective date pursuant to subdivision (c) of Section 110 or subdivision (c) of Section 5008, or a name that is under reservation for another corporation or social purpose corporation pursuant to this title, except that a social purpose corporation may adopt a name that is substantially the same as an existing

（d）公司章程依据本条规定一经备案，社会目的公司应自动继受被并入组织的所有权利和财产，并应承担其所有债务和责任，就像该社会目的公司自己的权利义务一样。现任的组织受托人应成为社会目的公司的初始股东并应继续任职到下一次年度股东会或其死亡、辞职或被解职。债权人和留置权人在组织财产中的全部权利应不被损害地保留。任何由该组织提出或针对该组织的未决诉讼或法律程序可被起诉至判决，该判决对社会目的公司具有约束力，或社会目的公司可以起诉或代替其位置。

（e）依据本条规定备案的公司章程，在州内该组织不动产所在县的县登记机构中的备案记录，经州务卿许可的，应能证明社会目的公司对组织位于该县的不动产的所有利益的名义所有权。

第 2601 条　名称中包含“银行”“信托”或“受托人”的备案；商业监督委员的批准证书；误导或虚假的名称；保留

（a）州务卿不应备案名称中有“银行”“信托”“受托人”或相关词语的公司章程，除非公司章程中附有商业监督委员的批准证书。本款规定不适用于受《银行法》调整的任何社会目的公司的公司章程，其公司章程应附由商业监督委员批准或商业监督委员许可的证书。

（b）（1）州务卿不应备案名称可能误导公众的章程，或名称与本州公司名称、本州社会目的公司名称、或依据第 2101 条规定被授权经营州内业务或已登记其名称的外州公司的名称、在依据第 110 条第 (c) 款或第 5008 条第 (c) 款规定已备案文件的生效日将成为公司或社会目的公司或外州公司登记名称的名称，或依据本编规定为另一个公司或社会目的公司保留的名称相同或相似以至于可能产生欺诈的名称。但是，社会目的公司可以证明本州或外州公司或社会目的公司同意并且州务卿认为在这种情况下公众不会被误导的除外，其可以采用一个与外州或本州的现存公司、社会目的公司、被许可经营州内业务的名称或依据第 2101 条规定登记的名称，实质相同的名称。尽管州务卿已对社会目的公司章程进行了备案，但社会目的公司违反本条规定使用名称的行为可被禁止。

corporation or social purpose corporation, foreign or domestic, which is authorized to transact intrastate business or has registered its name pursuant to Section 2101, upon proof of consent by the domestic or foreign corporation or social purpose corporation and a finding by the Secretary of State that under the circumstances the public is not likely to be misled.The use by a social purpose corporation of a name in violation of this section may be enjoined notwithstanding the filing of its articles by the Secretary of State.

(2) A corporation formed pursuant to this division before January 1, 2015, may elect to change its status from a flexible purpose corporation to a social purpose corporation by amending its articles of incorporation to change its name to replace "flexible purpose corporation" with "social purpose corporation" and to replace the term "flexible purpose corporation" with "social purpose corporation" as applicable in any statements contained in the articles. For any flexible purpose corporation formed prior to January 1, 2015, that has not amended its articles of incorporation to change its status to a social purpose corporation, any reference in this division to social purpose corporation shall be deemed a reference to "flexible purpose corporation."

(c) Any applicant may, upon payment of the fee prescribed in Article 3 (commencing with Section 12180) of Chapter 3 of Part 2 of Division 3 of Title 2 of the Government Code, obtain from the Secretary of State a certificate of reservation of any name not prohibited by subdivision (b), and upon the issuance of the certificate the name stated in the certificate shall be reserved for a period of 60 days. The Secretary of State shall not, however, issue certificates reserving the same name for two or more consecutive 60–day periods to the same applicant or for the use or benefit of the same person. No consecutive reservations shall be made by or for the use or benefit of the same person of names so similar as to fall within the prohibitions of subdivision (b).

§ 2602. Contents of articles of incorporation

The articles of incorporation shall set forth:

(a) The name of the social purpose corporation that shall contain the words "social purpose corporation" or an abbreviation of those words.

(b) (1) Either of the following statements, as applicable:

(A) "The purpose of this social purpose corporation is to engage in any lawful act or activity for which a social purpose corporation may be organized under Division 1.5 of the California Corporations Code, other than the banking business, the trust company business or the practice of a profession permitted to be incorporated by the California Corporations Code, for the benefit of the overall interests of the social purpose corporation and its shareholders and in furtherance of the following enumerated purposes ________________."

(B) "The purpose of this social purpose corporation is to engage in the profession of ________________ (with the insertion of a profession permitted to be incorporated by the

（2）依据本分编规定在 2015 年 1 月 1 日成立的公司可以通过修订公司章程，以“社会目的公司” 代替“灵活目标公司”来改变名称，选择将其形态从灵活目标公司变为社会目的公司，以适用于在公司章程中的任何声明。对于任何在 2015 年 1 月 1 日前成立的，没有选择修改其公司章程将其形态改变为社会目的公司的灵活目标公司，任何在本分编中提及“社会目的公司”之处应被认为是 “灵活目标公司”。

（c）任何申请人可以在支付政府法的第 2 编第 3 分编的第 2 节的第 3 章的第 3 分章（从第 12180 条开始）规定的费用后，从州务卿获得不被第（b）款规定禁止的任何名称的保留证书，并且一经发出，证书中的名称应保留 60 天。但是，州务卿不得向同一申请人或为同一人的使用或利益而签发连续两个或两个以上保留同一名称 60 日的证书。不应向同一人或为了同一人的使用或利益，连续保留过于相似以致被第（b）款规定禁止的名称。

第 2602 条　公司章程的内容

公司章程应规定：

（a）社会目的公司的名称应包含“社会目的公司”的词语或其缩写。

（b）（1）下列任何一项声明（如适用）：

（A）“社会目的公司的目的是从事《加利福尼亚州公司法典》的第 1.5 分编规定下社会目的公司可以从事的任何合法的行为或活动，除了银行业务、信托公司业务或依据《加利福尼亚州公司法典》允许的业务，为了社会目的公司及其股东的整体利益和促进以下的目的_________。”

（B）“社会目的公司的目的是从事______________的业务（《加利福尼亚州公司法典》允许的业务）和任何其他合法活动，除了银行或信托公司业务，不禁

California Corporations Code) and any other lawful activities, other than the banking or trust company business, not prohibited to a social purpose corporation engaging in that profession by applicable laws and regulations, for the benefit of the overall interests of the social purpose corporation and its shareholders and in furtherance of the following enumerated purposes ________________."

(2) A statement that a purpose of the social purpose corporation, in addition to the purpose stated pursuant to paragraph (1), is to engage in one or more of the following enumerated purposes, as also specified in the statement set forth pursuant to paragraph (1):

(A) One or more charitable or public purpose activities that a nonprofit public benefit corporation is authorized to carry out.

(B) The purpose of promoting positive effects of, or minimizing adverse effects of, the social purpose corporation's activities upon any of the following, provided that the corporation consider the purpose in addition to or together with the financial interests of the shareholders and compliance with legal obligations, and take action consistent with that purpose:

(i) The social purpose corporation's employees, suppliers, customers, and creditors.

(ii) The community and society.

(iii) The environment.

(3)(A) For any corporation organized under this division before January 1, 2015, that has not elected to change its status to a social purpose corporation, a statement that the corporation is organized as a flexible purpose corporation under the Corporate Flexibility Act of 2011. Such a corporation is not required to revise the statements required in paragraphs (1) and (2) to conform to the changes made by the act adding this subparagraph.

(B) For any corporation organized under this division on and after January 1, 2015, or that has elected to change its status to a social purpose corporation pursuant to paragraph (2) of subdivision (b) of Section 2601, a statement that the corporation is organized as a social purpose corporation under the Social Purpose Corporations Act.

(4) If the social purpose corporation is a social purpose corporation subject to the Banking Law (Division 1.1 (commencing with Section 1000) of the Financial Code), the articles shall set forth a statement of purpose that is prescribed by the applicable provision of the Banking Law.

(5) If the social purpose corporation is a social purpose corporation subject to the Insurance Code as an insurer, the articles shall additionally state that the business of the social purpose corporation is to be an insurer.

(6) If the social purpose corporation is intended to be a professional corporation within the meaning of the Moscone–Knox Professional Corporation Act (Part 4 (commencing with Section 13400) of Division 3), the articles shall additionally contain the statement required

止社会目的公司依据适当的法律法规，为了社会目的公司及其股东的整体利益和促进以下目的__________。”

（2）除依据第（1）项规定的目的外，声明社会目的公司的目的是下面列举的一个或多个目的，其可能也在依据第（1）项规定的声明中也有具体说明：

（A）非营利公共利益公司被许可实施的一项或多项慈善或公共目的活动。

（B）促进社会目的公司的活动对以下主体产生积极影响或最小化其负面影响的目标，前提是公司除了考虑股东的经济利益和遵守法律义务外，还要采取与目标一致的行动：

（i）社会目的公司的雇员、供应商、客户和债权人。
（ii）社区和社会。
（iii）环境。

（3）（A）对于任何在 2015 年 1 月 1 日前依据本分编规定组建的公司，如果该公司没有选择变更状态为社会目的公司，应声明该公司是依据 2011 年《公司灵活法案》成立的灵活目的公司。此等公司无须修订第（1）项和第（2）项规定的声明以符合增加本分项规定带来的改变。

（B）任何依据本分编规定在 2015 年 1 月 1 日组建的公司，或已经依据第 2601 条第（b）款第（2）项的规定选择改变其形态的社会目的公司，应声明公司是依据《社会目的公司法》成立的社会目的公司。

（4）如果社会目的公司是受《银行法》调整的［《金融法》的第 1.1 分编（从第 1000 条开始）］的社会目的公司，公司章程应列出《银行法》［《金融法》的第 1.1 分编（从第 1000 条开始）］相关条款规定的目的声明。

（5）如果社会目的公司是受《保险法》调整作为保险人的社会目的公司，公司章程应另外声明社会目的公司的业务是成为保险人。

（6）如果社会目的公司意图成为《莫斯康—诺克斯专业公司法》［第 3 分编第 4 节（从第 13400 条开始）］中规定的专业公司，公司章程应包含第 13404 条要求的声明。公司章程不得对社会目的公司的目的或权力作出任何进一步或额外的声

by Section 13404. The articles shall not set forth any further or additional statement with respect to the purposes or powers of the social purpose corporation, except by way of limitation or except as expressly required by any law of this state, other than this division, or any federal or other statute or regulation, including the Internal Revenue Code and regulations thereunder as a condition of acquiring or maintaining a particular status for tax purposes.

(7) If the social purpose corporation is a close social purpose corporation, a statement as required by subdivision (a) of Section 158.

(c) The name and street address in this state of the social purpose corporation's initial agent for service of process in accordance with subdivision (b) of Section 1502.

(d) The initial street address of the corporation.

(e) The initial mailing address of the corporation, if different from the initial street address.

(f) If the social purpose corporation is authorized to issue only one class of shares, the total number of shares that the social purpose corporation is authorized to issue.

(g) If the social purpose corporation is authorized to issue more than one class of shares, or if any class of shares is to have two or more series, the articles shall state:

(1) The total number of shares of each class that the social purpose corporation is authorized to issue and the total number of shares of each series that the social purpose corporation is authorized to issue or that the board is authorized to fix the number of shares of any such series.

(2) The designation of each class and the designation of each series or that the board may determine the designation of any such series.

(3) The rights, preferences, privileges, and restrictions granted to or imposed upon the respective classes or series of shares or the holders thereof, or that the board, within any limits and restrictions stated, may determine or alter the rights, preferences, privileges, and restrictions granted to or imposed upon any wholly unissued class of shares or any wholly unissued series of any class of shares. As to any series the number of shares of which is authorized to be fixed by the board, the articles may also authorize the board, within the limits and restrictions stated in the article or in any resolution or resolutions of the board originally fixing the number of shares constituting any series, to increase or decrease, but not below the number of shares of such series then outstanding, the number of shares of any series subsequent to the issue of shares of that series. If the number of shares of any series shall be so decreased, the shares constituting that decrease shall resume the status which they had prior to the adoption of the resolution originally fixing the number of shares of that series.

明，除非通过限制或本州法律另有明确要求（除本分编外）或任何联邦的或其他法律法规（包括《1986 年国内税收法典》及其规定）明确要求作为获得或维持税务目的特定地位的条件。

（7）如果社会目的公司是封闭社会目的公司，应作出第 158 条的第（a）款要求的声明。

（c）依据第 1502 条第（b）款规定设立的社会目的公司的初始代理人在本州的名称和街道地址。

（d）公司的初始街道地址。

（e）公司的初始邮寄地址，如果与初始街道地址不同。

（f）如果社会目的公司仅被批准发行一种类别股，社会目的公司被批准发行的股份数量。

（g）如果社会目的公司被批准发行多于一种的类别股，或任何类别的股份有两种或更多的系列，章程应声明：

（1）社会目的公司被批准发行的每种类别股的总体数量和社会目的公司被批准发行的每个系列股的总体数量或董事会被批准调整的任何该系列股的数量。

（2）每个类别的名称和每个系列的名称或董事会可以确定任何系列的名称。

（3）授予或施加给相关类别或系列股份或其持有者的权利、优先权、特权和限制，或董事会在规定的限制范围内，可以决定或改变授予或施加给全部未发行的类别股或类别股的全部未发行系列的权利、优先权、特权和限制。被批准由董事会调整股份数量的任何系列，公司章程可以批准董事会，在公司章程中规定的或董事会决议的调整任何系列的股份数量的限制范围内，增加或减少该系列股发行之后的任何系列股份的数量，但是不低于该系列当时已发行的股份数量。如果任何系列股的数量应减少，减少的股份应恢复到调整该系列股份数量的决议通过之前的状态。

§ 2603. Articles of incorporation; Optional provisions

The articles of incorporation may set forth:

(a) Any or all of the following provisions, which shall not be effective unless expressly provided in the articles:

(1) Granting, with or without limitations, the power to levy assessments upon the shares or any class of shares.

(2) Granting to shareholders preemptive rights to subscribe to any or all issues of shares or securities.

(3) Special qualifications of persons who may be shareholders.

(4) A provision limiting the duration of the social purpose corporation's existence to a specified date.

(5) A provision requiring, for any or all corporate actions, except as provided in Section 303, subdivision (b) of Section 402.5, subdivision (c) of Section 708, and Section 1900, the vote of a larger proportion or of all of the shares of any class or series, or the vote or quorum for taking action of a larger proportion or of all of the directors, than is otherwise required by Division 1 (commencing with Section 100) or this division.

(6) So long as consistent with the purpose of the social purpose corporation as set forth in the articles in accordance with subdivision (b) of Section 2602, a provision limiting or restricting the business in which the social purpose corporation may engage or the powers which the social purpose corporation may exercise, or both.

(7) A provision conferring upon the holders of any evidences of indebtedness, issued or to be issued by the social purpose corporation, the right to vote in the election of the directors and on any other matters on which shareholders may vote.

(8) A provision conferring upon shareholders the right to determine the consideration for which shares shall be issued.

(9) A provision requiring the approval of the shareholders (Section 153) or the approval of the outstanding shares (Section 152) for any corporate action, even though not otherwise required by Division 1 (commencing with Section 100) or this division.

(10) Provisions eliminating or limiting the personal liability of a director for monetary damages in an action brought by or in the right of the social purpose corporation for breach of a director's duties to the social purpose corporation and its shareholders, as set forth in Section 2700, subject to the following:

(A) The provision may not eliminate or limit the liability of directors (i) for acts or omissions that involve intentional misconduct or a knowing and culpable violation of law, (ii) for acts or omissions that a director believes to be contrary to the best interests of the social purpose corporation or its shareholders and its corporate purposes as expressed in its articles, or that involve the absence of good faith on the part of the director, (iii) for any transaction

第 2603 条　公司章程；任意条款

公司章程应规定：

（a）下列任何或所有的条款，除非在公司章程中有明确规定否则无效：

（1）有限制或无限制地授予对股份或任何类别股份进行评估的权力。

（2）授予股东优先认股权以认购任何或所有发行的股份或证券。

（3）成为股东的特别资格。

（4）限制社会目的公司存在期间持续至特定日期的条款。

（5）除第 303 条、第 402.5 条第 (b) 款、第 708 条第 (c) 款和 第 1900 条的规定外，要求任何或所有公司行为要通过任何类别或系列的多数或所有股份的投票，或法定多数或所有的董事投票，超过第 1 分编 (始于第 100 条) 或本分编中的规定。

（6）符合第 2602 条第 (b) 款规定的公司章程中的社会目的公司的目的，将限制或约束社会目的公司可能从事的业务或社会目的公司可能行使的权力，或两者兼有。

（7）授予由社会目的公司发出或将会发出的任何债务证明的持有人在董事选举和股东可投票的任何其他事项的表决权的条款。

（8）授予股东决定应发行何种股份的权利。

（9）要求股东批准（第 153 条）或已发行股份批准（第 152 条）的何公司行为的条款，即使在第 1 分编（始于第 100 条）或本分编没有其他要求。

（10）免除或限制董事因违反董事对社会目的公司及其股东的义务而在社会目的公司提起的诉讼中承担个人损害赔偿责任的条款，如第 2700 条的规定，应符合以下要求：

（A）该条款不得免除或限制基于以下行为的董事责任：（i）涉嫌故意违法的作为或不作为，（ii）董事认为与社会目的公司或其股东的最佳利益和其在公司章程中规定的公司目标相悖，或董事缺乏善意的作为或不作为；（iii）董事从交易中获得不适当的个人利益；（iv）行为表明，董事在履行董事义务的一般流程中，在董事明知或应知有严重损害社会目的公司、其股东或公司章程中规定的公司目标的

from which a director derived an improper personal benefit, (iv) for acts or omissions that show a reckless disregard for the director's duty to the social purpose corporation or its shareholders in circumstances in which the director was aware, or should have been aware, in the ordinary course of performing a director's duties, of a risk of serious injury to the social purpose corporation, its shareholders, or its corporate purposes as expressed in its articles, (v) for acts or omissions that constitute an unexcused pattern of inattention that amounts to an abdication of the director's duty to the social purpose corporation, its shareholders, or its corporate purposes as expressed in its articles pursuant to Section 2602, or (vi) under Section 310 or 2701.

(B) The provision shall not eliminate or limit the liability of a director for any act or omission occurring prior to the date on which the provision becomes effective.

(C) The provision shall not eliminate or limit the liability of an officer for any act or omission as an officer, notwithstanding that the officer is also a director or that his or her actions, if negligent or improper, have been ratified by the directors.

(11) A provision authorizing, whether by bylaw, agreement, or otherwise, the indemnification of agents of the social purpose corporation for breach of duty to the social purpose corporation and its shareholders, provided, however, that the provision may not provide for indemnification of any agent for any acts or omissions or transactions from which a director may not be relieved of liability as described in subparagraphs (A), (B), and (C) of paragraph (10).

Notwithstanding this subdivision, bylaws may require, for all or any actions by the board, the affirmative vote of a majority of the authorized number of directors. Nothing contained in this subdivision shall affect the enforceability, as between the parties thereto, of any lawful agreement not otherwise contrary to public policy.

(b) Reasonable restrictions upon the right to transfer or hypothecate shares of any class or classes or series, except that no restriction shall be binding with respect to shares issued prior to the adoption of the restriction unless the holders of those shares voted in favor of the restriction.

(c) The names and addresses of the persons appointed to act as initial directors.

(d) Any other provision, not in conflict with law, for the management of the business and for the conduct of the affairs of the social purpose corporation, including any provision that is required or permitted by this division to be stated in the bylaws.

§ 2604. Engagement in business activities

Subject to any limitation contained in the articles, to compliance with any other applicable laws, and to consistency with the special purpose of the social purpose corporation, any social purpose corporation other than a social purpose corporation subject to the Banking Law or a professional social purpose corporation may engage in any business

风险的情况下，不顾其对社会目的公司及其股东的义务；（v）构成不可原谅之疏忽的作为或不作为，视作未履行对社会目的公司、其股东或依据第 2602 条规定在公司章程中规定的公司目标的董事义务；或（vi）属于第 310 条或第 2701 条规定的情形。

（B）该条款不应免除或限制董事对在该条款生效前的作为或不作为承担的责任。

（C）该条款不应免除或限制高管作为或不作为的责任，即使高管也是董事或者其疏忽或不适当的行为已经被董事们批准。

（11）对代理人的任何行为或疏忽或交易进行赔偿，董事不得因此免除第（10）项第（A）、（B）、（C）分项规定的责任。

尽管本款有规定，章程细则可能要求所有或任何董事会的行为要由多数董事赞成通过。本款规定不影响任何当事人之间与公共政策不违背的合法协议的可执行性。

（b）对于转让或抵押任何类别或系列股份的权利的合理限制，除非股份的持有者支持该限制，否则对采纳限制前已发行的股票没有约束性。

（c）被任命为初始董事的人的名字和地址。

（d）与法律不冲突的，有关业务管理和社会目的公司事务执行的任何其他规定，包括本编规定要求或允许在章程细则中规定的任何条款。

第 2604 条　从事商业活动

除受《银行法》调整的社会目的公司或专业社会目的公司外，任何社会目的公司均可从事任何商业活动，但须遵守章程所载的任何限制、遵守适用的其他法律，并与社会目的公司的特殊目的保持一致。受《银行法》调整的社会目的公司或专业社会目的公司可从事其所遵守的相关法规和条例不禁止的任何商业活动。

activity. A social purpose corporation subject to the Banking Law or a professional social purpose corporation may engage in any business activity not prohibited by the respective statutes and regulations to which it is subject.

§ 2605. Powers

Subject to any limitations contained in the articles, to compliance with other provisions of this division and any other applicable laws, and to consistency with the special purpose of the social purpose corporation, a social purpose corporation shall have all the powers of a natural person in carrying out its business activities, including, without limitation, the power to:

(a) Adopt, use, and at will alter a corporate seal. Failure to affix a seal does not affect the validity of any instrument.

(b) Adopt, amend, and repeal bylaws.

(c) Qualify to do business in any other state, territory, dependency, or foreign country.

(d) Subject to the provisions of Section 510, issue, purchase, redeem, receive, take or otherwise acquire, own, hold, sell, lend, exchange, transfer or otherwise dispose of, pledge, use, and otherwise deal in and with its own shares, bonds, debentures, and other securities.

(e) Make donations, regardless of specific corporate benefit, for the public welfare or for a community fund, hospital, charitable, educational, scientific, civic, or similar purposes.

(f) Pay pensions, and establish and carry out pension, profit–sharing, share bonus, share purchase, share option, savings, thrift, and other retirement, incentive, and benefit plans, trusts, and provisions for any or all of the directors, officers, and employees of the social purpose corporation or any of its subsidiaries or affiliates, and to indemnify and purchase and maintain insurance on behalf of any fiduciary of these plans, trusts, or provisions.

(g) Subject to the provisions of Section 315, assume obligations, enter into contracts, including contracts of guaranty or suretyship, incur liabilities, borrow and lend money and otherwise use its credit, and secure any of its obligations, contracts, or liabilities by mortgage, pledge, or other encumbrance of all or any part of its property, franchises, and income.

(h) Participate with others in any partnership, joint venture, or other association, transaction, or arrangement of any kind, whether or not that participation involves sharing or delegation of control with or to others.

§ 2700. Duties of director

(a) A director shall perform the duties of a director, including duties as a member of any committee of the board upon which the director may serve, in good faith, in a manner the director believes to be in the best interests of the social purpose corporation and its shareholders, and with that care, including reasonable inquiry, as an ordinarily prudent person in a like position would use under similar circumstances.

第 2605 条　权力

受公司章程的限制，为了遵守本分编的其他条款和其他适用的法律，并符合社会目的公司的社会目的，社会目的公司应拥有自然人在进行商业活动时的所有权力，包括但不限于以下权力：

（a）承认、使用以及改变公司印章。未加盖印章不影响任何文件的效力。

（b）承认、修订以及废除章程细则。

（c）有资格在任何其他州、区域、属地或外州经商。

（d）依据第 510 条的规定，发行、购买、赎回、获得或以其他方式收购、所有、持有、出售、租借、置换、转让或以其他方式处分、抵押，使用以及以其他方式交易自己的股份、债券、信用债券以及其他证券。

（e）为了公共福利或社区基金、医院、慈善、教育、科学、市民或类似的目标进行捐赠，不用顾及特定公司利益。

（f）支付养老金，为社会目的公司或其任何子公司或附属机构的任何或所有董事、高管和员工建立和执行养老金、利润分配、股份分红、股份收购、股份期权、储蓄、节俭和其他退休、激励和福利计划、信托，并代表这些计划、信托或规定的任何受托人偿付、购买和维持保险。

（g）依据第 315 条的规定，承担义务，签订合同（包括担保或保证合同），承担责任，借款和贷款以及以其他方式使用其信用，以及通过抵押、保证或留置其全部或部分财产、特许权和收入为其义务、合同或债务进行担保。

（h）与他人在任何合伙、合资企业、其他组织、任何种类的交易或协议中合作，无论合作是否涉及分享或授予控制权。

第 2700 条　董事义务

（a）董事应善意地履行董事义务，包括作为董事会任何委员会成员的义务，以该董事认为符合社会目的公司及其股东最佳利益的方式，并且应有类似情况类似职位下一般谨慎人的注意，包括进行合理的调查。

(b) In performing the duties of a director, a director shall be entitled to rely upon information, opinions, reports, or statements, including financial statements and other financial data, in each case prepared or presented by any of the following:

(1) An officer or employee of the social purpose corporation whom the director believes to be reliable and competent in the matters presented.

(2) Counsel, independent accountants, or other persons as to matters which the director believes to be within that person's professional or expert competence.

(3) A committee of the board upon which the director does not serve, as to matters within its designated authority, which committee the director believes to merit confidence, so long as the director acts in good faith, after reasonable inquiry when the need therefor is indicated by the circumstances and without knowledge that would cause that reliance to be unwarranted.

(c) In discharging his or her duties, a director shall consider those factors, and give weight to those factors, as the director deems relevant, including the overall prospects of the social purpose corporation, the best interests of the social purpose corporation and its shareholders, and the purposes of the social purpose corporation as set forth in its articles.

(d) A person who performs the duties of a director in accordance with subdivisions (a), (b), and (c) shall have no liability based upon any alleged failure to discharge the person's obligations as a director. The liability of a director for monetary damages may be eliminated or limited by a social purpose corporation's articles to the extent provided in paragraph (10) of subdivision (a) of Section 2603.

(e) Notwithstanding any of the purposes set forth in its articles, a social purpose corporation shall not be deemed to hold any of its assets for the benefit of any party other than its shareholders. However, nothing in this division shall be construed as negating existing charitable trust principles or the Attorney General's authority to enforce any charitable trust created.

(f) Nothing in this section, express or implied, is intended to create or grant or shall create or grant any right in or for any person or any cause of action by or for any person, and a director shall not be responsible to any party other than the social purpose corporation and its shareholders.

§ 2701. Liability of director; Effect of abstention from voting; Suit; Damages; Subrogation

(a) Subject to Section 2700, directors of a social purpose corporation who approve any of the following corporate actions shall be jointly and severally liable to the social purpose corporation for the benefit of all of the creditors or shareholders entitled to institute an action under subdivision (c):

(1) The making of any distribution to its shareholders to the extent that it is contrary to

（b）在履行董事义务时，董事应有权在不同情况下依据由以下主体准备或提交的信息、意见、报告或报表，包括财务报表和其他财务数据：

（1）社会目的公司的高管或雇员，董事认为其在所提交的事项上是可靠和胜任的。

（2）律师、独立会计或董事认为该事项在其专业能力之内的其他人。

（3）该董事没有任职的，董事认为值得信任的，该事项在其被授予的权限之内的董事会委员会，只要董事在情况表明有此需要时，经过合理的调查，并在不知道会导致无根据的信赖的情况下，善意地行事。

（c）在履行其义务时，董事应考虑并重视其认为相关的因素，包括社会目的公司的整体预期，社会目的公司及其股东的最佳利益以及公司章程中规定的社会目的公司的目标。

（d）依据第（a）款、第（b）款和第（c）款规定履行董事义务的人不应对未能履行董事义务承担责任。董事的损害赔偿责任可以在第 2603 条的第（a）款第（10）项规定的范围内由社会目的公司的公司章程进行免除或限制。

（e）尽管公司章程中有公司目的的规定，社会目标公司不应被视为为其股东以外任何主体的利益持有其任何财产。但是，本分编规定不应被解释为否定现存的慈善信托原则或司法部长执行任何慈善信托的职权。

（f）本条规定的任何内容，无论是明示还是暗示，都无意于现在或将要创造或授予任何人的诉讼的权利或理由，并且董事不应对社会目的公司及其股东以外的任何主体负责。

第 2701 条　董事责任；弃权表决的影响；诉讼；损害赔偿；代位权

（a）依据第 2700 条的规定，批准以下任何公司行为的社会目的公司董事应就所有有权依据第（c）款规定提起诉讼的债权人或股东的利益与社会目的公司承担连带责任：

（1）超出第 500 条至第 503 条（包括该条）的规定向股东分红。

the provisions of Sections 500 to 503, inclusive.

(2) The distribution of assets to shareholders after institution of dissolution proceedings of the social purpose corporation, without paying or adequately providing for all known liabilities of the social purpose corporation, excluding any claims not filed by creditors within the time limit set by the court in a notice given to creditors under Chapter 18 (commencing with Section 1800) of Division 1, Chapter 20 (commencing with Section 1900) of Division 1, and Chapter 20 (commencing with Section 2000).

(3) The making of any loan or guaranty contrary to Section 2715.

(b) A director who is present at a meeting of the board, or any committee of the board, at which an action specified in subdivision (a) is taken and who abstains from voting, shall be deemed to have approved the action.

(c) Suit may be brought in the name of the social purpose corporation to enforce the liability as follows:

(1) Under paragraph (1) of subdivision (a) against any or all directors liable, by the persons entitled to sue under subdivision (b) of Section 506.

(2) Under paragraph (2) or (3) of subdivision (a) against any or all directors liable, by any one or more creditors of the social purpose corporation whose debts or claims arose prior to the time of any of the corporate actions specified in paragraph (2) or (3) of subdivision (a) and who have not consented to the corporate action, regardless of whether they have reduced their claims to judgment.

(3) Under paragraph (3) of subdivision (a) against any or all directors liable, by any one or more holders of shares outstanding at the time of any corporate action specified in paragraph (3) of subdivision (a) who have not consented to the corporate action, without regard to the provisions of Section 2900.

(d) The damages recoverable from a director under this section shall be the amount of the illegal distribution, or if the illegal distribution consists of property, the fair market value of that property at the time of the illegal distribution, plus interest thereon from the date of the distribution at the legal rate on judgments until paid, together with all reasonably incurred costs of appraisal or other valuation, if any, of that property or loss suffered by the social purpose corporation as a result of the illegal loan or guaranty, respectively, but not exceeding the liabilities of the social purpose corporation owed to nonconsenting creditors at the time of the violation and the injury suffered by nonconsenting shareholders.

(e) Any director sued under this section may implead all other directors liable and may compel contribution, either in that action or in an independent action against directors not joined in that action.

(f) Directors liable under this section shall also be entitled to be subrogated to the rights of the social purpose corporation:

（2）在社会目的公司的解散程序开始后，向股东分配财产，却没有充分偿付所有已知的社会目的公司的债务，不包括债权人在法院依据第 1 分编第 18 章（始于第 1800 条），第 20 章（始于第 1900 条）和第 20 章（始于第 2000 条）给出的债权人通知中的时限内未提出的主张。

（3）违反第 2715 条的规定进行借贷或担保。

（b）出席董事会或任何董事会委员会的董事采取第（a）款中规定的行为以及放弃投票，应被视为已经赞成了该行为。

（c）可以社会目的公司的名义提起诉讼，以执行以下责任：

（1）依据第（a）款第（1）项的规定，由有权依据第 506 条第（b）款规定诉讼的人向任何或所有有责任的董事提起诉讼。

（2）依据第 (a) 款第 (2) 或 (3) 项的规定，社会目的公司的任何一个或多个债权人，如果其债权是在第 (a) 款第 (2) 或 (3) 项规定的任何公司行为之前产生的，并且没有同意公司行为，则可向任何或所有有责任的董事提起诉讼，无论他们是否减少了诉讼请求。

（3）依据第 (a) 款第 (3) 项的规定，在第 (a) 款第 (3) 项规定的任何公司行为发生时，未同意公司行为的任何一个或多个已发行股票持有人，可向任何或所有有责任的董事提起诉讼，且与第 2900 条的规定无关。

（d）依据本条规定从董事处获得的损害赔偿应为非法分红的数额；或者如果非法分配的是财产，则为该财产在非法分配时的公平市场价值，加上从分配之日到支付日以法定利率计算的利息，和由对财产的评估或其他方式的评价所引发的合理成本（如有）；或社会目的公司由于非法借贷或担保遭受的损失，但是不超过社会目的公司在违法时对异议债权人的债务和异议股东遭受的损失。

（e）任何依据本条规定被诉的董事可以在该诉讼中或在针对未加入诉讼的董事的独立诉讼中起诉其他所有有责任的董事，并可以强制要求其分担赔偿数额。

（f）依据本条规定承担责任的董事也应有权代位向以下主体行使社会目的公司的权利：

(1) With respect to paragraph (1) of subdivision (a), against shareholders who received the distribution.

(2) With respect to paragraph (2) of subdivision (a), against shareholders who received the distribution of assets.

(3) With respect to paragraph (3) of subdivision (a), against the person who received the loan or guaranty.

Any director sued under this section may file a cross–complaint against the person or persons who are liable to the director as a result of the subrogation provided for in this subdivision or may proceed against them in an independent action.

§ 2702. Indemnification; Advance of expenses; Insurance; Applicability

(a) For the purposes of this section:

(1) "Agent" means any person who is or was a director, officer, employee, or other agent of the social purpose corporation, or is or was serving at the request of the social purpose corporation as a director, officer, employee, or agent of another foreign or domestic corporation, partnership, joint venture, trust, or other enterprise, or was a director, officer, employee, or agent of a foreign or domestic corporation which was a predecessor corporation of the social purpose corporation or of another enterprise at the request of the predecessor corporation.

(2) "Proceeding" means any threatened, pending, or completed action or proceeding, whether civil, criminal, administrative, or investigative.

(3) "Expenses" includes without limitation attorneys' fees and any expenses of establishing a right to indemnification under subdivision (b).

(b) Subject to the standards and restrictions, if any, set forth in its articles or bylaws, and subject to the limitations required by paragraph (11) of subdivision (a) of Section 2603, a social purpose corporation may indemnify and hold harmless any agent or any other person from and against any and all claims and demands whatsoever.

(c) Expenses incurred in defending any proceeding may be advanced by the social purpose corporation prior to the final disposition of the proceeding. The provisions of subdivision (a) of Section 315 do not apply to advances made pursuant to this subdivision.

(d) A social purpose corporation may purchase and maintain insurance on behalf of any of its agents against any liability asserted against or incurred by the agent in that capacity or arising out of the agent's status as an agent regardless of whether the social purpose corporation would have the power to indemnify the agent against that liability under this section. The fact that a social purpose corporation owns all or a portion of the shares of the company issuing a policy of insurance shall not render this subdivision inapplicable if either of the following conditions are satisfied:

(1) The insurance provided by this subdivision is limited as indemnification is required

（1）根据第（a）款第（1）项的规定，向收到分红的股东。

（2）根据第（a）款第（2）项的规定，向收到财产分配的股东。

（3）根据第（a）款第（3）项的规定，向收到贷款和担保的人。

依据本条规定被诉的董事可以基于本款规定的代位权向董事中有责任的人提出反诉，或在一个独立诉讼中起诉他们。

第 2702 条　赔偿；预付费用；保险；适用

（a）本条所称的：

（1）“代理人”，是指任何是或曾是董事、高管、雇员或其他社会目的公司代理人的人，或现在或曾经应社会目的公司要求担任其他外州或本州公司、合伙、合资企业、信托或其他企业的董事、高管、雇员或代理人，或曾是社会目的公司前身的外州或本州公司或经公司前身要求的其他企业的董事、高管、雇员或代理人。

（2）“程序”是指将要发生的、未决的或完成的诉讼或程序，无论是民事的、刑事的、行政的或调查的。

（3）“费用”包括但不限于律师费和依据第（b）款规定确立赔偿权利的任何费用。

（b）在依据公司章程或章程细则中的标准和限制，以及依据第 2603 条第（a）款第（11）项规定的限制的前提下，社会目的公司可以使任何代理人或其他人免于承担任何索赔或要求带来的损失。

（c）在程序中辩护产生的费用可以由社会目的公司在程序最终处置前垫付。第 315 条第（a）款的规定不适用于依据本款规定进行的垫付。

（d）社会目的公司可代表其任何代理人购买和维持保险，以应对代理人以该身份或因其代理人身份而被索赔或产生的任何责任，无论社会目的公司是否有权根据本款规定对该代理人的责任进行赔偿。社会目的公司拥有出具保险单的公司的全部或部分股份不应导致本款规定无法适用，如果满足以下任一条件：

（1）本款规定的保险受到限制，因为第 2603 条第（a）款第（11）项的规定要

to be limited by paragraph (11) of subdivision (a) of Section 2603.

(2) (A) The company issuing the insurance policy is organized, licensed, and operated in a manner that complies with the insurance laws and regulations applicable to its jurisdiction of organization.

(B) The company issuing the policy provides procedures for processing claims that do not permit that company to be subject to the direct control of the social purpose corporation that purchased that policy.

(C) The policy issued provides for some manner of risk sharing between the issuer and purchaser of the policy, on one hand, and some unaffiliated person or persons, on the other, such as by providing for more than one unaffiliated owner of the company issuing the policy or by providing that a portion of the coverage furnished will be obtained from some unaffiliated insurer or reinsurer.

(e) This section does not apply to any proceeding against any trustee, investment manager, or other fiduciary of an employee benefit plan in that person's capacity as such, even though the person may also be an agent as defined in subdivision (a) of the employer social purpose corporation. A social purpose corporation shall have power to indemnify a trustee, investment manager, or other fiduciary to the extent permitted by subdivision (f) of Section 2605.

§ 2800. Statements on certificates

(a) All certificates representing shares of a social purpose corporation shall contain, in addition to any other statements required by this section, the following conspicuous language on the face of the certificate.

"This entity is a social purpose corporation organized under Division 1.5 of the California Corporations Code. The articles of this corporation state one or more purposes required by law. Refer to the articles on file with the Secretary of State, and the bylaws and any agreements on file with the secretary of the corporation, for further information."

(b) There shall also appear on the certificate, the initial transaction statement, and written statements, unless stated or summarized under subdivision (a) or (b) of Section 417, the statements required by all of the following, to the extent applicable:

(1) The fact that the shares are subject to restrictions upon transfer.

(2) If the shares are assessable or are not fully paid, a statement that they are assessable or the statements required by subdivision (d) of Section 409 if they are not fully paid.

(3) The fact that the shares are subject to a voting agreement under subdivision (a) of Section 706 or an irrevocable proxy under subdivision (e) of Section 705 or restrictions upon voting rights contractually imposed by the social purpose corporation.

(4) The fact that the shares are redeemable.

(5) The fact that the shares are convertible and the period for conversion.

求对赔偿进行限制。

（2）（A）出具保险单的公司以符合其组织辖区内适用的保险法律法规的方式组建、许可和经营。

（B）出具保单的公司提供处理索赔的程序，不允许该公司受购买该保单的社会目的公司的直接控制。

（C）出具的保险单规定了保险单的出具者与购买者与一些独立的人之间的某种风险共担方式，例如通过规定出具保险单公司有不止一个独立的所有人或规定部分保额来自某些独立的保险人或再保险人。

（e）本条规定不适用于针对受托人、投资经理或雇员福利方案的其他受托人的任何程序，即使此人可能是在第（a）款中定义的社会目的公司的代理人。社会目的的公司应有权在第2605条第（f）款规定允许的范围内补偿受托人、投资经理或其他受托人。

第2800条　证书上的声明

（a）代表社会目的公司股份的证书，除了本条要求的其他声明，在证书的表面应明显记载以下的语句。

"该实体是依据加利福尼亚州公司法典第1.5编的规定组建的社会目的的公司。公司章程规定了一个或更多的法律要求的目标。更多的信息可以参考由州务卿备案的公司章程和公司秘书备案的章程细则和任何协议。"

（b）首次交易声明和书面声明也应该出现在证书上，依据第417条第（a）款或第（b）款的规定在适当的范围内声明或总结以下全部内容要求的声明除外：

（1）股份转让受限制的事实。

（2）如果股份是可评估的或未全额支付的，则应有可评估的声明或依据第409条第（d）款的要求进行声明。

（3）股份受制于第706条第（a）款规定下的投票协议或第705条第（e）款规定下不可撤销的投票权委托或社会目的的公司通过协议施加的投票权限制。

（4）股份是可赎回的。

（5）股份是可转换的以及转换的期限。

Statements or references to statements on the face of the certificate, the initial transaction statement, and written statements required by paragraph (1) or (2) shall be conspicuous.

(c) Unless stated on the certificate, the initial transaction statement, and written statements as required by subdivision (a), no restriction upon transfer, no right of redemption and no voting agreement under subdivision (a) of Section 706, no irrevocable proxy under subdivision (e) of Section 705, and no voting restriction imposed by the social purpose corporation shall be enforceable against a transferee of the shares without actual knowledge of the restriction, right, agreement, or proxy. With regard only to liability to assessment or for the unpaid portion of the subscription price, unless stated on the certificate as required by subdivision (a), that liability shall not be enforceable against a transferee of the shares. For the purpose of this subdivision, "transferee" includes a purchaser from the social purpose corporation.

(d) All certificates representing shares of a close social purpose corporation shall contain, in addition to any other statements required by this section, the following conspicuous legend on the face thereof:

"This social purpose corporation is a close social purpose corporation. The number of holders of record of its shares of all classes cannot exceed __________ (a number not in excess of 35). Any attempted voluntary inter vivos transfer which would violate this requirement is void. Refer to the articles, bylaws, and any agreements on file with the secretary of the social purpose corporation for further restrictions."

(e) Any attempted voluntary inter vivos transfer of the shares of a close social purpose corporation that would result in the number of holders of record of its shares exceeding the maximum number specified in its articles is void if the certificate contains the legend required by subdivision (c).

(f) Notwithstanding any other subdivision, the certificates representing shares of a corporation formed pursuant to this division as a "flexible purpose corporation" before January 1, 2015, shall continue to be valid even if the certificates reference a "flexible purpose corporation." A corporation formed pursuant to this division before January 1, 2015, may, but is not required to, reissue certificates to replace "flexible purpose corporation" with "social purpose corporation" as applicable. Any reference to a "flexible purpose corporation" or any abbreviation of that term in certificates representing shares of a corporation formed pursuant to this division before January 1, 2015, shall also be a reference to "social purpose corporation."

§ 2900. Institution of action; Pleadings; Bond; Hearing

(a) As used in this section:

(1) "Social purpose corporation" includes an unincorporated association.

在证书表面的声明或提及的声明，首次交易声明和第（1）项或第（2）项要求的书面声明应是显而易见。

（c）除非在证书、初始交易声明和第 (a) 款要求的书面声明中说明，否则，在不知道限制、权利、协议或委托书的情况下，社会目的公司施加的任何转让限制、赎回权和第 706 条第 (a) 款规定的投票协议、第 705 条 (e) 款规定的不可撤销的委托书以及投票限制都不能对股份受让人执行。对于评估的责任或认购费用的未支付部分，除按第 (a) 款的要求在证书上声明外，该责任对于股权受让人是不可执行的。本款所称的“受让人”是社会目的公司的买受人。

（d）所有代表封闭社会目的公司股份的证书应在表面上记载本条要求的任何其他声明之外的以下说明：

“社会目的公司是一个封闭社会目的公司。所有类别股份持有者的数量不超过_________（数量不超过 35）。任何违反该要求的自愿转让是无效的。进一步的信息请参见公司章程、章程细则和任何在社会目的公司秘书处备案的协议。”

（e）若证书上包含第（c）款要求的说明，将导致持股人数超过公司章程中规定的最高人数的，对封闭社会目的公司股份的自愿转让是无效的。

（f）尽管有其他款的规定，代表依据本编规定在 2015 年 1 月 1 日前成立的“灵活目的公司”股份的证书，应继续有效，即使证书提及“灵活目标公司”。依据本编规定在 2015 年 1 月 1 日前成立的公司可以，但是不被强制要求，重新发行证书以“社会目的公司”代替“灵活目标公司”。在代表依据本编规定在 2015 年 1 月 1 日前成立的公司股份的证书中提及“灵活目标公司”或该术语缩写，也应提及“社会目的公司”。

第 2900 条　诉讼制度；起诉；债券；审讯

（a）在本条中：

（1）“社会目的公司”包括非法人组织。

(2) "Board" includes the managing body of an unincorporated association.

(3) "Shareholder" includes a member of an unincorporated association.

(4) "Shares" includes memberships in an unincorporated association.

(b) Shareholders of a social purpose corporation may maintain a derivative lawsuit to enforce the requirements set forth in subdivision (c) of Section 2700.

(c) No action may be instituted or maintained in right of any domestic or foreign social purpose corporation under this section by any party other than a shareholder of the social purpose corporation.

(d) No action may be instituted or maintained in right of any domestic or foreign social purpose corporation by any holder of shares or of voting trust certificates of the social purpose corporation unless both of the following conditions exist:

(1) The plaintiff alleges in the complaint that plaintiff was a shareholder, of record or beneficially, or the holder of voting trust certificates at the time of the transaction or any part thereof of which plaintiff complains or that plaintiff's shares or voting trust certificates thereafter devolved upon plaintiff by operation of law from a holder who was a holder at the time of the transaction or any part thereof complained of.

Any shareholder who does not meet these requirements may nevertheless be allowed, in the discretion of the court, to maintain the action on a preliminary showing to and determination by the court, by motion and after a hearing, at which the court shall consider the evidence by affidavit or testimony, as it deems material, of all of the following:

(A) There is a strong prima facie case in favor of the claim asserted on behalf of the social purpose corporation.

(B) No other similar action has been or is likely to be instituted.

(C) The plaintiff acquired the shares before there was disclosure to the public or to the plaintiff of the wrongdoing of which plaintiff complains.

(D) Unless the action can be maintained the defendant may retain a gain derived from defendant's willful breach of a fiduciary duty.

(E) The requested relief will not result in unjust enrichment of the social purpose corporation or any shareholder of the social purpose corporation.

(2) The plaintiff alleges in the complaint with particularity plaintiff's efforts to secure from the board the action as plaintiff desires, or the reasons for not making that effort, and alleges further that plaintiff has either informed the social purpose corporation or the board in writing of the ultimate facts of each cause of action against each defendant or delivered to the social purpose corporation or the board a true copy of the complaint which plaintiff proposes to file.

(e) In any action referred to in subdivision (c), at any time within 30 days after service of summons upon the social purpose corporation or upon any defendant who is an officer

（2）“董事会”包括非法人组织的管理机构。
（3）“股东”包括非法人组织的成员。
（4）“股份”包括非法人组织中成员权。
（b）社会目的公司的股东可以提起派生诉讼以执行第2700条中第（c）款的要求。

（c）除了社会目的公司的股东，任何人不得以本州或外州社会目的公司的名义提起诉讼。

（d）任何社会目的公司的股份或表决权信托证书的持有者不得以本州或外州社会目标公司的名义提起诉讼，除非同时满足以下条件：

（1）原告在起诉书中宣称其在交易时或原告控告的任何阶段是名义或实质股东或表决权信托证书的持有人，又或原告的股份或表决权信托证书是通过运用法律在交易时或在原告控告的任何阶段从持有者处获得。

不符合这些要求的任何股东经法院裁量可以提起诉讼，基于动议和审理，法院应在宣誓和证言中考虑其认为重要的下列所有证据：

（A）有充分证据支持的以社会目的公司名义提出的索赔。

（B）没有其他类似诉讼已经或将要被提起。
（C）原告是在向公众或原告披露原告所诉的不法行为之前获得股份的。

（D）除非提起诉讼，否则被告可能由于故意违反信义义务而获得收益。

（E）请求的救济不会导致社会目的公司或其股东不当得利。

（2）原告在起诉书中特别指出，原告为确保董事会采取原告希望的行动所做的努力或未做此努力的原因，并进一步指出，原告已将针对每个被告的诉讼理由书面通知社会目的公司或董事会，或向社会目的公司或董事会交付原告拟提交的起诉书的真实副本。

（e）在第(c)款提及的任何诉讼中，在传票送达社会目的公司或社会目的公司高管或董事或在被诉行为发生时担任该职务的被告后30日内的任何时候，社会目

or director of the social purpose corporation, or held that office at the time of the acts complained of, the social purpose corporation or the defendant may move the court for an order, upon notice and hearing, requiring the plaintiff to furnish a bond as hereinafter provided. The motion shall be based upon one or both of the following grounds:

(1) There is no reasonable possibility that the prosecution of the cause of action alleged in the complaint against the moving party will benefit the social purpose corporation or its shareholders.

(2) The moving party, if other than the social purpose corporation, did not participate in the transaction complained of in any capacity.

The court on application of the social purpose corporation or any defendant may, for good cause shown, extend the 30–day period for an additional period or periods not exceeding 60 days.

(f) At the hearing upon any motion pursuant to subdivision (d), the court shall consider the evidence, written or oral, by witnesses or affidavit, as may be material to the ground or grounds upon which the motion is based, or to a determination of the probable reasonable expenses, including attorney's fees, of the social purpose corporation and the moving party that will be incurred in the defense of the action. If the court determines, after hearing the evidence adduced by the parties, that the moving party has established a probability in support of any of the grounds upon which the motion is based, the court shall fix the amount of the bond, not to exceed fifty thousand dollars ($50,000), to be furnished by the plaintiff for reasonable expenses, including attorney's fees, which may be incurred by the moving party and the social purpose corporation in connection with the action, including expenses for which the social purpose corporation may become liable pursuant to Section 2702. A ruling by the court on the motion shall not be a determination of any issue in the action or of the merits thereof. If the court, upon the motion, makes a determination that a bond shall be furnished by the plaintiff as to any one or more defendants, the action shall be dismissed as to the defendant or defendants, unless the bond required by the court has been furnished within such reasonable time as may be fixed by the court.

(g) If the plaintiff, either before or after a motion is made pursuant to subdivision (d), or any order or determination pursuant to the motion, furnishes a bond in the aggregate amount of fifty thousand dollars ($50,000) to secure the reasonable expenses of the parties entitled to make the motion, the plaintiff shall be deemed to have complied with the requirements of this section and with any order for a bond theretofore made, and any motion then pending shall be dismissed and no further or additional bond shall be required.

(h) If a motion is filed pursuant to subdivision (d), no pleadings need be filed by the social purpose corporation or any other defendant and the prosecution of the action shall be stayed until 10 days after the motion has been disposed of.

的公司或被告可在通知和听证后向法院申请命令，要求原告按下文规定提供保证金。该申请应依据以下一项或两项理由：

（1）依据起诉状中指控申请者的诉因进行起诉将不可能有利于社会目的公司或其股东。

（2）除社会目的公司外，申请者没有以任何身份参与被诉的交易。

在有充分理由的情况下，法院可根据社会目的公司或任何被告的申请，将 30 日的期间延长到不超过 60 天的期间。

（f）在对依据第（d）款规定提出申请的审理过程中，法院应考虑证人或宣誓书中的书面或口头的证据，其对该申请所依据的理由，或对决定社会目标公司和申请人在诉讼抗辩中可能产生的合理费用，包括律师费，有实质影响。在审理当事人提出的证据后，如果法院确定申请人依据的理由可能成立，法院应调整保证金的数额，不超过 50，000 美元，由原告承担以保证申请人和社会目的公司可能在诉讼中产生的合理费用，包括律师费和社会目的公司可能依据第 2702 条的规定承担责任而要负担的费用。法院对申请的裁决不应成为对诉讼中的问题或案情的决定。如果法院根据申请决定应由原告向一个或更多的被告提供保证金，则应驳回关于被告的诉讼，除非法院要求的保证金已在法院规定的合理时间内提供。

（g）在依据第（d）款规定提出申请或依据申请作出的命令或决定之前或之后，如果原告提供了总计 50，000 美元的保证金以确保有权提起申请的合理费用，则原告应被视为已遵守本条的要求和此前作出的任何保证金要求，并且待决的申请应被驳回并无须提交进一步或另外的保证金。

（h）如果依据第（d）款规定进行申请，社会目的公司或任何其他被告无须提交诉状并且起诉将暂停至申请被处理完毕后 10 天。

§ 3000. Approval of proposed amendment

(a) A proposed amendment to the articles of a social purpose corporation shall be approved by the outstanding shares of a class, regardless of whether that class is entitled to vote thereon by the provisions of the articles, if the amendment would:

(1) Increase or decrease the aggregate number of authorized shares of that class, other than an increase as provided in either subdivision (b) of Section 405 or subdivision (b) of Section 902.

(2) Effect an exchange, reclassification, or cancellation of all or part of the shares of that class, including a reverse stock split but excluding a stock split.

(3) Effect an exchange, or create a right of exchange, of all or part of the shares of another class into the shares of that class.

(4) Change the rights, preferences, privileges,or restrictions of the shares of that class.

(5) Create a new class of shares having rights, preferences, or privileges prior to the shares of that class, or increase the rights, preferences, or privileges or the number of authorized shares of any class having rights, preferences, or privileges prior to the shares of that class.

(6) In the case of preferred shares, divide the shares of any class into series having different rights, preferences, privileges, or restrictions or authorize the board to do so.

(7) Cancel or otherwise affect dividends on the shares of that class that have accrued but have not been paid.

(b) A proposed amendment shall be approved by an affirmative vote of at least two-thirds of the outstanding shares of each class, or a greater vote if required in the articles, regardless of whether that class is entitled to vote thereon by the provisions of the articles, if the amendment would materially alter any special purpose of the social purpose corporation stated in the articles pursuant to paragraph (2) of subdivision (b) of Section 2602, regardless of whether that purpose, as amended, would comply with the provisions of that paragraph.

(c) Different series of the same class shall not constitute different classes for the purpose of voting by classes except when a series is adversely affected by an amendment in a different manner than other shares of the same class.

(d) In addition to approval by a class as provided in subdivisions (a) and (b), a proposed amendment shall also be approved by the outstanding voting shares (Section 152).

§ 3001. Conversion to nonprofit corporation

(a) A social purpose corporation may, by amendment of its articles pursuant to this section, change its status to that of a nonprofit public benefit corporation, nonprofit mutual benefit corporation, nonprofit religious corporation, or cooperative corporation.

(b) The amendment of the articles to change its status to a nonprofit corporation shall revise the statement of purpose, delete the authorization for shares and any other provisions

第 3000 条　修订提议的批准

（a）如果对社会目的公司的章程提出的修订会导致以下情况，则应由某一类已发行股份批准，无论该类别的股份根据章程的规定是否有权对此进行投票：

（1）增加或减少该类别股份的总数，但依据第 405 条第（b）款或第 902 条第（b）款规定增加的除外。

（2）影响全部或部分该类别股份的置换、重新分类或取消，包括反向股票分割但不包括股票分割。

（3）将另一类别的全部或部分股份置换为该类别的股份，或创造一种置换权。

（4）改变该类别股份的权利、优先权、特权或限制。

（5）创建一个新的股份类别，其权利、优先权或特权优先于该类股份，或增加任何类别的权利、优先权或特权或授权股份的数量，其权利、优先权或特权优先于该类股份。

（6）针对优先股，将任何类别的股份分为具有不同权利、优先权、特权或限制的系列或授权董事会去这样做。

（7）取消或以其他方式影响已经产生但尚未支付的该类股份的利息。

（b）如果该修订将实质上改变社会目的公司依据第 2602 条第 (b) 款第 (2) 项的规定在公司章程中设定的特定目的，无论修订后该目标是否符合该项的规定，提议的修订应获得每个类别的已发行股份的至少 2/3 赞成票才能批准，或按照公司章程中更严格的表决要求批准，无论该类别依据公司章程的规定是否有权投票。

（c）同类别不同系列的股份在以类别进行投票时不应构成不同类别，除非一个系列受到修订不利影响的方式与同类别的其他股份不同。

（d）除由第（a）款和第（b）款规定的类别批准外，提议的修订应由已发行的表决权股（第 152 条）批准。

第 3001 条　转换为非营利公司

（a）社会目的公司可以通过依据本条规定修订公司章程，将其形态改为非营利公共利益公司、非营利互利公司、非营利宗教公司或合作公司。

（b）修改章程以改变其形态为非营利性公司，应修改目的声明，删除对股份的授权以及与授权或已发行股份有关的任何其他规定，进行其他必要或需要的修改，

relating to authorized or issued shares, make other changes as may be necessary or desired, and, if any shares have been issued, provide either for the cancellation of those shares or for the conversion of those shares to memberships of the nonprofit corporation. The amendment of the articles to change status to a cooperative corporation shall revise the statement of purpose, make other changes as may be necessary or desired, and, if any shares have been issued, provide for the cancellation of those shares or for the change of those shares to memberships of the cooperative corporation, if necessary.

(c) If shares have been issued, an amendment to change status to a nonprofit corporation shall be approved by all of the outstanding shares of all classes regardless of limitations or restrictions on their voting rights and an amendment to change status to a cooperative corporation shall be approved by the outstanding shares of each class regardless of limitations or restrictions on their voting rights.

(d) If an amendment pursuant to this section is included in a merger agreement, the provisions of this section shall apply, except that any provision for cancellation or conversion of shares shall be in the merger agreement rather than in the amendment of the articles.

(e) Notwithstanding subdivision (c), if a social purpose corporation is a mutual water company within the meaning of Section 2705 of the Public Utilities Code and under the terms of the status change each outstanding share is converted to a membership of a nonprofit mutual benefit corporation, an amendment to change status to a nonprofit mutual benefit corporation shall be approved by the outstanding shares of each class regardless of limitations or restrictions on their voting rights.

§ 3002. Conversion to business corporation

(a) A social purpose corporation may, by amendment of its articles pursuant to this section, change its status to that of a business corporation.

(b) The amendment of the articles to change status to a business corporation shall revise the statement of purpose to delete any provisions in the articles that are permitted by Section 2602, but that are not permitted to be in the articles of a domestic corporation.

(c) If shares have been issued, an amendment to change status to a business corporation shall be approved by an affirmative vote of at least two-thirds of the outstanding shares of each class, or a greater vote if required in the articles, regardless of whether that class is entitled to vote thereon by the provisions of the articles. If the status change is approved, shareholders with dissenting shares, as defined in subdivision (b) of Section 1300, may exercise dissenters' rights pursuant to Section 3305 and Chapter 13 (commencing with Section 1300) of Division 1.

(d) If an amendment pursuant to this section is included in a merger agreement, the provisions of this section shall apply, except that any provision for cancellation or conversion of shares shall be in the merger agreement rather than in the amendment of the articles.

如果已发行任何股份，则规定取消这些股份或将这些股份转换为非营利性公司的成员资格。为改变合作公司形态而对章程进行的修订应修改目的声明，进行其他必要或需要的修改，如果有任何已发行的股份，应规定取消这些股份或在必要时将这些股份转为合作公司的成员资格。

（c）如果股份已经发行，将公司形态改为非营利公司的修订应由全部类别的所有已发行股份批准，无论在投票权上是否有限制；将公司形态改为合作公司的修订应由每个类别的所有已发行股份批准，无论其在投票权上是否有限制。

（d）如果依据本条规定进行的修订包含在合并协议中，本条规定应适用，但任何关于取消或转换股份的条款应规定在合并协议中，而不是规定在公司章程的修正案中。

（e）尽管第（c）款有规定，如果社会目的公司是一个《公共设施法》中第 2705 条规定的共同水务公司且已发行股份根据形态变化条款转换为非营利互利公司的成员资格，公司形态改变为非营利互利公司的修订应由每个类别的已发行股份批准，无论其在投票权上是否有限制。

第 3002 条　转换为商事公司

（a）社会目的公司可以通过依据本条规定修订公司章程，将其形态改为商事公司。

（b）改变形态为商事公司的公司章程修订应删除公司章程中第 2602 条要求的任何条款以修订目标声明，以及在本州公司章程中不被允许的条款。

（c）如果股份已经发行，将公司形态改为商事公司的公司章程修订应获得每个类别已发行股份的至少 2/3 的赞成票，或由公司章程中更严格的表决要求批准，无论该类别股份依据公司章程是否有投票权。如果形态改变的修订被批准，有第 1300 条第（b）款规定的异议股份的股东，可以依据第 1 分编的第 3305 条和第 13 章（始于 Section 1300）的规定行使异议股东权。

（d）如果依据本条规定进行的修订包含在合并协议中，本条规定应适用，但任何关于取消或转换股份的条款应规定在合并协议中，而不是规定在公司章程的修正案中。

§ 3100. Transactions; Approval

(a) A social purpose corporation may sell, lease, convey, exchange, transfer, or otherwise dispose of all or substantially all of its assets when the principal terms of the transaction are approved by the board and are approved by an affirmative vote of at least two-thirds of the outstanding shares of each class, or a greater vote if required in the articles, regardless of whether that class is entitled to vote thereon by the provisions of the articles, either before or after approval by the board and before the transaction. A transaction constituting a reorganization shall be subject to Chapter 12 (commencing with Section 1200) of Division 1 and Chapter 10 (commencing with Section 3400) of this division and shall not be subject to this section, other than subdivision (d). A transaction constituting a conversion shall be subject to Chapter 11.5 (commencing with Section 1150) of Division 1 and Chapter 9 (commencing with Section 3300) of this division and shall not be subject to this section.

(b) Notwithstanding approval of two-thirds of the outstanding shares, the board may abandon the proposed transaction without further action by the shareholders, subject to the contractual rights, if any, of third parties.

(c) The sale, lease, conveyance, exchange, transfer, or other disposition may be made upon those terms and conditions and for that consideration as the board may deem in the best interests of the social purpose corporation. The consideration may be money, securities, or other property.

(d) If the acquiring party in a transaction pursuant to subdivision (a) or subdivision (g) of Section 2001 is in control of or under common control with the disposing social purpose corporation, the principal terms of the sale shall be approved by at least 90 percent of the voting power of the disposing social purpose corporation unless the disposition is to a domestic or foreign other business entity or social purpose corporation, the articles of incorporation of which specify materially the same purposes, in consideration of the nonredeemable common shares or nonredeemable equity securities of the acquiring party or its parent.

(e) Subdivision (d) shall not apply to a transaction if the Commissioner of Business Oversight, the Insurance Commissioner, or the Public Utilities Commission has approved the terms and conditions of the transaction and the fairness of those terms and conditions pursuant to Section 25142, Section 1209 of the Financial Code, Section 838.5 of the Insurance Code, or Section 822 of the Public Utilities Code.

§ 3200. Disappearing corporation is close social purpose corporation and surviving corporation is not close social purpose corporation

If any disappearing social purpose corporation in a merger is a close social purpose corporation and the surviving social purpose corporation is not a close social purpose corporation, the merger shall be approved by an affirmative vote of at least two-thirds of

第 3100 条　交易；批准

（a）社会目的公司可以出售、租赁、让与、置换、转让或以其他方式处置其全部或绝大部分财产，当董事会批准了交易的主要条款并获得每个类别已发行股份的至少 2/3 赞成票时，或按照公司章程中更严格的表决要求批准时，无论在董事会批准前后以及交易之前该类别股份依据公司章程是否有权投票，该交易都获得批准。构成重组的交易应受第 1 分编第 12 章（始于第 1200 条）和本分编第 10 章（始于第 3400 条）规定的调整，除了第（d）款外并不受本条规定的调整。构成转换的交易应受第 1 分编第 11.5 章（始于第 1150 条）和本分编第 9 章（始于第 3300 条）规定的调整，并不受本条规定的调整。

（b）尽管有 2/3 的已发行股份获得批准，董事会仍可放弃提议的交易，而无须股东采取进一步行动，但受第三方的合同权利（如有）的约束。

（c）出售、租赁、让与、置换、转让或以其他处置方式进行的交易可以依据董事会认为的符合社会目的公司最佳利益的条件和对价进行。对价可以是货币、证券或其他财产。

（d）如果依据第 2001 条第（a）款或第（g）款规定进行的交易中的收购方是处置的社会目的公司的控制方或共同控制方，出售的主要条款应由处置中社会目的公司至少 90% 的表决权批准，除非该处置是向一个本州或外州的其他商业实体或社会目的公司进行的，其在公司章程中规定了实质上相同的目标，以收购方或其母公司的普通股或不可赎回的股权证券为代价。

（e）第（d）款的规定不应适用于商业监督委员、保险委员或公共设施委员会依据《金融法》第 25142 条和第 1209 条、《保险法》第 838.5 条或《公共设施法》第 822 条的规定，批准了其交易的条款、条件和公平性的交易。

第 3200 条　消失公司是封闭社会目的公司并且存续公司不是封闭社会目的公司

如果任何合并中的消失公司是封闭社会目的公司并且存续公司不是封闭社会目的公司，该合并应由每个类别已发行股份的至少 2/3 的赞成票批准，或通过公司章程中更严格的表决要求批准，无论该类别股份依据消失社会目的公司的公司章程是

the outstanding shares of each class, or a greater vote if required in the articles, regardless of whether that class is entitled to vote thereon by the provisions of the articles, of the disappearing social purpose corporation. The articles may provide for a lesser vote, but not less than a majority of the outstanding shares of each class.

§ 3201. Disappearing corporation is social purpose corporation and surviving corporation is not social purpose corporation

If any disappearing corporation in a merger is a social purpose corporation and the surviving entity is not a social purpose corporation, or is a social purpose corporation the articles of incorporation of which set forth materially different purposes, the merger shall be approved by an affirmative vote of at least two-thirds of the outstanding shares of each class, or a greater vote if required in the articles, regardless of whether that class is entitled to vote thereon by the provisions of the articles, of the disappearing social purpose corporation. If the merger is approved, shareholders with dissenting shares, as defined in subdivision (b) of Section 1300, may exercise dissenters' rights pursuant to Section 3305 and Chapter 13 (commencing with Section 1300) of Division 1.

§ 3202. Disappearing corporation is social purpose corporation and surviving corporation is specified nonprofit corporation

If a disappearing social purpose corporation in a merger is a social purpose corporation governed by this division and the surviving corporation is a nonprofit public benefit corporation, a nonprofit mutual benefit corporation, or a nonprofit religious corporation, the merger shall be approved by all of the outstanding shares of all classes of the disappearing social purpose corporation, regardless of limitations or restrictions on their voting rights, notwithstanding any provision of Chapter 10 (commencing with Section 3400).

§ 3203. Merger of social purpose corporation with other business entity

(a) Any one or more social purpose corporations may merge with one or more other business entities. One or more domestic social purpose corporations not organized under this division and one or more foreign corporations may be parties to the merger. Notwithstanding this section, the merger of any number of social purpose corporations with any number of other business entities may be effected only if:

(1) In a merger in which a domestic social purpose corporation not organized under this division or a domestic other business entity is a party, it is authorized by the laws under which it is organized to effect the merger.

(2) In a merger in which a foreign corporation is a party, it is authorized by the laws under which it is organized to effect the merger.

(3) In a merger in which a foreign other business entity is a party, it is authorized by the laws under which it is organized to effect the merger.

(b) Each social purpose corporation and each other party that desires to merge shall

否有投票权。公司章程可以规定较宽松的表决要求，但是不能少于每个类别已发行股份的大多数。

第 3201 条　消失公司是社会目的公司并且存续公司不是社会目的公司

如果任何合并中的消失公司是社会目的公司并且存续公司不是社会目的公司，或存续公司是公司章程规定了实质上不同目标的社会目的公司，该合并应由每个类别已发行股份的至少 2/3 的赞成票批准，或按照公司章程中更严格的表决要求批准，无论该类别股份依据消失社会目标公司的公司章程是否有投票权。如果合并被批准，有第 1300 条第（b）款中的异议股份的股东，可以依据第 1 分编第 13 章（始于第 1300 条）和第 3305 条的规定行使异议股东权。

第 3202 条　消失公司是社会目的公司并且存续公司是特定非营利公司

如果任何合并中的消失公司是受本分编规定调整的社会目的公司并且存续公司是非营利公共利益公司、非营利互利公司或非营利宗教公司，合并应由消失社会目的公司的各类别的所有已发行股份批准，无论该类别股份的投票权是否受限，即使有第 10 章（始于第 3400 条）的规定。

第 3203 条　社会目的公司与其他商业实体合并

（a）任何一个或多个社会目的公司可以与一个或多个其他商业实体合并。一个或多个非依本分编规定组建的社会目的公司与一个或多个外州公司可以作为合并的一方。即使本条有规定，任何数量的社会目的公司与任何数量的商业实体的合并只有在以下情况才能实现：

（1）一个非依本分编规定组建的本州社会目的公司或本州其他商业实体是合并的一方，公司可依据其组建时所依据法律的授权完成合并。

（2）一个外州公司是合并的一方，则公司可依据其组建时所依据法律的授权完成合并。

（3）一个外州其他商业实体是合并的一方，则它可依据其组建时所依据法律的授权完成合并。

（b）每个社会目的公司和希望合并的其他各方都应批准合并协议，并应成为

approve, and shall be a party to, an agreement of merger. Other persons, including a parent party, may be parties to the agreement of merger. The board of each social purpose corporation that desires to merge, and, if required, the shareholders, shall approve the agreement of merger. The agreement of merger shall be approved on behalf of each party by those persons required to approve the merger by the laws under which it is organized. The agreement of merger shall state:

(1) The terms and conditions of the merger.

(2) The name and place of incorporation or organization of each party to the merger and the identity of the surviving party.

(3) The amendments, if any, subject to Sections 900, 902, 907, and 3002 to the articles of the surviving social purpose corporation, if applicable, to be effected by the merger. If any amendment changes the name of the surviving social purpose corporation, if applicable, the new name may be, subject to subdivision (b) of Section 2601, the same as or similar to the name of a disappearing party to the merger.

(4) The manner of converting the shares of each constituent social purpose corporation into shares, interests, or other securities of the surviving party. If any shares of any constituent social purpose corporation are not to be converted solely into shares, interests, or other securities of the surviving party, the agreement of merger shall state (A) the cash, rights, securities, or other property that the holders of those shares are to receive in exchange for the shares, which cash, rights, securities, or other property may be in addition to or in lieu of shares, interests, or other securities of the surviving party, or (B) that the shares are canceled without consideration.

(5) Any other details or provisions required by the laws under which any party to the merger is organized, including, if a domestic corporation is a party to the merger, Section 3203, if a public benefit corporation or a religious corporation is a party to the merger, Section 6019.1, if a mutual benefit corporation is a party to the merger, Section 8019.1, if a consumer cooperative corporation is a party to the merger, Section 12540.1, if a domestic limited partnership is a party to the merger, Section 15911.12, if a domestic partnership is a party to the merger, Section 16911, and if a domestic limited liability company is a party to the merger, Section 17551.

(6) Any other details or provisions as are desired, including, without limitation, a provision for the payment of cash in lieu of fractional shares or for any other arrangement with respect thereto consistent with the provisions of Section 407.

(c) Each share of the same class or series of any constituent social purpose corporation, other than the cancellation of shares held by a party to the merger or its parent, or a wholly owned subsidiary of either, in another constituent social purpose corporation, shall, unless all shareholders of the class or series consent and except as provided in Section 407, be

协议的一方。其他主体，包括母公司，可以成为合并协议的一方。意图合并的社会目的公司的董事会和股东（如有要求），应批准合并协议。合并协议应由合并所依据的法律规定的批准合并人员代表各方利益批准该合并。合并协议应说明：

（1）合并的条款和条件。

（2）合并各方的公司或组织的名称及地点，以及存续一方的身份。

（3）依据第900条、第902条、第907条和第3002条的规定对存续社会目的公司章程的修订将通过合并完成。如果修订改变了存续社会目的公司的名称，依据第2601条第（b）款的规定，新名称可以与合并中消失公司的名称相同或相似。

（4）将合并中社会目的公司的股份转换为存续一方的股份、权益或其他证券的方式。如果合并中社会目的公司的股份不能仅转换为存续一方的股份、权益或其他证券，合并协议应声明（A）股份持有人将收到现金、权益、证券或其他财产作为交换，这些现金、权益、证券或其他财产用以替代存续一方的股份、权益或其他证券，或（B）这些股份将被无偿取消。

（5）合并任何一方所依据的法律要求的任何其他细节或条款，包括：如果本州公司是合并的一方，则适用第3203条的规定；如果公共利益公司或宗教公司是合并的一方，则适用第6019.1条的规定；如果互利公司是合并的一方，则适用第8019.1条的规定；如果消费者合作公司是合并的一方，则适用第12540.1条的规定；如果本州有限合伙是合并的一方，则适用第15911.12条的规定；如果本州合伙是合并的一方，则适用第16911条的规定；以及如果本州有限责任公司是合并的一方，则适用第17551条的规定。

（6）任何其他需要的细节或条款，包括但不限于，规定支付现金以代替部分股份或符合第407条规定的任何其他安排。

（c）除合并一方或其母公司或两者的全资子公司在另一社会目的公司中持有的股份被注销外，任何社会目的公司的同一类别或系列的股份，在任何现金、权益、证券或其他财产的分配方面应被平等对待，除非该类别或系列的所有股东同意，但第407条另有规定的除外。尽管第（b）款第（4）项有规定，合并中的社会目的公司的

treated equally with respect to any distribution of cash, rights, securities, or other property. Notwithstanding paragraph (4) of subdivision (b), the nonredeemable common shares of a constituent social purpose corporation may be converted only into nonredeemable common shares of a surviving social purpose corporation or a parent party or nonredeemable equity securities of a surviving party other than a social purpose corporation if another party to the merger or its parent owns, directly or indirectly, prior to the merger shares of that corporation representing more than 50 percent of the voting power of that social purpose corporation, unless all of the shareholders of the class consent and except as provided in Section 407.

(d) Notwithstanding its prior approval, an agreement of merger may be amended prior to the filing of the agreement of merger or the certificate of merger, as is applicable, if the amendment is approved by the board of each constituent social purpose corporation and, if the amendment changes any of the principal terms of the agreement, by the outstanding shares, if required by Chapter 10 (commencing with Section 3400), in the same manner as the original agreement of merger. If the agreement of merger as so amended and approved is also approved by each of the other parties to the agreement of merger, the agreement of merger as so amended shall then constitute the agreement of merger.

(e) The board of a constituent social purpose corporation may, in its discretion, abandon a merger, subject to the contractual rights, if any, of third parties, including other parties to the agreement of merger, without further approval by the outstanding shares, at any time before the merger is effective.

(f) Each constituent social purpose corporation shall sign the agreement of merger by its chairperson of the board, president, or a vice president and also by its secretary or an assistant secretary acting on behalf of their respective corporations.

(g)

(1) If the surviving party is a domestic social purpose corporation, or if a domestic corporation or a foreign corporation, a public benefit corporation, a mutual benefit corporation, a religious corporation, or a corporation organized under the Consumer Cooperative Corporation Law (Part 2 (commencing with Section 12200) of Division 3) is a party to the merger, after required approvals of the merger by each constituent social purpose corporation through approval of the board and any approval of the outstanding shares required by Chapter 10 (commencing with Section 3400) and by the other parties to the merger, the surviving party shall file a copy of the agreement of merger with an officers' certificate of each constituent domestic social purpose corporation and foreign social purpose corporation attached stating the total number of outstanding shares of each class entitled to vote on the merger, and identifying any other person or persons whose approval is required, that the agreement of merger in the form attached or its principal terms, as required, were approved by that social purpose corporation by a vote of a number of shares of each class

不可赎回普通股只可以被转换为存续社会目的公司或母公司的不可赎回普通股或非社会目的公司的不可赎回股票，如果合并中另一方或其母公司在合并前直接或间接拥有代表该社会目的公司 50% 以上投票权，除非该类别所有股东同意并且第 407 条另有规定。

（d）尽管合并协议事先得到了批准，但在提交合并协议或合并证书（视情况而定）之前，如果该修订得到了每个社会目的公司的董事会的批准，并且如果该修订改变了协议的任何主要条款，如果第 10 章（始于第 3400 条）要求，以与原合并协议相同的方式得到了已发行股份股东的批准，则可以对合并协议进行修改。如果如此修订和批准的合并协议也得到了合并协议其他各方的批准，那么如此修订的合并协议应构成合并协议。

（e）在合并生效前的任何时间，合并中的社会目的公司的董事会可酌情放弃合并，但受第三方的合同权利（如有）的约束，包括合并协议的其他各方，而无须进一步获得已发行股份的批准。

（f）每个合并中的社会目的公司应由其董事会的董事长、主席或副主席以及其秘书或助理秘书代表各自的公司签署合并协议。

（g）

（1）如果存续实体是本州社会目的公司，或者本州或外州公司、公共利益公司、互利公司、宗教公司或依据《消费者合作公司法》（第 3 分编第 2 部分的规定（始于第 12200 条）组建的公司是合并中的一方，在通过每个合并中的社会目的公司的董事会批准和第 10 章（始于第 3400 条）及合并中的其他各方要求的已发行股份的批准后，存续方应备案合并协议的副本并附上每个合并中的本州社会目的公司和外州社会目的公司的高级管理人员证书，其应记载每个类别有权对合并进行投票的已发行股份总数并确认需由其审批的任何其他人，附上的合并协议或其主要条款由社会目的公司每个类别股份多于或等于要求的投票数批准，还要说明有权投票的每个类别和每个类别要求的投票比例及需由其审批的其他人，或者依据第 3401 条的规定合并协议可以由受该条规定调整的社会目的公司的董事会单独批准。如果母公司的股票将在合并中发行，被控制一方公司的高级管理人员证书应声明无须母公司股东的投票或已获得所需的投票。为代替高级管理人员的证书，合并证书应以州务卿要求的方式为每个合并中的其他商业实体备案。合并证书应经每个合并中的本州有限

that equaled or exceeded the vote required, specifying each class entitled to vote and the percentage vote required of each class and, if applicable, by that other person or persons whose approval is required, or that the merger agreement was entitled to be and was approved by the board alone, as provided in Section 3401, in the case of a social purpose corporation subject to that section. If equity securities of a parent party are to be issued in the merger, the officers' certificate of that controlled party shall state either that no vote of the shareholders of the parent party was required or that the required vote was obtained. In lieu of an officers' certificate, a certificate of merger, on a form prescribed by the Secretary of State, shall be filed for each constituent other business entity. The certificate of merger shall be executed and acknowledged by each domestic constituent limited liability company by all managers of the limited liability company, unless a lesser number is specified in its articles or organization or operating agreement, and by each domestic constituent limited partnership by all general partners, unless a lesser number is provided in its certificate of limited partnership or partnership agreement, and by each domestic constituent general partnership by two partners, unless a lesser number is provided in its partnership agreement, and by each foreign constituent limited liability company by one or more managers and by each foreign constituent general partnership or foreign constituent limited partnership by one or more general partners, and by each constituent reciprocal insurer by the chairperson of the board, president, or vice president, and by the secretary or assistant secretary, or, if a constituent reciprocal insurer has not appointed those officers, by the chairperson of the board, president, or vice president, and by the secretary or assistant secretary of the constituent reciprocal insurer's attorney–in–fact, and by each other party to the merger by those persons required or authorized to execute the certificate of merger by the laws under which that party is organized, specifying for that party the provision of law or other basis for the authority of the signing persons. The certificate of merger shall set forth, if a vote of the shareholders, members, partners, or other holders of interests of the constituent other business entity was required, a statement setting forth the total number of outstanding interests of each class entitled to vote on the merger and that the agreement of merger in the form attached or its principal terms, as required, were approved by a vote of the number of interests of each class that equaled or exceeded the vote required, specifying each class entitled to vote and the percentage vote required of each class, and any other information required to be set forth under the laws under which the constituent other business entity is organized, including, if a domestic limited partnership is a party to the merger, subdivision (a) of Section 15911.14, if a domestic partnership is a party to the merger, subdivision (b) of Section 16915, and, if a domestic limited liability company is a party to the merger, subdivision (a) of Section 17552. The certificate of merger for each constituent foreign other business entity, if any, shall also set forth the statutory or other basis under which that foreign other business entity

责任公司和有限责任公司的所有经理签署和确认，除非发生以下情形：在公司章程或组织经营协议上规定了较少的数量；由每个合并中的本州有限责任合伙的所有普通合伙人指定，除非有限合伙证书或合伙协议上规定了较少的数量；由每个合并中的本州普通合伙和两个合伙人指定，除非合伙协议上规定了较少的数量；由每个合并中的外州有限责任公司的一个或更多的经理；以及每个合并中的外州普通合伙或外州有限合伙和一个或更多的普通合伙人；以及每个合并中的互惠保险公司和董事会的董事长、主席或副主席和秘书或助理秘书，或者如果合并中的互惠保险公司没有任命那些高管，则由董事会的董事长、主席或副主席和互惠保险公司实际代理人的秘书或助理秘书；以及如果需要由合并中的其他商业实体的股东、成员、合伙人或其他权益持有人投票，则合并证书应载明一份声明，说明有权对合并进行投票的每一类别的已发行权益的总数，以及在所附表格中的合并协议或其主要条款（如有需要），列明有投票权的每一类别的权益数和每一类别的权益所需的投票百分比，以及根据组成其他商业实体的法律所需列明的任何其他资料，包括，如果国内有限合伙公司是合并的一方则适用第 15911.14 条第 (a) 款，如果合并一方为本州合伙则适用第 16915 条第 (b) 款，以及如果合并一方为本州有限责任公司则适用第 17552 条第 (a) 款。每个合并中的外州其他商业实体的合并证书，也应列出该实体组建时所依据的并授权其完成合并的法律或其他依据。该合并和被包含在合并协议中的存续社会目的公司的章程的修订，依据第 110 条第（c）款和第（j）款的规定，以及合并协议和每个合并中的本州公司和外州公司的高级管理人员证书和每个合并中的其他商业实体的合并证书经过备案生效，并且各方也成为一个实体。如果在 1974 年后组建的提供医疗事故保险的本州互惠保险公司是合并中的一方，合并协议或合并证书直至保险委员依据《保险法》第 1555 条的规定批准该合并及签发证书才完成备案。州务卿可以核证一份合并协议的副本，该副本独立于高级管理人员证书和合并证书高级职员证书和合并证书的副本。

is authorized by the laws under which it is organized to effect the merger. The merger and any amendment of the articles of the surviving social purpose corporation, if applicable, contained in the agreement of merger shall be effective upon filing of the agreement of merger with an officer's certificate of each constituent domestic corporation and foreign corporation and a certificate of merger for each constituent other business entity, subject to subdivision (c) of Section 110 and subject to the provisions of subdivision (j), and the several parties thereto shall be one entity. If a domestic reciprocal insurer organized after 1974 to provide medical malpractice insurance is a party to the merger, the agreement of merger or certificate of merger shall not be filed until there has been filed the certificate issued by the Insurance Commissioner approving the merger pursuant to Section 1555 of the Insurance Code. The Secretary of State may certify a copy of the agreement of merger separate from the officers' certificates and certificates of merger attached thereto.

(2) If the surviving entity is an other business entity, and no public benefit corporation, mutual benefit corporation, religious corporation, or corporation organized under the Consumer Cooperative Corporation Law (Part 2 (commencing with Section 12200) of Division 3) is a party to the merger, after required approvals of the merger by each constituent social purpose corporation through approval of the board and any approval of the outstanding shares required by Chapter 10 (commencing with Section 3400) and by the other parties to the merger, the parties to the merger shall file a certificate of merger in the office of, and on a form prescribed by, the Secretary of State. The certificate of merger shall be executed and acknowledged by each constituent domestic and foreign social purpose corporation by its chairperson of the board, president, or a vice president and also by its secretary or an assistant secretary and by each domestic constituent limited liability company by all managers of the limited liability company, unless a lesser number is specified in its articles of organization or operating agreement, and by each domestic constituent limited partnership by all general partners, unless a lesser number is provided in its certificate of limited partnership or partnership agreement, and by each domestic constituent general partnership by two partners, unless a lesser number is provided in its partnership agreement, and by each foreign constituent limited liability company by one or more managers and by each foreign constituent general partnership or foreign constituent limited partnership by one or more general partners, and by each constituent reciprocal insurer by the chairperson of the board, president, or vice president, and by the secretary or assistant secretary, or, if a constituent reciprocal insurer has not appointed those officers, by the chairperson of the board, president, or vice president, and by the secretary or assistant secretary of the constituent reciprocal insurer's attorney–in–fact.

The certificate of merger shall be signed by each other party to the merger by those persons required or authorized to execute the certificate of merger by the laws under which

（2）如果存续实体是一个其他商业实体，并且公共利益公司、互利公司、宗教公司或依据《消费者合作公司法》［第 3 分编第 2 部分（始于第 12200 条）］组建的公司均不是合并中的一方，在通过合并中的社会目的公司董事会批准和第 10 章（始于第 3400 条）及合并中的其他各方要求的已发行股份的批准后，合并中的当事人应在州务卿的办公室以其要求的形式备案合并证书。合并证书应由每个合并中的本州和外州社会目的公司及其董事会的董事长、主席或副主席和秘书或助理秘书签字和确认；以及由每个合并中的本州有限责任公司和有限责任公司的所有经理，除非在组织章程或组织经营协议上规定了较少的数量；以及由每个合并中的本州有限责任合伙的普通合伙人，除非在有限合伙证书或合伙协议上规定了较少的数量；以及由每个合并中的本州普通合伙的两个合伙人，除非在合伙协议上规定了较少的数量；以及由每个合并中的外州有限责任公司的一个或更多的经理；以及每个合并中的外州普通合伙或外州有限合伙的一个或更多的普通合伙人；以及每个合并中的互惠保险公司和董事会的董事长、主席或副主席和秘书或助理秘书，或如果合并中的互惠保险公司没有任命那些高级管理人员，则由董事会的董事长、主席或副主席和互惠保险公司实际代理人的秘书或助理秘书。合并证书应由合并中每个当事方中由该方组建时所依据的且规定该方签字人权力的法律条款或其他依据的法律要求或授权签署合并证书的人签署。

that party is organized, specifying for that party the provision of law or other basis for the authority of the signing persons.

The certificate of merger shall set forth all of the following:

(A) The name, place of incorporation or organization, and the Secretary of State's file number, if any, of each party to the merger, separately identifying the disappearing parties and the surviving party.

(B) If the approval of the outstanding shares of a constituent social purpose corporation was required by Chapter 10 (commencing with Section 3400), a statement setting forth the total number of outstanding shares of each class entitled to vote on the merger and that the principal terms of the agreement of merger were approved by a vote of the number of shares of each class entitled to vote and the percentage vote required of each class.

(C) The future effective date or time, not more than 90 days subsequent to the date of filing of the merger, if the merger is not to be effective upon the filing of the certificate of merger with the Secretary of State.

(D) A statement, by each party to the merger that is a domestic corporation not organized under this division, a foreign corporation or foreign other business entity, or an other business entity, of the statutory or other basis under which that party is authorized by the laws under which it is organized to effect the merger.

(E) Any other information required to be stated in the certificate of merger by the laws under which each respective party to the merger is organized, including, if a domestic limited liability company is a party to the merger, subdivision (a) of Section 17552, if a domestic partnership is a party to the merger, subdivision (b) of Section 16915, and, if a domestic limited partnership is a party to the merger, subdivision (a) of Section 15911.14.

(F) Any other details or provisions that may be desired.

Unless a future effective date or time is provided in a certificate of merger, in which event the merger shall be effective at that future effective date or time, a merger shall be effective upon the filing of the certificate of merger with the Secretary of State and the several parties thereto shall be one entity. The surviving other business entity shall keep a copy of the agreement of merger at its principal place of business which, for purposes of this subdivision, shall be the office referred to in Section 17057 if a domestic limited liability company, at the business address specified in paragraph (5) of subdivision (a) of Section 17552 if a foreign limited liability company, at the office referred to in subdivision (a) of Section 16403 if a domestic general partnership, at the business address specified in subdivision (f) of Section 16911 if a foreign partnership, at the office referred to in subdivision (a) of Section 15901.14 if a domestic limited partnership, or at the business address specified in paragraph (5) of subdivision (a) of Section 15911.14 if a foreign limited partnership. Upon the request of a holder of equity securities of a party to the merger, a

合并证书应规定以下内容：

（A）合并各方的名称，注册或组织地点以及州务卿的备案号（如有），分别标识消失方和存续方。

（B）如果第 10 章（始于第 3400 条）要求由合并中的社会目的公司中已发行股份进行批准，应有一项声明，说明每个类别有权对合并投票的已发行股份的总数和合并协议的主要条款，以及合并协议的主要条款的批准已符合有投票权类别股的数量和投票比例要求。

（C）如果合并协议经州务卿备案而合并却未生效，未来生效的日期和时间，在合并备案后的 90 天内。

（D）合并各方对其组建所依据的，授权其完成合并的法律或其他依据的记载，包括非依本分编规定组建的本州公司、外州公司或外州其他商业实体，或其他商业实体。

（E）各当事方组建时所依据的法律要求在合并证书中声明的任何其他信息，这些法律包括，若合并一方为本州有限责任公司则适用第 17552 条第（a）款；若合并一方为本州合伙则适用第 16915 条第（b）款；若合并一方为本州有限责任合伙则适用第 15911.14 条第（a）款。

（F）其他需要的任何细节或条款。

除非在合并证书中规定了未来的生效日期或时间，否则合并将在该未来的日期或时间生效，合并经州务卿对合并证书备案即应生效，并且其中各方成为一个实体。存续的其他商业实体依据本款规定应保留合并协议的副本在其主营业地，若为本州有限责任公司应是第 17057 条提及的办公室；若为外州有限责任公司应是第 17552 条第（a）款第（5）项规定的营业地址；若为应是第 16403 条第（a）款提到的办公室；若为外州合伙应是第 16911 条第（f）款规定的营业地址；若为外州合伙应是第 16911 条第（f）款规定的营业地址；若为本州有限合伙应是第 15901.14 条第（a）款提到的办公室；若为外州有限合伙应是第 15911.14 条第（a）款第（5）项规定的营业地址。经合并一方的股票持有者请求，有权代表存续的其他商业实体备案的人员应立即向该持有者提供一份合并协议副本。持有者对前述规定权利之放弃不可被强制执行。如果在 1974 年后组建的提供医疗事故保险的本州互惠保险公司是合并中的一方，合并协议或合并证书不应备案，直到保险委员依据《保险法》第 1555 条的规定批准该合并发出证书才完成备案。

person with authority to do so on behalf of the surviving other business entity shall promptly deliver to that holder, a copy of the agreement of merger. A waiver by that holder of the rights provided in the foregoing sentence shall be unenforceable. If a domestic reciprocal insurer organized after 1974 to provide medical malpractice insurance is a party to the merger the agreement of merger or certificate of merger shall not be filed until there has been filed the certificate issued by the Insurance Commissioner approving the merger in accordance with Section 1555 of the Insurance Code.

(h)

(1) A copy of an agreement of merger certified on or after the effective date by an official having custody thereof has the same force in evidence as the original and, except as against the state, is conclusive evidence of the performance of all conditions precedent to the merger, the existence on the effective date of the surviving party to the merger, and the performance of the conditions necessary to the adoption of any amendment to the articles, if applicable, contained in the agreement of merger.

(2) For all purposes for a merger in which the surviving entity is a domestic other business entity and the filing of a certificate of merger is required by paragraph (2) of subdivision (g), a copy of the certificate of merger duly certified by the Secretary of State is conclusive evidence of the merger of the constituent corporations, either by themselves or together with the other parties to the merger, into the surviving other business entity.

(i)

(1) Upon a merger pursuant to this section, the separate existences of the disappearing parties to the merger cease and the surviving party to the merger shall succeed, without other transfer, to all the rights and property of each of the disappearing parties to the merger and shall be subject to all the debts and liabilities of each in the same manner as if the surviving party to the merger had itself incurred them.

(2) All rights of creditors and all liens upon the property of each of the constituent social purpose corporations and other parties to the merger shall be preserved unimpaired, provided that those liens upon property of a disappearing party shall be limited to the property affected thereby immediately prior to the time the merger is effective.

(3) Any action or proceeding pending by or against any disappearing social purpose corporation or disappearing party to the merger may be prosecuted to judgment, which shall bind the surviving party, or the surviving party may be proceeded against or substituted in its place.

(4) Nothing in this section shall be construed to affect the liability a general partner of a disappearing limited partnership or general partnership may have in connection with the debts and liabilities of the disappearing limited partnership or general partnership existing prior to the time the merger is effective.

（h）

（1）合并协议副本在生效日或之后由有权官员认证，具有与原件相同的证据效力，除对国家不利外，是履行合并的所有先决条件、在合并的生效日存在的存续方以及履行通过合并协议中所载的任何条款修订的必要条件（如适用）的决定性证据。

（2）对于存续实体是本州其他商业实体并且合并证书的备案由第（g）款第（2）项规定的合并，由州务卿按时认证的合并证书的副本是各公司合并的决定性证据。

（i）

（1）在依据本条规定进行合并时，消失的合并方的单独存在即告终止，合并的存续方应继承每个消失的合并方的所有权利和财产，而无须其他转让，并应接受每个合并方的所有债务和责任，如同合并的存续方本身产生这些债务和责任。

（2）所有债权人的权利和每个合并中的社会目的公司和其他当事方所有财产上的留置权应完整保留，消失公司财产上的留置权应限于在合并生效前受影响的财产。

（3）由任何消失的社会目的公司或消失的合并方提起的或对其提起的任何诉讼或程序都可以被起诉至判决，这对存续一方具有约束力，或者存续方可以被起诉或被替代。

（4）本条规定不应被解释为影响在合并生效前存在的，与消失有限合伙或普通合伙的债务和责任有关的，消失有限合伙或普通合伙中普通合伙人可能承担的责任。

(j)

(1) The merger of domestic social purpose corporations with foreign corporations or foreign other business entities in a merger in which one or more other business entities is a party shall comply with subdivision (a) and this subdivision.

(2) If the surviving party is a domestic social purpose corporation or domestic other business entity, the merger proceedings with respect to that party and any domestic disappearing social purpose corporation shall conform to the provisions of this section. If the surviving party is a foreign corporation or foreign other business entity, then, subject to the requirements of subdivision (c), Section 407, Chapter 10 (commencing with Section 3400), and Chapter 13 (commencing with Section 1300) of Division 1, and, if applicable, corresponding provisions of the Nonprofit Corporation Law (Division 2 (commencing with Section 5002)) or the Consumer Cooperative Corporation Law (Part 2 (commencing with Section 12200) of Division 3), with respect to any domestic constituent corporations, Chapter 13 (commencing with Section 17600) of Title 2.5 with respect to any domestic constituent limited liability companies, Article 6 (commencing with Section 16601) of Chapter 5 of Title 2 with respect to any domestic constituent general partnerships, and Article 11.5 (commencing with Section 15911.20) of Chapter 5.5 of Title 2 with respect to any domestic constituent limited partnerships, the merger proceedings may be in accordance with the laws of the state or place of incorporation or organization of the surviving party.

(3) If the surviving party is a domestic social purpose corporation or domestic other business entity, the certificate of merger or the agreement of merger with attachments shall be filed as provided in subdivision (g) and thereupon, subject to subdivision (c) of Section 110 or paragraph (2) of subdivision (g), as applicable, the merger shall be effective as to each domestic constituent social purpose corporation and domestic constituent other business entity.

(4) If the surviving party is a foreign corporation or foreign other business entity, the merger shall become effective in accordance with the law of the jurisdiction in which the surviving party is organized, but, except as provided in paragraph (5), the merger shall be effective as to any domestic disappearing social purpose corporation as of the time of effectiveness in the foreign jurisdiction upon the filing in this state of a copy of the agreement of merger with an officers' certificate of each constituent foreign and domestic social purpose corporation and a certificate of merger of each constituent other business entity attached, which officers' certificates and certificates of merger shall conform to the requirements of paragraph (1) of subdivision (g). If one or more domestic other business entities is a disappearing party in a merger pursuant to this subdivision in which a foreign other business entity is the surviving entity, a certificate of merger required by the laws under which that domestic other business entity is organized, including subdivision (a) of Section 15911.14,

（j）

（1）本州社会目的公司与外州公司或外州其他商业实体的合并应遵守第（a）款和本款的规定。

（2）如果存续方是本州社会目的公司或本州其他商业实体，关于该方和消失社会目的公司的合并程序应遵守本条的规定。如果存续方是外州公司或外州商业实体，适用第10章（始于第3400条）的第407条第（c）款和第1分编第13章（始于第1300条）的要求，以及，如适用，关于本州公司则适用《非营利公司法》［第2分编（始于第5002条）］或《消费者合作公司法》［第3分编第2部分（始于Section 12200条）］的相关规定，关于本州有限责任公司则适用第2.5编第13章（始于第17600条）的相关规定，关于任何本州普通合伙则适用第2编第5章第6节（始于第16601条）的相关规定，关于任何本州有限合伙则适用第2编第5.5章第11.5节（始于第15911.20条）的相关规定，合并程序可以依据州法或存续方公司或组织所在地的法律。

（3）如果存续方是本州社会目的公司或本州其他商业实体，有附件的合并证书或合并协议应按第（g）款的规定进行备案，依据第110条第（c）款或第（g）款第（2）项的规定，合并应对合并中的本州社会目的公司和本州其他商业实体有效。

（4）如果存续方是外州公司或外州其他商业实体，合并依据存续方所在地的法律应有效，但是，第（5）项中另有规定的除外，合并应自其在外州管辖区域生效时对任何本州消失社会目的公司生效，经在本州备案合并协议的副本并附上符合第（g）款第（1）项规定的每个合并中的外州和本州社会目的公司的高级管理人员证书和每个合并中其他商业实体的合并证书。如果一个或多个本州其他商业实体是本款中的合并中的消失公司，其中外州其他商业实体是存续方，该本州其他商业实体组建时所依据的法律要求的合并证书也应在合并协议备案的同时进行备案，这些法律包括第15911.14条第（a）款、第16915的条第（b）款或第17552条第（a）款。

subdivision (b) of Section 16915, or subdivision (a) of Section 17552, as is applicable, shall also be filed at the same time as the filing of the agreement of merger.

(5) If the date of the filing in this state pursuant to this subdivision is more than six months after the time of the effectiveness in the foreign jurisdiction, or if the powers of a domestic disappearing social purpose corporation are suspended at the time of effectiveness in the foreign jurisdiction, the merger shall be effective as to the domestic disappearing social purpose corporation as of the date of filing in this state.

(6) In a merger described in paragraph (3) or (4), each foreign disappearing social purpose corporation that is qualified for the transaction of intrastate business shall by virtue of the filing pursuant to this subdivision, subject to subdivision (c) of Section 110, automatically surrender its right to transact intrastate business in this state. The filing of the agreement of merger or certificate of merger, as is applicable, pursuant to this subdivision, by a disappearing foreign other business entity registered for the transaction of intrastate business in this state shall, by virtue of that filing, subject to subdivision (c) of Section 110, automatically cancel the registration for that foreign other business entity, without the necessity of the filing of a certificate of cancellation.

§ 3300. Definitions

For purposes of this chapter, the following definitions shall apply:

(a) "Converted social purpose corporation" means a social purpose corporation that results from a conversion of an other business entity or a foreign other business entity or a foreign corporation pursuant to Section 3307.

(b) "Converted entity" means a domestic other business entity that results from a conversion of a social purpose corporation under this chapter.

(c) "Converting social purpose corporation" means a social purpose corporation that converts into a domestic other business entity pursuant to this chapter.

(d) "Converting entity" means an other business entity or a foreign other business entity or foreign corporation that converts into a social purpose corporation pursuant to Section 3307.

(e) "Domestic other business entity" has the meaning provided in Section 167.7.

(f) "Foreign other business entity" has the meaning provided in Section 171.07.

(g) "Other business entity" has the meaning provided in Section 174.5.

§ 3301. Conversion of social purpose corporation into domestic other business entity

(a) A social purpose corporation may be converted into a domestic other business entity pursuant to this chapter if, pursuant to the proposed conversion, each of the following conditions is met:

(1) Each share of the same class or series of the converting social purpose corporation

（5）如果依据本款规定在本州备案的日期晚于外州管辖区域生效后的 6 个月，或如果本州消失社会目的公司的权力在外州管辖区域生效时被暂停，该合并对于本州消失社会目标公司应在本州备案时生效。

（6）在第（3）项或第（4）项规定的合并中，每个有资格进行州内商业贸易的外州消失社会目的公司应依据本款规定进行备案，根据第 110 条第（c）款的规定，放弃其在本州进行州内商业贸易的权利。依据本条的合并协议或合并证书的备案，由在本州登记进行州内商业贸易的消失外州商业实体，通过备案，根据第 110 条第 (c) 款的规定，自动注销该外州商业实体的登记，无须备案注销证书。

第 3300 条　定义

本章中适用的定义如下：

（a）“已转换社会目的公司”是指由一个其他商业实体或外州其他商业实体或外州公司依据第 3307 条的规定转换而成的社会目的公司。

（b）“已转换实体”是指由本章规定下的社会目的公司转换而成的本州其他商业实体。

（c）“转换社会目的公司”是指依据本章规定转换为本州其他商业实体的社会目的公司。

（d）“转换实体”是指依据第 3307 条规定转换为社会目的公司的其他商业实体或外州其他商业实体或外州公司。

（e）“本州其他商业实体”与第 167.7 条中的含义相同。

（f）“外州其他商业实体”与第 171.07 条中的含义相同。

（g）“其他商业实体”与第 174.5 条中的含义相同。

第 3301 条　社会目的公司转换为本州其他商业实体

（a）社会目的公司可以依据本章规定转换为本州其他商业实体，若依据计划进行转换，则以下条件均需满足：

（1）除非该类别或系列的所有股东同意，否则股份持有人将会收到的任何现金、

shall, unless all the shareholders of the class or series consent, be treated equally with respect to any cash, rights, securities, or other property to be received by, or any obligations or restrictions to be imposed on, the holder of that share.

(2) The conversion is approved by an affirmative vote of at least two-thirds of the outstanding shares of each class, or a greater vote if required in the articles, regardless of whether that class is entitled to vote thereon by the provisions of the articles.

(3) Nonredeemable common shares of the converting social purpose corporation shall be converted only into nonredeemable equity securities of the converted entity unless all of the shareholders of the class consent.

(4) Paragraph (1) shall not restrict the ability of the shareholders of a converting social purpose corporation to appoint one or more managers, if the converted entity is a limited liability company, or one or more general partners, if the converted entity is a limited partnership, in the plan of conversion or in the converted entity's governing documents.

(b) Notwithstanding subdivision (a), the conversion of a social purpose corporation into a domestic other business entity may be effected only if both of the following conditions are met:

(1) The law under which the converted entity will exist expressly permits the formation of that entity pursuant to a conversion.

(2) The social purpose corporation complies with any and all other requirements of any other law that applies to conversion to the converted entity.

§ 3302. Approval of plan of conversion; Amendment; Abandonment

(a) A social purpose corporation that desires to convert to a domestic other business entity shall approve a plan of conversion. The plan of conversion shall state all of the following:

(1) The terms and conditions of the conversion.

(2) The jurisdiction of the organization of the converted entity and of the converting social purpose corporation and the name of the converted entity after conversion.

(3) The manner of converting the shares of each of the shareholders of the converting social purpose corporation into securities of, or interests in, the converted entity.

(4) The provisions of the governing documents for the converted entity, including the articles and bylaws, partnership agreement or limited liability company articles of organization and operating agreement, to which the holders of interests in the converted entity are to be bound.

(5) Any other details or provisions that are required by the laws under which the converted entity is organized, or that are desired by the converting social purpose corporation.

(b) The plan of conversion shall be approved by the board of the converting social

权益、证券或其他财产方面，或该股份持有人将会被施加的任何义务或限制，该转换中的社会目的公司的同一类别或系列的每股股份须获同等对待。

（2）该转换应通过每个类别已发行股份的至少 2/3 的赞成票或公司章程中更严格的表决要求的批准，无论该类别股份依据公司章程的规定是否有权投票。

（3）转换社会目的公司的不可赎回普通股应仅转换为已转换实体的不可赎回股票，除非该类别所有股东同意。

（4）第（1）项在转换方案或已转换实体的管理文件中不应限制转换社会目的公司的股东任命一个或多个经理（如果已转换实体是有限责任公司）或一个或多个普通合伙人（如果已转换实体是有限合伙）的能力。

（b）尽管第（a）款有规定，社会目的公司转换为本州其他商业实体需满足以下两项条件：

（1）已转换实体存在所依据的法律明确允许通过转换成立该实体。

（2）社会目的公司符合适用于转换为转换实体的其他法律的所有要求。

第 3302 条　转换方案的批准；修订；放弃

（a）要转换为本州其他商业实体的社会目的公司应批准其转换计划。该计划应规定以下内容：

（1）转换的条款和条件。

（2）已转换实体和转换社会目的公司的司法管辖权和转换后已转换实体的名称。

（3）将转换社会目的公司股东的股份转换为已转换实体的证券或权益的方法。

（4）已转换实体的管理文件的条款，包括公司章程和章程细则、合伙协议或有限责任公司的组织章程和经营协议，已转换实体的权益持有者将受其约束的所有文件。

（5）已转换实体组建时所依据的法律要求的或转换社会目的公司需要的任何其他细节或条款。

（b）转换方案应由转换社会目的公司的董事会批准，并且转换计划的主要条

purpose corporation, and the principal terms of the plan of the conversion shall be approved by at least two-thirds of the outstanding shares of each class, or a greater vote if required in the articles, regardless of whether that class is entitled to vote thereon by the provisions of the articles of the converting social purpose corporation. The approval of at least two-thirds of the outstanding shares may be given before or after approval by the board. If the plan is approved, shareholders with dissenting shares, as defined in subdivision (b) of Section 1300, may exercise dissenters' rights pursuant to Section 3305 and Chapter 13 (commencing with Section 1300) of Division 1.

(c) If the social purpose corporation is converting into a general or limited partnership or into a limited liability company, then in addition to the approval of the shareholders set forth in subdivision (b), the plan of conversion shall be approved by each shareholder who will become a general partner or manager, as applicable, of the converted entity pursuant to the plan of conversion unless the shareholders have dissenters' rights pursuant to Section 3305 and Chapter 13 (commencing with Section 1300) of Division 1.

(d) Upon the effectiveness of the conversion, all shareholders of the converting social purpose corporation, except those that exercise dissenters' rights as provided in Section 3305 and Chapter 13 (commencing with Section 1300) of Division 1, shall be deemed parties to any agreement or agreements constituting the governing documents for the converted entity adopted as part of the plan of conversion, regardless of whether a shareholder has executed the plan of conversion or those governing documents for the converted entity. Any adoption of governing documents made pursuant thereto shall be effective at the effective time or date of the conversion.

(e) Notwithstanding its prior approval by the board and the outstanding shares, or either of them, a plan of conversion may be amended before the conversion takes effect if the amendment is approved by the board and, if it changes any of the principal terms of the plan of conversion, by the shareholders of the converting social purpose corporation in the same manner and to the same extent as was required for approval of the original plan of conversion.

(f) A plan of conversion may be abandoned by the board of a converting social purpose corporation, or by the shareholders of a converting social purpose corporation if the abandonment is approved by the outstanding shares, in each case in the same manner as required for approval of the plan of conversion, subject to the contractual rights of third parties, at any time before the conversion is effective.

(g) The converted entity shall keep the plan of conversion at the principal place of business of the converted entity if the converted entity is a domestic partnership, or at the office at which records are to be kept under Section 15901.14 if the converted entity is a domestic limited partnership, or at the office at which records are to be kept under Section

款应通过每个类别已发行股份的至少 2/3 的赞成票或公司章程中更严格的表决要求的批准，无论该类别股份依公司章程的规定是否有权投票。至少 2/3 已发行股份的批准可以在董事会审批之前或之后给予。如果方案被批准，有第 1300 条第（b）款规定的异议股份的股东可以依据第 1 分编第 13 章（始于第 1300 条）和第 3305 条的规定行使异议股东权。

（c）如果社会目的公司正转换为一个普通或有限合伙或有限责任公司，在第（b）款规定的股东批准外，转换方案应由依据转换方案规定将成为已转换实体的普通合伙人或经理的每个股东批准，除非股东依据第 1 分编第 13 章（始于第 1300 条）和第 3305 条的规定享有异议股东权。

（d）转换一经生效，转换社会目的公司的所有股东，除依据第 1 分编第 13 章（始于第 1300 条） 和第 3305 条规定行使异议股东权的股东外，应作为转换方案一部分的已转换实体管理文件的协议当事方，无论股东是否签署转换方案或已转换实体的管理文件。根据该文件通过的任何管理文件应在转换的生效时间或日期生效。

（e）尽管有董事会和已发行股份或二者之一的事前批准，转换方案可以在转换生效前被修订，如果该修订被董事会批准并且其改变了转换方案的任何主要条款，则由转换社会目的公司的股东以原转换方案所要求的同样的方式和同样的范围进行批准。

（f）在转换生效前的任何时间，转换方案可以被进行转换的社会目的公司的董事会或股东放弃，如果该方案的放弃以批准转换方案要求的同样方式，被已发行股份批准，但受第三方的合同权利（如有）的约束。

（g）若已转换实体是本州合伙，已转换实体应在其主要营业地置备转换方案。若已转换实体是本州有限合伙，则应在依据第 15901.14 条的规定保存记录的办公室；若已转换实体是本州有限责任公司则应在依据第 17701.13 条规定保存记录的办公室。经转换社会目的公司的股东要求，代表可转换实体的被授权人应立即向股东提

17701.13 if the converted entity is a domestic limited liability company. Upon the request of a shareholder of a converting social purpose corporation, the authorized person on behalf of the converted entity shall promptly deliver to the shareholder, at the expense of the converted entity, a copy of the plan of conversion. A waiver by a shareholder of the rights provided in this subdivision shall be unenforceable.

§ 3303. Filing of documents

(a) After the approval, as provided in Section 3302, of a plan of conversion by the board and the outstanding shares of a social purpose corporation converting into a domestic other business entity, the converting social purpose corporation shall cause the filing of all documents required by law to effect the conversion and create the converted entity, which documents shall include a certificate of conversion or a statement of conversion as required by Section 3304, and the conversion shall thereupon be effective.

(b) A copy of the statement of partnership authority, certificate of limited partnership, or articles of organization complying with Section 3304, duly certified by the Secretary of State on or after the effective date, shall be conclusive evidence of the conversion of the social purpose corporation.

§ 3304. Statement and certificate of conversion; Effect of filing

(a) To convert a social purpose corporation:

(1) If the social purpose corporation is converting into a domestic limited partnership, a statement of conversion shall be completed on the certificate of limited partnership for the converted entity.

(2) If the social purpose corporation is converting into a domestic partnership, a statement of conversion shall be completed on the statement of partnership authority for the converted entity, or if no statement of partnership authority is filed, then a certificate of conversion shall be filed separately.

(3) If the social purpose corporation is converting into a domestic limited liability company, a statement of conversion shall be completed on the articles of organization for the converted entity.

(b) Any statement or certificate of conversion of a converting social purpose corporation shall be executed and acknowledged by those officers of the converting social purpose corporation as would be required to sign an officers' certificate, and shall set forth all of the following:

(1) The name and the Secretary of State's file number of the converting social purpose corporation.

(2) A statement of the total number of outstanding shares of each class entitled to vote on the conversion, that the principal terms of the plan of conversion were approved by a vote of the number of shares of each class which equaled or exceeded the vote required under

供合并协议的副本，由已转换实体付费。股东对本款规定的权利之放弃不可被强制执行。

第 3303 条　文件备案

（a）董事会和转换为本州其他商业实体的社会目的公司的已发行股份对转换方案依据第 3302 条规定进行批准后，转换社会目的公司应备案所有法律要求的文件以完成转换并创立已转换实体，该文件应包括第 3304 条要求的转换证书或转换声明，该转换随即生效。

（b）由州务卿在生效日或之后适时认证的符合第 3304 条规定的合伙授权声明、有限合伙证书或组织章程的副本，应成为社会目的公司转换的决定性证据。

第 3304 条　转换声明和证书；备案效力

（a）要对社会目的公司进行转换：

（1）如果社会目的公司要转换为本州有限合伙公司，转换声明应于已转换实体的有限合伙证书上完成。

（2）如果社会目的公司要转换为本州合伙公司，转换声明应于已转换实体的合伙授权声明上完成，如果没有备案合伙授权声明，那么转换证书应被单独备案。

（3）如果社会目的公司要转换为本州有限责任公司，转换声明应于已转换实体的组织章程上完成。

（b）转换社会目的公司的任何声明或转换证书应由转换社会目的公司的法律要求签署高级管理人员证书的高管签署和确认，并规定以下所有内容：

（1）转换社会目的公司的名称和州务卿备案号。

（2）一项声明，关于有权对转换进行投票的每个类别的已发行股份总数，转换方案的主要条款已由每个类别股份以等于或超过第 3302 条要求数量的投票批准，以及每个有权投票的类别和每个类别要求投票的比例。

Section 3302, specifying each class entitled to vote and the percentage vote required of each class.

(3) The name, form, and jurisdiction of organization of the converted entity.

(4) The name and street address of the converted entity's agent for service of process. If a corporation qualified under Section 1505 is designated as the agent, no address for it shall be set forth.

(c) The certificate of conversion shall be on a form prescribed by the Secretary of State.

(d) The filing with the Secretary of State of a statement of conversion on an organizational document or a certificate of conversion as set forth in subdivision (a) shall have the effect of the filing of a certificate of dissolution by the converting social purpose corporation and no converting social purpose corporation that has made the filing is required to file a certificate of election under Section 1901 or a certificate of dissolution under Section 1905 as a result of that conversion.

(e) Upon the effectiveness of a conversion pursuant to this chapter, a converted entity that is a domestic partnership, domestic limited partnership, or domestic limited liability company shall be deemed to have assumed the liability of the converting social purpose corporation to prepare and file or cause to be prepared and filed all tax and information returns otherwise required of the converting social purpose corporation under the Corporation Tax Law (Part 11 (commencing with Section 23001) of Division 2 of the Revenue and Taxation Code) and to pay any tax liability determined to be due pursuant to that law.

§ 3305. Shareholders with dissenting rights

The shareholders with dissenting rights, as defined in subdivision (b) of Section 1300, of a converting social purpose corporation shall have all of the rights under Chapter 13 (commencing with Section 1300) of Division 1 of the shareholders of a corporation involved in a reorganization requiring the approval of its outstanding shares, and the converting social purpose corporation shall have all of the obligations under Chapter 13 (commencing with Section 1300) of Division 1 of a corporation involved in the reorganization. Solely for purposes of applying the provisions of Chapter 13 (commencing with Section 1300) of Division 1, and not for purposes of this chapter, a conversion pursuant to Section 3301 or 3307 shall be deemed to constitute a reorganization.

§ 3306. Conversion fee

Notwithstanding any other provision of law, the Secretary of State shall charge an entity a fee not to exceed one hundred fifty dollars ($150) for its conversion made under this chapter.

§ 3307. Conversion of other business entity or foreign other business entity into social purpose corporation

(a) An other business entity or a foreign other business entity or a foreign corporation

（3）已转换实体的组织名称、形式和管辖权。
（4）已转换实体的代理人的送达名称和街道地址。

（c）转换证书应以州务卿规定的方式制作。

（d）由州务卿进行的对第（a）款规定的组织文件或转换证书上转换声明的备案，应有对转换社会目的公司的解散证书进行备案的效力，已进行备案的转换社会目的公司不被要求在转换完成后依据第 1901 条的规定备案选举证书或依据第 1905 条的规定备案解散证书。

（e）依据本章规定进行的转换一经生效，作为本州合伙、本州有限合伙或本州有限责任公司的已转换实体应被视为已经承担了转换社会目的公司的责任，即准备和备案或促使准备和备案《企业税法》[税收法第 2 分编的第 11 部分（始于第 23001 条）]要求的转换社会目的公司的所有税收和信息报表，并承担根据该法律确定的任何税收的责任。

第 3305 条　有异议权的股东

有第 1300 条第（b）款规定的异议权的转换社会目的公司股东，应有在第 1 分编第 13 章（始于第 1300 条）规定下的参与重组（要求已发行股份批准）的公司股东的所有权利，并且转换社会目的公司应有在第 1 分编第 13 章（始于第 1300 条）规定下的涉及重组的公司所有的义务。仅为了适用第 1 分编第 13 章（始于第 1300 条）的条款，而不是为了本章的目的，依据第 3301 条或第 3307 条规定进行的转换应被视为重组。

第 3306 条　转换费用

尽管法律有其他规定，但州务卿应向依据本章规定进行转换的实体收取不超过 150 美元的费用。

第 3307 条　其他商业主体或外州其他商业实体转换为社会目的公司

（a）其他商业实体，外州其他商业实体或外州公司可以依据本章规定转换为社

may be converted into a social purpose corporation pursuant to this chapter only if the converting entity is authorized by the laws under which it is organized to effect the conversion.

(b) An other business entity or a foreign other business entity or a foreign corporation that desires to convert into a social purpose corporation shall approve a plan of conversion or other instrument as is required to be approved to effect the conversion pursuant to the laws under which that entity is organized.

(c) The conversion of an other business entity or a foreign other business entity or a foreign corporation shall be approved by the number or percentage of the partners, members, shareholders, or other holders of interest of the converting entity that is required by the laws under which that entity is organized, or a greater or lesser percentage as may be set forth in the converting entity's partnership agreement, articles of organization, operating agreement, articles of incorporation, or other governing document in accordance with applicable laws.

(d) The conversion by an other business entity or a foreign other business entity or a foreign corporation shall be effective under this chapter upon the filing with the Secretary of State of the articles of incorporation of the converted corporation, containing a statement of conversion that complies with subdivision (e).

(e) A statement of conversion of an entity converting into a social purpose corporation pursuant to this chapter shall set forth all of the following:

(1) The name, form, and jurisdiction of organization of the converting entity.

(2) The Secretary of State's file number, if any, of the converting entity.

(3) If the converting entity is a foreign other business entity or a foreign corporation, the statement of conversion shall contain the following:

(A) A statement that the converting entity is authorized to effect the conversion by the laws under which it is organized.

(B) A statement that the converting entity has approved a plan of conversion or other instrument as is required to be approved to effect the conversion pursuant to the laws under which the converting entity is organized.

(C) A statement that the conversion has been approved by the number or percentage of the partners, members, shareholders, or other holders of interest of the converting entity that is required by the laws under which that entity is organized, or a greater or lesser percentage as may be set forth in the converting entity's partnership agreement, articles of organization, operating agreement, articles of incorporation, or other governing document in accordance with applicable laws.

(f) The filing with the Secretary of State of articles of incorporation containing a statement pursuant to subdivision (e) shall have the effect of the filing of a certificate of cancellation by a converting foreign limited liability company or foreign limited partnership,

会目的公司，只有在转换实体被其组建时所依据的法律批准时转换才得以生效。

（b）要转换为社会目的公司的其他商业实体、外州其他商业实体或外州公司，应依据实体组建时所依据的法律，批准转换方案或其他文件以完成转换。

（c）其他商业实体，外州其他商业实体或外州公司的转换，应按实体组建时所依据的法律要求的转化实体的合伙人、成员、股东或其他权益持有者的数量和比例批准，或者按转换实体的合伙协议、组织章程、经营协议、公司章程或符合所适用法律的其他管理文件中规定的更高或更低的比例批准。

（d）其他商事主体，外州其他商事实体或外州公司进行的转换，应在州务卿对包含符合第（e）款规定的转换声明的已转换公司章程进行备案后生效。

（e）依据本章转换为社会目的公司的实体的转换声明应规定以下所有内容：

（1）转换实体的名称、形式和管辖。
（2）转换实体的州务卿备案号。
（3）如果转换实体是外州其他商业实体或外州公司，转换声明应包含以下内容：

（A）声明转换实体已被组建时所依据的法律授权完成转换。

（B）声明转换实体已依据转换实体组建时所依据的法律批准了转换方案或其他文件以完成转换。

（C）声明转换已按实体组建时所依据的法律要求的转换实体的合伙人、成员、股东或其他权益持有人的数量或比例批准，或按转换实体的合伙协议、组织章程、经营协议、公司章程或符合所适用法律的其他管理文件中规定的更高或更低的比例批准。

（f）在州务卿处备案的包含第（e）款规定的声明的公司章程，应有备案进行转换的外州有限责任公司或外州有限合伙的注销证书的效力，并且进行备案的转换外州有限责任公司或外州有限合伙不被要求按照第 17708.06 条或第 15909.07 条的

and no converting foreign limited liability company or foreign limited partnership that has made the filing is required to file a certificate of cancellation under Section 17708.06 or 15909.07 as a result of that conversion. If a converting entity is a foreign corporation qualified to transact business in this state, the foreign corporation shall, by virtue of the filing, automatically surrender its right to transact intrastate business.

§ 3400. Approval of reorganization or share exchange tender offer

A reorganization or a share exchange tender offer shall be approved by the board of all of the following:

(a) Each constituent social purpose corporation in a merger reorganization.

(b) The acquiring social purpose corporation in an exchange reorganization.

(c) The acquiring social purpose corporation and the social purpose corporation whose property and assets are acquired in a sale–of–assets reorganization.

(d) The acquiring social purpose corporation in a share exchange tender offer.

(e) The social purpose corporation in control of any constituent or acquiring domestic or foreign social purpose corporation or other business entity under subdivision (a), (b), or (c) and whose equity securities are issued, transferred, or exchanged in the reorganization, hereafter a "parent party."

§ 3401. Approval of terms of reorganization; By outstanding shares; Where not required

(a) The principal terms of a reorganization shall be approved by the outstanding shares of each class of each social purpose corporation the approval of whose board is required under Section 3400, except as provided in subdivision (b) and except that, unless otherwise provided in the articles, no approval of any class of outstanding preferred shares of the surviving or acquiring social purpose corporation or parent party shall be required if the rights, preferences, privileges, and restrictions granted to or imposed upon that class of shares remain unchanged, subject to the provisions of subdivision (c). For the purpose of this subdivision, two classes of common shares differing only as to voting rights shall be considered as a single class of shares.

(b) No approval of the outstanding shares is required by subdivision (a) if the social purpose corporation, or its shareholders immediately before the reorganization, or both, shall own, immediately after the reorganization, equity securities, other than any warrant or right to subscribe to or purchase those equity securities, of the surviving or acquiring social purpose corporation or a parent party possessing more than five–sixths of the voting power of the surviving or acquiring social purpose corporation or parent party. In making the determination of ownership by the shareholders of a social purpose corporation, immediately after the reorganization, of equity securities pursuant to the preceding sentence, equity securities that they owned immediately before the reorganization as shareholders of another

规定备案作为转换结果的注销证书。如果转换实体是有权在本州进行交易的外州公司，备案后外州公司应自动放弃其进行州内交易的权利。

第 3400 条　重组或股份置换要约收购的批准

重组或股份置换要约收购应由以下主体的董事会批准：

（a）每个合并重组中的社会目的公司。

（b）在置换重组中的收购社会目的公司。

（c）在出售资产重组中的收购社会目的公司和财产及资产被收购的社会目的公司。

（d）在股份置换要约收购中的收购社会目的公司。

（e）控制任何子公司、收购本州或外州的社会目的公司或第（a）、（b）或（c）款规定下的其他商业实体的，以及其证券在重组中被发行、转让或置换的社会目的公司，以下称为“母公司”。

第 3401 条　重组条款的批准；通过已发行股份；没有要求之处

（a）除第（b）款另有规定外，重组的主要条款应由第 3400 条要求董事会批准的社会目的公司的每个类别的已发行股份批准，另外，除公司章程中另有规定外，如果依据第（c）款规定被授予或施加在该类别股份的权利、优先权、特权和限制保持不变，任何存续或收购社会目的公司或母公司的任何类别已发行优先股不应被要求进行批准。在本款规定中，仅在表决权上不同的两个类别的普通股应被视为一类股份。

（b）如果社会目的公司或其股东或二者均在重组之前或之后，除认购或购买那些证券的任何权证或权利外，拥有存续或收购社会目的公司或其母公司多于 5/6 表决权的证券，不再需要依第（a）款规定由已发行股份进行批准。在社会目的公司的股东依据前款决定证券的所有权时，他们在重组前作为交易另一方股东所拥有的权益证券应不予考虑。在本条中社会目的公司的表决权应通过假设所有可转换证券，立即或在未来的某个时间被转换为有权表决的股份的情况下进行计算，但假设中不包括认购或购买这些股份的任何认股权证或权利。

party to the transaction shall be disregarded. For the purpose of this section, the voting power of a social purpose corporation shall be calculated by assuming the conversion of all equity securities convertible, immediately or at some future time, into shares entitled to vote but not assuming the exercise of any warrant or right to subscribe to or purchase those shares.

(c) Notwithstanding subdivisions (a) and (b), the principal terms of a reorganization shall be approved by the outstanding shares of the surviving social purpose corporation in a merger reorganization, as otherwise required by Chapter 10 (commencing with Section 3400), if any amendment is made to its articles that would otherwise require that approval.

(d) Notwithstanding subdivisions (a) and (b), the principal terms of a reorganization shall be approved by the affirmative vote of at least two–thirds of each class, or a greater vote if required in the articles, of the outstanding shares of any class of a social purpose corporation that is a party to a merger or sale–of–assets reorganization if holders of shares of that class receive shares of the surviving or acquiring social purpose corporation or parent party having different rights, preferences, privileges, or restrictions than those surrendered. Shares in a foreign corporation received in exchange for shares in a domestic social purpose corporation shall be deemed to have different rights, preferences, privileges, and restrictions within the meaning of the preceding sentence.

(e) Notwithstanding subdivisions (a) and (b), the principal terms of a reorganization shall be approved by the affirmative vote of at least two–thirds of each class, or a greater vote if required in the articles, of the outstanding shares of any social purpose corporation that is a close social purpose corporation if the reorganization would result in the holders receiving shares or other interests of a corporation or other business entity that is not a close social purpose corporation. The articles may provide for a lesser vote, but not less than a majority of the outstanding shares of each class.

(f) Notwithstanding subdivisions (a) and (b), the principal terms of a reorganization shall be approved by a vote of at least two–thirds of the outstanding shares of each class, or a greater vote if required in the articles, of a social purpose corporation that is a party to a merger reorganization, regardless of whether that class is entitled to vote thereon by the provisions of the articles, if holders of shares of that class receive interests of a surviving other business entity in the merger that is not a social purpose corporation, or receive interests of a surviving social purpose corporation the articles of incorporation of which specify a materially different purpose as part of the reorganization.

(g) Notwithstanding subdivisions (a) and (b), the principal terms of a reorganization shall be approved by all shareholders of any class or series if, as a result of the reorganization, the holders of that class or series become personally liable for any obligations of a party to the reorganization, unless all holders of that class or series have the dissenters' rights provided in Chapter 13 (commencing with Section 1300) of Division 1.

（c）尽管第（a）款和第（b）款有规定，如果对其公司章程的任何修订需要得到批准，那么重组的主要条款应得到合并重组中存续社会目的的公司的已发行股份批准，如第 10 章（始于第 3400 条）所要求的那样。

（d）尽管第（a）款和第（b）款有规定，如果作为合并或资产出售重组一方的社会目的公司的任何类别的已发行股份的持有人，收到存续或收购社会目的的公司或母公司的股份，并有与让与股份不同的权利、优先权、特权或限制，则重组的主要条款应得到每个类别至少 2/3 的赞成票，或满足章程中规定的更高的表决要求。本州社会目的公司在股份置换中获得的外州公司的股份应被视为有前款中的不同权利、优先权、特权或限制。

（e）尽管第（a）款和第（b）款有规定，如果重组将导致持有者收到非封闭的公司或其他商业实体的股份或其他权益，重组的主要条款应由任何封闭社会目的公司的每个类别已发行股份至少 2/3 赞成票批准或满足公司章程中更严格的表决要求。公司章程可以规定更低的投票要求，但是不少于每个类别已发行股份的大多数。

（f）尽管第（a）款和第（b）款有规定，作为合并重组一方的社会目的公司，重组的主要条款应得到每一类已发行股份的至少 2/3 的投票批准，或满足公司章程规定的更高的表决要求，无论该类股份根据公司章程规定是否有权投票，如果该类股份的持有人获得合并中存续非社会目的的公司的其他商业实体的权益，或获得存续社会目的的公司的权益，而该公司作为重组一方在章程中规定了实质不同的目的。

（g）尽管第（a）款和第（b）款有规定，如果作为重组的结果，该类别或系列的股份持有者对重组的一方负有个人责任，重组的主要条款应由任何类别或系列的所有股东批准，除该类别或系列的持有者有第 1 分编第 13 章（始于第 1300 条）规定的股东异议权。

(h) Any approval required by this section may be given before or after the approval by the board. Notwithstanding approval required by this section, the board may abandon the proposed reorganization without further action by the shareholders, subject to the contractual rights, if any, of third parties.

§ 3500. Annual report; Management discussion and analysis; To be sent to shareholders

(a) The board of a social purpose corporation shall cause an annual report to be sent to the shareholders not later than 120 days after the close of the fiscal year. The annual report shall contain (1) a balance sheet as of the end of that fiscal year and an income statement and a statement of cashflows for that fiscal year, accompanied by any report thereon of independent accountants or, if there is no report, the certificate of an authorized officer of the social purpose corporation that the statements were prepared without audit from the books and records of the corporation, and (2) the information required by subdivision (b).

(b) The board shall cause to be provided with the annual report, a management discussion and analysis (special purpose MD&A) concerning the social purpose corporation's stated purpose or purposes as set forth in its articles pursuant to paragraph (2) of subdivision (b) of Section 2602, and, to the extent consistent with reasonable confidentiality requirements, shall cause the special purpose MD&A to be made publicly available by posting it on the social purpose corporation's Internet Web site or providing it through similar electronic means. The special purpose MD&A shall include the information specified in this subdivision and any other information that the social purpose corporation's officers and directors believe to be reasonably necessary or appropriate to an understanding of the social purpose corporation's efforts in connection with its special purpose or purposes. The special purpose MD&A shall also include the following information:

(1) Identification and discussion of the overall objectives of the social purpose corporation relating to its special purpose or purposes, and an identification and explanation of any changes made in those special purpose objectives during the fiscal year.

(2) Identification and discussion of the material actions taken by the social purpose corporation during the fiscal year to achieve its special purpose objectives, the impact of those actions, including the causal relationships between the actions and the reported outcomes, and the extent to which those actions achieved the special purpose objectives for the fiscal year.

(3) Identification and discussion of material actions, including the intended impact of those actions, that the social purpose corporation expects to take in the short term and long term with respect to achievement of its special purpose objectives.

(4) A description of the process for selecting, and an identification and description of, the financial, operating, and other measures used by the social purpose corporation during

（h）本条要求的任何审批可以在董事会批准之前或之后进行。即使本条要求批准，董事会可以无须股东进一步行动而放弃提议的重组，但受第三方的合同权利（如有）的约束。

第 3500 条　年度报告；管理讨论及分析；送交股东

（a）社会目的公司的董事会应在会计年度结束后的 120 日内将年度报告送交股东。年度报告应包含（1）该会计年度内的资产负债表和该会计年度的损益表和现金流表，附随独立会计的任何报告，如果没有报告，附随社会目的公司被授权的高管对这些报表中未经审计的公司账簿和记录的认证，以及（2）第（b）款要求的信息。

（b）董事会应提供一份年度报告，内容为社会目的公司依据第 2602 条第（b）款第（2）项的规定在公司章程中规定的目标的管理讨论及分析（特定目的管理讨论及分析），符合合理保密要求的情况下通过将特定目的管理讨论及分析公布于社会目的公司的网站或通过相似的电子方式使公众可获取。特定目的管理讨论及分析应包括本款规定的信息以及社会目的公司的高管和董事认为对理解社会目的公司在其特定目的上的努力合理必要或适当的任何其他信息。特定目的管理讨论及分析也应包括以下信息：

（1）确定和讨论社会目的公司与其特殊目的相关的总体目标，并确定和解释该会计年度期间这些特殊目的目标的任何变化。

（2）在该会计年度，社会目的公司为达到特定目的而采取的重要措施和那些措施的影响，包括措施和报告结果之间的因果关系，以及通过那些措施完成该会计年度特定目的的程度的确定和讨论。

（3）社会目的公司希望在短期和长期采取的与完成特定目的有关的重要措施，包括对那些措施意图达到的影响的确定和讨论。

（4）对选择程序的说明，以及社会目的公司在该会计年度为了评价其完成特定目的的情况所采取的财务、经营和其他措施，包括解释社会目的公司选择那些措

the fiscal year for evaluating its performance in achieving its special purpose objectives, including an explanation of why the social purpose corporation selected those measures and identification and discussion of the nature and rationale for any material changes in those measures made during the fiscal year.

(5) Identification and discussion of any material operating and capital expenditures incurred by the social purpose corporation during the fiscal year in furtherance of achieving the special purpose objectives, a good faith estimate of any additional material operating or capital expenditures the social purpose corporation expects to incur over the next three fiscal years in order to achieve its special purpose objectives, and other material expenditures of resources incurred by the social purpose corporation during the fiscal year, including employee time, in furtherance of achieving the special purpose objectives, including a discussion of the extent to which that capital or use of other resources serves purposes other than and in addition to furthering the achievement of the special purpose objectives.

(c) Except as may otherwise be excused pursuant to subdivision (h) of Section 1501.5, the reports specified in subdivisions (a) and (b) shall be sent to the shareholders at least 15 days, or, if sent by bulk mail, 35 days, prior to the annual meeting of shareholders to be held during the next fiscal year. This requirement shall not limit the requirement for holding an annual meeting as required by Section 600.

(d) If no annual report for the last fiscal year has been sent to shareholders, the social purpose corporation shall, upon the written request of any shareholder made more than 120 days after the end of that fiscal year, deliver or mail to the person making the request within 30 days following the request, the statements required by subdivisions (a) and (b) for that fiscal year.

(e) A shareholder or shareholders holding at least 5 percent of the outstanding shares of any class of a social purpose corporation may make a written request to the social purpose corporation for an income statement of the social purpose corporation for the three–month, six–month, or nine–month period of the current fiscal year ended more than 30 days prior to the date of the request and a balance sheet of the social purpose corporation as at the end of that period and, in addition, if no annual report for the most recent fiscal year has been sent to the shareholders, the statements referred to in subdivisions (a) and (b) relating to that fiscal year. The statements shall be delivered or mailed to the person making the request within 30 days following the request. A copy of the statements shall be kept on file in the principal office of the social purpose corporation for 12 months and shall be exhibited at all reasonable times to any shareholder demanding an examination of the statements or a copy shall be mailed to the shareholder. The quarterly income statements and balance sheets referred to in this subdivision shall be accompanied by the report thereon, if any, of any independent accountants engaged by the social purpose corporation or the certificate

施的原因以及确定和讨论在该会计年度那些措施任何实质改变的本质和原理。

（5）对于该会计年度社会目的公司为完成特定目的做出的任何重要的经营和资本支出的确定和讨论，善意评估社会目的公司为了完成特定目的希望在未来 3 个会计年度进行的任何另外的重要经营活动或资本支出，以及在该会计年度社会目的公司包括雇佣时间在内的其他重要的资源支出，在促进完成特定目的方面，包括对资本或其他资源的使用能在多大程度上服务于特定目的之外的其他目的的讨论。

（c）除依第 1501.5 条第（h）款的规定可能被另外免除的外，第（a）款和第（b）款规定的报告应在下一会计年度的年度股东会之前至少 15 天送交股东，若以大宗邮件方式送交则为年度股东会之前的至少 35 天。该要求不限制第 600 条规定的举行年度股东会的要求。

（d）如果上一会计年度的年度报告没有送交股东，在该会计年度结束 120 天后经任何股东书面申请，社会目的公司应将第（a）款和第（b）款要求的该会计年度报表在股东提交申请后 30 天内递送或邮寄给申请人。

（e）如果最近会计年度的年度报告没有送交股东，持有至少 5% 的社会目的公司任何类别已发行股份的股东可以对社会目的公司提交书面申请，索要申请日之前已结束 30 天以上的会计年度的 3 个月、6 个月或 9 个月的损益表和该申请期间结束后社会目的公司的资产负债表，以及第（a）款和第（b）款提到的关于该会计年度的报表。报表应在申请后 30 天内递送或邮寄给申请人。报表的副本应在社会目的公司的主营业地存档 12 个月，并在任何合理的时间向任何要求检查报表的股东展示或将副本寄送给股东。本款提及的季度损益表和资产负债表应附随社会目的公司聘用的独立会计的报告，或社会目的公司被授权的高管对这些报表中未经审计的公司账簿和记录的认证。

of an authorized officer of the social purpose corporation that the financial statements were prepared without audit from the books and records of the social purpose corporation.

§ 3501. Special purpose current report

(a) The board shall cause a special purpose current report to be sent to the shareholders not later than 45 days following the occurrence of any one or more of the events specified in subdivision (b) or (c), and, to the extent consistent with reasonable confidentiality requirements, shall cause the special purpose current report to be made publicly available by posting it on the social purpose corporation's Internet Web site or providing it through similar electronic means.

(b) Unless previously reported in the most recent annual report, the special purpose current report shall identify and discuss, in reasonable detail, any expenditure or group of related or planned expenditures, excluding compensation of officers and directors, made in furtherance of the special purpose objectives, whether an operating expenditure, a capital expenditure, or some other expenditure of corporate resources, including, but not limited to, employee time, whether the expenditure was direct or indirect, and whether the expenditure was categorized as overhead or otherwise where the expenditure has or is likely to have a material adverse impact on the social purpose corporation's results of operations or financial condition for a quarterly or annual fiscal period.

(c) Unless previously reported in the most recent annual report, the special purpose current report shall identify and discuss, in reasonable detail, any decision by the board or action by management to do either of the following:

(1) Withhold expenditures or a group of related or planned expenditures, whether temporarily or permanently, that were to have been made in furtherance of the special purpose as contemplated in the most recent annual report, whether those planned expenditures were an operating expenditure, a capital expenditure, or some other expenditure of corporate resources, including, but not limited to, employee time, whether the planned expenditure was direct or indirect, and whether the planned expenditure to be made would have been categorized as overhead or otherwise, in any case, where the planned expenditure was likely to have had a material positive impact on the social purpose corporation's impact in furtherance of its special purpose objectives, as contemplated in the most recent annual report.

(2) Determine that the special purpose has been satisfied or should no longer be pursued, whether temporarily or permanently.

§ 3502. Detailing or itemization; Presumption; Exclusion of information that would result in violation of laws; Exclusion from liability for forward looking statements; Reports to be understandable; Waiver; Satisfaction of requirements; Maintenance of reports

(a) Nothing contained in subdivision (b) of Section 3500 or Section 3501 shall require

第 3501 条　特定目的现况报告

（a）董事会应在第（b）款或第（c）款规定的一个或多个事件发生后的 45 天内将特定目的现况报告送交股东，并应在符合合理保密要求的范围内，将特定目的现况报告公布于社会目的公司的网站或通过相似的电子方式使公众可获取。

（b）除非在最近的年度报告中有讨论，否则特定目的现况报告应在合理的细节上确认和讨论促进特定目的的任何支出或相关计划的支出，不包括高管和董事的薪酬，无论是经营支出、资本支出还是公司资源的其他支出，包括但不限于雇佣时间，无论是直接还是间接支出，以及无论费用被归为日常费用还是该费用对季度或年度会计期间的社会目的公司的经营或财务状况有或可能有重大不利影响。

（c）除非在最近的年度报告中有讨论，否则特别目标现况报告应在合理的细节上明确和讨论以下董事会的任一决定或管理层的任一行为：

（1）扣留费用或相关计划的费用，如在最近的年度报告中预计用于促进特定目的的，无论暂时还是永久，无论费用是经营支出、资本支出还是其他公司资源支出，包括但不限于雇佣时间，无论计划费用是直接还是间接，以及无论费用被归为日常费用还是该计划费用对社会目的公司促进其特定目的的实现有或可能有重大积极影响，正如在最近的年度报告中所预期的那样。

（2）确定特定目的已实现或不再追求，无论是暂时的还是永久的目的。

第 3502 条　详述或逐条列举；推定；排除将导致违法的信息；排除前瞻性陈述的责任；可理解的报告；弃权；满足要求；报告的维护

（a）第 3500 条第（b）款或第 3501 条未要求详述或逐条列举公司产生的或计

a detailing or itemization of every relevant expenditure incurred, or planned or action taken or planned, by the corporation. Management and the board shall use their discretion in providing that information, including the reasonable detail that a reasonable investor would consider important in understanding the corporation's objectives, actions, impacts, measures, rationale, and results of operations as they relate to the nature and achievement of the special purpose objectives.

(b) Where best practices emerge for providing the information required by subdivision (b) of Section 3500 or Section 3501, use of those best practices shall create a presumption that the social purpose corporation caused all the information required by those provisions to be provided. This presumption can only be rebutted by showing that the reporting contained either a misstatement of a material fact or omission of a material fact.

(c) Notwithstanding subdivision (b) of Section 3500 and Section 3501, under no circumstances shall the social purpose corporation be required to provide information that would result in a violation of state or federal securities laws or other applicable laws.

(d) The social purpose corporation and its officers and directors are expressly excluded from liability for any and all forward looking statements supplied in the report required by subdivision (b) of Section 3500 and Section 3501, so long as those statements are supplied in good faith. Statements are deemed to be forward looking as that term is defined in the federal securities laws.

(e) The special purpose MD&A and any special purpose current report shall be written in plain English and shall be provided in an efficient and understandable manner, avoiding repetition and disclosure of immaterial information.

(f) Unless otherwise provided by the articles or bylaws, and if approved by the board of directors, the reports specified in Sections 3500 and 3501 and any accompanying material sent pursuant to this section may be sent by electronic transmission by the corporation.

(g) The financial statements of any social purpose corporation with fewer than 100 holders of record of its shares, determined as provided in Section 605, required to be furnished by Sections 3500 and 3501 are not required to be prepared in conformity with generally accepted accounting principles if they reasonably set forth the assets and liabilities and the income and expense of the social purpose corporation and disclose the accounting basis used in their preparation.

(h) The requirements described in Section 3500 shall be satisfied if a corporation with an outstanding class of securities registered under Section 12 of the Securities Exchange Act of 1934 both complies with Section 240.14a–16 of Title 17 of the Code of Federal Regulations, as amended from time to time, with respect to the obligation of a corporation to furnish an annual report to shareholders pursuant to Section 240.14a–3(b) of Title 17 of the Code of Federal Regulations, and includes the information required by subdivision (b) of

划采取的行动产生的任何相关支出。管理人员和董事会应酌情提供信息，包括理性投资者在理解公司为实现特定目的上的目标、行为、影响、措施、理由和经营结果时认为重要的信息。

（b）若存在提供第 3500 条第（b）款或第 3501 条要求的信息的最佳方法，使用那些最佳方法应推定社会目的公司已经提供了那些条款要求的所有信息。只有在表明报告包含对重要事实的虚假陈述或遗漏的情况下才能反驳这一推定。

（c）尽管有第 3500 条第（b）款和第 3501 条的规定，但是在任何情况下社会目的公司都不应被要求提供将导致违反州或联邦证券法或任何适用法的信息。

（d）社会目的公司及其高管和董事被免除在第 3500 条第（b）款和第 3501 条要求的报告中进行前瞻性陈述的责任，只要那些陈述是善意的。根据联邦证券法对该术语的界定，陈述被视为具有前瞻性。

（e）特定目的的管理层讨论与分析和制作任何特定目的现况报告应使用简明英语书写并应以有效和可理解的方式提供，避免重复和披露非重要信息。

（f）除公司章程或章程细则另有规定外，如果董事会批准，在第 3500 条和第 3501 条中规定的报告以及本条规定的任何附随的资料可以由公司进行电子传送。

（g）依据第 605 条的规定制作的，按照第 3500 条和第 3501 条要求提供的少于 100 个登记股份持有人的任何社会目的公司的财务报表，如果合理地列出了社会目的公司的财产、责任、收入和费用以及披露在编制报表中使用的会计基础，则不需要按照公认会计原则编制。

（h）如果公司有依据《1934 年证券交易法》第 12 条和联邦法规的第 17 编第 240.14a–16 条登记的已发行类别证券，有依据联邦法规的第 17 编第 240.14a–3（b）款向股东提供年度报告的公司义务，并且在年度报告中包含第 3500 条第（b）款要求的信息，则应满足第 3500 条规定的要求。

Section 3500 in the annual report.

(i) The requirements described in Section 3501 shall be satisfied if a corporation with an outstanding class of securities registered under Section 12 of the Securities Exchange Act of 1934 both complies with Section 240.13a–13 of Title 17 of the Code of Federal Regulations, as amended from time to time, with respect to the obligation of a corporation to furnish a quarterly report to shareholders, and includes the information required by subdivision (b) of Section 3501 in the quarterly report.

(j) In addition to the penalties provided for in this division, the superior court of the proper county shall enforce the duty of making and mailing or delivering the information and financial statements required by Sections 3500 and 3501 and, for good cause shown, may extend the time therefor.

(k) In any action or proceeding with respect to Section 3500 or 3501, if the court finds the failure of the social purpose corporation to comply with the requirements of those sections to have been without justification, the court may award an amount sufficient to reimburse the shareholder for the reasonable expenses incurred by the shareholder, including attorney's fees, in connection with the action or proceeding.

(l) Section 3500 and Section 3501 apply to any domestic social purpose corporation and also to a foreign social purpose corporation having its principal executive office in this state or customarily holding meetings of its board in this state.

(m) All reports and notices required by Section 3500 and Section 3501 shall be maintained by the social purpose corporation, in an electronic form for a period of not less than 10 years.

§ 3503. Liability with regard to reports and documents

Any officers, directors, employees, or agents of a social purpose corporation who do any of the following shall be liable jointly and severally for all the damages resulting therefrom to the social purpose corporation or any person injured by those actions who relied on those actions or to both:

(a) Make, issue, deliver, or publish any prospectus, report, including the reports required pursuant to Sections 3500 and 3501, circular, certificate, financial statement, balance sheet, public notice, or document respecting the social purpose corporation or its shares, assets, liabilities, capital, dividends, business, earnings, or accounts which is false in any material respect, knowing it to be false, or participate in the making, issuance, delivery, or publication thereof with knowledge that the same is false in a material respect.

(b) Make or cause to be made in the books, minutes, records, or accounts of a social purpose corporation any entry that is false in any material particular knowing it to be false.

(c) Remove, erase, alter, or cancel any entry in any books or records of the social purpose corporation, with intent to deceive.

（i）如果公司有依据《1934 年证券交易法》第 12 条和联邦法规的第 17 编第 240.13a–13 条登记的已发行类别证券，有向股东提供季度报告的公司义务，以及第 3501 条第（b）款要求的信息，则应满足第 3500 条规定的要求。

（j）除在本分编规定的处罚外，有关县的高等法院应履行第 3500 条和第 3501 条规定的制作、邮寄或递送信息和财务报表的义务，若有正当理由可以延期。

（k）在关于第 3500 条或第 3501 条的任何诉讼或程序中，如果法院发现社会目的公司未能遵守这些条款的要求而且没有正当理由的，法院可以判决充分赔偿股东与诉讼或程序相关的合理费用，包括律师费。

（l）第 3500 条和第 3501 条的规定适用于任何本州社会目的公司并适用于在本州有主营业地的或通常在本州召开董事会的外州社会目的公司。

（m）第 3500 条和第 3501 条要求的所有报告和通知应由社会目的公司以电子形式保存不少于 10 年的时间。

第 3503 条　关于报告和文件的责任

实施以下行为的社会目的公司的高管、董事、雇员或代理人应对以下行为导致的对于社会目的公司或任何人的所有损害承担连带责任：

（a）明知其为虚假，仍制作、发行、递送或公布在任何一个重要方面是虚假的招股说明书、报告，包括第 3500 条和第 3501 条要求的报告、通告、证书、财务报表、资产负债表、公告或关于社会目的公司或其股份、资产、责任、资本、红利、生意、收入或账目的文件，或参与制作、发行、递送或公布明知其为虚假的相同事项。

（b）明知其为虚假，仍将任何虚假的条目加入或使其加入社会目的公司的账簿、会议记录、记录或账目的任何重要的个别项目中。

（c）意图欺诈而移除、删除、改变或取消社会目的公司的账簿或记录中任何的条目。

(d) With respect to the reports required pursuant to subdivision (b) of Section 3500 and Section 3501, omit to state any material fact necessary in order to make the statements contained therein, in light of the circumstances under which those statements were made, not misleading in a material respect, knowing the omission to be misleading.

（d）在关于第3500条第（b）款和第3501条要求的报告中，根据陈述制作的情况，明知省略会产生误导，仍省略任何必要的重要事实。

THE STATE OF FLORIDA

Title XXXVI. Business Organizations. (Chs. 605–623).
Chapter 607. Corporations.
Part II. Social Purpose Corporations.

§ 607.501. Application and effect of part.

(1) This part applies to a social purpose corporation and does not affect a corporation that is not a social purpose corporation.

(2) Except as otherwise provided in this part, this chapter applies generally to all social purpose corporations.

(3) A social purpose corporation may be simultaneously subject to this part and to one or more chapters, including chapter 621. In such event, this part takes precedence with respect to a social purpose corporation.

(4) Except as authorized by this part, a provision of the articles of incorporation or bylaws of a social purpose corporation, or a shareholders agreement among shareholders of a social purpose corporation, may not limit, be inconsistent with, or supersede a provision of this part.

§ 607.502. Definitions.

As used in this part, unless the context otherwise requires, the term:

(1) "Benefit director" means:

(a) The director designated as the benefit director of a social purpose corporation under *s. 607.508*; or

(b) A person with one or more of the powers, duties, or rights of a benefit director to the extent provided in the articles of incorporation or bylaws under *s. 607.508*.

(2) "Benefit enforcement proceeding" means a claim or action for:

(a) The failure of a social purpose corporation to pursue or create a public benefit or a specific public benefit established in its articles of incorporation; or

(b) A violation of any obligation, duty, or standard of conduct under this part.

(3) "Benefit officer" means the individual designated as the benefit officer of a social

佛罗里达州

第 24 编　商业组织（第 605–623 章）
第 607 章　公司
第 2 节　社会目的公司

第 607.501 条　本节的法律适用与效力

（1）本节适用于社会目的公司，非社会目的公司不在本节调整范围内。

（2）除本节另有规定外，本章规定适用于所有社会目的公司。

（3）社会目的公司可能同时受本节和其他章节的调整，如第 621 章。对于社会目的公司，本节优先适用。

（4）除本节另有授权外，社会目的公司的公司章程、章程细则或股东间达成的股东协议，不得对本部分条款的内容产生限制、发生抵触，或替代本节的规定。

第 607.502 条　定义

除另有规定外，本节所使用的词语具有以下含义：

（1）“公共利益董事”是指：

（a）依第 607.508 条的规定所设立的社会目的公司的董事；或者

（b）有依第 607.508 条的规定所设章程中的一项或多项公共利益董事的权力、权利或义务的董事。

（2）“公共利益实施程序”是指因以下行为产生的任何主张或诉讼：

（a）社会目的公司未追求或实现公司章程所规定的公共利益或特定公共利益目的；或者

（b）社会目的公司违反本节规定的任何义务、责任或行为标准。

（3）“公共利益高管”是指社会目的公司依第 607.510 条规定所设立的高管。

purpose corporation under *s. 607.510.*

(4) "Independent" means not having a material relationship with the social purpose corporation or a subsidiary of the social purpose corporation. A person does not have a material relationship solely by virtue of serving as the benefit director or benefit officer of the social purpose corporation or a subsidiary of the social purpose corporation. In determining whether a director or officer is independent, a material relationship between an individual and a social purpose corporation or any of its subsidiaries will be conclusively presumed to exist, at the time independence is to be determined, if any of the following apply:

(a) The individual is or was within the prior 3 years an employee, other than a benefit officer, of the social purpose corporation or a subsidiary.

(b) An immediate family member of the individual is or was within the prior 3 years an executive officer, other than a benefit officer, of the social purpose corporation or a subsidiary.

(c) When ownership is calculated as if all outstanding rights to acquire equity interests in the social purpose corporation had been exercised, there is beneficial or record ownership of 5 percent or more of the outstanding shares of the social purpose corporation by:

1. The individual; or

2. An entity:

a. Of which the individual is a director, an officer, or a manager; or

b. In which, when ownership is calculated as if all outstanding rights to acquire equity interests in the entity had been exercised, the individual owns beneficially or of record 5 percent or more of the outstanding equity interests.

(5) "Minimum status vote" means:

(a) In the case of a corporation that is to become a social purpose corporation, whether by amendment of the articles of incorporation or by way of or pursuant to a merger, conversion, or share exchange; a social purpose corporation whose articles of incorporation are to be amended pursuant to *s. 607.506(2)*; or a social purpose corporation that is to cease being a social purpose corporation, in addition to any other required approval or vote, the satisfaction of the following conditions:

1. The holders of each class or series of shares shall be entitled to vote as a separate voting group on the corporate action regardless of any limitation on the voting rights of any class or series stated in the articles of incorporation or bylaws.

2. The corporate action is approved by vote of each class or series of shares entitled to vote by at least two-thirds of the total votes of the class or series.

(b) In the case of a domestic entity, other than a corporation, which is to be simultaneously converted to a social purpose corporation or merged into a social purpose corporation, in addition to any other required approval, vote, or consent, the satisfaction of

（4）“独立”是指与社会目的公司或其子公司没有实质性的关系。担任公共利益董事或公共利益高管并不当然丧失独立性。以下情形中，认为该个体与社会目的公司或其子公司存在实质性的关系：

（a）该个体是，或在过去的 3 年内是，社会目的公司或其子公司的公共利益高管以外的雇员。

（b）该个体的直系亲属是，或在过去的 3 年内是，社会目的公司或其子公司的公共利益高管以外的执行高管。

（c）在所有购股权都被视为已行使的情况下，下述持有社会目的公司 5% 以上已发行股份的登记股东或实际受益人：

1. 个人；或者

2. 实体。

a. 其中，该个人是该实体的董事、高管或经理；或者

b. 在所有购股权都被视为已行使的情况下，该实体中的个人为持有公共利益公司 5% 以上已发行股份的登记股东或实际受益人。

（5）“最低表决要求”是指：

（a）公司通过修改章程或采取兼并、财产转换或置换股权的方式转变成社会目的公司，社会目的公司依据第 607.506（2）款规定修改其公司章程，或社会目的公司终止其社会目的公司形态，除其他批准或表决的要求外，还应满足以下条件：

1. 每一类别或系列的股东应当有权作为一个独立的投票团体对公司行为进行投票，无论公司章程或章程细则是否对某一类别或系列股东的投票权作出了限制。

2. 公司行为必须获得每个类别或系列有投票权的所有股东的至少 2/3 的赞成票才能通过。

（b）非商事公司的实体转换为社会目的公司或通过兼并成为社会目的公司，除其他批准、表决或赞成的要求外，还应满足以下条件：

the following conditions:

1. The holders of each class or series of equity interest in the entity who are entitled to receive a distribution of any kind are entitled, as a separate voting group, to vote on or consent to the action regardless of any applicable limitation on the voting or consent rights of any class or series.

2. The action is approved by vote or consent of each class or series of equity interest described in subparagraph 1. who are entitled to vote by at least two-thirds of the votes or consent of the class or series.

(6) "Public benefit" means a positive effect, or the minimization of negative effects, taken as a whole, on the environment or on one or more categories of persons or entities, other than shareholders in their capacity as shareholders, of an artistic, charitable, economic, educational, cultural, literary, religious, social, ecological, or scientific nature, from the business and operations of a social purpose corporation. The term includes, but is not limited to, the following:

(a) Providing low-income or underserved individuals or communities with beneficial products or services.

(b) Promoting economic opportunity for individuals or communities beyond the creation of jobs in the normal course of business.

(c) Protecting or restoring the environment.

(d) Improving human health.

(e) Promoting the arts, sciences, or advancement of knowledge.

(f) Increasing the flow of capital to entities that have as their stated purpose the provision of a benefit to society or the environment.

(7) "Social purpose corporation" means a corporation that is formed, or has elected to become, subject to this part, the status of which as a social purpose corporation has not been terminated.

(8) "Specific public benefit" means a benefit identified as a purpose of the social purpose corporation which is set forth in the articles of incorporation and is consistent with a public benefit.

(9) "Subsidiary" means, in relation to a person other than an individual, an entity in which the person owns beneficially or of record 50 percent or more of the outstanding equity interests.

(10) "Third-party standard" means a recognized standard for defining, reporting, and assessing the societal and environmental performance of a business which is:

(a) Comprehensive, because it assesses the effect of the business and its operations upon the interests listed in s. *607.507(1)(a)*.

(b) Developed by an entity that is not controlled by the social purpose corporation.

1. 该实体的每一类别或系列的任何权益分配形式下的股权持有者有权对公司行为进行投票，即使存在对该类别或系列投票权的限制。

2. 公司行为必须获得第 1 分项规定的每个类别有投票权的所有股东的至少 2/3 的赞成票才能通过。

（6）“公共利益”是指公司的业务和运营在整体上对环境或一类或多类个人或主体（股东在股东权限内的受益除外）产生的实质性积极影响，或消极影响的最小化，具体包括艺术、慈善、经济、教育、文化、文学、宗教、社会、生态和科学性等方面。公共利益包括但不限于以下内容：

（a）向低收入、低福利人群或社区提供有益的产品或服务。

（b）在正常的业务过程中向个人或社区提供创造就业之外的经济机会。

（c）保护或改善环境。
（d）改善人类健康。
（e）促进艺术、科学或知识进步。
（f）促进资本流向拥有有利于社会或环境目标的实体。

（7）“社会目的公司”指根据本章规定设立或选择接受本章规定调整，且其社会目的公司的形态尚未终止的公司。

（8）“特定公共利益”指社会目的公司在其公司章程中表明的公司目的，其与公共利益相一致。

（9）“子公司”是指该实体 50% 以上已发行的股份的受益所有权或登记所有权被另一实体（不包括个人）所拥有。

（10）“第三方标准”是指用于定义、报告和评估公司社会和环境绩效的标准，其应满足以下条件：
（a）综合，根据第 607.507（1）（a）项中所列利益评估公司业务和经营绩效。

（b）其经独立于社会目的公司的第三方实体制定。

(c) Credible, because it is developed by an entity that has access to necessary expertise to assess the overall effect of the business and uses a balanced, collaborative approach to develop the standard, including a period for public comment.

(d) Transparent, because the following information is publicly available:

1. The criteria considered under the standard when measuring the overall effect of the business and its operations upon the interests provided in *s. 607.507(1)(a)* and the relative weights, if any, of those criteria; and

2. The process used in the development and revision of the third–party standard regarding the identity of the directors, officers, material owners, and governing body of the entity that developed and controls revisions to the standard; the process by which revisions to the standard and changes to the membership of the governing body are made; and an accounting of the revenue and sources of financial support for the entity with sufficient detail to disclose any relationships that could reasonably be considered to present a potential conflict of interest.

§ 607.503. Incorporation.

To incorporate as a social purpose corporation, an incorporator must satisfy the requirements of this chapter, and the articles of incorporation must state that the corporation is a social purpose corporation under this part.

§ 607.504. Election of social purpose corporation status.

(1) An existing corporation may become a social purpose corporation under this part by amending its articles of incorporation to include a statement that the corporation is a social purpose corporation under this part. The amendment must be adopted by the minimum status vote.

(2) A plan of merger, conversion, or share exchange must be adopted by the minimum status vote if an entity that is not a social purpose corporation is a party to the merger or conversion or if the exchanging entity in a share exchange and the surviving, new, or resulting entity is, or will be, a social purpose corporation.

(3) If an entity elects to become a social purpose corporation by amendment of the articles of incorporation or by a merger, conversion, or share exchange, the shareholders of the entity are entitled to appraisal rights under and pursuant to ss. 607.1301–607.1333.

§ 607.505. Termination of social purpose corporation status.

(1) A social purpose corporation may terminate its status as such and cease to be subject to this part by amending its articles of incorporation to delete the provision required under *s. 607.503* or *s. 607.504*. The amendment must be adopted by the minimum status vote.

(2) A plan of merger, conversion, or share exchange which has the effect of terminating the status of a corporation as a social purpose corporation must be adopted by the minimum status vote. A sale, lease, exchange, or other disposition of all or substantially all of the

（c）可信，该标准由拥有评估公司社会和环境综合绩效所需的专业知识的实体，使用平衡协调多方利益的方法制定，并设定听取公众意见的期间；

（d）透明，以下信息可公开获取：

1. 根据第 607.507（1）（a）项的规定衡量企业整体社会和环境绩效时所考虑的指标，及相应的权重（如有）；以及

2. 第三方标准制定和修改的程序，如制定、控制修改程序的董事、高管、主要股东和该实体的控制人员的身份，标准修改和控制人员变动的程序，收入和资金来源的计量，包括充分披露合理认知下存在利益冲突的所有细节。

第 607.503 条　设立

设立社会目的公司，公司创立人应满足本章的相关要求，公司章程中须说明公司为本节规定下的社会目的公司。

第 607.504 条　公共利益公司形态的选择

（1）已成立的公司可依据本节规定修改公司章程，转换为公共利益公司，并作出该公司为本节规定下公共利益公司的声明。公司章程的修改应满足最低表决要求。

（2）如果一家非社会目的公司是兼并或财产转换的一方，或者股权置换中一方和存续、新设或留存的实体是或即将成为社会目的公司，那么此等兼并、财产转换或股权置换的计划须满足最低表决要求才能通过。

（3）如果实体通过修改公司章程选择成为社会目的公司，或通过兼并、财产转换或股权置换的方式成为社会目的公司，则实体的股东享有第 607.1301–607.1333 条规定下的回购请求权。

第 607.505 条　社会目的公司形态的终止

（1）社会目的公司可通过删除第 607.503 条或第 607.504 条规定的公司章程中其作为公共利益公司的声明来终止公共利益公司形态并不再受本节规定的调整。公司章程的修改应满足最低表决要求。

（2）如果兼并、财产转换或股权置换计划有终止商业公司作为社会目的公司的效力，该计划应满足最低表决要求。社会目的公司的任何出售、出租、交换或者其他处置全部或主要财产的行为，须满足最低表决要求。但是，属于正常商业往来

assets of a social purpose corporation is not effective unless the transaction is approved by the minimum status vote. However, a minimum status vote is not required if the transaction is in the usual and regular course of business, is pursuant to court order, or is a sale pursuant to which all or a substantial portion of the net proceeds of the sale will be distributed to the shareholders within 1 year after the date of the sale.

(3) If a corporation's status as a social purpose corporation is terminated pursuant to subsection (1) or subsection (2), shareholders of the corporation are entitled to appraisal rights under and pursuant to ss. 607.1301–607.1333.

§ 607.506. Corporate purpose.

(1) A social purpose corporation has the purpose of creating a public benefit. This purpose is in addition to its purpose under *s. 607.0301*.

(2) The articles of incorporation of a social purpose corporation may identify one or more specific public benefits as its purpose in addition to its purposes under subsection (1) and *s. 607.0301*. A social purpose corporation may amend its articles of incorporation to add, amend, or delete the identification of a specific public benefit purpose; however, the amendment must be adopted by the minimum status vote.

(3) The creation of a public benefit and a specific public benefit under subsections (1) and (2) is deemed to be in the best interest of the social purpose corporation.

(4) A professional corporation that is a social purpose corporation does not violate *s. 621.08* by having as its purpose the creation of a public benefit or a specific public benefit.

§ 607.507. Standard of conduct for directors.

(1) In discharging their duties and in considering the best interests of the social purpose corporation, the directors:

(a) Shall consider the effects of any action or inaction upon:

1. The shareholders of the social purpose corporation; and

2. The ability of the social purpose corporation to accomplish its public benefit or any specific public benefit purpose.

(b) May consider the effects of any action or inaction upon any of the following:

1. The employees and work force of the social purpose corporation, its subsidiaries, and its suppliers.

2. The interests of customers and suppliers as beneficiaries of the public benefit or specific public benefits of the social purpose corporation.

3. Community and societal factors, including those of each community in which offices or facilities of the social purpose corporation, its subsidiaries, or its suppliers are located.

4. The local and global environment.

5. The short–term and long–term interests of the social purpose corporation, including benefits that may accrue to the social purpose corporation from its long–term plans and the

的交易、根据法院指令进行的交易，或出售全部或主要财产所获净收益将在出售一年内分配给股东的交易，无须满足最低表决要求。

（3）如果公司根据第（1）款或第（2）款的规定终止其社会目的公司形态，公司股东享有第 607.1301–607.1333 条规定下的回购请求权。

第 607.506 条　公司目的

（1）社会目的公司应当创设公共利益目的。该目的是在第 607.0301 条所规定的目的之外。

（2）除第 607.0301 条和本条第（1）款所规定的目的外，公司章程可设定一项或多项特定公共利益目的。社会目的公司可以增加、修改或删除公司章程中设定的特定公共利益目的。章程的修改须满足最低表决要求。

（3）依据第（1）款和第（2）款规定设定的公共利益和特定公共利益目的为社会目的公司的最佳利益。

（4）选择社会目的公司形态的专业公司并不因其有创设一般和特定公共利益的目的而违反第 621.08 条的规定。

第 607.507 条　董事行为标准

（1）在履行各自职责和考虑社会目的公司最佳利益的同时，董事：

（a）应当考虑对以下对象的影响：

1. 社会目的公司的股东；以及

2. 社会目的公司实现其公共利益和特定公共利益目的能力。

（b）可以考虑其作为或不作为对以下对象的影响：

1. 社会目的公司、其子公司和其供应商的雇员。

2. 作为社会目的公司公共利益或特定公共利益受益者的消费者和供应商的利益。

3. 社区和社会因素，包括社会目的公司及其子公司或其供应商的办公地或设施所在地的社区。

4. 当地和全球环境。

5. 社会目的公司的短期和长期利益，包括可能从其长期计划中产生的利益，以及社会目的公司继续保持独立可能产生的最佳利益。

possibility that these interests may be best served by the continued independence of the social purpose corporation.

(c) May consider other pertinent factors or the interests of any other group that they deem appropriate.

(d) Are not required to give priority to the interests of a particular person or group referred to in paragraph (a), paragraph (b), or paragraph (c) unless the social purpose corporation states in its articles of incorporation its intention to give such priority.

(e) Are not required to give equal weight to the interests of any particular person or group referred to in paragraph (a), paragraph (b), or paragraph (c) unless the social purpose corporation has stated in its articles of incorporation its intention to give such equal weight.

(2) Except as provided in the articles of incorporation, a director is not personally liable for monetary damages to the corporation, or to any other person, for the failure of the social purpose corporation to pursue or create a public benefit or a specific public benefit. A director is subject to the duties specified in s. *607.0830*.

(3) Except as provided in the articles of incorporation, a director does not have a duty to a person who is a beneficiary of the public benefit purpose or any one or more specific public benefit purposes of a social purpose corporation.

§ 607.508. Benefit director.

(1) If the articles of incorporation so provide, the board of directors of a social purpose corporation may include a director who is designated as the benefit director and, in addition to the powers, duties, rights, and immunities of the other directors of the social purpose corporation, has the powers, duties, rights, and immunities provided in this part.

(2) The benefit director shall be elected, and may be removed, in the manner provided by this chapter. Except as provided under subsection (5), the benefit director shall be independent and may serve as a benefit officer. The articles of incorporation or bylaws may prescribe additional qualifications of the benefit director.

(3) Unless the articles of incorporation or bylaws provide otherwise, the benefit director shall prepare, and the social purpose corporation shall include in the annual benefit report to shareholders required under s. *607.512*, the opinion of the benefit director on the following:

(a) Whether the social purpose corporation in all material respects acted in accordance with its public benefit purpose and any specific public benefit purpose during the period covered by the report.

(b) Whether the directors and officers complied with ss. *607.507(1)* and *607.509(1)*.

(c) Whether the social purpose corporation or its directors or officers failed to comply with paragraph (a) or s. *607.507(1)* or s. *607.509(1)*, including a description of the ways in which the social purpose corporation or its directors or officers failed to comply.

(4) The action or inaction of an individual in his or her capacity as a benefit director

（c）可考虑董事认为合适的其他相关因素或其他群体利益。

（d）不应将特定个人或群体的利益置于第（a）、（b）、（c）分项所设定的公共利益之上，公司章程赋予特定个人或群体利益优先权的除外。

（e）不应将特定个人或群体的利益置于第（a）、（b）、（c）分项所设定的公共利益同等重要的地位，公司章程赋予特定个人或群体利益同等重要地位的除外。

（2）除公司章程另有明确规定外，对于社会目的公司未能追求或实现公共利益或特定公共利益所造成的经济损失，董事不向公司或任何个人承担损害赔偿责任。董事行为应符合第 607.0830 条的规定。

（3）除公司章程另有明确规定外，董事不对社会目的公司公共利益或特定公共利益目的的受益人负责。

第 607.508 条　公共利益董事

（1）社会目的公司的公司章程中可以规定，董事会中包括一名公共利益董事，该董事除有社会目的公司的其他董事的权力、义务、权利和豁免权外，还有本节规定的权力、义务、权利和豁免权。

（2）公共利益董事应当依据本章的相关规定进行任免。除第（5）款的规定外，公共利益董事应当是独立的个体，其可同时担任公共利益高管。社会目的公司章程或章程细则可对公共利益董事的任职资格予以明确。

（3）除公司章程或章程细则中另有规定外，公共利益董事应当编写其对以下事项的意见，社会目的公司应当根据第 607.512 条将其附于年度公共利益报告中供股东查阅：

（a）在报告所述期间内，社会目的公司是否在所有重要事项上依一般和特定公共利益目的行事。

（b）董事和高级管理人员是否依第 607.507（1）款和第 607.509（1）款的规定行事。

（c）如果公共利益董事认为社会目的公司或其董事、高管未能依第（a）项、第 607.507（1）款或第 607.509（1）款的要求行事，应陈述社会目的公司或其董事、高管未能履行责任的情况。

（4）公共利益董事在职权范围内的任何个人作为或不作为应视为社会目的公

shall constitute for all purposes an action or inaction of that individual in his or her capacity as a director of the social purpose corporation.

(5) The benefit director of a corporation formed under chapter 621 is not required to be independent.

§ 607.509. Standard of conduct for officers.

(1) If an officer of a social purpose corporation reasonably believes that a matter may have a material effect on the ability of the corporation to create a public benefit or a specific public benefit identified in the articles of incorporation and the officer has discretion to act on the matter, the officer shall consider the interests and factors provided in *s. 607.507(1)*.

(2) The officer's consideration of interests and factors under subsection (1) does not constitute a violation of *s. 607.0841*.

(3) Except as provided in the articles of incorporation, an officer is not personally liable for monetary damages to the corporation or any other person for the failure of the social purpose corporation to pursue or create a public benefit or a specific public benefit; however, he or she is subject to *s. 607.0841*.

(4) Except as provided in the articles of incorporation, an officer does not have any duty to a person who is a beneficiary of the public benefit purpose or any specific public benefit purpose of a social purpose corporation arising from the status of the person as a beneficiary.

§ 607.510. Benefit officer.

(1) A social purpose corporation may designate an officer as the benefit officer.

(2) The benefit officer has the powers and duties set forth in the bylaws or determined by the board of directors, which may include, but are not limited to:

(a) Powers and duties relating to the public benefit or a specific public benefit purpose of the corporation; and

(b) The duty to prepare the annual benefit report required under *s. 607.512*.

§ 607.511. Right of action.

(1) (a) Except in a benefit enforcement proceeding, a person may not bring an action or assert a claim against a social purpose corporation or its directors or officers with respect to:

1. A failure to pursue or create a public benefit or a specific public benefit set forth in its articles of incorporation; or

2. A violation of an obligation, duty, or standard of conduct under this part.

(b) A social purpose corporation is not liable for monetary damages under this part for the failure of the social purpose corporation to pursue or create a public benefit or a specific public benefit.

(2) A benefit enforcement proceeding may be commenced or maintained only:

(a) Directly by the social purpose corporation; or

(b) Derivatively by:

司董事的作为或不作为。

（5）依据第 621 章的规定设立的公司，其公共利益董事不需要独立于社会目的公司。

第 607.509 条　高管行为标准

（1）如果高管有合理理由认为某事项对社会目的公司实现在章程中创设的公共利益或特定公共利益目的的能力有实质性影响，且高管就该事项有自由裁量权，则公司高管应考虑第 607.507（1）款所规定的利益和因素。

（2）高管对第（a）项中利益和相关因素的考虑不构成对第 607.0841 条规定的违反。

（3）除公司章程中另有规定外，对于社会目的公司未能追求或实现公共利益或特定公共利益所造成的经济损失，高管不向公司或任何个人承担损害赔偿责任。但是，高管的行为应符合第 607.0841 条的规定。

（4）除公司章程中另有规定外，高管不对社会目的公司公共利益或特定公共利益目的的受益人负责。

第 607.510 条　公共利益高管

（1）公共利益公司可任命一名公共利益高管。

（2）公共利益高管拥有公司章程细则和董事会决议中规定的权力和职责，包括但不限于：

（a）与公司公共利益和特定公共利益目的相关的权力和职责；以及

（b）根据第 607.512 条的规定编制年度公共利益报告的职责。

第 607.511 条　诉讼权利

（1）（a）非经公共利益实施程序，任何人不得因以下事项向社会目的公司或者其董事、高管提起诉讼或主张：

1. 未能追求或实现在其公司章程中设定的公共利益或特定公共利益；或者

2. 违反本节规定下的义务、责任或行为标准。

（b）社会目的公司不对本节规定下任何未能追求或实现公共利益或特定公共利益的事项承担损害赔偿责任。

（2）下列情形中，仅以下主体可提起公共利益实施程序：

（a）由社会目的公司直接提起；或者

（b）由以下主体派生提起：

1. A shareholder of record on the date of the action or inaction complained of in the benefit enforcement proceeding;

2. A director;

3. A person or group of persons that owns beneficially or of record 5 percent or more of the outstanding equity interests in an entity of which the social purpose corporation is a subsidiary on the date of the action or inaction complained of in the benefit enforcement proceeding; or

4. Any other person who is specified in the articles of incorporation or bylaws of the social purpose corporation.

§ 607.512. Preparation of annual benefit report.

(1) Unless it is prepared by a benefit director or benefit officer, the board of directors shall prepare an annual benefit report. The annual benefit report must include all of the following:

(a) A narrative description of:

1. The ways in which the social purpose corporation pursued a public benefit during the year and the extent to which a public benefit was created.

2. Any circumstance that has hindered the pursuit or creation of a public benefit by the social purpose corporation.

3. The process and rationale for selecting or changing the third–party standard used to prepare the benefit report, if the articles of incorporation of the social purpose corporation require, or the board of directors determines, that the annual benefit report must be prepared in accordance with a third–party standard.

(b) If the articles of incorporation of the social purpose corporation require, or the board of directors determines, that the annual benefit report must be prepared in accordance with a third–party standard, the third–party standard must be:

1. Applied consistently with any previous application in prior annual benefit reports; or

2. Accompanied by an explanation of the reasons for inconsistent application or any change in the standard from the immediate prior report.

(c) The name of the benefit director and the benefit officer, if those positions exist, and the respective addresses to which correspondence may be directed.

(d) If the corporation has a benefit director, his or her statement as provided in *s. 607.508(3)*.

(e) If the articles of incorporation of the social purpose corporation require, or the board of directors determines, that the annual benefit report must be prepared in accordance with a third–party standard, a statement of any connection between the organization that established the third–party standard, or its directors, officers, or any holder of 5 percent or more of the governance interests in the organization, and the social purpose corporation or its

1. 公共利益诉讼所针对的作为或不作为行为发生时的登记股东；

2. 董事；
3. 公共利益诉讼所针对的作为或不作为行为发生时，单独或合计持有社会目的公司母公司 5% 以上已发行股份的登记股东或实际受益人；或者

4. 社会目的的公司章程或章程细则中规定的其他人员。

第 607.512 条　年度公共利益报告的编制

（1）除公共利益董事或公共利益高管外，董事会也应编制社会目的公司的年度公共利益报告。报告应包括以下内容：

（a）对以下事项的说明：
1. 社会目的公司本年度追求公共利益的方法和公共利益的实现情况。

2. 阻碍社会目的公司追求或实现公共利益的情形。

3. 公司章程要求或董事会决议采用第三方标准编制年度公共利益报告的，报告中应说明选用或替换第三方标准的程序和原因。

（b）公司章程要求或董事会决议采用第三方标准编制年度公共利益报告的，应当：

1. 沿用先前公共利益报告中适用的标准；或者
2. 在选用新标准时，附一份说明以解释适用的差异和标准变化的原因。

（c）公共利益董事和公共利益高管的姓名，以及相应的通讯地址（如有）。

（d）公司设有公共利益董事的，报告中应包含公共利益董事依第 607.508（3）款规定应编写的陈述报告。

（e）公司章程要求或董事会决议采用第三方标准编制年度公共利益报告的，报告应包含设立第三方标准的组织或其董事、高管、享有 5% 以上管理利益的持有人，与社会目的的公司或其董事、高管或持有 5% 以上已发行股份的股东之间关系的声明，包括任何可能影响第三方标准可信度的财务或管理关系。

directors, officers, or any holder of 5 percent or more of the outstanding shares of the social purpose corporation, including any financial or governance relationship that might materially affect the credibility of the use of the third–party standard.

(2) If, during the year covered by an annual benefit report, a benefit director resigned from, or refused to stand for reelection to, his or her position, or was removed from his or her position, and he or she furnished written correspondence to the social purpose corporation concerning the circumstances surrounding his or her departure, that correspondence must be included as an exhibit in the annual benefit report.

(3) The annual benefit report and the assessment of the performance of the social purpose corporation in the annual benefit report required under paragraph (1)(b) are not required to be audited or certified by a third–party standards provider.

§ 607.513. Availability of annual benefit report.

(1) Each social purpose corporation shall send its annual benefit report to each shareholder:

(a) Within 120 days after the end of the fiscal year of the social purpose corporation; or

(b) At the same time that the social purpose corporation delivers any other annual report to its shareholders.

(2) A social purpose corporation shall post each annual benefit report on the public portion of its website, if any, and it shall remain posted for at least 3 years.

(3) If a social purpose corporation does not have a website, the corporation shall provide a copy of its most recent annual benefit report, without charge, to any person who requests a copy.

(4) If a social purpose corporation does not comply with the annual benefit report delivery requirement, the circuit court in the county in which the principal office of the social purpose corporation is located or, if no office is located in this state, the county in which its registered office is located, may, after a shareholder of the social purpose corporation requests a copy, summarily order the corporation to furnish the annual benefit report. If the court orders the annual benefit report to be furnished, the court may also order the social purpose corporation to pay the shareholder's costs, including reasonable attorney fees, which were incurred in obtaining the order and otherwise enforce his or her rights under this section.

（2）年度公共利益报告所述期间内，公共利益董事辞职、拒绝连任或被免职，且该董事就其离任与社会目的公司有过书面往来的，该书面往来应当作为年度公共利益报告的附件。

（3）年度公共利益报告及其中依据第（1）（b）项规定对社会目的公司绩效作出的评估，不需要经过第三方标准提供者的审计或证明。

第 607.513 条　年度公共利益报告的提供

（1）社会目的公司应当将公共利益报告送交各股东：

（a）在社会目的公司财政年度结束后 120 天内；或者

（b）社会目的公司向其股东送交其他年度报告的同一时间。

（2）若条件允许，社会目的公司应当将其所有公共利益报告发布于其网站的公共部分，且应至少保留 3 年。

（3）如果社会目的公司没有网站，则应向任何索取报告的个人免费提供最新公共利益报告的副本。

（4）社会目的公司未遵守送交年度利益报告的相关规定的，公司主要办公地所在县的巡回法院，可在股东向公司发出索取年度公共利益报告的请求后，立时指令公司提供年度利益报告。公司未在本州设办公地的，由公司注册地的巡回法院管辖。法院指令公司提供年度公共利益报告的，可要求公司支付股东为获取法院指令和实现本条规定下的权利所支出的费用，包括合理的律师费用。

THE STATE OF TEXAS

Business Organizations Code
Title 2 Corporations
Chapter 23 Special-purpose Corporations
Subchapter A General Provisions

Sec. 23.001. Determination of Applicable Law.

(a) A corporation created under this chapter or under a special statute outside this code, to the extent not inconsistent with a special statute regarding a particular corporation, is governed by:

(1) Title 1 and Chapter 21, if the corporation is organized for profit; and

(2) Title 1 and Chapter 22, if the corporation is organized not for profit.

(b) If a special statute does not contain any provision regarding a matter provided for in Title 1 or Chapter 21 or 22, or if the special statute specifically provides that the general laws for corporations supplement the statute, to the extent consistent with the special statute:

(1) Title 1 and Chapter 21 apply to a corporation organized for profit; and

(2) Title 1 and Chapter 22 apply to a corporation organized not for profit.

Sec. 23.002. Applicability of Filing Requirements.

Except as otherwise provided by the special statute, a document to be filed with the secretary of state under a special statute shall be executed and filed in accordance with Chapter 4.

Sec. 23.003. Domestic Corporation Organized Under Special Statute.

A corporation organized under a special statute other than this code is not considered a "domestic corporation" formed under this code, although this code may apply to the corporation.

Sec. 23.051. Definitions.

In this subchapter:

(1) "Corporation" means a business development corporation organized under this

得克萨斯州

商业组织法典
第 2 编　公司
第 23 章　特殊目的公司
第 A 节　一般条款

第 23.001 条　法律适用

（a）依据本章规定设立的公司接受以下法律的调整；依据本法典以外的特别法规设立的公司，在不与该特别法规冲突的前提下，也受以下法律的调整：

（1）营利性公司适用第 1 编和第 21 章的相关规定；以及

（2）非营利性公司适用第 1 编和第 22 章的相关规定。

（b）特别法规不包含第 1 编、第 21 章或第 22 章所规定的事项的，或特别法规明确为公司提供了一般性法律作为补充的，在不与该特别法规冲突的前提下，适用以下法律：

（1）营利性公司适用第 1 编和第 21 章的相关规定；

（2）非营利性公司适用第 1 编和第 22 章的相关规定。

第 23.002 条　备案要求

除特别法规中另有特别规定外，依据特别法规向州务卿备案的文件应当依照第 4 章的相关规定执行和备案。

第 23.003 条　依据特别法规设立的本州公司

依据本法典以外的特别法规设立的公司，不视为本法典下的“本州公司”，但本法典的相关规定可适用于该等公司。

第 23.051 条　定义

本节中所使用的词语，具有以下特定含义：

（1）“公司”指依据本节规定组建的商业发展性公司。

subchapter.

(2) "Financial institution" means a banking corporation or trust company, savings and loan association, governmental agency, insurance company, or related corporation, partnership, foundation, or other institution engaged primarily in lending or investing funds.

(3) "Loan limit" means the maximum amount permitted to be outstanding at one time on loans made by a member to a corporation.

(4) "Member" means a financial institution authorized to do business in this state that undertakes to lend money to a corporation.

Sec. 23.052. Organizers.

Subject to The Securities Act (*Article 581–1 et seq., Vernon's Texas Civil Statutes*), 25 or more persons, the majority of whom must be residents of this state, may form a business development corporation to promote, develop, and advance the prosperity and economic welfare of this state.

Sec. 23.053. Purposes.

(a) A business development corporation may be organized as a:

(1) for–profit corporation under Chapter 21; or

(2) nonprofit corporation under Chapter 22.

(b) In accordance with Section 3.005(a)(3), the certificate of formation of a business development corporation must state that the purposes of the corporation are to:

(1) promote, stimulate, develop, and advance the business prosperity and economic welfare of this state and the residents of this state;

(2) encourage and assist, through loans, investments, or other business transactions, new business and industry in this state;

(3) rehabilitate and assist existing industry in this state;

(4) stimulate and assist in the expansion of business activity that will tend to promote the business development and maintain the economic stability of this state, provide maximum opportunities for employment, encourage thrift, and improve the standard of living of the residents of this state;

(5) cooperate and act in conjunction with other public or private organizations in the promotion and advancement of industrial, commercial, agricultural, and recreational developments in this state; and

(6) provide financing for the promotion, development, and conduct of business activity in this state.

Sec. 23.054. Powers.

(a) The powers of a corporation include, in addition to the powers conferred on the corporation by Chapters 2 and 21 or 22, as applicable, the power to:

(1) elect, appoint, and employ officers, agents, and employees;

（2）“金融机构”指主要从事借贷或投资基金的银行、信托公司、储蓄贷款协会、政府机构、保险公司或其他相关公司、合伙、基金会和其他协会等。

（3）“贷款限额”指成员放贷时，一家公司在此成员处享有的最高未偿付额度。

（4）“成员”指本州内获得授权向公司放贷的金融机构。

第 23.052 条　发起人

根据证券法（《弗农的得克萨斯州民法典》第 581-1 条等）的规定，25 人以上可组建商业发展性公司以推动、发展和促进本州的繁荣和经济福利，其中一半以上的发起人须为本州居民。

第 23.053 条　目的

（a）商业发展性公司的组建应当受以下章节的规定调整：

（1）营利性公司依据第 21 章的相关规定；或者

（2）非营利性公司依据第 22 章的相关规定。

（b）依照第 3.005（a）（3）项的规定，商业发展性公司的设立证书须载明公司的目的，包括

（1）推动、刺激、发展和提高本州及本州居民的商业繁荣和经济福利；

（2）通过贷款、投资或其他商业往来，激励和协助本州新兴企业和产业的发展；

（3）帮扶并推动本州已有产业的复兴；

（4）对于有利于本州商业发展和经济稳定，能够最大化提供就业机会，鼓励节约和提高本州居民的生活水准的商业活动，协助其发展壮大；

（5）与旨在促进本州工业、贸易、农业和娱乐产业发展的其他私人组织或公共组织协同合作；

（6）为旨在推动、发展本州商业活动的事业提供融资。

第 23.054 条　权力

（a）除第 2 章、第 21 章和第 22 章赋予的公司权力外，公司拥有以下权力：

（1）选举、任命和聘用高管、代理人和职工；

(2) make contracts and incur liabilities for a purpose of the corporation;

(3) borrow money on a secured or unsecured basis to carry out a purpose of the corporation;

(4) issue for the purpose of borrowing money a bond, debenture, note, or other evidence of indebtedness, whether secured or unsecured;

(5) secure an evidence of indebtedness by mortgage, pledge, deed of trust, or other lien on a property, franchise, right, or privilege of the corporation, or any part of or interest in those items, without securing shareholder or member approval;

(6) make a secured or unsecured loan and establish and regulate the terms and conditions of that loan and the charges for interest or service connected with that loan;

(7) purchase, receive, hold, lease, or otherwise acquire, and sell, convey, transfer, lease, or otherwise dispose of, property and exercise those rights and privileges incidental and appurtenant to the acquisition or disposal of the property and to the use of the property, including any property acquired by the corporation periodically in the satisfaction of a debt or enforcement of an obligation;

(8) acquire improved or unimproved real property to construct an industrial plant or other business establishment on the property or dispose of the real property for the construction of an industrial plant or other business establishment;

(9) acquire, construct or reconstruct, alter, repair, maintain, operate, sell, convey, transfer, lease, or otherwise dispose of an industrial plant or business establishment;

(10) protect the corporation's position as creditor by acquiring the goodwill, business, rights, property, including a share, bond, debenture, note, other evidence of indebtedness, other asset, or any part of an asset or interest in an asset, of a person to whom the corporation loaned money and assume, undertake, or pay an obligation, debt, or liability of the person;

(11) mortgage, pledge, or otherwise encumber any property, right, or thing of value, acquired under Subdivision (7), (8), (9), or (10), as security for the payment of a part of the purchase price;

(12) promote the establishment of local development corporations in the various communities of this state, enter into agreements with those local development corporations, and cooperate with, assist, or otherwise encourage the local foundations; and

(13) participate with a properly authorized federal lending agency in the making of loans.

(b) A corporation may approve an application for a loan under Subsection (a)(6) only if the applicant demonstrates that:

(1) the applicant applied for the loan through ordinary banking channels; and

(2) the loan has been refused by at least two banks or other financial institutions.

（2）为公司利益订立合同和承担责任；

（3）为公司利益负担有担保或无担保的金钱债务；

（4）为借款而发行债券、无担保债券、票据以及其他有担保或无担保的债务凭证；

（5）不需公司股东或成员的批准，将公司的财产、特许经营权、权利、特权或以上项目的部分或其产生的利益以抵押、质押、信托契约或留置的方式来担保公司债务；

（6）发放有担保或无担保贷款，确立和规范贷款的条款和条件以及与贷款相关的利息和服务费用；

（7）购买、接收、持有、租赁或以其他方式取得财产，出售、让与、转让、出售或以其他方式处置财产，行使与取得、处置和使用财产相关的附属权利和特权，上述财产包括公司定期从债权收益和责任履行中获得的财产；

（8）获取和处置已改进或未被改进过的不动产，以建造工业厂房或其他工业设施；

（9）收购、建造、重建、改造、修理、维护、运营、出售、让与、转让、出租或以其他方式处置工业厂房和工业设施；

（10）从公司发放贷款的对象处，以及需要向公司承担义务、履行责任和偿还债款的对象处，获取商誉、业务、权利和财产，包括股票、债券、无担保债券、票据、其他债务凭证、其他资产、上述资产的部分或资产的利息等，以维护公司的债权人地位；

（11）为支付购买价款而设定担保，担保形式包括将依据第（7）、（8）、（9）、（10）款规定获得的财产、权利、有价物抵押、质押或设立其他负担；

（12）推动本州不同区域的当地发展性公司的建立，与当地发展性公司订立合同，以及协同、协助或以其他方式推动当地基金会的发展；

（13）与经授权的联邦贷款机构共同发放贷款。

（b）公司依据第（a）（6）项的规定发放贷款的，申请者应证明：

（1）申请者曾通过一般性的银行渠道申请贷款；并且

（2）贷款申请已经被至少两家银行或金融机构拒绝。

Sec. 23.055. Statewide Operation.

A corporation organized under this subchapter is a state development company as defined by Section 103, Small Business Investment Act of 1958 *(15 U.S.C. Section 662),* as amended, or similar federal legislation, and may operate on a statewide basis.

Sec. 23.056. Certificate of Formation.

(a) The certificate of formation of a corporation must state:

(1) the name of the corporation;

(2) the purpose or purposes for which the corporation is organized as required by Section 23.053; and

(3) any other information required by:

(A) Chapter 4; and

(B) Chapter 21 or 22, as applicable.

(b) The name of a corporation must include the words "Business Development Corporation."

Sec. 23.057. Management by Board of Directors; Number of Directors.

(a) The organization, control, and management of a corporation are vested in a board of directors. The board must consist of not fewer than 15 and not more than 21 directors.

(b) The board of directors may exercise any power of the corporation not conferred on the shareholders or members by law or by the corporation's bylaws.

Sec. 23.058. Election or Appointment of Directors.

(a) The organizers of a corporation shall name the directors constituting the initial board of directors of the corporation. Directors other than the initial directors shall be elected at each annual meeting of the corporation. If an annual meeting is not held at the time designated by the bylaws of the corporation, the directors shall be elected at a special meeting held in lieu of the annual meeting.

(b) At an annual meeting or special meeting held in lieu of the annual meeting, the members of the corporation shall elect two-thirds of the directors, and the shareholders of the corporation shall elect the remaining directors.

Sec. 23.059. Term of Office; Vacancy.

(a) A director of a corporation holds office until the next annual election of directors and until a successor is elected and qualified, unless the director is removed at an earlier date in accordance with the corporation's bylaws.

(b) A vacancy in the office of a director elected by the members shall be filled by the directors elected by the members, and a vacancy in the office of a director elected by the shareholders shall be filled by the directors elected by the shareholders.

Sec. 23.060. Officers.

The board of directors of a corporation shall appoint a president, a treasurer, and any

第 23.055 条　全州经营

依据本节规定组建的公司是 1958 年修订的《小型商业投资法案》(《美国法典》第 15 卷第 662 节)第 103 条或其他类似联邦立法中所定义的州发展性公司，可以在全州范围内经营。

第 23.056 条　设立证书

(a)公司的设立证书须载明：

(1)公司名称；

(2)依据第 23.053 条的要求组建的公司的一项或多项目的；以及

(3)以下条款要求的其他信息：

(A)第 4 章；以及

(B)第 21 章或第 22 章，如适用。

(b)公司名称应包含“商业发展性公司”。

第 23.057 条　董事会管理；董事数量

(a)董事会负责公司的组建、控制和管理。董事会成员数量应不少于 15 人，不超过 21 人。

(b)董事会可以依据法律或公司章程的规定，在未经股东和成员授权的情况下行使公司权力。

第 23.058 条　董事的选举或任命

(a)公司的发起人应当任命初始董事会的成员。除初始董事外，董事应在公司每年的年度会议中选举。年度会议未按公司章程的规定按期举行的，应当举行特别会议选举董事。

(b)在年度会议或为替代年度会议而召开的特别会议中，公司成员应选举产生 2/3 的董事，其余董事由公司股东选出。

第 23.059 条　任期；空缺

(a)除根据公司章程规定提前将董事免职外，董事的任期应当延续到下年度董事选举且有资格的继任者被选出之时。

(b)董事会中由成员选出的董事出现空缺时，应由成员选举董事填补；由股东选出的董事出现空缺时，应由股东选举董事填补。

第 23.060 条　高管

公司的董事会应当任命一名总裁，一名财务主管以及公司的其他高管或代理人，

other agent or officer of the corporation and shall fill each vacancy other than a vacancy on the board.

Sec. 23.061. Participation As Owner.

(a) An individual, corporation, or other organization authorized to conduct business in this state, including a public utility company, insurance and casualty company, or foreign corporation licensed to do business in this state, or a trust may acquire, purchase, hold, sell, assign, transfer, mortgage, pledge, or otherwise dispose of a bond, security, or other evidence of indebtedness created by, or shares of, the corporation.

(b) An owner of shares of the corporation may exercise any right, power, or privilege of that ownership, including the right to vote.

Sec. 23.062. Financial Institution As Member of Corporation.

(a) A financial institution may become a member of a corporation and may make loans to the corporation as provided by this chapter.

(b) A financial institution may request membership in the corporation by applying to the corporation's board of directors in the manner prescribed by the board. Membership in the corporation takes effect on the board's acceptance of the application.

(c) A financial institution that is a member of a corporation may acquire, purchase, hold, sell, assign, transfer, mortgage, pledge, or otherwise dispose of a bond, security, or other evidence of indebtedness created by, or a share of, the corporation. As owner of shares of the corporation, a financial institution may exercise any right, power, or privilege of that ownership, including the right to vote. A member of a corporation may not acquire shares of the corporation in an amount greater than 10 percent of the member's loan limit. The amount of shares of the corporation that a member may acquire is in addition to the amount of shares of corporations that the member may otherwise acquire.

(d) A financial institution that is not a member of the corporation may not acquire any shares of the corporation.

Sec. 23.063. Withdrawal of Member.

(a) On written notice to the corporation's board of directors, a member may withdraw from a corporation on the date stated in the notice. The date of a member's withdrawal must be at least six months after the date notice is given under this subsection.

(b) A member is not obligated to make a loan to the corporation pursuant to a call made after the date of the member's withdrawal from the corporation, but a member shall fulfill any obligation that has accrued or for which a commitment has been made before the withdrawal date.

Sec. 23.064. Powers of Shareholders and Members.

The shareholders and members of a corporation may:

(1) determine the number of directors and elect the directors as provided by Section

董事会应负责填补除董事会空缺外的所有职位空缺。

第 23.061 条　作为所有者参与

（a）个人、公司、其他经授权在本州经营商业的组织，包括经授权在本州经营的公用事业公司、保险公司、外国公司以及信托，可收购、购买、持有、出售、分配、转让、抵押、质押或以其他方式处置由公司发行的债券、证券、其他债务凭证以及公司股份。

（b）公司股份的所有者可以行使所有权包含的任何权利、权力或特权，包括投票权。

第 23.062 条　金融机构作为公司成员

（a）依据本章规定，金融机构能够成为公司成员并为其发放贷款。

（b）金融机构可以按照公司董事会规定的方式，向董事会申请取得成员资格。董事会接受该申请，成员资格即生效。

（c）作为公司成员的金融机构可以收购、购买、持有、出售、分配、转让、抵押、质押或以其他方式处置由公司发行的债券、证券、其他债务凭证以及公司股份。作为公司股份的所有人，金融机构可以行使所有权包含的任何权利、权力或特权，包括投票权。成员取得的公司股份不得超过其贷款限额的 10%。成员取得的公司股份数额应累积计算。

（d）不具备公司成员身份的金融机构不得获取公司股份。

第 23.063 条　成员的退出

（a）成员应按董事会发出的书面通知上所载明的退出时间退出公司。依据本款规定发送的书面通知，其签发日期与通知所载明的退出日期应至少间隔 6 个月。

（b）对于退出日期后的贷款请求，成员不再负有向公司发放贷款的义务，但成员应当履行退出日期前已发生或已承诺的贷款义务。

第 23.064 条　股东和成员的权力

公司股东和成员有权：

（1）依照第 23.058 条的规定决定董事数量和选举董事；

23.058;

(2) make, amend, and repeal bylaws of the corporation; or

(3) exercise any other power of the corporation that is conferred on the shareholders and members by the bylaws.

Sec. 23.065. Voting by Shareholder or Member.

(a) Each shareholder of a corporation has one vote, in person or by proxy, for each share held by the shareholder.

(b) Each member of a corporation has one vote in person or by proxy.

(c) A member with a loan limit that exceeds $ 1,000 has one additional vote, in person or by proxy, for each additional $ 1,000 the member may have outstanding on loans to the corporation at any one time as determined under Section 23.068.

Sec. 23.066. Loan to Corporation.

(a) When called on by a corporation to make a loan to the corporation, a member of the corporation shall make the loan on those terms and conditions periodically approved by the board of directors.

(b) A loan made to the corporation by a member shall be evidenced by a bond, debenture, note, or other evidence of indebtedness of the corporation that:

(1) is freely transferable at any time; and

(2) accrues interest at a rate of not less than one–fourth of one percent more than the rate of interest determined by the board of directors to be the prime rate prevailing on the date of issuance on unsecured commercial loans.

Sec. 23.067. Prohibited Loan.

(a) A member may not make a loan to a corporation if, immediately after the loan would be made, the total amount of the obligations of the corporation would exceed 50 times the capital of the corporation.

(b) For purposes of this section, the capital of the corporation includes the amount of the outstanding shares of the corporation, whether common or preferred, and the earned or paid–in surplus of the corporation.

Sec. 23.068. Loan Limits.

(a) A loan limit shall be established at the $ 1,000 amount nearest to the amount computed in accordance with this section.

(b) The total amount outstanding on loans made to a corporation by a member at any one time, when added to the amount of the investment in the shares of the corporation then held by the member, may not exceed:

(1) 20 percent of the total amount then outstanding on loans to the corporation by all members, including outstanding amounts validly called for a loan but not yet loaned; or

(2) the following limit, to be determined as of the time the member becomes a member

（2）制定、修改和废除公司章程；
（3）行使公司章程中规定的须取得股东和成员授权的公司权力。

第 23.065 条　股东和成员的投票权

（a）股东投票实行一股一票，可以直接行使或委托他人代理行使投票权；

（b）成员投票实行一人一票，可以直接行使或委托他人代理行使投票权；
（c）成员贷款限额超过 1000 美元的，依照第 23.068 条的规定向公司累计发放的贷款每超过 1000 美元时增加一个投票权，该投票权可以直接行使或委托他人代理行使。

第 23.066 条　公司贷款

（a）公司发出借款申请的，公司成员应当按照董事会定期制定的条款和条件向公司发放贷款。

（b）成员向公司发放的贷款应当有债券、无担保债券、票据或其他债务凭证：

（1）该凭证可在任何时间自由流通；并且
（2）成员贷款的利率水平应当不低于 0.25%，多于董事会依据贷款日当天的无担保商业贷款利率决定的最优惠利率。

第 23.067 条　禁止贷款

（a）如果提供一笔贷款后，公司负担的全部债务额将超过公司资本的 50 倍，则该成员不得向公司提供该笔贷款；

（b）为实现本条的目的，公司资本包括公司的全部流通股（普通股和优先股）以及资本盈余。

第 23.068 条　贷款限额

（a）贷款限额应确定为与依据本条规定计算的最接近的 1000 美元的数额。

（b）成员向公司的贷款总额，加上同一时间该成员持有的公司股份，不得超过：

（1）全体成员向公司提供的贷款总额的 20%，含公司已申请但成员尚未贷出的数额；或者
（2）成员在成为公司成员时设定的以下限额，或提交成员申请之前依据此前

of the corporation, or at any time requested by a member on the basis of the audited balance sheet of the member at the close of its fiscal year immediately preceding its application for membership or, in the case of an insurance company, its last annual statement to the Texas Department of Insurance:

(A) an amount equal to the lesser of $ 750,000 or two percent of the capital and surplus of a commercial bank or trust company;

(B) an amount equal to one percent of the total outstanding loans made by a savings and loan association;

(C) an amount equal to one percent of the capital and unassigned surplus of a stock insurance company other than a fire insurance company;

(D) an amount equal to one percent of the unassigned surplus of a mutual insurance company other than a fire insurance company;

(E) an amount equal to one–tenth of one percent of the assets of a fire insurance company; or

(F) the limits approved by the board of directors of the corporation for a government pension fund or other financial institution.

(c) Subject to Subsection (b), each call made by the corporation shall be prorated among the members of the corporation in substantially the same proportion that the adjusted loan limit of each member bears to the aggregate of the adjusted loan limits of all members.

(d) For purposes of Subsection (c), the adjusted loan limit of a member is the amount of the member's loan limit, reduced by the balance of outstanding loans made by the member to the corporation and the investment in shares of the corporation held by the member at the time of the call.

Sec. 23.069. Surplus.

(a) A corporation shall set apart as earned surplus not less than 10 percent of the corporation's net earnings each year until the surplus, with any unimpaired surplus paid in, is equal to one–half of the amount paid in on the shares then outstanding. The surplus shall be kept to secure against losses and contingencies. If the surplus becomes impaired, the surplus shall be reimbursed in the manner provided for its accumulation.

(b) Net earnings and surplus shall be determined by the board of directors after providing for the required reserves as the directors consider advisable. A good faith determination of net earnings and surplus by the directors under this subsection is conclusive.

Sec. 23.070. Depository.

(a) A corporation may deposit the corporation's funds in a banking institution that has been designated as a depository by a vote of the majority of the directors present at an authorized meeting of the board of directors of the corporation, excluding a director who is an

最近的财政年度的经审计的财务报表所设定的以下限额；如果是保险公司，则依据其向得克萨斯州保险部门提交的上年度报告设定以下贷款限额：

（A）对于商业银行和信托公司，取以下两者的较小值：75 万美元或资本与盈余之和的 2%；

（B）对于储蓄贷款协会，为该协会全部未偿还贷款的 1%；

（C）对于除火灾保险公司外的股份保险公司，为资本与未分配盈余之和的 1%；

（D）对于除火灾保险公司外的相互保险公司，为未分配盈余的 1%；

（E）对于火灾保险公司，为资产值的 0.1%；

（F）对于政府养老基金或其他金融机构，采公司董事会批准的限额。

（c）依据第（b）款的规定，公司发出的每一贷款申请数额均应在公司成员之间按比例分配，该比例须与每一成员调整后的贷款限额占全体成员调整后的总贷款限额的比重大体相同。

（d）第（c）款中调整后的贷款限额的计算方法为，成员的贷款限额，减去公司发出贷款申请时成员向公司已发放的贷款，再减去此时成员持有的公司股份。

第 23.069 条　盈余公积

（a）公司应当提取不少于公司年净利润的 10% 作为盈余公积，直到盈余公积（含未动用的盈余公积）达到公司流通股份的 50%。盈余公积应用于弥补亏损和应急。盈余公积减损的，应按照上述提取方式弥补盈余公积。

（b）董事会应在提取法定公积后，以其认为适合的比例确定净利润和盈余公积。董事根据本款规定确定净利润和盈余公积应当遵守信义义务。

第 23.070 条　托管

（a）公司应指定一家银行托管公司资金，董事会经授权后召开会议，以出席会议的董事过半数的投票选取公司的托管银行，担任托管银行的高管或董事的公司董事不得参与投票。

officer or director of the designated depository.

(b) The corporation may not receive money on deposit.

Sec. 23.071. Annual Report; Provision of Required Information.

(a) A corporation shall annually make a report of its condition to the banking commissioner and the Texas Department of Insurance.

(b) A corporation shall provide any information that is required by the secretary of state.

Sec. 23.102. Applicability of Chapter 22.

If this subchapter does not contain any provision regarding a matter provided for in Chapter 22, to the extent consistent with this subchapter, Chapter 22 applies to a corporation formed under this subchapter.

Sec. 23.103. Duration.

A grand body that incorporates under this subchapter may provide in the grand body's certificate of formation for the expiration of its corporate powers at the end of a stated number of years. If the certificate of formation does not provide for the duration of the grand body, the grand body has perpetual existence. The grand body may by its corporate name have perpetual succession of its officers and members.

Sec. 23.104. Subordinate Lodges.

(a) The incorporation of a grand body includes each of its subordinate lodges or bodies holding a warrant or charter under the grand body.

(b) A subordinate body has all of the rights of other corporations under and by the name given to the grand body in the warrant or charter issued to the grand body to which it is attached. Those rights shall be provided for in the charter of the grand body.

(c) A subordinate body is subject to the jurisdiction and control of its respective grand body, and the warrant or charter of the subordinate body may be revoked by the grand body.

Sec. 23.105. Trustees and Directors.

A grand body and a subordinate of the grand body may elect trustees and directors or may appoint trustees or directors from among their officers.

Sec. 23.106. Franchise Taxes.

A corporation formed under this subchapter is not subject to or required to pay a franchise tax, except that a corporation is exempt from the franchise tax imposed by Chapter 171, Tax Code, only if the corporation is exempted by that chapter.

Sec. 23.107. General Powers.

A grand body and a subordinate of the grand body may take action as directed or provided by law in the case of other corporations and may make constitutions and bylaws to govern their affairs.

（b）公司不得接收托管的银行存款。

第 23.071 条　年度报告；必要信息条款

（a）公司应当编制年度报告，向银行业委员会和得克萨斯州保险部门说明自身情况。

（b）公司应当按照州务卿的要求提供其所需的任何信息。

第 23.102 条　第 22 章的法律适用

在不与本节规定相抵触的前提下，对于本节未予规定的事项，依据本节规定设立的公司适用第 22 章的相关规定。

第 23.103 条　存续期间

根据本节规定设立的主体可以在其设立证书上载明公司权力的终止日期。如果设立证书未载明存续期间，则该主体可以永久持续经营。主体在使用同一公司名称时，其高管和成员可以继受。

第 23.104 条　下属分支机构

（a）主体的设立包括每一个下属分支机构和持有主体颁发的许可证或特许状的分部的设立。

（b）下属分支机构可依据其附属的主体所获发的许可证或特许状，享有与其他公司相同的权利。上述权利由主体颁发的特许状所规定。

（c）下属分支机构受其主体的管辖和控制，主体可撤回为其颁发的许可证或特许状。

第 23.105 条　受托人和董事

主体和主体的下属分支机构可以选举产生受托人和董事，或在高管中指定受托人和董事。

第 23.106 条　特许税

依据本节规定设立的公司不在特许税的调整范围内也无须缴纳特许税，除非公司对税收法典第 171 章规定的特许税享有豁免权。

第 23.107 条　一般权力

主体及其下属分支机构可以依照指示或法律规定向其他公司提起诉讼，其可以制定章程和细则来管理自身事务。

Sec. 23.108. Authority Regarding Property.

(a) A grand body or subordinate body may acquire and hold property as necessary or convenient for a site on which to erect a building for the use and occupancy of the body and to erect homes and schools for members' widows or orphans or elderly, disabled, or indigent members and may sell or mortgage the property.

(b) A conveyance must be executed by the presiding officer and attested to by the secretary with the seal.

(c) The authority of a subordinate body to sell or to mortgage property is subject to the conditions periodically prescribed or established by the grand body to which the subordinate is attached.

Sec. 23.109. Authority Regarding Loans.

(a) A grand body incorporated under this subchapter may:

(1) loan money held and owned by the grand body for charitable purposes, for the endowment of any of the institutions of the grand body, or otherwise; and

(2) secure loans by taking and receiving liens on real property or by another method elected by the grand body.

(b) On sale of real property secured by a lien, a grand body may become the purchaser of the real property and hold title to the property.

Sec. 23.110. Winding Up and Termination of Subordinate Body.

(a) On the winding up and termination of a subordinate body attached to a grand body, all property and rights existing in the subordinate body pass to and vest in the grand body to which it was attached, subject to the payment of any debt owed by the subordinate body.

(b) Notwithstanding a grand body's liability for the debt of a subordinate body under Subsection (a), the grand body is not liable for an amount greater than the actual cash value of the subordinate body's effects or authority.

第 23.108 条　财产相关的权力

（a）主体及其下属分支机构可以在必要时为自身便利获取和持有土地上的财产，包括建造供主体使用和居住的房屋，为成员中的遗孀、孤儿、老人、残疾人和贫困人口建造房屋和学校，售卖或抵押上述财产等。

（b）财产转让须由首席主管执行，并附有秘书的签章以作证明。

（c）下属分支机构出售或抵押财产的权力受制于其所附属的主体定期制定的条件。

Sec. 23.109.　贷款相关的权力

（a）依据本节规定设立的主体可以：

（1）以主体所持有和所有的具有慈善目的的款项，或以其接受的捐赠款项，对外发放贷款；或者

（2）通过不动产留置或主体选择的其他方式，发放担保贷款。

（b）出售留置的不动产时，主体可以成为该不动产的购买方，并获得财产的所有权。

第 23.110 条　下属分支机构的清算和终止

（a）主体的下属分支机构清算和终止时，分支机构所有的全部财产和权利应转让并归属于该分支机构所属的主体，分支机构的债务也一并转移。

（b）尽管主体承担第（a）款中所说的分支机构的债务，但仅以与分支机构作用和权限相当的实际现金价值以限，超出部分主体不承担责任。

THE STATE OF WASHINGTON

Chapter 23B.25 RCW

SOCIAL PURPOSE CORPORATIONS

23B.25.005 Becoming or ceasing to be a social purpose corporation.

(1) Any corporation may elect to be governed as a social purpose corporation by one of the following means:

(a) One or more persons may act as incorporator or incorporators of a social purpose corporation by delivering articles of incorporation that conform to the requirements of this chapter to the secretary of state for filing; or

(b) Any corporation which is not a social purpose corporation may elect to become a social purpose corporation by complying with RCW 23B.25.130.

(2) Any social purpose corporation may elect to cease to be governed as a social purpose corporation by complying with RCW 23B.25.140. [2012 c 215 § 1.]

23B.25.010 Powers, rights, and obligations — Definition — Application of RCW 23B.03.010.

(1) Except as otherwise expressly stated in this chapter, the provisions of this title and all powers, rights, and obligations thereunder shall apply to social purpose corporations organized under this chapter, and references in this title to the term "corporation" shall be read to include social purpose corporations organized under this chapter.

(2) Subject to any limitations contained in the articles of incorporation, a social purpose corporation may engage in any lawful business under RCW 23B.03.010. [2012 c 215 § 2.]

23B.25.020 General social purposes.

Every corporation governed by this chapter must be organized to carry out its business purpose under RCW 23B.03.010 in a manner intended to promote positive shortterm or long term effects of, or minimize adverse shortterm or longterm effects of, the corporation's activities upon any or all of (1) the corporation's employees, suppliers, or customers; (2) the

华盛顿州

《华盛顿州修订法》第 23B.25 章

社会目的企业

第 23B.25.005 条　选择或终止成为社会目的企业

（1）任何一家公司都可以通过以下任一种方式选择成为社会目的的公司：

（a）一人或多人可以公司或社会目的公司设立者的身份在办理登记时向州务卿递交符合本章要求的公司章程；或者

（b）任何一家非社会目的公司可以选择依据《华盛顿州修订法》第 23B.25.130 条的规定成为社会目的公司。

（2）任何一家社会目的公司可以选择依据《华盛顿州修订法》第 23B.25.140 条的规定终止其社会目的形态。

第 23B.25.010 条　能力、权利和义务——定义——《华盛顿州修订法》第 23B.03.010 条的适用

（1）除本章另有规定外，本编条款以及所规定的能力、权利和义务应适用于根据本章设立的社会目的公司，本编所提及的“公司”一词特指根据本章所设立的社会目的公司。

（2）在符合公司章程限制规定的情形下，社会目的公司可以根据《华盛顿州修订法》第 23B.03.010 条的规定从事合法的经营活动。

第 23B.25.020 条　一般社会目的

根据本章设立的公司必须以《华盛顿州修订法》第 23B.03.010 条规定的方式追求其商事目的，在促进受公司活动影响的以下群体的短期或长期利益的同时减少短期或长期负面影响：（1）公司员工、供应商或消费者；（2）本地、本州、本国或国际社会；（3）环境。

local, state, national, or world community; or (3) the environment. [2012 c 215 § 3.]

23B.25.030 Specific social purposes.

In addition to the general social purpose set forth in RCW 23B.25.020, every corporation governed by this chapter may have one or more specific social purposes for which the corporation is organized. [2012 c 215 § 4.]

23B.25.040 Articles of incorporation — Required and optional provisions — Notice — Availability of copies.

(1) In addition to the matters required to be set forth in the articles of incorporation pursuant to RCW 23B.02.020 (1) and (2), the articles of incorporation of a social purpose corporation must set forth:

(a) A corporate name for the social purpose corporation that contains the words "social purpose corporation" or "SPC" as an abbreviation of those words;

(b) A statement that the corporation is organized as a social purpose corporation governed by this chapter;

(c) A statement setting forth the general social purpose or purposes for which the corporation is organized pursuant to RCW 23B.25.020;

(d) If the corporation has designated one or more specific social purpose or purposes pursuant to RCW 23B.25.030, a statement setting forth such specific social purpose or purposes; and

(e) A provision that states the following: "The mission of this social purpose corporation is not necessarily compatible with and may be contrary to maximizing profits and earnings for shareholders, or maximizing shareholder value in any sale, merger, acquisition, or other similar actions of the corporation."

(2) In addition to the matters that must be set forth in the articles of incorporation in accordance with subsection (1) of this section and the provisions that may be set forth in the articles of incorporation pursuant to RCW 23B.02.020 (5) and (6), the articles of incorporation of a social purpose corporation may contain the following provisions:

(a) A provision requiring the corporation's directors or officers to consider the impacts of any corporate action or proposed corporate action upon one or more of the social purposes of the corporation;

(b) A provision requiring the corporation to furnish to the shareholders an assessment of the overall performance of the corporation with respect to its social purpose or purposes, prepared in accordance with a thirdparty standard;

(c) A provision requiring, for any or all corporate actions, the vote of a larger proportion or of all of the shares of any class or series, or the vote or quorum for taking action of a larger proportion or of all of the directors, than is otherwise required by this title or this chapter;

(d) A provision requiring the approval of the shareholders for any corporate action, even

第 23B.25.030 条　特殊社会目的

除《华盛顿州修订法》第 23B.25.020 条所规定的一般社会利益外，受本章规定调整的每个公司可为某个或多个特定社会利益而设立。

第 23B.25.040 条　公司章程——强制性和选择性条款——通知——副本的可获得性

（1）除《华盛顿州修订法》第 23B.02.020（1）款和第（2）款的内容必须规定于公司章程外，社会目的公司的章程还必须载明以下内容：

（a）社会目的公司的公司名称必须包含“社会目的公司”或其缩写“SPC”；

（b）公司章程必须作出公司是根据本章规定所设立的社会目的公司的声明；

（c）必须作出公司追求一般社会目的或者根据《华盛顿州修订法》第 23B.25.020 条所规定目的的声明；

（d）如果公司根据《华盛顿州修订法》第 23B.25.030 条的规定确定了一个或多个特定社会目的，必须对该特定目的予以声明；

（e）必须作出含有以下条款的声明：“本社会目的公司的宗旨可能与通过销售、并购或者其他类似方式追求股东利益或价值最大化的宗旨不符甚至相反。”

（2）除本条第（1）款和《华盛顿州修订法》第 23B.02.020（5）款和第（6）款规定的内容必须记载于公司章程的事项外，社会目的公司的章程还应包含以下条款：

（a）要求公司董事和管理人员考虑公司行为或计划是否会影响公司所设定社会目的的实现的条款；

（b）要求公司向股东呈交有关公司实现其社会目的情况的根据第三方标准编制的评估报告的条款；

（c）必须由超过本章所规定比例的绝大部分股东或全部股东或任何类别或系列股东或全体董事同意方可实施的行为；

（d）虽然本编并未规定，但必须经股东授权方可实施的其他行为；以及

though not otherwise required by this title; and

(e) A provision limiting the duration of the corporation's existence to a specified date.

(3) Prior to the issuance of shares, the corporation shall furnish a prospective shareholder with a copy of the articles of incorporation in the form of a record.

(4) Prior to the transfer of shares, the transferor shareholder shall give notice of the transfer to the corporation. Within a reasonable time after receiving notice, the corporation shall provide the prospective transferee with a copy of the articles of incorporation in the form of a record.

23B.25.050 Duties of director — Standards — Liabilities.

(1) A director of a social purpose corporation shall discharge the duties of a director, including duties as a member of any committee of the board upon which the director may serve, in good faith, with the care an ordinarily prudent person in a like position would exercise under similar circumstances, and in a manner the director reasonably believes to be in the best interests of the corporation in accordance with RCW 23B.08.300.

(2) Unless the articles of incorporation provide otherwise, in discharging his or her duties as a director, the director of a social purpose corporation may consider and give weight to one or more of the social purposes of the corporation as the director deems relevant.

(3) Any action taken as a director of a social purpose corporation, or any failure to take any action, that the director reasonably believes is intended to promote one or more of the social purposes of the corporation shall be deemed to be in the best interests of the corporation.

(4) A director of a social purpose corporation is not liable for any action taken as a director, or any failure to take any action, if the director performed the duties of the director's office in compliance with this section.

(5) Nothing in this chapter creates any liability or grants any right in or for any person or any cause of action by or for any person, and a director shall not be responsible to any party other than the corporation and its shareholders.

(6) Nothing in this chapter alters the general standards for any director of a corporation that is not a social purpose corporation.

23B.25.060 Duties of officer — Standards — Liabilities.

(1) An officer of a social purpose corporation with discretionary authority shall discharge the officer's duties under that authority in good faith, with the care an ordinarily prudent person in a like position would exercise under similar circumstances, and in a manner the officer reasonably believes to be in the best interests of the corporation in accordance with RCW 23B.08.420.

(2) Unless the articles of incorporation provide otherwise, in discharging his or her duties as an officer, the officer of a social purpose corporation may consider and give weight

（e）规定公司存续时间的条款。

（3）在发行股份之前，公司应该向潜在股东发放公司章程的副本，并对有关行为进行记录。

（4）在股份转让之前，转让股东应向公司递交转让通知。在收到通知后的合理期间内，公司应该向潜在受让方提供公司章程的副本，并对此进行记录。

第 23B.25.050 条　董事责任——标准——义务

（1）社会目的公司的董事包括董事可能任职的任何委员会成员应以如下方式履行董事义务：董事应尽到理性人在相似情形下应有的善意和合理注意，有合理理由认为该行为符合《华盛顿州修订法》第 23B.08.300 条的规定的最佳利益。

（2）除公司章程另有规定外，在履行董事义务时，社会目的董事可以酌情考虑一个或多个其认为相关的社会目的。

（3）社会目的公司的董事有合理理由认为有助于促进公司社会目的实现的作为或不作为将被视为符合公司的最佳利益的行为。

（4）如果社会目的公司的董事根据本条规定履行义务，则董事不因其作为或不作为承担责任。

（5）本章不应为任何个人或因任何个人的行为创设权利或义务，或成为任何人提起诉讼的理由，董事不应对除公司及其股东之外的第三人履行义务。

（6）本章中的任何内容不改变非社会目的公司董事的一般标准。

第 23B.25.060 条　高管责任——标准——义务

（1）享有自由裁量权的社会目的公司高管应该以善意和在相似情形下理性人所应有的注意来履行职责，同时，确信其行为符合《华盛顿州修订法》第 23B.08.420 条规定的公司的最佳利益。

（2）除公司章程另有规定外，高管履行其职责时应考虑其认为有关的公司的社会目的。

to one or more of the social purposes of the corporation as the officer deems relevant.

(3) Any action taken as an officer of a social purpose corporation, or any failure to take any action, that the officer reasonably believes is intended to promote one or more of the social purposes of the corporation shall be deemed to be in the best interests of the corporation.

(4) An officer of a social purpose corporation is not liable for any action taken as an officer, or any failure to take any action, if the officer performed the duties of the officer's office in compliance with this section.

(5) Nothing in this chapter creates any liability or grants any right in or for any person or any cause of action by or for any person, and an officer shall not be responsible to any party other than the corporation and its shareholders.

(6) Nothing in this chapter alters the general standards for any officer of a corporation that is not a social purpose corporation.

23B.25.070 Shares — Represented by certificate — Not represented by certificate.

(1) Shares issued by a social purpose corporation may but need not be represented by certificates.

(2) If shares are represented by certificates, in addition to the information required on certificates by RCW 23B.06.250 (2) and (3), each share certificate must state on its face the following language in a conspicuous manner:

"This entity is a social purpose corporation organized under Title 23B RCW of the Washington business corporation act. The articles of incorporation of this corporation state one or more social purposes of this corporation. The corporation will furnish the shareholder this information without charge on request in writing."

(3) If shares are not represented by certificates, within a reasonable time after the issue or transfer of such shares, the corporation shall send the shareholder a record containing the information required pursuant to RCW 23B.06.260(2) and the language required on certificates by subsection (2) of this section.

23B.25.080 Instituting or maintaining proceedings — Shareholders only.

(1) No proceeding may be instituted or maintained in the right of any social purpose corporation under this title by any party other than a shareholder of the social purpose corporation.

(2) A person may not commence a proceeding in the right of a social purpose corporation unless the person was a shareholder of the corporation when the transaction complained of occurred or unless the person became a shareholder through transfer by operation of law from one who was a shareholder at that time.

(3) Any proceeding instituted or maintained in the right of a social purpose corporation

（3）社会目的公司的高管有合理理由认为有助于促进公司社会目的的实现的作为或不作为将被视为符合公司的最佳利益的行为。

（4）如果社会目的公司的高管根据本条规定履行义务，则董事不因其作为或不作为承担责任。

（5）本章不应为任何个人或因任何个人的行为创设权利或义务，或成为任何诉讼的理由，高管不应对除公司及其股东之外的第三人履行义务。

（6）本章的任何内容不改变非社会目的公司高管的一般标准。

第 23B.25.070 条　股份——颁发股份证明书——未颁发股份证明书

（1）社会公共目的公司发行股份时可以不颁发股份证明书。

（2）如果颁发股份证明书，除《华盛顿州修订法》第 23B.06.250（2）款和第（3）款的内容必须记载于证明书外，每份证明书必须在其封面明显写明如下内容：

“本实体为根据《华盛顿州商事公司法》中《华盛顿州修订法》第 23B 编规定设立的社会目的公司。章程载明了本公司的社会目的，在股东提出书面申请时，本公司将免费向股东提供与公司社会目的有关的信息。”

（3）如果未颁发股份证明书，在发行或转让上述股份的合理期间内，公司应向股东递交载明《华盛顿州修订法》第 23B.06.260（2）款规定内容的记录，并在记录中写明本条第（2）款规定的内容。

第 23B.25.080 条　启动或维持程序——股东

（1）除社会目的公司的股东外，任何人都不能启动或维持本编规定下的社会目的权利的程序。

（2）除在争议交易发生时为社会目的公司股东或收购股份成为股东外，任何人不能启动社会目的程序。

（3）任何启动或维持社会目的的程序都要符合华盛顿州修订法第 23B.07.400

must comply with the procedure set forth in RCW 23B.07.400.

23B.25.090 Amendment to articles of incorporation — Change to social purposes — Voting requirements.

If a proposed amendment to a social purpose corporation's articles of incorporation would materially change one or more of the social purposes of the corporation, in addition to approval in accordance with RCW 23B.10.030, the amendment to be adopted must be approved by twothirds of the voting group comprising all the votes entitled to be cast on the proposed amendment, and by twothirds of the holders of the outstanding shares of each class or series, voting as separate voting groups, and of each other voting group entitled under the articles of incorporation to vote separately on the proposed amendment. The articles of incorporation may require a greater vote than that provided for in this section.

23B.25.100 Plan of merger or share exchange — Status as social purpose corporation— Voting requirements.

(1) In addition to approval in accordance with RCW 23B.11.030, a plan of merger or share exchange pursuant to which a social purpose corporation would not be the surviving corporation must be approved by twothirds of the voting group comprising all the votes of the corporation entitled to be cast on the plan, and by twothirds of the holders of the outstanding shares of each class or series, voting as separate voting groups, and of each other voting group entitled under the articles of incorporation to vote separately on the proposed plan. The articles of incorporation may require a greater vote than that provided for in this subsection.

(2) The additional approval described in subsection (1) of this section is not required if the surviving corporation of the plan of merger or share exchange is a social purpose corporation governed by this chapter and includes a specific social purpose or purposes that do not materially differ from the disappearing corporation's specific social purpose or purposes, if any.

23B.25.110 Selling, leasing, exchanging, or disposing of property — Voting requirements.

(1) In addition to approval in accordance with RCW 23B.12.020, a proposed transaction in which the social purpose corporation is to sell, lease, exchange, or otherwise dispose of all, or substantially all, of its property, otherwise than in the usual and regular course of business, must be approved by twothirds of the voting group comprising all the votes entitled to be cast on the transaction, and by twothirds of the holders of the outstanding shares of each class or series, voting as separate voting groups, and of each other voting group entitled under the articles of incorporation to vote separately on the proposed transaction. The articles of incorporation may require a greater vote than that provided for in this section.

(2) The additional approval described in subsection (1) of this section is not required if the acquirer of such property is a social purpose corporation governed by this chapter and

条的规定。

第 23B.25.090 条　公司章程的修改——改变社会目的——表决票数要求

如果一项改变社会目的公司章程的提案将在实质上改变公司的某项或多项社会目的，除满足《华盛顿州修订法》第 23B.10.030 条的规定外，对该提案的修改必须获得有投票权股东或根据章程规定享有独立投票权的类别股东的 2/3 以上多数票的同意。公司对章程的修改可以另行规定比本条规定更高的票数要求。

第 23B.25.100 条　收购或股份置换计划——社会目的企业形态——表决票数要求

（1）除根据《华盛顿州修订法》第 23B.11.030 条的授权之外，如果社会目的企业是兼并、收购、股权置换计划的一方，并且该计划会导致社会目的公司不再存续，则此等兼并或股权置换计划必须获得 2/3 以上有投票权的股东的同意。公司章程可以规定比本条更高的表决要求。

（2）如果兼并收购或股份置换计划的存续公司是受本章规定调整的社会目的公司，并且，其某一或某些特定社会目的与被兼并的公司的特定社会目的不存在实质性差异，则不适用本条第（1）款所规定的授权。

第 23B.25.110 条　出售、出租或者处置财产——投票权要求

（1）除《华盛顿州修订法》第 23B.12.020 条规定情形须获得授权外，公共利益公司的任何出售、出租或者其他处置全部或主要财产的行为，除满足正常的商事交易程序外，还应获得有投票权的股东 2/3 以上票数的同意。公司章程可以规定比本条更高的表决要求。

（2）若财产受让人是受本章规定调整的社会目的公司并有与处置财产公司的特定社会目的无实质区别的目标，则不要求满足本条第（1）款规定的额外批准要求。

includes a specific social purpose or purposes that do not materially differ from the disposing corporation's specific social purpose or purposes, if any.

23B.25.120 Shareholder dissent — Payment of fair value, when.

In addition to the corporate actions set forth in RCW 23B.13.020(1), a shareholder is entitled to dissent from, and obtain payment of the fair value of the shareholder's shares in the event of, any of the following corporate actions:

(1) An election by a corporation to become a social purpose corporation, which has become effective, to which the corporation is a party if shareholder approval was required for the election by RCW 23B.25.130 or the articles of incorporation;

(2) An election to cease to be a social purpose corporation, which has become effective, to which the corporation is a party if shareholder approval was required for the election by RCW 23B.25.140 or the articles of incorporation, and the shareholder was entitled to vote on the election; and

(3) An amendment of the social purpose corporation's articles of incorporation that would materially change one or more of the social purposes of the corporation.

23B.25.130 Corporation converting to a social purpose corporation — Conditions — Election.

(1) Any corporation that is not a social purpose corporation may elect to become a social purpose corporation if, pursuant to the proposed election, each of the following conditions are met:

(a) Each share of the same class or series of the electing corporation shall, unless all shareholders of the class or series consent, be treated equally with respect to any cash, rights, securities, or other property to be received by, or any obligations or restrictions to be imposed on, the holder of that share;

(b) The board of directors of the electing corporation must recommend the election to the shareholders, unless the board of directors determines that because of conflict of interest or other special circumstances it should make no recommendation and communicates the basis for its determination to the shareholders with the proposed election; and

(c) In addition to any other voting conditions imposed by the board of directors under subsection (2) of this section, the election must be approved by an affirmative vote of at least twothirds of the voting group comprising all the votes of the electing corporation's shareholders entitled to be cast on the corporate action, and by two–thirds of the holders of the outstanding shares of each class or series, voting as separate voting groups, and each other voting group entitled under the articles of incorporation to vote separately on the corporate action.

(2) The board of directors of a corporation electing to become a social purpose corporation may condition its submission of the proposed election on any basis, including

第 23B.25.120 条　股东异议——以公平价格回购

除《华盛顿州修订法》第 23B.13.020（1）款规定的公司行为外，股东对以下行为提出异议的，公司可以公允价格回购其股份：

（1）公司选择成为社会目的公司必须满足《华盛顿州修订法》第 23B.25.130 条的规定或者公司章程规定要求获得股东授权时；

（2）公司选择终止社会目的形态必须满足《华盛顿州修订法》第 23B.25.140 条的规定或者公司章程规定要求获得股东授权，并且异议股东对此议案享有投票权；

（3）社会目的公司章程的修改将实质性地改变其原来的社会目的。

第 23B.25.130 条　公司转换为社会目的公司——条件——选择程序

（1）如果选择程序满足以下所有条件的，任何非社会目的公司都可以选择成为社会目的公司：

（a）拟选择成为社会目的公司的公司股东，除非所有类别或者系列股东一致同意，否则每一系列或类别股东都应根据其投资数额、权利、持有的证券数额、财产数额或者其股份承担的义务而享受平等的待遇；

（b）除非董事会认为存在利益冲突或其他特殊情形，否则拟选择成为公共利益公司的董事会成员必须向股东汇报转换计划；并且

（c）除满足本条第（2）款规定的董事会投票条件外，转换计划必须获得 2/3 以上有投票权的所有股东的同意，包括每个系列或类别股票持有者 2/3 的投票，作为单独主体的投票以及根据公司章程对公司行为进行的其他投票。

（2）拟转换为社会目的公司的董事会可以规定提交转换议案的条件，包括对此议案有投票权的任一类别股特定比例的股东的同意。

the affirmative vote of holders of a specified percentage of shares held by any group of shareholders not otherwise entitled to vote as a separate group on the proposed election.

(3) To elect to become a social purpose corporation, an electing corporation must amend its articles of incorporation to include the matters required to be set forth in the articles of incorporation pursuant to RCW 23B.25.040(1).

(4) After an election to become a social purpose corporation is approved, and at any time prior to filing the articles of amendment to amend the electing corporation's articles of incorporation in compliance with subsection (3) of this section, the planned election may be abandoned by the electing corporation, subject to any contractual rights, without further shareholder approval, in the manner determined by the board of directors.

(5) The election to become a social purpose corporation shall be effective upon the later of the filing of the articles of amendment with the secretary of state or the effective date or time set forth in the articles of amendment.

(6) Upon the effective time of the election to become a social purpose corporation, the electing corporation shall thereafter be a social purpose corporation and shall be subject to all of the provisions of this chapter and the existence of the social purpose corporation shall be deemed to have commenced on the date the electing corporation was incorporated.

(7) The election to become a social purpose corporation shall not be deemed to affect any obligations or liabilities of the electing corporation incurred prior to its election to become a social purpose corporation or the personal liability of any person incurred prior to such election.

23B.25.140 Corporation ceasing to be a social purpose corporation — Conditions — Election.

(1) Any social purpose corporation may elect to cease to be a social purpose corporation if, pursuant to the proposed election, each of the following conditions are met:

(a) Each share of the same class or series of the electing social purpose corporation shall, unless all shareholders of the class or series consent, be treated equally with respect to any cash, rights, securities, or other property to be received by, or any obligations or restrictions to be imposed on, the holder of that share;

(b) The board of directors of the electing social purpose corporation must recommend the election to the shareholders, unless the board of directors determines that because of conflict of interest or other special circumstances it should make no recommendation and communicates the basis for its determination to the shareholders with the proposed election; and

(c) In addition to any other voting conditions imposed by the board of directors under subsection (2) of this section, the election must be approved by an affirmative vote of at

（3）选择成为社会目的公司的拟转换公司必须修改公司章程，将《华盛顿州修订法》第 23B.25.040（1）款规定的内容记载于公司章程中。

（4）转换为社会目的公司的议案获得通过后，在根据第（3）款规定修改公司章程前，在未获得股东授权的情况下，根据合同规定，拟转换公司董事会可以决定放弃成为社会目的公司。

（5）向州务卿递交修改的公司章程或者满足修改条件的公司章程规定了生效时间的，转换议案即告生效。

（6）在转换为社会目的公司的议案生效后，选择转换的公司即成为社会目的公司，并受本章所有规定的调整。社会目的公司的成立时间为公司最初的设立之日。

（7）转换为社会目的形态的公司并不影响其承担转换为社会目的公司之前的义务、责任或者个人责任。

第 23B.25.140 条　公司终止社会目的公司的公司形态——条件——选择程序

（1）如果终止议案满足以下全部条件，社会目的公司可以终止其社会目的的公司形态：

（a）除非所有类别或者系列股东一致同意，否则选举社会目的公司的每一系列或类别股份都应根据该股份持有人投资数额、权利、持有的证券数额、财产数额或者其股东承担的义务而受到同等对待；

（b）除非董事会认为存在利益冲突或其他特殊情形，否则拟终止社会目的形态的公司的董事会成员必须向股东汇报终止计划；并且

（c）除满足本条第（2）款规定的董事会投票条件外，转换计划必须获得每个类别或系列投票的 2/3 以上的赞成票的同意，包括社会目的公司有权对公司行为进

least twothirds of the voting group comprising all the votes of the electing social purpose corporation's shareholders entitled to be cast on the corporate action, and by twothirds of the holders of the outstanding shares of each class or series, voting as separate voting groups, and each other voting group entitled under the articles of incorporation to vote separately on the corporate action.

(2) The board of directors of a social purpose corporation electing to cease to be a social purpose corporation may condition its submission of the proposed election on any basis, including the affirmative vote of holders of a specified percentage of shares held by any group of shareholders not otherwise entitled to vote as a separate group on the proposed election.

(3) To elect to cease to be a social purpose corporation, an electing social purpose corporation must amend its articles of incorporation to remove the matters required to be set forth in the articles of incorporation pursuant to RCW 23B.25.040(1) (a) and (b).

(4) After an election to cease to be a social purpose corporation is approved, and at any time prior to the filing of the articles of amendment to amend the electing social purpose corporation's articles of incorporation in compliance with subsection (3) of this section, the planned election may be abandoned by the electing social purpose corporation, subject to any contractual rights, without further shareholder approval, in the manner determined by the board of directors.

(5) The election to cease to be a social purpose corporation shall be effective upon the later of the filing of the articles of amendment with the secretary of state or the effective date or time set forth in the articles of amendment.

(6) Upon the effective time of the election to cease to be a social purpose corporation, the electing social purpose corporation shall thereafter be a corporation which is not a social purpose corporation and shall be subject to all of the provisions of this title applicable to corporations generally and the existence of the corporation shall be deemed to have commenced on the date the electing social purpose corporation was incorporated.

(7) The election to cease to be a social purpose corporation shall not be deemed to affect any obligations or liabilities of the electing social purpose corporation incurred prior to its election to cease to be a social purpose corporation or the personal liability of any person incurred prior to such election.

23B.25.150 Social purpose report required — Timing — Information — Failure to comply.

(1) The board of directors of a social purpose corporation shall cause a social purpose report to be furnished to the shareholders by making such report publicly accessible, free of charge, at the corporation's principal internet web site address, not later than four months after the close of the corporation's fiscal year, and such report shall remain available on that

行的投票，每个系列或类别的流通股份持有人的 2/3 的赞成票，作为单独的投票组投票，以及根据公司章程有权对公司行为单独投票的其他投票组。

（2）拟终止社会目的形态的公司的董事会可以规定终止议案的提交条件，包括要获得任何对此议案有投票权的任一类别股份特定比例的股东的同意。

（3）选择终止社会目的公司形态的，拟终止形态的公司必须修改公司章程，从公司章程中删除《华盛顿州修订法》第 23B.25.040（1）（a）项和第（b）项规定的内容。

（4）终止公司社会目的形态的议案获得通过后，在根据本条第（3）款的规定修改公司章程前，拟终止社会目的形态的公司在未获得股东授权的情况下，根据合同规定，可以由董事会决定放弃终止议案。

（5）向州务卿递交已修改的公司章程后或者达到已修改的公司章程规定的生效时间的，终止议案即告生效。

（6）在公司终止社会目的形态的议案生效后，选择终止形态的公司即为非社会目的公司，受本编适用于普通公司的所有规定的调整。公司成立时间为社会目的公司设立之日。

（7）终止社会目的形态的公司并不影响其承担终止社会目的公司之前的义务、责任或者个人责任。

第 23B.25.150 条　社会目的报告的编写要求——时间——信息——未履行的责任

（1）社会目的公司的董事会应以公开、可获得、免费的方式在其网站上公布社会目的报告，使股东可以获得有关信息。社会目的报告应在公司财政年度结束后的 4 个月内递交，并且该报告在公司财政年度结束时应在该网站上保留。

web site through the end of the corporation's fiscal year.

(2) The social purpose report shall include a narrative discussion concerning the social purpose or purposes of the corporation, including the corporation's efforts intended to promote its social purpose or purposes. The narrative discussion may include the following information:

(a) Identification and discussion of the shortterm and longterm objectives of the corporation relating to its social purpose or purposes;

(b) Identification and discussion of the material actions taken by the corporation during the fiscal year to achieve its social purpose or purposes;

(c) Identification of material actions that the corporation expects to take in the future with respect to achievement of its social purpose or purposes; and

(d) A description of the financial, operating, or other measures used by the corporation during the fiscal year for evaluating its performance in achieving its social purpose or purposes.

(3) The requirements of subsection (1) of this section shall be satisfied if a social purpose corporation with an outstanding class of securities registered under section 12 of the securities exchange act of 1934 both complies with section 240.14a16 of Title 17 of the code of federal regulations, as amended from time to time, with respect to the obligation of a corporation to furnish an annual report to shareholders pursuant to section 240.14a–3(b) of Title 17 of the code of federal regulations, and includes the information required by subsection (2) of this section in the annual report.

(4) The failure to furnish to shareholders a social purpose report required by subsection (1) of this section does not affect the validity of any corporate action.

(5) The superior court of the county in which the social purpose corporation's registered office is located may, after notice to the corporation, summarily order a social purpose report to be furnished to shareholders on application of any shareholder of a social purpose corporation if a social purpose report was not furnished to shareholders for at least two consecutive fiscal years.

（2）社会目的报告包含对公司社会目的实施情况的描述，包括公司为促进其社会目的的实现所作的努力，社会目的报告中应包括以下内容：

（a）对与公司社会目的有关的短期目标和长期目标进行确定和讨论；

（b）确定和探讨公司在本财政年度为实现其社会目的而采取的措施；

（c）确定公司未来实现其社会目的的主要方式；以及

（d）描述公司在本财政年度用于评估其社会目的的实施情况的财务、运营或其他方法。

（3）如果社会目的公司有较大份额根据《1934 年证券交易法》进行注册的股份，还应遵守《联邦规制法典》第 17 编第 240.14a16 条的规定，应满足本条第（1）款规定的根据第 17 编第 240.14a3（b） 款的规定向股东提交年度报告，年度报告应满足本条第（2）款规定的要求。

（4）未能根据本条第（1）款的规定向股东提交社会目的报告的，并不影响公司其他行为的效力。

（5）如果社会目的公司连续两个财政年度未向股东提供社会目的报告，公司登记地的高等法院可以书面的方式，指令社会目的公司在股东提出申请时向股东提供社会目的报告。

BENEFIT LIMITED LIABILITY COMPANIES ACT

公共利益有限责任公司法

THE STATE OF MARYLAND

CORPORATIONS AND ASSOCIATIONS
TITLE 4A. LIMITED LIABILITY COMPANY ACT
SUBTITLE 12. BENEFIT LIMITED LIABILITY COMPANIES.

§ 4A-1201. Applicability of provisions to foreign and interstate commerce

(a) In general. -- In this subtitle the following words have the meanings indicated.

(b) Benefit limited liability company. -- "Benefit limited liability company" means a Maryland limited liability company that elects to be a benefit limited liability company in accordance with § 4A–1203 of this subtitle and has not ceased to be a benefit limited liability company through the operation of § 4A–1205 of this subtitle.

(c) General public benefit. -- “General public benefit” means a material, positive impact on society and the environment, as measured by a third–party standard, through activities that promote a combination of specific public benefits.

(d) Specific public benefit. -- “Specific public benefit” includes:

(1) Providing individuals or communities with beneficial products or services;

(2) Promoting economic opportunity for individuals or communities beyond the creation of jobs in the normal course of business;

(3) Preserving the environment;

(4) Improving human health;

(5) Promoting the arts, sciences, or advancement of knowledge;

(6) Increasing the flow of capital to entities with a public benefit purpose; or

(7) The accomplishment of any other particular benefit for society or the environment.

(e) Third–party standard. -- “Third–party standard” means a standard for defining, reporting, and assessing best practices in social and environmental performance that:

(1) Is developed by a person or entity that is independent of the benefit limited liability company; and

(2) Is transparent because the following information about the standard is publicly available or accessible:

马里兰州

公司和社团法
第 4A 章　有限责任公司法
第 12 节　公共利益有限责任公司

第 4A-1201 条　涉外及州际贸易条款的适用性

（a）一般性条款。——本节提及的用语的含义如下。

（b）公共利益有限责任公司。——“公共利益有限责任公司”是指选择按照本节第 4A-1203 条的规定设立，并按照本节第 4A-1205 条的规定作为公共利益有限责任公司持续经营的马里兰州有限责任公司。

（c）一般公共利益。——“一般公共利益”指根据第三方标准，公司促进特定公共利益实现的行为对社会和环境产生的实质性积极影响。

（d）特定公共利益。——“特定公共利益”包括：

（1）向个人或社区提供有益的产品或服务；

（2）在正常业务过程中向个人或社区提供创造就业之外的经济机会；

（3）保护环境；

（4）改善人类健康；

（5）促进艺术、科学或知识进步；

（6）促进资本流向拥有有利于社会或环境目标的实体；以及

（7）给予社会或环境其他特别的利益。

（e）第三方标准。——“第三方标准”是指用于定义、报告和评估公司行为的社会和环境绩效的标准，其应满足以下条件：

（1）经独立于公共利益公司的个人或实体制定；并且

（2）透明，该标准的以下信息可公开获取：

(i) The factors considered when measuring the performance of a business;

(ii) The relative weightings of those factors; and

(iii) The identity of the persons who developed and control changes to the standard and the process by which those changes were made.

§ 4A-1202. Severability

(a) Exceptions. -- The provisions of this title apply to benefit limited liability companies except to the extent that:

(1) The context of a provision clearly requires otherwise; or

(2) A specific provision of this title provides otherwise.

(b) In general. -- This subtitle applies only to a benefit limited liability company.

(c) Construction with other laws. -

(1) The existence of a provision of this subtitle does not of itself create any implication that a contrary or different rule of law is or would be applicable to a limited liability company that is not a benefit limited liability company.

(2) This subtitle does not affect any statute or rule of law as it applies to a limited liability company that is not a benefit limited liability company.

(d) Construction of articles of organization or operating agreement. -- A provision of the articles of organization or operating agreement of a benefit limited liability company may not be inconsistent with any provision of this subtitle.

§ 4A-1203. Short title

(a) Election to be benefit limited liability company. -- A limited liability company may elect to be a benefit limited liability company under this subtitle by including in its articles of organization a statement that the limited liability company is a benefit limited liability company.

(b) Name. -- The name of a domestic benefit limited liability company or a foreign benefit limited liability company authorized to transact business in this State must comply with Title 1, Subtitle 5 of this article.

§ 4A-1204. Clear references to status as benefit limited liability company

Clear reference to the fact that a limited liability company is a benefit limited liability company shall appear prominently:

(1) At the head of the articles of organization or an amendment to the articles of organization in which the election to be a benefit limited liability company is made;

(2) At the head of each subsequent articles of organization of the benefit limited liability company; and

(3) On each certificate representing outstanding membership interests in the benefit limited liability company.

（i）衡量企业绩效时所考虑的指标；
（ii）这些指标的相关权重；以及
（iii）制定、控制修改标准和程序的人员的身份。

第 4A–1202 条　可分割性

（a）例外条款。——本章条款适用于公共利益有限责任公司，但以下情形除外：

（1）条款内容明显规定不适用的；或者
（2）本章中的某一特定条款规定不适用的。
（b）一般性条款。——本节规定仅适用于公共利益有限责任公司。
（c）与其他法规的协调。——
（1）本节条款不应为非公共利益有限责任公司设定相反或不同的规则。

（2）本节规定不影响非公共利益公司有关条文和规则的适用。

（d）公司章程或经营协议的制定。——公共利益有限责任公司的公司章程或经营协议中的条款不得与本节有关规定相抵触。

第 4A–1203 条　标题

（a）公共利益有限责任公司形态的选择。——有限责任公司可通过在公司章程中增加该有限公司为公共利益有限责任公司的声明，成为本节规定下的公共利益有限责任公司。

（b）名称。——获得授权在本州开展商业活动的本州或外州公共利益有限责任公司，其名称须遵守本法第 1 章第 5 节的规定。

第 4A–1204 条　公共利益有限责任公司形态的明确标识

公司为公共利益有限责任公司形态的明确标识须在如下显著位置展示：

（1）公司章程或选择成为公共利益有限责任公司的章程修正案的标题部分；

（2）公共利益有限责任公司随后制定的公司章程的标题部分；

（3）公共利益有限责任公司的所有流通股份证书中。

§ 4A-1205. Termination of status

A benefit limited liability company may terminate its status as a benefit limited liability company and cease to be subject to this subtitle by amending its articles of organization to delete the statement required under § 4A–1203 of this subtitle that it is a benefit limited liability company.

§ 4A-1206. Purpose of creating general or specific public benefit

(a) In general.

(1) Each benefit limited liability company shall have the purpose of creating a general public benefit.

(2) The purpose described in paragraph (1) of this subsection is in addition to, and may be a limitation on, the purposes of the benefit limited liability company under § 4A–201 of this title.

(b) Additional specific public benefits.

(1) In addition to its purposes under § 4A–201 of this title and subsection (a) of this section, the articles of organization or operating agreement of a benefit limited liability company may identify as one of the purposes of the benefit limited liability company the creation of one or more specific public benefits.

(2) The identification in its articles of organization or operating agreement of a specific public benefit purpose under paragraph (1) of this subsection does not limit the obligation of a benefit limited liability company to create a general public benefit.

§ 4A-1207. Duties of manager

(a) In general. -- A person managing the business and affairs of a benefit limited liability company:

(1) Shall consider the effects of any action or decision not to act on:

(i) The members of the benefit limited liability company;

(ii) The employees and workforce of the benefit limited liability company and the subsidiaries and suppliers of the benefit limited liability company;

(iii) The interests of customers as beneficiaries of the general or specific public benefit purposes of the benefit limited liability company;

(iv) Community and societal considerations, including those of any community in which offices or facilities of the benefit limited liability company or the subsidiaries or suppliers of the benefit limited liability company are located; and

(v) The local and global environment; and

(2) May consider any other pertinent factors or the interests of any other group that the person determines are appropriate to consider.

(b) No duties to certain persons. -- A person managing the business and affairs of a benefit limited liability company does not have any duty on account of the factors or interests

第 4A–1205 条　公司形态的终止

公共利益有限责任公司可通过删除本节第 4A–1203 条规定的公司章程中其作为公共利益有限责任公司的声明，终止公共利益有限责任公司的形态并不再受本节规定调整。

第 4A–1206 条　实现一般或特定公共利益的公司目的

（a）一般性条款。

（1）公共利益有限责任公司应以实现一项一般公共利益作为公司目的。

（2）本款第（1）项所说的公司目的，应在本章第 4A–201 条规定的公共利益有限责任公司目的的基础上设立，但不限于该条规定的范围。

（b）其他特定公共利益。

（1）除本章第 4A–201 条和本条第（a）款规定的目的外，公共利益有限责任公司的公司章程或经营协议中可将一项或多项特定公共利益作为其公司目的。

（2）公共利益有限责任公司在公司章程或经营协议中将本款第（1）项规定的特定公共利益作为公司目的，不影响公司承担实现一般公共利益的责任。

第 4A–1207 条　经理职责

（a）一般性条款。——负责管理公共利益有限责任公司经营和事务的人员：

（1）其作为或不作为，应当考虑对以下对象的影响：

（i）公共利益有限责任公司的股东；

（ii）公共利益有限责任公司及其子公司和供应商的雇员；

（iii）作为公共利益有限责任公司一般或特定公共利益目的受益者的消费者的利益；

（iv）社区和社会因素，包括公共利益公司、其子公司或供应商的办公地或设施所在地的社区；以及

（v）当地和全球环境；以及

（2）可以考虑经理认为合适的其他相关因素或其他群体的利益。

（b）不对特定人员负责。——在本条规定的相关因素和利益范围内，负责管理公共利益有限责任公司经营和事务的人员不对以下人员承担责任：

set forth in this section to:

(1) A person that is a beneficiary of the public benefit purposes of the benefit limited liability company; or

(2) A member of the benefit limited liability company.

§ 4A-1208. Annual benefit report

(a) Contents. -- A benefit limited liability company shall deliver to each member an annual benefit report including:

(1) A description of:

(i) The ways in which the benefit limited liability company pursued a general public benefit during the year and the extent to which the general public benefit was created;

(ii) The ways in which the benefit limited liability company pursued any specific public benefit that its articles of organization or operating agreement states is the purpose of the benefit limited liability company to create and the extent to which that specific public benefit was created; and

(iii) Any circumstances that have hindered the creation by the benefit limited liability company of the public benefit; and

(2) An assessment of the societal and environmental performance of the benefit limited liability company prepared in accordance with a third-party standard applied consistently with the prior year's benefit report or accompanied by an explanation of the reasons for any inconsistent application.

(b) Time of delivery. -- The benefit report shall be delivered to each member within 120 days following the end of each fiscal year of the benefit limited liability company.

(c) Publication and posting. -

(1) A benefit limited liability company shall post its most recent benefit report on the public portion of its Web site, if any

(2) If a benefit limited liability company does not have a public Web site, the benefit limited liability company shall provide a copy of its most recent benefit report on demand and without charge to any person who requests a copy.

（1）公共利益有限责任公司公共利益目的的受益人；或者

（2）公共利益有限责任公司的股东。

第 4A-1208 条 年度公共利益报告

（a）内容。——公共利益有限责任公司应向其所有股东送交年度公共利益报告，内容包括：

（1）对以下事项的说明：

（i）本年度公共利益有限责任公司追求一般公共利益的方法和一般公共利益实现的情况；

（ii）公共利益有限责任公司追求公司章程或经营协议中规定的特定公共利益的方法及其实现情况；以及

（iii）阻碍公共利益有限责任公司实现公共利益的情形；以及

（2）沿用与上一年度公共利益报告相同的第三方标准，对公共利益公司的社会和环境表现作出的整体评价，如果适用的评价标准不一致，须附上说明以解释适用不一致标准的原因。

（b）送达时间。——公共利益报告应当在公共利益有限责任公司财政年度结束后 120 天内送交公司各股东。

（c）报告的发布和公示。——

（1）公共利益有限责任公司应当将其最新版的公共利益报告发布于公司网站的公共部分。如有

（2）如果公共利益有限责任公司没有公开的网站，则公司应向任何索取报告的个人免费提供最新版公共利益报告的副本。

SUSTAINABLE BUSINESS CORPORATION

可持续商事公司

THE STATE OF HAWAII

A BILL FOR AN ACT

RELATING TO BUSINESS REGULATION[1]

BE IT ENACTED BY THE LEGISLATURE OF THE STATE OF HAWAII

SECTION 1. The Hawaii Revised Statutes is amended by adding a new chapter to be appropriately designated and to read as follows:

[Chapter] __
SUSTAINABLE BUSINESS CORPORATIONS

§ -1 Purpose and findings.

This chapter authorizes a designation and code of conduct for a business corporation to offer entrepreneurs and investors the option to build and invest in businesses that operate in a socially and environmentally sustainable manner. Enforcement of those responsibilities comes not from governmental oversight but rather from new provisions on transparency and accountability included in this chapter.

§ -2 Definitions.

As used in this chapter:

"Benefit director" means the director designated as the benefit director of a sustainable business corporation under section –7.

"Benefit officer" means the individual designated as the benefit officer of a sustainable

1 BE IT ENACTED BY THE LEGISLATURE OF THE STATE OF HAWAII, THE SENATE TWENTY–SIXTH LEGISLATURE, 2011, STATE OF HAWAII. S.B.NO.298 S.D.3, H.D.3, C.D.1

夏威夷州

一项有关商业规则的法案[1]

由夏威夷州立法机构颁布

第 1 部分 《夏威夷州法典》增加如下新的章节，具体内容如下：

[章] ____
可持续商事公司

第 1 条 目的及规范路径

本章旨在为商事公司提供行为规则，企业家和投资者可选择在社会和环境方面以可持续发展的方式运行公司。这些责任的履行，并非依靠政府监督，而是依照本章有关透明度和责任义务的新规定。

第 2 条 定义

在本章中：

"公共利益董事"是指可持续商事公司根据第 7 条规定任命的董事。

"公共利益高管"是指可持续商事公司根据第 9 条规定任命的高管。

1 BE IT ENACTED BY THE LEGISLATURE OF THE STATE OF HAWAII, THE SENATE TWENTY-SIXTH LEGISLATURE, 2011, STATE OF HAWAII. S.B.NO.298 S.D.3, H.D.3, C.D.1

business corporation under section –9.

"General public benefit" means a material positive impact on society and the environment, taken as a whole and as measured by a third–party standard under section –12, from the business and operations of a sustainable business corporation.

"Independent" means having no material relationship with a sustainable business corporation or any of its subsidiaries.

"Material owner" means a shareholder who holds either beneficially or of record five per cent or more of the outstanding shares of a sustainable business corporation.

"Material relationship" means a relationship between a person and a sustainable business corporation where:

(1) The person is, or has been within the last three years, an employee other than a benefit officer of the sustainable business corporation or any of its subsidiaries;

(2) The person is related by blood, marriage, or adoption to; is a party to a civil union with; is a reciprocal beneficiary or household member of; or resides with an officer other than a benefit officer or director of the sustainable business corporation or any of its subsidiaries; or

(3) The person or an association of which the person is a director, officer, or manager or in which the person owns beneficially or of record five per cent or more of the outstanding equity interests or the outstanding shares of the sustainable business corporation; provided that percentage ownership in an association shall be calculated as if all outstanding rights to acquire equity interests in the association had been exercised.

"Minimum status vote" means that in addition to any other approval or vote required by this chapter or the by laws adopted by the shareholders:

(1) The holders of shares of every class or series shall be entitled to vote on the corporate action regardless of any limitation stated in the articles of incorporation or bylaws on the voting rights of any class or series; and

(2) The corporate action shall be approved by vote of the shareholders of each class or series entitled to cast at least two–thirds of the votes that all shareholders of the class or series are entitled to cast thereon.

"Subsidiary" of a person means an association in which the person owns beneficially or of record fifty per cent or more of the outstanding equity interests; provided that a percentage of ownership in an association shall be calculated as if all outstanding rights to acquire equity interests in the association had been exercised.

"Sustainable business corporation" means a domestic corporation, incorporated under chapter 414, that has elected to also become subject to this chapter and whose status as a sustainable business corporation has not been terminated as provided in this chapter.

"Third–party standard" means a standard for defining, reporting, and assessing overall corporate social and environmental performance that conforms to the requirements of this

“一般公共利益”是指根据第 12 条规定的第三方标准，可持续商事公司的业务和经营在整体上对社会和环境产生的实质性积极影响。

“独立性”是指与可持续商事公司或其子公司没有实质性的关系。

“实质所有者”是指持有 5% 以上可持续商事公司已发行股份的登记股东或实际受益人。

“实质性关联”是指与可持续商事公司存在以下关系的个体：

（1）该个体是，或在过去 3 年内是，可持续商事公司或其子公司除公共利益高管以外的雇员；

（2）除可持续商事公司及其子公司的公共利益高管或董事外，该个体与其他公司高管有血缘、婚姻或收养关系；或有民事联合关系；或是互惠受益人或家庭成员的；或共同居住的；或者

（3）持有可持续商事公司 5% 以上已发行股份的登记股东或作为实际受益人的个人或法人中的董事、高管或经理。计算法人中的所有权比重时，所有购股权应被视为已行使。

“最低表决要求”是指除本章或公司章程规定的其他批准或表决的要求外，还应满足以下条件：

（1）每一类别或系列的股东有权对公司行为进行投票，即使公司章程或章程细则对某一类别或系列股东的投票权作出了限制；并且

（2）公司行为必须获得每个类别或系列有投票权的所有股东至少 2/3 的赞成票才能通过。

“子公司”是指在所有购股权被视为已行使的情况下，该实体 50% 以上已发行的股份的受益所有权或登记所有权被另一实体所拥有。

“可持续商事公司”是指依第 414 章的规定设立，选择接受本章规定调整且其可持续商事公司形态并未终止的公司。

“第三方标准”是指符合本章要求的用于定义、报告和评估公司整体社会和环境绩效的标准。

chapter.

§ -3 Election of a domestic corporation to become a sustainable business corporation.

(a) A domestic corporation incorporated under chapter 414 may elect to become a sustainable business corporation under this chapter by including in its articles or amending its articles to include a statement that the corporation is a sustainable business corporation. An amendment pursuant to this subsection shall not be effective unless it is adopted by at least the minimum status vote.

(b) If a corporation that is not a sustainable business corporation is a party to a merger consolidation, or division, or is the exchanging corporation in a share exchange, and the surviving, new, or any resulting corporation in the merger, consolidation division, or share exchange is to be a sustainable business corporation, then the plan of merger, consolidation, division, or share exchange shall not be effective unless it is adopted by the corporation by at least the minimum status vote.

§ -4 Termination of sustainable business corporation status

(a) A sustainable business corporation may terminate its status as such and cease to be subject to this chapter by amending its articles to delete the statement that the corporation is a sustainable business corporation. An amendment pursuant to this subsection shall not be effective unless it is adopted by at least the minimum status vote.

(b) If a plan of merger, consolidation, division, or share exchange would have the effect of terminating the status of a business corporation as a sustainable business corporation, the plan shall not be effective unless it is adopted by at least the minimum status vote.

§ -5 Corporate purposes.

(a) Every sustainable business corporation shall have among its purposes the creation of a general public benefit.

(b) In addition to the general public benefit purpose required by subsection (a), the articles of a sustainable business corporation may identify one or more specific public benefits for which the sustainable business corporation was created. The identification of a specific public benefit under this subsection shall not limit the obligation of a sustainable business corporation to create a general public benefit. Allowable specific public benefits for sustainable business corporations subject to this chapter include:

(1) Providing low-income or underserved individuals or communities with beneficial products or services;

(2) Promoting economic opportunity for individuals or communities beyond the creation of jobs in the normal course of business;

(3) Preserving the environment;

(4) Improving human health;

第 3 条　本州可持续商事公司形态的选择

（a）依第 414 章规定设立的公司可根据本章的规定选择可持续商事公司形态，公司章程或修改后的章程须声明其为可持续商事公司。章程的修改应满足最低表决要求。

（b）如果一家本州的非可持续商事公司是兼并、合并或分立的一方，或者是股权置换中的一方，并且存续的实体属可持续商事公司，那么此等兼并、合并、分立或股权置换的计划须满足最低表决要求。

第 4 条　可持续商事公司形态的终止

（a）可持续商事公司可通过删除公司章程中其作为可持续商事公司的声明来终止可持续商事公司形态并不再受本章规定的调整。公司章程的修改应满足最低表决要求。

（b）如果兼并、合并、分立、股权置换行为会导致可持续商事公司形态终止，则该交易计划的通过应满足最低表决要求。

第 5 条　公司目的

（a）可持续商事公司必须设定一般公共利益目的。

（b）可持续商事公司章程可以在第（a）款规定外确定一项或多项特定公共利益目的。依本款设定的特定公共利益目的并不限制可持续商事公司在第（a）款规定下设定以下一般公共利益目的：

（1）向低收入、低福利人群或社区提供有益的产品或服务；

（2）在正常业务过程中向个人或社区提供创造就业之外的经济机会；

（3）保护环境；

（4）改善人类健康；

(5) Promoting the arts, sciences, or advancement of knowledge;

(6) Increasing the flow of capital to entities with a public benefit purpose;

(7) Accomplishing any other particular benefit for society or the environment; and

(8) Using the right to exclude, conferred by any and all patents in which the sustainable business corporation has an interest in this right through assignment, license, lien, security agreement, or obligation for the following purposes:

(A) Creating and retaining good jobs within the State as well as throughout the United States;

(B) Upholding fair labor standards nationally and internationally; provided that for purposes of this paragraph, "fair labor standards"shall be construed to prohibit child labor, forced or compulsory labor, discrimination in employment, restrictions on freedom of association, and denial of the right to collective bargaining; and

(C) Enhancing environmental protection nationally and internationally; provided that if the public benefit under this paragraph relating to the use of patents is specified, section –4 shall not apply to the corporation and the sustainable business corporation status shall be permanent, and this specific public benefit shall not be deleted from the articles of the corporation pursuant to subsection (d), unless the annual statement of the benefit director concludes that the sustainable business corporation has failed to pursue this specific public benefit, then the corporation shall have its status as a sustainable business corporation terminated.

(c) The creation of general and specific public benefits as provided in subsections (a) and (b) shall be in the best interests of the sustainable business corporation.

(d) A sustainable business corporation may amend its articles to add, amend, or delete the identification of a specific public benefit for which the sustainable business corporation was created.

An amendment pursuant to this subsection shall not be effective unless it is adopted by at least the minimum status vote.

§ -6 Standard of conduct for directors.

(a) In discharging the duties of their respective positions the board of director, committees of the board, and individual directors of a sustainable business corporation, in considering the best interests of the sustainable business corporation:

(1) Shall consider the effects of any action of the sustainable business corporation upon:

(A) The shareholders of the sustainable business corporation; and

(B) The accomplishment of general and specific public benefits set forth in the sustainable business corporations purposes; and

(2) May consider:

(A) The employees and workforce of the sustainable business corporation and its

（5）促进艺术、科学或知识进步；

（6）促进资本流向有利于社会或环境目标的实体；

（7）给予社会或环境其他特别的利益；以及

（8）可持续商事公司对其通过转让、许可、留置、担保协议或债务等方式取得的专利权，在行使专利排他权或将专利授权他人使用时，应符合如下目的：

（A）在本州或美国境内创造或保留工作岗位；

（B）提高国内或国际范围内的公平劳动标准；就本项目的而言，“公平劳动标准”指禁止使用童工，禁止强迫或强制劳动，禁止就业歧视，取消对结社自由的限制，禁止妨碍集体谈判的权利；以及

（C）推动国内或国际范围内的环境保护；如根据本项规定，与专利使用相关的公共利益是特定的，则第 4 条规定不适用于公司，并且可持续商事公司的形态应是永久的，不得删除依据本条（d）款规定的公司章程中的特定公共利益，公共利益董事在年度报告中声明可持续商事公司未能实现该特定公共利益的除外，此等情形下，公司应终止其可持续商事公司的形态。

（c）第（a）款和第（b）款所规定的一般和特定公共利益的创设应当是为了实现可持续商事公司的最佳利益。

（d）可持续商事公司可以增加、修改或删除公司章程中设定的特定公共利益目的。

根据本款规定对章程进行的修改须满足最低表决要求，否则该修改不发生效力。

第 6 条　董事行为标准

（a）在履行各自职责和考虑可持续商事公司的最佳利益时，公司的董事会、董事委员会和董事：

（1）其有关可持续商事公司的任何行动均应考虑对以下对象的影响：

（A）可持续商事公司的股东；以及

（B）可持续商事公司章程中设定的一般和特定公共利益目的的实现。

（2）可考虑对以下对象的影响：

（A）可持续商事公司及其子公司和供应商的雇员；

subsidiaries and suppliers;

(B) The interests of customers as beneficiaries of the general or specific public benefit purposes of the sustainable business corporation;

(C) Community and societal considerations including those of any community in which offices or facilities of the sustainable business corporation or its subsidiaries or suppliers are located;

(D) The local and global environment;

(E) The short–term and long–term interests of the sustainable business corporation including benefits that may accrue to the sustainable business corporation from its long–term plans and the possibility that these interests may be best served by the continued independence of the sustainable business corporation;

(F) The ability of the sustainable business corporation to accomplish its general public benefit purpose and any specific public benefit purpose;

(G) The resources intent and conduct of any person seeking to acquire control of the corporation; and

(H) Any other pertinent factors or the interests of any other group that they deem appropriate.

(b) A director shall not be personally liable for monetary damages for any action taken as a director if the director performed the duties of the director's office in compliance with the general standards of conduct pursuant to section 414–221.

§ -7 Benefit director.

(a) The board of directors of a sustainable business corporation shall include one director who shall be designated the "benefit director" and who shall have, in addition to all of the powers, duties, rights, and immunities of the other directors of the sustainable business corporation, the powers, duties, rights, and immunities provided in this section.

(b) The benefit director shall be elected pursuant to sections 414–193 and 414–194 and may be removed in the manner provided by sections 414–198 and 414–199. The benefit director may serve concurrently as the benefit officer. The articles or bylaws of a sustainable business corporation may prescribe additional qualifications of the benefit director; provided that the qualifications are consistent with this subsection.

(c) The benefit director shall prepare, and the sustainable business corporation shall include in the annual benefit report to shareholders required by section –11 a statement whether, in the opinion of the benefit director, the sustainable business corporation acted in accordance with its general, and any specific, public benefit purpose in all material respects during the period covered by the report and whether the directors and officers complied with sections –6(a) and –8 (a), respectively. If in the opinion of the benefit director the sustainable business corporation or its directors or officers failed to act according to the requirements of this chapter, then the statement

（B）作为可持续商事公司一般或特定公共利益受益者的消费者的利益；

（C）社区和社会因素，包括可持续商事公司及其子公司或供应商的办公地或设施所在地的社区；

（D）当地和全球环境；

（E）可持续商事公司的短期和长期利益，包括从其长期计划中产生的利益，以及可持续商事公司继续保持独立可能产生的最佳利益；

（F）可持续商事公司实现其一般和特定公共利益目的的能力；

（G）任何意图取得公司控制权的个人资源、意图和行为；以及

（H）董事认为合适的其他相关因素或其他群体的利益；

（b）若董事履行职务的行为符合第 414–221 条规定的一般行为标准，则董事不为其行为承担任何个人损害赔偿责任。

第 7 条　公共利益董事

（a）可持续商事公司的董事会应包含一名公共利益董事，该董事除有可持续商事公司的其他董事的权力、义务、权利和豁免权外，还有本条规定的权力、义务、权利和豁免权。

（b）公共利益董事应当根据第 414–193 条和第 414–194 条的相关规定选任，根据第 414–198 条和第 414–199 条的相关规定免职。公共利益董事可同时担任公共利益高管。可持续商事公司的章程或章程细则可对公共利益董事的资格作出附加规定，该附加规定须与本款规定相一致。

（c）公共利益董事应当编写其对以下事项的意见，可持续商事公司应当根据第 11 条的规定将该意见附于年度公共利益报告中供股东查阅：在报告所述期间内，可持续商事公司是否在所有重要事项上依一般和特定公共利益目的行事；董事和高管是否分别依第 6（a）款和第 8（a）款的规定行事。如果公共利益董事认为可持续商事公司或其董事、高管未能依本章要求行事，则其应在意见中陈述公司或其董事、高管未能履行责任的情况。根据第 11 条的规定开展的公共意见征集活动收集到的所有问题、关注点、评论和建议，公共利益董事在意见中均应对其作出回应，并附

of the benefit director shall include a description of the ways in which the sustainable business corporation or its directors or officers failed to act according to the requirements of this chapter. The benefit directors statement included in the final draft of the benefit report shall include formal responses to all questions, concerns comments, and suggestions raised through the public comment period required by section–11.

(d) A benefit director shall be independent of and shall have no material relationship with the sustainable business corporation.

§-8 Standard of conduct for officers.

(a) Each officer of a sustainable business corporation shall consider the interests and factors described in section –6 (a) in the manner provided in that section when:

(1)The officer has discretion to act with respect to a matter; and

(2)It reasonably appears to the officer that the matter may have a material effect on:

(A)The creation of a general or specific public benefit by the sustainable business corporation; or

(B)Any of the interests or factors referred to in section–6(a).

(b) An officer shall not be personally liable for monetary damages for any action taken as an officer if the officer performed the duties of the position in compliance with the general standards of conduct pursuant to section 414–233.

§-9 Benefit officer.

(a) A sustainable business corporation may have an officer designated as the benefit officer who shall have the authority and shall perform the duties in the management of the sustainable business corporation relating to the purpose of the corporation to create general or specific public benefit as may be provided by or pursuant to the bylaws or, in the absence of controlling provisions in the bylaws, as may be determined by or pursuant to resolutions or orders of the board of directors. If a sustainable business corporation has a benefit officer, the duties of the benefit officer shall include preparing the benefit report required by section–11.

(b) A benefit officer shall be independent of and shall have no material relationship with the sustainable business corporation.

§-10 Right of action.

The shareholders and directors of a sustainable business corporation shall have the right to bring direct or derivative claims to enforce corporate purposes and the standards for directors as set forth in section 414–221 (a) and shall have the right to bring direct or derivative claims to enforce the general or specific public benefit purposes of the sustainable business corporation and the standard of conduct for directors pursuant to section –6 (a) (1).

§-11 Annual benefit report.

(a) A sustainable business corporation shall deliver to each shareholder an annual benefit report including:

在最终版的公共利益报告中。

（d）公共利益董事应当保持独立，不得与可持续商事公司存在任何重大关联。

第 8 条　高管行为标准

（a）可持续商事公司高管应以第 6（a）款中规定的方式考虑该条中规定的利益和因素，如果：

（1）高管就该行为有自由裁量权；以及

（2）高管有合理理由认为该行为对以下事项有重大影响：

（A）可持续商事公司创设的一般或特定公共利益；或者

（B）第 6（a）款规定的任何利益或因素。

（b）高管履行其职责符合第 414–233 条规定的一般行为标准的，高管不对其行为承担损害赔偿责任。

第 9 条　公共利益高管

（a）可持续商事公司可将一名高管任命为公共利益高管，根据公司章程细则的规定，或者在公司章程细则中没有规定时根据董事会的决议或者命令，公共利益高管应当有创设一般或特定公共利益目的的权力和义务。公司有公共利益高管的，该高管的职责应包括根据第 11 条的要求编写公共利益报告。

（b）公共利益高管应当保持独立，不得与可持续商事公司存在任何重大关联。

第 10 条　诉讼权利

可持续商事公司的股东和董事有权为实现公司目的和执行第 414–221（a）款规定的董事标准而提起直接或代位诉讼，有权为实现公司的一般或特定公共利益目的和执行第 6（a）（1）项规定的董事的行为标准而提起直接或代位诉讼。

第 11 条　年度公共利益报告

（a）可持续商事公司应向其所有股东递交年度公共利益报告，其内容包括：

(1) A narrative description of:

(A) The ways in which the sustainable business corporation pursued general public benefits during the year and the extent to which general public benefit was created;

(B)The ways in which the sustainable business corporation pursued any specific public benefit that the articles state as a purpose of the sustainable business corporation and the extent to which that specific public benefit was created; and

(C)Any circumstances that have hindered the creation by the sustainable business corporation of general or specific public benefits;

(2)An assessment of the overall social and environmental performance of the sustainable business corporation, prepared in accordance with a third–party standard under section–12 applied consistently with any application of that standard in prior benefit reports or accompanied by an explanation of the reasons for any inconsistent application;

(3)The name of the benefit director and the benefit officer, if any, and the address to which correspondence to each of them may be directed;

(4)The compensation paid by the sustainable business corporation during the year to each director in the person's capacity as director;

(5)The name of each person who owns five per cent or more of the outstanding shares of the sustainable business corporation either beneficially to the extent known to the sustainable business corporation or of record;

(6)The statement of the benefit director described in section –7 (c);

(7)A statement of any connection to the organization that developed the third–party standard under section–12, or its directors, officers, or material owners from the sustainable business corporation, or its directors, officers, and material owners, including any financial or governance relationship that might materially affect the credibility of the objective assessment of the third–party standard; and

(8)A statement that, as a private corporation under the direction of its board and accountable to its shareholders and the articles and bylaws of the sustainable business corporation, including those governing the general or specific public benefit purpose and the activities of the sustainable business corporation, the sustainable business corporation and its activities are subject to the oversight of the board of the sustainable business corporation and are not subject to the direct oversight, regulation, or endorsement of any governmental body.

(b) A sustainable business corporation shall post a draft of its benefit report on the public section of its website, or make it otherwise available to the public, for a sixty–day public comment period prior to final publication of the benefit report. The deadline for a commentary shall be published in a publicly accessible manner.

(c) The benefit report shall be sent annually to each shareholder within one hundred twenty days following the end of the fiscal year of the sustainable business corporation.

（1）对以下事项的说明：

（A）可持续商事公司本年度追求一般公共利益的方法和一般公共利益实现的情况；

（B）可持续商事公司追求公司章程中规定的特定公共利益目的的方法，以及该特定公共利益实现的情况；以及

（C）阻碍可持续商事公司实现一般和特定公共利益的情形；

（2）由第三方根据第 12 条的规定，沿用先前公共利益报告中适用的标准，对可持续商事公司的社会和环境表现作整体评价，适用标准与先前报告采用的标准不一致的，还应附上解释说明。

（3）公共利益董事和公共利益高管的姓名和联系地址；

（4）可持续商事公司在上年度支付给每位董事的薪酬；

（5）拥有可持续商事公司 5% 及以上已发行股份的登记股东和实际受益人的姓名；

（6）第 7（c）款规定的公共利益董事意见；

（7）根据第 12 条的规定制定第三方标准的组织及其公司董事、高管或主要股东与可持续商事公司及其董事、高管或主要股东之间关系的声明，包括任何可能影响第三方标准可信度的财务或管理关系。

（8）可持续商事公司及其活动受其董事会监督，不受任何政府主体的直接监督、规制或支持的声明。可持续商事公司作为一家私人公司，由其董事会管理，对其股东负责，公司的一般或特定公共利益目的以及相应活动受其公司章程或章程细则的制约。

（b）可持续商事公司应将其公共利益报告的初稿发布在其网站的公开部分，或以其他方式向社会公开，终稿发布前应留出 60 天的公众评论期。公众评论的截止日期应当以公开方式发布。

（c）可持续商事公司应在其财政年度结束 120 天内向每位股东递送公共利益报告。

(d) A sustainable business corporation shall post its most recent benefit report on the public portion of its website, if any, except that the compensation paid to directors and any financial or proprietary information included in the benefit report may be omitted from the benefit report as posted. If a sustainable business corporation does not have a public website, it shall deliver a copy of its most recent benefit report upon request and without charge to any person who requests a copy.

§-12 Third-party standard.

A third-party standard for purposes of defining, reporting, and assessing overall corporate social and environmental performance of a sustainable business corporation subject to this chapter shall be:

(1) Comprehensive in its assessment of the effect of the business and its operations upon the interests listed in section-6(a);

(2) Developed by an organization that is independent of the sustainable business corporation; and

(3) Transparent because the following information is publicly available:

(A) The criteria considered when measuring the overall social and environmental performance of a business, as well as the relative weightings of those criteria;

(B) The identity of the directors, officers, any material owners, and the governing body of the organization that developed and controls revisions to the standard;

(C) The process by which revisions to the standard are made;

(D) The process by which changes to the membership of the governing body of the organization that developed and controls revisions to the standard are made; and

(E) An accounting of the sources of financial support for the organization that developed and controls revisions to the standard, with sufficient detail to disclose any relationships that could reasonably be considered to present a potential conflict of interest.

§-13 Ministerial role of department director.

Section414-16 shall apply to any filings made by a sustainable business corporation.

SECTION 2. This Act shall take effect upon its approval.

Report Title:

Business Regulation; Sustainable Business Corporations

Description:

Establishes an organizational and regulatory framework for sustainable business corporations.

（d）可持续商事公司应将其最新版的公共利益报告发布于其网站的公共部分，但可将公共利益报告中的董事薪酬和财务、所有权信息删除。公司没有公开网站的，应向所有索取报告的个人免费提供最新版公共利益报告的副本。

第 12 条　第三方标准

第三方标准是指依照本章规定，用于定义、报告和评估可持续商事公司整体社会和环境绩效的标准，其应满足以下条件：

（1）综合，根据第 6（a）款规定中所列利益评估公司业务和经营绩效；

（2）独立，由独立于可持续商事公司的第三方组织制定；以及

（3）透明，以下信息可公开获得：

（A）衡量企业整体社会和环境绩效时所考虑的指标，及指标的相关权重；

（B）制定和控制修改程序的董事、高管、主要股东和该实体控制人员的身份；

（C）标准的修改程序；

（D）第三方组织中标准修改和控制人员变动的程序；以及

（E）制定和修改标准的组织，其资金支持的来源的计量，包括充分披露合理认知下有利益冲突的所有细节。

第 13 条　部门主管的职责

第 414–16 条的规定适用于可持续商事公司的所有备案。

第 2 部分　本法案自通过之日起生效

报告标题：

企业监管；可持续商事公司

说明：

建立一套可持续商事公司组织和监管规则的框架。